A Companio

Blackwell Companions to Philosophy

This outstanding student reference series offers a comprehensive and authoritative survey of philosophy as a whole. Written by today's leading philosophers, each volume provides lucid and engaging coverage of the key figures, terms, topics, and problems of the field. Taken together, the volumes provide the ideal basis for course use, representing an unparalleled work of reference for students and specialists alike.

A Companion to Plato

Edited by
Hugh H. Benson

WILEY-BLACKWELL

A John Wiley & Sons, Ltd., Publication

This paperback edition first published 2009
© 2009 Blackwell Publishing Ltd
except for editorial material and organization © 2009 by Hugh H. Benson

Edition history: Blackwell Publishing Ltd (hardback, 2006)

Blackwell Publishing was acquired by John Wiley & Sons in February 2007. Blackwell's publishing program has been merged with Wiley's global Scientific, Technical, and Medical business to form Wiley-Blackwell.

Registered Office
John Wiley & Sons Ltd, The Atrium, Southern Gate, Chichester, West Sussex, PO19 8SQ, United Kingdom

Editorial Offices
350 Main Street, Malden, MA 02148-5020, USA
9600 Garsington Road, Oxford, OX4 2DQ, UK
The Atrium, Southern Gate, Chichester, West Sussex, PO19 8SQ, UK

For details of our global editorial offices, for customer services, and for information about how to apply for permission to reuse the copyright material in this book please see our website at www.wiley.com/wiley-blackwell.

The right of Hugh H. Benson to be identified as the author of the editorial material in this work has been asserted in accordance with the Copyright, Designs and Patents Act 1988.

Library of Congress Cataloging-in-Publication Data
A companion to Plato / edited by Hugh H. Benson.
    p. cm. — (Blackwell companions to philosophy)
  Includes bibliographical references and index.
  ISBN: 978-1-4051-9111-1 (paperback : alk. paper)   1. Plato.   I. Benson, Hugh H., 1956–
II. Series.

  B395.C64 2006
  184—dc22

                                                              2005034699

A catalogue record for this book is available from the British Library.

Set in 10/12.5pt Photina
by Graphicraft Limited, Hong Kong
Printed in Singapore by Fabulous Printers Pte Ltd

1 2009

Contents

Notes on Contributors

Sara Ahbel-Rappe is Associate Professor of Classical Studies at the University of Michigan. She is the author of *Reading Neoplatonism* (2000) and the co-editor of *The Blackwell Companion to Socrates* (Blackwell, 2006).

Hugh H. Benson is Professor and Chair of the Department of Philosophy at the University of Oklahoma, and was a Samuel Roberts Noble Presidential Professor from 2000 to 2004. He is the editor of *Essays on the Philosophy of Socrates* (1992) and author of *Socratic Wisdom* (2000) as well as various articles on the philosophy of Socrates, Plato, and Aristotle.

Thomas C. Brickhouse is a Professor of Philosophy at Lynchburg College and the co-author (with N. D. Smith) of four books and numerous articles on the philosophy of Socrates. He has also written on Plato and Aristotle.

R. M. Dancy is Professor of Philosophy at Florida State University. He is the author of *Sense and Contradiction: A Study in Aristotle* (1975), *Two Studies in the Early Academy* (1991), *Plato's Introduction of Forms* (2004), and editor of *Kant and Critique* (1993).

Daniel Devereux is Professor of Philosophy at the University of Virginia. He is the author of articles on the philosophy of Socrates, Plato's ethics and metaphysics, and Aristotle's ethics and theory of substance. He contributed a chapter, "Plato: Metaphysics," to *The Blackwell Guide to Ancient Philosophy* (2003). His most recent work has focused on the development of Plato's ethics.

Michael Ferejohn is Associate Professor of Philosophy at Duke University. He has held visiting positions at the University of Pittsburgh and Tufts University and a Mellon Faculty Fellowship at Harvard University. Ferejohn is the author of *The Origins of Aristotelian Science* (1991) as well as numerous articles on early Platonic ethics and metaphysics, and Aristotelian metaphysics, epistemology, and philosophy of science. He is currently working on a book on the place of definition in ancient epistemology.

Cynthia Freeland is Professor and Chair of the Department of Philosophy at the University of Houston. She has written articles on ancient philosophy and is the editor of *Feminist Interpretations of Aristotle* (1998). She also works in aesthetics, where her books include *Philosophy and Film* (co-edited with Thomas Wartenberg, 1995), *The Naked and the Undead: Evil and the Appeal of Horror* (1999), and *But Is It Art?* (2001).

Mary Louise Gill is Professor of Philosophy and Classics at Brown University. She is the author of "Method and metaphysics in Plato's *Sophist* and *Statesman*" in the *Stanford Encyclopedia of Philosophy* (2005), *Aristotle on Substance: The Paradox of Unity* (1989), and *Plato*: Parmenides, Introduction and co-translation (1996). She is co-editor of *A Companion to Ancient Philosophy* (Blackwell, 2006).

Christopher Janaway is Professor of Philosophy at the University of Southampton. He is the author of *Images of Excellence: Plato's Critique of the Arts* (1995) and has published extensively in aesthetics. His other publications include *Self and World in Schopenhauer's Philosophy* (1989), *Schopenhauer: A Very Short Introduction* (2002), and *Reading Aesthetics and Philosophy of Art* (Blackwell, 2006).

Charles Kahn is Professor of Philosophy, University of Pennsylvania. He is the author of *Anaximander and the Origins of Greek Cosmology* (1960), *The Verb "Be" in Ancient Greek* (1973; reprinted with new Introduction, 2003), *The Art and Thought of Heraclitus* (1979), *Plato and the Socratic Dialogue* (1996), and *Pythagoras and the Pythagoreans* (2001).

David Keyt has for many years been Professor of Philosophy at the University of Washington in Seattle, and has also taught at Cornell University, the University of Hong Kong, Princeton University, and the Los Angeles and Irvine campuses of the University of California, and held research appointments at the Institute for Research in the Humanities at the University of Wisconsin, the Center for Hellenic Studies in Washington, DC, the Institute for Advanced Study at Princeton, and the Social Philosophy and Policy Center at Bowling Green State University. He is the author of *Aristotle*, Politics *Books V and VI* (1999) and co-editor with Fred D. Miller, Jr. of *A Companion to Aristotle's* Politics (Blackwell, 1991).

A. A. Long is Professor of Classics and Irving Stone Professor of Literature at the University of California, Berkeley. His recent work, as author, includes *Stoic Studies* (1996) and *Epictetus: A Stoic and Socratic Guide to Life* (2002), and, as editor and contributor, *The Cambridge Companion to Early Greek Philosophy* (1999).

Gareth B. Matthews is Professor of Philosophy (emeritus) at the University of Massachusetts at Amherst. He taught previously at the University of Virginia and the University of Minnesota. He is the author of a number of books and articles on ancient and medieval philosophy, including *Socratic Perplexity and the Nature of Philosophy* (1999), and *Augustine* (Blackwell, 2005).

Mary Margaret McCabe is Professor of Ancient Philosophy at King's College London. She is the author of *Plato on Punishment* (1981), *Plato's Individuals* (1994), and *Plato and his Predecessors: The Dramatisation of Reason* (2000). She is also the general editor of the Cambridge University Press series *Studies in the Dialogues of Plato*. For 2005–8 she is a Leverhulme Trust Major Research Fellow.

Mark L. McPherran is Professor of Philosophy at the University of Maine at Farmington. He is the author of *The Religion of Socrates* (1996; pbk: 1999), the editor of *Wisdom, Ignorance, and Virtue: New Essays in Socratic Studies* (1997), *Recognition, Remembrance, and Reality: New Essays on Plato's Epistemology and Metaphysics* (1999), and a number of articles on Socrates, Plato, and ancient skepticism.

Susan Sauvé Meyer received her PhD in Philosophy at Cornell University in 1987 and taught at Harvard University before joining the faculty of the University of Pennsylvania in 1994, where she is now Associate Professor of Philosophy. Her current work focuses on Greek and Roman ethics, and she is presently completing a book, *Ancient Ethics*.

Fred D. Miller, Jr. is Professor of Philosophy and Executive Director of the Social Philosophy and Policy Center at Bowling Green State University. He is the author of *Nature, Justice, and Rights in Aristotle's* Politics (1995), co-editor with David Keyt of *A Companion to Aristotle's* Politics (Blackwell, 1991), and editor, in association with Carrie-Ann Khan, of *A History of the Philosophy of Law from the Ancient Greeks to the Scholastics* (2006). He has published many articles on ancient philosophy and on moral and political philosophy. He was President of the Society for Ancient Greek Philosophy from 1998 until 2004.

Deborah K. W. Modrak is a Professor of Philosophy at the University of Rochester. She is the author of two books, *Aristotle's Theory of Language and Meaning* (2001) and *Aristotle: The Power of Perception* (1987). She has also written numerous articles on topics in ancient Greek philosophy of mind, theories of cognition and language, and epistemology.

Debra Nails is Professor of Philosophy at Michigan State University. She is author of *The People of Plato: A Prosopography of Plato and Other Socratics* (2002), *Agora, Academy, and the Conduct of Philosophy* (1995); and articles on Socrates and Plato in various journals and collections. She also writes on Spinoza and pursues investigative work for the APA's Committee for the Defense of Professional Rights of Philosophers and the AAUP.

Terry Penner is Professor of Philosophy Emeritus, and was for a time Affiliate Professor of Classics, at the University of Wisconsin-Madison. In Spring 2005 he was the A. G. Leventis Visiting Research Professor of Greek in the University of Edinburgh. He has written numerous articles on Socrates, on Plato's psychology of action, and on Plato's Theory of Forms, as well as *The Ascent from Nominalism* (1987) and, with Christopher Rowe, *Plato's* Lysis (2005).

William J. Prior is Professor of Philosophy at Santa Clara University. He received his PhD from the University of Texas at Austin in 1975. He is the author of *Unity and Development in Plato's Metaphysics* (1985) and *Virtue and Knowledge* (1991), and the editor of *Socrates: Critical Assessments* (4 vols., 1996), and numerous articles in Greek philosophy. He is currently working on the Socratic problem and on Greek cosmology.

C. D. C. Reeve is Delta Kappa Epsilon Distinguished Professor of Philosophy at the University of North Carolina at Chapel Hill. He is author of *Love's Confusions* (2005) and *Substantial Knowledge: Aristotle's Metaphysics* (2000). His *Philosopher-Kings: The Argument of Plato's* Republic will be reissued in 2006.

Christopher Rowe is Professor of Greek at the University of Durham. He held a Leverhulme Personal Research Professorship from 1999 to 2004, and was co-editor of *Phronesis* (Leiden) from 1997 to 2003. He is the author of commentaries on several dialogues of Plato and has edited *The Cambridge History of Greek and Roman Political*

Thought with Malcolm Schofield (2000), completed a translation of Aristotle's *Nicomachean Ethics* (to accompany a philosophical commentary by Sarah Broadie, 2001), edited *New Perspectives on Plato* with Julia Annas (2002), and, with Terry Penner, written a monograph on Plato's *Lysis* (2005).

Gerasimos Santas is Professor of Philosophy at the University of California, Irvine. He is author of *Socrates: Philosophy in Plato's Early Dialogues* (1979; Greek edition, 1997; Italian edition, 2003), *Plato and Freud: Two Theories of Love* (Blackwell, 1988; Italian edition, 1990), *Goodness and Justice: Plato, Aristotle, and the Moderns* (Blackwell, 2001; Greek edition, 2006), and editor of *The Blackwell Guide to Plato's* Republic (Blackwell, 2006).

David Sedley is Laurence Professor of Ancient Philosophy at the University of Cambridge. He is author, with A. A. Long, of *The Hellenistic Philosophers* (1987), *Lucretius and the Transformation of Greek Wisdom* (1998), *Plato's* Cratylus (2003), and *The Midwife of Platonism: Text and Subtext in Plato's* Theaetetus, and editor of *The Cambridge Companion to Greek and Roman Philosophy* (2003). He was Sather Professor at University of California at Berkeley in 2004, and currently edits *Oxford Studies in Ancient Philosophy*.

Christopher Shields is Tutorial Fellow of Lady Margaret Hall and University Lecturer at the University of Oxford. He is the author of several books, including *Order in Multiplicity* (1999), *Classical Philosophy: A Contemporary Introduction* (2003), and *Aristotle* (forthcoming), as well as co-author, with Robert Pasnau, of *The Philosophy of Thomas Aquinas* (2003). He served as editor of *The Blackwell Guide to Ancient Philosophy* (Blackwell, 2003) and *The Oxford Handbook on Aristotle* (forthcoming).

Nicholas D. Smith is the James F. Miller Professor of Humanities, Chair of the Philosophy Department, and the Director of Classical Studies at Lewis and Clark College in Portland, Oregon. His publications with Thomas C. Brickhouse include: *Socrates on Trial* (1989), *Plato's Socrates* (1994), *The Trial and Execution of Socrates: Sources and Controversies* (2002), and the *Routledge Philosophy GuideBook to Plato and the Trial of Socrates* (2004).

Michael J. White is Professor of Philosophy and of Law at Arizona State University. His books include *Agency and Integrality: Philosophical Themes in the Ancient Discussions of Determinism and Responsibility* (1985), *The Continuous and the Discrete: Ancient Physical Theories from a Contemporary Perspective* (1992), *Partisan or Neutral?* (1997), and *Political Philosophy: An Historical Introduction* (2003). He has recently contributed to *The Cambridge Companion to the Stoics* (2003).

Nicholas White is Professor of Philosophy and Professor of Classics at the University of California, Irvine. He has been Professor of Philosophy at the Universities of Michigan and Utah. He is the author of *Plato on Knowledge and Reality* (1976), *A Companion to Plato's* Republic (1979), and *Individual and Conflict in Greek Ethics* (2002).

Charles M. Young is Professor of Philosophy at Claremont Graduate University. The author of a variety of articles on Plato and Aristotle, he is currently working on a monograph on Aristotle on virtue and the virtues and the Project Archelogos module on Book V of Aristotle's *Nicomachean Ethics*.

Preface

The essays collected in this volume are guided by four objectives. First, they are devoted to topics in Platonic philosophy rather than to individual Platonic dialogues. The assumption of this collection is that Plato is usefully approached by considering how positions advocated in one dialogue compare and contrast with positions advocated in others. Each individual author has been free to approach this assumption as he or she thinks is appropriate. Some have chosen to concentrate primarily on one dialogue, noting in passing how the topic is treated in other dialogues (for example, N. White), while other authors have chosen to focus their essay more broadly (for example, McPherran). Nevertheless, a common assumption of all of the essays is that it is appropriate, perhaps necessary, to ask whether Plato treats the relevant topic consistently throughout his corpus. This has inevitably resulted in some repetition and overlap from one essay to the next. The same Platonic text or doctrine sometimes gets explored on behalf of different topics. Such repetition, however, should be embraced as a reflection of the depth of individual Platonic texts and doctrines, and so of the diverse ways of approaching them.

Second, this collection aims to represent a range of views on Plato's philosophical development. Given the topic-oriented (as opposed to dialogue-oriented) approach, the debate about Plato's philosophical development is especially salient. If Plato treats a topic differently in one dialogue (or group of dialogues) than in another, it is natural to wonder whether this difference is to be explained by a change in context, a change in emphasis, or change in Plato's position. If change in position appears to be the best explanation, it then becomes natural to wonder which position Plato held first and so to trace his philosophical development on that topic. Here we have become embroiled in the ongoing debate between those scholars who see Plato's dialogues as reflecting his philosophical development and those who see them as displaying aspects, nuances, and subtleties of a single unified philosophical position throughout. In the essays that follow, some authors are committed to a fairly robust developmentalism (for example, McPherran, Penner, and Ferejohn), while others appear to be committed to a more moderate version (for example, Rowe), and still others appear to offer both developmentalist and non-developmentalist interpretations (for example, Modrak), or appear to allow a unitarian interpretation (for example, McCabe, Janaway, and Long). When the authors refer to the three chronological groups into which Plato's dialogues have often been thought to fall, they typically have in mind the following groupings – early dialogues (*Apology, Charmides, Crito, Euthydemus, Euthyphro, Gorgias, Hippias Major, Hippias Minor, Ion, Laches, Lysis, Menexenus, Meno, Protagoras*), middle dialogues (*Cratylus, Parmenides, Phaedo, Phaedrus, Republic, Symposium, Theaetetus*), and late dialogues (*Critias, Laws, Philebus, Politicus, Sophist, Timaeus*). But the collection as a whole does not presuppose that the dialogues are correctly seen as having been composed in this order, nor does it advocate either a developmentalist or unitarian approach to Plato.

Third, the topics have been selected with an ear to philosophical, as opposed to historical or philological significance. This distinction is of course vague and potentially misleading, but the focus has been philosophy – not history or philology. Consequently, I am sure the topics chosen reflect the biases of our time (and no doubt my own biases). Such a reflection is, I suppose, inevitable. But such a reflection will also, I hope, make the collection appealing to many individuals with current interests in philosophy.

Fourth, the authors of these essays were asked to compose their essays in a way accessible to the beginner or non-scholar and yet in a way that also advances the scholarly discussion. There is always, I suppose, a tension between serious scholarship and accessibility, but the authors are to be commended for their skill in navigating these waters. Consequently, the essays should be of interest both to those students approaching Plato for the first time and also to those students who have spent a good portion of their adult lives delving his inner depths. To this end the authors have either provided their own translations of key texts or have used the translations in *Plato: Complete Works*, edited by J. M. Cooper (Indianapolis: Hackett, 1997) which have now become the standard translations for scholars and non-scholars alike.

Finally, I would like to express my sincere appreciation to the fine scholars who have contributed the essays that follow. I appreciate their patience for my sometimes confusing instructions and frequent delays, their generosity for agreeing to contribute to the collection and foregoing the temptation of numerous notes, their grace in responding to my often obtuse comments, and especially their philosophical and scholarly skill in composing the essays that follow. In a very literal sense, this collection is theirs, not mine. I would especially like to thank Mary Louise Gill and M. M. McCabe for encouraging me through moments of uncertainty, desperation, and exasperation. Thanks also to Nick Bellorini, Jennifer Hunt, Gillian Kane, Kelvin Matthews, Mary Dortch, and the staff at Blackwell for their support, advice, and patience. My students Elliot Welch and Rusty Jones have also been invaluable contributors to this enterprise, doing much of the heavy lifting and saving me from some serious blunders. Finally, I cannot fail to thank Ann, Thomas, and Michael for helping me to remember where my priorities lie.

Abbreviations used in this Volume

Aristotle

APo.	*Posterior Analytics*
Cat.	*Categories*
de An.	*De Anima*
EE	*Ethics Eudemian*
EN	*Ethics Nicomachean*
GC	*Generation and Corruption*
Int.	*On Interpretation*
Metaph.	*Metaphysics*
Ph.	*Physics*
Poet.	*Poetics*
Pol.	*Politics*
SE	*Sophistici Elenchi*
Top.	*Topics*

Augustine

DCD	*City of God*

Diogenes Laertius

DL	*Lives of Eminent Philosophers*

Dionysius (Pseudo-Dionysius)

CH	*Celestial Hierarchy*
MT	*Mystical Theology*

Hesiod

Th.	*Theogony*
Op.	*Works and Days*

Homer

Il.	*Iliad*
Od.	*Odyssey*

Iamblichus

DM	*De Mysteriis Aegyptorum*

Pindar

N.	*Nemean Odes*
O.	*Olympian Odes*

Plato

Ap.	*Apology*
Chrm.	*Charmides*
Cra.	*Cratylus*
Cri.	*Crito*
Ep.	*Epistles*
Euthd.	*Euthydemus*
Euthphr.	*Euthyphro*
Grg.	*Gorgias*
Hp.Ma.	*Hippias Major*
La.	*Laches*
Lg.	*Laws*
Men.	*Meno*
Phd.	*Phaedo*
Phdr.	*Phaedrus*
Phlb.	*Philebus*
Plt.	*Politicus/Statesman*
Prm.	*Parmenides*
Prt.	*Protagoras*
R.	*Republic*
Smp.	*Symposium*
Sph.	*Sophist*
Tht.	*Theaetetus*
Ti.	*Timaeus*
VII	Seventh Letter

Plutarch

Per.	*Pericles*

Porphyry

Abst.	*de Abstinentia*
VP	*The Life of Pythagoras*

Proclus

In pr. Eucl.	*In primum Euclidis librum commentarius*

Sextus Empiricus

M.	*adversus Mathematicos*

Xenophon

Mem.	*Memorabilia*
HG	*Historia Graeca*

1

The Life of Plato of Athens

DEBRA NAILS

Plato died in the first year of the hundred and eighth Olympiad in the thirteenth year of the reign of Philip of Macedon – 347 BCE by contemporary reckoning – and was buried at the Academy.[1] So venerable and so widespread was the philosopher's reputation that mythologizing was inevitable and prolonged: Plato was sired by the god Apollo and born to the virgin Perictione; he was born on the seventh of Thargelion, Apollo's birthday, and the bees of Mount Hymettus dripped honey into the mouth of the newborn babe. Renaissance Platonists celebrated Plato's birth on the seventh of November, the same day his death was commemorated. Woodbridge's 1929 *The Son of Apollo* begins, "The demand of history that we be accurate contends with the demand of admiration that we be just. Caught between the two, biographers of Plato have written, not the life of a man, but tributes to a genius." Genius he certainly was, but he deserves better than a tribute and better than the standard *vita* cut to fit the pattern of the Alexandrian librarian Apollodorus who divided ancient lives into four twenty-year periods with an *akmē* at age 40.[2] By this scheme, Plato is duly born in 427, meets Socrates at age 20 (when Socrates is 60), founds the Academy at 40, voyages to Sicily at 60, and dies at the age of 80. Ample evidence belies the neat fit.

Plato of Collytus, son of Ariston – for that was his full legal name, under which he had rights of Athenian citizenship and by which his name will have been recorded on the Aegis tribal lists – was born in 424/3, the fourth child of Ariston of Collytus, son of Aristocles, and Perictione, daughter of Glaucon; Ariston and Perictione had married by 432. Leaving aside remote divine origins, both parents traced their ancestry to Athenian archons of the seventh and sixth centuries and, in Perictione's case, to kinship with the sage legislator, Solon (*Ti.* 20E1). Ariston and his young family were probably among the first colonists retaining Athenian citizenship on Aegina, when Athens expelled the native Aeginetans in 431 (Thucydides 2.27). When Ariston died around the time of Plato's birth, Athenian law forbade the legal independence of women, so Perictione was given in marriage to her mother's brother, Pyrilampes, a widower who had recently been wounded in the battle of Delium. Marriages between uncle and niece, as between first cousins, were common and expedient in Athens, preserving rather than dividing family estates. Plato's stepfather, Pyrilampes, had been Pericles' intimate friend (Plutarch, *Per.* 13.10) and many times ambassador to Persia (*Chrm.* 158A2–6); he brought to the marriage at least one son, Demos (*Grg.* 481D5, 513C7), whose name means "people": a tribute to the democracy under which Pyrilampes flourished in public life. When Pyrilampes and Perictione had another son, they did the more conventional thing, naming him Antiphon for his grandfather (*Prm.* 126B1–9). Thus Plato was reared in a household of at least six children, where he was number five: a stepbrother, a sister, two brothers, and a half brother. Pyrilampes died by 413, but Ariston's eldest son, Adeimantus, was old enough by then, about 19, to become his mother's guardian (*kurios*).

Plato's Youth in Athens

When Plato was a boy and old enough to be paying some attention to affairs of state affecting his family, Athens was embroiled in the Peloponnesian War, causing and enduring a horrifying sequence of disasters. In 416, when Plato was about 8 and the Peace of Nicias signed between Athens and Sparta in 421 had unraveled completely, Athens behaved with unprecedented cruelty toward Melos, using the might-makes-right arguments to be echoed by Thrasymachus in *Republic* I (Thucydides 5.84–116). The following year, as the city embarked on her catastrophic Sicilian campaign, an oligarchic political club smashed the city's herms one night, insulting the god of travel and setting off a superstitious hysteria that led to the summary execution, imprisonment, or exile of citizens accused of sacrilege, including members of Plato's family. One of the fleet's three commanders, the charismatic Alcibiades, was among the accused, and a terrible consequence of Athens' mass hysteria was Alcibiades' abandonment of the expedition and his betrayal of the city. With Athens' utter defeat in Sicily in 413, Sparta renewed the war. Plato would have been 12 when Athens lost her empire with the revolt of the subject allies; 13 when the democracy fell briefly to the oligarchy of the Four Hundred and when the army, still under the democrats, persuaded Alcibiades to return and lead it again; 14 when democracy was restored; 15 when his older brothers, Adeimantus and Glaucon, distinguished themselves at the battle of Megara (*R.* 368A3).

Despite the war and unrest, Plato and his male siblings would have received a formal education in gymnastics and music, but by "music" we are to understand the domains of all the Muses: not only dance, lyric, epic, and instrumental music, but reading, writing, arithmetic, geometry, history, astronomy, and more. A boy's informal induction into Athenian civic life was primarily the responsibility of the older males of his family. As illustrated in *Laches* and *Charmides*, a young male was socialized by his father, older brothers, or guardian, whom he accompanied about the city – while women remained discreetly indoors. In the company of his brothers, Plato was thus probably a young child when he became acquainted with Socrates. Both *Lysis*, set in early spring, 409, when Plato would have been 15, and *Euthydemus*, set a couple of years later, provide insight into Plato's school-age years since the young characters of those dialogues were Plato's exact contemporaries in real life. Lysis of Aexone, about whom we are lucky to have corroborating contemporaneous evidence independent of Plato's dialogues, probably remained an intimate of Plato's, since he is known to have lived to be a grandfather, at the very least 60 when he died.

2

Set at the time Plato would himself have been considering his educational prospects, *Euthydemus* illustrates the educational fashion of the day: the purported transfer of excellence (*aretē*, also translated "virtue") from teacher to student. Higher education in Athens in the late fifth century was dominated by sophists, foreign residents who achieved fame and wealth by professing techniques of persuasion and exposition, platitudes dressed up in high rhetorical style, the kind of skills that could help young men to become excellent *qua* successful in public life by speaking effectively in the Athenian Assembly (*ekklēsia*) and courts of law. Even the more respectable of these – Gorgias of Leontini and Protagoras of Abdera, who appear in dialogues named for them (cf. Socrates' impersonation of Protagoras in *Theaetetus*) – are represented as having done a poor job of transferring whatever excellence they had, however, for their students seem always to have trouble retaining and defending what their professors professed. In *Euthydemus*, two sophists of questionable character claim to be able to make any man good by calling him to philosophy and excellence (274D7–275A1), but their display is little more than a hilarious use of fallacies to abuse their respondents. The dialogue's denouement (from 304B6) is a serious reminder that, at the time of Plato's coming of age, Athenians were increasingly suspicious of sophists, rhetoricians, orators, and philosophers *alike*.

These were the closing years before Athens' surrender to Sparta in 404, when the Assembly was paying less and less attention to its written laws, and acting ever more irrationally, emotionally, and in vengeance. An older Plato would distinguish the lawful from the lawless democracy (*Plt.* 302D1–303B5) with good reason. Traditions were maintained, however, at the level of voting districts or demes, of which Athens had 139. Citizenship was passed strictly from father to son, so the sons of the deceased Ariston, each in his eighteenth year, would have been presented to the citizens of Collytus at *dokimasia* ceremonies, after which they would have been fully emancipated. It was in the year after Plato's *dokimasia* that Socrates attempted unsuccessfully to prevent the Assembly from unconstitutionally trying and executing six generals, including the son of Pericles and Aspasia, for failure to ensure the collection of casualties after winning the naval battle of Arginusae in 406. In the two years following his ceremony, Plato would have mustered with his fellow demesmen in the citizen militia, although confined to service within the borders of Attica. Afterwards, when called up, he would have served elsewhere. By both law and custom, greater maturity was required for participation in various other aspects of civic life. A citizen had to be 20 to enter public life without making a laughing-stock of himself, and 30 before his name was entered into the lotteries that determined the Athenian Council (*boulē*), juries, and archons, before he could be elected general, and before he was expected to marry.

As Plato came of age, he naturally imagined for himself a life in public affairs, as he says in a letter written in 354/3 (VII.324B9). The letter's authenticity was once much discussed, but even its detractors concede that its author, if not Plato, was an intimate of the philosopher with first-hand knowledge of the events reported. Many of its details are augmented and corroborated by contemporaneous historians of Greece and of Sicily, and its style – unlike other letters in the series – is that of *Laws* and *Epinomis* (Ledger 1989: 148–51).[3] Plato's extended family already included two men in Socrates' orbit, characters of the dialogues *Protagoras* and *Charmides*, who featured prominently in Athenian public life: Critias, Plato's first cousin once removed (Perictione's first cousin); and Critias' ward Charmides (Perictione's younger brother). Both were among fifty-one men for whom Plato had high hopes in 404 when, after the debacles and excesses of the sometimes lawless democracy, the Spartan defeat of Athens led to the election of the Thirty, charged with framing a post-democratic constitution that would return the city to the governing principles of the *patrios politeia*, the Athenian ancestral constitution. Critias was a leader of the Thirty, and Charmides was one of the Piraeus Ten municipal managers; the Eleven municipal managers of urban Athens completed the total of fifty-one. Although Plato was invited right away to join the administration, he was still young, he says (VII.324D4), and delayed, attending closely, and hoping to witness Athens' return to justice under the new leadership.

The Thirty disappointed him grievously, however, by attempting to implicate Socrates in their seizure of the democratic general Leon of Salamis for summary execution. Plato says of their oligarchy that it made the rule of the previous democracy appear a golden age by comparison (VII.324D6–325A5). According to Xenophon of Erchia, the constitutional framing was continually delayed (*HG* 2.3.11); and Isocrates of Erchia describes the Thirty as having quickly abused and exceeded their authority, summarily executing 1,500 citizens and driving some 5,000 more to the Piraeus during nine months in power (*Areopagiticus* 67). But the democrats in exile were able to regroup in Phyle whence, in 403, they re-entered the Piraeus and met the forces of the Thirty in the battle of Munychia, where both Critias and Charmides were killed. After months of further upheaval, the democracy was restored. Despite an amnesty negotiated with Spartan arbitration in 403–2 to reduce instances of revenge in the immediate aftermath of the civil war, the turmoil simmered. A provision of the reconciliation agreement was that all remaining oligarchic sympathizers would be allowed their own government in Eleusis, which they had earlier secured for themselves by putting to death the population on charges of supporting democracy (Xenophon, *HG* 2.4.8–10; Diodorus Siculus 14.32.5). The agreement was short-lived: as soon as the Spartans were distracted by a war with Elis, the oligarchs began hiring mercenaries; Athens retaliated by annexing Eleusis and killing all the remaining oligarchic sympathizers in the early spring of 401.

As in other revolutions spun out of control, the general level of disorder had made acts of retribution easier to perpetrate, violence easier to inflict without punishment. Yet the returned democrats, in Plato's account, showed seemly restraint during that period of revolutions (VII.325B1–5). Indeed, if the dialogues with dramatic dates from 402 to 399 (especially *Meno*, *Theaetetus*, *Euthyphro*, *Crito*, and *Phaedo*) can be counted as sources for the kinds of conversations Plato, in his early twenties, experienced in the company of Socrates, then at least some things about Athenian life were back to normal. That may be why Plato describes it as "by chance" (VII.325B5–6) that Anytus and Lycon, whose friend Leon Socrates had earlier refused to hand over to the Thirty, managed successfully to prosecute Socrates for impiety and to succeed in their proposed penalty of death. For Plato, this devastating event, together with his surmise that Athenian order was deteriorating into chaos, put an end to the desire to become politically active that had been rekindled briefly in him with the restoration of the democracy (VII.325A7–B1). Although continuing to contemplate how he might yet be able to effect an improvement of the laws and public life generally, at length he realized that every existing state suffered both bad governance and almost incurable laws and was forced in his mid-twenties to admit that without "right philosophy," one would be unable

> to determine what justice is in the *polis* or in the individual. The evils suffered by human-
> ity will not cease until either the right and true philosophers rule in the *polis* or the rulers
> in the *poleis*, by some divine turn of fate, become truly philosophical. (VII.326A5–B4;
> cf. *R.* V.473c11–E2)

Then, or soon after, Plato determined to make his contribution to public life as an educator. He was, in that role, to supplant the itinerant sophists and rhetoricians who had for so long been at the forefront of Athenian higher education.

Plato's First Visit to Sicily and the Founding of the Academy

After Socrates' execution, Plato remained in Athens for perhaps three years. During this time he associated with the Heraclitean Cratylus and with Hermogenes, bastard half-brother of the well-known Callias of Alopece, who had spent a fortune on sophists (see *Cra.*, *Prt.*, and *Ap.*). Then, from age 28 in 396, Plato resided for a while in Megara, half a day's walk from Athens, with Euclides and other Socratics in the pursuit of mathematics and philosophy (Hermodorus, quoted in Diogenes Laertius 3.6.2–6). Dubious hints of other travels appear only in late sources.

Turning 30 in 394, Plato would have been expected to set himself up as a house-holder and, although there is no hint that he did, to marry (despite *Laws* IV.721A–E and VI.772D). He was never among Athens' wealthiest citizens, but the agricultural income from his properties outside the city walls seems to have been adequate for his personal needs and for such familial obligations as dowries and funerals. Funding for operations of the Academy, still in the future, was probably supplemented by endow-ments; that Academic finances were distinct from Plato's personal accounts is witnessed by the absence of any mention of the Academy in Plato's will. Plato owned property in the deme of Iphistiadae, about 10 kilometers north-northeast of the ancient city wall, and 2 kilometers from the banks of the Cephisus river, a property he probably inherited (his will mentions no sum paid for it). The land can be precisely located because Plato describes it as bounded on the south by the temple of Heracles, a boundary stone for which was found in 1926. Plato was eventually to purchase another plot, in the deme of Eresidae, from an otherwise unknown Callimachus, a named executor in Plato's will; its location was roughly 3 kilometers north of the city wall, on the eastern bank of the Cephisus river. Plato's nephew, Eurymedon, another executor, owned the adjacent properties to the north and east. Although Plato's deme was Collytus, within the city walls, there were three brothers to divide Ariston's estate, and the laws of succession worked to preserve properties intact. Normally, the absence of a will required an initial apportionment of the assets of the estate (land under cultivation, structures, herds, precious metals, cash etc.) into equal portions; when these were agreed to be equal, the brothers might draw lots or choose their inheritance (MacDowell 1978: 93).

At about the same time that he was establishing himself, Plato and the mathemat-icians Theaetetus of Sunium, then 19, and dead five years later; Archytas of Tarentum, a Pythagorean, musical theorist, and enlightened political leader, who would remain close to Plato throughout his life; Leodamas of Thasos, and perhaps Neoclides (Proclus, quoted in Euclid, *Elements* 66.16) began congregating northwest of urban Athens in the grove of the hero Hecademus, between the rivers Cephisus and Eridanus, to pursue their studies. Speusippus of Myrrhinus, son of Plato's sister Potone, joined the group in about 390. The number of names of mathematicians that survives from a list originally compiled by Eudemus late in the fourth century BCE is a strong indication that the group of fellow students grew steadily in the early years. It is not until Eudoxus of Cnidos arrives in the mid-380s that Eudemus recognizes a formal Academy. The grove that would later become the Academy, however, had a gymnasium and commodious open spaces frequented by young intellectuals – not schoolrooms or lecture halls.

Plato had earned a reputation abroad by about 385, when he was invited to the court of the Sicilian tyrant, Dionysius I, who regularly asked notable Athenians to be his guests in the fortified royal compound on Ortygia, the peninsula jutting out into the harbor of Syracuse. This is a compelling indication that, apart from his mathematical and philosophical studies, Plato had begun writing dialogues that were copied and distributed. There is substantial evidence that a proto-*Republic*, comprising most of Books II–V of our current text of *Republic*, was published before 391 when Aristophanes' bawdy *Ecclesiazusae* parodied its central elements (Thesleff 1982: 102–10). *Apology*, an early draft of *Gorgias*, and what is now *Republic* I were likely also among the dialogues that were published in this early group. From time to time, both *Phaedrus* and *Lysis* have been thought to count there as well – especially in traditions outside Anglo-American analytic philosophy since the 1950s. There is abundant evidence of revision in several of the dialogues, an insuperable obstacle to definitive computer analysis of Plato's style, and thus to certainty about the order in which the dialogues were written, except for the very last ones (Ledger 1989: 148–51). Nevertheless, the impression of three major periods of productivity, edges blurred, persists in most interpretive traditions (Nails 1995: 97–114).

Plato says he was nearly 40 when he voyaged to Italy, where he probably visited Archytas in Tarentum, and to Sicily, where he was the guest of Dionysius I, tyrant of Syracuse. The journey was memorable despite Plato's disgust at both the tyranny and the decadent sensuality he encountered. He had no truck with the tyrant (strikingly like the tyrant in *Republic* IX), but met Dion, the tyrant's young brother-in-law. Here was an admirable if rather straight-laced youth of 20, quick to learn whatever Plato thought could help him achieve "freedom under the best laws" for the people of Sicily (VII.324B1–2). Their friendship – renewed by Dion's visits to Greece – was to last thirty years (VII.324A5–7). Late sources (Diodorus Siculus, Plutarch, Diogenes Laertius) offer varying details about the end of Plato's first trip to Sicily, though they agree that Plato's frank speaking so angered the tyrant that he was shipped off and sold into slavery. When he was purchased and set free by Anniceris of Cyrene, in Diogenes' account, Plato's friends tried to return the money, but Anniceris refused it and purchased for Plato a garden in Hecademus' grove.

The Academy, an Athenian center for advanced study including men and women from throughout the Greek-speaking world, the dialogues that were its textbooks, and the philosophical methods illustrated in them, are Plato's brilliant legacy. Founded after Plato's return from Sicily in 383, and with unbroken succession until about

79 BCE, the Academy is sometimes said to be the progenitor of the modern university, though Isocrates had established a permanent school for rhetoric in Athens in 390. The Academy's curriculum, grounded in mathematics and the *pursuit* of scientific knowledge – rather than its packaging – made it the first of its kind. Yet what can "founding" mean? Presumably, the Academy would publicize its readiness to welcome students, though no fees were charged. Members who had studied together for some years were perhaps ready now to share what they had learned, and to apply their knowledge in new areas. The Academy continued to attract sons of political leaders who were more interested in ruling than in the mathematics that was its prerequisite, but the beginnings are murky and it is difficult not to impose current categories (teacher, student) anachronistically – as in other centuries "master" and "disciple" were imposed. In any case, Plato appears to have spent the period from 383 to 366 in relative quiet, studying, discussing, writing, and contributing generally to Academic education. It is to this period that Plato's greatest productivity of dialogues is attributed; and it was during this time that the Academy's members and activities began to be spoofed on the Athenian comic stage. One might note the arrival in 367 of Aristotle of Stagira, the fragments of whose dialogues suggest that it was typical of academicians to write in that genre.

Plato's Sicilian Expeditions for Dion and Philosophy

In Letter VII, Plato minutely details his subsequent trips to Sicily. The brief summary below may be of interest if one keeps in mind the image of the philosopher of *Theaetetus*, an object of derision for being so perfectly inept at practical matters (172c3–177c2); Plato shows himself an innocent abroad, outmaneuvered at every turn, utterly incompetent to help his friend, much less to make the ruler a philosopher.

Plato was not eager to return when summoned back to Syracuse by Dionysius II in 366. The old Dionysius had died in 367, soon after hearing that his play, *The Ransom of Hector*, had won first prize at the Lenaean festival in Athens. Despite his reputation for learning and culture, he had not looked after the education of his son and heir. As a child, Dionysius II had been mostly kept out of sight, occupied with making wooden toys, but when he was called before his father, he was strip-searched for hidden weapons, like anyone granted an audience by the tyrant. An adult of about 30 by the time he summoned Plato, the younger Dionysius had married his paternal half-sister, Sophrosyne, with whom he had a son, and had recently been made an honorary Athenian citizen. Dion, meanwhile, had married his niece, Arete, daughter of the old tyrant, and had a son of 7, so Dion was brother-in-law and sometime adviser to the new tyrant.

Dion, at whose behest the summons had been issued, had difficulty overcoming Plato's reluctance to sail to Syracuse. He urged Plato on several grounds, including the young tyrant's passion for philosophy and for education generally. If Plato remembered the adolescent Dionysius from his first visit, he does not mention it, saying only that the passions of the young are apt to change radically. Dion persisted, exhorting Plato to help him influence Dionysius II, arguing *inter alia* that the death of the old tyrant might be that "divine turn of fate" required for the people's happiness in freedom under good laws to be realized at last; that there were already a few others in Syracuse who had come to the right views; that his young nephews likewise needed training in philosophy; and that the new tyrant might be led by Dion with Plato's help, as Dion had been led by Plato, to true philosophy, thereby effecting reforms and putting an end to the evils long suffered by the people. Besides, Dion added, if Plato did not come, worse men were waiting to undertake the young tyrant's education. Trusting more in Dion's steadfast character and intentions than in any hopes for success with Dionysius, fearing for Dion's safety, feeling a debt to his former host outweighing his present responsibilities at the Academy, a double reason finally proved decisive: it would be shameful in Plato's own eyes and a betrayal of philosophy if he proved after all to be a man of words who cowered at deeds. Plato finally embarked, in the first sailing season of 366, on a second trip to Sicily.

Factions in the royal court were suspicious of Dion and Plato from the start, assuming that Plato's secret aim was to put Sicily, then at war with Carthage, under Dion's rule. To check the philosopher's influence, they arranged for the savvy Philistus, an historian banished by the old tyrant, to be recalled from exile. After a few months in which both Plato and Dion attempted ceaselessly to make the life of moderation and wisdom attractive to Dionysius, whom they found not without ability (VII.338D7), Philistus gave evidence to Dionysius that Dion had been covertly negotiating peace with Carthage. Dion was summarily deported to Italy, dispossessed of his wife, son, and part of his property. Dion's friends feared retaliation, but the tyrant – mindful of both his reputation abroad and the need to placate Dion's supporters – made a show of begging Plato to stay while insuring against his escape by moving him into the fortress (VII.329D1–330A2). Plato persisted in the educational plan and even established ties between Dionysius and Archytas and other Tarentines. But Dionysius, attached to Plato, remained jealous of Plato's high regard for Dion. He desperately wanted Plato's praise, but not to work toward the wisdom that was the only way to earn it. Plato took every opportunity to persuade Dionysius to allow him to return to Athens, resulting finally in an agreement: Plato promised that, if Dionysius would recall both Dion and himself after securing peace with Carthage, both would come. On that basis, Plato took leave in an outwardly amicable way, and Dionysius removed restrictions on Dion's receipt of estate-income.

Dion had meanwhile traveled to Athens, where he had purchased an estate; the city remained his base and allowed study at the Academy and friendship with Speusippus. But he traveled widely in Greece, to a warm welcome in Corinth, and in Sparta, where he was given honorary citizenship. When Dionysius summoned Plato – but not Dion – in 361, and Dion implored him to go, having heard that Dionysius had developed a wondrous passion for philosophy (VII.338B6–7), Plato refused, angering both by pleading his advanced age. Rumors from Sicily were that Archytas, a number of friends of Dion, and many others had engaged Dionysius in philosophical discussions. When a second summons then arrived, Plato recognized in it the tyrant's jealous ambition (*philotimos*) not to have his ignorance of philosophy brought to light; and again Plato refused to return to Sicily. A third summons arrived, this one carried by a number of Plato's Sicilian acquaintances, including Archytas' associate, Archedemus, the Sicilian Dionysius believed Plato regarded most highly. Not only had they arrived by trireme to ease Plato's journey, Dionysius had written a long letter, saying that Dion's affairs, if Plato came, would be settled as Plato desired, but that, if he did not, Plato would not like the outcome for Dion's property or person. Meanwhile, Plato's Athenian connections were urging him strenuously to go at once; and letters were arriving from Italy and Sicily, making fresh arguments – Archytas reporting that important matters of state between Tarentum and Syracuse depended on Plato's return. As before, Plato's decision was that it would be a betrayal of Dion and his Tarentine hosts not to make the effort; as for the betrayal of philosophy, this time Plato reasoned (blindfolded, he would later say, VII.340A2) that perhaps Dionysius, having now discoursed with so many men on philosophical subjects, and come under their influence, may in fact have embraced the best life. At least Plato should find out the truth.

It was clear after their first conversation that Dionysius had no interest in discussing philosophy; indeed, the tyrant announced that he already knew what was important. Moreover, he canceled the payment of revenue from Dion's estates, whereupon Plato announced in anger that he was returning to Athens, meaning to board just any boat at harbor. Dionysius, his reputation in mind, entreated Plato to stay and, seeing that he could not persuade the angry philosopher, offered to arrange Plato's passage himself. But the next day he enraged Plato further by promising that, if Plato stayed through the winter, Dion would receive excellent terms, which he detailed, in the spring. Plato, without faith in these promises, considered various scenarios overnight and realized he had already been checkmated. He agreed to stay, with one stipulation, that Dion be informed of the terms so his agreement could be sought. Not only was the stipulation not honored, neither did the terms stay fixed: as soon as the harbor was closed and Plato could no longer escape the island, Dionysius sold off Dion's estates.

A crucial event involving Dion's friend Heraclides, leader of the Syracusan democratic faction, however, changed everything. A debacle over mercenary pay was blamed on Heraclides, who fled for his life and joined Dion. An inscription of the sanctuary of Asclepius at Epidaurus honors them together (*Inscriptiones Graecae* IV² 95.39–40). Dionysius meanwhile promised another of the democratic leaders special terms for Heraclides, if he would return to face charges, and Plato happened to be on hand to swear his oath as witness to the tyrant's promise. When, the next day, the tyrant seemed already to be breaking his word, Plato duly invoked the promise he had witnessed, which the tyrant duly denied, stinging Plato yet again. Taking Plato's action as a choice of Dion over himself, Dionysius moved Plato out of the fortress into the house of Archedemus, in the area of the city housing the tyrant's mercenaries.

If Plato had been a virtual prisoner before, now he was in danger: Athenian rowers among the mercenaries told him some of their number were plotting to kill him, so he began desperately sending letters for help. Through the intercession of Archytas, a Tarentine ship was sent to the rescue. But Plato did not return to Athens. He disembarked at Olympia and caught up with Dion at the games, delivering the news of the tyrant's further intransigence: in effect, the news that Plato had failed to accomplish anything worthwhile for Dion or for philosophy in seven years of Sicilian misadventure (VII.350D4–5). Dion's first reaction was to call for vengeance; and he wanted Plato's friends, family, and the old philosopher himself to join him. Plato refused on several grounds and offered instead his assistance in the event that Dion and Dionysius should ever desire friendship and to do one another good. That was never to be, although Dion's later actions show that his desire for revenge had been extinguished before the liberation of Syracuse, a mission he pursued "preferring to suffer what is unholy rather than to cause it" (VII.351c6–7).

Plato kept himself informed of his friend's efforts and continued to offer advice during the three years required to garner the necessary financial backing and to hire mercenaries covertly before Dion could finally set sail in 357, making a gift of his estate in Athens to Speusippus. Members of the Academy appear to have had high hopes for a philosopher-ruler: Plato had described them as "pushing" him into the third trip (VII.339D8–E1), and at least one member, Timonides of Leucas, went along to record Dion's operations for Speusippus and history. Heraclides remained behind to bring additional troops and triremes. Because Dion's contingent, including thirty Sicilian exiles, arrived while Dionysius' army was out of the city, Dion entered unopposed and was hailed as the liberator of the Sicilian Greeks. He was elected general-in-chief and enjoyed the support of all Syracuse – except the tyrant's fortress on Ortygia where Dion's wife and son were being held.

Dionysius feigned abdication, but sent his army to stealth-attack while negotiating the details; there were other deceptions, and military skirmishes that earned Dion a reputation for heroism. When Heraclides arrived with twenty additional triremes and 1,500 mercenaries, there was initial cooperation. The amity deteriorated, however, over Heraclides' official appointment as general, the tyrant's escape by sea on Heraclides' watch, and because Heraclides was more popular than Dion, causing strife among their respective followers. Heraclides and Dion had to make repeated attempts to bring their supporters together in common aims. Two turbulent years passed before Ortygia was finally open in the summer of 354, Dion's eleven-year separation from his family ended, and the citizen Assembly could debate domestic issues: redistribution of land and property, and whether there should be a Council. Within months, however, Heraclides was assassinated by some of Dion's supporters, and Dion was assassinated by an Athenian, Callippus, who had befriended him, hosted him in 366, and accompanied him to Sicily. Callippus, who, Plato insists, had no connection to the Academy, immediately declared himself tyrant. Plato, writing some six years after the meeting in Olympia, and some weeks or months after Dion's death, compares his friend of thirty years to a pilot who correctly anticipates a storm but underestimates its capacity for destruction: "that the men who brought him down were evil, he knew, but not the *extent* of their ignorance, their depravity and their greed" (VII.351D7–E2).

Plato's Final Years

After 360, Plato remained in Athens where there had been a number of changes in his family, and in the flourishing Academy. One of the letters with a small claim to authenticity mentions that two nieces had died, prompting Plato in about 365 to accept partial responsibility for four grandnieces ranging in age from not-yet-one to marriageable – which in Athens meant a year past puberty. The eldest was in fact on the verge of marrying her uncle Speusippus, then in his early forties and in line to be second head of the Academy (XIII.361c7–E5). Plato's mother had died some time after 365, but his sister Potone and at least one of his brothers had married and produced children and grandchildren. A "boy" Adeimantus, probably the grandson of Plato's brother of that name, was the recipient of Plato's estate. The elderly Plato was surrounded also by colleagues at the Academy: many names of his associates are extant. There was detailed record-keeping in the last decade of Plato's life, and the succession of Academy heads is preserved, so it is reasonable to suppose that rosters of students were drawn up from time to time during the nearly forty years of Plato's leadership. Besides those mentioned already – Aristotle, Eudoxus, Timonides, and Speusippus – notables in the late days include two women, Axiothea of Phlius, and Lasthenia of Mantinea; Heraclides of Pontus, historian; Hermodorus of Syracuse, biographer; Philippus of Mende, aka Philip of Opus, likely editor of Plato's late works; and Xenocrates of Chalcedon, who would succeed Speusippus.

We should reject the standard image of the old Plato, devoting his halcyon years to squinting with his stylus over *Timaeus-Critias*, *Sophist*, *Politicus*, *Philebus*, *Laws*, and Letter VII, for the image is as unrealistic as it is unnecessary. Although those works share statistically incontrovertible stylistic features that argue for their having been written or edited by one individual, *Epinomis* was uncontroversially written and published after Plato's death, yet it has the unmistakable, turgid prose of the others, suggesting that Plato enjoyed the assistance of a scribe whose responsibility it was to reformulate Academic productions into the approved Academic style. I say "productions" because there is good reason to suppose that Plato's Academy was like other ancient institutions (e.g., Hippocrates' and Aristotle's schools, Hellenistic Pythagoreans) in undertaking collaborative writing projects. *Laws* is almost certainly such a collective effort, with sustained dialectical argument confined primarily to Books I–II, and incomplete when Plato died (Nails and Thesleff 2003). A small number of brief passages in *Republic* appear to have suffered under the editor's hand too, suggesting that that great dialogue achieved its present form only very late in Plato's life.

Similarly, we should reject the image of a Plato who instructs initiates orally or gives doctrinal lectures (though Aristoxenus attributes to Aristotle an anecdote about a lecture on the good, *Harmonics* 30–1). In extant fragments, Plato's colleagues make no appeals to what the master *said*, though they engage in healthy disagreement about the nature of reality and knowledge, and about the meaning of obscure claims made by characters in dialogues (Cherniss 1945). We should reject these images for a strong epistemological reason. Plato

> remains convinced throughout that anything taken on trust, second-hand, either from others or from books, can never amount to a worthwhile cognitive state; knowledge must be achieved by effort from the person concerned. Plato tries to stimulate thought rather than to hand over doctrines. (Annas 1996: 1190)

Notes

All translations are the author's unless otherwise noted.

1   Most readers resist being buried in the exceptions, qualifications, citations, and asides that are necessary for a complete account; for more nuanced and more comprehensive arguments, and assessments of sources, see Nails 2002, including entries for Plato and all other persons mentioned herein.

11

2   Taylor's *Plato the Man and his Work* appeared first in 1927, sticking close to the Alexandrian model. Ryle (1966) and Randall (1970) challenged Apollodorus' just-so story, but did not reassess available evidence.
3   The letter is addressed to Dion's family and friends. Only if other letters, the will, and a few epigrams attributed to Plato are genuine is there additional autobiographical information about him.

References and further reading

Annas, J. (1996). Plato. In S. Hornblower and A. Spawforth (eds.) *Oxford Classical Dictionary* (pp. 1190–3). Oxford: Oxford University Press.
Cherniss, H. F. (1945). *The Riddle of the Early Academy.* Berkeley: University of California Press.
Davies, J. K. (1971). *Athenian Propertied Families 600–300 BC.* Oxford: Clarendon Press.
Jacoby, F. (1902). *Apollodors Chronik.* Berlin: Weidmann.
Ledger, G. R. (1989). *Re-Counting Plato: A Computer Analysis of Plato's Style.* Oxford: Oxford University Press.
MacDowell, D. M. (1978). *The Law in Classical Athens.* Ithaca, NY: Cornell University Press.
Nails, D. (1995). *Agora, Academy, and the Conduct of Philosophy.* Dordrecht: Kluwer.
—— (2002). *The People of Plato: A Prosopography of Plato and Other Socratics.* Indianapolis: Hackett.
Nails, D. and Thesleff, H. (2003). Early academic editing: Plato's *Laws.* In S. Scolnicov and L. Brisson (eds.) *Plato's Laws: From Theory into Practice* (pp. 14–29). Sankt Augustin: Academia.
Randall, J. H., Jr. (1970). *Plato: Dramatist of the Life of Reason.* New York: Columbia University Press.
Riginos, A. S. (1976). *Platonica: The Anecdotes Concerning the Life and Writings of Plato.* Leiden: Brill.
Ryle, G. (1966). *Plato's Progress.* Cambridge: Cambridge University Press.
Taylor, A. E. (1956). *Plato: The Man and his Work.* Cleveland: World.
Thesleff, H. (1967). *Studies in the Styles of Plato.* Helsinki: Suomalaisen Kirjallisuuden Kirjapaino.
—— (1982). *Studies in Platonic Chronology.* Helsinki: Societas Scientiarum Fennica.
Westlake, H. D. (1994). Dion and Timoleon. In D. M. Lewis, et al. (eds.) *The Cambridge Ancient History*, vol. 6: *The Fourth Century BC* (pp. 693–722). Cambridge: Cambridge University Press.
Woodbridge, F. J. E. (1929). *The Son of Apollo: Themes of Plato.* Boston: Houghton Mifflin.

2

Interpreting Plato

CHRISTOPHER ROWE

That Plato was a philosopher I take for granted, whatever else he may have been: for example, perhaps the greatest exponent of Greek prose writing, or a dramatist of the first order – a role whose importance for the present context will immediately become apparent. However the job of interpreting almost any other philosopher, ancient or modern, is easier than interpreting Plato. The chief reason for this – if it is reasonable also to assume that he is concerned to communicate with others, and is not merely writing for himself – is that he always addresses his reader in an indirect way: constructing dialogues, i.e. dramatized conversations, in which he never appears as a character himself. (Certain letters have come down to us in Plato's name, only one of which – the seventh – has much chance of being genuine. But even if it were by Plato, it would hardly help us; we would not even know from the letter *that* Plato wrote dialogues, let alone how to interpret them.) (See 1: THE LIFE OF PLATO OF ATHENS.) We then have to ask where, if anywhere, we find the author's authentic voice – and that is itself far from an easy question to answer, insofar as the central character in the majority of dialogues, Socrates, typically suggests that ideas he puts forward really come from some other source: just "someone I heard," or some named individual, like the priestess Diotima in the *Symposium* (probably herself a fiction); or else he suggests that they are merely provisional. (On the issues, see, e.g., Klagge and Smith 1992; Press 2000.) Add to that the point that a significant number of dialogues at least superficially end in *aporia* or impasse, and it is not difficult to see why some interpreters, ancient and modern, have proposed that Plato had no definitive proposals to make, no conclusions of his own to propound, to his readers: either, as the ancient Platonist (Academic) skeptics suggested, because he really was himself a skeptic, whose message was that we should look for the truth without any expectation of finding anything better than the merely probable; or because his chief or ultimate aim was to encourage us to *do philosophy*, and think things out for ourselves rather than supposing that we can get what we need from others, or from books. The latter is the view most congenial to the skeptics' natural modern successors, interpreters brought up in the analytical tradition.

Yet if we look at the whole history of Platonic interpretation, the dialogues have far more often been read as the source of a highly distinctive and connected set of views about human nature and existence, and about the world in general, held with a firmness that no skeptic could ever think justified. Either – so these more numerous, mostly "Neoplatonic," readers have held – these views are there in Plato's writings to be read off, by the expert interpreter, from each and every dialogue, or else (in a relatively recent variant of this same "dogmatic" mode of interpretation) they lurk behind the dialogues themselves, in the shape of what Aristotle calls the "unwritten doctrines"; for the latter approach, see, e.g., Krämer 1959; Szlezák 1985, 2004. ("Dogmatic" is here used merely as a convenient term to contrast with "skeptical." Few modern readers would in fact treat Plato as a "dogmatist," in view of the explicit descriptions of the philosophical process to be found in the dialogues.) The latter kind of reading is certainly attractive if, for example, one chooses to concentrate on the kinds of ideas that seem to have been put forward by Plato's immediate successors as head of the Academy, Speusippus and Xenocrates. What could be more natural than to suppose that they were following in Plato's footsteps, and that their perspectives were actually much like Plato's, only put more explicitly and directly, and no longer hidden behind fictional dialogues?

It must be said at once that the balance of probability seems to lie with the "dogmatic," or "doctrinal," sort of interpretation rather than with its "skeptical" counterpart. There are just too many occasions in the dialogues when even Socrates not only appears to commit himself to positive ideas (to the extent that he commits himself to anything), but offers no reason for rejecting them: about the unreliability of ordinary assessments of what is good and bad; about the importance for all human beings of knowledge, and of "virtue," i.e., the various "virtues" like justice, courage, and "moderation" or "self-control" (i.e., *sōphrosunē*, traditionally and unhelpfully translated as "temperance"); about the need for us humans to assimilate ourselves to the gods, whom Socrates typically treats as ideal knowers; and so on. While there is not much here that is actually incompatible with some moderate – Academic? – type of skepticism, still the skeptical reading is likely to strike most readers as getting the emphasis of the whole badly wrong. Important though the qualifications are that attach to (what appear to be) the outcomes of the dialogues, we are given every encouragement, by the way the dialogues are written, to suppose that those outcomes matter more to the author – or at least to his character Socrates – than the qualifications attaching to them; if the truth is ultimately inaccessible to us, nevertheless Plato continually suggests (as a skeptic surely could not) that we can to a greater or lesser degree *approximate* to it, acquire a greater or lesser grasp of it.

Yet "dogmatic" interpretations are by no means the only alternative to a skeptical reading; and indeed it will seem to many, even among those who are not skeptical readers themselves, already to take too much for granted. First, there are those, mainly literary theorists in the postmodern mode, who will protest that such a way of taking Plato, if it is put forward as the *right* way of taking him (as in the present context it certainly is), illegitimately presupposes the feasibility of a project that is by its very nature unfeasible: recovering the truth about Plato, as if there were some single way that Plato, or his texts, or anything, really *are*. No matter that – thanks especially to those centuries of "dogmatic" interpretation – Plato's name has become synonymous with this kind of error (call it "essentialism," and Plato will be the "essentialist" par excellence), still he too must be allowed to have many voices. This is not so much because of the difficulty of recovering the intention of an author, one who is not only dead but seems to have willfully avoided telling us what he was about; it is rather that texts in general are like that. (For a subtler and more nuanced version of the approach I describe so crudely here, see Blondell 2002.)

Here is the weakness of the postmodernists' objection: if they are ultimately relying on the unproven claim that no text is univocal, then unless the claim is merely trivial they will themselves be assuming too much. Literary texts may be impossible to pin down, and maybe we should not wish to pin them down; but why should not *philosophical* texts – and even highly literary philosophical texts – be different?

Much more threatening to any sort of "dogmatic" interpretation of Plato will be the charge that it takes for granted that *the interpreter is entitled to read any single dialogue in the light of others*, when the dialogues themselves (so the argument runs) rarely invite us to do any such thing, since they are for the most part independent artifacts. Occasionally, as with *Theaetetus*, *Sophist*, and *Statesman*, dialogues form a series, with each successive conversation referring explicitly to the one before, among the same set of interlocutors. *Timaeus* and *Critias* belong together in the same way as the *Theaeteus-Sophist-Statesman* group, and *Timaeus* seems to refer back to a conversation very like that represented in the *Republic*, though the interlocutors – apart from Socrates – are different. (*Timaeus* and *Critias* were evidently meant to be rounded off with a *Hermocrates*, *Statesman* to be followed by a *Philosopher*.) These, however, are the exceptions: the general rule, over the other thirty or so genuine dialogues, is that each starts afresh, and usually with a different interlocutor or set of interlocutors; sometimes Socrates is himself supplanted in the role of main speaker. Plato did not *have* to write like this, since in principle he might have written all his dialogues as a series of linked conversations between the same or similar casts, with references backwards and even perhaps forwards between them. It must be our business – so it may be said (see especially Grote 1865) – to recognize this fundamental feature of Plato's oeuvre, especially since to override it will leave us open to the charge of prejudging the admittedly controversial issue about whether or not there is anything like a unified system contained within the dialogues.

It must be said in any case that the attempt to apply a thoroughly "unitarian" approach to Plato's works immediately runs into considerable difficulties. Ancient interpreters, of whatever persuasion, tended simply to assume that Plato was always saying the same thing (whatever it was), and they could get away with it by virtue of simply ignoring those parts that might have appeared to say something different to a different, and perhaps more exacting, kind of reader. But the problem is that Plato often *does* seem to say – have his leading character(s) say – different things in different places, and indeed not infrequently to contradict himself. To meet this kind of problem, one of the commonest modern responses is to suppose that Plato's thinking underwent significant developments: that is, that he changed his mind on key issues (as indeed is the modern – as opposed to the ancient – expectation of a philosopher), in some cases abandoning what had come to seem to him untenable positions, in other cases refining what had earlier been put more crudely, and so on. This "developmentalist" approach to the interpretation of Plato has since the 1950s or before become standard at least in the Anglophone world, and has hardened into a particular thesis about Plato's intellectual career. The thesis is that he began by writing "Socratic" (or "early") dialogues, imitating the methods and preoccupations of his master Socrates; that he then broke free, in the "middle" dialogues, and introduced some of his most characteristic ideas, especially in metaphysics (more than anything I refer here, of course, to the "Theory of Forms"); but that in his "late" period he finally moved away from the optimistic "middle" constructions in the direction of a soberer kind of reflection. Looked at in this way, "developmentalism" is as much a strategy for *maintaining* a kind of "unitarian," or at least unifying, approach, as it is an alternative to it. "Developmentalism," that is, presupposes the same license to interpret one dialogue from another, or from others, except that that license is now more restricted or localized (reading between dialogues that happen to be located within any one period, but by and large not between dialogues falling in different periods). And just as the "dogmatic" reading has more initial plausibility than the "skeptical," not least because of the positive themes and ideas that *recur* in different dialogues, so the "developmentalist" approach seems initially more plausible than the plain "unitarian," just because it takes account of the way recurrence can appear to go hand in hand with reformulation – and indeed of the way themes and ideas, instead of recurring, may in fact disappear from the scene. (For some tastes, what I am now saying may well seem to take too little notice of dramatic, or more generally literary, form: see above. In common with many interpreters of Plato, I am presently speaking as if dramatic dialogue were merely another way of doing what could have been done through monologue. I shall, however, shortly be returning to these issues.) (See 4: FORM AND THE PLATONIC DIALOGUES.)

At the same time, the "developmentalist" approach – or at any rate the kind of "standard" version of "developmentalism" I have described – has its own weaknesses. A first objection, and perhaps the most important, is that it seems psychologically implausible that Plato should turn his back on Socrates intellectually (i.e., in the "middle" dialogues), and yet still continue to use him as main character – to introduce the very ideas that are *replacing* his (Socrates') own. Various ways can be found of mitigating this problem, but a problem it nevertheless remains. A second objection to the standard "developmentalist" approach is that it overstates the differences between the three groups of dialogues; a third is that the division into groups is itself uncertain and controversial.

An illustration of the second objection is Kahn 1996, which argues that the "early" dialogues are best read as somehow preparing the way for, and representing part of the same project as, the *Republic*, the quintessential "middle" dialogue for those who believe in a "middle," and newly metaphysical, Plato. I shall myself shortly propose a reading that is, in a way, a mirror image of Kahn's, but has the same effect of narrowing the gap between "early" and (supposedly) "middle." As for the division between "middle" and "late," the majority of those working on Plato's political dialogues probably now agree that *Republic* ("middle") and *Laws* ("late," and in fact latest of all) might just as well have been written at the same time, for all the "development" in political thinking that can be identified between them (see Laks 1990). And it is far from clear what "Forms" are, or how exactly their introduction changes the philosophical landscape (a point to which I shall return) (see 12: THE FORMS AND THE SCIENCES IN SOCRATES AND PLATO); and yet, according to the version of the "developmentalist" hypothesis in question, it is probably the most important single marker of the shift from "early"/"Socratic" to "middle" (see Vlastos 1991, and further below; for a subtler treatment Fine 2003: 298; *contra*, Rowe 2005).

As it happens, three of the dialogues in which Platonic Forms seem to figure – *Phaedo*, *Symposium*, and *Cratylus* – in fact belong, according to the best stylometric evidence, to the earliest group of dialogues (this is the third kind of objection to the standard "developmentalist" reading of the dialogues, namely that we ultimately have no good reason to accept the division of dialogues on which it depends; see Kahn 2002). ("Stylometry" is the study of the identifying features of an author's style, particularly features of which he or she may be presumed to be unconscious; if such features vary between different works or groups of works, one explanation may be that the works in question were written at different times. One might compare different "periods" in a painter's, or a composer's, output.) So, if stylometry is worth anything, and if stylistic differences here indicate dialogues written in different periods, some allegedly "middle" dialogues are "early."

Significant changes in Plato's thinking need not, of course, have coincided with changes in his style of writing. Nevertheless the so-called, standard, "middle" dialogues, including the stylistically earlier three, are as a group markedly different from the "early" ones in terms of structure, and above all of ambition. Only one of the dialogues that the standard "developmentalist" view tends to place before the "middle" period, namely the *Gorgias*, is written on the same sort of *scale* as the great (so-called) "middle" works like the *Republic* – to which the *Gorgias* is comparable in other respects too, even though unlike the *Republic* it lacks any mention of (allegedly "middle-period") Forms. "Early," "Socratic," dialogues like *Euthyphro*, *Charmides*, or *Lysis* by contrast tend to be short and to end in *impasse* (see above). So *something* about Plato's "style" in the (so-called) "middle" dialogues seems to be different, even if it does not show up at the level of the microscopic analyses of the stylometrists. However, if the larger kind of stylistic difference in question – the sheer size of the constructions involved – corresponds to no clear, and clearly significant, shift in terms of content (I here refer again to the issue about the difference that "Forms" make: see above), that larger stylistic difference ceases to add much to the "developmentalist" case, insofar as *this* case is couched in terms of content. Rather, Plato's turning to the bigger scale (in the case of the *Republic*, the monumental) might suggest a shift in his attitude to his *audience* – and/or in his view of the kind of audience he needs to address: perhaps a larger, less specialized one, to the extent that the larger works tend to be more accessible, and intelligible, at least at some level, than the shorter ones.

I shall return to this point in a moment. Here I wish merely to suggest, without arguing for it, an alternative and somewhat attenuated version of the "developmentalist" approach; a version which is indeed in some respects so attenuated that it may seem, in the end, hardly distinguishable from a moderate "unitarian" view.

The standard version of "developmentalism" sees various sorts of changes, not always connected, taking place in the thinking Plato is prepared to put in his character Socrates' mouth in the "middle" dialogues (see especially Vlastos 1991: ch. 2); nevertheless, as I have said, it is the changes relating to "Forms" – first introduced, then (allegedly) abandoned or rethought – that tend to be represented as the most significant. This way of understanding Plato in effect began with Aristotle, who was the first to identify Forms – or, strictly speaking, the "separation" of Forms – as the decisive break-point between Plato and Socrates: Plato made Forms "separate" while Socrates did not. (If "Forms" were universals, which is the only way Aristotle has of taking them, the difference might amount to something like Plato's treating them as real things while Socrates treated them as existing in name only, or only *in* particular things.) Now Aristotle started objecting to this move of Plato's early on in his writing, and he obviously thinks of it as pivotal; but we have no need to follow him and do the same (see 27: LEARNING ABOUT PLATO FROM ARISTOTLE). It may be that a commitment to separate Forms is, or becomes, an indispensable element in Plato's thought, and indeed it is hard to imagine the subsequent long history of Platonism without it. Yet it is at the same time unclear what difference it would have made to Socrates' own project; he seems not to have concerned himself with the ontological status of the things (the good, the just, the beautiful, and so on) he thought it so crucial for us to understand, and it is quite plausible to suppose that he would have greeted Plato's proposal to treat them as independent objects, if that is what "separation" amounted to, with equanimity. That Plato himself would have expected such a reaction might be suggested by the very fact that he actually has Socrates introducing the "Theory of Forms" as something familiar within the context of his philosophical discussions (though admittedly my argument thus far has left a large question mark over the issue of Socrates' being made to act as proponent of non-Socratic ideas: see above, and further below).

What really divides Plato from Socrates, on the non-standard version of "developmentalism" that I am advocating here, is that Plato came to think of human beings as a permanent combination of the rational and irrational. The standard version too acknowledges the same change, but takes it as one among many, occurring separately and independently as Plato asserts his independence from Socratic ideas and methods of argument. The version I prefer instead sees the introduction of irrational parts of the soul – argued for specifically in Book IV of the *Republic* (see 19: THE PLATONIC SOUL; 23: PLATO ON JUSTICE) – (a) as the *source* of many other changes (see especially Rowe 2003); and (b) as leaving other parts of the Socratic position to a surprising extent untouched. Socrates had held to the disconcerting, but – as one might think of it – optimistic, view that we are all fundamentally *rational* (see 18: THE SOCRATIC PARADOXES). ("Socrates" here is not merely the Socrates of Plato's dialogues, but also, at least in part, the historical Socrates. Aristotle's evidence is important here; see below and 3: THE SOCRATIC PROBLEM.) Each and every one of us desires his or her own good, or happiness, the nature of which – starting from where we are now – is in principle discoverable by philosophical reasoning; that is, through reasoning we may hope to determine what it is that is truly good and bad for us, and so achieve whatever degree of happiness may be available to us given our circumstances. What distinguishes us from each other is not our characters, our dispositions or desires (for our desire, or the one that is driving us as we act, is always the same: for what is truly good), but only the *state of our beliefs*. We go wrong, Socrates insisted, only because we are ignorant, that is, of what our true good is. So, if only we can get straight about that, we shall unerringly "do well," i.e., both be happy and – because, as he holds, acting justly, courageously, and so on will always turn out to be part of our own good – be just, courageous, and so on as well. This is the extraordinarily radical kind of account of human action that underlies not only the so-called "Socratic" dialogues, but also at least one of the so-called "middle ones": the *Symposium*, in which, strikingly, Socrates manages to give an extended description of what one might call "romantic" love without once bringing in irrational desires. ("Romantic" love, or *erōs*, from his point of view, will be just another expression of human desire for the good; what matters is that it should be directed towards the right objects, i.e., those that are truly beautiful and good. Contrast the account of *erōs* in the *Phaedrus*, evidently written after the *Republic*, where the story is dominated by the struggle between the charioteer of reason, and his white horse, with the black horse of appetite and lust.) (See 20: PLATO ON EROS AND FRIENDSHIP.)

In Book IV of the *Republic*, by contrast, Socrates argues for the existence of three parts to the soul, one rational and two irrational, the latter capable not only of preventing the agent from carrying through with decisions apparently made by the rational part, but of distorting it on a permanent basis, so diverting it from its natural projects. One of the two irrational parts is associated with anger, or more generally the competitive-aggressive aspects of human existence, the other with our appetitive drives for food, drink, and sex. No longer, on this model, is all desire – all desire, that is, that leads to action – for the (real) good, and no longer are human beings differentiated merely by the condition of their intellect; accordingly, it will take more than reasoning to change the behavior of those behaving in undesirable ways, insofar as it is caused, not by mere ignorance, but by irrational parts that are by their nature not open to reason. (They will need conditioning, or at least some form of training, of a sort that is sketched in *R*. II–III.) This view of human nature, or some variant of it (i.e., some view of human psychology which allows – to borrow more modern terms – that passion may overcome reason), is the one that operates not only in the *Republic* but in the *Phaedrus*, the *Timaeus*, the *Statesman*, the *Laws* – in fact, so far as we can tell, every dialogue likely to postdate the *Republic*. In short, Plato seems to have given up whatever commitment he may have had to that radical Socratic view (that the only cause of our going wrong, and doing what will harm us, is intellectual error) with which he was content to work in pre-*Republic* dialogues.

But why, then (one might reasonably ask), is this version of the "developmentalist" approach not vulnerable to exactly the same kind of objection as the standard version? How is it that Plato can have Socrates – still the main character in the *Republic*, and in thoroughly dominating form – putting forward views that are diametrically opposed to those that he has sponsored so enthusiastically before, as if nothing had changed? Maybe, after all, Socrates is no more than Plato's puppet, who will do whatever the puppet-master makes him do; this might be the sort of case that shows why we should not try reading off *Plato*'s convictions from what he has his characters say. The character Socrates, perhaps we should conclude, is meant just to be the typical philosopher, exploring the options. In that case, we will have gone back to a variety of what I earlier called a "skeptical" type of interpretation of Plato, one that leaves him committed to no particular view of things.

Yet in the *Republic* and in post-*Republic* dialogues, as much if not rather more than in earlier ones, Plato often writes, has his characters (and especially Socrates) speak, in a fashion that plainly exhibits a desire to *change his readers*. That is, he writes with evident conviction. This is not mere academic, theoretical musing. What is more, Aristotle's evidence unambiguously suggests that the theory of action I have attributed to the pre-*Republic* dialogues in fact belonged to the historical Socrates (which is, presumably, at least part of the reason why Plato has the character Socrates in those dialogues perpetually sponsoring it; for Socrates, at any rate, it is not just one possible option, whatever may be true of his author).

So the objection comes back again: if the Plato of the *Republic* is actually rejecting Socrates' core views, the ones he consistently put in his mouth in earlier dialogues, how can he go on blithely using this same highly distinctive character: ugly, erotic, penniless, barefoot (and so on) – even to the extent of having him announce, and argue for, that rejection of his own core views? The objection is a powerful one, but so limited is the attractiveness of the alternative interpretative options ("skeptical" readings; postmodern, or purely "literary," readings that treat the dialogues as essentially open texts; taking the dialogues one by one; and so on) that we have an equally powerful reason for expecting to be able to circumvent it.

The crucial point, if the objection is to be met, is that Plato must have thought the change less significant than it appears to us to be. Somehow or other, we must suppose, he thought of the introduction of irrational parts, capable of overturning and/or perverting reason, as an *improvement* on Socrates' position – a position which, it must be said, is likely to have seemed as implausible to any ancient audience as it is to a modern one. (Aristotle certainly regarded it as incredible.) At first blush this looks unlikely, just insofar as the introduction of irrational parts seems hardly to leave anything of that original Socratic position standing: acting in the best way *doesn't* just depend on the state of our beliefs; there *is* such a thing as character; and so on. But this is by no means the whole story. In the *Laws*, and so towards the very end of his life, Plato is still proposing – through the visitor (to Crete) from Athens who plays the main speaker – that *no one goes wrong willingly*. This the unwary reader is unlikely to have expected; after all, if Plato's diagnosis of error now includes the possibility (even the likelihood) that the agent has been "overcome by passion," or had his or her reasoning capacities perverted by irrational drives, surely such errors must be willing, i.e., voluntary? So they would be on the Aristotelian analysis; not, it seems, on Plato's. From an Aristotelian perspective, treating actions caused – directly or indirectly – by the "passions" as involuntary is a simple mistake; any action caused by what is internal to the agent must be willed by the agent. But Plato's perspective appears to be different (whether or not his pupil Aristotle would come to see it as a mistake). For Plato, post-*Republic*, actions done under the influence of the irrational parts, and contrary to what reason – in its unperverted state – would direct, are not properly wished for, desired, by the agent; any more than actions done as a result of straight intellectual error will be so desired. And this already takes us a long way back in the direction of the Socratic position, at the very core of which is precisely the claim that we never desire what it is not *in fact* good for us. (We may think we desire it, or want it, but that is entirely another matter.)

If all this is accepted, I believe that it should no longer be puzzling that Plato should have *Socrates* sponsoring the introduction of a soul divided between rational and irrational parts, with the irrational parts themselves capable of upsetting the applecart. Apart from cases of "weakness of will," or *akrasia* (i.e., cases where passion intervenes and actually cancels out decisions of reason – as, allegedly, in what are popularly called "crimes of passion"), which for Plato are I think likely to have been very much the exception rather than the rule, it will still be the case that we typically do what our reason tells us; the real difference from the Socratic position will be just that, along with sheer intellectual error (which on the new, Platonic, model might be seen as mere temporary, even immediately self-correcting, mistakes of calculation), there will also be errors of reasoning *caused by* irrational desires or drives. (So it is that the *Timaeus* can talk of intellectual error as actually stemming from bodily disease. Contrast the Socratic position, on which, since all desire that leads to action is for the real good, it is impossible that desire should distort anything; reason goes wrong by itself, e.g., by overreacting to felt desires.) And this difference, I suggest, seemed less important to Plato than his retention of that basic Socratic idea that we are all, as rational beings, oriented towards the real good; not least because his, Plato's, conception of that real good is also (I claim) still identical to that of Socrates.

Such an approach has immediate benefits. Take, for example, the way the argument goes at the end of Book IV of the *Republic*: just as healthy actions promote health in the body, Socrates argues, so just actions promote justice in the soul. So now (he says) we need to go back to our original question, about whether it is justice or injustice that pays. But Glaucon, his interlocutor at this point, says that no further argument is needed; clearly, given what Socrates has said, it's *justice* that's preferable – and Socrates agrees. While his argument, as he expounds it, might satisfy Glaucon, it is hard to see why it should satisfy us, and indeed many modern readers have felt distinctly short-changed; as they have felt short-changed by Socrates' assertion a few lines before that the person the parts of whose soul each do what belongs to them – his own distinctive, not to say peculiar, definition of justice in this context – will be less likely than anyone to do the things normally considered unjust. But the situation will be entirely different if we read the argument against the background of the kind of amended Socratic psychology that I have just imagined Plato as having in mind; for the "healthy" soul, in terms of *that* explanation of human action, will be exactly the one in which (a) reason sees correctly that the just thing is the best thing to do, and (b) there are no countervailing factors, in the shape of undisciplined irrational parts, that interfere with that correct understanding. And, if what all agents want is the maximum good (for themselves), then having and maintaining a "healthy" soul will obviously be preferable to coming to have an "unhealthy" one.

Since none of this is spelled out, it is unlikely to be what convinces Glaucon; his take on the argument seems to be altogether more superficial (we may suppose that for example he is attracted by the analogy between justice and health, especially after injustice in the soul has been associated with embezzlement, temple-robbery, theft, betrayal, the breaking of oaths, adultery, and so on). In this case, as in many others, Plato appears to operate on different levels, having Socrates offer his interlocutors, and perhaps those of his own readers who are on the same level as Socrates' interlocutors, a level – or at least a kind – of argument that is not the same as the one that would interest *him*, or Socrates. In the particular case in question, Socrates in fact said near the beginning of Book II that he himself was satisfied with the arguments he had already developed in Book I, in favor of justice, in response to Thrasymachus; but he says that he'll obviously have to try harder to persuade Glaucon and his brother Adeimantus, who have gone on, at the beginning of Book II, to restate the case for injustice. The whole of Books II–IV are thus designed to convince others about something Socrates says he himself is satisfied he has given sufficient grounds for believing. And if we look closely at the arguments in the two contexts (Book I, and Books II–IV), the difference we find is that those in the first rely on familiar Socratic premises (for example, that justice is wisdom), while those in the second do not – or at least, not on the surface, for as I have suggested, there are grounds for supposing that those Socratic premises are there lurking beneath the surface, providing the real justification for the argument as presented.

What is the reason for this kind of strategy (which I believe to be extremely common in Plato)? This brings us to the vexed question of Plato's use of dialogue, or more generally of dramatic form. It has often been proposed that one of the reasons why Plato writes in the way he does, using dialogue and drama, is that he wishes to avoid simply stating the truth, as if it could be conveyed directly from one mind to another. Intellectual progress (so he is imagined as reasoning) is just not like that; we have to work things out for ourselves. This is fair enough as far as it goes. But it misses out one crucial point: that Platonic, and Socratic, thinking is extraordinarily *radical* – so radical that, if it were presented to us simply and directly, it would strike us, as no doubt it strikes many readers even when it is spelled out, as purely and simply false, and so obviously false as not to be worth investigating. That seems to have been Aristotle's reaction to Socrates' position; Plato's he accommodates only at the cost of wholesale revision (see above). It will certainly matter to Plato that we work things out, rather than thinking that they can be handed to us on a plate. But the truth is that if they were handed directly to us, we should probably not wish to taste them at all. That this is so is shown by the willingness of the majority of modern interpreters to suppose that Plato *moved on* from Socrates (see above). So he has, in a way; but the thesis of the present chapter is that at bottom Plato remains a Socratic. At the same time, he recognizes the distance that is likely to separate himself, and his Socrates, from his audience, and the dialogues typically, if not exclusively, represent a conversation between two quite different positions: a conversation in which Plato's Socrates will frequently appear to take on the coloring, and the premises, of others, while actually trying to bring them round, as far as they can be brought round without a complete change of perspective. The new perspective would involve using the same language, but in a quite different way, so that – to take the most obvious example – a quite different set of things would be called "good" (because they *are* good, while the sorts of things normally called good will at best be neither good nor bad).

The variations that Plato plays on this strategy are almost as numerous as his dialogues, and cannot be described here. But there are some principles of reading which, I propose, will always need to be kept in mind by anyone attempting to read Plato. First, one should always be prepared to follow Plato's Socrates, or his other main speakers, where they lead, however paradoxical the outcomes may be. Secondly, one needs always to try to distinguish between several different things: Socrates speaking *in propria persona*; Socrates taking, or appearing to take, someone else's standpoint; and Socrates appearing to take an alien standpoint when actually – if the argument is to work at all – retaining his own. Above all, we need always to remember that Plato's Socrates *has* a standpoint (even if it subtly changes in the course of the dialogues, especially in relation to what he has to say about human action), and that it is always likely to be in play – even when he is not telling us about it. It is our failure to recognize this that frequently leads us to suppose that there are gaps, or simple fallacies, involved in his arguments, when we have simply misunderstood the premises he is using (because we expect him always to state them, and he does not).

In the present context, given the absence of extended demonstrations of the usefulness of these proposals, and of their capacity to illuminate Plato's text, they must be counted as no more than a set of suggestions for reading. Furthermore, it will be clear enough from the earlier parts of this chapter that they will be deeply controversial. Most controversial of all will be the last proposal, that Plato's Socrates, or his substitutes as chief speaker (who will *overall* speak for Plato) is typically relying on a determinate set of ideas – a "standpoint," as I called it, and a highly distinctive one at that – which he feels no obligation to make explicit even when he is relying on them. (I say "who will overall speak for Plato." There are issues here too, of course. We cannot *assume*, even on the approach I have proposed, that Socrates or any other character will always be expressing Plato's own mind: not only may Plato's characters be arguing *ad hominem*, they may also be presenting a strictly limited perspective, perhaps for a particular kind of audience; and so on.) Yet the chief speakers – as implied by the very possibility of referring to them as such – in Platonic dialogues always dominate the discussion, whether to a greater or to a lesser extent, and the more they keep bringing up the same sorts of substantive ideas (as they do), and doing battle against the same types of opponents (as they also do), the harder it becomes plausibly to propose distancing the author from them. Of course he might sometimes write, for example, in ironic mode; that he should adopt a permanently ironic stance stretches credulity.

To propose, as I have done, that in essence (despite some important divergences) Plato remains a Socratic throughout will hardly be more warmly welcomed than the proposal that he always has more up his sleeve than he declares, and is prepared to use it nonetheless. The idea that the so-called "middle" dialogues – that alleged constellation of dialogues announcing the "Theory of Forms," centered on the *Republic* – mark Plato's break with Socrates is thoroughly embedded in modern – Anglophone – perceptions of the corpus; and in a way the idea fits well with the version of the "dogmatic" Plato, elaborated lovingly by the Neoplatonists, that has predominated since the philosopher's death. The identification of an early, "Socratic," period, and a supposedly more realistic and analytical late one might be seen just as an appropriate modern refinement on a crudely unitarian – and insufficiently analytical – Neoplatonic approach. Yet this modern view is, and always has been, vulnerable, for the reasons I have suggested; among them are the ambiguities of the results reached by the stylometrists (the "middle" dialogues are *not* a stylistically unitary group), and the continuing unclarity about exactly what gains are made, what gains Plato thought were made, and what really is changed, by the introduction of (what used to be called) "middle-period" Forms.

Faced by all this controversy, readers may be tempted to abandon any attempt to read *Plato*, and instead just to concentrate on individual dialogues, or indeed cherry-pick particularly purple passages or contexts – whether in order to luxuriate in Plato's prose, or else to analyze the arguments, one by one. But intelligent readers who expose themselves in this limited way, on a regular basis, to different parts of the corpus are likely before long to notice two things: first, that there are many things in what they are reading that seem just to *fail to make sense* on the basis just of what the text has given them; and second, that there are some ideas, and arguments, which *go on cropping up, in one form or another*.

Plato is at once familiar, because he has been so fundamental to the growth of western culture, and totally unfamiliar: the closer one looks at him, the more peculiar and alien he is liable to appear. Perhaps he is just impenetrable to us. Yet the exchanges in the dialogues often look almost as far away from anything even his contemporaries might have felt comfortable with; indeed, when he portrays those contemporaries confronted with his, and Socrates', ideas we find them frequently disconcerted, uncomprehending. Or perhaps Plato is playing with us, his audience; or else he is merely quirky and provocative (a charge often made against his Socrates). But that is belied by the surely unmistakable earnestness – albeit typically laced with wit – that imbues so many Platonic contexts. (I earlier referred to the *conviction* behind Plato's writing.) There seems no option but to continue the attempt to trace the outlines of the Platonic *mindset*, whether that should turn out to be something that evolved over time or, as I now prefer, in most fundamentals remained faithful to its origins. In the latter case, the Neoplatonists will again have been proved right, in a way: there will be something (more or less) constant that may justly be called Platonism, even if it turns out to be rather more down-to-earth, and owing rather more to Socrates, than they bargained for.

References and further reading

Blondell, R. (2002). *The Play of Character in Plato's Dialogues*. Cambridge: Cambridge University Press.

Fine, G. (2003) [1984]. Separation. Repr. in *Plato on Knowledge and Forms* (ch. 11). Oxford: Oxford University Press.

Grote, G. (1865). *Plato and the Other Companions of Socrates* (3 vols.). London: John Murray.

Kahn, C. (1996). *Plato and the Socratic Dialogue: The Philosophical Use of a Literary Form*. Cambridge: Cambridge University Press.

—— (2002). On Platonic chronology. In J. Annas and C. Rowe (eds.) *New Perspectives on Plato, Modern and Ancient* (pp. 93–127). Cambridge, Mass.: Harvard University Press.

Klagge, J. and Smith, N. (eds.) (1992). *Methods of Interpreting Plato and his Dialogues*. *Oxford Studies in Ancient Philosophy*, supplementary volume. Oxford: Oxford University Press.

Krämer, H. J. (1959). *Arete bei Platon und Aristoteles*. Heidelberg: C. Winter.

Laks, A. (1990). Legislation and demiurgy: on the relationship between Plato's *Republic* and *Laws*, Classical Antiquity 9, pp. 209–29.

Penner, T. and Rowe, C. (2005). *Plato*: Lysis. Cambridge: Cambridge University Press.

Press, G. A. (ed.) (2000). *Who Speaks for Plato? Studies in Platonic Anonymity*. Lanham, Md.: Rowman and Littlefield.

Rowe, C. (2002). Comments on Penner (T. Penner, The historical Socrates and Plato's early dialogues: some philosophical questions). In J. Annas and C. Rowe (eds.) *New Perspectives on Plato, Modern and Ancient* (pp. 213–25). Cambridge, Mass.: Harvard University Press.

—— (2003). Plato, Socrates and developmentalism. In N. Reshotko (ed.) *Desire, Identity and Existence: Studies in Honour of T. M. Penner* (pp. 17–32). Kelowna, BC, Canada: BPR Publishers.

—— (2005). What difference do forms make for Platonic epistemology? In C. Gill (ed.) *Virtue, Norms, and Objectivity* (pp. 215–32). Oxford: Oxford University Press.

Szlezák, T. (1985). *Platon und die Schriftlichkeit der Philosophie. Interpretationen zu den frühen und mittleren Dialogen*. Berlin: de Gruyter.

—— (2004). *Das Bild des Dialektikers in Platons späten Dialogen (Platon und die Schriftlichkeit der Philosophie, Teil 2)*. Berlin: de Gruyter.

Vlastos, G. (1991). *Socrates: Ironist and Moral Philosopher*. Ithaca, NY: Cornell University Press; Cambridge: Cambridge University Press.

3

The Socratic Problem

WILLIAM J. PRIOR

Introduction

Socrates is one of the most famous and influential figures in the western intellectual tradition; but who was he? His disciples included the most influential philosophers of his time, who are credited by historians of philosophy with founding several schools; but what did he teach them? These questions constitute the "Socratic Problem," the attempt to discover the historical individual behind the ancient accounts of Socrates and his philosophy.

Socrates wrote nothing; for our information we depend on four major sources. The earliest source is Greek comedy, primarily Aristophanes' *Clouds*, produced in 423 BCE. Two other associates of Socrates, Plato and Xenophon, wrote extensively about him; their writings, unlike those of several others who also wrote Socratic works, have survived. Unlike these three authors, our fourth source, Aristotle, was not a contemporary of Socrates. Born fifteen years after Socrates' death, Aristotle was a member of Plato's Academy and was presumably familiar with the ancient literature and lore concerning Socrates. He included remarks about Socrates in his systematic treatises on various aspects of philosophy. The Socratic Problem stems in part from questions about the reliability of these sources.

I shall argue below that we know a good deal about the life, character, philosophical interests and method of the historical Socrates. Unfortunately, our knowledge does not extend to what doctrines, if any, he may have professed, which is just what contemporary philosophical scholars most want to know. The uncertainty about Socrates' doctrines is traceable to our earliest sources, and in fact to the portraits of Socrates in our most weighty source, Plato. Socrates was apparently something of a mystery even to his closest associates. I shall begin by discussing the problem of the reliability of our sources; I shall continue by describing what we can safely extract from these sources about Socrates; I shall conclude with a discussion of the problem of the teaching of Socrates.

The Reliability of our Sources

The Socratic Problem arises in part from the fact that none of our sources has impeccable credentials as a biographer. The earliest source of information about Socrates is Greek comedy. Our only complete surviving play featuring Socrates as protagonist is Aristophanes' *Clouds*, the only one of our primary sources that dates to Socrates' own lifetime. Aristophanes portrays Socrates as a "new intellectual," a disbeliever in the gods of traditional Greek religion and a sophist who teaches "unjust argument" to his pupils. Scholars have found reason to minimize the importance of, or ignore, Aristophanes' portrait of Socrates. Comedy is not biography; the relevant question was not, "Is it true?" or "Is it fair?" but "Is it funny?" Aristophanes' portrait looks to many scholars like a composite picture of Athenian intellectuals in the latter part of the fifth century; they have therefore rejected the idea that it contains accurate information about Socrates.

On the other hand, the *Clouds* gives us some important information about Socrates. It says that he was a public figure in Athens, and that Aristophanes thought that the audience would not be able to distinguish his views from those of the sophists and natural philosophers with whom he was, in the public view, associated. If Plato's *Apology* is to be trusted on this point, this is proved to be true. Plato has Socrates cite this play in the *Apology* (18d1–2, 19c2–5) as a major source of prejudice against him. In Plato's eyes, the *Clouds* is, if not an accurate portrait of Socrates, an important source for the popular understanding of Socrates in the late fifth century.

Xenophon wrote his Socratic works in part to defend Socrates against the charges of Aristophanes and others. He wrote four Socratic works: the *Apology*, *Memorabilia*, *Oeconomicus*, and *Symposium*. Xenophon was a companion of Socrates for some time (exactly how long is unclear) during the last decade of Socrates' life. A charming anecdote from later antiquity shows Socrates seeking him out, asking him if he knows where various foods are found, and concluding by asking where men are made gentlemen (*kalos k'agathos*, "fine and good"). When Xenophon can't answer the question, Socrates says, "follow me and learn" (*DL* II.48). Whether or not the anecdote is historical, it reflects Xenophon's interest in Socrates: he saw Socrates as one who made his associates "fine and good." Xenophon did not associate with Socrates to become a philosopher, but to become a gentleman. Unlike Plato, he apparently saw no difficulty in becoming one without becoming the other.

Xenophon was eager to show that Socrates was innocent of the official charges raised at his trial: impiety and corrupting the youth. He devoted the first chapter of his *Memorabilia* to arguing that Socrates was a believer of the most pious and traditional sort. He devoted the bulk of the *Memorabilia* to showing that Socrates was beneficial to everyone who associated with him. Xenophon's Socrates is first and foremost a dispenser of practical moral advice (see, e.g., *Mem.* II.7). He gives this advice not only to his close associates, but to virtually everyone he meets, including cavalry commanders and courtesans. Xenophon rarely shows Socrates in the kind of antagonistic confrontation with an interlocutor that is prominent in Plato's work. He does, however, show Socrates in conversation with sophists (Antiphon and Hippias, in *Mem.* I.6, IV.4), in search of definitions (*Mem.* III.9, IV.6), and as a devotee of *erōs* (*Symposium* 6.8) – all aspects of Socrates that Plato emphasizes. Xenophon's Socrates does not insist on his ignorance, as does Plato's, but he points out to his interlocutors their ignorance, as a preliminary stage of their education. (Hippias does mention Socrates' refusal to answer the questions he asks of others at *Mem.* IV.4.9, but for the most part Xenophon's Socrates is only too willing to state his views.)

Xenophon's portrait of Socrates is valuable for two reasons. First, it corroborates several aspects of Plato's portrait. Second, it emphasizes an aspect of Socrates' life that Plato does not concentrate on: his relations with his disciples. Both Plato and Xenophon depict Socrates as a man who had passionately devoted disciples; Xenophon offers a more extensive explanation than does Plato of how Socrates may have elicited that devotion. Xenophon wrote with a polemical intent: he wanted to show that Socrates was completely innocent of the charges lodged against him by his accusers and the popular prejudice against him. He has been criticized for making Socrates appear bland and uncontroversial; Gregory Vlastos stated that the Athenians never would have indicted Xenophon's Socrates (Vlastos 1971a: 3). Xenophon also attributes to Socrates interests that can only have been Xenophon's own, such as military science and estate management. The length and closeness of his association with Socrates have been questioned by scholars. Because he was not primarily interested in Socrates' philosophy, he is not our best witness to the content of that philosophy. Still, I think it undeniable that Xenophon knew and associated with Socrates, that he was inspired by him, and that he was concerned enough with his reputation to devote a considerable portion of his literary production to his defense.

Unquestionably, our main source of information about Socrates is Plato. Plato became a follower of Socrates in the last decade of Socrates' life, and was one of his closest associates. Unlike Xenophon, Plato was a philosopher; his works emphasize Socrates' philosophical activity. Like Xenophon, he was concerned to show that Socrates was not guilty of the charges raised against him by his accusers; unlike him, he does not downplay the controversial elements of his character and method. Plato's Socrates is a relentless questioner, bent on revealing the interlocutor's ignorance to him. He also insists on his own ignorance, often in explanation of his refusal to answer the questions he raises. In spite of this insistence, Plato's Socrates does put forward, on occasion, philosophical views. At the end of the *Gorgias* (523A–527C) for instance, he presents an account of the immortality of the soul. In the *Crito* (from 47C to the end) he presents both a theory of moral action and a defense of obedience to the law. Reconciling Socrates' advocacy of these theories with his profession of ignorance is a problem for scholars (see 8: SOCRATIC IGNORANCE).

Plato was a great philosopher in his own right, a thinker who developed his own answers to the questions Socrates asked. This raises a question: where, in his works, does Plato present Socrates' views, and where does he present his own? Scholars have hoped to solve this question by dividing Plato's dialogues into three groups: an early group, containing dialogues that (it is argued) present a faithful portrait of the historical Socrates; a middle group, containing dialogues that represent Plato's own philosophical views; and a late group, containing a further stage of Plato's development. This tripartite division, however, has been criticized; both the membership of the respective groups and the order of the dialogues within them have been questioned

(Kahn 2002). Even if we accept the tripartite grouping of the dialogues, however, and the general developmental picture that goes with them, it seems there is no decisive reason to believe that the dialogues of the early group represent the views of the historical Socrates rather than an early stage of Plato's own philosophical thought (see 2: INTERPRETING PLATO).

To solve this problem scholars have turned to the works of our fourth source, Aristotle. As noted above, Aristotle was a member of Plato's Academy during the last twenty years of Plato's life. He would have been able to discuss Socrates with Plato, had he desired, and he would have had access to the Socratic works of other philosophers that are now lost. Though he was not born when Socrates died, his intellectual world was much closer to Socrates' than is ours. Nonetheless, scholars have questioned Aristotle's general credibility as a historian of philosophy (for a negative assessment, see Kahn 1996: 79–87; for more positive evaluations, see Guthrie 1971: 35–9, and Lacey 1971: 44–8). It may be unfair to describe Aristotle as a historian of philosophy, though, rather than as a philosopher writing about other philosophers. His interest in philosophy was systematic, but in developing his own views he made reference to those of his predecessors, including Socrates. His primary aim in doing so was to show that, while earlier thinkers may have anticipated some aspects of his thought, they did not bring it to perfection. His tendency to see earlier thinkers as forerunners of his own view has raised questions about the objectivity of his historical account. Also, as in the case of Plato, the question arises whether Aristotle is reporting what Socrates said, or what he thought Socrates meant. Finally, some critics of Aristotle as a source for Socrates have questioned whether there is anything in his account that is not traceable to Plato's dialogues (Burnet 1912: xxiv).

Aristotle's comments on Socrates are confined to his philosophy, and he gives us several very important pieces of information about it. Here I shall focus on two. First, he confirms Plato's picture of Socrates as one who professed ignorance (*SE* 183b6–7). Second, he tells us that, although Socrates sought definitions and focused attention on universals, he did not "make the universals . . . exist apart" as Plato did (*Metaph.* XIII.4, 1078b29–30). Scholars have taken this passage to provide a crucial distinction between Plato, with his doctrine of separate Forms, and Socrates. They have used the distinction to divide the dialogues into developmental stages: a Socratic group that does not contain the doctrine of separate Forms, and a later Platonic group that does. Aristotle's testimony raises more questions than it answers, however. It is not clear what he is attributing to Socrates: a theory of unseparated universals, such as his own (which would be hard to reconcile with the Socratic profession of ignorance), or merely a methodological interest in universal definition (see 6: PLATONIC DEFINITIONS AND FORMS). Aristotle's testimony on the authorship of the theory of separate Forms contradicts two passages in Plato's dialogues in which Socrates claims to be the author of the theory: *Phd.* 100b1–7 and *Prm.* 130b1–9. This led John Burnet and A. E. Taylor, early in the last century, to reject Aristotle's testimony. Most scholars have sided with Aristotle on this question, but the tension between Plato's portrayal of Socrates and Aristotle's testimony is significant. Aristotle's testimony on Socrates appears to be more objective than that of Plato and Xenophon, but it reflects his own interests, and as it was not based on personal experience it relied, inevitably, on earlier sources, especially Plato.

What our Sources tell us about Socrates

Despite their differences of emphasis, our sources agree about several aspects of Socrates' life, character, philosophical interests and method. Where they concur, we have the best historical evidence about Socrates that we are likely to have. If we reject this evidence, we shall have nothing on which to base our account of the historical Socrates. Where our sources disagree, we may be unable to reconcile them, but in some cases we may not need to: both sides may present aspects of Socrates we ought not to dismiss.

Our sources tell us a good deal about the life of Socrates. He was born in Athens in about 469 BCE, and was a citizen of the city, of the deme Alopece. His father, Sophroniscus, was a stonecutter; Socrates claimed that his mother, Phaenarete, was a midwife. He was married to one Xanthippe and had three sons. Growing up during the Golden Age of Athens he witnessed her disastrous decline and fall in the Peloponnesian War (431–404). During that war he served in the Athenian army as a hoplite (a heavily armed infantryman), a position that suggests a certain level of family wealth. According to Alcibiades and Laches (as reported by Plato), he displayed conspicuous courage in battle. Plato and Xenophon both report two incidents that attest to Socrates' courage in other contexts. First, in the latter stages of the war, when the Athenians wished to try *en masse* ten generals who had abandoned either dead or wounded soldiers after the battle of Arginusae, Socrates, who was serving at the time on the Council, alone refused to put the motion to do so to a vote, on the (correct) ground that it was illegal. Second, when the Thirty Tyrants, who ruled Athens in 403–402, ordered Socrates and several others to arrest Leon of Salamis, he alone in the group refused. Both episodes put his life in considerable danger. The best-known episodes in Socrates' life came at its very end. In 399 Socrates was tried on charges of impiety and corrupting the youth. His prosecutors were Meletus, Anytus, and Lycon. He was found guilty and sentenced to death. He refused to escape from prison, and died by drinking hemlock. Socrates claimed that he had a divine voice that spoke to him on occasion; according to Plato, it only forbade him to undertake actions he was considering. He expressed great interest in, and according to Plato knowledge of, erotics (see 20: PLATO ON EROS AND FRIENDSHIP).

Some of the information I have just given about Socrates' life, such as that concerning his military service, is found in only one source (in this case Plato), but most is found in more than one (chiefly in Plato and Xenophon) and is contradicted by none. It has formed the basis of our historical understanding of Socrates, and it is as certain as anything about an historical figure can be. Uncertainty about Socrates enters the picture when we consider his character. For ancient comedy, Socrates was an eccentric underminer of traditional Athenian values, a "crackpot." He was associated in the public mind with Alcibiades, the most flamboyant figure in Athenian public life in the Peloponnesian War era, and with Critias, the widely despised leader of the Thirty. For his followers, he was a man of the highest moral quality, an inspirational figure. Both Plato and Xenophon refer to him as the most just man of his time. (Plato, *Ep.* VII.324E and *Phd.* 118A; Xenophon, *Mem.* IV.8.)

This controversy cannot be resolved by reference to the agreed-upon facts of Socrates' life. Socrates *was* something of an eccentric in the context of Athenian life, and his threadbare cloak and unkempt appearance were subjects of comic treatment. More importantly, both Critias and Alcibiades were among his associates, and Xenophon and Plato had to argue that he was not responsible for their conduct. Socrates was associated with the pro-Spartan oligarchic elements of Athenian life, and he was a critic of at least some aspects of Athenian democracy, such as election of magistrates by lot; but he chose to die rather than to leave Athens when he had been convicted. If those who knew him best are to be believed, Socrates' personal piety was exemplary; but his willingness to question every traditional belief would have encouraged those who, like Critias and Alcibiades, scoffed at popular religious views. Two features of Socrates' character seem uncontroversial and amply attested by our ancient sources: his courage and his personal integrity. Socrates demonstrated his courage both in battle and on trial, and he showed his integrity (what Xenophon calls his freedom) both by refusing to teach for money and by refusing to compromise his standards when his life was in danger.

Socrates was undoubtedly a complex person. He could not have attracted followers like Xenophon and Plato had he not been a man of virtue, of deep moral seriousness; he could not have attracted followers like Alcibiades if he had not been something of an iconoclast. Moreover, Socrates' virtue must have seemed somewhat enigmatic even to his admirers. It was displayed in action, not in words; as Xenophon has Socrates say to Hippias, "I demonstrate my knowledge of justice by my conduct" (*Mem.* IV.4.10). Unquestionably, Socrates' associates were attracted to him because of the way he lived his life. But what theoretical account of virtue, if any, lay behind that conduct? Did Socrates have anything like a moral philosophy?

Our sources agree that Socrates was primarily interested in ethical questions. They disagree only on whether he was *exclusively* interested in them. Aristophanes portrays Socrates as a teacher of "just and unjust argument," rival views of human conduct, but also as a scientific investigator. Xenophon gives us a Socrates interested in a wide variety of topics, including military tactics and farming, as well as ethics; it seems reasonable to assume, though, that the first two topics represent Xenophon's interests rather than Socrates'. Plato and Aristotle describe him as primarily an ethicist, but Aristotle also attributes to Socrates a theoretical interest in definition and inductive argument (*Metaph.* XIII.4, 1078b27–9), and Plato attributes to him views on the soul.

All of our sources agree again about Socrates' primary method of inquiry: he philosophized by asking questions. No doubt part, at least, of the controversy over Socrates' doctrines stems from this fact about his philosophical method. Whether his aim was to refute a supposed expert or to offer practical moral advice to someone, Socrates' method was to elicit his interlocutor's views by a series of questions and then critically examine them. Aristophanes shows Socrates questioning Strepsiades (*Clouds* 636–99, 723–90); Aristotle, as noted above, says that Socrates only questioned others and refused to answer, for he said he did not know; and Plato and Xenophon show Socrates constantly questioning others. This method of questioning was so character-istic of Socrates that it gave rise to a genre of literature, the *Sokratikoi logoi,* or "Socratic conversations" (see Kahn 1996: 1–35). We derive the "Socratic method" of examina-tion from this source.

It is easy to imagine, when one is participating in or witnessing a Socratic examina-tion, that Socrates must know the answers to the questions he asks. Here again our sources disagree. Plato's Socrates repeatedly insists that he does not know, that he is inquiring just like his interlocutor. This claim is endorsed by Aristotle, but Aristophanes does not mention it and Xenophon writes as if it is not true (though he does have Hippias remark on Socrates' famous refusal to give his own view). It is often easy, even if Socrates does disavow knowledge of the answers to his questions, to treat this disavowal as ironic. That is the response of Thrasymachus in *Republic* I, and it is closely related to some remarks of Alcibiades that we shall consider below. Thus, though there is unanimity among our sources concerning Socrates' method of inquiry, there is no agreement about the sincerity of his profession of ignorance that (on Plato's account, at least) lies behind it.

The Problem of Socrates' Doctrines

This brings us to our final question, the one that, more than any other, has given rise to the Socratic Problem. However much we may know about Socrates' life, his character, his interests, and his method, scholars will be disappointed unless they can determine what, if any, philosophical doctrines Socrates held. Here again, our sources differ; moreover, there is conflict within our most significant source, Plato. Our inability to answer this question concerning doctrine, I shall argue, stems from this conflict. Of our sources, Plato offers us the philosophically richest portrait of Socrates. Not just in the early dialogues, but in the middle and later works, Plato returns again and again to the question of the philosophical significance of Socrates. Three of the most significant Platonic portraits of Socrates occur in dialogues generally *not* regarded by scholars as Socratic.

The first portrait I shall consider occurs in the *Sophist*, a late dialogue. In a series of attempts to define the nature of the sophist, a character named "the Eleatic Visitor" finally suggests that a sophist is someone who cross-examines his interlocutors with the aim of removing from them the false belief that they know something of which they are really ignorant. His intent is to make them angry with themselves and gentle toward others, and to purify their souls so that they might be ready to receive knowledge (230B–D). The Eleatic Visitor's description is an accurate summary of Socrates' activity as described in the early, "Socratic" dialogues. Neither the Eleatic Visitor nor any other character says that the person thus described is Socrates, but it hardly could be anyone else. Socrates on this account is not a propounder of doctrine, but an examiner of the views of others. If he has beliefs of his own, they do not enter into the picture, for his concern is entirely with the purification of others. If there is a philosophical truth to be learned, this Socrates contents himself for preparing the ground for it.

The great advantage of this portrait is that it is largely faithful to the method of the Socratic dialogues, if not to all of their content. If Socratic doctrines do emerge in these dialogues, they do so indirectly, in the context of Socrates' examination of others. A second advantage is that it makes sense of a historical fact about Socrates' disciples. Socrates, as noted above, was surrounded by several philosophers who held very different views. Aristippus was a proponent of the view that pleasure is the good, and founder of the Cyrenaic school of philosophy. Antisthenes' philosophy was the polar

31

opposite of Aristippus'. Simmias and Cebes were Pythagoreans; Euclides was known for some unusual logical doctrines. Then there was Plato, with his own distinctive constructive views. If Socrates espoused no doctrines but only questioned others, it is easy to understand how such a variety of thinkers could have chosen to associate with him, and how they might well have thought that *their* answers to the questions he raised were ones of which he would have approved. If the historical Socrates possessed and taught any positive doctrines, it is less easy to understand how this constellation of disciples could have arisen.

A disadvantage of the portrait of Socrates as a purely critical dialectician is that it does not explain very well his attraction to those young men such as Xenophon who did not go to Socrates for philosophical instruction but for practical counsel, for advice on how to become *kalos k'agathos*. For such young men, the endless repetition of the Socratic technique for twisting his interlocutors into knots would soon have lost its appeal. A better account, from this perspective, is the one Plato puts in Socrates' own mouth in the *Theaetetus* (149A–151D). According to this story, Socrates is an intellectual midwife, after the manner of his mother Phaenarete. He himself is barren: "The common reproach against me is that I am always asking questions of other people but never express my own views about anything, because there is no wisdom in me," he says, "and that is true enough" (150c4–7). Despite his barrenness, Socrates is able to help his associates give birth to intellectual offspring. Some of these are phantoms; they don't withstand his examination. On the other hand, some of his associates "discover within themselves a multitude of beautiful things, which they bring forth into the light" (150D7–8). Socrates complains that some who find their offspring exposed as phantoms have been "literally ready to bite when I take away some nonsense or other from them" (151c6–7). They don't understand that his motive is benevolent. On the other hand,

> With those who associate with me it is different. At first some may give the impression of being ignorant and stupid; but as time goes on and our association continues, all whom God permits are seen to make progress – a progress which is amazing both to other people and to themselves. And yet it is clear that this is not due to anything they have learned from me. (*Tht.* 150D2–7)

The midwife analogy offers an account of what the *Sophist* passage did not. It explains why some people would choose to associate with Socrates for a long period of time. Under his tutelage, they bring to birth "a multitude of beautiful things" (D7–8) which they have discovered within themselves. The language of the midwife analogy is reminiscent of the doctrine of recollection in the *Meno*. In the *Meno* Socrates claimed that everyone has the truth within himself, and that this truth can be elicited by his critical questioning (see 9: PLATO ON RECOLLECTION).

The *Theaetetus* preserves the picture of truth latent within the soul, but with this variation: not all are pregnant with wisdom. Some who come to him are not, and he sends them to other teachers (151B). Most importantly, Socrates himself is barren: he has no wisdom in his soul. One problem with this analogy is that it is not clear exactly *how* Socratic questioning, which is essentially critical, can elicit truth from another's soul. Another is that we almost never see this process at work in Plato's dialogues. The interlocutors in the early dialogues, with the exception of the slave-boy in the *Meno*, never produce a conception that survives Socratic criticism; and, when we do see constructive philosophical positions introduced, they all seem to come from Socrates.

Despite the difficulty of reconciling the midwife analogy with the Platonic dialogues, it forms, with the description of the "noble Sophist" in the *Sophist*, a consistent and highly attractive portrait of the historical Socrates. Both accounts show a Socrates who has no philosophical doctrines, only a method. Though this method is critical in its operation, and designed to make people aware of their ignorance, according to the midwife analogy it leads to the disclosure of true beliefs, and indeed wisdom, in the souls of his companions. Now if we apply this analogy to the case of Plato himself, we get the following analysis: the elenctic method of the early dialogues is the contribution of Socrates, but the positive philosophical doctrines that may be found there, as well as in later dialogues, are the contribution of Plato (see 7: PLATO'S METHOD OF DIALECTIC). It is Plato, not Socrates, who is responsible for the account of the nature and immortality of the soul found in the *Gorgias* and *Meno*, for the theory that virtue is knowledge, for the doctrine of (unseparated) Forms that appears in the *Euthyphro* and *Meno*, and for the theory of moral and political obligation found in the *Crito*. One could argue that, in the midwife analogy, Plato is providing us with a key for the proper interpretation of his dialogues (see Sedley 2004: esp. 37).

As I have said, I find this picture a very attractive account of the historical Socrates. It coheres with the portrait in the *Sophist* while going beyond it to offer an account of the positive side of Socratic philosophy. It explains that positive side, and Socrates' appeal to his disciples, without attributing to him any philosophical theories. It shows us a Socrates whose disciples were philosophers of the most divergent views. It reinforces an intuition that many readers of Plato and Xenophon, have, including myself: that his unique appeal is not to be explained in terms of his doctrines, but in terms of his character and the spirit of inquiry that he unquestionably manifested. It shows what is wrong with all attempts, from the most ancient to the most recent, to fit Socrates into the "doxographical" form of the history of philosophy, which understands philosophers in terms of their theories.

Why, then, should we not simply say that the historical Socrates has been found, and found in his own self-portrait in a dialogue from our weightiest ancient source, Plato? The problem is that Plato offers us another portrait, one that is flatly inconsistent with this one. According to this portrait, Socrates is anything but barren. The portrait is drawn by Alcibiades in the *Symposium*, and it is as vivid and persuasive as the portraits we have already seen. Arriving at Agathon's party late and highly intoxicated, Alcibiades is asked to eulogize Socrates. He begins by comparing him with a Silenus – a statue of a satyr that, when opened, reveals images of gods within (215A–B). The significance of the Silenus analogy is that the outer appearance of Socrates contrasts sharply with what lies within:

> To begin with, he's crazy about beautiful boys; he constantly follows them around in a perpetual daze. Also, he likes to say he's ignorant and knows nothing. Isn't that just like Silenus? Of course it is! And all this is just on the surface, like the outsides of those statues of Silenus. I wonder, my fellow drinkers, if you have any idea what a sober and temperate man he proves to be when you have looked inside . . . In public, I tell you, his whole life is one big game – a game of irony. I don't know if any of you have seen him when he's really serious. But I once caught him when he was open like Silenus' statues, and I had a

33

glimpse of the figures he keeps hidden within; they were so godlike – so bright and beautiful, so utterly amazing – that I no longer had a choice; I just had to do whatever he told me. (*Smp.* 216D2, 216E–217A2)

After a lengthy and comical account of his failed attempts to seduce Socrates, combined with stories of Socrates' courage in combat and of one of his legendary trances, Alcibiades returns to the Silenus analogy at the end of his encomium:

> Even his ideas and arguments are just like those hollow statues of Silenus. If you were to listen to his arguments, at first they'd strike you as totally ridiculous; they're clothed in words as coarse as the hides worn by the most vulgar satyrs. He's always going on about pack asses, or blacksmiths, or cobblers, or tanners; he's always making the same tired old points in the same tired old words. If you are foolish, or simply unfamiliar with him, you'd find it impossible not to laugh at his arguments. But if you see them when they open up like the statues, if you go beyond their surface, you'll realize that no other arguments make sense. They're truly worthy of a god, bursting with figures of virtue inside. They're of great – no, of the greatest – importance for anyone who wants to become a truly good man. (*Smp.* 221D7–222A6)

Alcibiades' Silenus analogy is as masterful a depiction of the power of Socrates as is the midwife analogy. It explains why Socrates should appear a figure suitable for comic treatment, and why he should be dismissed by slow-witted interlocutors. It explains his professed erotic interest in beautiful teenage boys, and at the same time his profession of ignorance, as cases of irony (see 8: SOCRATIC IGNORANCE). It does not go so far as to depict Socrates as a propounder of philosophical doctrines, but it says that he contains within him godlike arguments, uniquely sensible, that are constructive in character: they lead one to true goodness. If you look within Socrates' arguments, says Alcibiades, you will find them rich in images of virtue; and the same is true if you look within Socrates himself.

The midwife analogy and the Silenus analogy are powerful and persuasive, and they are found in our most weighty source for the historical Socrates. But they could not be more at odds. One tells us that Socrates is barren, that he elicits truths from others that he does not possess himself. The other tells us that he is filled with divine arguments and images of virtue in a way that is unique among humans. Each image explains the central feature of the other as a kind of illusion: according to the midwife analogy, Socrates appears to be fertile because he elicits offspring from others; according to the Silenus Analogy, Socrates appears to be sterile because he cloaks his fecundity in a mask of irony.

I see no way of resolving this conflict. One might argue that the two analogies are compatible, in that neither requires us to attribute particular philosophical theories to Socrates. All the Silenus analogy requires, it could be claimed, is that Socrates possesses arguments that can be used to test the philosophical claims presented by others. Thus, the richness of those arguments lies solely in their power to lead the interlocutor toward the truth. Unfortunately, I think this attempt fails. It ignores the fact that the midwife analogy must take Socrates' professions of ignorance as sincere, while the Silenus analogy requires us to take them as ironic. It also ignores the fact that, according to Alcibiades, Socrates, as well as his ideas and arguments, is filled with godlike images of virtue.

We face a "Socratic Problem," in the end, because Plato has left us these two irreconcilable images of Socrates' philosophy, images that our other sources do not enable us to harmonize. It is possible that the historical Socrates was what the midwife analogy tells us he was: a barren exposer of human ignorance whose followers none-theless made progress in discovering philosophical truths. It is also possible that he was what the Silenus analogy tells us he was: an ironist containing within himself uniquely powerful constructive arguments and images of virtue. It is finally possible that he was an inconsistent, paradoxical, mixture of both (see 18: THE SOCRATIC PARADOXES). We are not in a position to resolve this conflict. Nor, apparently, were Plato's ancient interpreters. The skeptical Academy, under the leadership of Carneades and Arcesilaus, took the barren Socrates as their philosophical model. The Middle Academy and Neoplatonic interpreters of Plato saw Socrates as the constructive philo-sopher described by Alcibiades. Our inability to resolve this conflict should in no way undermine the confidence we have in our knowledge of Socrates' life, character, and philosophical interests and method, as sketched in the early part of this paper. It should, however, give pause to those interpreters who have been eager to tell us exactly what philosophical doctrines the historical Socrates held. For before we can answer that question we must be able to say, at least with a high degree of plausibility, that he held any doctrines at all; and this, because of the conflict between the midwife and Silenus analogies, we are in no position to do.

Note

Translations of Plato are taken from J. M. Cooper (ed.) *Plato: Complete Works* (Indianapolis: Hackett, 1997).

References and further reading

Burnet, J. (1912). Introduction. In *Plato's* Phaedo (pp. ix–lix). Oxford: Clarendon Press.

Guthrie, W. K. C. (1971). *Socrates*. Cambridge: Cambridge University Press.

Kahn, C. (1996). *Plato and the Socratic Dialogue*. Cambridge: Cambridge University Press.

—— (2002). On Platonic chronology. In J. Annas and C. Rowe (eds.) *New Perspectives on Plato, Modern and Ancient* (pp. 93–127). Cambridge, Mass.: Harvard University Press.

Lacey, A. R. (1971). Our knowledge of Socrates. In G. Vlastos (ed.) *The Philosophy of Socrates* (pp. 22–49). Garden City, NY: Doubleday.

Patzer, A. (1987). *Der Historische Sokrates*. Darmstadt: Wissenschaftliche Buchgesellschaft.

Prior, W. J. (1996). *Socrates: Critical Assessments* (4 vols.), vol. 1. London and New York: Routledge.

Sedley, D. (2004). *The Midwife of Platonism*. Oxford: Clarendon Press.

Vlastos, G. (1971a). The paradox of Socrates. In G. Vlastos (ed.) *The Philosophy of Socrates* (pp. 1–21). Garden City, NY: Doubleday.

—— (ed.) (1971b). *The Philosophy of Socrates*. Garden City, NY: Doubleday.

—— (1991). *Socrates: Ironist and Moral Philosopher*. Ithaca, NY: Cornell University Press; Cam-bridge: Cambridge University Press.

Part I

PLATONIC METHOD AND THE DIALOGUE FORM

4

Form and the Platonic Dialogues

MARY MARGARET MCCABE

Plato wrote dialogues. Indeed, of his surviving works, almost all depend in some way or another on the dialogue form. And yet there may well be no such thing as a single dialogue form; instead Plato uses dialogue in a multiplicity of ways. Why does he do that – even on those occasions where it seems least successful? How – if at all – does the form of the dialogues relate to their philosophical purposes?

Direct Conversations

Many of the dialogues are *direct* conversations, in densely described settings. In the *Gorgias* Socrates and Chaerephon, coming from the market, encounter Callicles, who has been listening to the rhetorical display just delivered by Gorgias. A three-part discussion develops between Socrates and Gorgias, then Socrates and Polus, and finally Socrates and Callicles; the dialogue ends with a grand myth of the soul's fate in the underworld. The *Meno* refers back to the encounter in the *Gorgias*, and starts without preamble in a debate between Socrates and Meno – himself a follower of Gorgias – about the teachability of virtue. In the *Euthyphro* Socrates and Euthyphro meet just outside the court, each on their way inside: Euthyphro to prosecute his father for impiety, Socrates to defend himself against the charge of corrupting the young. The *Crito* takes place in the prison after Socrates has been condemned to death; Socrates and Crito discuss whether Socrates should attempt to escape before sentence is carried out. The *Cratylus* and the *Philebus* each begin in the midst of a vigorous dispute. The *Phaedrus* describes a riverside meeting between Socrates and Phaedrus, and their discussion about love, about rhetoric, about writing, and about the soul. (*Hippias Major*, *Hippias Minor*, *Laches*, *Menexenus*, *Ion*, and *Alcibiades* are similarly direct.)

These encounters are dramas, and their protagonist is Socrates. But the *Sophist* and the *Statesman* describe an occasion when Socrates met a Stranger from Elea. This Stranger takes the leading role; and his interlocutor is, in each case, a young, and amenable, companion of Socrates. Likewise the central role of the *Timaeus* is taken, not by Socrates, but by the cosmologist Timaeus; and the *Critias* is a speech by Critias on the story of Atlantis. The *Laws* leaves Socrates out altogether: this is a conversation between Cleinias, Megillus, and the Athenian Stranger, who takes the protagonist's role.

As Socrates recedes into the background the dialogues themselves seem to lose their dramatic character. They were written, many think, late in Plato's career; perhaps the dialogue form has become banal. Originally, Plato may just have followed the example of others; there seems to have been an industry in writing Socratic dialogues in the period after Socrates' death. Or he may have followed a rather different tradition, influenced, no doubt, by the democratic institutions of classical Athens; the presentation of abstract thought moved from plodding verse (à la Parmenides) or neat aphorism (à la Heraclitus), towards adversarial argument (e.g., in the sophistic *Dissoi Logoi*, "Double Arguments," parodied in Aristophanes' *Clouds*). Plato may have used dialogue instrumentally, a way of presenting argument in a dramatic format, congenial to the theater-loving Athenians. So perhaps the dialogue form is merely the outcome of cultural forces; and as such, just a formal matrix into which some philosophical arguments are placed. Its purpose, on such a view, would be to blandish the reader, to make acceptable abstract argument, to slake the aridity of pure philosophical discourse (whatever that might be).

This account of the relation between philosophy and how it is written suggests that there is no direct philosophical function to the dialogue form. But the characterization of the *form* as corresponding to one genre ("literary," "oratorical," and so forth) and the *argument* as corresponding to another ("philosophical," "logical," and so forth) is tendentious. What is more, it seems to shove Plato into his own trap. For Socrates frequently attacks rhetoric for substituting blandishment and persuasion for reason (*Grg.* 453A1–461A1). If the form of a dialogue is designed to persuade, where its arguments are designed to reason, does the dialogue form take the disgraceful part of the orator? Does it take the wrong side in the ancient quarrel between poetry and philosophy (*R.* 607B5)?

Frames and Framed

But not so fast. For Plato's use of the dialogue form is less uniform than the examples above might suggest – less uniform and composed in rich, resonant ways. Consider a different group of dialogues, whose setting is more complex than the last.

Five dialogues (*Charmides, Lysis, Protagoras, Euthydemus,* and *Republic*) are narrated by Socrates himself; the dialogue is the story that he tells. Here, therefore, one of the protagonists (Socrates) speaks of his own contributions in the first person. The engagement with the interlocutors seems all the more immediate – and the views of Socrates seem privileged over those of the other characters. That might tempt us to suppose that Socrates represents Plato; sometimes it is easy to assume that "I" in the *Republic* is the author himself, in this dialogue which is often taken to be Plato's magnum opus, his own account of pretty much everything to which he might turn his philosophical attention.

But sometimes this assumption comes under attack, as we are forced to notice the way the dialogue is composed, and to pay critical attention to the exact role of Socrates. Consider an incident in the *Protagoras*. The main part of the dialogue is narrated by Socrates to an unnamed friend. The friend asks him to describe his encounter the day before with the great sophist Protagoras. Socrates agrees, with alacrity, and recounts the whole lengthy meeting. Protagoras turns out to be a tricky interlocutor, reluctant to abandon his habit of making long speeches and elaborate comments. Socrates, however, insists on short question and answer discussion. Protagoras, notable for his ability to keep it short (329B1–5), agrees to Socrates' request, but soon relapses into verbiage. Socrates complains:

> Protagoras, I tend to be a forgetful sort of person, and if someone speaks to me at length I tend to forget the subject of the speech. Now, if I happened to be hard of hearing, and you were going to converse with me, you would think you had better speak louder to me than to others. In the same way, now that you have fallen in with a forgetful person, you will have to cut your answers short if I am going to follow you. (*Prt.* 334C8–D5; trans. Lombardo and Bell)

Socrates' remark comes at the end of a series of points about method and procedure, but its extraordinary nature should not escape us: how could the Socrates who can give us an apparently verbatim account of the whole encounter claim that he is forgetful? There is irony here, for sure – but why? The bad fit between Socrates' account of himself and his ability to tell the whole tale calls attention to just how the dialogue itself is being set up: why?

Other dialogues are similarly self-conscious. We might think the *Phaedo* a tragedy, a moving account of Socrates' last day, of his arguments about the immortality of the soul, and of the devastation of his friends at his death. The dialogue has a pietistic air, and that again might suggest that Plato sees himself as Socrates. What, then, are we to make of the rare reference to Plato himself, at the beginning when Phaedo, recounting the story to his friend Echecrates, lists those who were present? Many prominent Socratics are named – then Phaedo says, "but Plato, I think, was ill" (59B10). We should be brought up short: if Plato was ill, how are we to take this record of what happened? Now this is pointedly a story, an elaboration, even a fiction, not a set of minutes of the meeting in the prison. And that renders problematic Plato's relation to Socrates if, unlike the other Socratics, he did not hear the final arguments of his master. Is the relation more complex, less direct, less easy to read than as the recording of doctrines heard from the mouth of his master? A further feature of the *Phaedo*'s drama reiterates the question. The "frame" dialogue is the direct encounter between Phaedo and Echecrates, within which Phaedo narrates the events in the prison. But twice the frame breaks in on the narration. On the first occasion (88C8–89A9), the frame reflects the framed argument, as Echecrates comments that he is convinced by an objection to Socrates' claim that the soul is immortal. On the second (102A3–B1), after an extremely convoluted (and hotly disputed) passage, Echecrates suddenly pronounces himself satisfied by the utter clarity of Socrates' account. Good for Echecrates: but Plato's readers may be less sanguine – and the interruption itself surprises us: why does the frame suddenly obtrude at these very moments?

The interruptions undoubtedly call attention not only to individual points in the argument, but also to the way in which the dialogue is written. The same effect occurs in the *Euthydemus*, again a dialogue told within an outer frame. Socrates recounts to Crito a meeting he had the previous day with the brother sophists Euthydemus and Dionysodorus (Crito was present, but unable to hear what happened). Here again, the

41

frame erupts into the narrated discussion (290E1), as Crito comments with incredulity on Socrates' account of how the framed argument is proceeding. Thenceforth the argument is carried on in the frame for a while, as a direct discussion between Socrates and Crito. Once again, the interruption calls attention both to a particular moment in the argument itself; and to the very fact that the discussion is narrated. Is there a philosophical purpose here?

Fiction and Reporting

Consider three more complicated cases: *Theaetetus*, *Symposium*, and *Parmenides*. The *Theaetetus* is a dialogue between Euclides and Terpsion, anticipating the death of Theaetetus, wounded in battle. Euclides mentions the meeting years ago between Theaetetus, then a young man, and Socrates shortly before his death. Euclides himself was not present on that previous occasion; but Socrates told him of it. Euclides confesses that while he is unable to reproduce Socrates' tale from memory (unlike Socrates, then), he has a written record, whose accuracy he checked with Socrates. He has set the conversation down in direct speech, to avoid the elaborations of "and then he said" and so forth. This extraordinarily elaborate introduction foregrounds not only the dialogue's claims to truthfulness (Euclides makes a great fuss about the accuracy of his report) but also, by emphasizing the reader's distance from the action, its fictionality.

Compare the beginnings of the *Symposium* and the *Parmenides*, both of which embed the central dialogue in an elaborate reportage. In the *Symposium* the story is told by Apollodorus to an unknown listener, the day after he had recounted it to Glaucon (who had heard about it from Phoenix). Apollodorus heard it from Aristodemus, who had accompanied Socrates to the symposium at Agathon's house; like Euclides, Apollodorus subsequently checked the detail with Socrates. The *Parmenides* is narrated by Cephalus (to an unspecified listener – the reader?), who went to Athens expressly to find out about the encounter between Socrates and the great Eleatic philosophers, Parmenides and Zeno. Cephalus asks Adeimantus and Glaucon about their half-brother Antiphon, who apparently heard (and learned by heart) the story from Pythodorus, a friend of Zeno's. They go together in search of Antiphon, who eventually relates the story that Pythodorus gave him. In both dialogues we seem to hear a story that is well-attested: repeated, checked, learned by heart – although emphatically distanced from us by the chain of narrators. But that reportage also has the reverse effect, for it makes us hesitate about the truth of the account. What does happen, after all, when a story is passed from one person to another, but distortion, exaggeration, the loss of vital detail?

In all of these cases, the story is put at arm's length, its accuracy, and its point, subject to question. As a consequence, the relation between the frame and the framed becomes increasingly problematic. It is all the more surprising, then, that when each of these three dialogues closes, the outer frame has disappeared. The *Theaetetus* ends ominously as Socrates goes to meet the charges which lead to his death: a telling match to the imminent death of Theaetetus, the promising young mathematician who looks like Socrates, in the frame. The *Symposium* ends when Socrates outtalks the others at the party; they fall asleep, and he goes off to his usual pursuits. The *Parmenides* – perhaps most striking of all – ends a dense discussion between Parmenides and a young man (who happens to be called Aristotle) with a contradiction:

> It seems that whether the one is or is not, both it and the others are and are not, and appear to be and not to be all manner of things in all manner of ways, with respect to themselves and to one another. (*Prm.* 166c2–5)

To this, astonishingly, Aristotle replies "Very true." Are we to take this as the conclusion? And if this is the conclusion, how did Parmenides and Aristotle allow us to reach it? How did Socrates, standing by, allow it to happen? Didn't any of the narrators notice?

Socrates on Question and Answer

If the relation between the frame and the framed is hard to settle, what of the framed dialogues themselves? Socrates explains why he engages in dialogue in the speech he purportedly made in his own defense, the *Apology*. He describes to his audience of jurors how he has acquired the reputation for wisdom in Athens, and how the charges have come to be brought against him. His friend Chaerephon went to the oracle at Delphi to ask whether there was anyone wiser than Socrates. The oracle said there was not; Socrates, on hearing this outcome, was puzzled, and tried to discover just what the oracle could mean (21B3–9). He talked to various groups of pretenders to knowledge: politicians (who turn out to know nothing at all); poets (inspired to tell the truth, but unable to explain it), and craftsmen (who have expertise, but fail to see its limitations). By posing questions to them Socrates asked the pretenders to explain their claims to knowledge; and in each case they turned out to be unable to give an account of what they were supposed to know. This inability to give an account constituted, in Socrates' view, a failure of knowledge, so that their pretension to be wise failed too. Socrates concluded that he was indeed wiser because he alone understood that he was not wise.

The pretenders were asked to give an account of what they knew, and their failure was demonstrated by the process of question and answer with Socrates. Socrates takes the asking and answering of questions to be somehow central to explanation, to knowledge, and to wisdom. Thus midway through his defense (24c9) he is imagined having a direct conversation with one of his accusers, Meletus, and exposes him as being unable to explain coherently what he means in accusing Socrates of corrupting the young. There is a parallel between the ways in which Socrates sought to examine the pretenders to knowledge, and the direct dialogue we are asked to imagine with his accuser. This way of proceeding, in turn, is replicated in other dialogues, where the sequence of question and answer is connected to a demand for explanation, and where in conversation the interlocutor is seen to fail to meet that demand (e.g., *Euthphr.* 11A5–B1; *La.* 193E1–7); (see also 6: PLATONIC DEFINITIONS AND FORMS).

Fair enough: philosophical inquiry regularly searches for explanation by asking "why?" Likewise the sequence of thought represented by a sequence of questions and answers may well be structured by the relation of explanation. If one party makes a claim, and the other questions it, the answer will be connected to the original claim as an explanation is to what it explains. If the explanation fails (or is incomplete) the next question will extend the demand for explanation, and the answer will try to supply it, still in relation to the original claim. Such, indeed, is the method which Socrates is represented as using in many dialogues; it is a model for written dialogue. The interlocutor offers a view about some topic or other (often in response to a question from Socrates: "What is courage?," "What is piety?"); Socrates asks him to explain; and they proceed by question and answer. Unfortunately for the interlocutor, the investigation of his claim usually ends up in trouble; and the interlocutor himself collapses into embarrassment, anger, accusation (e.g., *Chrm.* 169c3–d1; *Men.* 70e7–80b4; *Grg.* 505c1–d9). We may find it easy to see how Meletus would ask for the death penalty.

If this is how Socrates thought philosophy should work, perhaps Plato uses the dialogue form to *represent* the Socratic way of doing philosophy. If, however, the dialogue form shows us the Socratic method at work, how does that account for the *Parmenides*, where Socrates is portrayed as young, in awe of Parmenides and Zeno – and silent for the major part of the work? How does it account for dialogues where Socrates is replaced by others such as the Eleatic Stranger, or where the interlocutors complain of the aridity of the Socratic method (notably at *Phlb.* 20a1–8)? How, in short, does it explain the many ways in which the dialogues do not *portray* a terse Socratic interrogation? Furthermore, is *portraying* all that happens even in those dialogues where Socrates does seem to be "Socratic"?

Socratic *Aporia*

In dialogues such as *Euthyphro*, *Charmides*, and *Laches* the conversation regularly ends in an argumentative impasse, in *aporia*: the interlocutor (and often Socrates too) finds himself unable to decide what to say, or even what to think, and the discussion comes to a stop (see 2: INTERPRETING PLATO). And it is catching; if one of the interlocutors gets stuck, so often does the other (e.g., *Chrm.* 169c3–4): Socrates rightly concludes that he too knows nothing. If these dialogues *are* intended to be representations of Socrates and his ways of doing philosophy, then these impasses seem essential to them, just because this is where his conversations always end up. Meno, at the end of such a sequence of argument, complains that Socrates numbs people like a stingray (*Men.* 80a6). Worse, impasse may be lethal to any kind of philosophical progress. He challenges Socrates to show us how, from a position of ignorance, we may inquire into anything; and how, even if we can, we can ever reach the end of inquiry (see 8: SOCRATIC IGNORANCE). This – Meno's paradox of inquiry – may provide the model for two rather different ways of interpreting the ways in which the dialogues regularly end.

If, on the one hand, even Socrates is unable to reach an end to his inquiries, if his method produces only negative results, perhaps there is a general principle that inquiries *can* only be negative. Then the failure of these dialogues to go beyond an impasse may imply some kind of skepticism: nothing can be known, perhaps, or that nothing can be demonstrated definitively (see also 5: THE SOCRATIC *ELENCHUS*). If skepticism of this kind is true, it cannot itself be demonstrated (to do so begs the question). Instead, it can only be exemplified in the repeated failure of philosophical inquiries to be conclusive. And this may generalize: not only the "Socratic" dialogues, but other dialogues too fail to produce conclusions that are absolute or decisive. We should notice – such an interpretation urges – that each dialogue, no matter how different it may be from any other, ends on a note of indecision. The *Theaetetus*, for example, after exhaustive inquiry fails to explain what knowledge is; the *Philebus* closes with the account of the best life still unfinished; even the *Republic* marks its failure to produce a demonstration by resorting in the end to myth. The dialogue form, on this interpretation, bears witness to a skeptical Plato.

On the other hand, perhaps the important thing is the inquiring itself. Even if extreme skepticism is not the point of the dialogue form – after all, not everything said or claimed in any dialogue is refuted or reduced to an impasse – the prevalence of *aporia* may suggest that each dialogue is somehow or other "open-ended." Like the skeptical account, this too is thought to be generalizable: the activity of philosophy is constantly ongoing; inconclusive, perhaps, but nonetheless "the unexamined life is not worth living." This, like the skeptical interpretation, rests its generality on the very fact that the dialogues are multiform, different, focused in ways that differ widely one from another. And it treats the philosophical issues discussed within the dialogues as somehow or other secondary to the open-endedness of the process of discussing them. The dialogue form, on this account, is at the heart of Plato's account of philosophy.

The Paradox of Writing

Their open-endedness gives us an account, further, of how the written dialogues are to be read. The dialogues, as we have seen, do not lay claim to expressing the views of Plato; instead they express the views of the characters portrayed by Plato. What is the reader to make of this? The position of the reader, indeed, may be deeply problematic, not least because what he reads is intractably fixed:

> You'd think that [written words] were speaking as if they have some understanding, but if you question anything that has been said because you want to learn more, it continues to signify just that very same thing forever. When it has once been written down, every discourse rolls about everywhere, reaching indiscriminately those with understanding no less than those who have no business with it, and it doesn't know to whom to speak and to whom it should not. And when it is faulted and attacked unfairly, it always needs its father's support; alone it can neither defend itself nor come to its own support. (*Phdr.* 275D7–E5, trans. Nehamas and Woodruff)

Socrates' remarks are paradoxical, of course, since their attack on the written word is itself written in words. But many have thought that the puzzle about writing under-pins Plato's authorial strategies, and the enigmatic nature of the arguments, the encounters, and the conclusions he presents. For the dialogues, complex as they are, repeatedly demand interpretation; this form (this form alone?) can be mobile enough for a full dialectical engagement with its readers. So the dialogues are inconclusive in order to provoke the reader into thinking for herself. All their peculiar features and ostentatious inconcinnities, then, are to be explained as weapons in Plato's armory to force reflection on the person who seems entirely outside the dialogue's action: the person who reads it. If philosophy demands conversation and dialogue, written philosophy can after all engage with that by indirect means – by the dialogue form.

This explains, then, why Plato does not figure in the dialogues: it is so that he may be distanced from what his characters say, and thus better provoke a dialogue with his reader. It may even explain, as has been suggested, those works where the dialogue form seems to have become an empty formality. Plato may have a dialogue propose a view, even a view which retains plausibility when the dialogue is finished (the account of falsehood in the *Sophist*, for example), without committing himself absolutely to its truth, without declaring in his own voice that he *knows* this to be true. This distancing of Plato from the direct claims of his characters (remember, in the *Phaedo*, Plato was sick) dovetails well with his designing the dialogues to make the reader think for herself; and it may rescue works such as the *Sophist* and the *Statesman* from the charge that Plato is just losing his touch.

But still, does either the general claim that the dialogues are open-ended just to provoke, or the more specific one that they distance their author from their conclusions, explain enough about the dialogue form? Does it account for the intricate detail of the dialogues, or for their striking differences in presentation? Even the disavowal of authority recedes at times. Consider, for example, the first words of the *Republic*: Socrates says, "I went down yesterday to the Piraeus." Banal, of course, and hardly striking, at the first reading. But if we read and reread the *Republic* – as Plato turns out to have been right to expect – we realize that the business of descent is heavily loaded. For it is the philosophers who, having seen the truth illuminated by the good, go back down to the city, and rule. If Socrates is on his way down (and if, in what follows, he proves full of convictions, albeit claims that cannot be fully transmitted to his companions) does he really disavow authority? And even if he does, does the further thought that the dialogue is open-ended explain why there is a complex relation between the setting of the dialogue and its content?

Drama and the Ethical Dimension

In the drama of the dialogues, the personalities and the destinies of Socrates and his companions are brought to life. Some are figures of comedy – Prodicus booming from under the bedclothes (*Prt.* 316A1–2); Aristophanes hiccupping (*Smp.* 185c5–7); the slapstick eroticism of the admirers of Charmides (*Chrm.* 155c1–4). Some are figures of tragedy: the trial and death of Socrates overshadows many of the dialogues (*Apology*, *Crito*, *Phaedo*, of course, but also *Euthyphro*, *Meno*, even *Theaetetus*); the flawed Alcibiades; Theaetetus, the mathematical talent who dies too young. Socrates himself suggests that there is but a narrow distinction between tragedy and comedy (*Smp.* 223D3–5); and the dialogues bear him out. These characters are vividly portrayed living some kind of life, whether trivialized by their pursuit of victory in argument (the sophist brothers Euthydemus and Dionysodorus of the *Euthydemus*) or by their mindless attraction to pleasure (*Philebus*); or made meaningful, as Socrates' is, by philosophy. If Socrates is right, it is the examination represented in the dialogues that transcends both tragedy and comedy. The point, then, of the dialogues may be to display the infinite variety of characters and the range of their different responses to philosophy, to display that the unexamined life is not worth living.

So, the dialogue form has an ethical purpose. Plato's passionate account of Socrates' death – and Socrates' own impassivity to it – is a defense of the philosophical life. Contrariwise, the lives of those driven by the desire to win in argument, no matter what the truth of the matter is, are somehow empty and valueless (Callicles, for example, or Euthydemus). Plato presents them to insist on the connection between how we live our lives and how we account for them; and he portrays them in dialogue to ask how our defence of how we live stands up to the scrutiny of others. The frame of the dialogues, then, is continuous with the framed, instantiating the relation between the life that is lived and its accountability.

This amounts to a strong philosophical thesis: what we might call ethical rationalism. On this view, the way someone lives and his or her character are directly connected to the actual claims this person advances in argument, even if those claims turn out not to support the life in question. This connection will be thoroughgoing. If the dialogue form represents this character thus and so *and* as involved in an argument about, for example, the nature of relations (e.g., *Phd.* 74A9–D7) or the distinction between knowledge and belief (e.g., *Men.* 97A6–98A8), or the scope of ontology (*Prm.* 130B1–135c2), the representation denies that there are lines of demarcation between one part of philosophy and another. If arguments about logic, or metaphysics, or epistemology are lodged in a context which is manifestly ethical; and if that context is philosophically relevant to the arguments themselves, then Plato evidently denies that metaphysics has nothing to do with ethics, nor ethics with logic (see 11: KNOWLEDGE AND THE FORMS IN PLATO). This integration, if it can be supported, between the living of an examined life and the arguments and principles required to do so – between the principles of ethics and those of metaphysics, of epistemology, of logic – constitutes a striking and important claim about the seamless nature of philosophy.

We might see this at work in some conversions, for better and for worse. Lysis develops his philosophical acuity in ways that will matter for his relations with others. Protarchus in the *Philebus* is induced by argument to see that mindless hedonism, which excludes argument, is untenable, and so he is converted away from the hedonism he originally expounds. In the *Euthydemus*, Ctesippus, too eager to emulate the sophists, ends up no better than their clone. In the *Gorgias*, Callicles is taken over by his own admiration of the use of force, reduced to a baleful presence, in whom, as Socrates predicts, Callicles does not agree with Callicles. In cases such as these the dialogues show us lives being lived well or poorly just by virtue of the principles that govern them.

Limitations of the Ethical

But then do these examples simply beg the question? Are the principles which Plato already adjudges bad ones, made to seem worse by the characters who put them up? We know some principle to be wrong – this view might have it – just because we can see that its exponent is the villain of the piece. The drama of character, then, encodes the arguments and their premises, and disposes us to reject them out of hand. The seamlessness of ethics with metaphysics and the rest would then be just a trick of Platonic rhetoric.

Two thoughts may amplify this disquiet. Firstly, what of the characters *not* articulated in a rich ethical manner? This account tells us little of the Eleatic Stranger, let alone young Socrates; little of Parmenides' meek interlocutor Aristotle; little indeed of Zeno and Parmenides themselves. As a consequence, we may be hard put to see just how the explanation of falsehood, or even the Theory of Forms, is relevant to how best to live. Must we posit some kind of dividing line between the dialogues which are thus ethically elaborate, and those which are not? Whatever that dividing line might be, it had better not be a merely chronological one; the *Philebus*, commonly agreed to have been written late in Plato's life, is as ethically pregnant as you might wish.

Secondly, this emphasis on drama may not explain the relation between the frame and the framed. Think of the practice of irony (Socratic or Platonic). When Socrates is – or is accused of being – ironical, something about the tone of what is said, or some oddity in its context, indicates that somehow Socrates is concealing what he really thinks from his companion (whatever one might mean by saying that this fictional character "really thinks" anything at all). Consider, for example, his disconcerting deception of young Charmides into thinking that he has a magic leaf which will cure Charmides' headache; the reader, but not Charmides, may think that perhaps curing headaches is trivial, compared to acquiring virtue. Or recall the occasions when Socrates expresses extravagant amazement at someone's claim to expertise. Euthyphro, for example, is oblivious to the barbs of Socrates' comments; and Euthydemus and Dionysodorus miss Socrates' suggestions throughout the *Euthydemus* that they are barren of what we should really aspire to know. These ironical moments are not directly representative, because they work by offsetting what is represented with how the reader understands it to be meant. They demand interpretation beyond the confines of the dialogue itself; and they do so by means of the dramatic frame.

Another point of detail extends the scope of a dialogue beyond the confines of the represented conversation: the (often deep and complex) connections that are made between one dialogue and another. At *Phd.* 72E3–73A3, for example, Cebes alludes to the demonstration of recollection in the *Meno* (82B9–86B4). The cross-reference serves, not merely as a footnote, but towards a deeper philosophical aim. For Socrates next argues for the theory of recollection by means of a discussion of the phenomenon of ordinary remembering. But the detailing of that phenomenon is immediate to the reader just if she recalls the *Meno* passage which we are asked to bear in mind, and so herself instantiates that very phenomenon. Indeed, just as irony works in the dialogues by remaining unnoticed by its target, so these intertextual connections are not for the interlocutor, but for the reader. The dense references, for example, to the autobiography of "Socrates" (*Phd.* 96A6–100A7) in a passage of the *Philebus* where the interlocutor, Protarchus, exhibits Socratic tendencies (11A1–21D5) invite us to compare and contrast the methodologies discussed in the two passages thus brought into scrutiny. The same effect is achieved by the opening pages of the *Timaeus*, which both recall the *Republic* and resile from a direct connection with it when the account that Socrates gives in the *Timaeus* of the ideal state notably leaves out the central metaphysics of the *Republic*. The cross-references are inexact; their intertextuality has therefore a significantly critical, comparative role. It plays that role by transcending the dialogue in question, and inviting the reader to do all the hard work. It would be a mistake, then, to see the frame as inert, a mere decoration to the philosophy represented within.

This might reduce the account of the dialogue form, however, once again to mere generality. Is the point of all these devices just to make the reader into an active philosopher, whatever that might be? Are all the dialogues alike in their open-ended provocation, all designed just to have us puzzle and worry about problems philosophical? The dialogues would differ, therefore, in order to ensure that if one puzzle doesn't get us another will; the variety of the dialogues has the scattergun effect of the persistent paradox-monger. To that end, we might complain, the inordinate length and complexity of some of the arguments (not to mention their poverty) is just unwarranted (why not just go for a good paradox instead? "I am lying" alone could perhaps do all the work of provocation done by a whole dialogue). This thought, in turn, serves to unhitch any direct connection between lives and particular arguments in favor of generating a thoroughgoing puzzlement. It will not matter, on this account, which questions we ask ourselves just so long as they are philosophically worrying, intractable enough to keep us thinking. Is there, then, any more to be said about the connection between the ethical outer frame of the dialogues, and the motley collections of arguments, topics, puzzles, difficulties, and counterarguments found within?

The Soul's Silent Dialogue

If the dialogues are meant to get us to think, what does that involve? In the *Theaetetus* (also at *Phlb.* 38c5–E7) Socrates offers some general remarks about the nature and importance of dialogue by suggesting that thinking is like an inner, silent dialogue:

> A talk which the soul has with itself about the objects under its consideration . . . It seems to me that the soul when it thinks is simply carrying on a discussion in which it asks itself questions and answers them, affirms and denies. And when it arrives at something definite, either by a gradual process or a sudden leap, when it affirms one thing consistently and without divided counsel, we call this its judgment. (*Tht.* 189E6–190A4, trans. Levett and Burnyeat)

Thinking, on this account, is a conversation within us between two different points of view. The conversation is imagined to take place by means of question and answer; and it terminates when the soul (the mind) says "one thing consistently," or comes to a unified point of view. Coming to a judgment is not merely the arbitrary choice of one point of view: it is arrived at by inner interrogation, and by thinking *about* those two points of view.

Aristotle picks up on this in his description of dialectic (*Metaph.* 995a24–b4). Both Aristotle and Plato think that the play between the two sides of a case, between the two points of view, is essential to making progress in our understanding. How might this inform our understanding of Plato's use of the dialogue form? (See also 7: PLATO'S METHOD OF DIALECTIC.)

Perhaps (as has been suggested) the link between the dialogue form and the silent dialogue is a psychological one: the dialogue form echoes or imitates our own trains of thought, so that reading something like this will come easily. But does that fully account for the prescriptive features on philosophical conversation which the dialogue form imposes, on the nature of philosophical dialectic there outlined?

Question and answer is regularly (though not always) insisted upon by Socrates, and occasionally by his interlocutors (Protarchus at *Phlb.* 24D8–E2) and it is a prominent feature of the soul's silent dialogue. The formalities of question and answer figure largely in the examination of the slave-boy in the *Meno*, designed to show that knowledge is recollection. In the frame dialogue, Socrates and Meno offer comments on Socrates' exchange with the slave-boy. Socrates insists that he has only asked questions (and not imparted knowledge); en route he induces the boy to see that he did not know what he thought he knew; and then to be in a state of bewilderment, *aporia*. When, in the end, the boy comes up with the right answer, Socrates comments to Meno:

> These opinions have now been stirred up like a dream, but if he were repeatedly asked these same questions in various ways, you know that in the end his knowledge about these things would be as accurate as anyone's. (*Men.* 85c9–D1, trans. Grube)

Other interrogations are embedded in a frame. In the *Hippias Major*, for example, Socrates describes a conversation that he has, offstage, with another man, who turns out to be just like (or to be) Socrates himself. So we imagine Socrates in conversation with himself; and we are invited to inspect his own failings to himself. Similarly, Socrates engages a different point of view as if in dialogue with Meletus in *Ap.* 24c9–26A7; with the man who believes at *R.* 476E4–480A13; or with "the many" at *Prt.* 352D4–357E8. In these dialogues within dialogues, the relation between frame and framed becomes mobile, so that the framed becomes the frame. When that happens, the frame itself provides the locus for comment and reflection upon what happens in the framed dialogue.

This feature occurs most strikingly in those (late?) dialogues whose conversational style seems to have become arid and perfunctory. For they still contain some vivid imaginary encounters embedded in the main discussion: notably, three discussions that are imagined to take place with Plato's philosophical predecessors, Protagoras, Heraclitus, and Parmenides. In the *Theaetetus* Socrates imagines Protagoras defending his extreme relativist claim that "man is the measure of all things" (152A1–179D1) and later offers an imaginary encounter with Heraclitus and the exponents of total flux (181B8–183B6). In the *Sophist* (244B6–245E2) the Eleatic Stranger portrays himself as committing parricide on his philosophical progenitor, Parmenides, who claimed that all there ever is, is one thing. In each of these imagined conversations, the argument begins as it means to go on: by question and answer. But in each case the imagined interlocutor is unable to engage, because the very theory he advances makes the extended sequence of question and answer, and the different points of view that such a sequence demands, impossible. It is to display these theories (relativism, total flux, strong monism) as incapable of engaging in dialectical exchange that they are represented within the dialogues in which they appear; and they provide us with a paradigm case of the constraints of philosophical dialogue. Further, by being embedded in a framing dialogue, they expose those constraints to our reflective attention, as the focus of comment in the frame itself.

First, there needs to be a process, a sequence of answers to connected questions. If the interlocutor sulks, or is too shy to answer, or too arrogant to pay attention, the process breaks down. If the interlocutor holds a position that precludes dialogue, the process breaks down: he needs to be able to sustain more than just the first answer to the first question. Indeed, the process needs to be somehow continuous. Consider – as the dialogues regularly invite us to do – how questions may be related to their answers; and how this generates the next question along. This occurs repeatedly just because the questioner seeks to understand the position of the answerer: the dominant questions are "What does this mean?" or "Why do you think that?" or "What follows from this?" or "How does that fit with what you said before?"

Second, the process goes forward by virtue of some kind of contrast between two points of view, between assertion and denial. Why? The outer conversations make the point clear; while the process continues, one point of view has not yet convinced the other; the questioner continues to refuse his agreement until the answers have fully satisfied him. The process, then, takes place between these two points of view, and it is their difference (due either to two views being directly opposed, or to one view not being convinced by the other) that provides the dynamic. Sometimes the two views occur within the represented conversation; sometimes they are embedded within it; and sometimes they occur between the framed argument and its frame, when the frame itself asks questions of what is said within it (e.g., *Euthd.* 290E1–293A9).

These demands themselves, third, reveal an underlying assumption which is brought out in the slave-boy episode: that understanding (whether of one's own point of view or of another's) is a matter of relating together all the things one believes, connecting them with their reasons and consequences. Understanding, that is to say, takes place across a large web of belief, and never piecemeal. That is how the silent dialogue will end up with a single view, but only after the process of question and answer has been carried out. This is a *judgment* just because it is based on reasons, and fits with the process of thought that has led up to it (the silent dialogue notably does not describe the mind as just plumping for one or another of the points of view presented to it).

But then the correlation between the silent dialogue and the process imagined, represented, failing to be represented, repudiated, scorned, but never ignored in the Platonic dialogues themselves, shows us one further feature of the portrayal of dialogue. Whether the dialogue portrayed be written, spoken, enacted, or imagined, the dialogue form repeatedly invites reflection upon the arguments in question. That is to say, the points of view in play are seen from within, as if one occupied one of the points of view; but they are also seen from without, with the detached stance of the observer, the person who (like Socrates) is not yet convinced of either point of view, but who reflects upon their interplay, their explanatory power, and their integration with other principles that we might hold. This reflection on the arguments is offered to Plato's reader by the complexity of his use of the dialogue form, by the relation between frame and framed. It is, moreover, both a formal feature of the nature of dialectical exchange, and particular to the arguments and discussions upon which the reflection operates.

Reflection and its Content

This reflectiveness of the dialogue form is determined by the constraints upon it from the frame of individual dialogues, and it is, consequently, both broad and varied in its content. Consider two examples where the relation between the frame and the framed is essential to our understanding of the arguments. First, Philebus, in the eponymous dialogue, espouses a life of extreme hedonism, devoid of reason and thought. But such a life cannot sustain talk about itself, or reflection upon it. Philebus' position refutes itself just if he tries to speak, and he falls silent before the dialogue is half way through (28B6). Second, Dionysodorus maintains that consistency does not matter (*Euthd.* 287B2–5). Socrates cannot refute him (because such a refutation would assume that consistency matters), but the dialogue makes clear that without consistency we have no coherent account to give of personal identity, nor of the life that a person might live.

In these two cases, the principles of ethics (how best to live) connect with the principles of metaphysics and logic: in the first the frame makes logical demands on an ethical claim; in the second the frame makes ethical and metaphysical demands on a logical one. But we see this only by virtue of the reflective distance between the frame dialogue and what it frames. Both Philebus and Dionysodorus take positions that are untenable (extreme hedonism, the sophistic denial of consistency). The frame, by comparing the untenable position with its denial in a dialectical exchange, shows just what assumptions the untenable position would force us to forsake (personal identity, consistency), and how that would impact on our ethical purposes. This can work both ways: sometimes the ethical position is framed, and shown in the frame to be unbearable (as in the *Philebus*); sometimes it is the frame which offers an ethical account of what seems quite neutral in the framed dialogue (as in the *Euthydemus*). Cases like these are extreme examples of the way that ethical rationalism works, by supposing the principles of logic and metaphysics to sustain ethics (there must be a persistent person to live a life) and the principles of ethics to sustain those of logic and metaphysics (consistency must matter, if we are to have a coherent account of the life we live). It is a constant feature of the dialogue form to make possible this dialectical interplay between the foundational principles of philosophy, and to bring it into reflective focus.

Plato's dialogue form is not uniform, nor are its purposes either evident or singular. But these are its virtues. For these dialogues provoke us to reflect on the dialogue itself: on how it works and why it should. In reading we occupy the position of Meno observing the examination of the slave-boy, or of Theaetetus hearing about Socrates' imaginary conversations with Protagoras. We stand outside the action even where we may agree with what is said, and in that way we can think *about* just how the arguments work. And so a dialogue may reflect on the principles of argument itself. For underlying Plato's interest in the dialogue form is his concern to explain how understanding is shaped and constrained, and his concern to show why it matters. The drama of the dialogues – these people in these situations, there and then – makes clear that understanding is something that matters in their lives, or if it does not, it should. That the dialogues repeatedly fail is part of their challenge – a challenge which the reader is invited to take up. But the challenge is formed in such a way as to show us what it would be to meet it: to develop, as the dialogue invites, a systematic and unified account of what it is we are endeavoring to understand – an account which integrates the problems of philosophy with the unity of a life. In the interplay between the represented dialogues and their presentation in their frames, Plato formulates this seamless account of the reflection that constitutes philosophy.

Notes

All translations are the author's own, or are taken from J. M. Cooper (ed.) *Plato: Complete Works* (Indianapolis: Hackett, 1997).

I should like to record my thanks to those with whom I had conversations about Platonic conversation while I was writing this paper, especially David Galloway, Owen Gower, Verity Harte, Alex Long, James Warren, and my gratitude for the exemplary skills of the editor.

References and further reading

Annas, J. and Rowe, C. (2002). *New Perspectives on Plato, Modern and Ancient*. Cambridge, Mass.: Harvard University Press.

Benson, H. H. (1992). *Essays on the Philosophy of Socrates*. New York: Oxford University Press.

Beversluis, J. (2000). *Cross-examining Socrates: A Defense of the Interlocutors in Plato's Early Dialogues*. Cambridge: Cambridge University Press.

Blondell, R. (2002). *The Play of Character in Plato's Dialogues*. Cambridge: Cambridge University Press.

Burnyeat, M. (1985). Sphinx without a secret? *New York Review of Books*, May 30, pp. 30–6.

Cossuta, F. and Narcy, M. (eds.) (2001). *La forme dialogue chez Platon: évolution et receptions*. Grenoble: J. Millon.

Ferrari, G. R. F. (1987). *Listening to the Cicadas: A Study of Plato's* Phaedrus. Cambridge: Cambridge University Press.

Gadamer, H. (1980). *Dialogue and Dialectic: Eight Hermeneutical Studies of Plato*, trans. P. C. Smith. New Haven, Conn.: Yale University Press.

Gill, C. and McCabe, M. M. (eds.) (1996). *Form and Argument in Late Plato*. Oxford: Oxford University Press.

Griswold, C. L. (1988). *Platonic Writings, Platonic Readings*. New York: Routledge.

Hart, R. and Tejera, V. (eds.) (1997). *Plato's Dialogues: The Dialogical Approach*. New York: Edwin Mellen.

Kahn, C. H. (1996). *Plato and the Socratic Dialogue: The Philosophical Use of a Literary Form*. Cambridge: Cambridge University Press.

Klagge, J. and Smith, N. (eds.) (1992). *Methods of Interpreting Plato and his Dialogues. Oxford Studies in Ancient Philosophy*, supplementary volume. Oxford: Oxford University Press.

McCabe, M. M. (2000). *Plato and his Predecessors: The Dramatisation of Reason*. Cambridge: Cambridge University Press.

Nehamas, A. (1998). *The Art of Living: Socratic Reflections from Plato to Foucault*. Berkeley: University of California Press.

Nightingale, A. (1995). *Genres in Dialogue: Plato and the Construct of Philosophy*. Cambridge: Cambridge University Press.

Nussbaum, M. (1986). *The Fragility of Goodness: Luck and Ethics in Greek Tragedy and Philosophy*. Cambridge: Cambridge University Press.

Press, G. A. (2000). *Who Speaks for Plato? Studies in Platonic Anonymity.* Lanham, Md.: Rowman and Littlefield.

Rutherford, R. (1995). *The Art of Plato.* London: Harvard University Press.

Sayre, K. (1995). *Plato's Literary Garden: How to Read a Platonic Dialogue.* Notre Dame, Ind.: University of Notre Dame Press.

Sedley, D. (2004). *Plato's* Cratylus. Cambridge: Cambridge University Press.

Smiley, T. (1995). *Philosophical Dialogues: Plato, Hume, Wittgenstein.* Oxford: Oxford University Press.

Stokes, M. C. (1986). *Plato's Socratic Conversations.* London: Johns Hopkins University Press.

Szlezák, T. A. (1999). *Reading Plato,* trans. G. Zanker. London: Taylor and Francis. (Original work published 1993.)

5

The Socratic *Elenchus*

CHARLES M. YOUNG

Introduction

Socrates – if not the man himself, then the character in most of Plato's shorter dialogues and, perhaps, a few of the longer ones as well – was up to something special. Believing that he was acting under the instructions of Apollo, the god of the oracle at Delphi, Socrates spent his time talking to people, both ordinary people and more sophisticated thinkers, asking them questions about human life and how it is to be lived. When his interlocutors proved unable to defend their opinions on such questions, Socrates offered his own radical positive agenda in their place. We are happy, he thought, when our souls are in their best condition – when, as he believed, we have the virtues of character: courage, temperance, piety, and especially justice. Since we all want to be happy, we shall inevitably do what is virtuous if only we know what it is (see 18: THE SOCRATIC PARADOXES; 21: PLATO ON PLEASURE AS THE HUMAN GOOD). Hence our path to happiness is the removal of ignorance and vice from our souls and their replacement with virtue and knowledge (see 8: SOCRATIC IGNORANCE).

Nearly everyone agrees with that characterization of Socrates' life and thought, or with something like it. Hardly anyone, however, agrees about the details. Why, exactly, does Socrates believe that he is acting under divine orders? Why does he believe that Apollo instructed him to ask people questions about how we should live our lives? What does he think happiness is? What does he think a soul is? Why does our happiness turn on *its* good condition? Why does he think that the virtues of character have anything to do with the soul's good condition? Is Socrates' critical agenda in questioning his fellows connected to his constructive agenda involving the virtues and happiness? Nothing close to a consensus on the answers to any of these questions exists.

Nor is there a consensus on what Socrates was up to in his questionings of others about the virtues of character and how we are to live. A central feature of Socrates' examinations is, however, commonly identified by a particular name nowadays: it is called the Socratic *elenchus* ("cross-examination"). But again, scholars disagree about the details; witness a 2002 collection of articles on the *elenchus* (Scott 2002). They disagree about what, exactly, is involved in the arguments that employ the *elenchus*, and about what its distinctive features are, if indeed it has any. They disagree over which passages in Plato's dialogues involve the *elenchus* and over which dialogues are relevant to its study. They disagree on whether and how Socrates can reach positive conclusions by means of the *elenchus*. They even disagree over whether Socrates actually *has* a method, that is, a characteristic way of doing philosophy. And many more points of disagreement could be mentioned.

I cannot settle any of these questions here. Instead, I shall consider passages that have been neglected in discussions of the *elenchus*, at least in the aspects of them on which I shall focus. All involve points that need to be taken into account if we are to achieve any consensus on what is going on in the Socratic dialogues, with the *elenchus*, and with Socrates.

Preliminaries

It will be useful to have some of the history of the noun "*elenchus*" and its cognate verb *elenchō* (following Lesher 2002) on the table. "*Elenchus*" begins life with the meaning of "shame" or "disgrace," typically of the sort that arises from a failure in a martial or athletic test: "For it will be a disgrace (*elenchus*), if Hector of the flashing helm captures the ships" (*Il.* XI.314–15). Later, the meaning shifted from the idea of shame or disgrace per se to the idea of the tests in which shame or disgrace was incurred or avoided: "The bow is no test (*elenchus*) of a man: it is a coward's weapon" (Euripides, *Heracles* 162). Subsequently, the meaning expanded to include tests or contests other than martial or quasi-martial ones: e.g., the test of a poem's merits by public opinion (see, e.g., Pindar, *N.* VIII.20–1). By mid-fifth century BCE, the term began commonly to designate any sort of examination of the true nature of a particular person or thing (see, e.g., Aeschylus, *Suppliant Women* 993). Then the word came to focus more narrowly on the examination of a person's words for truth or falsity (see, e.g., Herodotus, *History* II.115), or the negative result of such an examination (see, e.g., *Grg.* 473B9–10). That brings us up to Plato.

It is nowadays common to deny that Socrates has anything that might be called a *method* that goes beyond his usual, self-avowed modes of inquiry: examining (*exetazō*), investigating (*skopeō* and its cognates), questioning (*erōtō* and its cognates), seeking, (*zētō* and its cognates), talking over (*dialegō*), and sometimes cross-examining or refuting (*elenchō*), etc., his fellows. This denial of a method to Socrates may well be right. But the Socratic dialogues, and even some other dialogues, contain several passages that must be taken into account in coming to a final view of this claim and similar ones. A few of these passages are as follows: In his opening remarks in the *Apology*, Socrates contrasts his way of making a case with that of his accusers, and he says that he's going to use the same sort of arguments that he was accustomed to using in the marketplace (17A1–18A6). In the *Crito*, Socrates says he's the sort of person who decides what to do by reference to the "argument" or "principle" (*logos*) that looks best to him on reflection (46B4–6), and the personified Laws of Athens give as their reason for cross-examining him the fact that he cross-examines others (50c8–9). In the *Gorgias*, Socrates contrasts his way of arguing (*tropos elenkou*) with that of forensic orators (472c2–4). Two characters in the dialogues take special notice of aspects of Socrates' argumentative technique: Alcibiades (*Smp.* 221D1–222A6) and, with contempt,

Callicles (*Grg.* 491A1–3). Finally, in the *Sophist*, the Athenian Stranger draws attention to a "noble sophistry" that is concerned with "the refutation (*elenchus*) of the empty belief in one's own wisdom" (231B5–8); this sort of sophistry is a kissing cousin, at least, of whatever it is that Socrates seems to have been doing. Whether or not Socrates has what we should be prepared to call a "method," then, it is clear from the Socratic dialogues that Plato regards Socrates' conduct of his examinations of others as in some way distinctive.

A relatively simple illustration of an *elenchus* occurs at *La.* 192B9–D11. Here Laches ventures this definition of courage:

A. Courage is endurance (192B9).

Socrates then elicits from him a claim about courage:

B. Courage is among the very fine or admirable things (192c5–6).

He also elicits two claims about endurance:

C. Endurance with wisdom is fine or admirable and good (192c9–10).
D. Endurance with folly is harmful and injurious (192D1–2).

Then comes a general truth about what is harmful and injurious:

E. The sort of thing that is harmful and injurious is not fine or admirable (192D4–5).

Finally, we get two inferences. Since

F. Endurance with folly is not fine or admirable (192D8),

and

G. Courage is a fine or admirable thing (192D8),

Socrates and Laches conclude first that

H. Endurance with folly is not courage (192D7),

and second that "according to [Laches'] argument,"

I. Wise endurance is courage (192D10–11)

Presumably, (F) follows from (D) and (E), (G) follows from (B), and (H) from (F) and (G). Where (I) comes from is unclear.

This argument exemplifies a pattern that Gregory Vlastos, in a classic paper on the *elenchus* (Vlastos 1983; see also Vlastos 1994), called the "standard" *elenchus*. It begins with Socrates' interlocutor's asserting some claim, here (A). Socrates then secures the interlocutor's agreement to further claims: (B) through (E). Socrates then infers, with the interlocutor's acceptance, that the original claim is false: in this instance, (H). The original claim may, however, survive in some qualified form, as here, in (I). In a "standard" *elenchus*, the original claim, according to Vlastos, plays no role in the argument, apart from providing Socrates with a target. This is in contrast to "indirect" *elenchus*, in which the original claim does play a role.

Vlastos's distinction between these two modes of *elenchus* is spurious. If we have a set of claims – P, Q, and R, say – that entails the negation of an interlocutor's original claim, C, it doesn't matter, from a logical point of view, whether the set includes the original claim or not: If the entailment obtains, then there is no situation in which P, Q, R, and C are all true, whether or not C is one of the claims P, Q, and R. So it would be better not to distinguish two modes of *elenchus* but instead to characterize the *elenchus* simply as an argument in which an interlocutor's original claim is rejected when it is seen to be inconsistent with other things that the interlocutor believes.

Apology 21B9–23c1: The Origins of the Socratic *Elenchus*

Socrates' account in the *Apology* of the origins of his philosophical mission is familiar, but certain of its details will repay scrutiny here. Socrates begins his defense against the charge of impiety by drawing his audience's attention to a set of "earlier" and "more dangerous" accusers, whose traducements against him, he maintains, created an atmosphere of prejudice towards him that his current, "later," accusers are using to their advantage in bringing their charges against him (18A7–19D7). At the heart of the prejudice, he tells us, is his possession of what he calls *sophia tis* (20D7). Here *sophia tis* must be "wisdom of a sort," and not "a sort of wisdom" (as it is at, e.g., *La.* 194D9) – not a branch of wisdom, but an understanding that offers part of what wisdom offers, without being the real thing. For Socrates immediately (20D8) identifies his "wisdom of a sort" with "human wisdom" (*anthrōpinē sophia*), and this proves to consist in knowing that one doesn't know anything, in particular that one doesn't know anything "fine and good" (21D4). In fact, "human wisdom" is worth "little or nothing" (23A6–7). Socrates' possession of "human wisdom," however, gave rise to the prejudice against him, inasmuch as it made him appear to people, despite his denials, as if he really thought he knew something important.

Socrates came to believe in his "human wisdom" through various conversations he had with other people in an effort to understand the statement of the oracle at Delphi that no one was wiser than he. He approached three different groups of people: politicians, poets, and artisans. He had different experiences with each group. His discussions with politicians revealed that although they were thought by others and by themselves to be wise, they in fact were not (21B9–22A8). The poets presented a more complicated case. In their poems, Socrates concedes, the poets had "many fine things" to say, but because they could not explain themselves adequately, he thought that they did not *know* the things they said in their poems, but instead composed their works through natural talent or through inspiration. In addition, because of their poetic talents, the poets believed they knew other things, but in fact they did not know them (22A8–c8). The artisans, finally, did prove to know "many fine things," but because of what they knew, they thought that they also knew other, important things (22c8–E5). Famously, Socrates went away convinced that he was wiser than any of those he talked to. He was wiser, however, not because he knew things that they did not, but because they thought they knew things that in fact they did not know, whereas he had no such thought. This is what his "human wisdom" consists in. As he tells us,

> What is probable, gentlemen, is that in fact the god is wise and that his oracular response meant that human wisdom is worth little or nothing, and that when he says this man, Socrates, he is using my name as an example, as if he were to say, "This man among you, mortals, is wisest who, like Socrates, understands that his wisdom is worthless." (23A5–B4, trans. Grube, modified slightly)

What we need to understand, for present purposes, are the epistemic similarities and differences Socrates claims to find among the three groups he confronted and how he detected these differences. He doesn't tell us, so we shall have to make some guesses. One obvious guess is that Socrates subjected members of all three groups to questioning of the sort that is familiar to us from the Socratic dialogues, and which we have been calling the "*elenchus.*" This suggestion is borne out by the fact that in the passage under discussion Socrates uses all the terminology, noted in the previous section, that he regularly uses in describing his philosophical activities, and if the suggestion is right, then the similarities and differences Socrates notes must reflect similarities and differences in how his respondents fared in his cross-examinations of them. But an *elenchus* can have only two results: either the interlocutor's initial claim fails, or it survives. It fails if Socrates can show it to be inconsistent with other things the interlocutor believes; it survives if he cannot. Socrates concludes that the people in all three groups think they know things about certain subjects that in fact they do not know. Since Socrates himself knows nothing about these subjects, he cannot be inferring his interlocutors' ignorance from the fact that he, Socrates, knows better. He must, instead, draw this inference from the fact that his interlocutors cannot consistently maintain their claims to knowledge. That's a reasonable guess: If I cannot consistently defend my beliefs in some area, it is fair for Socrates to conclude that I do not know what I am talking about in that area, even if he himself doesn't know what I am talking about, either.

So much for the similarities among the three groups. What about the differences? Socrates says that the poets had "many fine things" to say in their compositions, that they could not explain themselves adequately, and that they did not know the fine things they said. In the case of the artisans, Socrates concedes that they did know the "many fine things" they had to say. It is reasonable to guess that the things the artisans knew were things that fall within their crafts: that's what they know. But Socrates would not have conceded that the artisans *knew* the fine things they had to say if they had not survived his questioning about those things: As we have seen, Socrates takes failure to survive the *elenchus* as proof of ignorance. So we may reasonably guess that the artisans did survive the *elenchus* so long as Socrates' questions fell within their areas of competence. We can go further: Socrates denied that the poets *knew* the fine things they said on the grounds that they could not adequately explain themselves. Presumably he would have said the same thing about the artisans if they, too, had been unable to explain themselves adequately. So it is a fair inference that the artisans *were* able to explain themselves adequately on issues that fell within their areas of expertise. We can go further still: all three groups failed to survive the *elenchus* in certain areas. The artisans pass the test within their areas of expertise. What are we to say about the poets when they were asked about their poems? Did they pass or did they fail? If they failed, there would have been no difference between the poets and the politicians, and Socrates could have claimed that the poets did not know what they said in their compositions on that basis, without appealing to their inability to explain themselves. Since he does not do this, it is not unreasonable to guess that the poets did not fail the elenctic test when talking about their compositions. They may not have been able to explain themselves, but at least they didn't contradict themselves.

What sorts of explanations does Socrates think an artisan can give that a poet cannot? Taking a cue from *Grg.* 464B2–465A7, we might reasonably speculate that a fifth-century doctor, for example, would have had a theory about human health that gave him the conceptual resources with which to frame explanations. He might have thought, for example, that human bodies are made up of earth, air, fire, and water; that human beings are healthy when the heat, cold, wetness, and dryness associated with these elements are in the appropriate balance, and sick when that balance is lacking; and that the aim of medical treatment is to restore appropriate balance to people who are sick and lack balance. Thus: "My patient is feverish; this must mean that she is suffering from an excess of heat; bleeding her will remove the excess heat and restore her to health." So the difference between the poets and the artisans, on this suggestion, is that the artisans have a supporting theory and the poets do not. Why, exactly, the poets lack a supporting theory is left unclear. It might be that the "many fine things" the poets say aren't the kinds of thing that can have a supporting theory at all, as *Grg.* 464B2–465A7 would have us believe, e.g., about the claim that while cookies are good with milk, and doughnuts with coffee, neither is good with Scotch whiskey. Or it might be that the poets' claims can be adequately explained, but not by their proponents, as an idiot savant might believe that $761,838,257,287 \times 193,707,721 = 2^{64} - 1$ without being able to carry out the relevant calculations.

The suggestion that this is indeed the difference Socrates sees between the poets and the artisans is confirmed by the fact that he thinks it is in order to give an alternative explanation, in terms of natural talent and inspiration, for the poets' ability to say "many fine things" in their compositions. This is standard Socratic practice in cases in which someone is apparently in some sort of control of some subject matter but cannot explain himself adequately. Thus in the *Gorgias* (464B2–465A7), Socrates claims that pastry baking fails the explanation test, since it "has no account of the nature of whatever things it applies by which it applies them, so that it's unable to state the cause of each thing [it does]" (465A3–5, trans. Zeyl). But he is prepared, even so, to call pastry baking a "knack," acknowledging that pastry bakers can achieve more or less regular success. Similarly, Socrates does not challenge Ion's ability to say "many fine things" about Homer (*Ion* 542A5), but he does question whether that ability can be attributed to Ion's possession of knowledge, and when Socrates establishes that it cannot, he accounts for the ability by crediting Ion with a "divine gift" (542A4). And in the *Meno*, he attributes the abilities of politicians, soothsayers, prophets, and poets to get things right without knowledge to the gods' influence and possession (99B11–100B5).

To sum up: Socrates in the *Apology* distinguishes three levels of epistemic involvement. If I claim knowledge in some area, Socrates will claim that I am wrong to say I know if I cannot consistently defend my beliefs in that area. He will also claim I am wrong to say I know, even if he cannot convict me of inconsistency in some area, if I cannot explain my beliefs in the area in a certain way. If I can explain my beliefs in the right way, however, then Socrates, not being himself an expert in the area in question, has no choice but to let my claim to knowledge stand.

Inconsistency

The *elenchus* thus aims to expose false claims to knowledge by convicting claimants to knowledge of holding inconsistent beliefs. Inconsistency matters, according to many accounts of the *elenchus*, because it seems that if I believe A, B, and C, and I then come to believe that A, B, and C are inconsistent, then (a) at least one of A, B, and C must be false, and (b) if I wish to maintain my belief in A and my belief in B, say, I must give up my belief in C. Here (a) is true, but (b) is not. This is so for at least two reasons.

In the first place, I might retain my belief that A, B, and C are each true and give up my belief that A, B, and C are inconsistent. Consider in this connection the refutation of Charmides' first try at defining temperance at *Chrm.* 159B5–160D3. Charmides ventures that

A. Temperance is quietness (159B5–6).

Socrates then secures Charmides' agreement to

B. Temperance is among the fine or admirable things (159c1).

Socrates then runs through any number of cases in which

C. Doing things quickly is finer or more admirable than doing them quietly (159c3–4, c8–9, etc.).

This is a claim that Socrates puts in a variety of ways. In (C) Socrates uses adverbs and comparative adjectives. Elsewhere, though, he uses superlative adverbs and adjectives:

D. Doing things as quickly as possible, not doing them as quietly as possible, is the finest or most admirable (160A5–6).

Sometimes he mixes superlative and comparative adjectives:

E. The quickest things, not the quieter, are the finest or most admirable (159D4–5).

Sometimes he uses abstract substantives:

F. Quickness is finer or more admirable than quietness (160B4–5).

And sometimes his formulations are simply bizarre:

G. Quickness is more temperate (!) than quietness (159D10–11).
H. The quiet life (!) is not more temperate than the quick life (160c7–D1).

At any rate, the formulation with which Socrates wraps up the argument is:

I. Quick things are no less fine or admirable than quiet things (160D2–3), claiming that from (I) and
B. Temperance is among the fine or admirable things,

it follows that

J. Temperance is not quietness (160B7).

And this is the denial of (A), Charmides' original definition.

Well. Socrates' claim that (I) and (B) are inconsistent with Charmides' original definition, though it is asserted by Socrates and accepted by Charmides (160D4), plainly depends on something rather more sophisticated than *modus ponens*, and Charmides is not given any reason, much less any good reason, for accepting the inference. He could reasonably retain his belief that temperance is quietness, even given his acceptance of (B) and (I), by claiming that Socrates' claim of inconsistency does not succeed, or at least that it has not been made out. Charmides does not have to give up his definition of temperance.

61

So it does not follow that if I believe A, B, and C, and I come to believe that A, B, and C are inconsistent, then I must give up my belief in C if I wish to retain my belief in A and B. I can instead give up my belief that A, B, and C are inconsistent. Matters are actually worse than that: In certain circumstances, I can believe A, B, and C, and believe that A, B, and C are inconsistent, and still retain my belief in all three of A, B, and C. Suppose, for example, that I am rolling a fair die. Consider these three claims:

A. Something other than 1 or 2 will come up.
B. Something other than 3 or 4 will come up.
C. Something other than 5 or 6 will come up.

Since the probabilities of each of these claims is 0.67, I should believe that each of them is more likely than not. But plainly I should reject the conjunction of A, B, and C. For that conjunction amounts to

D. Something other than 1, 2, 3, 4, 5, or 6 will come up,

and that's impossible. So I should accept all three of A, B, and C, even though I recognize that they cannot all be true together. To be sure, I would know that one of A, B, and C is false, but I would not know which one. So this is a case in which I accept A and accept B, and accept that A, B, and C are inconsistent, but I should not reject C. Quite the contrary, I should accept C as well.

The possibility just described is, moreover, not a merely logical possibility, especially in philosophical contexts, where anything like certainty is hard to achieve. And indeed, Richard Kraut drew attention over twenty years ago to the fact that Socrates (in the Socratic dialogues, including the *Protagoras*, for the purposes of this point) thinks he has good reasons for accepting all three of these propositions:

A. Virtue is unteachable.
B. Virtue is knowledge.
C. If virtue is knowledge, then virtue is teachable,

even though he recognizes that (A), (B), and (C) are inconsistent (see Kraut 1984: 285–8). Again, Socrates knows that at least one of (A), (B), and (C) must be false, but he has no reason to give up any one of them in particular.

Does Socrates Cheat?

So. Socrates himself holds sets of beliefs that he knows cannot all be true. But in conducting the *elenchus*, he regularly insists that his interlocutor jettison the claim that he has targeted once it emerges that that claim is inconsistent with other things the interlocutor believes. Is that fair? Is that cheating, to frame the question as it has come to be framed since the publication of Vlastos 1991, esp. ch. 5, "Does Socrates cheat?" If to cheat is to offer arguments that one recognizes to be of questionable soundness, or to encourage one's interlocutors to abandon claims when they are not required to, it seems to me clear that Socrates does cheat. He probably cheated in the *Charmides* argument just discussed, in supposing that formulations (C) through (I) are equivalent to one another and in supposing that (I) and (B) entail that temperance is not quietness, without giving Charmides, or us, any reason to accept these far from trivial suppositions. And, as many have observed over the years, Socrates' argument probably trades on the thought that the contrary of *quiet* is *quick*, and not, as Charmides surely intended, *tumultuous, over the top*, or something similar. It is hard to believe that Plato was not aware of either point, and if he was aware, it's hard to believe that he is not representing Socrates as cheating.

But sometimes what's hard to believe is true, so let me take up a couple of examples from the *Ion* that are, I believe, clearer. In that dialogue, Ion the rhapsode claims two related competences, one performative and one critical. He claims, first, the ability to recite Homer's poetry with power, feeling, and effectiveness (530D4–5; cf. 535B2–3). And he claims, second, the ability to understand the substance of Homer's thought (530c5) and to offer sound critical observations on that thought (530D1–2). Ion also accepts Socrates' suggestion that his critical competence is based on knowledge of what Homer is talking about (530c7), and it is this idea that Socrates targets in the *elenchus* that follows. In the course of that argument, Ion comes to admit that his critical competence is restricted to Homer (532B6–c4). Even though, as he concedes, other poets talk about pretty much the same things that Homer talks about (531c1–D2), he, Ion, has nothing at all to say about the other poets (532B8–c2). Socrates then concludes that Ion's critical competence with respect to Homer is not based on possession of knowledge: "If you were able to talk about Homer through knowledge, you would be able to talk about all the other poets as well" (532c7–8).

Ion accepts this (532c10). But he insists that his critical competence with respect to Homer, even if limited, is, by common opinion, real, and he accordingly asks Socrates to explain the basis for his competence, given that it cannot be explained by his possession of knowledge (532B8–c4). Socrates responds, famously, with the simile of the magnet and the theory of divine inspiration, supplemented with facts drawn from the phenomenology of poetic experience (533c9–536B5). The simile and the theory are reasonable as an explanation of Ion's performative competence, and it is as such that they are presented by Socrates (note "sing" at 535B4 and 536B6, and "song" at B7) and accepted by Ion (535A3–5, A8, A10, c4–D1, D6–7, E1–6). But Socrates goes on, beginning at 536B6, to turn his explanation of Ion's performative competence into an explanation of his critical competence. The shift occurs within a single sentence: "When any *song* of that poet [namely, Homer] *is sounded*, you are immediately awake . . . and you have plenty *to say*" (536B7–c1, my emphasis; trans. Woodruff). Socrates then concludes, "It's not because you're a master of knowledge about Homer that you can say what you say [about him], but because of a divine gift, because you're possessed" (536c1–2; trans. Woodruff). This is unfair of Socrates, and Ion understandably balks: "You're a good speaker, Socrates. But I would be amazed if you were good enough to convince me that I am possessed or crazed when I praise Homer" (536D4–6). So Ion accepts Socrates' theory as an explanation of his performative competence but rejects it as an explanation of his critical competence, and the dialogue goes on. Socrates tried to cheat, in attempting to pass off a plausible explanation of Ion's performative competence as an explanation also of his critical competence, and Ion refused to let him get away with it.

Socrates' second try for the same conclusion also depends on a cheat – one that, this time, succeeds. The nub of the argument begins at 540B3. Socrates is engaged in trying to determine what it is that Ion, as a rhapsode, knows. Ion ventures that "he'll know what sorts of things it's fitting for a man or a woman to say – or for a slave or a freeman, or for a follower or a leader" (540B3–5). Socrates takes Ion to be talking not about men, slaves, or women as such, but about men who are also navigators in a storm or doctors treating the sick, or slaves who are also cowherds who need to calm their cattle, or women who are also wool-workers spinning their yarn – all of them artisans at work on their crafts (540B6–8, c1–2, c4–6, c6–D1). And Ion must of course deny that a rhapsode will know what it is fitting for artisans to say about their craftwork, and so indeed he does (540B8, c2–3, c6, D1). But then Socrates gives Ion an opening: "Will a rhapsode know what sorts of things a man should say, if he's a general, to encourage his troops?" (540D1–2). Ion seizes his opportunity: "Yes! A rhapsode will know those sorts of things" (540D2–3). Socrates then says that Ion must be a general (540D4), and that's a hook he's not allowed to wiggle off of for the rest of the dialogue.

This again is a cheat. What Ion is trying to say is that a rhapsode knows human character, that a rhapsode can, say, compose the St Crispin's Day speech in *Henry V*. He knows, that is, the sort of speech a man who learned in his teens that he was the future King of England is apt to deliver, now that he is King, before a decisive battle in a questionable war undertaken at his own initiative. But Socrates won't allow Ion to make any such claim. The only sort of person one can be, so far as the logic of Socrates' argument goes, is an artisan, and the argument has it that a rhapsode isn't able write the St Crispin's Day speech without also being able to win the Battle of Agincourt. Ion is not given a chance to say what he means.

The *Ion* even ends with still another cheat, and by thematizing cheating. "You're doing me wrong," Socrates says to Ion, "if what you say is true that what enables you to praise Homer is knowledge . . . you're cheating me" (541E1–5). But "if . . . you're possessed by a divine gift . . . then you are not doing me wrong" (542A3–6). Socrates then gives Ion the option of being regarded "as a man who does wrong, or as someone divine" (A6–7; trans. Woodruff); not surprisingly Ion plumps for the latter (B1–2). Socrates is famous for his indifference to what others may think of one elsewhere (see, e.g., *Cri.* 48c2–6); here he bullies Ion into saying something that Ion does not believe by appealing to what others may think of him.

Some Stabs at Explanations

I have raised various questions about the *elenchus*, in particular about what it can be said to have established, given that consistency in belief lacks the importance it has usually been taken to have, and given that Socrates regularly cheats. Here I shall try to explain why Plato allows Socrates to cheat on so many occasions, although I don't claim to know in every case why he does.

I have raised questions about seven passages in the Socratic dialogues:

(a) Socrates' claim at *La.* 192B9–D11 that the dialectic of his refutation of Laches' definition of courage as endurance supports the conclusion that courage is wise endurance.

(b)   Socrates' assumption in the argument at *Chrm.* 159B5–160D3 that his various formulations of principle (I) (namely, that quick things are no less fine or admirable than quiet things) are equivalent to one another.

(c)   His belief, in the same argument, that from (I) and the claim that temperance is among the fine or admirable things, it follows that temperance is not quietness.

(d)   His treatment, in the same argument, of "quick" as the opposite of "quiet."

(e)   Socrates' bullying Ion in the *Ion* to agree that his (Socrates') plausible explanation of Ion's performative competence via the theory of divine inspiration applies as well to Ion's critical competence.

(f)   His refusal, again in the *Ion*, to allow Ion to say what he manifestly is trying to say.

(g)   His accusation that Ion is cheating him at the end of the *Ion*.

I have little to say about (g) that is not merely speculative. Perhaps Plato is aware that he is having Socrates cheat and is worried that his readers will sense that cheating is going on, and he hopes to make those feelings come to rest on Ion, not on Socrates. Perhaps, alternatively, it is the other way round: Plato wants us to appreciate that Socrates is cheating and hopes that if he raises the question of cheating in connection with Ion, we will raise it ourselves in connection with Socrates. Or perhaps he wants us clearly to distinguish Ion's two very different competencies, and to think seriously about the topic of poetry and human character.

I likewise have little to say about (d) and (e). On treating "quiet" and "quick" as contraries, I suggest that Plato has other items on his agenda in the *Charmides* (especially to distinguish Socrates from Critias, some of whose views seem similar, at least verbally, to some of Socrates' own views) and gives Socrates the argument he does *faute de mieux*. As for Socrates' assuming without argument in the *Ion* that the theory of divine inspiration, plausible as an explanation for Ion's performative competence but not for his critical competence, nonetheless applies to both competences, I would guess that Plato had worked out the theory of divine inspiration for poetic composition and performance, needed a forum for it, and didn't come up with a better way to get it into a dialogue.

I can be more helpful, I think, with regard to (f), Socrates' refusal to allow Ion to say what he means. I believe Ion means to be claiming that he – or the poet whose stand-in he is – is an expert on human character. Here are Ion's words again: "[A rhapsode will] know what sorts of things it's fitting for a man or a woman to say – or for a slave or a freeman, or for a follower or a leader" (540B3–5). Compare those words with these, from Aristotle's explanation in the *Poetics* of his claim that poetry is more philosophical and serious than history, since it is concerned with universals, not particulars: "By a universal statement I mean one as to what such or such a kind of man will probably or necessarily do; which is the aim of poetry; though it affixes proper names to the characters" (*Poet.* 9, 1451b8–10; trans. Bywater, modified slightly). It's the same idea. Plato takes up the poets elsewhere, in the *Republic*. But he saves his big guns in the "ancient battle between poetry and philosophy" for Book X, after he has developed in Books IV and Books VIII–IX a theory of human character that makes it the province of philosophy, not poetry (see 26: PLATO AND THE ARTS). He doesn't have such a theory in the *Ion*, or he cannot, for whatever reason, lay it out there. So the reason that Ion is not allowed to say what he wants and claim expertise on human character is that Plato is not in a position, in the *Ion*, to answer him.

As for (a), (b), and (c), I can only offer suggestions (some of them following Johnson 1977). But I believe that while part of Plato's agenda in the Socratic dialogues is to explore and develop various ideas about explanation or causation and abstraction that drive the dialectic, he omits, with only a few exceptions (e.g., *Euthphr.* 5D1–5), to give official notice of these ideas until the *Phaedo*. For example, at *Chrm.* 159B5–160D3, as we have seen, Socrates takes it that

I. Quick things are no less fine or admirable than quiet things (160D2–3),

and

B. Temperance is among the fine or admirable things (159c1),

entail the falsity of Charmides' original definition of temperance:

A. Temperance is quietness (159B5–6).

Why? (B) is about temperance understood as a *state of character*: it is thought of as something that is (or may be) in Charmides (see, e.g., 158E6–159A1). It is clear from the arguments in support of (I), in contrast, that it is about quick and quiet *actions*. What connects them? If (I) and (B) are to be at all relevant to the truth of (A), we shall have to read (I) as saying something about the actions that temperance produces, and not about the state of character that temperance is. And we shall also have to read (B) and Charmides' original definition:

A. Temperance is quietness (159B5–6),

as entailing something like:

K. Quiet actions are finer or more admirable than quick ones.

What principles such readings might depend upon is very far from clear.

A second, more striking example is the argument at *La.* 192B9–D11, with which we began. Recall that Socrates represents his refutation of Laches' definition of courage as endurance as giving Laches, at least, reason to believe:

I. Wise endurance is courage (192D10–11).

But all we have in the argument that might be supposed to be relevant to (I) are these two claims:

B. Courage is among the very fine or admirable things (192c5–6).
C. Endurance with wisdom is fine or admirable and good (192c9–10).

One way to understand what is going on here is this: Laches has defined courage as endurance. Socrates has argued that endurance with folly is not courage. So all that is left, so to say, of the endurance that Laches identified with courage is wise endurance. Hence, Laches has some reason to believe that wise endurance is courage.

I do not deny that this explanation may well be correct. But a more interesting explanation is available. The relevant claims, again, are:

B. Courage is among the very fine or admirable things (192c5–6).
C. Endurance with wisdom is fine or admirable and good (192c9–10).

(B) presumably means or at least entails:

G. Courage is a fine or admirable thing (192D8).

(G) and (C) can be given a *causal* reading. That is, we can read (G) and (C) as saying that it is the courage in courageous actions that makes those actions fine or admirable, and the wise endurance in wisely enduring actions that makes them fine or admirable, just as we read "love is blind" (with apologies to Jessica at *Merchant of Venice*, II. vi. 36–9) as saying that the love in those who love makes them blind to the faults of those they love. If we do read (G) and (C) in this way, and if we are drawn to the idea that

H. Similar features must be explained by reference to similar explanatory factors (cf. *Phd.* 97A2–B3),

we shall be inclined to conclude, with Socrates, that:

I. Wise endurance is courage (192D10–11).

And if we were to note that just actions, temperate actions, etc., are also fine or admirable, we should find ourselves, given (H), well down one road to the unity of virtues in action.

I believe, then, that it may well be possible to give plausible rationales to the inferences in passages (a), (b), and (c) listed at the start of this section. But to give them we shall have to devote much more study than we have so far to the dialectic of the Socratic dialogues. (Major steps in this direction are taken in Dancy 2004. See also 6: PLATONIC DEFINITIONS AND FORMS.)

Concluding Remarks

As I have described the Socratic *elenchus*, it uses cross-examination to extract contradictions from interlocutors in order to expose their false claims to knowledge. Socrates was interested in exposing such claims because he believed that false convictions about the important questions of human life stood in the way of the happiness of the people who held those convictions, and that their false convictions must be removed if they are to have a chance at happiness. But the agenda of Plato's Socratic dialogues extends well beyond Socrates' critical agenda. A few of the items on it are: to memorialize Socrates, and to understand both the man and his positive views; to mark Socrates off from others with whom he might be confused (sophists, eristics, Critias, etc.); to examine the credentials of various people who claim to know how we should live (politicians, soldiers, rhetoricians, sophists, and poets). And, as I have suggested, Plato has a serious concern with argumentation: how it works, when it succeeds, what principles it depends upon, etc. These constitute a wide spectrum of concerns that Plato had to balance in composing his dialogues. Sometimes, as in the *Apology*, Plato succeeded in weaving his various concerns into a single artistic and philosophical whole. Other times he was less than fully successful. Those who think that we may expect a thinker of Plato's literary and philosophical gifts to score a complete success every time out are wishful thinkers; I would advise them to take a look at Burke 1941 and think again. Plato often has to distort, push, shove, maul, gouge, stretch, chip, and avert his gaze (to paraphrase Nozick 1974: x), just like the rest of us, if at a higher level.

Note

All translations are the author's unless otherwise noted.

References and further reading

Benson, H. H. (1987). The problem of the *elenchus* reconsidered. *Ancient Philosophy* 7, pp. 67–85.

—— (1990). The priority of definition and the Socratic *elenchus*. In *Oxford Studies in Ancient Philosophy*, vol. 8 (pp. 19–65). Oxford: Oxford University Press.

—— (1995). The dissolution of the problem of the *elenchus*. In *Oxford Studies in Ancient Philosophy*, vol. 13 (pp. 45–112). Oxford: Oxford University Press.

—— (2000). *Socratic Wisdom*. New York and Oxford: Oxford University Press.

Brickhouse, T. C. and Smith, N. D. (1984). Vlastos on the *elenchus*. In *Oxford Studies in Ancient Philosophy*, vol. 2 (pp. 185–96). Oxford: Oxford University Press.

—— (1991). Socrates' elenctic mission. In *Oxford Studies in Ancient Philosophy*, vol. 9 (pp. 131–61). Oxford: Oxford University Press.

—— (1994). *Plato's Socrates*. New York: Oxford University Press.

Burke, K. (ed.) (1941). Antony on behalf of the play. In *The Philosophy of Literary Form* (pp. 279–90). New York: Vintage Books.

Dancy, R. M. (2004). *Plato's Introduction of Forms*. Cambridge: Cambridge University Press.

Irwin, T. (1977). *Plato's Moral Theory: The Early and Middle Dialogues*. Oxford and New York: Clarendon Press.

Johnson, T. E. (1977). Forms, reasons, and predications in Plato's *Phaedo*. Unpublished PhD dissertation, Claremont Graduate School, Claremont, Calif.

Kraut, R. (1983). Comments on Gregory Vlastos, "The Socratic *elenchus*". In *Oxford Studies in Ancient Philosophy*, vol. 1 (pp. 59–70). Oxford: Oxford University Press.

—— (1984). *Socrates and the State*. Princeton, NJ: Princeton University Press.

Lesher, J. H. (2002). Parmenidean *elenchos*. In G. A. Scott (ed.) *Does Socrates Have a Method? Rethinking the* Elenchus *in Plato's Dialogues and Beyond* (pp. 19–35). University Park, Pa.: Pennsylvania State University Press.

Nozick, R. (1974). *Anarchy, State, and Utopia*. New York: Basic Books.

Polansky, R. (1985). Professor Vlastos' analysis of Socratic *elenchus*. In *Oxford Studies in Ancient Philosophy*, vol. 3 (pp. 247–60). Oxford: Oxford University Press.

Robinson, R. (1953). *Plato's Earlier Dialectic*. Oxford: Oxford University Press.

Scott, G. A. (ed.) (2002). *Does Socrates Have a Method? Rethinking the* Elenchus *in Plato's Dialogues and Beyond*. University Park, Pa.: Pennsylvania State University Press.

Vlastos, G. (1983). The Socratic *elenchus*. In *Oxford Studies in Ancient Philosophy*, vol. 1 (pp. 27–58). Oxford: Oxford University Press.

—— (1991). *Socrates, Ironist and Moral Philosopher*. Ithaca, NY: Cornell University Press.

—— (1994). The Socratic *elenchus*: method is all. In M. F. Burnyeat (ed.) *Socratic Studies* (pp. 1–28). Cambridge: Cambridge University Press.

6

Platonic Definitions and Forms

R. M. DANCY

Aristotle tells us (*Metaph.* I.6.987a29–b14, XIII.4.1078b12–32 and 9.1086a24–b4) that Socrates was concerned with definitions in the domain of "ethical matters" (broadly construed, to include virtually any matter of evaluation), and that Plato took over this concern from him. And many of the dialogues of Plato classified as "early" or "Socratic" show an overarching concern with matters of definition. I see no very good reason for doubting Aristotle (on the other side see, e.g., Kahn 1996) and am strongly inclined to suppose that the Socratic dialogues give us something of the flavor of Socratic discourse. In other words, I think of those dialogues as historical fiction, especially in connection with definitions. Even in Xenophon Socrates shows an occasional predilection for pursuing definitions (see, e.g., *Mem.* I.i.16; IV.vi), although when it comes to reconstructing Socrates' practice, Xenophon provides us with nothing on the order of Plato's Socratic dialogues.

Aristotle also tells us that Plato's adoption of Socrates' quest for definitions took a special turn: Plato made the objects of definition, "forms," *distinct* or *separate* from perceptible things. And we shall find this taking place, not in the Socratic dialogues, but in the *Phaedo* and *Republic*. These are among what are commonly referred to as the "middle" dialogues.

The Socratic dialogues that are considered here are: *Charmides, Euthyphro, Hippias Major, Laches, Lysis*, the *Protagoras*, and Book I of the *Republic* (for controversy over the *Hippias Major, Lysis*, and *Republic* I, see references in Dancy 2004: 7–9). Those who question the historical veracity of these dialogues may take the following reconstruction as pertaining only to Plato himself. Hence occurrences of the name "Socrates" need only be taken as referring to the character in Plato's dialogues.

This applies a fortiori to the use of the name "Socrates" as it occurs in discussion below of the middle dialogues, *Phaedo, Symposium*, and *Republic*, and of the *Meno*, which I take to be transitional. In my view (which is hardly mine alone) these latter dialogues involve a good deal more of Plato and less of Socrates than the Socratic dialogues do: on this view, the Socrates of the Socratic dialogues tends to represent the historical Socrates, while that of the others tends to represent Plato, and there is a development over time from one to the other (see 2: INTERPRETING PLATO; 3: THE SOCRATIC PROBLEM).

You need not share any of these views to follow this chapter. The development of which I speak is in the first instance a logical one: Socrates' arguments in the Socratic dialogues do not commit him, as I see it, to the metaphysical position standardly called the "Theory of Forms"; his arguments in the "middle" dialogues do. But the latter arguments emerge from the previous ones. In particular, one crucial argument that emerges is what I'll be calling the "Argument from Relativity" (AR). In the middle dialogues this contrasts a Form, the Beautiful, say, with its mundane participants, the ordinary beautiful things, on the ground that the latter are beautiful only relatively, whereas the Beautiful is just plain beautiful (see 12: THE FORMS AND THE SCIENCES IN SOCRATES AND PLATO). It effects this contrast in the following way (further commentary below):

(ARE) There is such a thing as the Beautiful.
(ARO) Any ordinary beautiful [thing: Greek does not require this word] is also ugly.
(ARBeautiful) The Beautiful is never ugly.
∴(ARC) The Beautiful is not the same as any ordinary beautiful [thing].

Here (ARE) assumes the Existence of the Beautiful, (ARO) is a premise (but to be argued for) to the effect that Ordinary beautiful things are only relatively beautiful, (ARBeautiful) is one about the Form, the Beautiful, according to which it is not merely relatively beautiful, and (ARC) is the Conclusion.

This argument does not appear in the Socratic dialogues, although there is a clear anticipation of it in the *Hippias Major* (see below). It does appear in the middle dialogues. That is the main development of which I am speaking, and it is there, whatever the chronology or personnel may be.

We're going to construct a Theory of Definition for Socrates. This theory does not pretend to be Socrates' Theory of Definition, or Plato's, since there is no explicit Theory of Definition in these dialogues, by contrast with the later dialogues *Phaedrus*, *Sophist*, *Statesman*, and *Philebus*, in which there is something more by way of a theory (sometimes referred to as the "Method of Collection and Division"). Rather than laying down Socrates' pronouncements on what a definition needs to be, the Theory of Definition relies on Socrates' refutation of various specific attempts to define terms; we ask, in the case of each such refutation, how specifically it fails, and then what a definition that avoided that failure would have to be like.

That Theory of Definition will contain one fairly straightforward condition of adequacy for a definition, below called the "Substitutivity Requirement," another more difficult one, the "Explanatory Requirement," and a third quite puzzling one, the "Paradigm Requirement." The latter two especially will feed into the Theory of Forms. They do not, however, entail that theory; where Socrates is concerned with definitions, he is not concerned with metaphysics at all (against this see, e.g., Allen 1970). We shall see the turn toward metaphysics when we get to the *Phaedo*.

A Socratic Theory of Definition

Perhaps the first thing to notice is that Socrates does not have a word that straightforwardly means "definition"; one term he uses means, in the first instance, "boundary," but the primary weight of his discussions falls on the question "what is . . . ?": "what is the pious?" (*Euthyphro*), "temperance?" (*Charmides*), "the beautiful?" (*Hippias Major*), etc.

Before introducing our theory, we must consider why Socrates is after definitions, answers to his "what is . . . ?" questions, in the first place.

In *Republic* I he asks what justice is; he expects this to make it clear whether just people are happier than unjust people, and so (352D1–7) to help us to see how we ought to live our lives. This practical concern is quite visible in other dialogues in which definitions are being sought. The first two-thirds of the *Laches* has to do with the question whether or not learning to fight in heavy armor helps build character, especially courage; the question "what is courage?" is raised in 190D to resolve that question. The *Lysis* comes around to the question what a friend is (212A8–B2: for the phrasing see 223B7–8) after consideration of how friends should treat each other (this consideration accounts for half of the dialogue). In the *Euthyphro* the question "what is piety?" comes in at 5C–D (quoted below) after Euthyphro has claimed to be prosecuting his father for murder on the basis of claims about what it is pious to do. Perhaps the most striking dialogue in this connection is the *Protagoras*, which begins by raising the question whether studying with a sophist such as Protagoras will conduce to virtue or excellence, pursues an astonishing number of wide-ranging ramifications, and ends with Socrates telling everyone that all the difficulty has been due to their failure to answer the question "what is excellence?" Everyone turns out to be too busy for that, and so the dialogue stops.

So Socrates wants definitions because he thinks they are essential to figuring out how to live rightly, and quite often in these dialogues the "preliminaries" leading up to the question of definition occupy more space than the discussion of that question.

Nonetheless, the definition question is clearly of great importance, and Socrates gives us a reason for insisting on it when we are trying to determine how to live. He is presupposing (against this see, e.g., Beversluis 1987), as he explicitly says, something I shall refer to as the "Intellectualist Assumption" (often referred to elsewhere as the "Socratic Fallacy" or the "Principle of the Priority of Definition"; see esp. Benson 1990, and 2000: 112–63; and Dancy 2004: 35–64 for further comment and references), which we may write as:

(IA) To know that . . . F —, one must be able to say what the F, or F-ness, is.

Here ". . . F —" is to be any declarative sentence containing "F" (or "F-ness," or "the F"); e.g., where "F" is "pious," ". . . F —" could be "this action is pious" or "piety is a good thing." Saying what the F or F-ness is is defining it. So, for example: to say whether prosecuting one's father for murder under circumstances such as Euthyphro's is the pious thing to do, one must define the pious or piety (see *Euthphr.* 4D9–E8, 5C8–D5, 6D6–E7, 15C11–E1); to say whether something is fine or beautiful (alternative translations of the same Greek word, *kalon*; I'm going to stick with "beautiful") one must define the beautiful (see *Hp.Ma.* 286C5–D2, 298B11–C2, 304D4–E3); to say whether just people are happier than unjust ones, one must define justice (see R. I, 354A12–C3).

So far I have been using the lower case, as in "the beautiful," to label the subject about which Socrates is asking "what is it?" In the middle dialogues, the beautiful is reconstrued as a Form, "the Beautiful." I'll adhere to this convention: the capitals come in when we are talking about Forms.

The convention also applies to the word "form" itself; in the Socratic dialogues, Socrates more than once speaks of what he is after as a "form" (*eidos*) or an "idea" (*idea*). There is no discernible difference in force between these two words, both derived from the root "*id---*," associated with a verb for seeing; I shall stick to "form." The words in question were common enough in Greek as a term for characters or qualities of things (initially, *visual* characters or qualities), used by people who had no profound ideas about the ontological status of characters or qualities. So I shall speak of "forms" in the Socratic dialogues and "Forms" in the middle ones.

Socrates sometimes sets off on his quest for definition by checking to see whether he and his interlocutor agree that there is something to talk about. In the *Hippias Major* (287c8–D2) he asks whether there is such a thing as the beautiful, and Hippias readily concedes that there is. Such concessions, when we get to the Theory of Forms, are construed as claims about Forms, to the effect that there is such a thing as the Beautiful, the Form. But plainly when Hippias makes his ready concession, he is not thinking of it as carrying that kind of metaphysical weight. And Socrates immediately cashes the concession in on what he wants it for: "Say then, friend, what is the beautiful?" (287D2–3). He does nothing by way of elaborating on the ontological status of the beautiful. The dialogue is concerned with defining, not with ontology. When we talk in an ordinary way about animals, say, and ask what distinguishes the lion from the tiger, we are usually not in the slightest interested in the metaphysical question whether the lion is something over and above ordinary lions. And Socrates seems to show no interest in the parallel question whether the beautiful is anything over and above beautiful things – at least, not at this point. From the point of view of this chapter, that is the difference between the Socratic and the middle dialogues.

The Theory of Definition we are going to construct for Socrates looks like this. We start with a candidate *definiens*: an expression that purports adequately to define some term, the *definiendum*. The Socratic dialogues ask of an adequate definition that it satisfy:

the Substitutivity Requirement: its *definiens* must be substitutable for its *definiendum* without upsetting the truth or falsehood of the sentence containing the *definiens* (*salva veritate*);

the Paradigm Requirement: its *definiens* must give a paradigm or standard by comparison with which cases of its *definiendum* may be determined; and

the Explanatory Requirement: its *definiens* must explain the application of its *definiendum*.

The first of these three requirements may conveniently be broken down into two, according to the schema that formalizes it:

(SR) $w =_{df} abc \rightarrow (\ldots w — \leftrightarrow \ldots abc —)$

understanding "$\ldots w —$" as earlier with "$\ldots F —$" and reading "$\rightarrow$" as "only if" and "$\leftrightarrow$" as "if and only if". Then (SR) can be understood as the conjunction of

(Nec) $w =_{df} abc \rightarrow (\ldots w — \rightarrow \ldots abc —)$,

73

which tells us that the *definiens* "*abc*" gives a necessary condition for something's satisfying the *definiendum* "*w*," and

(Suf) $w =_{df} abc \rightarrow (\dots abc \longrightarrow \dots w \longrightarrow)$,

which tells us that the *definiens* gives us a sufficient condition for something's satisfying the *definiendum*. E.g., if "vixen" is correctly defined as "female fox," then (Nec) tells us that if Vickie is a vixen, she's a female fox, and (Suf) that if she's a female fox she's a vixen.

The bald statement of the requirements in one important respect fails to mirror Socrates' practice, for Socrates does not always treat these as isolated requirements: rather, he is prone to running more than one of them together.

As an example of this phenomenon, consider a couple of passages from the *Euthyphro*. First, at 5C8–D5 Socrates says:

> So now, by Zeus, tell me what you just now affirmed you clearly know: what sort of thing do you say the reverent [i.e., pious: see 5D2 below] and the irreverent [i.e., impious] are, both concerning murder and concerning the other [matters]?
> Or isn't the pious the same as itself in every action, and the impious, again, the contrary of the pious in its entirety, but like itself and everything whatever that is to be impious having, with respect to its impiety, some one idea?

(When at the beginning Socrates speaks of Euthyphro's having "just now" affirmed that he clearly knew what the reverent is, he is pointing to 4D–E, in which the Intellectualist Assumption is deployed.) In my terms, this is telling us that (Nec) is satisfied, and if we read "impious" as "not pious," it is also telling us that, by contraposition, (Suf) is also satisfied.

Euthyphro accepts this, and Socrates adverts to it, after Euthyphro has made a stab at defining the pious as "prosecuting one who commits injustice, whether [it is] about murders, or temple robberies, or does wrong in any other such way, whether it is actually one's father or mother or anyone else, and not prosecuting is impious" (5D9–E2). We may put this as:

(D₁pious) *x* is pious $=_{df}$ *x* is a case of prosecuting someone who does wrong in one way or another.

Before we get any farther, it should be noted that (D₁pious) is completely typical of all the dialogues under consideration in that, despite generations of commentary, Socrates' interlocutors, in their first attempts at definition, do not cite "particulars" as opposed to a "universals" (see Nehamas 1975/6). In the case of (D₁pious), prosecuting bad guys is a perfectly good "universal," instantiated many times over in courts of law even today. Socrates' interlocutors always give universals, albeit often, as in this case, universals that are not universal *enough*, as Socrates points out. What he says is (6D6–8):

> . . . But, Euthyphro, many other things you would say are pious as well.
> *Euthyphro*: For they too are (pious).

74

So far, all we have is Substitutivity, in particular, (Nec): there are other pious things besides prosecuting evildoers, so that does not give us a necessary condition for piety.

What Socrates next says goes beyond this (6D9–E7):

> *Socrates*: Then do you remember that I did not direct you to teach me some one or two of the many pious things, but that form itself by which all the pious things are pious? For you said, I think, that it is by one idea [= form: see above] that the impious things are impious and the pious things pious; or don't you recall?
> *Euthyphro*: I certainly do.
> *Socrates*: Then teach me this idea, what it is, so that looking to it and using it as a paradigm, whatever is such as it is among the things either you or anyone else does, I shall say is pious, and whatever is not such, I shall say [is] not.

Here we are not only getting Substitutivity, but also the Explanatory Requirement (that "form itself *by which* all the pious things are pious") and the Paradigm Requirement as well ("*using it as a paradigm*, whatever *is such as it is* . . . I shall say is pious, and whatever is not such, I shall say [is] not"). But all Socrates requires in the argument against (D₁pious) is (Nec); he makes no use of these additional requirements. He will, later, and they get separate employments (see below).

In other dialogues, the Substitutivity Requirement is employed without mention of the others. In the *Laches*, the first attempt (190E5–6) to define courage as standing one's ground fails because there are courageous actions that do not involve standing one's ground, but, in fact, retreating (191A5–C6); Socrates wants, he says, "what is the same in all the cases" (191E10–11). Here the *definiens* fails Substitutivity by failing to give a necessary condition. Laches' next attempt (192B9–C1) defines courage as perseverance, and Socrates objects by pointing out that there are cases of perseverance that do not count as courage (192C5–D9; Socrates' argument is more complicated than this, but this is its basis). Here the *definiens* fails Substitutivity because it does not give a sufficient condition. And all the other attempts in that dialogue fail on one or the other of these grounds, without the help of the other requirements. And the same holds for many other cases in other dialogues.

The Explanatory Requirement is a different story. I can find only one case in which it is used in a context that mentions no other requirements. But it bears the primary weight in more than one of Socrates' arguments against proposed definitions; sometimes, although the other requirements appear in the background, they are irrelevant to the actual course of Socrates' argument.

It will help to consider the initial plausibility of the Explanatory Requirement. The idea is that an adequate definition should not just give us a term uniformly substitutable for the defined term, but should also explain the application of the defined term. But this is initially plausible only if "explain" is read fairly weakly. Perhaps it makes sense to say that what explains the fact that this is a vixen is that it is a female fox. But this explanation is not in any obvious way "causal," even if we can rephrase the claim by saying that this is a vixen because it is a female fox: what is being explained is merely what we mean by calling it a "vixen"; we are merely explaining the content of the claim "this is a vixen."

In the single context in which the Explanatory Requirement appears solo, the very complex argument of *Euthphr.* 9D1–11B1, this is ultimately all that is at stake. The definition to be defeated is:

(D$_3$pious) x is pious $=_{df}$ x is loved by all the gods

(for (D$_2$pious), see below). The crucial claim that operates against this is Euthyphro's concession that

(EC) what is pious is not pious because it is loved by all the gods; rather it is loved by all the gods because it is pious.

And Socrates' contention is that if (D$_3$pious) were correct, it would follow that what is pious is so because it is loved by all the gods. On the face of it, this just amounts to saying that if (D$_3$pious) were correct, it would follow that the content of the claim "this is pious" could be unpacked as "this is loved by all the gods": there is nothing more going on here than there was in the case of "vixen" and "female fox." At any rate, there is no suggestion that some super-physical entity labeled "the Loved by All the Gods" would be *causing* various actions or people to be pious.

Full substantiation would require detailed analysis of Socrates' actual argument, which is quite a bit more complex than the above sketch indicates, but there is no space for that here.

More often, the Explanatory Requirement appears in conjunction with the Paradigm Requirement. So let us first have a look at that.

The general idea is that what is cited by way of defining a term "F" must be a paradigm for "F" in the sense that it bears no admixture of the contrary term "con$F$": what defines "beautiful" can have about it nothing of ugliness. For Socrates in the dialogues we are considering, this is not true of a great many things that are beautiful; they are also ugly, in different respects, at different times, in the eyes of different people, and so on. They are, in this sense, only *relatively* beautiful: they are beautiful, or ugly, relative to certain contexts of evaluation, and the beautiful cannot be that.

There is one case in which the Paradigm Requirement is employed virtually on its own, again in the *Euthyphro* (and again the argument is more complex than the following indicates). At 6E11–7A1 Euthyphro tries defining the pious as that which is loved by the gods; this is

(D$_2$pious) x is pious $=_{df}$ x is loved by the gods.

It is Socrates' revision of this that leads to (D$_3$pious), which additionally requires unanimity on the part of the gods, and that revision is required by the argument against (D$_2$pious). For that turns on Euthyphro's belief (already registered at 6B7–C7, and appealed to by Socrates in 7B2–4, D9–E4) that the gods disagree, and some approve of ("love") what others do not. Socrates generalizes this, whether legitimately or not, to the claim that all the same things are loved and hated by the gods, and concludes that all the same things are pious and impious (7E10–8A9). We need Substitutivity for this, but what really undermines (D$_2$pious) is this (8A10–12):

> *Socrates*: Then you did not answer what I asked, Amazing Fellow. For I wasn't asking for
> that which is, while it is the same [thing], in fact both pious and impious; but what-
> ever is god-loved is also god-hated, as it seems.

The complaint is not that there is a contradiction in the conclusion that the same things are both pious and impious; it is, rather, that (D$_2$ pious) fails the Paradigm Requirement: the god-loved is not through and through pious, that is, pious and under no circumstances impious.

The Paradigm Requirement is puzzling: it is not at all obvious that a definition can satisfy both it and Substitutivity. Clearly, if a *definiens* gives us something that is non-relatively pious, or beautiful, or whatever, whereas any or all ordinary cases of pious or beautiful things are merely relatively pious, that *definiens* is not going to be substitutable for "pious" or "beautiful" in those ordinary cases, for that *definiens* does not give us a term co-extensive with the defined term, but one that designates a single instance of the defined term, albeit a perfect one.

One of the features of Socrates' discourse that tends to support the Paradigm Requirement is his not invariable but common habit of referring to what he wants to define using generically abstract noun phrases such as "the pious" or "the beautiful" instead of the abstract nouns "piety" or "beauty." (For example, the abstract noun "beauty" occurs only once or twice in the *Hippias Major* at 292D3, and possibly in a quotation from Heraclitus at 289B5; everywhere else in that dialogue he speaks of "the beautiful.") This makes the claim that the beautiful is beautiful sound like a tautology, and the claim that the beautiful is ugly a contradiction. So the "Self-Predication" (this term goes back to Vlastos 1954) (see also 13: PROBLEMS FOR FORMS)

(SP) The *F* is *F*

has a more natural sound than perhaps it should, as does its strengthened form

(SPs) The *F* is always *F* and never con*F*.

Socrates buys into both, as do his metaphysically innocent interlocutors (for example, Euthyphro at *Euthphr.* 6E4–9 and 8A10–B9, and Protagoras at *Prt.* 330B7–E2, where the assumption is carried over to abstract nouns of the form F-ness).

At any rate, it is (SPs) that connects the Paradigm Requirement with the Explanatory Requirement, and begins to bring in a piece of metaphysics (although not yet the Theory of Forms). For Socrates occasionally operates with what I shall call a "Transmission Theory of Causality" (the term descends from Lloyd 1976), which can be broken down as follows:

(TT1) It is the *F* (or *F*-ness) because of which anything counts as *F*.
(TT2) Whatever it is because of which anything counts as *F* is itself always *F* and never con*F*.
∴ (TT3) The *F* (or *F*-ness) is itself always *F*.

(TT1) is a rewritten version of the Explanatory Requirement, (TT3) is (SPs), and is here made a consequence of (TT1) and the new claim, (TT2); this makes this a Transmission Theory: whatever causes x to be F is itself F and makes x F by transmitting F to x.

This was for centuries a popular view about causality; it can be found, for example, in Anaxagoras, in Aristotle, in Thomas Aquinas' first way of proving the existence of God, and in Descartes's *Third Meditation*. (These days its popularity may seem difficult to explain: a lot of things cause pain without, unfortunately, themselves being in pain.) That it is a metaphysical theory is undeniable, since it is a theory about causality (see also 14: THE ROLE OF COSMOLOGY IN PLATO'S PHILOSOPHY). But its acceptance by all those philosophers shows that it is not yet the Theory of Forms, since none of them accepted that theory. And in the dialogues here under discussion, Socrates does not connect it with any questions having to do with the ontological status of the F: it is accepted by interlocutors who have never given a thought to such questions, such as (again) Protagoras in *Protagoras* (332B6–E2), or, in definition-seeking contexts, Charmides and Hippias.

Charmides tries defining temperance as modesty (*Chrm.* 160E3–5). Socrates invokes against this (161A8–9) the claim that what makes men good must itself be good and never bad. This is an instance of (TT2), and Charmides unhesitatingly accepts it. He also agrees that temperance makes men good, and that modesty is sometimes bad. So temperance is not modesty. (This condenses a very difficult argument, but that is its guiding thread.)

In *Hp.Ma.* 287E2–4, Hippias defines "the beautiful" as follows:

(Dbeautiful) x is beautiful $=_{df}$ x is a beautiful girl,

where what is meant is any beautiful girl at all. Socrates begins, ignoring the obvious objection of circularity, by stating another obvious objection: there are lots of other beautiful things, such as horses and pots (288B8–E5), so it looks as if he is headed for Substitutivity. But he doesn't go there. Instead, he points out that a beautiful girl, although beautiful when compared with an ape, is ugly when compared with a god (289A1–B7), and turns this into the following objection (289C3–D5, omitting some complications):

> when asked for the beautiful, do you give in reply, as you yourself say, what is in fact no more beautiful than ugly? . . . But . . . if I had asked you from the beginning what is both beautiful and ugly, if you'd given me in reply what you just now did, wouldn't you have replied correctly? But does it still seem to you that the beautiful itself, by which all the other [things] are adorned and show themselves as beautiful when this form is added, is a girl, or a horse, or a lyre?

And Hippias moves on, without comment. Clearly, what disqualifies "a beautiful girl" as a *definiens* for the beautiful is that it cannot explain why other things are beautiful, and it cannot do this because a beautiful girl is not just beautiful, but also ugly (here in comparison with other things). This at least connects the Explanatory Requirement with the Paradigm Requirement, where that is understood as incorporating (SPs) and the Transmission Theory.

78

Subsequent arguments in the *Hippias Major* (289D6–291C9, 291D1–293C8) have essentially the same structure, although they trade on different ways in which something can be only relatively beautiful: beautiful in one context, ugly in another, and beautiful in the eyes of some, ugly in the eyes of others.

The argument for which we are headed, the "Argument from Relativity" is very nearly with us in the *Hippias Major*. What we have, concentrating on the first of the refutations, is this much:

(arE) There is such a thing as the beautiful.
(arG) Any beautiful girl is also ugly.
(arbeautiful) The beautiful cannot be ugly.
∴ (arC) The beautiful is not the same as any beautiful girl.

This is not quite the Argument from Relativity, for that requires a generalization Socrates does not give us in the *Hippias Major*, to the effect that (arG) is not just true of girls, horses, or lyres, but of any mundane beautiful thing whatever. And Socrates says nothing whatever to indicate that he has an overarching interest in the transcendental existence of the Form of the Beautiful; he is merely trying to defeat attempts to define the beautiful.

The *Meno*: Between Definitions and Forms

In the *Meno* there is a massive shifting of gears.

At first it does not seem so. The dialogue begins with an abbreviated Socratic dialogue of definition on the question "what is excellence?" (or "what is virtue?"). The Intellectualist Assumption is heavily emphasized: Meno's opening question is whether excellence can be taught, and Socrates professes himself unable even to start on that since he does not know at all what excellence is (70A5–71C4). Meno essays three attempts, all shot down by Socrates, in pretty much the ways we have come to expect, although with a new twist: Socrates insists that the correct *definiens* for excellence must display the unity that makes all the various excellences (justice, temperance, etc.) *one*. Nothing much is said by way of elaboration, but the emphasis is new.

But there is more that is new than this. Meno grinds to a halt after his third attempt goes out the window, and becomes obstreperous. He asks (80D5–9) how Socrates thinks he could ever get an answer to the question "what is excellence?" if he really doesn't know anything at all about it. How could he recognize that any given answer was the correct one? This is often referred to as "Meno's Paradox."

The question is one many of us have been wanting to ask for a long time. In real life, we manage to arrive at definitions, when we do, on the basis of some background knowledge about the application of the *definiendum*. If we really know nothing of decacumination or esurience, there can be no hope of our defining them.

In those cases, remembering Latin would help some. And what Socrates offers Meno is a little like that. He introduces (81A10–B6) a view, the "Doctrine of Recollection," according to which we never in fact do learn the answers to Socrates' definition-questions (see here Scott 1995), at least not in this life. What we do instead is recollect the answers, the knowledge of which we have possessed in a period before this life (see 9: PLATO ON RECOLLECTION). It is a difficult question whether we should say that that knowledge was acquired prenatally, in which case there was a point at which we learned it, or that our souls have been so constituted that they always had the knowledge; some of what Socrates says points one way (81c5–e2) and some another (86a6–b4).

Either way, it is that background knowledge that makes it possible to cope with Socratic questions. Socrates does not quite make it clear precisely how Meno's Paradox is met by the Doctrine of Recollection. He illustrates the doctrine in a sub-dialogue (81e–86c) with one of Meno's slaves, who is asked the rather complex question: given a square with sides two feet long, what is the length of the side of a square double the area? Socrates leads him to the correct answer, which is: the diagonal of the original square. On his account, he elicits this answer from the slave rather than supplying it to him. There is room to differ about this, but it is pretty clear that Socrates is pointing toward what is now called a priori knowledge, and that there is such knowledge has had many defenders apart from Plato (for the best exposition of the *Meno* from this point of view, see Vlastos 1965).

Meno's Paradox and the Doctrine of Recollection are completely new to the *Meno*. The doctrine is going to reappear in the *Phaedo* (and in the *Phaedrus*, but, in my view, nowhere else). There it is associated with the Theory of Forms. Is it so associated here in the *Meno*? There is no mention of that theory in the *Meno*, but there are a couple of things that suggest it may not be far off. There is first the above-mentioned emphasis on the idea that the thing being defined is somehow *one*, and perhaps this suggests that the *definiendum* is being thought of as an object, with a unity of its own. And second there is the fact that in the preliminary dialogue on the question "what is excellence?" Socrates twice (in 72d8, e5) refers to what he is after as a "form." This counts for little by itself, since Meno himself uses the term, unprompted, in 80a5, and nothing suggests that he is in on the Theory of Forms. But if we ask: What is it that the slave is recollecting, and what is it that we recollect in successfully answering Socrates' "what is it?" questions, and if we expect the Doctrine of Recollection to have any bearing on the question what excellence is, what had better be recollected is the form, excellence.

Of course, this is a far cry from an explicit Theory of Forms; we must wait for the *Phaedo* for that. But we are not done with the novelties introduced in the *Meno*. Two call for present attention.

As for the Doctrine of Recollection as illustrated by the sub-dialogue with the slave, Meno professes qualified conviction, and accordingly Socrates encourages him to have another go at the question what excellence is (86b6–c6). But Meno abruptly returns to his opening question, whether excellence is teachable, and Socrates, with only a grumble, simply abandons the Intellectualist Assumption and agrees to pursue that question (86c7–e1).

This is striking: in subsequent dialogues the Intellectualist Assumption, as stated above, plays no role. (It is not that there are no further requests for definition, but the suggestion that in the absence of a definition one can say nothing whatever is gone.) And with that goes the other novelty to which we must briefly attend: the abandonment of the Intellectualist Assumption carries with it a method of approach to non-definition questions such as whether excellence is teachable, the "Method of Hypothesis," of which Socrates now gives a short and quite obscure description (86E1–87B2). The method plainly has its roots in mathematics, in a geometrical Method of Analysis employed by Greek mathematicians (for an exposition see Menn 2002). The geometrical method involves beginning with a question to which the answer is at the outset unknown and working backwards, towards assumptions which (if everything works right) eventually derive from things that are known, such as the geometrical axioms. Socrates wants to apply this to Meno's question about excellence by asking what assumptions would be sufficient to give us the conclusion that excellence is teachable (87B2–c3). He works back to the assumption that excellence is a sort of knowledge, and then to the assumption that knowledge is the only good thing that there is (87c5–89A7) (see also 7: PLATO'S METHOD OF DIALECTIC).

But then he undermines his own argument by suggesting that, apart from knowledge, true belief would also be a good thing (96D7–97c10). This is mitigated by the further suggestion that true belief is not *as* good as knowledge (97c11–98B6), but then this in turn is at least partially retracted (98B7–D3), and the dialogue ends, in Socratic fashion, inconclusively.

The Doctrine of Recollection, the retraction of the Intellectualist Assumption, and the Method of Hypothesis are hardly Socratic, if we take the dialogues discussed above as our touchstone of Socraticism. So it looks very much as if, in the *Meno*, we have Plato striking out on his own. He is, it appears, now prepared to allow that we can use terms in the absence of an explicit definition, and that, when definitions *are* required, our way of getting at them is due to our prenatal grasp of what is to be defined.

Forms

If the *Meno* shows Plato stepping out from behind his lead character Socrates, the *Phaedo* has him emerging farther still, for the Method of Hypothesis will appear again there, and now tied to the Theory of Forms.

In the *Phaedo*, we first encounter the Forms (as opposed to forms) at 65A9–66A10, without argument, and without even the word "form." At 65D4, Socrates asks his interlocutor Simmias whether there is "something itself just," "something beautiful and good"; he shortly (65D12–13) adds "largeness, health, strength." So far, there is nothing to indicate that we have been launched into the realm of Forms. But Simmias also readily accepts that we have not made contact with these things through the senses, but only through "pure thought" (66A1–2). These striking claims are new: they find no parallel in the Socratic dialogues. But they are just what Aristotle had led us to expect. And this is what leads to my capitalization of "Form."

The argument that we miss in 65A9–66A10 appears in the course of *Phd.* 72E11–78A9. The overall undertaking in that passage is the presentation of a new argument for the Doctrine of Recollection (as a step toward establishing the immortality of the soul), but embedded in it, and detachable from it, is the Argument from Relativity. What Socrates wants to show is that our ability to answer "what is it?" questions of the sort he had been asking in the Socratic dialogues depends on our prenatal acquaintance with a special realm of objects not encountered by the senses. These objects are the Forms, and in successfully answering Socratic questions we are being led by things we often do encounter in sense-experience to recollect those objects.

Socrates' example of a Form in this passage is "the equal itself" (74A12 *et passim*), and he says that this is one example among others, of which he mentions "the large," "the small," "the beautiful," "the good," and all the things we're always talking about, raising about them "what is it?" questions (75c7–D5, 76D7–E7). In other words, "equal" is here being treated as in some way parallel to "beautiful," and this, to our ears, is peculiar because with "that's equal" we expect a complement unpacking "equal to what" whereas we expect no such complement with "that's beautiful." But perhaps this is not the way things sounded to Plato, for, as we have already seen in connection with the *Hippias Major*, he would have required fleshing out "that's beautiful" with a clause explaining what it was beautiful relative to, in what context, in the eyes of whom, and so on. Shortly put: we think of "equal" as a term of relation; Plato thought of "beautiful" as a term of relation also.

Why the switch to "equal"? Why not "beautiful" all the way through? Here we must attend to what Simmias says. In 74B2–3, he says he knows what the equal is; that should mean that he is in a position to give a definition for it (which definition, regrettably, he does not state: for one possibility, see *Prm.* 161D). In 76B5–c5, he gives vent to the fear that, once Socrates has died, there won't be anyone left who can give definitions for such terms as "the beautiful" (just mentioned along with the other cases in 75c10–D4). Now Socrates, as everyone knows, is going to die at the end of the *Phaedo*, and Simmias is not. So it must be that he does not know what (say) the beautiful is, and cannot define it. And then it must be that the reason for picking "the equal" is just the contrast between it and "the beautiful" on that score. And perhaps that has to do with Simmias' previous familiarity with the Pythagorean Philolaus (see 61D6–E4); the Pythagoreans were much exercised over the notion of equality. (This is, of course, conjecture; the contrast between Simmias' knowledge of the definition for "equal" and his lack of knowledge of the definition for "beautiful" is not.)

At any rate, in 74B4–c6, having elicited from Simmias the claim that he knows what the equal is, Socrates goes on to argue that the equal is distinct from any of the ordinary sticks, stones, or whatever that prompt us to recollect it. The argument is, to put it sketchily (the details get rather complex), that given above as an example of the Argument from Relativity, but with "equal" replacing "beautiful":

(ARE) There is such a thing as the Equal.
(ARO) Any ordinary equal [thing] is also unequal.
(AREqual) The Equal is never unequal.
∴ (ARC) The Equal is not the same as any ordinary equal [thing].

Here (ARO) is presumably to be supported by the fact that what counts as a stick that is equal depends on the situation in which the comparison is being made.

The argument is admittedly easier going with "beautiful," and when Diotima in the *Symposium* states its upshot, she does so in terms of "beautiful." She is talking about someone who is becoming initiated in the mysteries of love, and this involves his contemplation of beautiful things. In 210E2–211B5 she tells Socrates that once the initiate has got far enough:

82

he will suddenly discern something beautiful, wondrous in its nature, this, Socrates, [being] that for the sake of which were all his labors hitherto, which, first, always is: it neither comes-to-be nor perishes, neither waxes nor wanes; then too, [it is] not beautiful in one way, ugly in another, nor [beautiful] at one time and not at another, nor beautiful relative to one thing, ugly relative to another, nor beautiful at one place, ugly at another, as being beautiful to some and ugly to others; nor, again, will the beautiful appear to him as some face or hands or anything else of which body partakes, nor as a certain account or a certain knowledge, nor as being somewhere in something else, e.g. in an animal, in the earth, in heaven, or in anything else, but itself by itself with itself, always being singular in form, while all the other beautiful [things] are partakers of that [beautiful] in such a way that, while the others are coming-to-be and passing-away, that in no way comes-to-be any larger or smaller or undergoes anything.

Diotima is here describing at length the Form, the Beautiful. We may note at this point that it fits with two of the conditions we ran into in constructing a theory of definition for Socrates: it covers all the cases, in that whatever is beautiful partakes of it (and, presumably, nothing that is not beautiful does), and it is a paradigmatically beautiful thing. So Substitutivity and the Paradigm Requirement are echoed in the Theory of Forms.

And so is the Explanatory Requirement. This emerges in the final argument for immortality in the *Phaedo* (99D4–103c4). There Socrates constructs a theory of causality by adverting to the Method of Hypothesis outlined in the *Meno*. Now the Hypothesis becomes the Theory of Forms itself (100B1–9), and Socrates extends that into a theory of causality when he says (100c4–6, D3–8):

it seems to me that, if there is anything else beautiful besides the beautiful itself, it is not beautiful because of any other single [thing] than because it partakes of that beautiful . . . but simply, artlessly, even perhaps foolishly, I hold this close to myself, that nothing else makes it beautiful other than the presence or communion or however and in whatever way it comes on of that beautiful; for I don't make any further claims about that, but [I do claim] that [it is] by the beautiful that all beautiful [things are] beautiful.

This "simple" theory requires elaboration to turn it into an argument for immortality, but the elaboration has no real impact on the Theory of Forms.

This is the Theory of Forms, and its heritage is pretty clearly Socrates' quest for definitions. At any rate, "simply, artlessly, even perhaps foolishly, I hold this close to myself," however controversial it may be.

Notes

All translations are the author's unless otherwise noted.

Virtually everything in this chapter is a matter of controversy; there are brief indications of where to go for dissenting views, but for detailed defense and further references see Dancy 2004 (in particular, for all the cases in which I have said that the argument is more complex than the present analysis indicates, a full analysis will be found there).

References and further reading

Allen, R. E. (1970). *Plato's* Euthyphro *and the Earlier Theory of Forms.* London: Routledge and Kegan Paul; New York: Humanities Press.

Benson, H. H. (1990). The priority of definition and the Socratic elenchus. In *Oxford Studies in Ancient Philosophy*, vol. 8 (pp. 19–65). Oxford: Oxford University Press.

—— (2000). *Socratic Wisdom: The Model of Knowledge in Plato's Early Dialogues.* New York and Oxford: Oxford University Press.

Beversluis, J. (1987). Does Socrates commit the Socratic fallacy? *American Philosophical Quarterly* 24, pp. 211–23. Repr. in H. H. Benson (ed.) *Essays on the Philosophy of Socrates* (pp. 107–22). New York and Oxford: Oxford University Press.

Dancy, R. M. (2004). *Plato's Introduction of Forms.* Cambridge: Cambridge Univesity Press.

Kahn, C. H. (1996). *Plato and the Socratic Dialogue: The Philosophical Use of a Literary Form.* Cambridge: Cambridge University Press.

Lloyd, A. C. (1976). The principle that the cause is greater than its effect. *Phronesis* 21, pp. 146–56.

Menn, S. (2002). Plato and the method of analysis. *Phronesis* 47, pp. 193–223.

Nehamas, A. (1975/6). Confusing universals and particulars in Plato's early dialogues. *Review of Metaphysics* 29, pp. 287–306. Repr. in *Virtues of Authenticity: Essays on Plato and Socrates.* (pp. 159–75). Princeton, NJ: Princeton University Press.

Scott, D. (1995). *Recollection and Experience: Plato's Theory of Understanding and its Successors.* Cambridge: Cambridge University Press.

Vlastos, G. (1954). The third man argument in the *Parmenides. Philosophical Review* 63, pp. 319–49. Repr. in R. E. Allen (ed.) (1965) *Studies in Plato's Metaphysics* (pp. 231–63). London: Routledge and Kegan Paul; G. Vlastos (1995) *Studies in Greek Philosophy*, vol. II: *Socrates, Plato, and their Tradition*, ed. D. W. Graham (pp. 166–90). Princeton, NJ: Princeton University Press.

—— (1965). *Anamnesis* in the *Meno. Dialogue* 4, pp. 143–67. Repr. (1995) in *Studies in Greek Philosophy*, vol. II: *Socrates, Plato, and their Tradition*, ed. D. W. Graham (pp. 147–65). Princeton, NJ: Princeton University Press.

7

Plato's Method of Dialectic

HUGH H. BENSON

Richard Robinson, in his classic work *Plato's Earlier Dialectic* (1953), describes the following difference between dialogues which he takes to represent Plato's "early period" and dialogues which he takes to represent Plato's "middle period":

> The early gives prominence to method but not to methodology, while the middle gives prominence to methodology but not to method. In other words, theories of method are more obvious in the middle, but examples of it are more obvious in the early. Actual cases of the *elenchus* follow one another in quick succession in the early works; but when we look for discussions of the *elenchus*, we found them few and not very abstract. The middle dialogues, on the other hand, abound in abstract words and proposals concerning method, but it is by no means obvious whether these proposals are being actually followed, or whether any method is being actually followed. (Robinson 1953: 61–2)

Robinson goes on in what follows to soften this distinction between the two sets of dialogues, but scholarly discussion of Platonic method in the latter set of dialogues has continued to focus more upon Plato's explicit proposals than on Plato's actual practice in those dialogues. No doubt part of the explanation for this tendency is Robinson's suggestion that in the latter dialogues Plato appears not to practice what he preaches. The philosophical method that Plato has Socrates recommend in dialogues such as the *Meno*, *Phaedo*, and *Republic* is apparently not the method that Plato has Socrates practice in those dialogues. In this chapter I resist such a conception of Platonic dialectic.

I will begin by looking briefly at Plato's explicit recommendations of philosophical method in three key middle dialogues: the *Meno*, the *Phaedo*, and the *Republic*. We will see that while differences in the methods recommended in these three dialogues are apparent, certain core features remain invariant. These core features can be reduced to two processes: a process of identifying and drawing out the consequences of propositions, known as hypotheses, in order to answer the question at hand, and a process of confirming or justifying those hypotheses. I will then maintain that in three pivotal and extended stretches in these three dialogues Plato has Socrates practice one or the other of these processes of the method he has had Socrates recommend. Such a view of Platonic dialectic has two immediate consequences. First, there is more continuity and commonality to Plato's discussion of method, his "methodology" to use Robinson's word, than has often been supposed. The methods of hypothesis introduced in the *Meno* and again in the *Phaedo* and the method of dialectic explicitly introduced in the *Republic* are versions of a single core method. Second, in order to understand Plato's recommended philosophical method in the so-called middle dialogues we should not restrict ourselves to Plato's explicit discussions of that method. Just as in the so-called early dialogues we look at both Socrates' explicit discussions of method and his actual practice in order to understand the *elenchus* (see 5: THE SOCRATIC *ELENCHUS*), so in the so-called middle dialogues we should look at both Socrates' explicit discussions of method and his actual practice in order to understand dialectic. We should, that is, look at both his "methodology" and his "method," to use Robinson's words. Nevertheless, we will see that the philosophical method that emerges from both of these sources remains by Plato's own lights in some way inadequate. I will conclude by offering an explanation of this apparent inadequacy – an explanation that points in the direction of further study.

Dialectic with a Small "d"

Let us begin with the word "dialectic." Robinson, again, famously maintained that

> the word "dialectic" had a strong tendency in Plato to mean "the ideal method, whatever that may be." In so far as it was thus merely an honorific title, Plato applied it at every stage of his life to whatever seemed to him at the moment the most hopeful procedure. . . . This usage, combined with the fact that Plato did at one time considerably change his conception of the best method, has the result that the meaning of the word "dialectic" undergoes a substantial alteration in the course of the dialogues. (Robinson 1953: 70)

One might be surprised to learn, however, that the Greek substantive *hē dialektikē* and its cognates occur only 22 times in the Platonic corpus and only once in dialogues that Robinson considers early (*Euthd.* 290c5). Moreover, more than a third of those occurrences are concentrated within six Stephanus pages in the *Republic* (531D9, 532B4, 533c7, 534B3, 534E3, 536D6, 537c6, 537c7). The substantival infinitive *to dialegesthai* occurs much more frequently and can sometimes carry a technical sense as opposed to its more ordinary meaning of "to converse" or "to discuss." But it is often difficult to determine when the technical sense is being employed. Nevertheless, when the technical sense is plausibly employed, Robinson correctly calls attention to its instability. For example, twice in the *Gorgias* Socrates appears to be drawing a quasi-technical contrast between *to dialegesthai* and rhetoric where the contrast appears little more than a preference for a shorter question and answer style of philosophical discussion over longer displays of philosophical prowess (*Grg.* 447B9–c4 and 448D1–449c8; see Kahn 1996: 303). In the *Republic*, however, Socrates contrasts the power of *to dialegesthai* with a method apparently sometimes employed by mathematicians, where the contrast appears highly technical, making use of specialized notions like hypotheses, conclusions, first principles, and so on (510B2–511D5). Nevertheless, throughout this instability one feature remains invariant: Socrates' preference for the method he picks out by *to dialegesthai, dialectikē* or their cognates (Gill 2002: 150).

In discussing Plato's dialectical method, then, I take myself to be discussing Plato's preferred or recommended philosophical method whatever that may be. The method he recommends and practices in the so-called early dialogues has already been discussed in a previous chapter – the method of *elenchus*. The method Plato introduces and apparently recommends in the *Meno* and the *Phaedo* has come to be known as the method of hypothesis. In the middle books of the *Republic* (VI–VII), Plato recommends as the culmination of the educational process of the philosopher-rulers an apparently distinct method often understood as dialectic strictly so-called (see *Republic* 531D– 537c mentioned above; "Dialectic" with a cap "D"). The method of collection and division is introduced and recommended in the *Phaedrus* and apparently practiced in the *Sophist*, *Politicus*, and *Philebus*. While Plato's dialectical method (at least "dialectic" with a small "d") includes all these methods, my focus will be on the method or methods discussed and, I maintain, practiced in the *Meno*, *Phaedo*, and *Republic*. Connections with Plato's *elenchus* and his method of collection and division are abundant and important, but cannot be pursued here.

Plato on Dialectic in the *Meno*, *Phaedo*, and *Republic*

The questions of this chapter, then, are: What is the method that Plato recommends in the central dialogues of the *Meno*, the *Phaedo*, and the *Republic*, and does he practice it in those dialogues? Consider, first, Socrates' response to Meno's desire to return to the question of the teachability of virtue prior to answering the question of the nature of virtue approximately two-thirds of the way through the *Meno*. Socrates has just responded to Meno's paradox that it is either impossible or unnecessary methodically to attempt to acquire knowledge of something. Either one fails to know what one is attempting to know, in which case the attempt cannot be successfully begun or concluded; or one knows what one is attempting to know, in which case the attempt is unnecessary. Socrates' response consists first in appealing to the theory of priests and priestesses, which has come to be known in the literature as the theory of recollection (see 9: PLATO ON RECOLLECTION), and then illustrating that theory by means of a conversation with a slave concerning doubling the area of an original four-square-foot square. Socrates concludes that while he would not vouchsafe the details of his response, he would vouchsafe that we ought methodically to seek the knowledge that we lack rather than accept that such an inquiry is impossible. Apparently having been persuaded, Meno expresses his desire to return to the question with which the dialogue began, the teachability of virtue. Surprisingly, and despite some misgivings, Socrates accedes to this desire on the condition that Meno permit him to pursue the question according to the method of the geometers, which he immediately explains with the following example:

> if they are asked whether a specific area can be inscribed in the form of a triangle within a given circle, one of them might say: "I do not yet know whether that area has that property, but I think I have, as it were, a hypothesis that is of use for the problem, namely this: If that area is such that when one has applied it as a rectangle to the given straight line in the circle it is deficient by a figure similar to the very figure which is applied, then

I think one alternative results, whereas another results if it is impossible for this to happen. So, by using this hypothesis, I am willing to tell you what results with regard to inscribing it in the circle – that is, whether it is impossible or not." (86ε6–87β2)

While the details of this example are notoriously obscure and controversial, the idea seems to be that the method of the geometers is to first propose a hypothesis which attributes to the given area a property such that, if the area has that property such an inscription can be made, and if it does not, then such an inscription cannot be made. So if the hypothesis is true, the inscription can be made; and if the hypothesis is false, it cannot be made. Then, the geometers turn their attention to inquiring whether or not the hypothesis is true. Here, then, we have Socrates proposing a method that consists of two processes. First, it consists of the process of identifying a hypothesis such that its truth is necessary and sufficient for a determinate answer to the question under consideration. In the case of the geometrical example, the hypothesis appears to be that the area is "such that when one has applied it as a rectangle to the given straight line in the circle it is deficient by a figure similar to the very figure which is applied," while in the case of the teachability of virtue the hypothesis is that virtue is a kind of knowledge (see 87β5–c7). The second process is to determine whether the hypothesis in question is true. One seeks to determine whether the given area is "such that when one has applied it as a rectangle to the given straight line in the circle it is deficient by a figure similar to the very figure which is applied" or whether virtue is a kind of knowledge. The two-part method that Plato has Socrates propose here in the *Meno* has come to be called the method of hypothesis. (For further discussions of the method proposed here in the *Meno* see Robinson 1953: ch. 8; Bluck 1961; Bedu-Addo 1984; and Benson 2003.)

This so-called method of hypothesis makes its appearance at a similar stage in the *Phaedo*. Socrates has been offering a series of three arguments designed to establish the immortality of the soul, each of which has met with formidable objections (see 19: THE PLATONIC SOUL). In response to the last objection to the third argument Socrates explains that an adequate response will require "a thorough investigation of the cause of generation and destruction" (95ε9–96α1), and he offers to recount his own investigation. He began in his youth, he tells us, by following the method of the natural scientists, but he quickly came to learn that rather than acquire the knowledge he lacked he actually lost some of the knowledge he formerly thought he had (96c–97β). Next, he turned to the method of Anaxagoras (see 97β3–7), which consisted of attempting to determine what is best (97c–98β). Unfortunately, Socrates was unable to acquire the knowledge he lacked by this method either, for he was able neither to discover what is best on his own nor to learn it from the writings of Anaxagoras. Consequently he explains that he set out to acquire the knowledge of the cause of generation and destruction – which he lacked – by means of the following "second-best" method.

I thought I must take refuge in discussions [*tous logous*] and investigate the truth of things by means of words. . . . I started in this manner: taking as my hypothesis in each case the theory that seemed to me the most compelling, I would consider as true, about cause and everything else, whatever agreed with this, and as untrue whatever did not so agree. (99ε4–100α7)

Socrates next explains that the hypothesis he has in mind in the present case is what has come to be called in the literature his Theory of Forms: "the existence of a Beautiful, itself by itself, of a Good and a Great and all the rest" (100B5–7) (see also 12: THE FORMS AND THE SCIENCES IN SOCRATES AND PLATO). Socrates indicates that it follows from this theory that the cause of a thing's having a given property is that thing's participation in the relevant Form. For example, "it is through Beauty that beautiful things are made beautiful" (100E2–3). Socrates concludes his discussion of this method by explaining how one should react when one's hypothesis is "questioned" (*echoito*; see Kahn 1996: 318 n. 35):

> you would ignore him and would not answer until you had examined whether the consequences that follow from it agree with one another or contradict one another. And when you must give an account of your hypothesis itself you will proceed in the same way: you will assume another hypothesis, the one which seems to you best of the higher ones until you come to something acceptable, but you will not jumble the two as the debaters do by discussing the hypothesis and its consequences at the same time, if you wish to discover any truth. (101D3–E3)

Once again at a crucial stage in the argument of a dialogue, Plato has Socrates propose a method employing hypotheses in order to continue the inquiry. Again, he distinguishes two processes of the method. In describing the first process Socrates stresses the process of drawing out the consequences of the proposed hypothesis rather than the process of identifying the hypothesis (100A3–7), and in describing the second process Socrates explains in more detail precisely how one is to carry it out. First, one should determine whether the consequences of the hypothesis are consistent with other background beliefs or information concerning the topic under discussion. Second, one should employ the method of hypothesis on the hypothesis itself – identifying a further hypothesis whose truth is necessary and sufficient for the truth of the original hypothesis and testing the consistency of the consequences of this new hypothesis with one's background beliefs or information – until one reaches a hypothesis that is "acceptable" (*hikanon*). (For further discussions of the method proposed here in the *Phaedo*, see Robinson 1953: ch. 9; Gallop 1975; Bostock 1986; Rowe 1993a; van Eck 1994; and Kanayama 2000.)

Finally, in the central books of the *Republic* Plato provides an extended discussion of the appropriate philosophical method. Two passages are especially salient. In the first passage Plato has Socrates distinguish two methods. One method is practiced by mathematicians and can at best lead one to acquire thought (*dianoia*). The other is the one he recommends and that leads one to acquire knowledge (*epistēmē* or *noēsis*). In the second Plato has Socrates explicitly describe the discipline of dialectic as the culmination of a lifetime of philosophical education.

At 509C–511D Socrates asks the interlocutors of the *Republic* to imagine a line cut into two unequal portions. The smaller portion, he says, represents the things that participate in Forms, for example, the beautiful things, and the larger portion the Forms themselves, for example, the Beautiful itself. Each of these two portions of the line is similarly divided into two unequal subsections. The portion representing the things that participate in Forms consists of a smaller subsection representing images of the things that participate in Forms – shadows, reflections in pools of water, etc. – while the larger subsection represents the originals of the things imaged in the smaller subsection. The portion representing the Forms, however, is not divided according to objects like the two lower subsections, but according to the methods employed in each subsection. According to Socrates, in the smaller subsection of the portion representing the Forms [A1] the soul uses as images the originals of the previous subsection, [A2] is forced to investigate from hypotheses, and [A3] proceeds to conclusions, not to a first principle (510B4–6), while in the larger subsection the soul makes "[B1] its way to a first principle that is not a hypothesis, [B2] proceeding from a hypothesis [B3] but without images used in the previous subsection, using forms themselves and making its investigation through them" (R. 510B6–9). Corresponding to these four subsections of the line are four conditions of the soul: imaging (*eikasia*), belief (*pistis*), thought (*dianoia*), and understanding or knowledge (*noēsis*).

Notice that Plato's description of the two methods distinguished in the top two subsections appeals to three features which appear to correspond as follows: [A1]/ [B3], [A2]/[B2], and [A3]/[B1]. That is, both the method that leads to *dianoia* – the dianoetic method, and the method that leads to knowledge – the dialectical method, make use of hypotheses: [A2] and [B2]. The two methods are distinguished not by the fact that they employ hypotheses but by the way they employ hypotheses. The dianoetic method uses the originals from the preceding subsection in proceeding from its hypotheses [A1], while dialectic does not [B3], and dianoetic proceeds from hypotheses to conclusions and not first principles [A3], while dialectic proceeds from hypotheses to first principles [B1]. Socrates' subsequent elaboration of these features suggests that the former difference amounts to a difference between the use of sense-experience (by the dianoetic method: 510D5–511A2 and 511A6–8) as opposed to the a priori method of dialectic (511B7–c2), while the latter difference amounts to a distinction between treating hypotheses as though they were confirmed and not in need of justification or an account (by the dianoetic method: 510c1–D4 and 511A3–6) and treating hypotheses as unconfirmed stepping-stones requiring justification or an account until one reaches "the unhypothetical first principle of everything" (511B3–7), which is plausibly identified with the Form of the Good. What is important to notice for our present concerns is the continuity between the methods proposed in the *Meno* and *Phaedo* and the method of dialectic in the *Republic*. All three consist of two fundamental processes of, on the one hand, identifying and drawing out the consequences of hypotheses and, on the other hand, verifying or confirming the truth of the hypotheses. The failure of the dianoetic method – in large part – lies in its failure to focus attention on the latter process.

The three features of dialectic specified here in the *Republic* – the use of hypotheses, the unsuitability of sense-experience, and the necessity of confirming the hypotheses employed until one reaches the "unhypothetical first principle of everything" – are repeated in the last of the passages we will be looking at, although the last feature is the focus of attention. At R. 531D7–535A2 (which contains five of the 22 occurrences of *hē dialektikē* in the Platonic corpus) Socrates describes dialectic as the completion of a lifetime of philosophical education (531D, 534E–535A). He says "dialectic (*hē dialektikē*) is the only inquiry that travels this road, doing away with hypotheses (*tas hupotheseis anairousa*) and proceeding to the first principle itself, so as to be secure"

(533c7–d1). While the claim that dialectic does away with hypotheses might be understood as indicating that Plato is here recommending against the use of hypotheses, it is more plausible to suppose (especially in light of the passages we have just been examining) that Plato is recommending the manner in which they should be used (see, for example, Robinson 1953: 161–2; and Gonzalez 1998: 238–40). They need to be confirmed, explained, and justified ultimately "proceeding to the first principle itself, so as to be secure." It is this aspect of the use of hypotheses that is emphasized throughout the discussion of dialectic in this passage. Socrates explains that dialectic can give an account (*ho logos*) of what it knows (531d6–e6, 534b, and 534c), doesn't give up until the first principle or the Form of the Good is grasped (532a–b, 534b–c), and can survive against all refutations (*elenchōn*) (534c). But Socrates also refers to the other feature of the use of hypotheses mentioned in the divided line passage: the unsuitability of sense-experience. He explains that the dialectician "tries through argument (*tou logou*) and apart from all sense perceptions to find the being itself of each thing" (532a6–7).

In these three key dialogues, then, we find Plato having Socrates describe a methodology he appears to be endorsing. All three passages feature the use of hypotheses, but each provides a different perspective. The *Meno* introduces the method in general terms, describing it as a method employed by geometers and identifying its two fundamental processes (identifying hypotheses necessary and sufficient for resolving the question at hand and determining the truth of the hypotheses). The *Phaedo* recognizes two processes as well but stresses drawing out the consequences of the hypotheses rather than identifying the hypotheses, and it provides additional details for how one should go about determining the truth of the hypotheses – (testing their consistency with other background beliefs and information and attempting to confirm them by employing the method on the hypotheses themselves). Finally, the *Republic* adds that the process of determining the truth of hypotheses should be independent of sense-experience and carried on until one hits upon the "unhypothetical first principle of everything." Having discovered the rough outlines of the method Plato has Socrates discuss and propose in the *Meno*, *Phaedo*, and *Republic*, we can now consider whether Plato has Socrates practice what he preaches.

Plato's Practice of Dialectic in the *Meno*, *Phaedo*, and *Republic*

Let us begin with perhaps the easiest case. Immediately following Socrates' introduction of the method at *Men.* 86e6–87b2, Socrates proposes to "investigate whether it is teachable or not by means of a hypothesis" (87b3–5). He immediately identifies a hypothesis such that its truth is necessary and sufficient for the teachability of virtue, namely that virtue is a kind of knowledge, and then sets out to determine the truth of this hypothesis. He does this by employing the second of the two procedures mentioned in the *Phaedo*: employing the method of hypothesis on the hypothesis itself. First, he identifies further hypotheses whose truth is necessary and sufficient for the truth of the hypothesis that virtue is a kind of knowledge, namely that virtue is good (87d2–3) and that nothing else is good other than knowledge (87d4–8). The former he justifies only by claiming that it "remains" or "stands firm for us" (*menei hēmin*;

87D3). The latter he defends by means of a brief argument (87E5–89A1), after which he concludes that since wisdom is beneficial and virtue is beneficial, "Virtue then, as a whole or in part, is wisdom" (89A3–4). (If we are not to find Socrates guilty of an irrelevant conclusion here, we must assume that he is using "wisdom" (*sophia*) and "knowledge" (*epistēmē*) interchangeably.)

That this portion of the *Meno* is an instance of the method of hypothesis has been generally recognized. But the portion is short – little over two Stephanus pages long – and it is often thought that the method is dropped for the rest of the dialogue. Thus, Robinson assumes that the method ends here at 89c (Robinson 1953: 117), confirming his view that Plato seldom depicts Socrates practicing the method he discusses in the so-called middle dialogues. But the method of hypothesis is not abandoned at this point in the *Meno*. Rather, Socrates takes up the first of the two procedures the *Phaedo* mentions for confirming a hypothesis: testing its consistency with other background beliefs and information. (For a longer defense, see Benson 2003; see also Kahn 1996: 313.)

After concluding at 89c2–4 that the answer to Meno's question is that virtue can be taught, on the hypothesis that virtue is knowledge, Socrates expresses doubt, saying

> I am not saying that it is wrong to say that virtue is teachable if it is knowledge, but look whether it is reasonable of me to doubt whether it is knowledge. Tell me this: if not only virtue but anything whatever can be taught, should there not be of necessity people who teach it and people who learn it? (*Men.* 89D3–8)

Notice that Socrates here expresses doubt about the hypothesis – that virtue is a kind of knowledge – from which the positive answer to Meno's question has been inferred, revealing that he is still operating within the confines of the method of hypothesis. He is expressing doubt about the truth of the hypothesis. Its truth has been supported by the second of the two procedures mentioned in the *Phaedo*, but the results of the first procedure – testing its consistency with other background beliefs and information – which Socrates is about to perform go in the other direction. An immediate consequence of the hypothesis that virtue is knowledge is that virtue is teachable (the positive answer to Meno's question), but a consequence of this (at least given the background belief expressed above that for everything that can be taught there are people who teach and people who learn it) is that there are teachers and learners of virtue. But the subsequent discussion with Meno and Anytus from 89E6 to 96D4 reveals background beliefs and information concerning the educational practice of sophists and the gentlemen of Athens that entail that there are no teachers nor learners of virtue. While the second procedure from the *Phaedo* tended to confirm the truth of the hypothesis that virtue is a kind of knowledge, the argument from 89D3 to 96D4 has revealed that the first procedure from the *Phaedo* has controverted it.

Thus, contrary to the suggestion that Plato tends not to depict Socrates practicing the method he proposes in the middle dialogues, here in the *Meno* we have Socrates depicted as practicing the method he has just proposed at length (for nearly a third of the dialogue as a whole and for more than three-quarters of the dialogue following the introduction of the method). What is unique about this portion of the *Meno* – as we will see in a moment – is not that we are presented with an extended instantiation of the method Socrates proposes, but that we are presented with the portion of the method aimed at determining the truth of the hypothesis. Indeed, we are presented with this portion of the method having conflicting results: the first procedure of the *Phaedo* controverting the hypothesis, the second procedure confirming it. Socrates provides no guidance in either the *Phaedo* or the *Republic* for how one is to proceed when this two-part process has conflicting results. *Men.* 96D5–100B4 suggests that one should review the arguments presented in each part to determine whether they contain any flaws. Socrates claims that the flaw is to be found in the argument for the claim that nothing else is good other than knowledge. True belief, Socrates professes, is no less beneficial than knowledge (97A9–D3 and 98B7–c3). Whether we take this profession seriously or not, we should not conclude that Socrates fails to practice the method he proposes.

As I mentioned above, however, the *Meno* may be the easiest case to make out. Nearly everyone would grant that Plato depicts Socrates practicing the method he proposes at least briefly in the *Meno*. But what about the *Phaedo*? Does Plato depict Socrates practicing the method he proposes in the *Phaedo*? Obviously I believe that the answer to this question is yes, but the way in which Socrates practices the method he proposes in the *Phaedo* is different from the way in which he practices it in the *Meno*. Recall that all three dialogues – the *Meno, Phaedo*, and *Republic* – propose and discuss a method that consists of two distinct processes: the process of identifying hypotheses and drawing out their consequences and the process of verifying, confirming, or otherwise determining the truth of the hypotheses. We saw that in the *Meno* Plato depicted Socrates concentrating on the latter process: verifying or confirming the hypotheses, depicting only briefly Socrates' attention to the former (87B5–c7). The converse is the case in the *Phaedo*. Despite providing more detail about the process of verifying hypotheses at 101D3–E3, Plato depicts Socrates concentrating on the process of identifying hypotheses and drawing out their consequences.

After the general description of the method at 99E4–100A7, Socrates provides content by turning to the case at hand. He identifies the hypothesis that the Forms exist (100B5–9), and infers from it, together with various subsidiary premises concerning the nature of cause (perhaps the three laws or requirements of "cause"; see Gallop 1975: 186; Bostock 1986: 137; and Kanayama 2000: 54), that each thing comes to be what it is by sharing in a Form. For example, something becomes beautiful because it shares in the Form of Beauty (100D4–8), something becomes two because it shares in the Form of Twoness (101c1–6), and something becomes big because it shares in the Form of Bigness (100E5–101A5). From this "safe" causal principle (again presumably together with various subsidiary premises) Socrates infers a "more subtle" causal principle according to which a thing comes to be what it is, say F, by possessing something that entails *F-ness*. For example, three comes to be odd by possessing Oneness which entails Oddness, or the body comes to be hot by possessing fire which entails Heat (105B5–c6). At this point Socrates begins his final argument for the immortality of the soul, which can be summarized as follows. The "more subtle" causal principle entails that if the presence of a thing makes x F, then that thing cannot be not-F. For example, if the presence of fire in water makes water hot, then fire cannot be not hot. Since the presence of the soul makes a body alive, it follows that the soul cannot be not alive. It cannot die. It is immortal. After acknowledging the

93

appropriateness of Simmias' continued "private misgivings," Socrates concludes the argument as follows:

> our first hypotheses require clearer examination, even though we find them convincing. And if you analyze them adequately, you will, I think, follow the argument as far as a man can and if the conclusion is clear, you will look no further. (107B5–9)

This last passage makes it explicit that Socrates supposes that he has been practicing all along the method he proposed. He has, to be sure, been focused on the first of the two processes which characterize the method: the process of identifying and drawing out the consequences of the hypotheses for the question at hand, in this case the immortality of the soul. But he here maintains that the method will not be complete until one turns to the second process of verifying or confirming the hypotheses employed. Thus, here in the *Phaedo* for the crucial final argument for the immortality of the soul, Plato appears to be depicting Socrates practicing the method he proposes, just as in the *Meno*.

Of course, this having been said, my sketch of this final argument for the immortality of the soul runs roughshod over a variety of difficulties surrounding the argument and the interpretation of the method proposed. For example, it might be objected that one cannot derive interesting or substantive consequences from a single hypothesis (as the general description at 99E4–100A7 would suggest that one can), and indeed, it will be noticed that in describing the argument that follows as an instance of deriving such consequences I frequently had recourse to additional hypotheses and/or auxiliary premises. Moreover, I have simply assumed without argument that the notion of "agreement" (*sumphōnein*) employed in the general description is roughly the notion of logical entailment despite all of the difficulties that surround such an assumption (see, for example, Robinson 1953: 126–8; Gentzler 1991; and Kanayama 2000: 62–4). And, of course, finally, I have hardly offered anything like a definitive and problem-free interpretation of the structure of Plato's final argument in the *Phaedo* (for a more detailed interpretation of which see, for example, Kanayama 2000). Nevertheless, as we seek to address these difficulties surrounding the method Socrates proposes in *Phaedo*, we need not, and indeed, should not restrict ourselves to Socrates' explicit statements concerning it. We should look to the final argument for the immortality of the soul that follows Socrates' explicit statements. In coming to understand his method of *elenchus* one would not – and indeed does not – restrict oneself to Socrates' explicit statements concerning it, but one looks to his actual practice in dialogues such as the *Euthyphro*, *Laches*, *Charmides*, and *Protagoras*. Similarly, while the last third of the *Meno* should be seen as evidence of what Socrates has in mind by verifying or confirming hypotheses, so the final argument for the immortality of the soul in the *Phaedo* should be seen as evidence for what Socrates has in mind by identifying and drawing out their consequences.

A similar point applies to the method practiced in the *Republic*, although our discussion will necessarily be more sketchy. The *Republic* can be read as an extended argument aimed at showing that justice is a good welcomed for its own sake as well as its consequences (357A1–358A8). (See, for example, White 1979; Annas 1981; see also 23: PLATO ON JUSTICE.) To show this, Socrates proposes first to determine the nature of justice, and immediately points out that the investigation they are about to begin is not easy, but requires "keen eyesight."

> Therefore, since we aren't clever people, we should adopt the method of investigation that we'd use if, lacking keen eyesight, we were told to read small letters from a distance and then noticed that the same letters existed elsewhere in a larger size and on a larger surface. We'd consider it a godsend, I think, to be allowed to read the larger ones first and then to examine the smaller ones, to see whether they really are the same. (368D1–7)

Like the geometer in the *Meno* Socrates here proposes to reduce the question he is concerned with – the nature of individual justice – to a question that is supposed to be easier to answer: the nature of civic justice. That is, he proposes to identify a hypothesis from which he can infer an answer to his original question. Such a hypothesis, however, is not ready to hand and so he turns to two other hypotheses from which he infers such a hypothesis. Socrates proposes to construct the ideal city, or Kallipolis, on the basis of two hypotheses: that "none of us is self-sufficient, but we all need many things" (369B6–7) and that "each of us differs somewhat in nature from the others, one being suited to one task, another to another" (370A8–B2). (See, for example, White 1979: 84–5; Annas 1981: 73; and Pappas 1995: 61.) From these two hypotheses and numerous auxiliary premises and arguments Socrates infers that civic justice is each class of Kallipolis – the craftsmen class, the soldier class, and the ruler class – performing the task for which it is best suited (433E–434c, esp. 434c7–10). Next, on the basis of the hypothesis that "the same thing will not be willing to do or to undergo opposites in the same part of itself, in relation to the same thing, at the same time" (436B8–9; see also 436E8–437A2), together with various psychological premises, Socrates infers that the soul too consists of three parts arranged like the parts of Kallipolis, and so, on the basis of the presumed reduction with which the argument begins, individual justice is seen to be each part of the soul – appetite, spirit, and reason – performing the task for which it is best suited. From this account of the nature of justice Socrates goes on in Books VIII through X to show that justice is a good welcomed for its own sake and for its consequences. Given this admittedly hurried and imperfect reconstruction of the main argument of the *Republic*, Plato may be seen as depicting Socrates practicing the method he has been proposing. Socrates proceeds by attempting to identify and draw out the consequences of hypotheses in order to answer the question at hand.

Even if we grant this reconstruction of the argument, it must be admitted that the evidence that Plato depicts Socrates as practicing the dialectical method as proposed in the *Meno*, *Phaedo*, and *Republic* in the central argument of the *Republic* is at best circumstantial. Indeed, it might be wondered whether any argument could be seen as an instantiation of this aspect of the dialectical method – at least to the extent that the main argument of the *Republic* can. But the evidence becomes more compelling when we turn to two passages in which Socrates describes the argument he has provided.

The first is a short passage following the account of civic justice, as Socrates turns to the question of individual justice. He says

> But you should know, Glaucon, that, in my opinion, we will never get a precise answer using our present methods of argument – although there is another longer and fuller road that does lead to such an answer. But perhaps we can get an answer that's up to the standard of our previous statements and inquiries. (R. 435c9–d5)

Plato here has Socrates express misgivings about the force of the argument to this point. The answer it has arrived at appears in some way uncertain. Knowing what we know about the dialectical method Plato has been proposing in the *Meno*, *Phaedo*, and *Republic* and its difference from the dianoetic method, we might speculate that the difficulty with the argument is that it has only employed one of the processes that constitute the dialectial method. It has only identified and drawn out the consequences of hypotheses necessary and sufficient to answer the question at hand. It has not attempted to verify or confirm the truth of those hypotheses. The longer road would be to employ this process as well – all the way to "the unhypothetical first principle of everything." A longer road, indeed! What Plato appears to be indicating here, however, is that Socrates is not practicing the dianoetic method, but the dialectical method, though incompletely. Socrates is aware that his hypotheses are in need of confirmation. Unlike the dianoetic mathematician, he does not take his conclusions as secure when they are based on unconfirmed hypotheses.

This speculation is confirmed when Plato has Socrates return to his distinction between the shorter and longer road when discussing the education of the future rulers. Socrates says, referring back to the passage we have just been discussing,

> Do you remember when we distinguished three parts in the soul, in order to help bring out what justice, moderation, courage, and wisdom each is?
> . . . We said, I believe, that, in order to get the finest possible view of these matters, we would need to take a longer road that would make them plain to anyone who took it but that it was possible to give demonstrations of what they are that would be up to the standard of the previous argument. And you said that that would be satisfactory. So it seems to me that our discussion at that time fell short of exactness, but whether or not it satisfied you is for you to say. (504a4–b7)

After Glaucon expresses his satisfaction, Socrates explains that the future rulers, however,

> must take the longer road and put as much effort into learning as into physical training, for otherwise, as we were just saying, he will never reach the goal of the most important subject and the most appropriate one for him to learn. (504c9–d3)

Here we are told that the longer road is the road to that leads to the most important subject. We go on to learn that this subject is the knowledge of the Form of the Good. Given the identity of the Form of the Good and "the unhypothetical first principle of everything" our speculation is confirmed. The shorter road being pursued in the main argument of *Republic* is defective because it has failed to employ the process of verifying the hypotheses employed up to "the unhypothetical first principle of everything." The method Socrates employs in the main argument of the *Republic* is one half of the dialectical method he describes in the *Meno*, the *Phaedo*, and the *Republic*.

The Second-Best Method

Thus far I have maintained that is it a mistake to view Socrates as failing to practice the method Plato has him propose in the central dialogues of the *Meno*, the *Phaedo*, and the *Republic*. In these dialogues Socrates is made to propose a method that consists of two processes: a process of identifying and drawing out the consequences of hypotheses necessary and sufficient for resolving the question at hand, and a process of verifying or confirming such hypotheses. The method undergoes development and/or elaboration throughout the course of these three dialogues, but these two fundamental processes remain invariant. In the *Meno* Socrates is depicted as employing the process of verifying or confirming hypotheses to an apparently unsatisfactory result. In the *Phaedo* and *Republic*, Socrates is depicted as employing the process of identifying and drawing out the consequences of the hypotheses necessary and sufficient for determining, on the one hand, the immortality of the soul and, on the other hand, whether justice is a good welcomed for its own sake as well as for its consequences. Nevertheless, throughout these passages there remains something unsatisfactory about the method Socrates is depicted as proposing and employing. We have just seen that in the *Republic*, Socrates reproaches the method he has employed in Books II through IV as taking the shorter rather than the longer, superior road. In the *Phaedo* he describes the method he proposes and then employs as in some way "second best" (*deuteros plous*; see, for example, Gentzler 1991: 266 n. 4; Rowe 1993b: 238–9 and 68–9; and Gonzalez 1998: 192 and 351 n. 3; *pace* Kanayama 2000: 87–95). And, in the *Meno* many have taken Socrates to propose and employ the method he does only because of Meno's refusal to pursue the nature of virtue rather than its teachability (Brown 1967: 63–5; Seeskin 1993: 45–7; and Kahn 1996: 318–19). How are we to explain this apparent reluctance to endorse the method Plato has had Socrates propose and employ?

It might be thought that this reluctance indicates that for Plato genuine philosophical method or genuine dialectic cannot be depicted in the dialogues. It is in some way ineffable or non-discursive. It must be practiced, not described or depicted. What Plato describes and depicts is the second-best method of hypothesis. In fact, something like this may be supported by Plato's apparent disparagement of writing as a way of practicing philosophy in the *Phaedrus* (275c5–277A4). Nevertheless, this same dialogue offers yet another account of the nature of dialectic – this time characterized as the method of collection and division (265D3–266c1), which many think Plato goes on to depict in some detail in dialogues such as the *Sophist*, *Politicus*, and *Philebus*. (See, for example, Stenzel 1973: xliii and Kahn 1996: 300.) It is difficult then to take Plato to be committed to the impossibility of depicting genuine dialectic as such in the dialogues.

Others have suggested that Plato's reluctance to endorse the method employed and proposed in our three dialogues is precisely to distinguish that method from the method of dialectic endorsed in the middle books of the *Republic* (and employed in the so-called early dialogues; see Gonzalez 1998). The method that Plato employs and proposes prior to the middle books of the *Republic* is the method of hypothesis, and that method is to be identified with the dianoetic method. But the dianoetic method's second-best status in Plato's eyes is straightforward. Of course, I have maintained that such a view of the method of hypothesis needs re-examination. Both the dialectical and dianoetic methods of the *Republic* employ hypotheses. What distinguishes these two methods is the way they employ hypotheses. Dianoetic uses sense-experience in dealing with hypotheses and treats them as though they were confirmed, while dialectic does not use sense-experience and treats its hypotheses as unconfirmed until it reaches "the unhypothetical first principle of everything" or the Form of the Good. We have not focused on the use of sense-experience in the methods proposed in the *Meno* and *Phaedo* and practiced in all three dialogues. But we have seen that Socrates does not describe the method he proposes in the *Meno* and *Phaedo* as verifying or confirming its hypotheses until one reaches "the unhypothetical first principle of everything," nor does the method he practices in any of the three dialogues confirm its hypotheses to this point. Indeed, Socrates' description of his practice in the *Republic* as the shorter road reveals that he does not takes his hypotheses as so confirmed.

Perhaps this indicates how we should understand Plato's apparent reluctance to endorse the method he has had Socrates propose and employ prior to the middle books of the *Republic*. Plato's failure to depict Socrates practicing a method that confirms its hypotheses to the point of "the unhypothetical first principle of everything" explains the second-best status of Socrates' practice in these dialogues. The method resides some place between dianoetic and dialectic. It fails to confirm its hypotheses to the point of "the unhypothetical first principle of everything." But it recognizes its need to do so.

Why Plato chooses not to depict Socrates confirming his hypotheses up to such a principle, given his recognition that he needs to, calls for an answer. To begin such an answer requires detailed study of Plato's account of the Form of the Good, including why he chooses to discuss it by means of an analogy in the middle books of the *Republic* (see 24: PLATO'S CONCEPT OF GOODNESS). It also requires distinguishing between practicing philosophy as a method of philosophical discovery and practicing philosophy as a method of philosophical instruction and considering how writing philosophy (whether in dialogue form or not) is related to both (see 4: FORM AND THE PLATONIC DIALOGUES). Finally, it requires making sense of an "unhypothetical first principle of everything" – something which on the face of it simply seems beyond the pale. For now, however, we can conclude that a thorough examination of Plato's method of dialectic should not confine itself to Socrates' explicit statements concerning method in Plato's central dialogues. It should also look to Socrates' practice in those dialogues. To return to the quotation from Robinson with which we began this chapter, in the *Meno*, *Phaedo*, and *Republic* Plato gives prominence to method *as well as* methodology.

Note

Translations of Plato are taken from J. M. Cooper (ed.) *Plato: Complete Works* (Indianapolis: Hackett, 1997).

References and further reading

Annas, J. (1981). *An Introduction to Plato's* Republic. Oxford: Clarendon Press.
Bedu-Addo, J. D. (1984). Recollection and the argument from a hypothesis in Plato's *Meno*. *Journal of Hellenic Studies* 104, pp. 1–14.

Benson, H. H. (2003). The method of hypothesis in the *Meno*. *Proceedings of the Boston Area Colloquium in Ancient Philosophy* 18, pp. 95–126.

Bluck, R. S. (1961). Plato's *Meno*. *Phronesis* 6, pp. 94–101.

Bostock, D. (1986). *Plato*: Phaedo. Oxford: Oxford University Press.

Brown, M. S. (1967). Plato disapproves of the slaveboy's answer. *Review of Metaphysics* 20, pp. 57–93.

Gallop, D. (1975). *Plato*: Phaedo. Oxford: Oxford University Press.

Gentzler, J. (1991). *Sumphonein* in Plato's *Phaedo*. *Phronesis* 36, pp. 265–77.

Gill, C. (2002). Dialectic and the dialogue form. In J. Annas and C. Rowe (eds.) *New Perspectives on Plato, Modern and Ancient* (pp. 145–71). Cambridge, Mass.: Harvard University Press.

Gonzalez, F. J. (1998). *Dialectic and Dialogue: Plato's Practice of Philosophical Inquiry*. Evanston, Ill.: Northwestern University Press.

Kahn, C. H. (1996). *Plato and the Socratic Dialogue*. Cambridge: Cambridge University Press.

Kanayama, Y. (2000). The methodology of the second voyage and the proof of the soul's indestructibility in Plato's *Phaedo*. In *Oxford Studies in Ancient Philosophy*, vol. 18 (pp. 41–100). Oxford: Oxford University Press.

Pappas, N. (1995). *Plato and the* Republic. New York: Routledge.

Robinson, R. (1953). *Plato's Earlier Dialectic*, 2nd edn. Oxford: Oxford University Press.

Rowe, C. (1993a). Explanation in *Phaedo* 99c6–102a8. *Oxford Studies in Ancient Philosophy*, vol. 11 (pp. 49–70). Oxford: Oxford University Press.

—— (ed.) (1993b). *Plato*: Phaedo. Cambridge: Cambridge University Press.

Seeskin, K. (1993). Vlastos on elenchus and mathematics. *Ancient Philosophy* 13, pp. 37–54.

Stenzel, J. (1973). *Plato's Method of Dialectic*, trans. D. J. Allen. New York: Arno Press.

van Eck, J. (1994). *Skopein en logois*: On *Phaedo* 99d–103c. *Ancient Philosophy* 14, pp. 21–40.

White, N. P. (1979). *A Companion to Plato's* Republic. Indianapolis: Hackett.

Part II

PLATONIC EPISTEMOLOGY

8

Socratic Ignorance

GARETH B. MATTHEWS

According to the picture we have of Socrates from the early Platonic dialogues, Socrates believed that recognizing a certain ignorance[1] in himself was a form of wisdom, in fact a form of wisdom that otherwise intelligent people seem to lack. But what kind of ignorance? And what form of wisdom? As the considerable commentary on Socratic ignorance so eloquently testifies, it is difficult to be clear about (1) what exactly Socrates thought he did not know that, as he says, other people around him mistakenly thought they did know. It is equally difficult to be clear about (2) why Socrates thought that recognizing this ignorance in himself is actually a form of wisdom. It will be my aim in what follows to get a little clearer about both these two matters.

According to Plato's *Apology*, Socrates first came to appreciate the wisdom of recognizing his own ignorance in response to an assertion of the oracle in the Temple of Apollo at Delphi. According to the oracle no one was wiser than Socrates (*Ap.* 21A). When Socrates heard from his friend, Chaerephon, what the oracle had said, he set out, he tells us, to determine if the claim the oracle had made could possibly be true. His way of trying to determine whether it might be true was to question Athenians thought by their fellow citizens to be wise. He would try to discover if these people actually did know things he himself did not know.

Socrates began his investigation, he tells us, by questioning a public figure considered by others – and, Socrates adds, slyly, by the man himself – to be wise. Socrates quickly established, he says, that this man was in fact not wise at all. Socrates even tried, unsuccessfully, to convince the man that he was not wise. As could have been anticipated, those efforts only made the man dislike Socrates. So Socrates withdrew from this encounter and made the following well-known judgment:

> **T1.** I am wiser than this man; it is likely that neither of us knows anything worthwhile, but he thinks he knows something, when he does not, whereas when I do not know, neither do I think I know; so I am likely to be wiser than he to this small extent, that I do not think I know what I do not know. (*Ap.* 21D3–7)

Socrates, as he goes on to relate, did not end his investigation with this first reputedly wise man, but went on to cross-examine others as well. He examined politicians, poets, tragedians, and, eventually, artisans. He found, he says, that "those who had

103

the highest reputations were nearly the most deficient, while those who were thought to be inferior were [actually] more knowledgeable" (*Ap.* 22A3–6).

The Divine Mission

Here it is well to keep in mind that Socrates seems not to conceive the examination process he had begun as a contest between himself and other Athenians to see who would get top honors for wisdom. Instead he thinks of it as a way of carrying out a divine mission:

> **T2.** So even now I continue this investigation as the god bade me – and I go around seeking out anyone, citizen or stranger, whom I think wise. Then if I do not think he is, I come to the assistance of the god and show him that he is not wise. (*Ap.* 23B4–7)

Thus, whatever it is that Socrates and those he questions fail to know when they fail to know anything "worthwhile," it is, as he supposes, something the god thinks it important that they realize they do not know. And it is something such that, failing to realize that one lacks knowledge of it shows that one is, for that very reason, not wise.

These are tantalizing hints as to what it might be to know something "worthwhile." But they are not enough, by themselves, to give us any very clear conception of what Socrates might mean by "worthwhile" knowledge.

At this point it might be well to focus on the expression that the translator of **T1**, G. M. A. Grube, has rendered "worthwhile," *kalon k'agathon.* I suspect that, in this context at least, "worthwhile" is something of an under-translation of that expression. The first word of the phrase, *kalon,* means "noble," or "beautiful," or, more generally, "fine." And the second word is an elision of the word for "and" and the word for "good." Plato commonly uses the whole phrase, especially with masculine endings, for a person who is noble and good, but ideally for someone both beautiful and good (see, for example, *Ly.* 207A2–3), where the message seems to be that nobility of character is also beauty of character, as well as beauty of person (see 20: PLATO ON EROS AND FRIENDSHIP). In his dialogues, Plato often links the beautiful and the good (see, for example, *Smp.* 201c1–2). Thus his justification, in the *Republic,* for including music and poetry in the curriculum for future guardians is that, learning to appreciate beauty in art and nature is an essential part of moral education.[2] Perhaps, then, we should understand the claim in **T1** to be this:

(A) Socrates claims not to know anything fine and good.

Yet (A) does not get us much further in the effort to determine what it is that Socrates insists he does not know. What would Socrates consider a case of knowing something fine and good?

Knowing Something Fine and Good

Perhaps the most promising way to approach that question is to consider what questions Socrates asked other Athenians when he tried to determine whether they knew something he himself claimed not to know. We have a pretty good idea of what those questions were. We do, at least, if we can accept the early Platonic dialogues as a fairly accurate portrayal of the people Socrates interrogates and a good representation of the kind of question he asks them. What Socrates asks his interlocutors in the early dialogues, are such questions as these: "What is piety?" "What is bravery?" "What is friendship?" "What is beauty?" "What is justice?" and "What is temperance?" And what Plato presents Socrates as not himself knowing in these "definitional" dialogues is how to answer these "What is F-ness?" questions in a satisfactory way, where a satisfactory answer apparently must provide informatively necessary and sufficient conditions for x to be F (see 6: PLATONIC DEFINITIONS AND FORMS).

Euthyphro, for example, thinks he knows what piety is. Socrates doesn't think he himself knows. One thing the dialogue *Euthyphro* makes clear is that Euthyphro does not, in fact, know what piety is any more than Socrates does. That is, Euthyphro cannot offer informatively satisfactory conditions for some action or some person to count as being pious. I'm adding the caveat that the answer needs to be informative because Socrates says this:

> **T3.** Tell me then what this form itself is, so that I may look upon it, and using it as a model [or template or pattern, *paradeigma*], say that any action of yours or another's that is of that kind is pious, and if it is not that it is not. (*Euthphr.* 6E3–6)

To understand the import of the requirement stated in **T3** consider what would happen if one were to answer Socrates by saying,

1 Piety is what all and only pious actions necessarily have in common.
  or by saying,
2 Piety is just what makes pious things pious.

In both cases one would have said something Socrates accepts as true. But one would not have identified the form of piety in such a way that we could use it to determine which things are pious and which are not, as **T3** stipulates. The "model" or "pattern" that **T3** asks for must be something that makes apparent the criteria for an action or person to count as being pious. And neither (1) nor (2) would be of any use in determining which actions are pious and which are not. And so they cannot be examples of what Socrates is seeking and has not yet found. What he wants is something that can serve as an "inner template" to lay on candidate actions or persons to see if they qualify for being pious.

In the dialogue, *Charmides*, Socrates asks what *sōphrosunē* ("temperance" or "prudence") is. Late in that dialogue Critias offers "self-knowledge" as his answer to the question, "What is *sōphrosunē*?" He challenges Socrates: "But now I wish to give you an explanation of this definition, unless of course you already agree that temperance is to know oneself" (165B). Socrates replies:

T4. But Critias . . . you are talking to me as though I professed to know the answers to my own questions and as though I could agree with you if I really wished. This is not the case – rather, because of my own ignorance, I am continually investigating in your company whatever is put forward. However, if I think it over, I am willing to say whether I agree or not. Just wait while I consider. (165B4–C2)

In the dialogue Socrates makes clear that he does not think he knows how to answer satisfactorily the question, "What is *sōphrosunē*?" However, and this is an interesting point that needs to be kept in mind, he is willing to say whether he agrees with Critias' suggestion or not, that is, whether he thinks it is a satisfactory account of what *sōphrosunē* is, once he has had a chance to think about it.

A little later in the same dialogue Socrates ties the search for what temperance is to his resolve not to think he knows what he does not know. Again he is addressing his interlocutor, Critias:

T5. Oh come . . . how could you possibly think that even if I were to refute everything you say, I would be doing it for any other reason than the one I would give for a thorough investigation of my own statements – the fear of unconsciously thinking I know something when I do not. And this is what I claim to be doing now, examining the argument for my own sake primarily, but perhaps also for the sake of my friends. (166c7–D4)

My suggestion is that to know what piety or temperance is, in the sense of being able to supply informatively necessary and sufficient conditions for some act or person to count as being pious, or temperate, would be, according to Socrates, to know something fine and good. If this suggestion is along the right lines, then several features of the oracle story fall nicely into place.

The subsequent history of philosophy has shown how maddeningly difficult it is to arrive at a satisfactory analysis of any philosophically interesting concept. Among the philosophically interesting concepts we should include ethical ones, such as bravery, virtue, piety, and temperance, all of which Socrates was himself interested in. But we should also include metaphysical notions, such as cause, time, and number, for which later philosophers have sought with great ingenuity to find informatively necessary and sufficient conditions, as well as epistemological concepts, such as truth and knowledge itself. Alas! None of their efforts has found universal acceptance. We should therefore not be surprised that the Athenian citizens Socrates questions are unable to supply informatively necessary and sufficient conditions for an action to count as being brave, or pious, or just. On the other hand, we should not be surprised either to find Socrates thinking that being able to supply satisfactory accounts of this sort for moral concepts in particular would be so important to the moral life that our inability to supply such conditions is a crucial piece of ignorance. Even recognizing that one cannot supply such accounts for virtue and the individual virtues, such as bravery and piety, could itself be counted as a form of wisdom. And it would be plausible to suppose that "the god" might give Socrates the mission of nurturing such wisdom in others.

At this point a very important question arises. If Socrates does not know what piety or bravery or temperance is, at least not in the strong sense of being able to offer an informatively satisfactory set of necessary and sufficient conditions for a person or an action to count as pious, brave, or temperate, how can he know of any token persons or actions that they are pious, brave, or temperate?

Priority of Definitional Knowledge

Socrates himself asks this very question in several dialogues, including the *Hippias Major*, where the question under discussion is "What is *to kalon*?" (that is, "What is the beautiful, or the fine, or the noble?"). Here is part of Socrates's final speech to Hippias:

> **T6.** If I make a display of how stuck [that is, how perplexed] I am to you wise men, I get mud-splattered by your speeches when I display it. You all say what you just said, that I am spending my time on things that are silly and small and worthless. But when I'm convinced by you and say what you say, that it's much the most excellent things to be able to present a speech well and finely, and get things done in court or any other gathering, I hear every insult from that man (among others around here) who has always been refuting me. He happens to be a close relative of mine, and he lives in the same house. So when I go home to my own place and he hears me saying those things, he asks if I'm not ashamed that I dare discuss fine activities when I've been so plainly refuted about the fine, and it's clear I don't even know at all what *that* is itself! "Look," he'll say, "How will you know whose speech – or any other action – is finely presented or not, when you are ignorant of the fine? And when you're in a state like that, do you think it's any better for you to live than die?" (304c1–E3)

Many commentators think that this speech and others like it commit Socrates to what Hugh Benson calls "the Priority of Definitional Knowledge." Benson formulates part of the Principle of Priority of Definitional Knowledge this way:

(P) If A fails to know what *F*-ness is, then A fails to know, for any *x*, that *x* is *F*. (Benson 2000: 113)

According to (P), if Socrates fails to know what *to kalon* is (that is, what the fine or beautiful or noble is), in the sense of not being able to give informatively necessary and sufficient conditions for someone or something to be *kalon*, then Socrates fails to know of any speech (for example) that it is fine (or beautiful or noble).

Benson and other commentators think that the Priority of Definitional Knowledge extends even further than (P). They think it includes what Benson formulates this way:

(D) If A fails to know what *F-ness* is, then A fails to know, for any *G*, that *F*-ness is *G*. (Benson 2000: 113)

According to (D), if Socrates fails to know what "the fine" is, again, in the sense of being unable to supply informatively necessary and sufficient conditions for someone or something to be fine, then Socrates does not even know whether fineness is a virtue, or a good thing to have.

107

On the issue of whether Socrates is committed to (D) in particular, it is worth noting how that final speech of the *Hippias Major* ends. Here is what immediately follows **T6** and ends the dialogue (Socrates is speaking):

> **T7.** That's what I get, as I said. Insults and blame from you, insults from him. But I suppose it is necessary to bear all that. It wouldn't be strange if it were good for me. I actually think, Hippias, that associating with both of you has done me good. The proverb says, "What's fine is hard" – I think I know *that*. (304E3–9)

On a natural, and I think correct, reading of **T7**, Socrates here says he thinks he *knows* that what is fine is hard (more literally: that "noble things are difficult" – *chalepa ta kala*). So he thinks he knows something about the fine or the noble, namely, that fine or noble things are difficult. But if he does *know* this, he rejects (D). This passage alone should make one hesitate to attribute (D) to Socrates.

In fact, there are other passages that should make one doubt whether Socrates is committed to either (P) or (D), let alone to their conjunction. Consider this one from the *Apology*:

> **T8.** And surely it is the most blameworthy ignorance to believe that one knows what one does not know. It is perhaps on this point and in this respect, gentlemen, that I differ from the majority of men, and if I were to claim that I am wiser than anyone in anything, it would be in this, that, as I have no adequate knowledge of things in the underworld, so I do not think I have. I do know, however, that it is wicked and shameful to do wrong, to disobey one's superior, be he god or man. (29B1–7)

This passage includes a qualified claim of ignorance ("I have no adequate knowledge of things in the underworld") as well as a clear, even insistent, claim of knowledge ("I do know, however, that it is wicked and shameful to do wrong, to disobey one's superior, be he god or man"). Socrates does not explain why his knowledge of the underworld is "not adequate." We can speculate that it might be inadequate simply because, up to that time, he had had no experience of the underworld at all. But what about his claim to know "that it is wicked and shameful to do wrong [and] to disobey one's superior"? If this is indeed something Socrates knows, why should it not count as something "fine and good"? Moreover, why should it not count as a clear counterexample to (P)?

I suggest that the "ground-level" knowledge Socrates claims here to have could be subjected to the same kind of questioning that Socrates poses to his interlocutors in the "definitional" dialogues we have been talking about. That is, Socrates could ask, "What is the wicked?" or "What is the shameful?" If he were to ask himself, or others, those questions, one can be quite certain that neither he nor his interlocutors would be able to come up with informatively necessary and sufficient conditions for an action to count as being wicked or shameful. Lacking this understanding, he and his interlocutor would both be lacking the kind of knowledge he admits he lacks, and is wise for admitting that he lacks, whereas others do not even think they lack it. And yet, for all that, Socrates clearly claims to know that it is wicked and shameful to do wrong and to disobey one's superior.

So here is an example of Socrates claiming knowledge that some action is wicked and shameful even though, as we suspect, he would have to admit that he lacks the (fine and good) knowledge of what makes that action wicked and shameful. Thus **T8** seems to flout (P), just as **T7** seemed to flout (D).

The Aporetic Reading

Is there then another way of reading those passages in which Socrates seems to commit himself to (P) and (D)? I think there is. In fact, the reading I have in mind is a very natural one. We can understand Socrates to be, not *asserting* that definitional know-ledge is prior to knowledge of instances and to knowledge of essential connections, but only *asking* how it can be possible to know, for example, that *x* is pious and *y* is just, or that piety and justice are virtues, unless one already knows in an informative, that is, non-trivial way, what piety and justice are. I shall call this reading of such passages an "aporetic reading." My idea is that Socrates uses the question to express a perplexity (*aporia*) about how one could have knowledge that *x* is *F* or that *F*-ness is *G* without having prior knowledge of what *F*-ness is.

We have seen that Socrates is attracted to the idea that we recognize instances of *F*-ness by appeal to a paradigm or template that we have in our minds. Given this model of instance recognition, it is only a short step to the conclusion that I can know that *x* is *F* if, and only if, (1) I have immediately available to me, informatively neces-sary and sufficient conditions for someone's or something's being *F* and (2) I believe correctly that *x* satisfies those necessary and sufficient conditions.

Here it is important to note that, characteristically, those passages in which Socrates is taken to be committing himself to the Priority of Definitional Knowledge do have the form of a question. Thus, in **T6**, Socrates says his relative will ask him:

> **T9.** How will you know whose speech or other action is finely [or beautifully] presented, when you are ignorant of the fine [that is, the beautiful]? (*Hp.Ma.* 304D8–E2)

Commentators have tended to take this question to be a rhetorical one. That is, they have taken its import to be this: *You cannot know* whose speech or other action is fine [or beautiful] when you are ignorant of the fine [or the beautiful], that is, when you cannot supply informatively necessary and sufficient conditions for something's being fine [or beautiful]. But it needn't be understood this way. It can be taken to be a genuine question, one which expresses a puzzlement or perplexity about how one could possibly know that *x* is an instance of *F*-ness without having determined that *x* satisfies the criteria for being *F*. Thus on my aporetic reading, Socrates is not actually asserting that definitional knowledge is prior; instead he is expressing puzzlement about how it could be otherwise, that is, how one could recognize instances without prior knowledge of the appropriate criteria.

If we give the Priority of Definitional Knowledge the aporetic reading I am propos-ing, then we needn't be surprised to find Socrates sometimes flouting (P) or (D), or both, as in **T8** above. And consider another passage from the *Apology*. It comes after the jury at his trial has ruled that Socrates is guilty as charged. To understand this passage we must understand a certain feature of the Athenian system of justice (see 25: PLATO ON THE LAW). According to that system, if the defendant in court is found guilty, the party who brought charges proposes a penalty and the party found guilty proposes an alternative penalty. The jury then has to accept one of the two proposals; it cannot choose a penalty of its own devising. Meletus, Socrates's accuser, proposes death, and Socrates needs to propose an alternative. Should he propose some sort of prison term? The jury might accept that. This is part of what Socrates says:

> **T10.** Since I am convinced that I wrong no one, I am not likely to wrong myself, to say that I deserve some evil and to make some such assessment against myself. What should I fear? That I should suffer the penalty Meletus has assessed against me, of which I say I do not know whether it is good or bad? Am I then to choose in preference to this something that I know very well (*eu oida*) to be an evil and assess the penalty of that? Imprisonment? Why should I live in prison, always subjected to the ruling magistrates the Eleven? (37B2–c2)

Socrates gives reasons at the end of the trial for explaining his uncertainty about whether death is good or evil. But he thinks he knows very well that imprisonment would be an evil. He must think he can know this, even though he cannot give informatively necessary and sufficient conditions for something's being evil. Thus on my aporetic reading of the Principle of the Priority of Definitional Knowledge, Socrates would have been free to follow up his assertion in **T10** with this question: "How can I know that imprisonment would be an evil, if I cannot say what it is for something to be an evil?" But he would *not* have been forced, on pain of inconsistency, to *deny* that he had such knowledge.

Telling a Lie

My own favorite way of illustrating the aporetic use of the Principle of Definitional Priority is to tell a personal story about an attempt to come up with informatively necessary and sufficient conditions for telling a lie. In my own classroom my students and I usually come up with what I call the "Standard Analysis of Lying" (SAL), which goes like this:

(SAL) In saying to B that *p*, A tells a lie iff (i) it is false that *p*;
(ii) A believes that it is false that *p*; and
(iii) in saying to B that *p* A means to deceive B.

After my class and I have agreed that this is the best analysis we can give of what it is to tell a lie, I offer the following story.

When I was at Boy Scout camp one summer, all eight of the Scouts in my tent got along well with each other, except for one, Delbert. Delbert didn't get along with any of the rest of us. None of us liked him.

One night my best friend, James, put a garter snake under the sheet of Delbert's cot. I saw him do it. Later that night, when Delbert slipped his feet under the sheets and felt the slimy snake, he let out a shriek and fled the tent. The next day, much to the pleasure of Delbert's tent-mates, Delbert phoned his mother and got taken home.

The Scoutmaster had overwhelmingly good reason to suspect that James, who was the only snake fancier in camp, had done the mischievous deed. But he didn't think he could punish James unless he had an eyewitness to the deed. So he asked me, James's best friend, whether I had seen James do it. I said, "No, I didn't see James do any such thing."

My class and I agreed that, in saying what I did, I lied. But in saying that, I did not intend to deceive the Scoutmaster. I knew he had overwhelmingly good evidence that James was the perpetrator. But I also realized that he didn't think it would be fair to punish James unless he had the word of an eyewitness that James had done the deed. So I said that I had not seen James put the snake under Delbert's cot sheet simply to protect James from punishment, not to deceive the Scoutmaster about whether, in fact, James had done the deed. Thus what I did does not satisfy the third condition of (SAL).

Neither my class nor I can improve on (SAL) so as to accommodate the Delbert case. Thus we *cannot say what makes this case a case of telling a lie*. Yet I did tell a lie. In fact, I would say that I *know* I told a lie. But how can I know that I told a lie if I cannot supply informatively necessary and sufficient conditions for telling a lie? I do not know. I am in perplexity, *aporia*.

On my interpretation of the Socratic disavowals of knowledge in the early dialogues of Plato, the fine and good knowledge Socrates denies having is knowledge of what makes x an F – that is, what makes x pious, or temperate, or brave, or whatever it is that is under discussion in that dialogue. Given the prima facie plausibility of the Priority of Definitional Knowledge, it seems that one couldn't recognize instances of F-ness or essential facts about F-ness without having available what eludes him and his interlocutors in those dialogues, namely, an informative set of necessary and sufficient conditions for someone or something to count as an F. Yet it seems he can and does recognize instances, just as I recognize that what I said to the Scoutmaster was a lie without being able to supply a satisfactory analysis of what it is to tell a lie.

Recollection

Eventually, in the *Meno* and the *Phaedo*, Plato has his literary figure, Socrates, introduce the Doctrine of Recollection, according to which we all have latent knowledge of the Forms that Socrates, in the early dialogues, had been trying to get his interlocutors help him "define" (see 9: PLATO ON RECOLLECTION). In the *Phaedo*, at 100D, Socrates says that he no longer even understands his efforts in the *Hippias Major* to find informatively necessary and sufficient conditions for *to kalon* (beauty, or fineness). He is there content to say that it is by beauty that beautiful things are made beautiful. He calls this style of explanation "safe but foolish." Moreover, Plato has Socrates go on to offer another style of explanation that, like the first, does not require definitional knowledge either.

Most commentators are agreed that the Socrates of the *Phaedo* is a rather different character from the historical Socrates (see 2: INTERPRETING PLATO). The situation with regard to the dialogue *Meno* is somewhat more complicated. But many, if not most, commentators consider it to be a transitional dialogue, one that begins to move away from the figure we get to know in the *Apology*. In any case, the idea of Recollection presented in those two dialogues allows for the possibility that we might, latently at least, know what Equality, Beauty, Justice, and Piety are without being able to offer informatively necessary and sufficient conditions for two things to count as equal, or for something or someone to be beautiful or just or pious.

Our own contemporaries today who undertake to offer analyses of philosophically problematic concepts are well advised *not* to accept the Priority of Definitional Knowledge. Consider, for example, attempts in the late twentieth century to provide a satisfactory analysis of what it is to know something. These attempts continue a project begun by Plato. In both the *Meno* and the *Theaetetus*, Plato has Socrates offer the suggestion that knowledge is true belief with an account (*logos*). The modern descendant of this Platonic suggestion is the idea that knowledge is justified true belief (the "JTB analysis"). After Edmund Gettier published his celebrated counterexample to the JTB analysis of knowledge many philosophers proposed amendments to, or substitutes for, the original JTB analysis. The motivation behind this flurry of analytic activity has been, I think, genuinely Socratic. How *can* we really know that we know something unless we can supply informatively necessary and sufficient conditions for a belief to count as knowledge? Yet the response to the Gettier problem strongly suggests that no one is able to supply the desired necessary and sufficient conditions.

On the other hand, it is quite striking that the various alternative analyses offered to replace the original JTB analysis of knowledge have all been rejected on the basis of counterexamples, indeed, counterexamples that almost all philosophers seem to have been able to recognize as either (1) genuine cases of knowledge that fail to fit the suggested analysis or else (2) cases that fit the suggested analysis but that are not genuine cases of knowledge. It is hard to understand this situation without assigning some sort of priority to non-definitional knowledge of what knowledge itself is. In the same way, it is hard to understand the claims of Socrates to know this and that without supposing that he, too, assigns some sort of priority to non-definitional knowledge.

I turn finally to a brief review of what other philosophers have said recently about Socratic ignorance. I begin with the position on Socratic ignorance taken by the dean of twentieth-century Socratic studies, Gregory Vlastos.

Vlastos

Vlastos begins his article, "Socrates' disavowal of knowledge," by setting up two opposed positions on the question of how we are to understand the Socratic claims of ignorance. He writes:

> In Plato's earliest dialogues, when Socrates says he has no knowledge, does he or does he not mean what he says? The standard view has been that he does not. What can be said for this interpretation is well said in Gulley, 1968: Socrates' profession of ignorance is "an expedient to encourage his interlocutor to seek out the truth, to make him think that he is joining with Socrates in a voyage of discovery" (p. 69). More recently the opposite interpretation has found a clear-headed advocate, Terence Irwin in his *Plato's Moral Theory*

holds that when Socrates disclaims knowledge he should be taken at his word: he has renounced knowledge and is content to claim no more than true belief. (Vlastos 1994: 39)

After discussing these two alternatives – (1) Socrates is being insincere as a way of drawing his interlocutor into discussion and (2) Socrates really means that he knows nothing – Vlastos proposes a third alternative. He distinguishes two senses of the relevant Greek verbs for "to know." In what we might call the "strong sense" of these verbs, which Vlastos marks with a subscript "c," we know all and only what we are infallibly certain of. In the weak sense, which he marks with a subscript "E," we can know whatever has survived elenctic examination.

According to the Vlastos proposal, this is how we are to understand Socrates' knowledge claims and disawowals of knowledge:

> when he says he knows something he is referring to knowledge$_E$; when he says he is not aware of knowing anything – absolutely anything, "great or small" . . . – he refers to knowledge$_c$; when he says he has no knowledge of a particular topic he may mean *either* that in this case, as in all others, he has no knowledge$_c$ and does not look for any *or* that what he lacks on that topic is knowledge$_E$, which, with good luck, he might still reach by further searching. (Vlastos 1994: 58)

Vlastos's disambiguation suggestion has an immediate appeal. But there are several difficulties with it. In the first place, Socrates never says anything in the early Platonic dialogues to suggest that he thinks of himself as using a verb for "to know" in two different senses. Specifically, he never says anything like this: "In one sense I know, but in another I do not." Moreover, he never says, "I know and I don't know," which would be a natural way to signal that one is using "know" in two different senses.

Here is a second difficulty. The disambiguation of a strong and a weak sense of "know" offers us two ways of understanding this implication of **T1**:

(a)   Neither Socrates nor his interlocutor knows anything worthwhile.

On the first interpretation of "knows," (a) means

(a1)   Neither Socrates nor his interlocutor is infallibly certain of anything worthwhile.

No doubt Socrates could well agree to (a1). But, as Vlastos himself makes clear, the Socratic examination of interlocutors is not aimed at determining whether they are infallibly certain of anything. Instead, it is focused on determining whether any of the interlocutor's beliefs can survive elenctic examination. So (a1) does not really capture a significant part of the result reported in **T1**.

The other disambiguation option Vlastos offers us for understanding "knows" in (a) is captured in this elucidation:

(a2)   Neither Socrates nor his interlocutor has any beliefs about anything that has survived elenctic examination.

113

This time the problem is that, according to Vlastos, (a2) is not a true statement. In fact, his attempt to resolve, as he supposes the "paradox" of Socratic "disavowals of knowledge," rests in part on isolating a weak sense of Greek verbs for "to know" in which Socrates does know a variety of things, in fact, all the things that have survived elenctic examination. Thus (a2), according to Vlastos, would simply be false. He insists that there are many things Socrates can admit he knows in the weak sense.

Benson

Hugh Benson, in his authoritative study of Socrates' epistemology, *Socratic Wisdom*, marks out a clear and plausible position on how to understand Socratic claims of ignorance. "I maintain," he writes, "that Socrates' profession of ignorance is indeed sincere and that while its scope is rather broad, perhaps broader than many scholars would accept, I see little reason or evidence to understand its scope to be universal" (Benson 2000: 168). Benson adds that he leaves underdetermined "the precise nature of the knowledge Socrates disavows."

As we have already seen, Benson maintains that Socrates accepts the Priority of Definitional Knowledge in its fullest form, that is, as the unqualified conjunction of (P) and (D). Thus, on his view, Socrates cannot consistently claim to know of any case, x, that x is F unless he can supply informatively necessary and sufficient conditions for something or someone to be F. Nor can he consistently claim to know of any F-ness that it is G, unless, again, he can supply informatively necessary and sufficient conditions for being F.

Benson's position comes out particularly clearly in the way he handles the passage in the *Apology* where Socrates reports on his examination of the craftspeople, or artisans. Here is the passage:

> **T11.** Finally I went to the craftsmen, for I was conscious of knowing practically nothing, and I knew that I would find that they had knowledge of many fine things. In this I was not mistaken; they knew things I did not know, and to that extent they were wiser than I. But, gentlemen of the jury, the good craftsmen seemed to me to have the same fault as the poets: each of them, because of his success at his craft, thought himself very wise in other most important pursuits, and this error of theirs overshadowed the wisdom they had . . . (22c9–E1)

And here is the core of Benson's reading of **T11**:

> Again, what distinguishes Socrates from the craftsmen . . . is his correct assessment of what he does not know. He is not wiser than they because he knows more than they do . . . Rather, he is wiser than they because they think they know things, in particular, "other most important things" . . . that they do not, while Socrates does not think so [i.e., does not think he knows these important things]. (Benson 2000: 170)

On Benson's reading Socrates is a skeptic, not in the sense of believing that nothing can be known, but in the sense that, as he believes, he knows almost nothing and he has found only a few others who do know something, namely the artisans. They know "many fine things." However, even the artisans have, Socrates thinks, less wisdom than he, since they think they know many things that they do not know, whereas he does not think he knows what, in fact, he does not know.

Brickhouse and Smith

In their fine study of the philosophy of Socrates, *Plato's Socrates*, Thomas C. Brickhouse and Nicholas D. Smith discuss at great length what they call the "paradox of Socratic ignorance." By identifying Socratic claims of ignorance as "paradoxical" Brickhouse and Smith give weight to what Socrates actually claims to know and also to what he acts as if he knows, as well as to what he denies knowing. As they point out, "For someone who claims to be ignorant himself, Socrates has an astonishing capacity to discern ignorance and confusion in others" (Brickhouse and Smith 1994: 31–2). And they also discuss a variety of passages in which Socrates actually claims to have knowledge, several of which we have already discussed here.

Instead of supposing, as Vlastos does, that Plato uses his words for "know" in two different senses, Brickhouse and Smith maintain that Socrates recognizes two different sorts of knowledge, "one which makes its possessor wise and one which does not" (1994: 31). In view of the fact that Socrates does claim to have a sort of wisdom, even though it consists only in realizing that he fails to know what others think they know, Brickhouse and Smith also need to recognize two kinds of wisdom, the merely human and the divine. So, on their reading, when Socrates denies having knowledge, the sort of knowledge he disclaims having is the kind that would give him the higher sort of wisdom. What he admits he has carries with it the recognition that he lacks the higher sort of knowledge.

Picking up on a Greek phrase for "how these things are," which Socrates uses in the early dialogues, Brickhouse and Smith characterize the knowledge Socrates denies having as knowledge of "how something is," that is, what makes something to be the case (1994: 38–45). What they have in mind seems to be very close to what we have been calling "definitional knowledge." So their idea is that Socrates can know, perhaps by divination, or by perception, or perhaps somehow through elenctic examination, that something is the case without having the wisdom that would come with knowing what makes it to be the case.

Brickhouse and Smith put another restriction on the sort of knowledge they think Socrates disclaims having. According to them, it is knowledge of virtue. They read Socrates in the *Laches* as claiming to know how to define "quickness" (192A–B) and in the *Meno* as claiming to know how to define "figure" (76A). But he cannot do the same for "virtue."

As for the Principle of the Priority of Definitional Knowledge, Brickhouse and Smith deny that Socrates is committed to any strong version of such a principle. They write:

> We have argued that there is a sense in which Socrates does not believe that one knows nothing of justice unless one knows the definition. On the contrary, he thinks one can have a kind of knowledge – the kind that does not make one wise – through divination, through elenctic examination, and through everyday experience. (1994: 60)

115

Conclusion

In conclusion I want to say a little about the philosophical significance of Socratic ignorance on each of the interpretations I have discussed. Each of these interpretations, it should be noted, takes Socratic claims of ignorance to be sincere. Many commentators, however, from ancient times down to the present, have supposed those claims to be insincere and merely ironic. Thus Charles Kahn writes of Socrates:

> If he successfully examines his fellow Athenians concerning virtue and the good life, Socrates must himself know something about human excellence and, more generally, something about what is good and what is bad. He must possess the kind of knowledge that is beneficial for human beings and that makes for a happy life. In the *Apology* [however] any claim to such knowledge remains hidden behind the ironic mask of ignorance. (Kahn 1996: 201)

Although this ironic way of understanding the claims of Socratic Ignorance is certainly worth examining and assessing, I have not tried to do that here.

Of the four interpretations of the Socratic claim of ignorance I have discussed above, the interpretation Gregory Vlastos offers is, one could say, the most deflationary. It is also the simplest. According to his reading, all Socrates means when he makes his striking pronouncements of ignorance is that there is a sense of "know" expressed by various Greek verbs in which neither he nor his interlocutors knows anything fine and good. In that sense, what one knows one is infallibly certain of. The wisdom Socrates lays claim to, on the Vlastos reading, is the awareness that he does not know, in that strong sense of "know," what others think they know.

The chief philosophical moral to be drawn from the Vlastos interpretation of the various claims of Socratic ignorance arises from the philosophical importance of looking out for shifts in meaning. If a philosopher really does use a key expression, such as "know," in two significantly different senses, then it is certainly important to recognize this shift.

The chief philosophical significance of Socratic ignorance on Benson's interpretation seems to lie in a recognition that there can be wisdom in understanding the skeptical implications of holding firmly to the Priority of Definition. The Principle of the Priority of Definitional Knowledge may be initially plausible, given the natural thought that one could never get beyond examples of, say, bravery or piety, to identify new cases unless one had in mind informatively necessary and sufficient conditions for an act or a person to count as being brave, or pious. On the other hand, however, unless we can first know that certain acts or persons are brave, it is hard see how we could ever come to learn what bravery is. Benson calls this latter puzzle the "acquisition problem." On Benson's understanding of Socratic epistemology, Socrates holds fast to the Priority of Definitional Knowledge, and finds consolation in the oracle's pronouncement by interpreting it to mean that he at least has the wisdom of not thinking he knows anything very important.

According to Brickhouse and Smith, the philosophical significance of claims of Socratic ignorance includes the pressure it puts on us to realize that there must be other routes to knowledge besides applying informatively necessary and sufficient conditions for being *F* to new cases. They mention specifically that we might receive knowledge as a gift from the gods and that we might have some knowledge from everyday experience.

The aporetic interpretation of Socratic ignorance I have argued for here includes calling attention to the fact that the Principle of the Priority of Definition is characteristically put as a question: "How can you know that x is F, if you do not know what F-ness is?" The perplexity this question can give expression to is something that both motivates and plagues philosophical analysis. It motivates analysis by encouraging us to search for the epistemic validation of having informatively necessary and sufficient conditions for saying that x is F. It plagues analysis when we fail in our efforts to come up with such conditions by suggesting that, even for what we had thought of as a standard case of an F, we don't really know what *makes* it F.

In my own example, after my class and I have done our best to offer informatively necessary and sufficient conditions for something to count as telling a lie, we have to concede that we have encountered a counterexample. In this case I want to resist skepticism and say that I know I have told a lie, even though what I did would not count as a lie according to my best attempt to offer an analysis of what it is to tell a lie.

My situation with respect to telling a lie is, I think, typical of what happens in philosophical analysis. If I investigate the matter diligently enough, I can expect to find some counterexample or other to my very best attempt to say what a cause is, what free will is, what justice is, or what F-ness is, for any philosophically interesting F-ness. I can even expect to be entirely confident that I *know* the counterexample to be a counterexample. Socratic professions of ignorance are important for pointing up this perplexity: If I cannot offer informatively necessary and sufficient conditions for x to be F, how can I either (1) know that x is F or (2) know that F-ness is G? But it also invites this related perplexity: How can I hope to find out what are informatively necessary and sufficient conditions for being F unless I already at least know of certain cases, x, y, and z, that they are all F, and of instructively similar cases, u, v, and w, that they are not F? In this way Socratic wisdom leads to a form of the Paradox of Inquiry (see 11: KNOWLEDGE AND THE FORMS IN PLATO).

Notes

Translations of Plato are taken from J. M. Cooper (ed.) *Plato: Complete Works* (Indianapolis: Hackett, 1997).

1 In this essay I shall follow the commentary tradition and use "ignorance" to mean simply lack of knowledge. Thus even someone with only true belief might be said to be ignorant in this sense.

2 . . . Because anyone who has been properly educated in music and poetry will sense it acutely when something has been omitted from a thing and when it hasn't been finely crafted or finely made by nature. And since he has the right distastes, he'll praise fine things, be pleased by them, receive them into his soul, and, being nurtured by them, become fine and good. He'll rightly object to what is shameful, hating it while he's still young and unable to grasp the reason, but, having been educated in this way, he will welcome the reason when it comes and recognize it easily because of its kinship with himself. (*R.* III.401E1–402A4)

References and further reading

Benson, H. (2000). *Socratic Wisdom: The Model of Knowledge in Plato's Early Dialogues*. New York: Oxford University Press.

Brickhouse, T. C. and Smith, N. D. (1994). *Plato's Socrates*. New York: Oxford University Press.

Geach, P. T. (1966). Plato's *Euthyphro*: an analysis and commentary. *The Monist* 50, pp. 369–82.

Gulley, N. (1968). *The Philosophy of Socrates*. London: Macmillan.

Irwin, T. (1977). *Plato's Moral Theory: The Early and Middle Dialogues*. Oxford: Oxford University Press.

Kahn, C. H. (1996). *Plato and the Socratic Dialogue*. Cambridge: Cambridge University Press.

Vlastos, G. (1994). Socrates' disavowal of knowledge. In M. Burnyeat (ed.) *Socratic Studies* (pp. 39–66). Cambridge: Cambridge University Press.

9

Plato on Recollection

CHARLES KAHN

The doctrine of recollection plays a central role in three Platonic dialogues, *Meno*, *Phaedo*, and *Phaedrus*; but the doctrine is formulated each time differently, and in the context of a different problem. Hence the interpreter must decide whether Plato presents three essentially distinct doctrines of recollection or three partial statements of a single theory. On either view a further task will be to relate recollection, so understood, to the accounts of knowledge given in other Platonic dialogues such as the *Republic* and the *Theaetetus*.

First of all, a word about the philosophical relevance of this doctrine. Platonic recollection is the ancestor of the theory of innate ideas developed by Descartes and Leibniz in the seventeenth century, both of whom claimed Plato as their predecessor. Thus Leibniz said that he would endorse the doctrine of the *Meno* "stripped of the myth of pre-existence" (*Discourse on Metaphysics*: 26). More remotely, recollection is also a precedent for the Kantian distinction between a priori and a posteriori knowledge. As a consequence of these complex influences, the legacy of Plato's doctrine can be recognized today in two distinct areas of contemporary discussion: in epistemology in the question of a priori knowledge, which focuses on the cognitive status of logic and mathematics; and in psychology in questions of innateness, for example in language acquisition. These two problems are entirely distinct from one another, even if there may be some important connection between them. (For an interesting suggestion that the a priori status of mathematics and logic might be explained in terms of psychological innateness, see Horwich 2000: 168.) As an issue in epistemology, the a priori is a matter of the justification or entitlement for a certain kind of knowledge claim: are there any true propositions, whose verification does not rely on empirical evidence? Innateness on the other hand is a problem in psychology: how does one explain the complex behavior involved in language acquisition? What is the specifically human cognitive capacity that accounts for the fact that babies normally do, but puppies and kittens do not, learn the language spoken in the house where they grow up? The problem of innateness in psychology is of course more general than the question of language acquisition, but this example makes clear that we are dealing with an empirical question in cognitive or developmental psychology, and not with the epistemic status of logic and mathematics. We need to recognize not only that these two questions are entirely distinct, but also that the distinction was not drawn either in Plato's time or in the seventeenth century. It was Kant who first clearly distinguished the issue of a priori knowledge claims from questions in empirical psychology. We need to bear in mind that Plato, in raising such issues for the first time, cannot take for granted this post-Kantian distinction between epistemology and psychology, or between philosophy and natural science. Hence we cannot simply identify Plato's theory either with issues in epistemology or with questions in developmental psychology. Plato's discussion is located in some neutral territory, providing seeds from which both of the modern questions will emerge.

Recollection in the *Meno*

The topic of recollection is introduced for the first time in response to Meno's paradox of inquiry: how does one seek for what one does not know? (The priority of the *Meno* is indicated by what amounts to a backward reference at *Phd.* 73A.) Meno's challenge arises in the context of a search for the definition of virtue, a search governed by the principle of priority of definition – the principle that claims you cannot know anything about X unless you know *what X is* (see 8: SOCRATIC IGNORANCE). But the actual discussion of recollection follows Meno's challenge in leaving behind this question of defining virtue and shifting to the wider question of learning anything at all.

Socrates' illustration of successful recollection concerns a problem in geometry: how to double the area of an arbitrary square. The learner (or "recollector") is an uneducated slave-boy. The distinct stages of recollection are as follows: (1) the slave-boy falsely believes that he knows the solution, (2) the slave-boy recognizes the falsity of this belief and realizes his ignorance, (3) the slave-boy is led to see that a certain line (namely, the diagonal of the original square) solves the problem; he now has the true belief that the square on this line is twice the size of the first square. This is as far as the illustration goes, but Socrates offers the possibility of a further stage: (4) "if someone questions him often and in many different ways about these same matters, he will end by having accurate knowledge of them inferior to no one" (*Men.* 85c10). So the stages of recollection move from false belief to the recognition of ignorance, from there to true belief, and (if fully carried out) from true belief to complete knowledge, in this case to the knowledge of plane geometry. (It is not clear from Socrates' brief account whether he envisages a stage of knowledge for a particular proposition independently of the knowledge of geometry as a whole.) So scientific knowledge, as represented here by geometry, is held out as the final goal of the process. But the only recollection actually illustrated is the acquisition of a true belief about the solution to a particular problem.

How are we to interpret this example? And what is the content of "these true *doxai* that were in him" (85c4)? Skeptics have claimed that the slave-boy is simply using his eyes to see that the new square is twice as big. Vlastos has made the more plausible suggestion that recollection here means "any enlargement of our knowledge which results from the perception of logical relationships" (Vlastos 1995: 157). I think this is correct in principle, but too narrow. To cover what is going on in the geometry lesson, recollection must mean not only the perception of formal relationships but also the capacity to make judgments of truth and falsity, of equality and similarity. It is these judgments that are "the *doxai* that were in him" and that are brought out by Socrates' questioning. More generally, we can say that recollection stands here for rationality or *logos* in the Aristotelian sense, as the distinctively human capacity to comprehend discourse and to make rational use of sense-perception. What is required of the slave-boy is precisely to understand Socrates' questions and to respond by making judgments of equality and inequality on the basis of what he sees. And it is this same capacity that (as Socrates claims) would permit him to master geometry if the lessons were to continue. So if recollection is illustrated in the geometry lesson as interpreted by Socrates, it is a process that begins with the capacity to understand simple questions and make simple numerical calculations and potentially ends with the acquisition of full scientific knowledge. Furthermore, the capacity which makes this process possible belongs generally to every mature human being, as is demonstrated here by the choice of an untutored slave-boy.

In an influential discussion, Dominic Scott has proposed an interpretation of recollection that draws a sharp distinction between two levels of learning: between ordinary thinking, performed by everyone, and philosophic knowledge of transcendent Forms. Scott wishes to restrict recollection to the latter, but he recognizes that the *Meno* is not explicit on this, since it makes no mention of Forms. He correctly recognizes that the text of the *Meno* is "indeterminate"; the dialogue contains only "a provisional sketch of the theory" (Scott 1995: 34). What is clear is that the choice of a slave-boy shows that the capacity in question is quite ordinary, and the recollection represented in the geometry lesson reaches only to the merest beginning of specialized knowledge. If our goal is to interpret the *Meno* in a way that is compatible with the *Phaedo* and the *Phaedrus*, we can take recollection in all three dialogues as a theory of human rationality, with rationality understood as articulated in the classical account of the three acts of the intellect: (1) grasping concepts, (2) forming judgments, (3) following inferences. All three capacities are implied by the mastery of a natural language like Greek, and all three acts are illustrated by the slave-boy's answers to Socrates' questions. On the one hand, this example does not illustrate the original acquisition of concepts by a child; on the other hand, it does not present the full achievement of specialized knowledge. Socrates' lesson in the *Meno* represents an intermediate stage in the realization of cognitive capacity, after the mastery of a language and before the mastery of geometry. But there is no suggestion in the text that the capacity itself would be different for different stages.

Plato does not connect language comprehension with recollection in the *Meno*; he simply notes as a prerequisite the slave boy's knowledge of Greek (82B4). In the *Phaedrus*, on the other hand, understanding language is said to be an essential element in recollection (249B7). So we meet here, for the first time, the need to choose between the hypothesis of unity and the hypothesis of development in dealing with discrepancies between the dialogues (see 2: INTERPRETING PLATO). The text of the *Meno* cannot decide this issue. But the text contains nothing to rule out the view that language comprehension is part of recollection broadly construed, as the *Phaedrus* maintains.

Also absent from the *Meno* is any hint of an ontology for the objects of recollection. The text says only that the soul in its many births "has seen all things, both things here and things in Hades" (81c6), and that accordingly "we possess the truth of realities (*ta onta*) in our soul" (86B1). What kind of realities are available to the discarnate

121

soul? The *Meno* does not tell us. But a moment's reflection will show that, to offer a solution to Meno's paradox, such prenatal seeing of all things must be radically different from the ordinary learning that is to be accounted for by recollection. (If prenatal cognition is not radically different, recollection offers only a regress, not an explanation.) So the *Meno* presupposes something like direct knowledge by acquaintance, something corresponding to the vision of disembodied souls described in the *Phaedrus*. What the *Meno* does not tell us is that such cognition must take as its object noetic Forms (see 11: KNOWLEDGE AND THE FORMS IN PLATO). Here again we must choose between the assumptions of unity or development. What does Plato have in mind when, later in the *Meno*, he distinguishes knowledge from right opinion by the "binding" which consists in *aitias logismos*, the calculation of the cause? What kind of causal explanation or *aitia* does Plato invoke in order to separate knowledge from true opinion, and to characterize the final goal for recollection? ("This, namely the binding of *doxai* by *aitias logismos*, is recollection, as we have agreed," 98A4.) Could the goal of recollection and the criterion of knowledge be simply the logical *logos* of definition, the account of whatness given in question and answer, rather than the corresponding ontological Form? Here once more the text is compatible with either assumption (see 6: PLATONIC DEFINITIONS AND FORMS).

If we ask now how recollection in the *Meno* relates to the two modern issues of the a priori and innateness, the connection with innateness is the clearer of the two. It is in virtue of some natural and universal human capacity, independent of explicit learning, that the slave-boy is able to follow Socrates' geometric reasoning, correct his own mistakes, and recognize the proposed solution. Of course language learning is presupposed in this example. Plato's theory of recollection is extended to the broader notion of innateness, including the capacity to comprehend language, only in the *Phaedrus*. On the other hand, any link between recollection and the epistemic notion of a priori knowledge is much more remote, since there is no explicit concern here with the justification of knowledge claims. It is nonetheless noteworthy that the example of true belief (and potentially knowledge) developed in the *Meno* is an important proposition in mathematics, namely, a fundamental instance of the Pythagorean Theorem. So what the slave-boy "recollects" is in fact an item of a priori knowledge, although he has realized it only at the level of true opinion. Thus we can see how questions of both innateness and the a priori are present in germ in the account of recollection in the *Meno*, although the notion of innateness is closer to the concerns of the text. There is a strikingly similar blend of issues of innateness and non-empirical justification in the corresponding doctrine of Descartes: "Mathematical truths reveal themselves with such evidence and agree so well with my nature that, when I begin to discover them, it does not seem to me that I am learning something new but rather that I am remembering what I already knew, that is to say, that I perceive things that were already in my mind, although I had not yet turned my thought to them" (*Fifth Meditation*).

Recollection in the *Phaedo*

In the *Meno* the immortality and pre-existence of the soul was taken for granted on the authority of wise priests and priestesses. In the *Phaedo* immortality is an issue and will be systematically argued for. A central argument will take recollection as its premise: since we are born with some knowledge already present in the soul, the soul must have acquired that knowledge in a previous existence. (The explicit issue, then, is innateness, but the argument for innateness is based on a knowledge claim.)

The discussion of recollection in the *Phaedo* begins with a mention of diagrams and skillful questioning that invokes the geometry lesson of the *Meno* (73A7–B2). However, the argument itself begins from a position unknown to the *Meno*, namely the existence of Forms and the discrepancy between Forms and their sensible homonyms. The doctrine of Forms pervades the whole dialogue; it was implied earlier in the description of the philosopher's goal as "beholding the things themselves with the soul itself" (*Phd.* 68E). The Forms are introduced from the beginning in epistemic terms, as the realities (*ta onta*) that are known in thought and reasoning rather than in sense-perception (65c–66A). (This distinction between two kinds of cognition will be standardized in the *Republic* as the distinction between sense and intellect, between *aisthēsis* and *nous*. The distinction itself is older than Plato; see Democritus B11 DK.) It is only in the argument from recollection that Socrates begins to specify the ontological distinction between Forms and participants (74B–C). This discrepancy in the level of reality is crucial for the conception of the psyche implied in the argument for immortality (see 19: THE PLATONIC SOUL). Like knows like, and the transcendence of the soul is entailed by its epistemic link, via recollection, to the nature of the Forms. As Socrates insists, "necessarily, just as these Forms exist, just so must our soul exist even before we were born" (76E2–4, echoed at 76E5, 76E9–77A2, and again at 92D7). Literally, then, the argument from recollection shows only the pre-existence of the soul, which is required for the semi-mythical framework of reincarnation. But the philosophical point is deeper. The ultimate function here of the theory of recollection (like the argument from affinity which follows) is to establish the transcendental status of the soul by its cognitive link to the transcendent being of the Forms.

So much is clear. Problems arise when we seek to specify precisely how recollection connects the soul with the Forms. Is recollection of Forms involved in ordinary acts of thinking and perceptual judgment? Or only in explicit comparisons between a Form and the corresponding participants? It is the latter that is emphasized in the text of the argument, which begins with a recognition of the deficiency of equal sticks and stones in contrast to the Equal itself (74D–75B) (see 12: THE FORMS AND THE SCIENCES IN SOCRATES AND PLATO). Now this recognition of a disparity between Forms and sensible participants belongs only to Platonic philosophers, since most people have no explicit knowledge of the Forms at all. If such recognition is required for recollection, most human beings could not recollect. (The slave-boy of the *Meno* certainly could not.) On the other hand, the argument from recollection is clearly intended to support the claim of immortality for human souls generally, and not only for philosophers. How are we to interpret an argument that begins with a premise applying only to Platonic philosophers and ends with a conclusion concerning all human beings? Is Socrates generalizing here from a small and privileged sample?[1] If so, the argument seems extraordinarily weak.

There is clearly something defective in this argument, but I suggest a different diagnosis. I believe Socrates is running together two claims that ought properly to be distinguished, one concerning recollection for philosophers and one concerning cognition for all human beings. Only philosophers *know what they are doing* when they recollect, because only philosophers can distinguish Forms from particulars and recognize the deficiency of the latter. But all human beings implicitly refer to the Forms in every perceptual judgment. Thus they unwittingly refer to the Equal itself in judging sticks and stones to be equal. That is why Socrates can conclude the argument from recollection by asserting that "we refer all our sensory input (*ta ek tōn aisthēseōn panta*) to the being of the Forms" (76D9). This referring to Forms involves two recognitions: (1) that sensible equals all want to be like the Equal itself, but (2) that they fall short (75B5–8). The first recognition is made implicitly by all humans, for example by the slave-boy in making judgments of equality. The second judgment is the privilege of philosophers. The distinction is carefully prepared at 74A6, where the judgment of deficiency is described as an additional step (*prospaschein*) after the judgment of similarity. In the course of the argument, however, this distinction is blurred. Socrates begins with the deficiency judgment, since that is essential for establishing the transcendental nature of the Forms as objects of recollection. But we end with "referring all our sensory input to Forms" because that is what all human beings must do in making perceptual judgments.

On this reading, the argument is still imperfect, but its generality is justified by the quasi-Kantian view of human cognition as involving the application of universal concepts to particular sensory input. This principle is much more clearly stated in the account of recollection in the *Phaedrus*, as we shall see in a moment. But I believe the same notion of an implicit reference to Forms in ordinary perceptual judgment is also presupposed in the *Phaedo* argument, and this accounts for its generality. It is just such a view that is reflected in the repeated mention of referring (*anoisein, anapheromen*) the deliverance of the senses to Forms (75B6, 76D9). And this view is also suggested by the focus on the Forms of Equal, Greater, and Less. In the context of recollection, the mention of these Forms can be seen as a commentary on the geometry lesson of the *Meno*, where it is precisely judgments of equality and inequality that are cited as evidence that the slave-boy is recollecting "the opinions (*doxai*) that are in him." Thus the discussion of recollection in the *Phaedo*, which is clearly introduced as a continuation of the topic treated in the *Meno*, can be seen as a fuller statement of the doctrine of that dialogue. The crucial innovation is the connection between perceptual judgment, as illustrated in the *Meno*, and the implicit cognition of Forms. Such implicit reference to Forms in all perceptual judgment is the epistemic correlate to the ontological dependence of sensible qualities on the corresponding Form (*Phd.* 100D: "nothing makes it beautiful other than the presence or sharing or other form of connection with the Beautiful itself") (see 11: KNOWLEDGE AND THE FORMS IN PLATO). This structural parallelism between cognition and ontology, between referring to Forms and participating in Forms, probably seemed so obvious to Plato that he is not always careful to make it explicit (see 27: LEARNING ABOUT PLATO FROM ARISTOTLE).

Recollection in the *Phaedrus*

The final statement of recollection in the *Phaedrus* is also the fullest and most precisely formulated. (The *Phaedrus* must be later than the *Meno* and *Phaedo*, since it belongs to the group of dialogues roughly contemporary with the *Republic* – stylistic Group II, whereas *Meno* and *Phaedo* belong to the pre-*Republic* group – stylistic Group I. See Kahn 2002.) The doctrine is introduced here not to explain how learning takes place (as in the *Meno*), nor to prove the immortality of the soul (as in the *Phaedo*), but rather to give a metaphysical explanation for the experience of falling in love (see 20: PLATO ON EROS AND FRIENDSHIP). This version of the theory is the fullest because, on the one hand, Socrates offers a mythical account of the prenatal vision of the Forms that is somehow presupposed in the *Meno* and the *Phaedo*, while on the other hand, this dialogue also contains an explicit statement of the notion of human rationality that is, I suggest, implied by the account of recollection in the other two dialogues. On this view, what is specific to the human soul is the capacity to understand conceptual language and to make unified judgments on the basis of sense-perception. Only a soul that has had the prenatal vision of the Forms can be reborn in a human body.

> For a human being must comprehend what is said by reference to a form (*kat' eidos legomenon*), proceeding from many sense perceptions to a unity gathered together by reasoning (*logismos*). This is recollection of those things which our soul once saw when it was traveling together with a god. (*Phdr.* 249B6–c3)

This is as close as Plato comes to anticipating the modern notion of innateness, by specifying, as a requirement of human nature, the capacity to learn and understand language and to carry out conceptual thought. The doctrine of recollection serves to tie this epistemic capacity to Plato's metaphysics by representing the capacity symbolically as the recall of a mythical glimpse of non-sensible reality on the part of discarnate souls. So the shock of falling in love is explained as the effect of visible beauty serving as an unconscious reminder of the transcendent Beauty that our soul once beheld in its prenatal vision, "when it traveled together with a god" in a magnificent extra-celestial chariot parade.

Some prenatal cognition is presupposed by the very notion of recollection, even in the *Meno* and *Phaedo* where no such cognition is described. But an account of prenatal experience can be given only in mythic form, just as myth is the only vehicle for describing the fate of souls after death. The myth of pre-existence in the *Phaedrus* thus answers to the myths of judgment in the *Phaedo* and *Republic*. As in the other cases, the imaginative splendor of the mythical framework is purchased at the expense of some doctrinal inconsistency. For example, if the horses in the *Phaedrus* represent the irrational elements in Plato's tripartite soul, as is clearly implied by the struggle for chastity with which the speech ends, then it is not clear why they have any place at all in the soul of gods, or even in discarnate human souls. (It is clear from the *Timaeus* that only the rational soul is immortal, and the argument from recollection in the *Phaedo* similarly applies only to the soul that is cognizant of Forms. The *Republic* is less explicit on this point, but it points in the same direction in Book X, when the soul disfigured by community with the body is contrasted with the pure soul revealed in philosophical activity; it is only the latter that is "akin to the divine and the immortal and the being that is eternal" (611E).) So if only the rational soul is immortal, then the horses should not belong to a soul after death. But of course horses are required for the mythic machinery: how else could the souls travel with the gods?

CHARLES KAHN

We may detect a similar inconsistency in regard to recollection, which is on the one hand attributed to all human beings as a necessary condition for embodiment in human form, whereas the next sentence might be thought to designate recollection as a prerogative of philosophers: "Hence only the thought of a philosopher is rightly winged, for he is always connected by memory as far as possible with those things by connection with which a god is divine" (249c4).[2] If we read on, however, we see that recollection of the Forms is a matter of degree. All lovers recollect to some extent, not only the philosophic followers of Zeus but also the followers of Hera or Ares or Apollo (252c–253B). But it is the philosophers who use such recollections correctly (*orthōs* 249c7) and hence become the perfect lovers.

Thus the view of the *Phaedrus* is in principle the same as that of the *Phaedo*, on the reading proposed above: there is a weak notion of recollection applying to all human cognition and a stronger notion that is distinctive of philosophers. All humans with linguistic competence must be able to recognize the general kinds of things signified by words, and this is what permits them to unify their sense-experience under concepts. It is noteworthy that *eidos* in the key passage cited above ("a human being must comprehend what is said according to an *eidos*") is not a special term for Form but a less technical word for kind or type of thing. (So, rightly, Bobonich 2002: 313.) The reference to Forms is implicit in ordinary cognition, which simply recognizes kinds of things, just as a reference to the Beautiful itself is implicit in the ordinary experience of falling in love. That is recollection in the weak sense. Recollection in the strong sense, on the other hand, requires philosophy. The philosopher is the perfect lover because only he has, or can regain, a sufficiently vivid memory of the prenatal vision to understand correctly the metaphysical dimension of his erotic experience. His situation is parallel to that of the philosopher in the *Phaedo*; although in the weak sense all humans must recollect the Forms, only a philosopher can recognize the discrepancy between sensible equals and the Equal itself.

Notice that the account of weak recollection in the *Phaedrus* (and in the *Phaedo* too, if my interpretation is correct) implies that Plato has already reached the conclusion that is so carefully argued for in the *Theaetetus*, namely that sense-perception alone cannot account for belief or perceptual judgment (*doxa*), much less for knowledge. The mind must contribute something of its own. That was the point of recollection, from the beginning: beyond sensory input, another source of cognition is required for the slave-boy to follow Socrates' demonstration. (As Leibniz said, emending the medieval formula: there is nothing in the intellect that was not previously in the senses – except the intellect itself!) For human beings to make propositional judgments, they must be able to organize the manifold of sense-perceptions into conceptual unities, the components of the internal *logos* that constitute thinking. This insight is systematically developed in the *Theaetetus* and the *Sophist*, where thought is interpreted as silent *logos*, and *logos* in turn analyzed into subject and predicate (*onoma* and *rhēma*, *Sph.* 262A–E). But the germ of this insight is here, in the reference to language and conceptual unity as a requirement for the human soul (*Phdr.* 249B).

Thus the *Meno*, *Phaedo*, and *Phaedrus*, despite the different philosophical problems they address, can be seen as successive stages in the exposition of a single doctrine. The *Meno* presents us with a sample of ordinary perceptual judgment on its way to becoming scientific knowledge. The prenatal sources on which such cognition must draw are not identified in the *Meno*, beyond the claim that "the truth of beings is present in the soul." In the *Phaedo* the beings in question are identified as the Forms, in particular the Forms of Equal, Greater, and Less, which must somehow have been made available to the slave-boy's soul before its human birth. The *Phaedrus* adds a mythical account of the soul's prenatal contact with such Forms, together with a more precise description of the cognitive capacities that make perceptual judgment possible, as judgment according to concepts or kinds of things. In both the *Phaedo* and the *Phaedrus* the existence of transcendental Forms is taken for granted, and their sensible homonyms are conceived as images (*homoiōma* at Phdr. 250A6, *eidōlon* 250D5) or participants (in the *Phaedo*). The doctrine of recollection is thus closely tied to the theory of Forms in its classical version.[3] It may therefore seem paradoxical that in the *Republic*, where the theory of Forms is most fully stated, there is no mention made of recollection. We will return to this question in a moment.

The Place of Recollection in Plato's General Theory of Knowledge

Recollection dominates the discussion of knowledge in the *Meno* and *Phaedo*; it disappears from the *Republic* entirely but reappears in a central role in the *Phaedrus*. There is no explicit reference to recollection either in the *Theaetetus* or in the *Timaeus*, although we can recognize echoes or analogues to recollection in both dialogues. Has Plato's theory of knowledge undergone a fundamental change, or has he found a new expression for what is fundamentally the same conception? The choice between unity and development, which was posed by the variation between the three versions of recollection, confronts us now on a larger scale in the diversity between the various Platonic discussions of knowledge, with and without the doctrine of recollection. In order to locate the role played by recollection in Plato's epistemology, we must briefly survey the account of knowledge in other dialogues, above all in the *Republic* and *Theaetetus*.

In the *Meno*, opinion (*doxa*) and knowledge are recognized as distinct stages in recollection. This distinction is neglected in the *Phaedo* and *Phaedrus*, but it returns to center stage in *Republic* Book V, where (without reference to recollection) the distinction between knowledge and opinion serves to introduce the doctrine of Forms. Knowledge and right opinion were distinguished in the *Meno* by their relative stability (opinion tends to run away) and by the fact that knowledge must include the account (*logos*) of a cause or explanation (*aitia*). This latter condition will now be satisfied by the Theory of Forms. In the *Republic* opinion as such (not just *right* opinion!) is distinguished first in terms of its fallibility (477E6) and then systematically in terms of its object. Whereas knowledge (*gnōsis*, *epistēmē*) takes as its object eternal Being or What-is (in other words, the Forms), opinion cognizes What-is-and-is-not, that is to say, the realm of sensory appearance and change (477A–479E), which is also characterized as Becoming (e.g., 508D7). The epistemic dichotomy of the *Meno* is now given an ontological basis in the distinction between Forms and participants. Our cognition of the Forms, which in the *Phaedo* involves recollection, is expressed in the *Republic* in terms of direct noetic vision.

The distinction between knowledge and opinion, introduced in *Republic* Book V, is developed and refined in the famous Divided Line of Book VI. The two kinds of objects are now distinguished as the intelligible and the visible, by reference to two parallel faculties: intellect (*nous*) and sight, with sight serving as representative of sense-perception generally (509D). The Forms, identified in Book V as the objects of knowledge, are here located in the uppermost subdivision of the intelligible section of the Line; the realm assigned to *doxa* in Book V is now described as coextensive with the visible section, that is, with the sensible world. This new equation between *doxa* and sense-perception explains why the *Republic* has abandoned the *Meno's* restriction to *right* opinion. It also reflects the fact that, in epistemic contexts before the *Theaetetus*, Plato's discussion of *aisthēsis* is generally concerned with perceptual judgment and not with bare sensation.

Thus the Divided Line of Book VI introduces a more complex picture than the simple distinction between knowledge and opinion in the *Meno* and in Book V. The wider division between intellect and sense allows Plato to distinguish two levels of noetic cognition, only one of which will ultimately count as knowledge (*epistēmē*). It is only the highest level of cognition, using the method of dialectic to comprehend the Forms and their unconditional source, that represents knowledge proper, whereas the lower level of noetic cognition, which relies on the mathematical method of deduction from assumed premises (*hypotheses*), is labeled by the humbler term of "art" or "craft" (*technē*) (511B2, 533B4). Thus while the primary dichotomy between the intelligible and the sensible relies upon a distinction between two faculties of cognition, the noetic subdivisions are distinguished by their scientific method or mode of inquiry: dialectic is the method of the highest segment, deduction from hypotheses is the method for the second intelligible level (see 7: PLATO'S METHOD OF DIALECTIC).

It is sometimes claimed that, in the curious passage about perceiving a finger that introduces the study of mathematics in *Republic* Book VII, Plato is guilty of assuming that the senses alone, without other assistance, could make perceptual judgments such as "This is a finger." Hence it would be a correction introduced in the *Theaetetus* to recognize that unaided *aisthēsis* can make no judgments at all (where a judgment means something that can be true or false) (Sedley 2004: 113, citing Burnyeat). I do not think the text of *Republic* VII supports this view. The contrast at 523A–525A is between two kinds of perceptual attributes or predicates, those that do and those that do not pose conceptual problems (by being accompanied by the opposite attributes) and hence do or do not call on *noēsis* to ask questions about being, questions such as "What is X?" There is no claim here that in the non-problematic cases the sense is operating alone, without the collaboration of any other faculty such as *doxa*. Here as often, Plato uses the term *aisthēsis* loosely for perceptual judgment. Adam notes (in his commentary on 523c2) that it is typical of Plato in this section of the *Republic* to make no sharp distinction between *aisthēsis* and *doxa*; thus, "the sort of contradictory judgments that are here ascribed to . . . *aisthēsis* have already been attributed to *doxa* in [Book V] 479B–479E." As Adam says, "the relevant consideration is that in such cases [as 'This is a finger'] the intellect is not, as a rule, aroused, and this is equally true whether we regard the judgment as the act of *aisthēsis* alone or as the joint product of *aisthēsis* and *mnēmē*" (Adam 1902, II: 109. Adam is alluding to the suggestion made at *Phlb.* 38B12 that *doxa* is derived from sense and memory together).

In this connection, one of the major achievements of the *Theaetetus* is to distinguish clearly between the occurrence of a sensory affect, via a bodily change, and the corresponding perceptual judgment (see 10: PLATO: A THEORY OF PERCEPTION OR A NOD TO SENSATION?). It is here for the first time that Plato systematically distinguishes *doxa* from *aisthēsis*. In the first part of the *Theaetetus* the speakers attempt to define knowledge in terms of sense-perception. This proposal is finally abandoned, and in the second half there is an equally unsuccessful attempt to define knowledge in terms of *doxa*, judgment or opinion. (The *Theaetetus* thus has the structure of a double reductio, rejecting first *aisthēsis* and then *doxa* as candidates for knowledge.) The final refutation of sense-perception is based upon a fundamental distinction between two kinds of predicates or attributes: those which the soul perceives through a bodily instrument, such as the eye or the ear, and those that it considers by itself, not through a bodily instrument (185D–E). The latter, called *koina* or common, include basic concepts such as being, same, and other, numbers, and also good and bad, honorable and shameful. The decisive point here is that sense-perception through the body cannot grasp being and hence not truth, and so it cannot be knowledge (186c–D). Therefore we must move on to the rational activity of the soul itself, which leads us to the subject of *doxa* or judgment in the rest of the dialogue.

This distinction in the *Theaetetus* between sensory and non-sensory attributes has been compared to a distinction between the a priori and the empirical, since it isolates "a set of predicates to which we have access independently of the use of our sense-organs" (Sedley 2004: 106). If we interpret the *Theaetetus* distinction ontologically, these non-sensory attributes correspond to Forms and the sensory predicates refer to the phenomenal realm. So we have a kind of analogue here to recollection in the capacity of the soul to consider a certain range of concepts without direct dependence on the body. In cases where (according to the *Theaetetus*) the soul relies wholly on its own resources, we can think of it as independent of the body and hence potentially discarnate, as in the prenatal state posited by recollection. The *Theaetetus* makes no use of the notion of recollection. But since the context in the *Theaetetus* is explicitly epistemological (what kind of cognitive activity can count as knowledge?), this passage may reasonably be regarded as Plato's closest approximation to the modern, post-Kantian concept of a priori cognition, as a kind of knowledge claim that is logically independent of empirical evidence.

If we return now to the topic of recollection, its absence from the *Republic* and later dialogues is quite striking. As we have seen, the analysis of knowledge and opinion, which began in the *Meno* in the context of recollection, proceeds without this context in the rest of the corpus. What has happened?

One suggestion would be that recollection has been replaced in the *Republic* by the notion of noetic vision. It might even be thought that Plato, after relying on the notion of recollection to explain our ability to acquire knowledge that transcends ordinary experience, had decided that there was a better way to account for this cognitive capacity. Hence (on this view) he abandoned the semi-mythical notion of innate knowledge acquired in some previous existence, and adopted instead the more rational concept of noetic intuition or *Wesenschau*, an intellectual "seeing" of the Forms accessible to those whose minds have been properly prepared by dialectic. We could then interpret the epistemology of the *Republic*, centered on the imagery of light and the climactic vision of the Forms, as successor and replacement for the innatist theory of the *Meno* and the *Phaedo*.

129

However, this hypothesis that Plato, when he wrote the *Republic*, had given up the doctrine of recollection for the notion of noetic vision is not defensible on chronological grounds. For there is no reason to suppose that the *Phaedrus* comes before the *Republic*, and some reason to suppose that it is later. (For example, the account of dialectic in the *Phaedrus* is much closer to the dialectic of the *Sophist* and *Statesman* than to that of the *Republic*.) Furthermore, the *Phaedrus* shows that recollection and noetic vision can appear side by side; in the *Phaedrus* version recollection is the consequence of a direct vision of the Forms. Such a vision is also suggested in dialogues earlier than the *Republic*, for example a vision of the Form of Beauty in Socrates' speech in the *Symposium*. Similarly in the *Phaedo*, where recollection plays such an important role, Socrates also holds out the possibility of "beholding the things themselves with the soul itself" (66D8). In this series of dialogues from the *Meno* to the *Phaedrus*, there is no sign of a linear development, in which one epistemology replaces another. It is rather that different conceptions of knowledge are used in different contexts for different purposes.

Why then does recollection not appear in the *Republic*? (Actually, something like recollection is presupposed in the Myth of Er at 619Bff. and also in the suggestion at 498D that Thrasymachus might eventually benefit from the current conversation in a later reincarnation. But recollection does not appear in an epistemological context.) It is not because Plato has changed his mind about knowledge. On the contrary, the passage on the conversion of the soul in the Allegory of the Cave has often been recognized as close in spirit to the doctrine of recollection. There Socrates denies that one can put knowledge into a soul that lacks it, "as if one were putting sight into a blind eye." On the contrary, "this capacity [to see the truth], and this instrument by which everyone learns, is present in everyone's soul." But the whole soul needs to be turned around in order for the eye of the soul to be directed towards reality, towards the clarity of true being (VI.518c). Plato here is clearly a kind of innatist: the turning of the eye of the soul towards the light is a close analogue to the process of recollection.

Why then are the prisoners in the Cave not said to be recalling some prenatal exposure to the daylight? My explanation is that the obstacle here is not conceptual but rhetorical. It would spoil the drama and difficulty of the escape from the Cave if Plato had ascribed to the prisoners a previous acquaintance with the world outside. There is no philosophical reason for the omission of recollection from the *Republic*, but there is an excellent artistic reason. Recollection does not fit into the parallel between *nous* and vision, between knowledge and light, which dominates the imagery of the central books, from the introduction of the Forms in Book V to the culminating vision of the Good at the end of Book VII (540A).

It is important to recognize that the theme of noetic vision remains metaphorical throughout and never hardens into a fixed doctrine. Plato's distinction between the sense and the intellect (in *Republic* VI and elsewhere) can be seen as the ancestor of the faculty theory of the mind that extends from Aristotle to Kant; but Plato himself does not have such a theory. The term *nous* serves as a name for "the capacity of every soul [to see the truth] and the instrument by which everyone learns." But Plato frequently employs other, more periphrastic expressions to make clear the non-technical status of this concept of *nous*: "seeing Beauty itself by that to which it is visible" (*Smp.* 212A3); "grasping the nature of each essence with the appropriate part of the soul" (*R.*

VI.490B3); "leading the finest thing in the soul to the vision of the best thing among beings" (*R.* VII.532c5). All we learn about the capacity called *nous* is that it is not sense-perception but involves language (*logos*) and reasoning or calculation (*logismos*). Beyond that we have a claim, but no schema of the mind, in the passage quoted above from the *Phaedrus*: that a human soul must be able to derive rational concepts from many sense-perceptions. Recollection serves only as a mythical narrative to identify a transcendental source for this capacity to transcend sensory experience. If we separate out the myth of reincarnation, the prosaic thesis of recollection reduces to the formula of the *Meno*: the truth of beings is in the soul. This thought is most fully worked out in the construction of the soul in the *Timaeus*. Thus at *Ti.* 35A the ingredients of the world soul include the basic Forms of Being, Same, and Different, together with the corresponding kinds of corporeal substance. The implication is that the soul is capable of knowing in virtue of its kinship with the known. This doctrine in the *Timaeus* gives us the physical (or metaphysical) equivalent of recollection: for knowledge to be possible, the objects of knowledge must be *already present in the soul*. This was what was implied by recollection from the beginning: "the truth of realities (*ta onta*) is in our soul" (*Men.* 86B1).

Ultimately, then, Plato's epistemology merges into his ontology. It is because reality has some definite structure that the soul must have a version of *the same structure*. I suggest that this notion of kinship or formal identity between the mind and the world, between the soul and the Forms, is the deep meaning of recollection (see also 23: PLATO ON JUSTICE). There is no Platonic theory of *nous* because for Plato the mind has no independent structure: it is simply the capacity of a human soul to cognize, and thus to identify with, the structure of objective Being. For Plato knowledge and understanding are simply psychic reflections of the nature of reality. Epistemology is grounded in ontology. Recollection and noetic vision serve as alternative construals of the same phenomenon, our access to the place of concepts, which is, for Plato, the place of true Being and eternal Form. But the notion of recollection is philosophically deeper, more explanatory than the metaphor of vision. It claims that the objective structure of reality is not only accessible to us but that it is accessible precisely because it is already ours, because the intrinsic nature of our mind is structured to reflect, and hence identify with, the structure of reality itself. Whether triggered by Socratic questioning (in the *Meno*), by reflection on the deficiencies of sense-experience (in the *Phaedo*), or by falling in love (in the *Phaedrus*), the awakening of the soul to the understanding of noetic form is so exciting because it is a return to our own deep self, to the primordial nature of the soul.

Nevertheless, neither recollection nor noetic vision gives us any reliable indication of what such Forms are like. It would be a mistake to take the metaphor of vision too literally, and hence to conclude that Plato is committed to an ontology that can ground a theory of intellectual intuition. Philosophers from Ryle to Heidegger have made this mistake, and have claimed that Plato must have conceived the Forms as "simple nameables" (Ryle) or quasi-visible "objects." But the *Phaedo* is there (with other texts, including many in the *Republic*) to warn us against this error, and to remind us that the Forms are primarily conceived as the kind of reality (*ousia*) "of whose being (*einai*) we give and receive an account (*logos*) in questioning and answering" (*Phd.* 78D1), and whose most proper designation is "the X itself, what it is" (*auto to ho estin*, 74D6 and *passim*). In other words, the nature of the Forms is to be understood not from the perspective of vision or recollection but from the perspective of *logos*, where *logos* is conceived as the dialectical pursuit of definition, the pursuit of clarity and understanding by way of linguistic exchange, by means of question and answer concerning *what* things are and *how* they are. That is why, despite its changed configuration in the later works, dialectic remains the best description – in the *Philebus* as well as in the *Phaedrus* and *Republic* – for the highest form of knowledge, the cognition of what is ultimately real.

Notes

All translations are the author's.

1 This is the suggestion of Scott (1995: 69). Plato generalizes from a limited sample "on the assumption that it is more plausible that all human beings are fundamentally of the same type than of two radically different types." Hence "most people, though they do indeed have the knowledge latently, do not manifest it," i.e., do not recollect (p. 71). For criticism of Scott's view see Kahn 2003.
2 For the view that in the *Phaedrus* only philosophers recollect, see Scott 1995: 74–80; for a critique, see Bobonich 2002: 554f. n. 36.
3 I find no evidence for the "farewell to the theory of Forms" that Alexander Nehamas attributes to Socrates' great speech (Nehamas 1999: 352). Of course the account of Forms in the *Phaedrus* is vague, in accord with the mythic setting. But it would be strange, if (as Nehamas suggests) Plato were abandoning the so-called fallacy of paradigmatism, that he should base his most brilliant theory of love on a stellar example of this very fallacy.

References and further reading

Adam, J. (1902). *The* Republic *of Plato* (2 vols.). Cambridge: Cambridge University Press.
Bobonich, C. (2002). *Plato's Utopia Recast: His Later Ethics and Politics*. Oxford: Oxford University Press.
Diels, H. and Kranz, W. (DK) (1985). *Die Fragmente der Vorsokratiker*. Zurich: Weidmann.
Horwich, P. (2000). Stipulation, meaning and apriority. In P. Boghossian and C. Peacocke (eds.) *New Essays in the A Priori* (p. 168). Oxford: Oxford University Press.
Kahn, C. H. (2002). On Platonic chronology. In J. Annas and C. Rowe (eds.) *New Perspectives on Plato, Modern and Ancient* (pp. 93–127). Cambridge, Mass.: Harvard University Press.
—— (2003). On the philosophical autonomy of a Platonic dialogue: the case of recollection. In A. N. Michelini (ed.) *Plato as Author* (pp. 299–312). Leiden and Boston: Brill.
Nehamas, A. (1995). *Plato: Phaedrus*, trans. A. Nehamas and P. Woodruff (pp. xlii–xlv). Indianapolis: Hackett.
—— (1999). *Virtues of Authenticity: Essays on Plato and Socrates*. Princeton, NJ: Princeton University Press.
Scott, D. (1995). *Recollection and Experience: Plato's Theory of Learning and its Successors*. Cambridge: Cambridge University Press.
Sedley, D. (2004). *The Midwife of Platonism: Text and Subtext in Plato's* Theaetetus. Oxford: Oxford University Press.
Vlastos, G. (1995). *Anamnesis in the* Meno. In D. W. Graham (ed.) *Studies in Greek Philosophy*, vol. 2 (pp. 147–65). Princeton, NJ: Princeton University Press.

10

Plato: A Theory of Perception or a Nod to Sensation?

DEBORAH K. W. MODRAK

The challenge when writing about Plato on perception is showing that Plato had anything to say on this topic that is both interesting and constructive. His frequent denigrating remarks about perceptible objects, particularly in the middle period dialogues, have led many scholars to conclude that he allows perception little or no epistemic role in cognition and that its only role is to contribute to delusory opinions. This is not to say that Plato rejects the phenomena of sensation, but rather to say that he rejects any notion of perception as a full-fledged cognition that might constitute knowledge or be a state upon which knowledge might be based. Is this his position or do his critical remarks belie an acceptance of perception as a source of true beliefs?

Socratic Dialogues

If we turn to the early Socratic dialogues for answers to these questions, we find very little discussion of perception. These dialogues tend not to engage in much critical reflection about the nature of human cognition. Typically Socrates is energetically pursuing questions about the nature of virtue; he often defends (or seems to defend) various theses about wisdom, which he identifies with virtue (see 22: THE UNITY OF THE VIRTUES). He seeks the knowledge that would be constitutive of virtue and shows that many who claim to have this knowledge lack it. Questions about the reliability (or lack thereof) of perception simply do not arise. Perception is only occasionally mentioned and when it is, it is not the focus of the discussion. Perception is invoked to illustrate certain points in various arguments about virtue. In the *Charmides*, while challenging the thesis that temperance is a science of science, Socrates secures agreement to the claim that if hearing hears itself, it will hear itself possessing sound (168D2–E1). Socrates uses the example of the eye seeing itself in *Alcibiades* I to provide insight into how the soul might come to know itself (132D2–133c6). In the *Laches*, he argues that in order to add sight to the eyes to make them better, we must know what sight is (190A1–B1). In the *Lysis*, he appeals to the difference between hair looking white because it is white with age and its looking white because it has been painted white (217D1–E3). In none of these contexts is perception as such subjected to critical scrutiny, and its general reliability is taken for granted.

The *Meno*, a transitional dialogue, raises the question, what is virtue? But much of the discussion addresses a different question: is virtue teachable? And the related question: is virtue knowledge? Perception is not explicitly discussed but assumptions about its veracity figure in these arguments. Socrates uses a drawing in the sand to lead a slave-boy away from the boy's false beliefs about squaring the diagonal to his innate correct belief (82B9–85D1). While the slave-boy does not learn the right answer from the diagram but recollects it, the prominent role assigned a visual aid in a dialectical effort to uncover the truth is striking (see 9: PLATO ON RECOLLECTION). It shows how perception in concert with reasoning may be a tool for recognizing the truth. The discussion of recollection is followed by a discussion of the respective roles of true belief and knowledge in guiding behavior (97A3–99C10). Both are equally sound but the former, unlike the latter, is unstable. The person who has actually made the trip to Larissa is said to have knowledge, whereas the person who has been told the way has, at best, true belief (97A3–B3). This illustration of the difference between knowledge and true belief implicitly privileges direct perception over information acquired through verbal reports (see 11: KNOWLEDGE AND THE FORMS IN PLATO). Despite differences in context, a later dialogue, the *Theaetetus*, also privileges direct experience in relation to inferential judgment. The eyewitness to a crime is said to have knowledge whereas the jurors have, at best, true belief based on the reports of eyewitnesses (201A7–C2).

In the early dialogues, then, Socrates takes the reliability of perception for granted but he otherwise pays scant attention to it. Questions about the nature of perception or its limitations are not to be found. In the *Meno*, perception even plays a key but unacknowledged role in grounding the distinction between knowledge and true belief.

Phaedo

More than any other dialogue, the *Phaedo* advocates the separation of the soul and its powers from the body. In this context, we would expect to find a very critical assessment of perception and we do. Socrates argues for the importance of the intellect separating itself from the body in order to grasp the truth (65A9–66A8; cf. 99E1–6). To make clear what it is to grasp realities that are inaccessible through the senses, Socrates asks rhetorically, "Do men find any truth in sight or hearing?" He and Simmias agree that the soul is deceived whenever it examines anything to do with the body. This description of perception seems to leave little room for any of the senses playing a constructive role in inquiry. Perception appears to be a source of worthless information at best and to have little share in clarity or precision. It is worth noting, however, that this passage occurs in the context of an argument to show that the philosopher has been pursuing a goal throughout his life – the separation of soul from body – that can only be achieved fully in death.

In a subsequent argument for the existence of ideal objects such as the Equal-itself, Socrates seems to take a somewhat different line on perception. While perception grasps that two objects are equal, it does so by employing a concept of equality that could not have arisen on the basis of perceptions of equal things (74D4–75B8). It is striking that in this context Socrates allows the application of concepts in perception that are not acquired through perception. He assumes that things are seen and heard as equal.

This assumption is or appears to be in conflict with the earlier claim that the senses are wholly unreliable. As portrayed in the discussion of equality, the perceiver perceives equal things by applying a concept of absolute equality to them and at the same time recognizes that perceptible equals fall short of absolute equality (74D3–E4). That a typical percipient would recognize the difference between absolute equality and the equal things that she perceives is essential to the argument that the concept of equality is not acquired through perception. To have the required argumentative force, the claim must be a general one, i.e., that any self-reflective and reasonably astute perceiver can and will recognize the difference. Although the intellect would be deceived were it to confuse perceptible equals with absolute equality, it seems in no danger of doing so. The possibility of deception remains, but not the certainty of it, as is suggested by the earlier passage. A similar acceptance of perceptually based beliefs figures in the defense of teleological explanation (96A6–99D2). Pre-Socratic physicalism is rejected on the grounds that physical causes cannot explain many phenomena satisfactorily. Both cosmic order and deliberate action can, Socrates argues, only be adequately explained by an appeal to teleological causes. At no point in this critique does Socrates challenge the veracity of sense-perception or empirically based beliefs.

While arguing for the immortality of the soul on the basis of the difference between the body and the soul, Socrates again emphasizes the differences between physical objects and ideal ones (78B4–81A2). The former are constantly undergoing change; the latter are unchanging. The former are grasped through the senses; the latter, by the mind alone. The changeable nature of physical objects is such that the intellect becomes confused when it makes use of the body. Because the objects that are perceptible are unstable, philosophy persuades the soul to withdraw from the senses (83A1–c3). The goal of philosophy is to grasp unshakeable truths.

Even while voicing reservations about perceptible objects and perceptual powers, the *Phaedo* allows perception to play a significant role in cognition. Perception provides reliable information about the physical world. A human perceiver is even able to apply general concepts such as equality in perception. The limitations of perception are a reflection of the limitations of concrete objects in comparison with ideal objects.

Republic

At first blush with respect to cognition, the *Republic* may seem to proceed in much the same way as the *Phaedo*. It does not appear to be a very likely place to find support for the thesis that perception grasps the truth about perceptibles. Many well-known passages contrast unreliable opinings to steadfast knowledge. The objects of opinion are accessible through perception; the objects of knowledge are accessible only through thought unaided by the senses. Lovers of sights and sounds are found to be wanting in comparison to lovers of truth (474D3–480A13). In a famous illustration, Socrates divides a line drawn on the sand to display the relative rankings of cognitive powers and their objects (509D1–511E3). The main division of the line is between the visible realm and the intelligible realm. The activity of dialectic that makes no use of perceptibles but proceeds through intelligibles alone is praised as the highest cognitive power (511B3–c1; 533A8–534D1).

Yet, on a closer reading of these and related passages, we find a subtle distinction between the grasp of genuine perceptibles and the apprehension of more general features.

> I'll point out, then, if you can grasp it, that some sense perceptions don't summon the understanding to look into them, because the judgement of sense experience is itself adequate, while others encourage it in every way to look into them, because sense perception seems to produce no sound result. (523A10–B4, trans. Grube)

When we perceive the same finger as large in one context and small in another, the intellect is prodded by the puzzle to think about the nature of the great and the small (523B10–525A2). This case is contrasted with the simple perception of a finger. Sight is capable of providing fully adequate information about the color and shape of its objects and of applying certain unproblematic concepts such as that of being a finger. Certain general features, however, for instance, being beautiful or being large are such that they are grasped in perception in a way that is ambiguous. It is always possible to perceive the same object as having general features that are opposed to the initially perceived features. For instance, a sound that is beautiful in one context may be discordant and ugly in another. A finger that is large in relation to one finger may be small in relation to another. As a consequence, any attempt to make general claims on the basis of perceptions alone about such features is problematic.

This explains the difference in tone between the passage at 523A10–B4 and the description of the lovers of sights and sounds as living in a dream state at 474D3–480A13. Here, too, the role of perception is implicitly a prompt to further philosophizing; philosophers are said to be like the lovers of sights and sounds (475E2), in that both groups are lovers of beauty. Unfortunately, however, the lovers of sights and sounds do not recognize that the physical manifestations of beauty that they love are but likenesses of beauty. They confuse the likeness with the thing itself. Plato does not describe their cognitive condition in terms of having false perceptions but rather as a case of false opinion. What makes the opinion problematic is the generalization from the core perception to a further identity claim about the object, i.e., that it is Beauty-itself. The lover of sights and sounds makes an error that the hypothetical perceiver of equality in the *Phaedo* avoids. Because the object of opinion is a conflation of a likeness with a reality, it is said to be halfway between what is and what is not (478D3).

The picture of human cognitive powers illustrated by the divided line is also in evidence in the discussion of the education of the guardians in *Republic* VII (see 16: PLATO AND MATHEMATICS). Socrates distinguishes between astronomy as it is practiced by his contemporaries and true astronomy (528D5–530c1). The former seeks to explain the movements of the celestial bodies precisely as they appear to the observer. This means that the model will include irregular movements with imperfect orbits. The latter explains observable motions on an idealized geometrical model in terms of perfect spheres and regular motions. A similar distinction is drawn in the case of harmonics; the true harmonics offers a mathematical model of audible sounds. To the extent that it is possible to understand observables, a mental shift away from the visible and audible to the purely intelligible is required. The use of vision to grasp observable motions or of hearing to grasp audible musical notes is not challenged here

136

but rather Plato stresses the importance of moving beyond observables. Genuine understanding can only be achieved by the study of problems, i.e., by the mental construction of models that are purely mathematical.

Perceptual powers used in relation to appropriate objects are treated with respect in the *Republic*. The model for intellection is vision under good conditions. Plato draws an analogy between the sun as the source of light and the Form of the Good (508A4–509A4). Light makes the potentially visible actually visible; the Form of the Good makes potentially intelligible objects fully intelligible. Even perceptions that produce confusion, such as those of largeness and beauty, have an important role to play in cognition as prods to further reflection (see 7: PLATO'S METHOD OF DIALECTIC). Philosophical investigation begins with perceptions of qualities such as beauty and largeness. In the *Symposium*, although "Diotima's speech" about love quoted by Socrates does not mention perception as such, the same progression from perceptibles to intelligibles is envisaged. The true lover of beauty begins with the beauty of a single male body, moves on to all beautiful bodies, then on to beauty as manifested in laws and customs, and finally arrives at Beauty-itself (210A4–211D1).

In the *Republic*, perception is the starting point for a cognitive process that, when successful, terminates in the apprehension of ideal objects. The divided line provides a vivid picture of the difference between perception and its objects and intellection and its objects. Nevertheless, human cognizers begin in the world of physical objects as presented in and conceptualized through perception and, on the basis of questions prompted by perceptions, the inquiring mind moves beyond observable objects.

Timaeus

The creation myth that frames the discussion of the *Timaeus* spawns a detailed description of perceptual mechanisms, especially those of vision (see 14: THE ROLE OF COSMOLOGY IN PLATO'S PHILOSOPHY).

> When light surrounds the visual ray, then like falls upon like and they coalesce, and one body is formed by affinity in the line of vision, wherever the light that falls from within presses firmly against an external object it has encountered. And the whole visual ray, being similarly affected, in virtue of similarity transmits the motions of what it touches or what touches it over the whole body, until they reach the soul, causing that perception which we call seeing. (45C2–D2)

The attention to detail is striking in this account. It also makes clear that for Plato perception is a psycho-physical activity that begins with a series of purely physical changes – in the medium between the organ and the object and in the perceptual organ. Hearing and smell, like sight, are caused by changes in a medium; only the organ of sight interacts with the medium to create the conditions required in order for seeing to take place. Sight, the sense that seems the least amenable to explanation in terms of bodily contact, is described in terms that seem to make it a case of contact. A body is formed that extends through the medium to the organ and causes changes in it. The terminology makes it clear that we are to understand the perceptual process solely in terms of physical causality up to the point where the changes in the percipient's body cause changes in the soul. A process that begins in physical changes outside the body of the percipient and ends in changes in the percipient's mind is constitutive of perception. All components of the process are necessary for perception to take place.

According to Timaeus, the eyes were the first organs to be fashioned by the gods (45B2–4). Sight is of supreme benefit to human beings; without it "none of our present statements about the universe could have been made" (47A1–4). The investigation of the universe led thinkers to philosophy (47A4–B2). Despite the importance of vision, Plato continues to circumscribe the range of objects that are accessible through perception. The familiar distinction between understanding and true opinion is invoked in order to establish that Forms by themselves are not objects of perception (51D2–52D1). Were true opinion identical to understanding, it is argued, then the objects perceived through our senses would be the most stable things that are. Since there is a distinction, Forms are more stable than perceptibles.

When Timaeus turns to the properties of the elemental bodies, he says that it will be necessary to appeal to sense-perception at every step in the discussion (61c3–D1). Fire is hot because its shape is such that it cuts bodies into small pieces; moisture is cold because it compresses our bodies (61D5–62B6). Whatever our flesh gives way to is hard; whatever gives way to our flesh is soft (62B6–c2). Other perceptible characteristics are explained in terms of more basic qualities. Roughness is due to a combination of hardness and non-uniformity; smoothness is due to a combination of uniformity and density (63E8–64A1). Since these characteristics are a consequence of the shapes of the elemental bodies, the perceptible properties mentioned have an objective basis in the things causing them. A similar account is given of tastes, odors, sounds, and color (65c1–68B2).

"Color is a flame which flows forth from bodies of all sorts, with its parts proportional to our sight so as to produce perception" (67c4–D1). Timaeus goes on to explain that differences in color are due to differences in size between the flame emanating from external bodies and the flame emanating from the eye. If there is no difference between the two, the result is transparency. White dilates the ray of sight, and black contracts it. Similar accounts are given of brightness and the other colors, many of which are due to the mixture of more basic colors. Green, for instance, is a mixture of amber and black.

The description of perceptible qualities, like the earlier description of the visual ray, underscores the importance of the physical mechanisms involved in perception. The character of a simple perception of a proper object is fully determined by the physical interaction between the body of the percipient and external bodies. The content of the perception is explicated in terms of the fit or lack of fit between the relevant physical characteristics of an external body and the organ.

When Timaeus turns his attention to situating the soul in the body, he places the immortal soul, the seat of rationality, in the head, and the mortal soul in the chest and trunk. Sense-perception, pleasure and pain, emotion, and appetite are mentioned in connection with the mortal soul initially, but then sense-perception drops out of the account (69D4–6). The descriptions already given of four of the five senses (sight, hearing, smell, and taste) appear to place them in the head. Perception, even on Timaeus' account, challenges a strict division between mortal and immortal soul. While a story might be told about a central sensorium in the chest to which all the individual sense organs attach, this story is not told by Plato. We are left with a puzzling omission of a faculty that seems to challenge the physical compartmentalization of different types of soul, despite its having been much discussed prior to the compartmentalization.

Theaetetus

The topic under discussion is knowledge and Theatetus makes various attempts to define knowledge by identifying it with other cognitive faculties, namely, perception and opinion. These are variously characterized. Three different accounts of what it might mean to say that knowledge is perception are explored. In the end, all are found unsatisfactory, and the thesis that knowledge is perception is laid to rest at 186E. The focus then shifts to various attempts to define knowledge in terms of opinion. For our purposes, the *Theaetetus* is a very important work, because it is the one dialogue in which perception is discussed at length in its own right as a cognitive power.

The thesis that knowledge is perception is given three different interpretations and, on each interpretation, the thesis is refuted. On the first interpretation, the thesis is said to be equivalent to the Protagorean claim that man is the measure of all things. On the second interpretation, it is explicated in terms of a Heraclitean world where everything and everyone are in a constant state of flux. Neither the Protagorean version of the thesis nor the Heraclitean version holds up under scrutiny. Yet Plato revisits the claim that knowledge is perception. The third refutation, found at 184B4– 186E7, is aimed at an unadorned version of the thesis as interpreted by Socrates and Theaetetus. Socrates begins the refutation by distinguishing between objects that are perceived through one faculty and those that are common.

> *Socrates*: Now will you also agree that with respect to the objects you perceive through one faculty it is impossible to perceive them through another – for instance, to perceive objects of hearing through sight or objects of sight through hearing?
> *Theaetetus*: Of course.
> *Socrates*: So, if there's something which you think about both of them, it cannot be something which you are perceiving about both, either by means of one of the instruments or by means of the other. (184E8–185A6)

Theaetetus and Socrates agree that since there is no organ through which the common features (sameness, difference, and being) are perceived, these objects are apprehended directly by the mind. Since knowledge involves the apprehension of common features, it cannot be perception. This whole argument, however, depends upon the claim made above that restricts each sense, and hence perception in general, to objects that are not accessible through more than one sense. The challenge for us is to uncover the reasons that explain why Theaetetus readily assents to this restriction on perception. More important, does the dialogue offer any justification for this position?

The answer (and the justification of the crucial premise) is found not in the final argument at 184B4–186E7 but earlier in the dialogue (Modrak 1981). At 156A1– 157C2, Socrates puts forward a theory of perception in the context of the Heraclitean flux doctrine. Whether Plato accepts this theory, the so-called "secret doctrine," has been a matter of controversy. It is noteworthy, however, that critical support for the

139

thesis that each sense is limited to its own proper object is found there. According to this theory, the object of perception is dependent upon the act of perceiving and the structure of the external object.

> When an eye and something else commensurate with it come within range, they give birth to whiteness together with its cognate perception, which would not have occurred, had either one of these not encountered the other.... Then the eye becomes filled with sight and now sees and becomes not sight but a seeing eye; while the other parent of the color is filled with whiteness and becomes not whiteness, but a white thing, be it stick or stone or whatever else may happen to be so colored. (156D3–E7)

The object of perception is a phenomenal object; it is created through the interaction of the sense organ and the external object. A later passage reaffirms the identification of a sense with a capacity of a specific bodily organ (185C3–E1). Taking both passages together, we have the justification needed for the claim that no sense can grasp another's object. The interaction that takes place between a specific organ, e.g., an eye, and an external object, e.g., a stone, were it to occur in a different organ through different means, would be a different interaction. Crucially, the product of the interaction would be a different phenomenal object, e.g., a hard thing. The characteristics of a sense object reflect its "parentage."

As developed in the Heraclitean framework of the second part of the *Theaetetus* (151D7–183A7), this account of perception has the consequence that phenomenal objects are totally unstable, because both the organ and the external object are constantly changing in a Heraclitean universe. As a result, the white thing is wholly ephemeral. The same theory of perception, however, in a non-Heraclitean universe where both organ and external object were fairly stable would yield phenomenal objects that were also fairly stable.

Perception is identified with the mind's apprehending sensible features through bodily faculties at 184B8–186E10. Included in perception is not only the passive reception of sensibles but so also is the active investigation of sensible features by the mind. When asked through what the mind would think about the saltiness of color and sound, Theaetetus responds that were it possible for the mind to decide the question whether a color or a sound were salty it would do so through the faculty of the tongue. Simple judgments of the form, *X* is *S*, where *S* is some sensible characteristic, e.g., saltiness, are made through perception. But then what is the difference between judgments of this form and knowledge? The difference, according to Socrates, is that knowledge requires the apprehension of certain common features, namely truth and *ousia* (being). These features the mind grasps after a long and arduous effort of reasoning about them and thinking about them in relationship to each other over time (186B6–D5). To grasp the *ousia* of *X* is to grasp *X* embedded in the larger causal and ontological context that provides a fully adequate understanding of *X*. The simple perceptual judgment, "this is salty," is not knowledge, because it does not address the character of the salty item. For knowledge, a non-perceptual recognition that the perceptual judgment is about a phenomenal feature would be required. Unlike the perception of a sensible feature, knowledge would not allow its possessor to confuse the phenomenal object with an object having intrinsic stability, a Form.

The *Theaetetus* account of perception is quite compatible with the description of the causal processes involved in perception in the *Timaeus*. It also explains Timaeus' reservations about theories about physical objects. The object-as-perceived is accessible through perception but the object-as-perceived is a product of the interaction between the sense and the external object. We do not have direct access to physical objects. In the *Timaeus*, the sensible features of objects are analyzed in terms of their underlying geometrical structures. But Timaeus is cautious in presenting his findings and reminds his audience that the account is only probable. The *Theaetetus* gives us an account of perception that allows the perceiver to grasp phenomenal objects in a way that provides reliable information about the world as perceived but that, nonetheless, falls short of knowledge.

Sophist

Perception as such is barely mentioned in the *Sophist*. In the battle between the Friends of Forms and the Giants, the antagonists stake out positions that include diametrically opposed attitudes toward the visible and tangible (246A7–249D4). The Friends of Forms relegate perceptions to the domain of coming to be in contrast to that of being. The Giants insist that nothing is except that which possesses tangibility. The Stranger argues that neither position is defensible and that, besides being, the philosopher must embrace both the unchanging and that which changes (251D5–254D5). Since the changing nature of physical objects and perceptibles has been the primary reason for rejecting the evidence of the senses in other contexts, making change ontologically respectable would seem to allow perception to be epistemically respectable.

Throughout the discussion of sophistry, the notions of likeness and likeness-making figure importantly. A further distinction is drawn between a likeness (*eikon*) that maintains true proportions and another kind of likeness, an appearance (*phantasma*), that does not, and between likeness-making and appearance-making (235c8–236c7, 266D2–E4). The elements, animals, and other natural bodies are created by divine art and are likenesses. Sophistry produces appearances in words. The difference between divine and human art and the existence of copies that maintain the true proportions of their originals would provide a basis for granting the physical world as grasped in perception epistemic legitimacy. This possibility is not explored in the dialogue but is, nonetheless, significant. The causal account of perception in the *Timaeus* makes the character of the perception a consequence of the elemental shapes causing it. This account could be developed in light of the *Sophist* in a way that made the contents of perceptions likenesses rather than mere appearances. Under these conditions, perceptions would provide accurate information about stable objects, the characteristics of which would mirror realities (Forms).

Philebus

Pleasure, not perception, is the topic under consideration in the *Philebus*, but quite a bit is said about perception in the course of the discussion (see 21: PLATO ON

PLEASURE AS THE HUMAN GOOD). Pleasures and pains have cognitive content; perception is the source of this content. Socrates describes a kind of pleasure that belongs to the soul itself. This type of pleasure is dependent upon memory, which in turn is defined in terms of perception. Perception is the motion that occurs when the soul and body are affected together (34A3–5). Memory is the preservation of perception. On particular occasions, memory and perception write words (*logous*) in our soul (39A1–7). In addition, perceptual experiences also often give rise to pictures corresponding to the verbal inscriptions. Socrates explains how this occurs: "A person takes his judgments and assertions directly from sight or any other sense and then views the images in himself of those judgments and assertions" (39B9–c2; trans. Frede). The inscriptions and the associated pictures are true if they give a correct account, or false if they do not. This is a complex and provocative account of human cognitive life. It envisages the transformation of perceptual information into verbal form as well as the retention of sensible features. The latter mirror the characteristics of the original perception. A simpler picture would envisage neither an internal writer nor an internal painter. The function of both writer and painter is the transfer of incoming perceptual information into other media for its preservation in the soul. Perceptions spontaneously issue in judgments and internal images. This maximizes the amount and kinds of information that the perceiver has access to for current and future use. It is noteworthy that this process, when all goes well, allows perception to be a source of completely reliable information.

In the *Philebus*, perception is defined in a way that covers the awareness of internal states as well as perception through the senses. Not only does the soul have awareness of its own pleasures and pains but it is also aware of the pleasures and pains of the body. As a consequence, a person sometimes experiences a psychic pleasure that opposes a bodily pain and a psychic pain that opposes a bodily pleasure (41D1–3). Just as the relative distance of objects from the eyes distorts our perception of their actual size, so too does the relative temporal proximity of pleasures and pains distort our perception of them (41E2–42c2; cf. *Prt.* 356A3–357B2). In both cases, it is possible for a discerning perceiver to distinguish between appearance and reality. What distinguishes a false pleasure from a true one is an accurate perception of its content. Socrates appeals to this picture in order to argue against Protarchus' restriction of truth and falsity to belief (*doxa*). False pleasures are said to be ridiculous imitations of true ones (40c4–6). Here the familiar Platonic distinction between appearance and reality that sometimes seems to separate perception from intellection is being applied to perceptions of pleasures and pains as well as to judgments. Some perceptions are correct and give us information about realities; some are not and present us only with misleading appearances.

Seventh Letter *and* Definitions

The authorship of the *Seventh Letter* is disputed, and the *Definitions* are undoubtedly a Platonic handbook not written by Plato (see 1: THE LIFE OF PLATO OF ATHENS). Yet since in both works perception is discussed, a brief look at these passages seems appropriate. The author of the *Seventh Letter* defends the importance of an oral tradition

142

in which the preferred method of philosophy is that of dialectical discussion. It is "only when names, definitions, visual and other perceptions are rubbed together" and tested in discussion that the nature of anything can be understood (344B1–c1). In the *Definitions*, sight is defined as a state of being able to discern bodies (411c9); and perception, as a movement of the soul by the body (414c5–7). In both works, we find the assumption that perceptions are often veridical.

Overview

Our survey of the dialogues has revealed certain consistent themes in Plato's handling of perception, both in the few explicit discussions of it and in the assumptions, implicit as well as explicit, made about perception. One constant feature is the identification of perception with a psycho-physical activity in which changes in the body are communicated to the soul. This activity is the result of the external world's impacting the body in various ways. In some cases, for instance, hearing, the body is fairly passive while being acted upon by the world; in others, the body contributes to the conditions that enable perception to occur, for instance, the visual ray sent out by the eye. Typically, the causal sequence begins in the external world when an object or event acts on the sense organ and the movement in the organ is then communicated to the soul. A similar sequence of events takes place internally in the case of the awareness of bodily sensations, for instance, the awareness of a toothache or an aching back.

Another common feature is Plato's conception of a cognitive faculty. All cognitive faculties, perceptual and intellectual alike, are distinguished by their objects (see 19: THE PLATONIC SOUL). Sight is distinct from hearing, because color is distinct from sound. The objects that we perceive lack the inherent stability that characterizes objects of thought. Since the object-as-perceived is a consequence of an interaction between the perceiver and the external object, the object-as-perceived shares many characteristics of the external object causing the perception. The object-as-perceived is as stable or as unstable as its cause.

In the *Republic* and other middle period dialogues, the direct apprehension of an object, such as is found in vision, is the model for intellectual apprehension at its best. Moreover, according to Plato, in the acquisition of information about the world, it is always epistemically better to have been a percipient than to have been merely a recipient of information from others about the same events or objects. Perceiving the world directly through the senses is a prerequisite for being in the best epistemic position one can be in with respect to physical objects.

Other features of perception, however, seem to change from one dialogue to another. This is especially true of the value attached to cognitive graspings of physical objects through perception and the related issue of whether the information that is presented through perception can serve as the basis for true beliefs. The *Phaedo*'s claim that the soul is always deceived when relying upon the body contrasts with the *Philebus*' acceptance of perception as a source of true opinion.

There are several strategies for resolving these tensions (see 2: INTEPRETING PLATO). On one plausible story line, Plato's views about perception evolve. They evolve from a fairly uncritical acceptance of sense-perception in the Socratic dialogues to considerable disenchantment with its capacity to yield anything of any epistemic value in the early middle period to a more nuanced acceptance of its critical capacity in the late dialogues. There is also an alternative story available that does not assume any particular order of the dialogues while still attributing a coherent story to Plato. Plato emphasizes different aspects of a nuanced account of perception throughout. He is always willing to concede a role for perception as a reliable source of information about the physical world. One reason why perceptions cannot be relied upon to grasp unshakeable truths firmly is that the objects presented in perception are always somewhat unstable. This flaw is rooted in the nature of bodies and the physical world. Plato's apparent skepticism about the senses is driven by his skepticism about physical objects. It is not that the character of the senses is such that we cannot know physical objects through the senses but rather that the character of physical objects is such that we cannot fully know them. Thus, in order to grasp objects that are fully intelligible, the intellect must separate itself from the presentation of physical objects through perception. When Plato's attention shifts to the requirements of knowledge, he emphasizes the importance of apprehensions that are integrated into a whole network of consistent, true beliefs. From this vantage point, knowledge of perceptibles is possible, although perceptions would still not be instances of knowledge. On either one of these story lines, true opinion and even justified true opinion in our sense, but not Plato's sense, can be based upon perception and often is.

A closely related issue is that of the difference between perception and knowledge. Perceptions sometimes provide misleading information; knowledge never does, but what distinguishes the true perception from an instance of knowledge? In many passages, knowledge is described in terms of the immediate grasp of an object. Thus described, knowledge seems very like an instance of perception of a special sort of object. The lover of Beauty-itself seems to stand in the same cognitive relation to Beauty-itself, as does the lover of beautiful sights, when he gazes upon a beautiful body. The difference as developed by Socrates in *Republic* V (474D3–480A13) is purely in terms of the features of Beauty-itself, its unchanging nature, its being essentially beautiful in every respect. Yet, as Socrates goes on to make clear in the discussion of the divided line, the objects of knowledge, the Forms, are interrelated. We have knowledge when we grasp a whole conceptual network and possess a number of interconnected, true propositions. This conception of knowledge and understanding is quite evident in later works such as the *Theaetetus* and *Sophist*. If knowledge is not simply the immediate, perception-like grasp of independent objects of the right type, namely Forms, then perception, even though it has immediacy, provides at best an accurate snapshot. It is always going to fall short of knowledge. Knowledge requires a contextualized understanding based on grasping all the relevant concepts. The evaluation of the truth of a perceptual judgment requires the mind to embed the perceptual judgment in a network of beliefs, some of which will employ concepts that are beyond the grasp of perception.

We set out to investigate Plato's views about the nature of perception. We wondered whether Plato allowed perception a role in the acquisition of true beliefs. It is now clear that an affirmative answer to that question is in order. Plato allows perceptions to constitute true beliefs, but he does not allow perception by itself to issue directly in judgments about the truth of these beliefs. This is a nuanced position that does not fit particularly well with the standard modern use of "true." Perhaps the best way to express Plato's position in familiar terms is to say that perceptions may constitute veridical beliefs that are true in the sense that they get it right about the perceived object, but true perceptual beliefs do not meet Plato's criteria for justification. A justified true belief, according to Plato, requires a full understanding of the phenomenon in question. This is the force of the statement in the *Theaetetus* that perception cannot make judgments about truth (186B–D). This may also explain those occasional statements scattered throughout the Platonic corpus that seem to express sweeping skepticism about the reliability of perception. As we have seen, even in dialogues where such statements are found, other descriptions of perception belie a sweeping condemnation of perception and suggest that perception is reliable with respect to certain kinds of objects. Despite our initial worries, as it turns out, Plato does have an interesting and coherent account of perception as a full-fledged cognitive power.

Note

All translations are the author's unless otherwise noted.

References and further reading

Bedu-Addo, J. (1991). Sense-experience and the argument for recollection in Plato's *Phaedo*. *Phronesis* 36, pp. 27–60.

Bondeson, W. (1969). Perception, true opinion and knowledge in Plato's *Theaetetus*. *Phronesis* 14, pp. 111–22.

Burnyeat, M. (1976). Plato on the grammar of perceiving. *Classical Quarterly* 70, pp. 29–51.

Cooper, J. (1970). Plato on sense-perception and knowledge: *Theaetetus* 184–186. *Phronesis* 15, pp. 123–46.

Fine, G. (1990). Knowledge and belief in *Republic* V–VII. In S. Everson (ed.) *Companions to Ancient Thought*, vol. I: *Epistemology* (pp. 85–115). Cambridge: Cambridge University Press.

Frede, M. (1987). Observations on perception in Plato's later dialogues. In *Essays in Ancient Philosophy* (pp. 3–8). Minneapolis: University of Minneapolis.

Holland, A. (1973). An argument in Plato's *Theaetetus*: 184–186. *Philosophical Quarterly* 23, pp. 97–116.

Kanayama, Y. (1987). Perceiving, considering, and attaining being (*Theaetetus* 184–186). *Oxford Studies in Ancient Philosophy* 5, pp. 29–82.

Modrak, D. K. (1981). Perception and judgment in the *Theaetetus*. *Phronesis* 26, pp. 35–54.

Nakhnikian, G. (1955). Plato's theory of sensation. *Review of Metaphysics* 9, pp. 129–48, 306–27.

Schipper, E. (1961). Perceptual judgments and particulars in Plato's later philosophy. *Phronesis* 6, pp. 102–9.

Turnbull, R. (1978). The role of the "Special Sensibles" in the perception theories of Plato and Aristotle. In P. Machamer and R. Turnbull (eds.) *Studies in Perception* (pp. 3–26). Columbus: Ohio State University Press.

11

Knowledge and the Forms in Plato

MICHAEL FEREJOHN

Grades of Epistemological Involvement

It is generally agreed among historians of the western philosophical tradition that the roots of epistemology reach no further back than the Platonic dialogues. This, however, prompts the narrower question of exactly where and how this field of study emerged within that large body of works. More specifically, on the common "developmental" interpretation of the dialogues as representing progressive stages of Plato's thought, a question that naturally arises is whether Plato's early, or "Socratic," dialogues contain contexts that can reasonably be counted as epistemological by modern lights (see 2: INTERPRETING PLATO).

As is often the case with such historical classificatory questions, the answer should properly take the form of a set of conditionals specifying different possible ways of understanding what is required for a context to qualify as properly epistemological in character (but see Benson 2000: 3–10, for a defense of an affirmative categorical answer). Starting from the simple observation that modern epistemology takes its name from the ancient Greek verb *epistamai* and its derivative noun-form *epistēmē*, to set a baseline we first might agree that basic linguistic competence in the use of these and roughly synonymous expressions does not by itself qualify one as an epistemologist, any more than the ability to use the term "bird" competently would make one an ornithologist. We might therefore isolate a special set of applications that might be termed "principled" or "reflective" because they are supported by reasons invoking allegedly necessary conditions upon correct uses of the term. On this minimal conception, the character of Socrates in the early Platonic dialogues would be classified as an epistemologist, since it is quite common in those works to find him concluding that others around him fail certain tests for the possession of genuine knowledge that he himself administers.

But of course, not all reasons someone might give for applying or withholding a term are equally sound, and since epistemology is essentially a *philosophical* enterprise, it would perhaps be unduly generous to admit into its domain the invocation of bad or irrelevant reasons, such as those based on subjective reactions or appeals to baseless authority. To exclude these we might strengthen our conception of epistemology by requiring that the reasons given be *philosophical* reasons that plausibly bear some objective connection to conditions that anyone in possession of genuine knowledge would reasonably be expected to satisfy. As will emerge, the stronger conception of epistemology generated by this qualification is also detectable in the early Platonic dialogues. But this, I believe, is the strongest conception that can be found in those works, and it falls far short of epistemology, as it is currently practiced. To begin with, the early dialogues betray no concern with developing a set of necessary and *sufficient* conditions for the possession of knowledge, and so cannot be said to contain an *analysis* of knowledge (see 6: PLATONIC DEFINITIONS AND FORMS). Moreover, since Socrates doesn't offer any analyses of knowledge whatsoever in the early dialogues, he is in no position to undertake the most recognizable aspect of modern epistemology, the *comparative assessment* of different and competing analyses. In the next section I will offer an account of how, during the course of Plato's philosophical career, theoretical activities more akin to contemporary epistemology arise out of relatively modest Socratic beginnings. After that I will consider how Plato's epistemology is subsequently developed and transformed in his middle and late periods.

The Socratic Certification Program

By most accounts, the Socratic conversations depicted in the early Platonic dialogues are devoted almost entirely to the practical ethical issues of identifying, embracing, and promulgating the best possible, i.e., the most virtuous, form of human life. The problem, however, is that Socrates recognizes that there is no shortage of people in Athens who are thought by themselves or others to possess sufficient expertise to speak authoritatively on such matters. His principal project, then, is to find ways to distinguish effectively between the genuine moral expert – the authentically wise person whose advice should be followed in ethical matters – and various pretenders to this position.

In approaching this task, Socrates quite naturally endeavors to formulate necessary conditions, or *tests*, for the possession of genuine expertise in any field whatever. However, in many instances the actual tests employed in this Socratic "certification program" are almost entirely unreported. Perhaps the earliest relevant text is *Ap.* 20E8–21D7, a well-known passage where Socrates describes his reaction at being told of the Delphic oracle's pronouncement that "no one is wiser than Socrates." According to Socrates, he is initially puzzled by this report, since he believes himself to be "wise on no subject, neither great nor small" (21B1–5). However, recognizing that the oracle's statements cannot be false, he sets out to investigate this conundrum by seeking out individuals in the city with reputations for wisdom, and interrogating them to determine whether, *per impossibile*, they really are wise and the oracle was mistaken, or that they lack the wisdom they are thought to possess.

Given the unquestioned infallibility of the oracle, the outcome of Socrates' investigation is entirely predictable: he reports that every single one of his subjects was revealed upon examination not really to be wise. One of the most striking things about these passages, however, is how little we learn from them about Socrates' *grounds* for these negative conclusions. To take just one representative example, in the case of a certain unnamed politician he questions, Socrates says merely at 21c5–8 that after "conversing with him" (*dialegomenos autō(i)*), he concluded that this man seemed wise, *but was not actually so* (*einai d'ou*). But Socrates does not say what happened during the course of this "conversation" to give him that impression. Thus, even though these passages in the *Apology* make it clear enough that Socrates is applying certain tests (and so presupposing certain necessary conditions) for the possession of knowledge and wisdom, they simply don't contain sufficient information about what transpires during these interrogations to reveal anything of substance about the nature or content of these tests. Fortunately, passages in some of the other early dialogues provide considerably more information on this score.

The General Account-Requirement

Perhaps the most common and best known and of Socrates' tests for knowledge is a product of his well-documented tendency to regard "crafts" (*technai*) such as medicine or ship-navigation as providing the clearest examples of genuine expertise. For one particularly potent ramification of this "craft-model" of knowledge is a crucial insight that eventually goes deep into the heart of Platonic (and Aristotelian) epistemology, namely that a real expert can authenticate his claim to knowledge by producing the appropriate sort of "account" (*logos*) upon demand. This idea will no doubt seem portentous to anyone familiar with the subsequent history of epistemology. However, as it appears in the early dialogues, the requirement is actually quite amorphous, and is evidently understood by Socrates and his interlocutors very differently in different contexts.

To begin with, what I shall call the "account-requirement" is sometimes invoked in passages where the Socratic certification project takes on a distinctly *ad hominem* tone. In such places, Socrates appears to be much more concerned with trying to determine whether some reputed sage before him is a genuine expert than with directly adjudicating any particular knowledge claim that his respondent happens to make during the course of the interrogation. (Perhaps Socrates thinks that the pronouncements of a *certified* expert could generally be accepted as reliable. Such an authoritarian attitude in ethical matters seems thoroughly non-Socratic, but it is perhaps suggested at *Cri.* 47A12–D5.) One particularly vivid description of this is given at *La.* 187E6– 188A2 when Nicias describes what he thinks is the inevitable effect of prolonged exposure to Socratic questioning:

> Whoever comes into close proximity to Socrates and converses with him . . . will not be able to stop until he is led into giving *an account of himself*, of the manner in which he now spends his days, and the kind of life he has lived.

In this and similar passages, Socrates' certification procedure appears to rest on the rather loose idea that a true expert should be able to respond fully and candidly to Socrates' questioning without being caught up in doctrinal inconsistencies or other, "practical," sorts of incongruencies. But these passages tell us nothing at all about the form such an "account of oneself" should take, and so they do not constitute much of an advance over the *Apology* passages discussed earlier.

In addition to these *ad hominem* contexts, the early dialogues also contain other passages where Socrates seems to think of his certification program in a much more "impersonal" manner, and to be asking what conditions *anyone* would have to satisfy to be counted as knowledgeable on a given subject. Typically this is done by the use of first-person plural pronouns. For example, when Socrates launches his certification procedure at *La.* 186A2–B5, he conspicuously includes himself among those who must be tested for expertise in the matter of identifying and imparting courage – even though he had never claimed to have any expertise whatsoever in this field. Similarly, at the very end of *Republic* I (which I take to be a "Socratic" context; see Irwin 1995: 376 n. 1), at 354A12–c3 Socrates chides the entire company – again, including himself – for trying to say things about justice without first having discovered what justice is.

I believe this "depersonalization" of the Socratic tests for expertise is one of two crucial contributing factors to the development of later Platonic epistemology. For whereas I suggested above that in its *ad hominem* form, the account-requirement amounts to a rather vague test of "elenctic survival" (for an unspecified length of time) in the rough and tumble of Socratic interrogation, in "impersonal" settings it takes on comparatively specific and precise forms much more in line with what could reasonably be viewed as plausible *philosophical* conditions on the possession of genuine knowledge (see 5: THE SOCRATIC *ELENCHUS*).

Definitional and Explanatory Accounts

There is, however, an additional complication that must now be added to the proceedings. In this section I intend to show that in different "impersonal" certification-contexts within the early dialogues, the general account-requirement is given two distinct specifications. As we shall see, these come to play major roles, both individually and in combination, in later Platonic epistemology.

Each of these two different ways of understanding the account-requirement might plausibly be thought to flow out of what one would reasonably expect of genuine experts. One of these variants is that genuine experts will know – and be able to say – *what is* the subject matter of their expertise. In what I have described as *ad hominem* contexts, the requirement perhaps amounts to little more than the truism that to speak knowledgeably you must know *what* you are talking about. This seems to be Socrates' attitude at *Euthphr.* 4E3–8, when he reacts incredulously to his interlocutor's brash announcement that he intends to indict his own father for murder on questionable factual grounds:

> In the name of Zeus, Euthyphro, do you think your knowledge of divine laws, and of piety and impiety, is so exact that, the facts being as you describe, you do not fear doing something impious by prosecuting your father for murder?

By contrast, in what I am calling "impersonal" contexts, the requirement is apparently presented as a methodological principle dictating the proper *order* of Socratic investigations (see Benson 2000: chs. 5–7). This so-called "priority of definition" principle is at work, for instance, at *La.* 190B7–c2, when Socrates insists that it will not be possible to speak knowledgeably about the best way to acquire virtue unless we *first* know "what virtue is" (*ti estin pote aretē*) (see 8: SOCRATIC IGNORANCE). Similarly, in *Republic* I, at 354B1–c1 he declares that it had been a mistake to try to discover facts about justice *before* determining "what justice is" (*to dikaion ho ti pot' estin*). But these differences aside, it is reasonably clear that in both sorts of contexts Socrates understands the account-requirement as the reasonable demand that anyone knowledgeable on a given subject, *X*, must be able to produce and defend a satisfactory answer to the question, "What is *X*?" In this specification, the sort of account Socrates demands from a reputed expert is a *definitory* account – that is to say, a *definition* – of the subject matter of the alleged expertise.

The second variant of the Socratic account-requirement also stems from capacities that one might naturally associate with genuine expertise. In this case, the leading idea is that true experts do not rest their beliefs and decisions merely on their presumed authority; instead, they stand ready to support those judgments with *explanations* of their correctness. That is to say, in later, Aristotelian, terms true experts know (and can show) not just *that* certain things are so, but also *why* they are so (*APo.* I.2,71b9–16). As it happens, the textual evidence for this second variant of the account-requirement is less direct, since Socrates never in those works formulates it explicitly, but I believe it is decisive. The key passages are those in which Socrates elaborates upon his demand that reputed experts produce (and defend) definitory accounts of the subjects on which they are supposed to be authorities. For example, at *Euthphr.* 6D9–E1, shortly after asking Euthyphro to tell him "what piety is," Socrates expands upon this request in the following manner: "I asked you to tell me . . . that essential form *by which* (*hō(i)*) all pious things are pious."

In using a causal idiom here and in parallel passages (cf. esp. the occurrences of *dia* throughout *Euthphr.* 9E–11B and at *Men.* 72c8), Socrates cannot be committing himself to the eccentric view that the "essential form" of piety literally *causes* a person or action to be pious. In view of his keen interest in the *impartation* of virtue, he is surely aware that such factors as upbringing and training are what play those causal roles. Charity therefore recommends that we interpret these passages not as concerned with causal responsibility, but with *explanatory priority*, and that he expects that the correct answer to his question, "what is piety" will explain why certain acts or persons are properly *classified* as pious. It will, in other words, provide "logically sufficient" rather than "causally necessitating" grounds for something being pious. (Note that the expression "logically sufficient" is used here and below in a broad sense to include "analytic" as well as strictly "logical" implications.)

Chronic and Episodic Perspectives on Knowledge

If, as I have just argued, Socrates relies on the explanatory variant of account-requirement in the early dialogues, it may be wondered why he never explicitly formulates it in those works, as he does the definitory version. The explanation, I suggest, is that it is not until the *Meno* that the Socratic certification program undergoes a second key transformation that can be regarded as a natural extension of the "depersonalization" discussed earlier, but without which the role of "explanatory" accounts remains partially obscured.

In such early dialogues as the *Ion* and *Laches* Socrates had been exploring the issue of what *standing* characteristics an alleged expert must possess in order to be certified as genuine. By contrast, in the last part of the *Meno* Socrates begins to focus more narrowly on the question of what conditions must obtain in order for a person – *on a given occasion* – to be said to possess knowledge, as opposed to merely having a true belief. This *episodic* perspective appears quite suddenly at 96D5–97c2, when Socrates challenges his earlier conclusion that virtue – considered as a *chronic* psychological condition – should be classified as "a sort of wisdom" (88D2–3). He now argues that if one were simply interested, on a given occasion, in getting from one place to another, it would not make any difference, from a purely *practical* point of view, whether one consulted someone who really *knew* the route or someone who merely had an ill-founded opinion that happened to be true.

However, just as soon as he concludes that there is no *practical* difference between knowledge and mere true belief, Socrates immediately reverses himself yet again by suggesting a *conceptual* distinction between the two. He does this by invoking the image of the self-moving statues of Daedalus, to which he likens mere true belief on the grounds that, insofar as they are not "fastened" (*dedemena*), they do not "remain" (*paramenei*) but instead tend to "run away" (*apodidraskei*) and therefore "are not of much value" (*ou pollou axiai eisin*). By contrast, he declares, genuine knowledge would be analogous to such a statue that had been "fastened," and therefore stays put. He then expands upon this metaphorical "tying up" by making an explicit connection between knowledge and the possession of "explanatory" accounts: "[Mere] true beliefs are not worth much until one 'fastens them' (*dēsē(i)*) with 'causal accounts' (*aitias logismō(i)*)" (98A1–4).

Here Socrates is clearly concerned with the conditions under which someone (indeed, *anyone*) can be said to possess knowledge on a particular occasion. Hence the ultimate reason for the difference in visibility between the two understandings of Socrates' account-requirement should now be clear. Unlike the definitory variant, which attaches primarily to the *cognitive subject* as a condition of expertise, the explanatory variant constitutes a necessary condition for the attribution of knowledge *on a particular occasion*. This is why it is not articulated until the *Meno*, when Plato begins to investigate the nature of knowledge from the episodic perspective.

The Formal *Aitia*

In the last section I have been at pains to distinguish these two Socratic variants of the general account-requirement, but I have not meant to suggest that they are entirely unconnected. In fact, quite to the contrary, I believe that they are often brought together in the early dialogues to form a very special sort of explanatory scheme that Aristotle later refers to in *Ph.* II.3 (194b24–195a3) as the "formal *aitia*." (Traditionally, the noun *aitia* has been translated as "cause," which gives the misleading impression that it is limited to the modern notion of "efficient" cause. Since, for both Plato and Aristotle, *aitiai* are ultimately modes of explanation, some recent translations make barbarous use of the conjunction "because" to translate this noun. Probably the most accurate translation, though hardly the most elegant, would be something like "the most salient entity mentioned in a distinctive form of explanation.")

As I argued above, at *Euthphr.* 6D9–E1, when Socrates describes the essence of piety as that *by which* pious things are pious, he is not suggesting that possession of the essence of piety somehow *induces* someone to be pious, but only that something satisfying the definition of piety would explain, in a very special way, why that thing should be *classified* as pious. Now it is well documented that Socrates never discovers the correct definition of piety or any other virtue throughout the early dialogues, and so those works cannot display any samples of the sort of explanation he has in mind. Nevertheless, if we let *XYZ* stand in for the (unknown) correct definition of piety, and *A* denote some pious act, I believe the sort of explanation Socrates is after can be represented by the following syllogistic schema.

$XYZ =_{df}$ Piety,
A is *XYZ*,
Therefore, *A* is pious

The key thing to notice here is that while this syllogism as a whole is an *explanatory* account of the piety of *A*, its minor premise is at the same time a *definitory* account (i.e., a definition) of piety itself. In other words, the connection between the two different sorts of accounts distinguished above is that definitory accounts can function as explanatory principles *within* a very special sort of explanatory account, namely the sort Aristotle later describes as the "formal *aitia*." (Besides the "efficient" and "formal" sorts already mentioned, this passage also catalogs two others, the so-called "final" and "material" *aitiai*.)

According to my earlier argument, Socrates is not in a position to formulate the explanatory variant of the account-requirement explicitly in the early dialogues because he has not there yet begun to think about knowledge from the episodic perspective. That said, it is worthwhile to consider whether, from his position in the *Meno* (after he *had* made that advance) he would regard these "formal" explanations retrospectively as instances of what he calls "causal accounts" at *Men.* 98A1–4. In my view, not only would Socrates be agreeable to this suggestion, but quite possibly he would regard "formal" explanations as the *only* admissible sort of "causal account" capable of transforming mere true belief into knowledge. Certainly, neither the early dialogues nor the *Meno* contain the faintest scent of the other three modes of explanation (*aitiai*) later distinguished by Aristotle in *Ph.* II.3. By contrast, we shall see that as Plato moves beyond the *Meno* and through his middle period, his thinking undergoes two important developments. For one thing, the range of legitimate forms of explanation he envisions expands significantly. But even more importantly, he comes to see a need to supplement his theory of knowledge with a metaphysical underpinning (see 27: LEARNING ABOUT PLATO FROM ARISTOTLE).

Metaphysics and Epistemology in the *Republic*

The *Republic* can certainly stand on its own as a classical sourcebook in both epistemology and metaphysics. All the same, Plato's investigations into these areas are never undertaken simply for their own sake. For even though this remarkable dialogue touches on topics in nearly every area of philosophy, all of its doctrines ultimately subserve its central ethical project. In particular, Plato's ethics and political theory both require the real possibility of an exceptionally reliable human capacity to make correct ethical judgments, which can then be utilized in the proper sort of governance of a well-functioning political state or a well-developed ethical person (see 12: THE FORMS AND THE SCIENCES IN SOCRATES AND PLATO). The novel idea of the *Republic* is that if such ethical judgments are not to be "fleeting" in the manner of Daedalus' statues, they must have as their objects entities with natures that are sufficiently fixed, stable, and determinate. (Notice that Plato may be fudging the distinction between a cognitive state *itself* being fixed and stable in the *Meno*, and a cognitive state having an *object* with a fixed and stable nature in the *Republic*.) Now since Plato both believes that such knowledge is possible, and endorses the Heraclitean view that the sensible world is utterly lacking in this sort of entity, he is led in *Republic* VI and VII to postulate the existence of such stable entities "elsewhere" – in a place "separated" from the world presented by the senses. It is not clear whether Plato's reasons for thinking that sensible things are not suitable objects of knowledge stem from the fact that they are constantly changing their properties through time, or from a very different consideration, which has been called the "compresence of opposites," that any predicate that applies to them can also be shown, with equal plausibility, not to apply. (On this, see Irwin 1995: ch. 10.) It thus appears that Plato's best-known philosophical invention, the Theory of Forms, was designed specifically for this epistemological purpose (see 13: PROBLEMS FOR FORMS).

One thing that will strike a careful reader of the *Republic* already familiar with Plato's earlier work is the virtual absence of the account-requirement on knowledge that is so prominent both in the early dialogues and the last part of the *Meno*. So, for example, in presenting his theory by means of the famous Cave Allegory in *Republic* VII, Socrates doesn't show any interest in whether his protagonist (a philosopher who has acquired genuine knowledge of the Forms and then returned to the cave) could pass the *Socratic* test for knowledge by giving an account – of any sort – to his unenlightened cohabitants. He merely says that the philosopher, once habituated to the cave, will be "infinitely better" at discerning what is presented there (520c3–6), and therefore will be more capable of "acting wisely in private and public affairs" (517c4–5) because he had come to see "the cause of all that is right and beautiful" (namely, the Form of the Good). To be sure, in describing the higher, "intelligible" section of the Divided Line in *Republic* VI, at 510B2–D3 Socrates does speak about geometers reasoning from postulated first principles to establish their theorems. However, this passage is pervaded by idioms of investigation (e.g., *zētein* at 510B5 and *skepsin* at 510D2), which suggests that this passage is concerned primarily with how the geometer discovers his theorems, not with how he justifies them to others.

This virtual lack of interest in the account-requirement in the *Republic* can easily give the impression that Plato has abandoned the *Meno's* project of grounding the distinction between knowledge and belief by formulating an epistemological condition – the ability to give the right sort of account – and decided instead to achieve this objective by proposing a metaphysical distinction between the respective objects of the two forms of cognition. This, I believe, is a mistaken impression generated by the different dramatic frameworks of the dialogues in question (see 4: FORM AND THE PLATONIC DIALOGUES).

The early dialogues, as well as the *Meno*, are written from what we might call the "Socratic" perspective, i.e., from the point of view of a critical inquirer who recognizes that he himself does not possess genuine knowledge, and then sets about to discover whether anyone around him is any better off in this respect. From this point of view, it is incumbent on someone who genuinely possesses knowledge to demonstrate that fact to Socrates, and the account-requirement is a proposal about what form such a demonstration should take. By contrast, in the *Republic* the figure of Socrates is a theoretician engaged in constructing a comprehensive philosophical system that will support an objective theory of justice. But since, as that theory is articulated, the operation of a hyper-reliable cognitive faculty (knowledge) is seen to be necessary for the possibility of justice, Socrates is required in the middle books to provide a supplementary epistemological theory on which differences in reliability of different kinds of cognition are ultimately grounded in ontological differences between their respective objects. On this general line of interpretation, the *Republic* is written from a detached *theoretical* perspective. For that reason, such "Socratic" questions as "How can the other prisoners determine whether the returning philosopher really knows what he claims to know?" lie outside its purview.

The Simple and Subtle *Aitiai* in the *Phaedo*

By contrast, what I am calling the "Socratic perspective," and with it the account-requirement for knowledge, is very much in evidence in the *Phaedo*, the other middle-period work in which the Theory of Forms is explicitly formulated and deployed for epistemological purposes. Socrates' central objective in that work is to establish the immortality of the soul. To do this, however, it would not be sufficient for him to demonstrate (in the manner of the *Republic*) that souls will turn out to be immortal on *his proposed theory*. Rather, he wants to show they *really are* immortal. Consequently, he must argue from true premises that are available to Socrates and his interlocutors in their benighted condition, or from what I have called the "Socratic" perspective. To be sure, elements of the Theory of Forms sometimes appear in the course of these arguments. But unlike in the *Republic*, where the theory is apparently offered as a hypothesis to be explored, in the *Phaedo* Socrates attempts to provide philosophical reasons for thinking that the theory is actually true (see especially 72E2–76A7; see also 7: PLATO'S METHOD OF DIALECTIC).

The relevant section of the *Phaedo* is a long "autobiographical" stretch of text that begins when Socrates complains that his attempt to determine whether the soul is indestructible has been impeded by his complete ignorance of *aitiai*, i.e., of why (*dia ti*) anything is generated (*gignetai*), or is destroyed (*apollutai*), or exists (*esti*) (*Phd.* 96A6–10, with 97B3–7). For immediately following this Socrates undertakes a critical survey of various patterns of explanation, which amounts to a systematic investigation into different possible ways of interpreting the phrase "causal account" (*aitias logismos*), which occurs at *Men.* 98A1–4. As we shall see, one intriguing aspect of this survey is that it touches on all four of the *aitiai* distinguished by Aristotle in *Ph.* II.3.

Socrates commences this survey at *Phd.* 97B8–99C6 by recounting a youthful encounter with the doctrines of Anaxagoras. He says that he was initially encouraged

154

by a second-hand report that this natural philosopher made heavy use of the concept of *mind* (*nous*), which Socrates took to be a good thing. He says, however, that his high hopes vanished when he subsequently read Anaxagoras' treatise and discovered that it merely paid lip service to *nous* (by containing frequent occurrences of the expression), but did not actually make theoretical use of that concept in any form that Socrates recognized (namely, as the repository of beliefs, desires, etc.) (see 19: THE PLATONIC SOUL). It was, Socrates complains, as if someone had tried to explain why he is currently in prison awaiting execution by referring to the structure and movements of his "bones and sinews" (97c6–7), and in so doing neglected the "real causes" (*tas hōs alēthōs aitias*, 98E1) of his predicament: "that it seemed best to Athenians to condemn me, and that as a result it seemed best to me to sit here and submit to the punishment they ordered" (98E2–5).

Socrates is here expressing a clear and categorical preference for "teleological" explanations (the Aristotelian "final cause") in terms of goals, intentions, and so forth, over those that make reference only to "efficient" causes (Aristotle's "moving cause"). At this point, however, Socrates' account takes a surprising turn. At 99c6–D1 he abruptly declares that at some point he realized that his preferred teleological explanations were *unavailable*, and that it therefore became necessary for him to commence what he calls a "second sailing" (*deuteron ploun*), a search for a "second-best" mode of explanation that is at least within his reach. (Presumably Socrates is not here reversing his earlier judgment about the "real causes" of his imprisonment. Perhaps Plato thinks that adequate teleological explanations of physical phenomena would only be knowable to a divine mind.)

In the course of his description of this "second voyage" Socrates introduces the Platonic Forms for the first time into his survey of types of explanation. At 100B1–9 he shifts temporarily out of the "autobiographical" mode and asks Cebes to reaffirm his earlier commitment to the existence of the Forms. After Cebes does so, Socrates then asks for and receives his further agreement to an aspect of his theory that had not come to light earlier in the dialogue.

> It seems to me that if anything is beautiful besides the Beautiful-itself, [that other thing] is beautiful for no other reason than *because* (*dioti*) it participates in the Beautiful-itself, and that this applies to all [these other] things. Do you assent to *this cause* (*tē(i) toiade aitia(i)*)? (100c3–8)

The idioms of explanation in this passage suggest a form of explanation that Socrates refers to at 100E1 as the "safe *aitia*". Letting *A* be any beautiful particular thing, the "safe" explanation of its beauty would be as follows.

Anything that participates in the Form of Beauty is beautiful.
A participates in the Form of Beautiful,
So, *A* is beautiful.

Presumably, Socrates characterizes this explanation as "safe" (*asphales*) on the grounds that, assuming the truth of Socrates' theory, its explanans will without exception provide necessary and sufficient conditions for the truth of its explanandum.

However, Socrates' recognition that there can be no counterexamples to this explanatory scheme does not mean that he ultimately judges it to be adequate. On the contrary, his later characterization of it at 105B8–c1 as "simple-minded" (*amathes*), along with his proposal of what he describes at 105c2 as a "more subtle" (*kompsoteran*) alternative, strongly suggest that he has serious reservations about it. Unfortunately Socrates doesn't say why he calls this "safe" mode of explanation "simple-minded," but most likely it is because he thinks it is *so* "safe" that it is vacuous, i.e., entirely devoid of explanatory force. Here one should keep in mind that the existence of the Forms, along with the relationship of participation between the Forms and sensibles, are *theoretical* conditions posited to explain observed facts about the sensible world (e.g., that a certain particular is an instance of beauty). This is to say that, at least from what I am calling the "Socratic" perspective, there is no access to Forms save through acquaintance with their participants. In view of this, the "safe" explanation sketched above really says nothing more than that a thing will be beautiful when and only when the conditions responsible for its being beautiful are satisfied. But plainly this is no explanation at all.

Now inasmuch as the participation relation is the Platonic counterpart to the Aristotelian condition of a thing satisfying a certain definition (or having a certain essence), the "safe" *aitia* of the *Phaedo* would undoubtedly count as a "formal" *aitia* according to the Aristotelian classification of types of explanation in *Ph.* II.3. Nonetheless, it doesn't follow that Socrates' displeasure with the "safe" *aitia* would extend to *all* "formal" explanations without exception. For the vacuity problem noted above arises not because the relation between explanans and explanandum in the safe *aitia* is one of "logical" (rather than "causal") sufficiency, but because the conditions posited in the explanans are not conceptually *independent* of the facts they are intended to explain. (Indeed, neglect of the fact that "logical" sufficiency is consistent with conceptual independence is what gives rise to the "paradox of analysis" formulated, but not named, in Moore 1933.) But this is not a universal feature of "formal" explanations. For example, in Aristotle's own pet example, the fact that the interior angles of a certain figure equal two right angles is explained by its satisfaction of the definition of triangle, but he surely doesn't believe that knowing the definition of triangle by itself brings familiarity with this consequence. And it is not just Aristotelian examples of the "formal" *aitia* that are exempt from Plato's reservations about the safe *aitia*, but "Socratic" ones as well. For instance, even though the *Euthyphro* never reveals the correct definition of this virtue, it is plausible to infer from the proposed definitions that Socrates considers there that it would not only give conditions jointly necessary and sufficient for a thing being pious, but would also constitute an *analysis* of piety. That is to say, it would employ concepts that are not just independent of piety, but explanatorily prior to it as well (see 6: PLATONIC DEFINITIONS AND FORMS).

At any rate, it appears that some such misgivings about the "safe" *aitia* lead Socrates to propose a final, and presumably better, form of explanation, which he labels the "more subtle" *aitia*. As with its "safe" cousin, the Forms also play a principal role in this type of explanation, but some additional players are introduced as well. At 103D2–3 Socrates now asks Cebes to acknowledge the existence not just of Forms, but also of such items as snow and fire. There is some indeterminacy about how exactly Socrates is conceiving of these new entities, in particular whether he is postulating additional

Forms for these things. Here I will follow a plausible line of interpretation on which he is thinking of snow and fire and so forth simply as the physical "stuffs" or materials. At 105c1–2, Socrates then indicates how these figure in his more "subtle" style of explanation,

> If you ask me what causes anything to be hot, I will not give you that [earlier] safe but simplistic answer by saying that it is heat [i.e., Heat Itself], but I can now give you a more subtle answer, and say that it is fire.

The first part of this remark constitutes a clear rejection of the following, "safe and simplistic" explanation of why a certain body, *A*, is hot.

Whatever participates in the Form of Heat is hot.
A participates in the Form of Heat.
So *A* is hot.

In its place, Socrates then proposes his "more subtle" alternative by relying on the plausible idea that there are conceptual connections between participation in certain Forms (e.g., Heat), and the presence of certain materials, such as fire.

Whatever contains [much] fire [greatly] participates in the Form of Heat.
Whatever [greatly] participates in the Form of Heat is hot.
A contains [much] fire.
So, *A* is hot.

To be more precise, Socrates adds a further wrinkle by interposing between Forms and their sensible participants an additional sort of entity, "forms-in-things," which bear a clear resemblance to what were called "tropes" in the early twentieth century (on which, see Moore 1923, and Stout 1923). With this addition, the "subtle" *aitia* then takes the following, more complicated, form.

Whatever contains fire participates in the Form of Heat.
Whatever participates in the Form of Heat possesses a Heat-trope.
Whatever possesses a Heat-trope is hot.
A contains fire.
So, *A* is hot.

(This may be an attempt by Plato to avoid the "one-over-many" problems with the participation relation raised by Plato himself at *Prm.* 132A–135C. If so, the ploy is unsuccessful, since it relocates rather than avoids those difficulties. For a discussion of the ontological status of these "forms-in-things" and their theoretical malfunction in the *Phaedo*, see Silverman 2002: ch. 3.)

In Aristotelian terms, what Socrates is proposing here is a "hybrid" form of explanation that incorporates elements of both the "formal" and the "material" *aitiai* of *Ph.* II.3. The first and most important thing to notice is that it avoids the problem about vacuity noted above with the "safe" *aitia*. For whereas the Forms are theoretical entities, such things as snow and fire, on the present interpretation, are physical materials whose existence is detectable by means of sensory perception (at least when they are present in sufficient quantities). Hence, I suggest, unlike the "safe" explanation displayed above, it is genuinely explanatory to reason from the observable presence of fire in a body to its theoretical participation in the Form of Heat, and thence to the observable fact that it is hot.

There is also a second and closely related advantage to this "hybrid" form of explanation that is perhaps not so obvious. Whatever defects Socrates perceived in Anaxagoras' theories, they at least had the virtue of offering "local" explanations of *particular* events and circumstances. So, for example, the pseudo-explanation floated at *Phd.* 98c2–D6 in terms of "bones and sinews" does not purport merely to explain why people generally are sometimes imprisoned, nor why Socrates was imprisoned at some place or other, or at some time or other. Rather, it purports to explain how a certain *particular* collection of bones and sinews came to be at a certain *particular* physical location at a certain *particular* moment in time. This is a virtue not shared by the "safe" *aitia*, which is conceived entirely within the theoretical constraints of the Theory of Forms. For there are no theoretical resources within the simple metaphysics of Forms and participation to explain how any particular body comes to participate (or continues to participate) in a certain Form at the particular place that it does and at the particular time that it does. By contrast, if, as I have suggested, Plato conceives of such things as fire and the like in the *Phaedo* as observable physical materials, it is easy to see how he could think that a fully explicit instance of his "subtle" *aitia* would include a local explanation of how fire came to be at a certain place, or entered into a particular body, at one particular time rather than another.

It is something of a mystery that, despite the apparent merits Plato sees in this "hybrid" form of explanation, his attraction to it seems not to have endured. For even though its appearance is the culmination of the "second sailing" in the *Phaedo*, which suggests that it is the favored form of available explanation there, it is never mentioned again in the later dialogues. Instead, it appears that in his late works Plato redirects his efforts towards rehabilitating the purely "formal" mode of explanation that he had disparaged in the *Phaedo*.

"Analytic" Formal Accounts in the Late Dialogues

One instructive way to understand Plato's disposition of the "safe" *aitia* in the *Phaedo* is as a consequence of his epistemology outrunning his metaphysics. I argued earlier that one principal motivation for the Theory of Forms was to provide a metaphysical basis on which to distinguish knowledge from true belief, and that this strategy was supposed to supplement, rather than replace, his earlier attempts to ground the same distinction by means of the "account-requirement" on genuine knowledge. The "safe" *aitia* of the *Phaedo* can be interpreted as Plato's initial and somewhat crude attempt to bring these two strands of thought together by specifying a very special sort of "explanatory account" (*logismō aitias*) that is purely "formal" because it involves reference to nothing other than Forms, sensible particulars, and the participation relation. As we have seen, however, the problem is that the only sort of such "purely formal" explanatory account that can be constructed with the limited metaphysical resources of the *Republic* and the *Phaedo* is patently vacuous.

Recall now that I also argued above that the "safe" *aitia* of the *Phaedo* doesn't even respect Plato's recognition back in the early dialogues that an adequate definition – and therefore an adequate "formal" explanation – will provide an *analysis* of its definiendum by means of other concepts that are independent of it. In my view, these two shortcomings are not unrelated. At bottom, what makes the "safe" *aitia* "simplistic" is that it purports to explain the possession of a given property wholly by reference to participation in a *single* Form associated with that property. However, in the *Euthyphro* Plato is already aware that the correct definition of piety will have to explain why things have this property by reference to *other* properties with which it is analytically connected. The way out of this quandary should be obvious. If, in the original spirit of the "safe" *aitia*, the Theory of Forms is still to provide the metaphysical underpinning for this more sophisticated, type of "formal" explanation, it will need to be augmented by the addition of "analytic" principles linking participation in certain Forms necessarily with participation in certain others. In this augmented metaphysical scheme, the piety of a thing will not then be explained "safely" by participation in the Form of Piety alone, but rather by participation in *other* Forms associated with the properties that figure in the correct analysis of piety, together with such "analytic" principles. Since we never meet with any correct analyses in the Platonic dialogues, I will resort here to a familiar, neo-Aristotelian example to illustrate this more complex, *analytic* version of the "formal" *aitia*.

Whatever participates in the Forms of Rational and Animal necessarily participates in the Form of Human.
Whatever participates in the Form of Human is human.
Socrates participates in the Forms of Rational and Animal.
So, Socrates is human.

I propose that essentially this same solution occurs to Plato himself by the time he writes the *Sophist* and the *Statesman* during his late period. (I omit any discussion here of the *Theaetetus*, the only Platonic dialogue devoted entirely to an investigation of the nature of knowledge. This is because I do not endorse the influential view in Cornford 1957, that the dialogue presents a series of epistemological difficulties that Plato believes can be overcome only by postulating the Forms, and that the dialogue as a whole in effect therefore constitutes an indirect argument for their existence. On the interpretation I prefer, the Forms are properly absent from the *Theaetetus* because Plato there conducts a *metaphysically unbiased* investigation into the nature of knowledge that leaves open the question of how well its results fit with his general ontological commitments.)

The centerpiece of both the *Sophist* and the *Statesman* is the Platonic method of defining by "collection and division," which is taken over by Aristotle as definition by "genus and differentia." To be sure, the language of the passages where this method is executed gives the superficial impression that Plato is describing a more or less "empirical" procedure of making natural divisions among *classes* of objects on the basis of their observed features, and that his Forms play no role whatsoever in the method. There is reason to be suspicious of this interpretation even prior to a consideration of the evidence. For it would be odd, to say the least, to find Plato expounding a doctrine with such "empiricist" (not to mention "nominalist") undertones. It is therefore fortunate that this superficial interpretation is undercut by passages in the *Sophist* that strongly suggest a more appropriate, "realist" interpretation of Platonic division.

The overarching objective of this dialogue is to deploy the method of division to develop a definition of sophistry, Plato's chief intellectual nemesis throughout his career. This procedure is temporarily interrupted, however, by a long digression at 237–64 intended to establish the possibility of false judgment. Near the end of this digression, at 254D4–5 the Stranger introduces a quintet of Forms he calls the "greatest of the kinds" (*megista tōn genōn*) (namely, Being, Sameness, Difference, Motion, and Rest), and then describes a "dialectical" procedure that consists in determining which of these kinds can "participate in," "blend with," or "commune with" which of the others (251D5–9). However, it is clear from the surrounding context that Plato does not intend this "dialectical" method to be confined to the "simplified" Platonic universe of the "greatest kinds" alone, but to *all* Forms across the board. Moreover, on the present interpretation, this generalized dialectic, i.e., the charting of necessary relations amongst *all* Forms, is what ultimately drives the "divisions of kinds" in the *Sophist* and the *Statesman* beneath their "empirical" facades. In addition, these necessary relations include not just necessary inclusions (e.g., between human and animal), but also necessary exclusions (e.g., between animal and plant), which gives Platonic (as well as Aristotelian) divisions their characteristic tree-like structure.

From a broader perspective, this section of the *Sophist* can be interpreted as supplying the final piece of Plato's vindication of the "formal" *aitia*. For in discerning the necessary relations that obtain among the Forms, the dialectician of the *Sophist* can at the same time be viewed as collecting a corresponding set of "analytic" principles expressing those necessary relations. But according to my earlier arguments, the addition of such principles is precisely what is needed to convert "safe" and vacuous "formal" explanations into the more complex, "analytic" sort that do constitute genuine explanations.

Thus, to return to the classificatory question with which I began, the central concerns of the *Sophist* could hardly be classified as epistemological in nature. Nonetheless, on the general line of interpretation I have been developing here, this dialogue occupies a central place in the development of Plato's thinking in that field. For according to my earlier arguments, the pivotal moment of that development is Plato's decision in his middle period to deploy a metaphysical theory to ground the distinction between knowledge and belief. My closing suggestion is that his conception of dialectic in the *Sophist* gives him the means to refine and augment that metaphysical theory to the extent that it finally becomes adequate to fulfill its original epistemological purpose.

Note

All translations are the author's.

References and further reading

Benson, H. (2000). *Socratic Wisdom*. Oxford: Oxford University Press.

Cornford, F. M. (1957). *Plato's Theory of Knowledge*. New York: Macmillan.

Irwin, T. (1995). *Plato's Ethics*. Oxford: Oxford University Press.

Moore, G. E. (1923). Are the characteristics of particular things universal or particular? *Proceedings of the Aristotelian Society*, supplementary volume III, pp. 95–113. Repr. in G. E. Moore (1962) *Philosophical Papers* (pp. 17–32). New York: Collier Books.

—— (1933). The justification of analysis. *Analysis* 1, pp. 28–30.

Silverman, A. (2002). *The Dialectic of Essence: A Study of Plato's Metaphysics*. Princeton, NJ: Princeton University Press.

Stout, G. F. (1923). Are the characteristics of particular things universal or particular? *Proceedings of the Aristotelian Society*, supplementary volume III, pp. 114–22.

Vlastos, G. (1991). *Socrates: Ironist and Moral Philosopher*. Cambridge: Cambridge University Press.

Part III

PLATONIC METAPHYSICS

The Forms and the Sciences in Socrates and Plato

TERRY PENNER

The truth about Plato's Forms is, I think, quite straightforward. Unfortunately, for lack of proper context in presentation, and some hostility to any tincture of metaphysics – not to mention Aristotle's dismissal of the Forms – it has in modern times been crusted over with misinterpretation. This article makes a beginning at providing some useful context.

The "What is X?" Question, the Sciences, Virtue, and the Forms

"How extraordinary that the world should contain – objectively and quite independently of our thought, language, and culture – not just people, animals, plants, trees, buildings, chairs, and the like – but also (objective, abstract) objects that unify and structure individuals of the first group in various scientifically helpful ways, and that are, accordingly, whatever else Forms may be, objects of the sciences."

So we may imagine Plato musing as he considered the entities Socrates presupposed – apparently *without* wonder – as the objects about which he asked his famous "What is X?" questions: What is courage? What is piety? What is the experience called "being overcome by pleasure"? What is virtue – and is it [the kind of thing that is] teachable?

I presuppose two things here. The first is commonly granted: that the Theory of Forms emerges from Socrates' concern with what Richard Robinson famously called the "What is X?" question – a question said to be prior to any other question about X (for example, whether X has a certain property or attribute), in that Socrates holds, notoriously, that one cannot know the answer to any question of the sort "Is X Y?" ("Is X an F thing?") unless one already knows the answer to the "What is X?" question. (See 6: PLATONIC DEFINITIONS AND FORMS; 11: KNOWLEDGE AND THE FORMS IN PLATO.) The second presupposition is not at all commonly granted – or even so much as considered. This is that the importance of the "What is X?" question is intimately connected with Socrates' view that

VS Virtue is a science (knowledge or expertise: also sometimes referred to as a craft or an art), that is, the science of good and bad (the science of goods and bads: also a *metrētikē*, a science of measuring goods and bads (and even pleasures and pains) against each other, especially when at different distances in time from the present).

Notice that the question "Is virtue teachable?," which I have formulated above as "Is virtue the kind of thing that is teachable" (*Men.* 86D3–E4, 87A1–3, B2–C3), is really a variant on the "What is *X*?" question, namely, "Is virtue identical with (some form of) knowledge or a science?" (*Men.* 89A2–3: though the Greek may also be translated as "knowledge is some part of virtue." The point is that virtue is *one* of the sciences, namely the science of good and bad; for confirmation, see 87C5, D6–7, E5, 88D2–3. The point is *not* that virtue is partly knowledge and partly something else, say, character-dispositions, as it certainly is in Aristotle.)

But what is the connection between the most important of the things asked about in "What is *X*" questions (courage, piety, temperance, justice, virtue, and the like) and the view that virtue is a science? To see this connection, consider only the extraordinary way in which Socrates forces on his interlocutors' accounts of such things as courage, piety, and the like, what used to be called the "analogy of the arts" and more recently the "craft analogy." (If it is just to return what you owe to a friend on condition that doing so will benefit and not harm your friend, who, Socrates asks, will be best able to benefit their friends in the matter of health? As if the issue were a certain skill or expertise rather than a matter of, say, what is right, or fairness!) This "analogy" which Socrates so regularly forces on his interlocutors expresses Socrates' view that these objects he is always asking about – the (human) good, courage, piety, virtue, and the like – stand to the science of virtue as does

> health to the science of medicine;
> the bed, the table, and the shuttle (and various particular kinds of shuttle) to carpentry;
> the sandal, the buskin, and the like, to cobblery;
> food, the olive, the grape, barley, and the like to the expertise of farming;
> the sheep to shepherding; and so forth

That is, Socrates treats this science (knowledge, expertise) of the good as just as much a science as those others which he used as stalking horses for this science. My argument below will suggest that the principal object of *this* science would, in the *Republic*, show up as the Form of the Good.

Notice here that human health, as even Socrates will have been thinking of it, is a single object – the very same thing that is studied in all medical schools, for purposes of dealing with a multiplicity of patients anywhere. The science of medicine is not about *my* health, or *your* health, but about health in general – an abstract object, a "universal," as Aristotle puts it (using a word that he coined). Just so, virtue is a single object, and so too justice is a single object. It is because such single objects are not anywhere visible or spatially isolated, that I speak of them as *abstract objects* – once more, even for Socrates (and for Aristotle).

Notice also that this "craft analogy" is in fact no mere analogy. For Socrates, virtue is not just *analogous* to knowledge of other kinds, or to other sciences or expertises: it is itself knowledge of a particular kind (a science, an expertise). This should be clear enough from the way in which, in the *Apology*, Socrates speaks of artisans (in contrast to politicians and poets) as finally in possession of *some* forms of knowledge (*some* sciences, *some* expertises) – though not the particular science or expertise of good which he was looking for.

To sum up so far, the things being asked about in the "What is *X*?" questions, if there *exist* any such things to be asked about, turn out to be the objects of the sciences – the good being, in the crucial case, the principal object of the knowledge, science, or expertise which is virtue. Aristotle certainly thinks that Socrates and Plato share this view of the objects of the sciences, though Aristotle also thinks that these new objects of the sciences that Plato believed in were wrongly identified by Plato with certain extraordinary, even preposterous, entities, the Forms; while if we avoid such an over-reaction, Aristotle continues, what we get are simply those (abstract) objects, universals, which are precisely what the objects of the sciences should be. These objects Aristotle himself accepts (and thinks he has been anticipated in by Socrates' attempts to answer the "What is *X*?" questions) (see 27: LEARNING ABOUT PLATO FROM ARISTOTLE).

Plato's "Argument from the Sciences" for the Existence of Forms, as Apparently Represented by Aristotle, and Aristotle's Criticism of that Argument

These important similarities and differences between Plato and Aristotle can perhaps be best brought out by looking at an argument for the Forms which is attributed to Plato in Aristotle's (alas, lost) treatise, *On the Ideas* (Forms). For this argument reveals both how well Aristotle grasped what I shall call the *Parmenidean* view of existence with which Plato works, and also shows (unwittingly), in Aristotle's own comments on what he presents as Plato's own "argument from the sciences," the difficulties he must fall into in agreeing with Socrates and Plato (to the considerable extent that he does) about the sciences and their objects. Thanks to the Aristotelian commentator, Alexander of Aphrodisias, writing more than four centuries later, but with a copy of Aristotle's treatise in front of him, we have a long paraphrase of three versions Aristotle gave of this argument in the original. All three may be argued to proceed by way of reducing to absurdity a certain natural *reductionist* account of what health (the principal object of the science of medicine) is. Here, for brevity's sake is my own shorter paraphrase of this argument:

Suppose that (human) health reduces to nothing more than healthy people, i.e., that all there is to health is healthy people. Then to come from Manitowoc to Madison to study medicine, in order to return to Manitowoc to practice medicine, is to study the (current) healthy (and sick) patients in Madison in order to practice on healthy (and sick) patients in Manitowoc.
– But then how would these students be any further forward by studying one group of people if what they want to do is to deal with another group of people?
– You're missing the point. They're studying something common to both groups.
– Precisely: something *other than* either of these two groups of people! But then it can't be that all there is to human health is healthy people. There will have to exist, if there is to be such a thing as a science of medicine, such a thing as health, which is the object of that science. An abstract object indeed.

167

About this argument, Aristotle says that it *does* show that there exists *something* in addition to the healthy people; but that it does *not* show that the something else in question is a Form. It could be a simple universal (as, according to Aristotle, both he and Socrates thought). The problem is that Aristotle thinks universals are *such*-es, not *this*-es (again, Aristotle's coinages). And in bringing Socrates under his tent, Aristotle implies – wrongly – that for Socrates too, the objects of the sciences are (what Aristotle calls) *such*-es.

What are these supposed *this*-es and *such*-es? Consider the sentence "Socrates is wise" as Aristotle would treat it. This sentence (a) is *about* (or *refers to*) the object which the word "Socrates" refers to, i.e., Socrates; and (b) *predicates of* Socrates the quality or attribute which the predicate ". . . is wise" stands for, i.e., wisdom. The idea of giving the predicate as simply the rest of the simple sentence in question, and using the dots to show where the subject term goes, is not Aristotle's, but Frege's. But as Wilfrid Sellars has noted, it is highly suggestive not just of Frege's view of how these "gappy" predicates stand to subjects (and of the parallel way in which, at the level of what the words stand for, *concept* stands to *object*), but also of the Aristotelian view of how attributes relate to particular objects.

The object, Socrates, referred to by the name "Socrates," is a particular individual and so a "this" (the kind of thing to which you would refer using the word "this"). The attribute of wisdom, Aristotle tells us, is not a particular individual; rather, it is the kind of thing that may be predicated of *many* different particular individuals (in parallel with the way in which the *expression* ". . . is wise" may take many different subject-expressions in the gap indicated by the dots). If "such" is a word that designates or stands for a relevant *kind* of particular individuals (the wise ones, the foolish ones, the strong ones, the healthy ones, and the like), then it will be appropriate, Aristotle thought, to say that wisdom is a "such" and not a "this." (The Latin *quali-tas* – mimicking the Greek word *poio-tēs* which Plato coined – is, in construction, simply *such*-ness.)

So far, there is nothing much to criticize in this distinction between *this*-es and *such*-es. Plato himself could almost have gone along with it. The problem comes in certain further things that Aristotle goes on to say about *this*-es and *such*-es – in particular, that a group of words such as "exists," "one," "same" (i.e., the very same thing), "different" (i.e., *not* the very same thing) are irretrievably ambiguous. That is, these words mean one thing for *this*-es (e.g., Socrates) and quite another (derivative) thing for *such*-es (e.g., wisdom). Aristotle's doctrine of the categories – substances, qualities, quantities, relations, places, times, and the like – goes even further and affirms that these words have different senses for *each category*. I say Aristotle makes these words irretrievably ambiguous between *this*-es and *such*-es (or across categories), since Aristotle also holds that there is not, in addition to the sense in which qualities exist and the sense in which substances exist, a further, unifying sense, in which one can say "Substances (e.g., Socrates) *and* qualities (e.g., wisdom) *both* exist" (so that each would be one, and taken together they would be two, and not the same thing as each other). For if Aristotle were to grant the possibility of a further unifying sense, he would undermine his own criticism of Plato as failing to see that *this*-es and *such*-es do not exist in the same sense, that is, in any single sense. Thus the point is not that Socrates and wisdom both exist in some one sense, with, in addition, Socrates being a particular, and wisdom being an attribute. The point is that there is no sense of "exist" in which it would be anything but meaningless to say "Socrates *and* wisdom *both* exist". As Ryle puts it, using his brilliant synthesizing of Aristotelian metaphysics with Russell's theory of logical types, and applying it to modern philosophy of mind: minds exist, and bodies exist, but it is (neither true nor false but) *meaningless* to say minds *and* bodies exist. This idea of "logical types" (under different names) has been evident throughout the history of philosophy, quite apart from Ryle's use for so-called "category errors". It appears already, for example, as the "analogy of being" in Aquinas.

This further move on Aristotle's part was undertaken to oppose the idea, which he accuses Plato of falling into, of "separating" the Forms from particulars. The content Aristotle assigns to "separation" is a matter of some dispute; but I take this charge, once put into the invented language of *this*-es and *such*-es, to amount precisely to the charge of treating *such*-es as if they were *this*-es – treating universals as if they were yet other particulars (*Metaph.* XIII.9.1086a32–3, III.6.1003a5–9). This, Aristotle thinks, would make universals and particulars exist in the same sense – contrary to the results of the preceding paragraph. Aristotle thought that his alleged error would make the "Third Man Argument" fatal to the Forms. (See 13: PROBLEMS FOR FORMS. See also *Metaph.* VII.13.1038b34–1039a3; *SE* 22.178b36–9, 179a8–9, and also *Cat.* 3b10–21.)

In sum, when Aristotle charges Plato with "separating" universals or *such*-es from particular substances or *this*-es, and says that Socrates did *not* commit himself to this view, he is implicitly – and indefensibly – attributing to Socrates Aristotle's own view of existence. It's as if Plato, not understanding what existence is, did something that took him beyond Socrates' implicit grasp of the vast difference between *this*-es and *such*-es. Such a charge is mistaken, I shall argue directly. Plato had a very clear idea of what existence is – what I have referred to above as a Parmenidean view of existence. Such a view seems to me not only far superior to Aristotle's, but also one which Aristotle himself cannot escape.

Plato the Parmenidean

For Plato the Parmenidean (as no doubt for Socrates too), "exists" or "be" is not ambiguous, meaning something different for different categories of things. Rather "exists" always stands for the same thing. Let us begin with what it is to *not exist*. Plato held, following Parmenides, that

NEXNOTH: To not exist is to be *nothing at all,*

so that, switching from the negative to the positive, we may also attribute to Plato the view that

EXOB: To exist is to *not be nothing at all,* and therefore to be *something* (some *one* thing) – some *object.*

In Plato it is not required, for example, that for something to be an object it cannot be a quality or a universal, or a number. (If this were required, one would be making

169

"object," "one," and "exist" irretrievably ambiguous. Should anyone really be supposing, as Aristotle will have to, that "nothing at all" is ten-ways ambiguous – and
irretrievably thus ambiguous?) If wisdom or the number 4 *are not nothing at all*, then
each of them is an object. From this we can even derive a criterion for whether one
can candidly declare that something does not exist (a negative criterion for ontological
commitment).

NEGONTCOMM: If you claim a certain alleged object does not exist, then stop talking
about it, for you should not be referring to anything of which you say that it is nothing
at all.

(This is very much in the spirit of both Parmenides and Plato.) Here is the similar
positive criterion for ontological commitment:

POSONTCOMM: If you find you cannot avoid referring to an alleged object, then be
candid and admit that you think it exists.

Thus, unless you are prepared to deny that there is anything common to the healthy
people of Madison and the healthy people of Manitowoc, you should be prepared to
admit that you think there exists, in addition to healthy people, a further thing, health.
These Parmenidean and Platonic modes of thought were brilliantly reinvented by
Quine's "On what there is" of 1948, although in Quine there is also a totally un-
Platonic "linguistic turn" (reducing what *you* are committed to, to what *your language*
commits you to). The Platonic/Parmenidean modes of thought are implicit also in Frege
and in many serious workers in the foundations of mathematics, many not supposing
they were going anything like so far as Quine in relativizing ontology to language.

Given this description of the distinction Aristotle tries to draw between universals
and particulars, let us return to the argument from the sciences, and Aristotle's objection to it. Aristotle tells us that

1   Plato is right that there does exist something, health, in addition to all the healthy
    people; there is one more thing in the universe than the reductionists suppose; on
    the other hand,
2   Plato is wrong to think that health exists in the same sense as the many healthy
    people.

Now in fact, (1) and (2) cannot, without incoherence, both be held by Aristotle. For
(1) *requires* that health and healthy people both exist: health is one *more* thing in the
universe, and so there is no ambiguity in "one" either; but (2) denies it.

Here is a parallel difficulty: for Aristotle, it should be neither true nor false but
meaningless that health is one more thing besides (something not the same thing as)
all the healthy things. But surely any theory that makes meaningless the obviously
true claim that Socrates and health are two different things is *not* meaningless! And
surely any theory that says it is will be dubious at best. So Aristotle's anticipation of
the theory of logical types (Beth 1965) and of Frege's concept/object distinction (Sellars
1963) is (a) inconsistent with methods of argumentation he himself is committed to,
and is in any case (b) very dubious indeed as metaphysics.

170

If Aristotle is wrong on this point, the question still arises: what in Plato's dialogues (or in anything Aristotle might have gathered from Plato in conversation with him during Aristotle's twenty years in the Academy) leads Aristotle to suppose that there *is* some important difference between Socrates and Plato on the Forms? Another passage in Aristotle (*Metaph.* XIII.9.1086a21–b13) shows that Aristotle correctly identifies one difference between the early dialogues (excepting *Symposium, Cratylus,* and *Phaedo*) and all the other dialogues. This is that Plato argued for the Forms by claiming that perceptible particulars are in constant flux, while knowledge requires universals (that are not in constant flux; see 10: PLATO: A THEORY OF PERCEPTION OR A NOD TO SENSATION?). This contrast involving flux, I am suggesting, may be what leads Aristotle – though he agrees that the sciences require universals – to think that Plato is "separating" universals from particulars (a36–b5), or, as he describes it at a32–4, to treat universals as "separate, i.e. (*kai*), as particulars." In that case, Aristotle's error is to misidentify Plato's use of Heracleitean flux in perceptible particulars with the supposed error of treating *such*-es with *this*-es. (There *is* no error for it to be identified with.)

Two things show that this use of the flux of perceptibles does represent a development of the views of Socrates: (a) there is arguably no mention of flux in the Socratic parts of the early dialogues; and (b) Aristotle tells us that Plato studied with Cratylus, disciple of Heraclitus, that great proponent of the view that the perceptible world is in constant flux. I conclude that it was this contrast between the ever-changing perceptibles in the world of "becoming" and the eternally existing Forms in the world of "being" which was a principal source of Aristotle's deceiving himself into thinking that he had skewered Plato by suggesting that Plato was wrongly "separating" the Forms from perceptible particulars.

Aristotle may also have been misled by the fact that Socrates' *emphasis* is on the objectivity of the sciences – as one might expect from the effort to show that virtue is a science or expertise – while *Plato's* emphasis, perhaps because he felt an increasing need to defend Socrates' views against sophistic counterattack, came to shift to validating the objectivity of the sciences by way of validating the *objects* of the sciences. These differences in emphasis, together with Plato's use of flux as a way of arguing for the Forms, lead Aristotle to find here – mistakenly – fundamental differences in metaphysical belief.

Both the "argument from the sciences" and this argument from flux (which is itself an appeal to the existence of objects of knowledge or science) presuppose the characteristic Parmenidean/Platonic anti-reductionism. That is, both argue against the view that there is nothing more to health than healthy people, arguing that there exists one more thing in the universe than reductionists suppose. The "one more" thing *cannot* be understood in terms of the Aristotelian theory of logical types and so it is meaningless to say that health and the healthy people each exist and are one in different senses.

Here is a striking example of Plato's Parmenidean approach to existence: an important little argument at R. 475E–476E. Plato has Socrates give Glaucon an argument he thinks many would not grant him, but Glaucon will. It is this:

Beautiful and ugly are opposites.
So, they're two.
So each is one.

Now what is so difficult here that many will not grasp? Don't we all believe that *beautiful* and *ugly* are opposites, and so two, and so each one? It turns out immediately that whether they recognize it or not, there are certain people who *cannot* grant that beautiful and ugly are opposites – not without incoherence in their views. For the "lovers of sights and sounds," Socrates tells us, are "dreamers" – where dreaming is identified with thinking (whether awake or asleep) that $x = y$ when the truth is that x merely *resembles* y. (For example, you may dream that the falling-sensation you are having in the dream is an experience of actually falling.)

So, then, what about the alleged "dreaming" done by the lovers of sights and sounds? Here the text tells us that the y and the x are the beautiful itself and beautiful sights and sounds. But how can they think that

the beautiful itself is identical with beautiful sights and sounds?

They don't even *believe in* the Forms! The view Socrates is attributing to them here is surely only comprehensible if we take them to hold that what the beautiful itself is reduces to nothing more than the many beautiful sights and sounds!

I take it here that beautiful "children" or "temples" is meant to contrast with "the beautiful itself" – "beautiful" just by itself without the "children" or "temple" parts. (Compare the expression "beautiful children" with the first word of this expression just by itself.) As will be seen below, I take "the Beautiful itself" as mere shorthand for the attribute "being beautiful."

How, then, for such reductionists, there could not be two *further* entities, the opposites beautiful and ugly, each being one, in addition to the many beautiful sights and sounds? What Plato is having Socrates point out here is that such reductionists may *think* they can refer to opposites; but they cannot; see NEGONTCOMM above. (Incidentally, this argument also shows that the Form of Beauty *is* the opposite "beautiful.")

The reductionist view Plato combats here is a comprehensible hard-nosed, down-to-earth position, akin to nominalism and materialism – being a position held both by intellectuals and by quite unintellectual people, impatient with certain positions of intellectuals and the religious, for example on unseen forces and gods. It seems a view well worth engaging with at Plato's time and place, especially for one who, like Socrates and himself, is committed to there being real truths which our own good requires pursuing systematically, even if with limited success.

I should mention two further examples of this sort of anti-reductionist argument that arise in connection with the "What is X?" question. They appear in two of the most celebrated passages of the *Republic*: the Simile of the Divided Line and the Allegory of the Cave. (For these, see Penner 2006.)

Sciences and Pseudo-Sciences

I have spoken about a difference between Socrates and Plato in the relative *emphasis* given to the sciences and to the objects of the science. (This is no difference in doctrine: the objectivity of the sciences is interdependent with that of their objects. It's just that Plato begins to look for arguments for the *existence* of objects of the sciences – a need which Socrates apparently had not yet felt.) If we ask *why* this difference in emphasis occurs, the answer may cast further light on the importance of the sciences and of the Forms to both thinkers.

Socrates' claim that there *are* objective sciences shows no idle intention to cover just any old discipline or profession that someone might *choose* to call an expertise or a science. On the contrary, Socrates often insists that certain disciplines often *thought of* as sciences are not sciences at all. Socrates numbered amongst these pseudo-sciences (as I shall refer to them), rhetoric à la Gorgias, sophistic, cookery, cosmetics, and literary interpretation à la Ion.

I may capture the flavor of Socrates' opposition to these pseudo-sciences by mentioning here the one Socrates discusses most: rhetoric. What rhetoric is, according to its proponents, is

RHET: a science of great power in public life, enabling one to persuade most people on any subject whatever, without oneself having to acquire any knowledge on that subject.

Implicit in this appears to be the following account of "power":

POWR: Power is being able to accomplish whatever one wants.

Clearly, modern universities, like Aristotle before them, suppose there are such sciences (and corresponding subject matters). For we have professors of rhetoric, speech, advertising, communication and the like. Not Socrates – and not Plato. It is true that Socrates thinks there *could be* people who are experts at persuasion on a particular subject, but not unless they are also experts on (have actual *knowledge* of) the subject they are persuading on. Not quite the usual idea of rhetoric! Here Plato stands with Socrates and against such neutral sciences as Aristotle's rhetoric.

In the time of Socrates and Plato, the subject of rhetoric, taught by itinerant teachers known as "sophists," was presented as a means to possessing great power, and to getting on in life – especially within direct democracies, such as that in Athens, where success of this sort was heavily dependent on persuading the *demos*, or citizenry. Here persuasion is persuasion concerning matters of justice, wisdom, war, public (and private) life, and is designed to get orators (rhetors) what they *want* in life – as is implied by POWR.

One more detail needs to be added here: for the sophists, what one wants is taken, in a familiar way, to be identical with "whatever one decides one wants," or "settles on as what one wants." This, as will be seen, has something to do with Socrates' reasons for denying it is a science.

What would be the *object* of this supposed science of rhetoric? Socrates suggests it would be "what is persuasive on any subject whatever," taken as "successfully usable even by those without knowledge of the subject." This suggests, in those (such as the sophists) who see this supposed science as giving one power, and as getting what one decides one wants in life, certain reductionist lines of thought, almost entirely new to Greek culture of the time. These new lines of thought introduce innovative sophistic alternatives to traditional views of the good, justice, and the like; and they underlie the sophistic view of what the objects of the supposed science might be.

Sph1: All there is to the human good is what you (*decide* you) want, so that all there is to power is the ability to do what you (decide you) want;

Sph2: All there is to justice is what those in power *declare* to be "just" (which of course they will do with a view to what they suppose is in their own interest);

Sph3: All there is to justice in your *own* case is what *you* declare to be "just" (which of course you will do in the belief that it is in your interest, whether or not you attend to the interests of others);

and, slightly differently,

Sph4: All there is to justice in human affairs, as in the animal world, is simply the decisions of the strong imposed upon the weak (whether or not with any regard to the interests of the weak) – the *pleonexia* which, in the *Gorgias* and the *Republic*, Socrates comes to see as a serious challenge.

This gets us the following sophistic view (as held by Gorgias and Protagoras) both of virtue and of the science of rhetoric,

SOPH: All there is to virtue or human goodness is being good at getting what you decide you want,
i.e., whatever you *think* you want,
i.e., whatever you *think* advantageous to yourself,
i.e., your *apparent* good;
so that the supposed science which sophistic education can offer is the science of gaining whatever you settle on as what you want.

Here, the sophists and rhetoricians treat the techniques of persuasion as the *hard* part, the easy, even trivial, part being to decide what it is you want. For Socrates, as for Plato, this has the cart before the horse: *the hard part is in seeing what that real good is that one wants*. In opposing such "reductionist" suggestions as (Sph1)–(Sph4) and (SOPH), Socrates was once again Plato's inspiration, constantly engaging people, especially the young, in conversation and argument ("dialectic") that was apparently designed to bring his interlocutors to confront the possibility that what wisdom, justice, or the human good are is not a matter of what people *decide* to want, or *declare* to be good, but a matter of what is objectively *so*. For Socrates and Plato, when not speaking with the vulgar, what one wants is:

what is objectively good – even if that is quite different from what people *say* (or what the conventions of their language say) or what an agent decides is his or her own good.

Questions of what is objectively so are questions of objective science or expertise, not matters of opinion or definition or decision, or of what one *says* one wants or of what the strong say they want. A pseudo-science, by contrast, gives methods for getting what one *declares* one wants – *without* the need for the science of good, or of any other science. With this official indifference to the sciences, there can be little doubt (in the real world) that sophists, rhetoricians, and those who are persuaded by them, will get not the real good, but something far worse. Such is the Socratic/Platonic argument against rhetoric and sophistic.

This argument of course presupposes that there *is* a real good, a real nature of the good, as even Aristotle presupposes. (As there is a real nature of health and a real nature of the shuttle, so there is a real nature of the good.) It also presupposes that the real nature in question is *always* what desirers want (exception in Plato: irrational desires), even when they don't know what it is (see 18: THE SOCRATIC PARADOXES; *Grg.* 466–8; *R.* 505E–506B, 504E–505B.) So when a sophist or an orator trumpets his supposed science as a way of getting whatever one wants, the Socratic (and Platonic) reply is that without a science of what is really good (and is what the person *does* want, even if it is different from what he or she *thinks* it is), a science for getting that by way of finding good means to pursue what one merely *thinks* is best will necessarily be incoherent – and disastrous. For those without knowledge, there is no such object as

what the real good is, i.e., what I *think* the real good is

since the two parts of the description go against each other. So there can be no science of any such thing.

Socrates' *conclusion* here, in its opposition to rhetoric and sophistic, is at any rate *closer* to traditional religious culture than to sophistic. But in Socrates' unyieldingly dialectical/scientific (and distinctly non-traditional, even anti-traditional) *pursuit* of knowledge of that real nature, he came to be viewed by the traditionalists – understandably, and fatally, though wrongly – as himself a sophist.

How far should Socrates have been depending on the objectivity of those sciences he found in his time and place? Surely Socrates could not have failed to notice that then, as now, there are many questions medicine, say, cannot answer convincingly. So by what right does he say there *are* such sciences as medicine, farming, and so forth? Or does it not matter just how adequate the sciences are in their current state? What is important to Socrates is the *ideal* or (looked at in another way) the *possibility* of such a science as medicine being had by the relevant expert, even if no one at that time *has* a complete grasp on the answers to all the questions that fall under that science. The point about Socrates' interest in possibility may be put slightly differently as follows. It may be reasonable to suppose that:

3 there *is* such a science as medicine even if no one is currently in possession of such a science.

But this supposition implies that

4 there is a real nature of health, and so an objective truth about all matters falling under the science of medicine, even if no one currently is in possession of knowledge of those truths.

The reason for thinking the real issue about the sciences is given by (3) and (4) is that the point of the so-called "analogies" of particular sciences with knowledge of the good was precisely to bring out the nature of a science of the good, and of the good which is the object of that science. For

5   Socrates thought that there is such an objective science as the science of (the human) good, even if no one currently has it, and this is exactly the human condition, since Socrates is the wisest person there is, and he has no such science. He also thought that there is an objective truth about all matters falling under the science of good, even if no one is in possession of knowledge of those truths.

This science of the good Socrates identifies with virtue (or human goodness), so that

6   to be a good human being is to have that science of the good.

The answer to the question why Socrates would think that it was sufficient for a person to be a good person that they should simply have knowledge lies beside our path here (see 22: THE UNITY OF THE VIRTUES). It involves Socratic intellectualism (see, e.g., Penner and Rowe 2005: ch. 10). The idea is that

7   even if no human has ever *had* the science of the good, nevertheless the mere belief in the existence of (unknown) objective truths makes it reasonable to suppose that one's chances of coming closer to those real objective truths are greater if one pursues them every day in the conviction that the unexamined life is not worth living.

Somewhere here, I believe, lies the motivation of Socrates' concern for the idea of the existence of the sciences (and so the possibility of an expert *having* the relevant science). Plato's theory is very close to this, though it involves some modification, owing to Plato's belief that sometimes we act in accordance with something like brute, irrational desires.

The Good and the Sciences

The primary object of the science of medicine, namely, health, is also the good or end of the science of medicine, and it is the function or work of the science to bring about that state in patients; so that a good doctor is one who thus heals his or her patients. (Aristotle says that there is the same science of opposites, so that, as Socrates says, the doctor is not only the expert at producing health, but also an expert at producing sickness, should he or she, as a person, wish to do so. But presumably, because the function of medicine is to heal, medicine is the science of health and not of sickness.) Just so, food (and nutrition) is the good or end of farming; safe and efficient sea voyage the good or end of sea voyages; and the shuttle one of the goods of the science of carpentry.

From the good or end of farming, we can determine that the good farmer is the person who finds good means to the end of his or her expertise; and similarly for good doctors, good carpenters, and the like. Thus Socrates often speaks of the function of medicine in terms of health (the end), and of the function of the doctor in terms of healing (the means to health).

There will also be a teleological hierarchy of sciences, and so of goods: the good of the shuttle is weaving, the good of weaving is clothes, the good of clothes is protection, and so forth all the way up to the good of the human being. This teleological hierarchy reappears in the means/end Socratic theory of desire, which Plato continues to hold for *rational* desires only. This parallel between the hierarchy of the sciences and the hierarchy of means and ends in desire is one which Aristotle does not hesitate to exploit in the opening chapter of the *Nicomachean Ethics*.

In fact, *all* sciences, for Socrates and Plato, have their own good and end, even, as the teleology of the *Timaeus* shows, subjects such as biology, chemistry, and physics. Does that show that whatever a doctor does is good? It does not. Sometimes, the *Laches* tells us, it is *not* better that the patient live rather than die. So, then, what is the relation between the good of any given science and the good *simpliciter* (in Socrates, the human good)? The answer appears to be that we have particular sciences because we have found that there are, objectively, ways to achieve certain things of a sort that are *usually* or *standardly* good for humans – for example, health, wealth, strength, and so forth. Though *standardly* goods, they can become very bad for the humans involved if used unwisely. (No wonder that "the unexamined life is not worth living".) Only one thing is unconditionally good, to gain which is, in my case, to gain my own maximum happiness over the remainder of my life, starting from where I am now; in your case, your own maximum happiness . . . and so forth for anyone whatever.

All of this suggests that in order to have a given science, and so know the good and end of that science, one will have to know *why* that end is a good; and that will require knowing what the good is *simpliciter*. So it is that Plato, in the simile of the Sun at R. 506E–509D, says that no other Form can be known, or can even *exist*, unless one knows the Form of the Good (just as no perceptible object can either exist in the world of becoming, or be perceived, without the Sun which both nourishes and reveals to perception). What it is for a shuttle to *be* is for a certain standard good to be, standing in the appropriate relation to the good *simpliciter*. So both the existence and knowability of the standard good (for example, the real nature of the shuttle) depends upon the existence and knowability of the good *simpliciter*. (It may seem that Socrates' "analogy of the arts" ("craft analogy") presupposes that one can have autonomous knowledge of each of the sciences, that is, knowledge of a science *without* having knowledge of the good. But clearly no such autonomy needs to be presupposed if the purpose of the "analogy" is to bring Socrates' interlocutors to the idea of a science of the good.)

Now the *Republic* makes it clear that the Form of the Good is the centerpiece of the Theory of Forms. What is more, the Form of the Good is intimately connected with the ethics of the *Republic* (see 24: PLATO'S CONCEPT OF GOODNESS). Thus I have argued elsewhere that a proper understanding of Plato's dividing the soul into three parts, analogously to his division of the ideal city into intellectual rulers, soldiers (police), and workers, is supposed to be illuminated by a certain "longer road" (IV.435C–D, VI.503E–504B) in the following way. The division of the soul is to enable us to say what the virtues are: for example, that justice in the individual soul is each of the three parts fulfilling its own function. But then to understand adequately this account, we need to know what the functions are of the parts, and especially of the rational part. This, we learn, is to look to the advantage (good) of each of the parts and of the whole (that is, the entire soul: the individual). So our story about justice is incomplete until such time as we discover, via the "longer road" – and to the extent one can – what the Form of the Good is; that one thing it is most important to get to know. The taking of the longer road takes up most of Books VI and VII of the *Republic*, by any account, the central and climactic part of the *Republic*.

As for what the Form of the Good *is*, that will of course be as difficult to come to know (*R.* 506B–507A, *Phd.* 97B–100c), as it is difficult, in Socrates, to know what virtue or the good *are*. Nonetheless, a proper interpretation of the "longer road" does make it clear that the Form of the Good is the Form of Advantage, or Benefit; it is not, as it *is* in most influential interpretations since about the 1920s, such as by Morris, White, Irwin, Cooper, and Annas, the Form of some impersonal or quasi-moral good.

This said, the question of course remains for Socrates and Plato, "What *is* advantage (or benefit)?" But even without a full answer to this question, it is reasonable to suppose that the best life is to proceed with one's dialectical inquiries into the good in the conviction that there *is* such a thing as what the good really is, even if it does not correspond with any of our present convictions.

A Proposal: The Forms are Attributes; and There are No Attributes that are not Forms

We learn from both the *Lysis* and from the *Symposium* that

8   the attribute of being beautiful *is* the attribute of being good,

just as

9   the desire for the good *is* erōs (erotic love) for the beautiful.

These two identities may seem bizarre in the extreme. But Plato explains fairly clearly what he thinks on this point, at *Smp.* 205A–D. Here he says – no doubt for historical reasons, including the fact that so few people have (so far) accepted these identities – that we use *erōs* and "the beautiful" for situations where sexual desire is involved, and "desire" and "the good" for non-sexual desires. But that does not make *erōs* and "desire for good" distinct. It's just a matter of decent respect to conventional word usages. (Similarly, at this point in history, we point at "the morning star" in the morning, and at "the evening star" in the evening, even while fully realizing that it is one and the same heavenly body, the planet Venus, that we are pointing at on the two occasions. Thus, as Frege urges philosophers not to confuse "reference" with "meaning," Plato is here urging us not to confuse reference with historical associations of the words we use to pick out those references in particular contexts.)

The question now arises what the relation is between the *Form* of Beauty and the *Form* of the Good. My analysis above of how Plato argues for the Forms suggests that there is every reason to suppose that

10   the Forms just *are* those attributes which are the objects of the sciences.

178

So, above, the argument at *R.* 475E–476E requires that the beautiful itself just *is* the beautiful. (This should surprise no one who, like me, thinks the Theory of Forms is the first systematic theory of abstract objects in the history of western thought. Universals that are *not* Forms come only later, with Aristotle.) To say this is to say that in spite of Aristotle's charge of massive duplication, Plato does not believe there are Forms *and* attributes. I shall go even further, and claim that Plato also thinks (as Socrates would have) that

11   there *are* no attributes which are not Forms.

Thus one might think that there is such an attribute as "the interest of the stronger" as conceived by Thrasymachus, i.e., "the interest of the stronger, to be gained at least sometimes by taking away the good of the weaker" – even if Plato would not grant that there is such a Form. But (contrary to some scholars who believe that, numbered amongst the many sights and sounds is this supposed Thrasymachean universal), I am denying Plato would have granted that there is any such entity, or any of the supposed objects noted above in (Sph1)–(Sph4), or the supposed *apparent good* in (SOPH) above. If it be asked how we come to talk about them, the answer is: for purposes of rejecting these misbegotten creatures of sophistic imaginations, "hoked up" with such things as *interest, strength,* and the like, which *do* exist, although only outside of these combinations. Talk about such pseudo-attributes is really no more than talk of certain illusions of the sophists, with which we may compare more familiar illusions, such as Satanism, phlogiston, witchcraft, or Santa Claus.

What about Plato's Other Reasons for Believing in Forms (Logical, or Mystical-Metaphysical-Theological)? And Won't These Reasons Make of Forms Something Rather More than Simply Attributes?

In *On Ideas* and elsewhere, Aristotle also attributes to Plato a "One over Many" Argument for the Forms, which in modern times might have been referred to as an argument from predication: an argument necessary, indeed, to the science of logic which Aristotle himself invented. (For Aristotle will undoubtedly have thought of Plato as *trying* – unsuccessfully and too unsystematically – to articulate a science of logic.) Here, the idea is that in predicating *anthrōpos* (man, i.e., human being) or "tallness" of each of many things, e.g., Alcibiades, Callias, and Aspasia, we are predicating something in common of these three. But this something is not identical with any of the three. So this thing predicated in common is something *else*: the Form. This argument would quickly yield all sorts of "hoked-up" predicates, such as the supposed Thrasymachean universal noted above. (And it could use this predicate in syllogisms, as indeed Socrates does in the *Republic*. For Aristotle, this will be enough to make it a universal.)

But does Plato ever make such an argument, or an argument that will commit him to attributes corresponding to such "hoked-up" predicates? Or is the argument a product of Aristotle's extraordinary creativity in offering formal arguments for positions that need explanations telling us where the positions come from? I believe so; but, for reasons of space, that belief will need to be defended elsewhere.

Second, many scholars think Plato also had mystical, metaphysical, or quasi-theological reasons for believing in the Forms. Here I need to admit that in the *Meno* and the *Phaedo* Plato did flirt with *recollection from a previous life of the soul* as a way of acquiring knowledge (see 9: PLATO ON RECOLLECTION). Fortunately, such a source of knowledge is ignored in every other important dialogue that discusses the Forms. (Recollection from a previous life of the soul *does* show up in the *Phaedrus* myth: but not as a source of *knowledge*.)

At the same time, many other things Plato seems to say do give the impression that the purpose of the Forms must extend beyond the purposes of science or logic. Augustine and Aquinas, for example, treat the Form of the Good in the Similes of the Sun and Line, and in the Allegory of the Cave, as practically identical with God. And some modern interpreters have urged that Plato was telling us that all Forms are "self-predicational," so that the Form of the Good is the best of all objects, the Form of the Beautiful (often thought of as different from the Form of the Good) the most beautiful object, the Form of Largeness the largest of all objects, the Form of the Bed the most perfect and most real of beds. On this view, the Forms constitute a kind of celestial museum, containing all the best examples of every universal.

The most powerful texts usually cited for this view consist in those which speak of Forms as "paradigms" (patterns, standards) which perceptible particulars imperfectly "imitate," so that if a large person imperfectly imitates Largeness itself, then Largeness itself must itself be a large object (*very* large).

This sort of view of the Forms was invented – and in my opinion could only have originated – in a period during which positivists and Wittgensteinians spent much of their time not so much *addressing* metaphysical claims about truth, existence, and the like, as *reducing* them to claims about scientific or more ordinary observations. (To paraphrase Protagoras, "the observational is the measure of all things.") Either that, or they were *diagnosing* supposedly observationally incoherent claims as flowing from misunderstanding "the logic of our language."

Rather more plausible than Self-Predication is the view that this "imitation" of "paradigms" is like imitation of gods, so that, for example, if these quasi-gods, the paradigms, are just and always at peace (*R.* 500B–D), humans strive to be just and at peace. What is more, this semi-mystical, semi-theological picture may seem to be strongly supported by the glorious myth of the soul's journey to the place of the Forms in the *Phaedrus* – and indeed in other myths. On the other hand, I do not myself see why the Form of the Shuttle, by being the real nature of the shuttle, which itself is what it is by virtue of the real nature of weaving, the real nature of clothing, and so forth, should not be a quite adequate paradigm which the carpenter "looks to." Why would it need to be a perfect shuttle, or a quasi-god? And similarly for the real nature of good. But I must stop here.

Objections to the Theory of Forms

I shall deal only with the most famous of many objection to the Forms: the argument Aristotle took over from Plato himself and called "The Third Man Argument" (see 13:

PROBLEMS FOR FORMS). This argument develops out of the "One over Many" Argument already discussed above, by suggesting that if one comes to believe in a Form of Largeness by this means, the Form itself will have to be a large object (self-predication?). But then, by parity of reasoning, if all the many non-Forms that are large need the existence of a Form of Largeness to explain the ways we predicate attributes of objects, that will itself have to be large (self-predication?). And then we will need a further Form to explain why the other large things and the Form of Largeness are all large. This embarks us on an infinite regress, which suggests the Form is no longer one. As I see it, this is one of a series of five arguments, each giving different accounts of what the relation is between Forms and particulars. Plato gives every indication of thinking that all five accounts are in different ways inadequate, without himself offering an account of the correct relation. Since he goes on to suggest that we cannot do without the Forms, it is evident that he thinks there must be such an account – though he is not yet in possession of it. Similarly, at *Phd.* 100D he leaves it entirely open what the relation is. As for those who think that we lose all reason to believe in Forms if we cannot give an account of the relation to particulars, consider what a clever analytical philosopher could do with the relations between mental images and the objects they are images of. These difficulties would hardly show that the mental images do not exist. No, the main question is: Do the Forms *exist?* And if they do, as mental images certainly do, then the relations they stand in to particulars will be whatever they have to be.

As for the troubles with the development of the Third Man Argument from the One Over Many Argument, I have already suggested that Plato would not have accepted this latter argument from predication. That Plato himself introduces difficulties in the supposed relation (of predication) between the Forms and particulars is no surprise to me.

The Theory of Forms in Later Dialogues

The Theory of Forms undergoes important developments in later dialogues, such as the *Sophist, Statesman,* and *Philebus.* The most frequent means by which Plato has his characters affirm the existence of Forms in the *Republic,* the *Parmenides,* the *Phaedo* and the like, is in terms of "each is *one*" and the closely related "each itself." (Incidentally, to take "each is one" as sufficient to bring out what it is to be a Form is surely to suggest that what is in question is the existence of *something additional* to the spatial and perceptible particulars, such as a genuine attribute. It certainly does not suggest that for there to be a Form is for there to be some mystical, quasi-theological entity.)

But there is a later development in the fundamental idea that "each is one." In the later dialogues (and the *Parmenides*), we tend to get instead an insistence that each is one "and many." One example of being one "and many" would be knowledge (science) being one, though because the sciences of mathematics, medicine, and astronomy are distinct, knowledge is also many (three so far). Thus the idea that we should also say that knowledge (science) comprises, for example, these three sciences brings us closer to the idea of the "method of division": saying what things are (such as knowledge, or pleasure) by searching for natural divisions into genera and species.

The need for "natural" divisions leads Plato to the view that there is no Form "not-beautiful," for example, or "non-human" or "non-crane," or of "barbarian," i.e., non-Greek-speaker. Plato's rejection of such pseudo-attributes would also go against the modern position that if two given properties, or extensions, exist, it follows that all Boolean combinations of those properties, or extensions, exist. Plato's way does not leave his theory open to the paradoxes of logic, semantics, and set theory in the same way as the modern position on properties and extensions.

What motivates this development in the Theory of Forms? One possibility is that early on, Plato emphatically marks off the one Form the Beautiful *itself* from the many beautiful things – especially in the *Phaedo* and the *Republic* with such Forms as "Beautiful" and "Ugly," which are also opposites. (This could even lead to the idea, as in the recollection passage at *Phd.* 72A–77A, that we have incorrigible knowledge of such simple and unstructured Forms as Equality and Inequality. This incorrigibility, produced by the idea of knowledge via recollection, is, I believe, resisted at *Tht.* 189B–190E, 195E–196c, esp. 196c7–8, together with 187E–188c, 199c–D, 200A–c, 167A8.) This emphasis on the contrasts between Forms being one and perceptibles being many might explain how little *theoretical* attention Plato, before the *Parmenides*, pays to the relations amongst the Forms themselves. But he could not have failed already to notice that he would eventually have to elaborate on such relations if he were to account for such central matters as the relations between standard goods, such as the real nature of health and the real nature of the shuttle, and that real nature of the Good which is the Form of the Good. The Method of Division, then, making the Forms both one and many, would direct attention to the locus of each Form within much larger structures. The emphasis on "natural" divisions will also explain Plato's opposition to treating "barbarian" or "non-human" as objects of science, and the *Sophist*'s introduction of the Form of Other to cover all these negative predicates at a stroke, without any of the supposedly corresponding pseudo-attributes.

Some of this work is still relevant to modern logic and philosophy. Thus, in an extremely important discussion in the *Sophist*, Plato has the Eleatic Visitor (a Parmenidean!) argue that there is no Form of "non-being," even while there *is* a Form of Being. Plato thus stands in contradiction with modern logical and philosophical doctrine that "existence is not a predicate," that is, not an attribute. For Plato, non-existence is *not* an attribute, while existence is. Philosophers and logicians, in a fit of – understandable – zeal for logical form and the Law of the Excluded Middle, insist, by contrast, that if *non*-existence is not an attribute, then existence too may not be an attribute. I do not believe that this zeal for logical form and the Law of the Excluded Middle is much of a justification for such a fundamental metaphysical position, however much it may seem necessary to resist the Ontological Argument.

Space not allowing for further discussion of the later Theory of Forms, let me simply conclude that there is still much in the Theory of Forms to challenge us philosophically today.

Note

I would like to thank Antonio Chu for his invaluable comments on an earlier draft.

182

References and further reading

Beth, E. W. (1965). *Foundations of Mathematics.* Amsterdam: North-Holland.

Irwin, T. (1995). *Plato's Ethics.* Oxford: Oxford University Press.

Morris, C. R. (1934–5). Plato's theory of the good man's motives. *Proceedings of the Aristotelian Society* 34, pp. 129–42.

Penner, T. (1987). *The Ascent from Nominalism.* Dordrecht: Reidel.

—— (1988). Socrates on the impossibility of belief-relative sciences. *Proceedings of the Boston Area Colloquium in Ancient Philosophy* III, pp. 263–325.

—— (1991). Desire and power in Socrates: the argument of *Gorgias* 466A–468E that orators and tyrants have no power in the city. *Apeiron* 24, pp. 147–202.

—— (2006). Plato's Theory of Forms in the *Republic.* In G. Santas (ed.) *The Blackwell Guide to Plato's* Republic (pp. 234–62). Malden, Mass. and Oxford: Blackwell.

—— (forthcoming). The Form of the Good: what it is, and how it functions within the ethical programme of the *Republic.* Part I: A question about the plot of the *Republic.* In D. Cairns, F. G. Herrmann, and T. Penner (eds.) *The Good and the Form of the Good in Plato's* Republic (Proceedings of the fourth biennial Leventis conference). Projected publisher: Edinburgh University Press.

—— (forthcoming). The Good and the Form of benefit or advantage in the *Republic.* In D. Cairns, F. G. Herrmann, and T. Penner (eds.) *The Good and the Form of the Good in Plato's* Republic (Proceedings of the fourth biennial Leventis conference). Projected publisher: Edinburgh University Press.

Penner, T. and Rowe, C. J. (1994). The desire for good: Is the *Meno* consistent with the *Gorgias? Phronesis* 39, pp. 1–25.

—— and —— (2005). *Plato's Lysis.* Cambridge: Cambridge University Press.

Prichard, H. R. (1968) [1928]. Duty and interest. In *Moral Obligation,* 2nd edn. (ch. 3). Oxford: Oxford University Press.

Quine, W. V. O. (1948). On what there is. In *From a Logical Point of View* (pp. 1–19). Cambridge, Mass.: Harvard University Press.

Robinson, R. (1953). *Plato's Earlier Dialectic.* Oxford: Clarendon Press.

Ryle, G. (1949). *The Concept of Mind.* London: Hutchinson.

Sellars, W. (1963). Grammar and existence: a preface to ontology. In *Science, Perception, and Reality* (pp. 247–81). London: Routledge and Kegan Paul.

White, N. P. (1970). *A Companion to Plato's* Republic. Cambridge, Mass.: Hackett.

13

Problems for Forms

MARY LOUISE GILL

Plato's Theory of Forms is his most famous contribution to philosophy. Forms are eternal, unchanging objects, each with a unique nature, which we grasp with our minds but not with our senses. Forms are supposed to explain the properties things have in our changing world. For instance, the Form of Beauty, which is eternally and unqualifiedly beautiful, is supposed to explain the beauty of things we experience in the world around us. But works such as the *Phaedo* and *Republic*, which appeal to Forms, raise more questions than they answer. Neither dialogue gives a systematic account of Forms but simply refers to them in the course of treating other topics, such as the immortality of the soul (*Phaedo*) or the education of the philosopher-king (*Republic*). The *Parmenides* is the only dialogue that sets out a Theory of Forms as the explicit focus of its attention. Yet this dialogue's aim is to show the ways in which Forms are problematic.

In the first part of the *Parmenides*, Plato has Socrates, as a youth, set out a Theory of Forms, which is then subjected to intense and sustained scrutiny by the master-philosopher Parmenides. Socrates' proposals seem to fare badly when put to the test, and by the end of the cross-examination we might think that Forms should be abandoned. What are we to make of this apparent failure? Are the objections answerable, and is Socrates simply too inexperienced to answer them? Or did Plato regard the objections as fatal to his own previous views? Or did he think the objections were answerable but only by substantially revising his views? Does the *Parmenides* mark a turning point in Plato's philosophy, recording a crucial stage of reflection and self-criticism after his self-assured masterpiece, the *Republic*? If so, where should we look for his revisions? Should we look for his answers in dialogues such as the *Theaetetus*, *Sophist*, *Statesman*, and *Philebus*, which most scholars date after the *Parmenides*? What about the *Timaeus*, which has traditionally been regarded as a late dialogue, which appears consistent with the *Phaedo* and *Republic* in its treatment of Forms? Does it ignore the objections in the *Parmenides* and so indicate that those objections were not regarded as serious? Or are scholars wrong to date the *Timaeus* after the *Parmenides*? Alternatively, does the *Timaeus* actually respond to the *Parmenides* (on the status of the *Timaeus*, see 14: THE ROLE OF COSMOLOGY IN PLATO'S PHILOSOPHY)? Or should we look for his answers in the long second part of the *Parmenides* itself, where Plato presents an elaborate philosophical exercise? These questions indicate why the

Parmenides is pivotal for understanding Plato's philosophy more generally. The fact that there is no general agreement about the answers is one reason why the dialogue continues to puzzle and fascinate its readers.

In this chapter we shall focus on the main problems for Forms raised in the first part of the *Parmenides*. My own view, which I cannot defend in detail here, is that the *Parmenides* as a whole, including the philosophical exercise, has a single overall purpose: to show that there must be Forms, or intelligible objects of some sort, if we are to explain the world at all.[1] Thus the objections to Forms raised in the first part of the dialogue are to be taken very seriously. The presentation of Forms and their relations to sensible things in the late dialogues is therefore likely to differ in some important respects from that in dialogues such as the *Phaedo* and *Republic*. This chapter will focus, not on those further developments, but on singling out the main problems for Forms Plato thought he needed to address.

Theory and Critique of Forms in the *Parmenides*

The main discussion in the *Parmenides* begins after Zeno, Parmenides' younger colleague, has completed a reading of his book. His book apparently contained a series of arguments that aimed to defend Parmenides' thesis, "the all is one" (*Prm.* 128A8–B1), from critics who believed in a plurality of things. Zeno's arguments probably had the following shape: If things are many, they must be both F and not-F (e.g., like and unlike, or limited and unlimited). This is impossible, because the same things cannot have incompatible properties.

Socrates responds to Zeno in a long speech, arguing that Zeno's problem can be dissolved: Socrates has a theory that explains the compresence of opposites in ordinary things. He himself can be both one and many (e.g., one person among the seven people present but many parts) because he partakes of two Forms, the Form of Oneness and the Form of Multitude. Similarly, he can be like Simmias in one respect and unlike him in another respect by partaking of the Forms of Likeness and Unlikeness. The Forms of opposites are supposed to explain the opposite features he has (we'll call these features "immanent characters"). According to Socrates, it is no surprise that a single sensible object has opposite features. The Forms explain this. It would be astonishing, however, if such compresence occurred in the Forms themselves. Obviously, if Forms are supposed to explain the compresence of opposites in ordinary things, they cannot themselves be subject to the same problem. Otherwise we would need to appeal to further entities to explain the compresence in them, and the original Forms would fail to be explanatory.

We might well ask why anyone should think we need a theory of eternal immaterial Forms to explain the compresence of opposites. The same thing can of course be both F and not-F, if it is F in one respect or relation and not-F in another, or F at one time and not-F at another. There is a problem only if the same thing is F and not-F at the same time, in the same respect, and in relation to the same thing. Plato regularly mentions the qualifiers, yet it is an interesting fact that the speakers in his dialogues nonetheless find it troubling that the same thing is both F and not-F, even if it is F and not-F in different respects, comparisons, or whatever. The reason for this puzzlement appears to be that, whereas we moderns regard predicates like "large" and "small," "like" and "unlike," as *incomplete*, requiring something further to complete the sense, Plato regarded those predicates as *complete* – as specifying genuine properties an object has. For that reason he takes a statement like "Simmias is large (in comparison with Socrates) and small (in comparison with Phaedo)" to be as troubling as the statement "the same object is round and square": the properties are felt to be incompatible with each other. Forms are supposed to remove a feeling of paradox we do not share.

One of the main problems for Forms, as Parmenides repeatedly shows in the *Parmenides*, is that the Form *F* is itself both *F* and not-*F* – for instance, the One is both one and many. This is a serious problem, since Forms are supposed to explain the compresence of opposites in other things. How can they explain, if they are themselves subject to the same problem?

Parmenides' critique of Forms divides into six movements, which I label for convenience: Scope of Forms (130B1–E4), Whole–Part Dilemma (130E4–131E7), Largeness Regress (132A1–B2), Forms are Thoughts (132B3–c11), Likeness Regress (132c12–133A7), and Separation Argument (133A11–134E8).[2] Parmenides focuses on two fundamental questions: First (Scope of Forms), what Forms are there? What are the reasons for positing Forms in some situations but not others? Are they good reasons? And second (Whole–Part Dilemma and Likeness Regress), what is the nature of the relation between physical objects and Forms – the relation known as "participation"? Connected with this second question is another: What sort of entities are Forms anyway? Are they universals? Immaterial stuffs? Perfect particulars (paradigms)? Socrates' inability to explain participation also prompts a further question: On what grounds does he regard each Form as one, and are those grounds viable (Largeness Regress and Forms are Thoughts)? Parmenides reveals the inadequacy of Socrates' position by repeatedly showing that Forms are not one but many.

When Socrates finally recognizes that he lacks an adequate account of participation, Parmenides suggests, in the final movement (Separation Argument), that perhaps there is no relation between physical objects and Forms. Entities in each group are related only to other entities in their own group. But then, if we in our realm have no relation to Forms and they in theirs have no relation to us, what import can they have for us? Socrates in his opening presentation of Forms had claimed that physical objects have the properties they have by partaking of Forms. It now appears that if Forms exist but have no relation to us then they don't explain anything. Nor do they ground our knowledge, since we have no access to them. So the question we are left with at the end of Parmenides' interrogation (*Prm.* Part I) is: Why posit Forms at all?

Here we will discuss four of Parmenides' objections: Scope of Forms, Whole–Part Dilemma, Largeness Regress, and Likeness Regress.

Scope of Forms (*Prm.* 130B1–E4)

Parmenides' interrogation in this first movement proceeds in four stages, and the guiding question is: What Forms are there? The deeper, unexpressed question is: What grounds are there for positing Forms in some cases but not in others? Socrates is quite sure that there are Forms of the sorts Parmenides lists at stages (1) and (2), he begins to have doubts about the Forms mentioned at stage (3), and seems quite sure there aren't Forms of the sorts mentioned at stage (4), though he is troubled by the possibility that the reasons for positing Forms in the other cases might apply here as well.

Stage (1) asks about Forms of opposites, apparently in reference to those Socrates mentioned in his long speech: "likeness and unlikeness, multitude and oneness, rest and motion, and everything of that sort" (129D8–E1). Parmenides opens stage (1) by asking for clarification, not only about this list but also about the relation between Forms and their participants:

> Tell me. Have you yourself distinguished as separate, in the way you mention, certain forms themselves, and also as separate the things that partake of them? And do you think that likeness itself is something, separate from the likeness we have? And one and many and all the things you heard Zeno read about a while ago?
>   I do indeed, Socrates replied. (130B1–6)

Here Parmenides gets Socrates to confirm two points that were not explicit in his presentation. First, separation is a symmetrical relation. Socrates said in his speech that Forms are distinguished as separate from the things that partake of them (129D6–8). He now agrees that things that partake of Forms are also separate from them. Second, Socrates agrees that likeness itself is separate from the likeness we have – the immanent character that a Form is invoked to explain. As we shall see, his agreement on this point will later be a source of trouble for his theory.

Parmenides does not ask, and so we do not yet know, precisely what Socrates understands by "separation." The expression could indicate merely that Forms are distinct from their participants and immanent characters and vice versa (as we might say that any two non-identical entities are distinct from each other). Or it might mean something stronger, for instance, that Forms exist apart from their participants and the immanent characters and vice versa (as we might say of two objects in space, such as a table and a chair not in contact, that they are spatially separate, or of two events in time, such as the writing of the *Parmenides* and the stabbing of Julius Caesar, that they are temporally separate). Two objects are separate in this way if they have no common parts. Alternatively, separation might be construed as ontological independence. Two items are separate in this sense if the nature of the one does not involve the nature of the other. For example, two chemical elements, say copper and tin, are not only distinct from but also ontologically independent of each other. Bronze, on the other hand, is ontologically dependent on both, since its nature involves the natures of copper and tin. This third notion is unlikely to be what Socrates means by separation in his speech. If it is, he makes a serious mistake agreeing with Parmenides that separation between Forms and their participants is symmetrical. Forms can be ontologically independent of their participants, but their participants depend on Forms for what they are. The notion of separation is important in the *Parmenides*, and its meaning is left vague at this stage of the argument.

Included at stage (1), apparently, are Forms for all the opposites mentioned in Zeno's arguments. Plato does not give us a complete list, and we are left to wonder how extensive the list should be. At stage (2) (130B7–10) Parmenides asks whether Socrates thinks there are Forms of Just, Beautiful, and Good, and everything of that sort. Moral and aesthetic concepts were the focus of Socrates' interest in the early dialogues, and they are regularly cited as Forms in the *Phaedo* and *Republic*. At stage (3) (130c1–4) Parmenides asks whether there is a Form of Human Being, separate from us all, and Forms of Fire and Water.

At this point Socrates begins to hesitate. If we recall Socrates' speech, the reason for his hesitation may not be far to seek. He introduced Forms to explain the compresence of opposites. He posited Forms of Likeness and Unlikeness to explain how the same thing can be both like and unlike. Moral and aesthetic concepts can occasion similar discomfort. Duchamp's *Fountain* (a urinal) might strike me as beautiful, but you as ugly. An action regarded as just in one society might seem unjust in another society. The predicate "human being" does not occasion the same uneasiness as those at stages (1) and (2).

In *Republic* VII (523A10–524D6) Socrates says that some of our sense-perceptions do, whereas others do not, provoke our thought to reflection (see 10: PLATO: A THEORY OF PERCEPTION OR A NOD TO SENSATION?). Perceptions that prompt our reflection are those that yield an opposite perception at the same time. He holds up three fingers, the little finger, ring finger, and middle finger, and points out that each of them appears to be a finger. Since sight gives no opposite impression, ordinary people aren't stimulated to ask: What is a finger? Perception of a finger does not compel them to call upon their intellect. The situation is different with largeness and smallness, hardness and softness, and other perceptual features, because sight reports, for example, that the ring finger is large compared to the little finger but small compared to the middle finger. Here the visual report seems inadequate, telling us as it does that the same thing is both large and small. So we are provoked to call upon our intellect and to ask: What is largeness? What is smallness?

This passage does not say that there is a Form of Largeness and not a Form of Finger, but it corroborates the impression, given by his long speech in the *Parmenides*, that Socrates posits Forms to explain the compresence of opposites. In the case of physical objects like human beings, and stuffs like fire and water, perception does not raise an immediate problem about what they are. He therefore feels no comparable need to posit a Form. Socrates is represented in the *Parmenides* as young and inexperienced. At the end of the first movement of the cross-examination (130E1–4) and again in the transition to Part II (135c8–D6), Parmenides attributes Socrates' difficulties to his youth and lack of training. As a novice he is provoked to reflection by the obviously difficult cases, like largeness and smallness, without fully appreciating that perception on its own may also be inadequate in cases that involve no obvious perceptual conflict, like human being, fire, and water.

At stage (3) we, as readers, are invited to ask why Forms are posited in some cases but not in others. What are the reasons for positing Forms of physical objects and stuffs (*Phlb.* 15A4–5 mentions a Form of Human Being, and *Ti.* 51B8 mentions a Form of Fire)? Does Zeno's problem – the compresence of opposites – infect these cases too? Is Zeno's problem just one reason among others for positing Forms? Is it even perhaps the wrong reason for positing them? Maybe Socrates should go back to stages (1) and (2) and reconsider his justification for positing Forms in those cases.

The mandate to consider when and why Forms are needed is repeated with greater force at stage (4), where Socrates balks at the proposal that there may be Forms of things that seem undignified and worthless, like hair, mud, and dirt (130c5–D9). At 130E1–4 Parmenides says that Socrates' reluctance is a sign of his inexperience. Is he suggesting that there is a Form whenever we call a number of things by the same name, and is he saying that Socrates will eventually recognize that fact (cf. *R.* 596A6–7; see 12: THE FORMS AND THE SCIENCES IN SOCRATES AND PLATO)? In the *Statesman* the Eleatic Visitor, in discussing the method of division, says that divisions should be made at the proper joints (*Plt.* 262A8–263A1; cf. *Phdr.* 265E1–266B1). For instance, it is a mistake to divide the class of human beings into Greek and barbarian. The latter is not a proper group because it includes all persons who are non-Greek. Although there is a common name "barbarian," this passage suggests that it would be inappropriate to posit a corresponding Form. Or is he merely calling to Socrates' attention that he needs a better reason for denying that there are Forms of hair, mud, and dirt than that they seem base and worthless? What problem or problems are Forms supposed to solve? Does a Platonist need a Form of Mud, for instance, if there are Forms of Earth and Water (cf. *Tht.* 147c4–6, where the word here translated "mud" is usually translated "clay" and defined as "earth mixed with liquid")? If Forms perform an explanatory role, perhaps mixtures of stuffs could be explained by reference to the Forms of stuffs that compose the mixture. And what about the functional parts of a thing, for instance, a human finger or human hair? Does the Platonist need a Form of Finger or Hair, if there is a Form of Human Being? Could one perhaps explain what a finger or hair is, if one understood what a human being is (see *Ti.* 76c1–D3 for a functional account of hair)?

This movement invites further questions: If an entity is composed of parts (as mud is composed of earth and water, and a human being of various functional and non-functional parts), what is the relation between the whole and its parts? Is the whole the same as the aggregate of the parts? If so, perhaps there must be Forms corresponding to each of the parts, so that an account of the whole can be given by enumerating the parts. Or is the whole different from all the parts? If so, what relevance do the parts have to an account of the whole? In that case perhaps we need only a Form of the Whole. Or is the relation between whole and parts of some special sort? If so, that too would affect our decision about what Forms there are (see Harte 2002; *Tht.* 203c4–205E8; Burnyeat 1990: 191–209).

Whole–Part Dilemma (*Prm.* 130E4–131E7)

Parmenides now turns to the question: What is the relation between physical objects and Forms? Socrates' own proposals in this and the arguments that follow, as well as Parmenides' suggestions on Socrates' behalf, also bear on another question: What sort of entities are Forms?

Parmenides starts, as he did at the beginning of the first movement, by clarifying what he takes to be Socrates' position and asking for confirmation:

> But tell me this: is it your view that, as you say, there are certain forms, from which these other things, by getting a share of them, derive their names – as, for instance, they come to be like by getting a share of likeness, large by getting a share of largeness, and just and beautiful by getting a share of justice and beauty?
>   It certainly is, Socrates replied. (130E4–131A3)

Socrates said nothing expressly about names in his speech, but Parmenides' proposal spells out Socrates' claim that things that get a share of Likeness come to be like. If some sticks and stones come to be like by getting a share of Likeness, then by having a share of Likeness they can be called by the name "like," derived from the name of the Form (see 15: PLATO ON LANGUAGE).

Parmenides' opening statement, with its reference to names, is highly reminiscent of the opening move in the final argument for the immortality of the soul in the *Phaedo*, suggesting that our present argument could helpfully be read in the light of that discussion. In the *Phaedo* Socrates gives what he calls a "safe" explanation of why beautiful things are beautiful. He claims that their beauty is not explained by their bright color or shape or anything like that. The one thing he is sure of is that the Form of the Beautiful makes them beautiful. He admits that he is unclear about precisely how the Form makes them beautiful; that is, he is vague about what the relation is between the Form and the things whose character it explains. He says:

> Nothing else makes it beautiful except the presence or communion, or whatever the manner of its occurrence, of that beautiful. I stop short of affirming that, but affirm only that it is by the beautiful that all the beautiful things are beautiful. (100d4–8)

To understand how the Beautiful makes things beautiful, we need to understand the relation between the Form and the things whose character it explains. The converse relation, between physical objects and a Form, is known as "participation." In our dialogue Parmenides presses Socrates for an account of participation.

Parmenides proposes two alternatives, and Socrates agrees that they are exhaustive (in the Likeness Regress, Socrates will propose another alternative). Does each thing that gets a share of a Form get as its share the whole Form or only a part of it?[3] Let us reformulate the question in terms of immanent characters: When something partakes of a Form, does it get as its immanent character the whole of the Form or only a part of it? For instance, when Simmias partakes of the Form of Largeness, is the largeness in him the whole of Largeness or merely a part of it?

Consider the first side of the dilemma: Can a whole Form – one thing – be in each of a number of things? If so, won't the Form be separate from itself by being, as a whole, in things that are separate from each other (131A8–B2)?

Socrates suggests that a Form could simultaneously be, as a whole, in each of a number of things, if it is like one and the same day (131B3–6). One and the same day, he says, is in many places at the same time without being separate from itself. If a Form is like that, it could be one and the same in all.

Just what is this proposal? What does Socrates mean by "day"? Does he mean one and the same day*time*: some definite period between sunrise and sunset, which is simultaneously present in Athens and Thebes? Or one and the same day*light*: an invisible, homogeneous stuff that covers many different places at the same time? Perhaps Plato is prodding us, as readers, to consider the implications of these alternatives (see 2: INTERPRETING PLATO). One question we might ask is why Socrates proposes an analogy at all. If he had been born a century later and had attended Aristotle's lectures in the Lyceum, he might have retorted, "Parmenides, if you think a form is separate from itself, by being simultaneously in a number of things, you misunderstand the nature of forms. Forms are universals, and the nature of a universal just is to be present in many places at the same time and to be predicated in common of a number of things. (see Aristotle *Int.* 7, 17a39–40; *Metaph.* VII.16, 1040b25–6). Universals are not thereby separated from themselves." But Aristotle's distinction between universals and particulars had not yet been formulated, and Socrates may not appreciate the distinction. On one interpretation of his analogy, he seems to conceive of Forms as abstract objects, on the other as homogeneous invisible stuffs.

Readers sometimes fault Parmenides for not taking Socrates' proposal seriously and for intimidating him into accepting his own less auspicious analogy instead. Perhaps Parmenides recognizes that Socrates' analogy can be interpreted in more than one way and proposes his own to see if that is what Socrates had in mind. In any case, Parmenides switches the analogy from the day to a sail (131B7–9), and Socrates hesitantly accepts the replacement. If we cover a lot of people with a sail, we might say that one thing is over many. This analogy, though less provocative than Socrates' own, has the one advantage of removing the previous ambiguity. Like one and the same daylight, which is simultaneously in many places, or like a sail that covers a lot of people, one and the same Form is in many participants.

Parmenides' analogy leads into the second side of the dilemma. If a Form is like a sail, isn't a part of it over each person? When Socrates concedes that different parts of the sail are over different people, Parmenides points out that in that case Forms are divisible, and things that partake of them partake of a part. Contrary to what Socrates intended with his own analogy, only part of the Form is in each thing. In that case Forms are not merely divisible but actually divided into parts. If a Form is divided into parts, will it still be one?

The Whole–Part Dilemma treats Forms as though they were quantities of stuff that things get a share of. The question is whether a participant gets the whole of the stuff as its share or whether it gets a part of it. If Simmias gets a share of Largeness, is the largeness he gets – the character immanent in him – Largeness as a whole or a part of Largeness? Think of a proper stuff like gold. If we conceive of gold as the element with atomic number 79, we could say that gold, as a whole, is in each of the golden things, because the nature of gold is wholly present in each instance. So gold is separate from itself by being, as a whole, in things that are separate from each other (first side of the dilemma). If, on the other hand, we conceive of gold, as a whole, as the totality of gold, it is the sum of all the instances of gold in the world, whether in coins or jewelry, dust or nuggets, or still in the ground. Gold, as a whole, is split up into bits and scattered around in the various golden things (second side of the dilemma). We can accept both alternatives in the case of material stuffs, because we mean different things by "whole" in the two situations, and both seem to make good sense. But Socrates finds both sides of the dilemma disturbing. How can Forms, each of which he takes to be one, be separate from themselves or be aggregates of scattered parts?

In the next section (131c12–E5) Parmenides makes fun of the view that Forms are analogous to quantities of stuff by focusing on Forms of quantities. He states a series of paradoxes that turn on two conceptions of Forms and immanent characters that come into blatant conflict in these cases. First, Parmenides and Socrates appear to agree that Forms and immanent characters have the same property – the property

191

whose presence in things the Form is invoked to explain – just as the stuff gold and portions of gold are both golden. So both Largeness itself and largeness in Simmias are large. Second, on the conception of Forms and immanent characters as wholes and parts, the whole is larger than each of its parts, and each part is smaller than the whole. Given these two conceptions, there are paradoxes in the case of Largeness, Equality, and Smallness.

Consider the Small. The paradoxical result in the case of the Small turns on the assumption that the Form of Smallness is small: the Small is small, because that is its proper character, but also large, because it is a whole, which is larger than each of its parts. Parmenides also says, in discussing Largeness, that things are large "by a part of largeness smaller than largeness itself" (131D1–2), which clearly implies that Largeness is large. Largeness is large for two reasons: both in the way that Smallness is small, because that is its proper character, and in the way that Smallness is large, because it is a whole, which is larger than each of its parts. The assumption that Smallness is small, that Largeness is large, and generally that F-ness is F is known as the "Self-Predication Assumption" (see Malcolm 1991) and will figure in the two regress arguments that follow.

At the end of the Whole–Part Dilemma, Parmenides asks: "Socrates, in what way, then, will things get a share of your forms, if they can do so neither by getting parts nor by getting wholes?" (131E3–5). Socrates admits that he is stumped. In the next argument, Parmenides shifts the focus from the problem of participation, with its unwelcome result that each Form is many, to Socrates' ground for thinking that a Form is one. And once he establishes Socrates' ground, he will use that ground to show, to Socrates' dismay once again, that the Form is after all many.

Largeness Regress (*Prm.* 132A1–B2)

This time Parmenides does not start his argument by asking for clarification. In proposing a reason why Socrates might think each Form is one, he goes beyond anything Socrates said in his speech. Here is the argument:

> (1) I suppose you think each form is one on the following ground: whenever some number of things seem to you to be large, perhaps there seems to be some one character, the same as you look at them all, and from that you conclude that the large is one.
> That's true, he said.
> (2) What about the large itself and the other large things? If you look at them all in the same way with the mind's eye, again won't some one thing appear large, by which all these appear large?
> It seems so.
> (3) So another form of largeness will make its appearance, which has emerged alongside largeness itself and the things that partake of it, and in turn another over all these, by which all of them will be large. Each of your forms will no longer be one, but unlimited in multitude. (132A1–B2)

What is the proposal at stage (1)? Is Parmenides saying that whenever Socrates looks at a number of things – temples and elephants, say – all of which seem to him to be large, he notices that they share one common character, largeness, and from that concludes that the Large is one? Is Parmenides suggesting that Socrates takes the character he observes in the various large things to be the Form? If so, then he takes Socrates to identify the Form with the immanent character. At the same time, Parmenides' claim that Socrates observes some *one* character exhibited in *many* large things might indicate that he takes Socrates to regard the Form as a universal: one thing present in many places at the same time.

This interpretation has one serious drawback. The passage suggests that Socrates makes an inference. He is supposed to conclude that the Large is one on the basis of what he notices about the many large things. What he noticed was some one character. If the one character he notices just is the Form, what inference has he made when he concludes that the character is one?

The Largeness Regress should be considered in its context, following the Whole–Part Dilemma. In the Whole–Part Dilemma Parmenides and Socrates both assumed that the Form is one, and Parmenides asked how one Form could be in many things (131A8–9). He argued that if the Form is in many things then it is not one but divided into many (131c9–10). This conclusion prompts him now to ask: Why does Socrates assume that a Form is one? Are his grounds for that assumption adequate? Parmenides will show that Socrates' grounds are inadequate by arguing once again that his Form is many, this time by reduplication.

Parmenides is probably making the following suggestion at stage (1): Whenever Socrates looks at a number of things that all seem to him to be large, he thinks that some one character (call it "the large in us") is the same in all the cases, and from that he infers that the Form, which corresponds to that character, is one. In the rest of the argument Parmenides reveals the inadequacy of Socrates' grounds for that conclusion.

At stage (2) things start to get peculiar. Socrates is asked to repeat what he did at stage (1), but this time with his mind's eye: just as he looked at the many large things at the outset, he is to look in the same way (but with his mind's eye) at the Large itself, together with the other large things. Why does Parmenides propose this as a possible performance, and why does Socrates allow him to derive the consequences he does? If on the first round Socrates took the Form simply to be the common character (as in the first interpretation of stage (1) above), why does he now agree to look at it together with its instances? A common character is what we now call a universal. Is the common character that temples and elephants share itself large? Except for certain unusual universals, like oneness and being, most universals are not instances of themselves.

We saw in the Whole–Part Dilemma that Parmenides derived paradoxes in the case of the Large, the Equal, and the Small by relying on two conceptions of Forms and immanent characters that come into conflict in the case of Forms of quantities. One of those was a Self-Predication Assumption: both *F*-ness itself and *F*-ness in us are *F*. For example, both Largeness itself and largeness in Simmias are large. That discussion, however, treated Forms not as universals but as analogous to material stuffs. It is not odd to think that the stuff gold is golden, but it is quite odd to think that the universal gold is golden or that the universal largeness is large. (Self-predication claims occur occasionally in the dialogues: *Prt.* 330c2–E2, *Hp.Ma.* 292E6–7, *Phd.* 100c4–6.)

If Forms are universals but self-predicating, perhaps the relation between subject and character differs from that in ordinary predications. For instance, perhaps "justice is just" is not a predication but an identity-statement, in which the predicate reidentifies the subject. Or perhaps it is shorthand for "justice is whatever it is to be just," where what follows the first "is" (of identity) could be replaced by a definition once we have it (Nehamas 1979). But if we are to understand the "is" in "the Large is large" as the "is" of identity, Socrates has no reason to group the Form together with the large things. For in that case the Large has no feature in common with them.

Socrates does agree to the grouping, however. The Form of Largeness is probably regarded in this passage as a cause, though not a cause in our modern sense. A Form is not an event, nor does a Form do anything to bring about an effect. Nonetheless a Form is somehow responsible for the effect, and appeal to the Form is thought to explain it. In this sense a Form can be regarded as a cause. Notice that at stage (2) Parmenides mentions some one thing *by which* the Large itself and the other large things appear large, and at stage (3) he speaks of a Largeness *by which* the collection, Largeness$_1$, Largeness$_2$, and the other large things are large. This causal language recalls Socrates' "safe" explanation in *Phaedo* discussed above: "[I] affirm only that it is by the beautiful that all the beautiful things are beautiful" (100D7–8).

Plato probably attributes to Socrates a view about causes that Aristotle would later espouse: a cause has the character that an effect has in virtue of it. Both Plato and Aristotle probably inherited the idea from their predecessors. Consider this passage from the *Phaedo*:

> It appears to me that if anything else is beautiful *besides the beautiful itself*, it is beautiful for no other reason than because it partakes of that beautiful; and the same goes for all cases. Do you assent to that sort of explanation? (100c4–7)

Here Socrates appears to be claiming that the Beautiful itself is beautiful, and that other things are beautiful because they partake of it. The Form of the Beautiful, which is itself beautiful, explains the beauty of other things.

If Socrates thinks of Forms as causes that have the character they explain in other things, then he should be prepared to view (with his mind's eye) the Large itself together with the other large things, since it shares with them a common character.

But now we must ask why he permits Parmenides to generate a regress. If Socrates believes that a Form *explains* the character that other things have, he should insist that the Form itself needs no further explanation. Otherwise his theory is indeed subject to the regress Parmenides describes. In his long speech Socrates mentioned "a form, itself by itself, of likeness," and he said that other things get a share of it (128E6–129A3). It is by getting a share of Likeness that things come to be like and by having a share that they are like. Does he think that Likeness itself is like by having a share of Likeness? Notice that Socrates says that a Form is "itself by itself." This phrase can be understood in more than one way. In one construal it means "separate." On another construal something is itself by itself, if it is itself responsible for its own proper being, independently of other things. If Socrates thinks that Forms are causes, he should think that Forms are what they are by – in virtue of, because of – themselves, not by, or because of, something other than themselves. Yet if that is what he thinks, why in our argument does he allow the regress? He should object that other things are large because of Largeness but Largeness itself is large because of itself.

Socrates does not challenge the regress, however, apparently agreeing that the large itself is large because of something other than itself. Scholars have supposed that he is relying on a tacit Non-Identity Assumption, which they formulate in various ways, and perhaps most usefully as: nothing is *F* in virtue of itself (Petersen 1973; Fine 1993). Obviously he does need to rely on some such assumption, since he permits the regress. The question is why he would make that assumption, given that it so obviously defeats the explanatory theory he was defending in his long speech.

We find a reason earlier in the dialogue. Recall Parmenides' initial request for clarification at the beginning of the Scope of Forms (130B1–5, quoted above, p. 187). Parmenides made two points explicit that were not explicit in Socrates' long speech: first, separation between Forms and participants is symmetrical; and second, Forms are separate not only from their participants, but also from the immanent character they explain.

Separation was repeatedly discussed in the Scope of Forms. While Socrates agreed at stages (1), (2), and (3) that the Forms mentioned are separate from things, at stage (4) he balked at the idea that Forms of undignified stuffs are separate, saying that hair, mud, and dirt are just what we see (130D3–5). This reaction suggests that, in the case of those Forms he accepts, he envisages them as existing apart from the things they explain and not as features we perceive in them.

If separate existence is what Socrates means by separation, then in assenting to Parmenides' second proposal at 130B3–4, that Likeness itself is separate from the likeness we have, he has agreed to a premise that Parmenides can use in the Largeness Regress. Socrates' causal Theory of Forms commits him to regarding Largeness itself as large (because it explains that character in other things). Accordingly, Largeness itself can be added to the group of things that have a common immanent character. An immanent character does not exist apart from the objects whose character it is. But now, since Socrates thinks that since the Form exists apart from the character it explains, the Form cannot explain its *own* immanent character. So he must posit a further Form to account for the immanent character the first Form shares with its participants. As a cause, the second Form will then have that same character, and so there must be a third Form, separate from the second, that accounts for it. And so the regress proceeds. The Forms generated by the regress are qualitatively identical but numerically distinct, because each exists apart from its predecessor.

This unwanted consequence results from Socrates' commitment to two theses: first, the view that Forms have the character that others things have in virtue of them; and second, the view that Forms are separate – exist apart – from the immanent character they explain. Given these two beliefs, each of Socrates' Forms, which he regarded as one, turns out to be not one but unlimited in multitude. This time a Form is many, not by division, as in the previous argument, but by reduplication.

Likeness Regress (*Prm.* 132c12–133A7)

In this movement Socrates offers a proposal, which squarely addresses the problem of participation with a new alternative. This proposal is important, because it is a view favored elsewhere in Plato's dialogues, including the *Timaeus*. So we may presume that it is a conception Plato himself took very seriously. Socrates says that what appears to him most likely is that Forms are like patterns (*paradeigmata*) set in nature, and other things resemble them and are likenesses (*homoiomata*). Partaking of Forms, he says, is simply being modeled on them.

The current proposal about participation is very different from that envisaged in the Whole–Part Dilemma. On that view, if something partakes of a Form, it gets a share of it, as though the Form were a quantity of stuff that is parceled out to the various participants. On the present view, a Form is comparable to an artist's model, and the participants are comparable to the images the artist makes. Participation in the Form *F*-ness, as Socrates describes it, is being a likeness or copy of *F*-ness. Notice that *being a likeness of* is an asymmetrical relation. If *x* is a likeness of *F*-ness, *F*-ness is not a likeness of *x*. A portrait is a likeness of Simmias; Simmias is not a likeness of it. Parmenides makes trouble for Socrates' proposal by arguing that the asymmetrical relation is based on an underlying symmetrical relation, the relation of *being like*. If *x* is like *F*-ness, *F*-ness is like *x*. If a portrait of Simmias is like Simmias, Simmias is like it.

There are two general ways to construe the argument that follows. On one reading, Parmenides generates a regress in much the same way as he did in the earlier argument about Largeness. Take any Form, say the Form of Beauty. According to Socrates' proposal, the many beautiful things are beautiful because they are likenesses of the Beautiful itself. Parmenides then points out that, if the many beautiful things are likenesses of Beauty, not only are they like Beauty, but Beauty is like them. Since they are like, Beauty and its Likenesses have a feature in common on the basis of which they are like, namely their beauty. (This time, instead of assuming self-predication, Parmenides infers it from Socrates' proposal.) But since the Form that accounts for that character is separate from it (Separation Assumption), a regress follows as before. Another Form of Beauty will make its appearance to account for the beauty shared by the first Form and the other beautiful things. And so on. There is an unlimited multitude of Forms that are qualitatively the same but numerically distinct.

The second way to read the argument is to take it as concerning the Form of Likeness (see Schofield 1996; Allen 1997). Read in this way, the regress is quite different from the previous one. Socrates gets into trouble by failing to recognize that likeness is a relation between entities, not an item that stands in a further relation to the entities it relates. We start as before with any Form, say the Form of Beauty. Both Beauty and its likenesses are like each other, so they have a feature in common, namely (both beauty and) likeness. Socrates claimed in his long speech that things are like by getting a share of Likeness. He therefore believes that if the Form of Beauty and the many beautiful things are like each other, they are like by partaking of Likeness. If the many beautiful things and the Beautiful itself all partake of Likeness, then on the present proposal they are likenesses of Likeness. Now the Form of Likeness, as pattern, is like things that are like it; so it can be grouped together with them on the basis of their common feature, likeness. What ties together this new group? There is no logical reason why a relation should not relate itself to other things, but once more Socrates' commitment to the Separation Assumption prevents him from recognizing this. He agrees that since the Form of Likeness is like other things, there must be a further

Form, Likeness$_2$, to relate the members of the new collection. And since this new Form shares a feature with its participants, likeness, there must be a fresh Form, Likeness$_3$, to relate them, and so on indefinitely.

There are textual reasons to prefer this interpretation of the argument to the previous one (Schofield 1996). An advantage of the interpretation is that the Likeness Regress does not simply repeat the Largeness Regress but exposes a different problem. The Largeness Regress derived a regress by focusing on a Form things partake of, showing that if something partakes of one, it partakes of an unlimited number. The Likeness Regress derives a regress by focusing on the relation between an object and the Form it partakes of, treating the relation as standing to its relata in an analogous relation. At each step the relation that bundled the previous group must itself be bundled together with them. There must then (given the Separation Assumption) be a further relation that bundles them, and so on indefinitely. So an unlimited number of relations are needed to connect an object and its character. The regress resembles one made famous by F. H. Bradley (1897: 18; cf. Ryle 1939: 107).

Conclusion

The argument of the *Parmenides* as a whole shows that one of the most serious problems for Forms is Socrates' assumption in his long speech that Forms cannot themselves be both *F* and not-*F*, for instance, that the One is not both one and many. The second part of the dialogue suggests that a way to preserve the explanatory power of Forms, even though they themselves admit their own opposite, is to distinguish what a Form is in virtue of itself and what it is in virtue of something other than itself: e.g., the one is one in virtue of itself but many in virtue of its participation in multitude (see Meinwald 1991). The problem of participation is not so easily solved, though one might argue that in the *Timaeus* Plato introduces the Receptacle (the spatial medium in which sensible things come to be and pass away but Forms cannot enter) to save the paradigm-copy model of participation (Gill 2004). But that will not solve the problem of participation among Forms themselves. Aristotle complained that Plato did not solve the problem, and he himself pursued a different kind of answer (see 27: LEARNING ABOUT PLATO FROM ARISTOTLE).

Notes

1 Gill 1996. This chapter is an adaptation of parts of the first half of that longer work. All translations of the *Parmenides* come from the translations by Gill and Ryan 1996, reprinted in J. M. Cooper (ed.) *Plato: Complete Works* (Indianapolis: Hackett, 1997). Translations from works other than the *Parmenides* are my own.

2 Since Vlastos 1954, the primary attraction of the *Parmenides* has been the two regress arguments, which Aristotle later referred to under the blanket title "Third Man" (neither version of Plato's argument concerns man, but Aristotle's version does).

3 For an interpretation of the *Phaedo* that finds there the model of participation criticized here, see Denyer 1983.

197

References and further reading

Allen, R. E. (1997). *Plato's* Parmenides, 2nd edn. New Haven, Conn.: Yale University Press.

Bradley, F. H. (1897). *Appearance and Reality*, 2nd edn. Oxford: Clarendon Press.

Burnyeat, M. F. (1990). *The* Theaetetus *of Plato*. Indianapolis: Hackett.

Cohen, S. M. (1971). The logic of the third man. *Philosophical Review* 80, pp. 448–75. Repr. in G. Fine (ed.) (1999) *Plato*, vol. 1: *Metaphysics and Epistemology* (pp. 275–97). Oxford: Oxford University Press.

Denyer, N. (1983). Plato's theory of stuffs. *Philosophy* 58, pp. 315–27.

Devereux, D. (1994). Separation and immanence in Plato's Theory of Forms. In *Oxford Studies in Ancient Philosophy*, vol. 12 (pp. 63–90). Oxford: Oxford University Press. Repr. in G. Fine (ed.) (1999) *Plato*, vol. 1: *Metaphysics and Epistemology* (pp. 192–214). Oxford: Oxford University Press.

Fine, G. (1986). Immanence. In *Oxford Studies in Ancient Philosophy*, vol. 4 (pp. 71–97). Oxford: Oxford University Press.

—— (1993). *On Ideas*. Oxford: Clarendon Press.

Gill, M. L. (1996). Introduction. In M. L. Gill and P. Ryan (eds.) *Plato*: Parmenides (pp. 1–109). Indianapolis: Hackett.

—— (2004). Plato's first principles. In A. Pierris (ed.) *Aristotle's Criticisms of Plato: The Metaphysical Question* (pp. 155–76). Patras: Institute for Philosophical Research.

Harte, V. (2002). *Plato on Parts and Wholes*. Oxford: Clarendon Press.

Malcolm, J. (1991). *Plato on the Self-Predication of Forms*. Oxford: Clarendon Press.

Meinwald, C. (1991). *Plato's* Parmenides. Oxford: Clarendon Press.

Nehamas, A. (1979). Self-Predication and Plato's Theory of Forms. *American Philosophical Quarterly* 16, pp. 93–103.

Petersen, S. (1973). A reasonable self-predication premise for the third man argument. *Philosophical Review* 82, pp. 451–70.

Ryle, G. (1939). Plato's *Parmenides*. *Mind* 48, pp. 129–51. Repr. with Afterword in R. E. Allen (ed.) (1965) *Studies in Plato's Metaphysics* (pp. 97–147). London: Routledge and Kegan Paul.

Schofield, M. (1996). Likeness and likenesses in the *Parmenides*. In C. Gill and M. M. McCabe (eds.) *Form and Arguments: Studies in Late Plato* (pp. 49–77). Oxford: Clarendon Press.

Strang, C. (1963). Plato and the third man. *Proceedings of the Aristotelian Society* 37, pp. 147–64. Repr. in G. Vlastos (ed.) (1971). *Plato: A Collection of Critical Essays*, vol. 1: *Metaphysics and Epistemology* (pp. 184–200). Garden City, NY: Anchor Books.

Vlastos, G. (1954). The third man argument in Plato's *Parmenides*. *Philosophical Review* 63, pp. 319–49. Repr. with Addendum in R. E. Allen (ed.) (1965). *Studies in Plato's Metaphysics* (pp. 231–63). London: Routledge and Kegan Paul.

Waterlow, S. (1982). The third man's contribution to Plato's paradigmatism. *Mind* 91, pp. 339–57.

14

The Role of Cosmology in Plato's Philosophy

CYNTHIA FREELAND

Introduction

It is always tricky to discern Plato's own opinion on any specific issue, given his choice of the dialogue format, complex views about speaking and writing, and masterful literary craftsmanship (see 2: INTERPRETING PLATO). A further problem in trying to give an account of Plato's cosmology is that all of his cosmological views are set out in passages explicitly described as "myths" or stories. This holds true of the three most important presentations of such views: toward the end of the *Phaedo* when Socrates tells a myth of the afterlife; in the *Phaedrus'* account of the lives of souls before birth and embodiment; and, finally, in the *Timaeus*, where cosmology is presented in the guise of an *eikos muthos* or "likely story." Is cosmology important per se in Plato, or just as a backdrop for accounts of the soul, the Forms, and the good life? And what was the influence of Plato's own cosmological ventures upon later, quite serious, investigations of astronomy in the Academy?

To begin tackling these questions, we first need to clarify just what is meant by a "cosmology." *Logos* is an account or reasoned statement about something, and the Greek word "*kosmos*" has as its primary meaning order or arrangement. Scholars have argued that the term "*kosmos*," used to describe the world in the sense of the universe as a whole, is derivative upon a primary meaning of "order," and that in fact the first broadened use of the term was developed by Plato (Finkelberg 1998). In this broader sense the *Timaeus'* narrator, a famous astronomer, describes the order of the *kosmos* when referring to the structure of the heavens (*ouranos*). Thus the use of the word "*kosmos*" to designate the world in the sense of universe reflects a shift first from its use to describe "order" in the sense of "heavenly arrangement," and second to "order of the world (*ouranos* or heaven) as a whole." "*Kosmos*" is used in this sense in what are generally taken as Plato's later dialogues: in addition to the *Timaeus* (for example, at 28b3), also in the *Politicus* (269d8) and *Philebus* (29e1, 59a3).

Cosmology in ancient times also typically encompassed *cosmogony*, or an origin story: an account of how the universal order was created and came to be (the *genesis* of the *kosmos*). This association was common in earlier pre-Socratic theories of the *archē* or universe's first principle, and we shall find it is also true in Plato.

For purposes of this article, I shall sidestep some of the hard issues about how to construe Plato's writing strategies. I will instead present the theories that can be gleaned from the relevant dialogues, taking the view that something like the most developed view given in them, that of the *Timaeus*, is close to Plato's own belief. To appreciate Plato's contributions to cosmology as a discipline we shall need to understand something of the pre-Socratic backdrop for his theories; and in the end I will also sketch a bit of the subsequent influence of his views (particularly from the *Timaeus*) for later studies in the Academy and beyond.

Pre-Socratic Cosmologies and the *Phaedo*

The *Phaedo* is the story of the last day of Socrates' life, during which he discussed the nature of soul and the question of its afterlife with his close friends. Here Socrates denies having much interest in cosmology or physical theory. It is surprising, then, to read that Socrates claims having had an interest in such matters at a young age. (Whether this is true of the historical Socrates is a matter of debate, but seems unlikely.) Most of the cosmologies Socrates would have encountered, i.e., those of the pre-Socratics, were accounts built upon some kind of *archē* or first principle of the universe. Usually the *archē* was described in terms we might suppose refer to a material entity, such as water, air, fire, "seeds," or atoms. However, such material was usually conceived as in some sense active, and not a mere "stuff." It also was typically invoked in accounting for the nature of soul. Thus Anaximenes' air, for example, was associated with a person's life-breath, and also understood as the major active force in the universe, something we might link with wind. In some few cases the *archē* was something more abstract, such as the "One Being" of Parmenides. Parmenides almost put an end to cosmology by arguing forcefully that non-being could not exist, thus disallowing the possibility of change, which seems to require non-being in some sense. That is, when something changed, it changed to what was not before. But non-being could not itself be. This is an issue Socrates does not mention as worrying in the *Phaedo* story, but we shall see it becomes central in the *Timaeus* account. Here is a strong reason to argue for Plato's own independent interest in constructing an adequate cosmology: in order to give a coherent metaphysical response to Parmenides' challenge.

As Aristotle summarizes them in his *Physics*, pre-Socratic cosmologies aimed to answer various fundamental questions: Where did our world come from? How did it evolve? What is it made of? What are the mechanical and physical principles underlying processes of change we observe, especially orderly ones? How can we account for the nature and movements of the heavenly bodies? And, after Parmenides, there needs to be some explanation or answer to his problem about non-being, to account for the underlying ontology of change. Perhaps surprisingly, cosmology also included some account of the nature of life or soul. Typically the cosmos itself was regarded as a living being animated by the same principle or substance that brought life to the animals within it. That is, the macrocosm was an analogue of the microcosm. (We can see this same principle at work in the later Stoic account of the entire universe as a *zōon* or living animal.)

In the *Phaedo*, Socrates complains that his early forays into cosmology left him disappointed because the philosophers who had made relevant proposals neglected one key thing: the "why" or reason for various cosmological processes to occur. They all, he said, focused only on the physical reasons or mechanical causes without accounting for the aims or goals of nature. Socrates tells about being particularly disappointed when he realized that Anaxagoras, who made Mind a first principle, nevertheless failed to explain its aims or purposes. He says that he wanted to know "in the same way about the sun and the moon and the other heavenly bodies, about their relative speed, their turnings and whatever else happened to them, how it is best that each should act and be acted upon" (98A2–6). But no answer was forthcoming from Anaxagoras.

Just as the pre-Socratic cosmologies failed to supply any purpose at the general cosmic level, so also for the microcosmic level of an individual person. Here, Socrates gives the example of his own case of staying in prison: a purely physicalist theory could not explain why his body had remained in prison, when this was in fact due to his moral beliefs about what was right and wrong (98c8–99A4).

The *Phaedo* makes it clear that a chief criterion of success in a Platonic cosmological theory is that it will provide such a purposive explanation, both for the cosmos as a whole and for the individuals within it. It is striking, then, that the metaphysical theory Socrates goes on to set forth in the *Phaedo* – the canonical presentation of Plato's theory of Forms – does *not* provide any such account of universal purposes. Socrates insists, in his search for reasons, that the "simple *aitia*" or explanation of why something is beautiful is the presence of the Form of Beauty. Similarly, a thing is cold because of Cold, or sick because of Sickness. But these claims do nothing to answer the "why" question in each case.

There are numerous other problems with the Theory of Forms if we regard it as a sketch of a kind of cosmology. First, it is not at all clear from the *Phaedo* presentation just how many Forms there are, or how they are connected. Socrates hints that there must be some sort of internal or "essential" link between Forms like One and Oddness or Snow and Coldness, but just what this is is not explained. The metaphysical Theory of Forms in the *Phaedo* thus fails to provide answers to some of the most fundamental questions of cosmology, such as how the universe was caused or created, what explains the heavenly bodies and ongoing regularity of natural processes, and – most importantly, given Socrates' own criterion – what is the purpose of it all.

Toward the end of the *Phaedo*, when Socrates is nearing the moment when he must drink the hemlock, he seems to sense the lingering doubts of his friends about his philosophical arguments for the immortality of the soul. So he changes gears and offers them instead a kind of fairy tale or comforting story, presented in the form of an elaborate account of the soul's fate after death (107D–115A). A person's soul journeys into a physical afterlife where it is submitted to judgment and undergoes a process of purification. This process differs for different types of crimes or "sins." Souls must spend time in Hades, sometimes suffering for a long period by being tossed about in fiery rivers. But some souls can achieve a higher form of existence.

To understand this higher existence, we are given a fairly complex physical account of the nature of our world. This is so despite the fact that Socrates says he doesn't have the skill or the time to prove what things are true about the earth, its nature and size (108c6). He says, "However, nothing prevents my telling you what I am convinced of is the shape of the earth, and what its regions are" (108D9–E2). What ensues is a quite elaborate account of the earth. It is described as a rough sphere at the center of heaven, where it rests in the middle through equilibrium (it "has no need of air or any other force to prevent it from falling" (109A2–3). The earth is very large and we dwell on only a small part of it, since it has many hollows filled with water, mist, and air. These hollows are interconnected by tunnels; in some of these, water flows, but in the deeper ones, there are fiery rivers like streams of lava. Humans live in these hollows (109C3–5), but the actual surface of the earth is set in the pure heaven, along with the stars (in the *aether*, 109B–C). And if we could rise to that surface, and endure the contemplation, then we would see things in the true heaven (*ouranos*) (109E2–7).

Life on the true surface of the earth is described as a utopian existence. There is a perfect climate with no sickness. There are numerous higher beings who also live in this region, with aether as their natural element, just as air is for us (111A8–B1). These higher beings have superior eyesight, hearing, and intelligence. Indeed, they are said to communicate directly with the gods: "They see the sun and moon and stars as they are, and in other ways their happiness is in accord with this" (111c1–3).

The physical cosmos in the *Phaedo* tale is a stage setting for the judgment of human souls (113D–114c). Here Socrates teaches his friends that virtue will be rewarded and vice punished. The tale is a consequentialist one that suggests we should be good in life because of concerns about our fate in the afterlife. Those who have led exceptionally holy lives are free and move up to dwell above ground (114c1–2). In stark contrast to the jewel-strewn, crystalline existence of these higher souls is the dire fate of the souls caught and tossed in the terrifying rivers and streams of fire that pulse threateningly deep in the hollows of the earth, in the region called Tartarus (112E–113B). Here there are terrible winds and winding rivers compared to serpents (112D8). A soul can be tortured in this way for thousands of years.

At the conclusion of this quite elaborate digression about the afterlife, Socrates sums up as follows: "Those who have purified themselves sufficiently by philosophy live in the future altogether without a body; they make their way to even more beautiful dwelling places which it is hard to describe clearly, nor do we now have the time to do so" (114c2–6).

What are we to make of this story? It is flagged by Plato himself as something told to comfort listeners, like a child's bedtime story. In his thinly veiled comments on the status of this story, Plato has Socrates remark that no one sensible should believe the story, but that nevertheless, "a man should repeat things like this to himself as if it were an incantation" (114D6–7), because belief in this or something like this is a "noble risk" (114D6). We can compare this to Socrates' discussion of the "noble lie" in the *Republic*, and also to Socrates' briefer story in the *Gorgias* of the just and pious soul's journey in the afterlife to the Isles of the Blessed (523A1–524A7).

There are numerous philosophical problems with the *Phaedo* myth if we try to assess it as serious cosmology. First, it does not cohere in any obvious way with the Theory of Forms. Where would Forms "be" in the physical universe it describes? Second, the possibility that some souls escape the cycle of bodily reincarnation does not fit with earlier parts of the *Phaedo* that seem to insist on opposites always coming from, and turning into, their opposites (71A6–7). An endless disembodied life is not compatible with assertion of repeated cycles between carnate and discarnate states, given that earlier we were told that the soul must come from its opposite, being dead (77c9–d3) (see 19: THE PLATONIC SOUL). A third major problem is metaphysical: the myth does not address the problem of how to explain change, so it fails to respond to Parmenides' challenge about non-being.

The fourth very serious problem with the *Phaedo* myth, given Socrates' earlier complaint about Anaxagoras, is that the physical universe as a whole is not set within any teleological framework. We are given no broad account of the creation of the universe and of its physical constitution that would explain its larger purposes. What the myth *does* do is supply a certain sense of purpose to our human lives as set within very vast cosmological processes. In this story, although souls and their fates do seem very central, we see that humans are not the central goal, since there are various "higher" and "more intelligent" creatures whose condition we can only aspire to. Whether these creatures somehow play a larger role in cosmic teleology – and just what they are – is not explained. Plato has used the excuse of Socrates' impending death to reduce the cosmology to a sketch here, a kind of fable told to encourage virtuous behavior in its listeners. For a serious attempt at cosmological theorizing, he needs to supply a more complete, coherent, all-encompassing cosmological theory that will do all of these things: explain the universe's process of creation, its physical structure, its orderly processes of change, and its goal or purpose, integrating the metaphysics of the Forms into the overall framework.

The Soul and the Universe in the *Phaedrus*

Another elaborate mythical account of the soul is presented in the *Phaedrus*, which also foregrounds the soul's moral life as a central factor in the structure of the universe. But the *Phaedrus* myth makes one significant advance over that of the *Phaedo*: it begins to integrate Forms into the story. Socrates begins the relevant section of the dialogue by describing his view that every soul is immortal, at 245c5. He says that there is a self-mover or source in each soul, which itself has no source; so can't be destroyed either. (This may be a response to Parmenides, making each soul a complete, indestructible "one being" like his One.) Again, as in the *Phaedo*, Socrates hedges the truth of his tale when he remarks that "to describe what the soul actually is would require a very long account . . . but to say what it is like is humanly possible and takes less time" (246a3–6).

At this point we are given the famous metaphor of the soul as a charioteer with two winged horses. Socrates suggests that at some kind of starting point of physical creation – or at least before any soul's physical embodiment – Zeus drives his winged chariot at the head of a large procession of all souls, "looking after everything and putting all things in order" (246e5–6). At this time the eleven other gods (i.e., all except Hestia) are arranged in formation. The shape of the universe resembles a Greek theater or big open bowl. The souls, all in their chariots, take a steep climb up the aisles of the theater to get to the rim of heaven. "But when the souls we call immortals reach the top, they move outward and take their stand on the high ridge of heaven, where its circular motion carries them around as they stand while they gaze upon what is outside heaven" (247b6–c2).

And what of the place beyond heaven? Socrates says this is risky to talk about. Here the souls see "what really is," and are treated to a vision of all of the Forms (247c–d). As the soul is carried around on top of the ridge of the "bowl" they have climbed, it has a view of Forms, such as Justice, Self-control, and Knowledge. Of course what Socrates has in mind is not real, literal vision, since, "what is in this place is without color and without shape and without solidity . . . visible only to intelligence, the soul's steersman" (247c6–8).

The *Phaedrus*, like the *Phaedo*, describes incarnation of the soul in a body as a sort of fall – the loss of the soul's wings – and supposes that most souls will be repeatedly reincarnated in the flesh. However, it also allows for a time during which the soul is bodiless, and perhaps, even for permanent escape. Plato writes, "No soul returns to the place from which it came for ten thousand years . . . except the soul of the man who practices philosophy or who loves boys philosophically" (248e5–249a2). If such souls choose this sort of right life three times in a row, "they grow their wings back, and they depart in the three-thousandth year" (249a4–5). Only the soul of a wise and virtuous philosopher will grow back these precious wings (249c4–5). As we saw in the *Phaedo* myth, there is a curious problem about the chance of a soul escaping reincarnation, since one might suppose that unless the fresh supply of souls is endless, they would eventually run out, bringing all mortal life to an end.

The *Phaedrus* myth complements that of the *Phaedo* by providing an account of the soul's pre-existence (something also presupposed, but not described, in the *Phaedo's* Theory of Recollection), but it supplements the *Phaedo* by its inclusion of the Forms. If we were to combine the physical story of the two myths, we might imagine that the souls of virtuous humans, like those of the higher beings that naturally inhabit the earth's surface, are able to rise even higher, "flying" up into a kind of Platonic Heaven where they are able to glimpse the Forms. This process can scarcely be a real physical flight, nor is the relevant vision an actual kind of sight. Without another persuasive account to offer, Plato typically describes contact with Forms as sight and uses visual imagery to convey what it is like. For example, in *Symposium* he famously discusses seeing the true Form of Beauty, and in the *Republic* he talks about seeing in a new way in the light of the sun-like Form of the Good (*R*. VI.508b–509d). In the *Phaedrus* as in the *Phaedo*, the physical senses are said to be so murky that only a few people down here are able to glimpse the originals of the likenesses we now see, the originals encountered before our embodiment, of Justice and Self-Control, etc. Vision is our sharpest sense, but it does not see Wisdom. But Beauty is different, and an exception. It prompts a stronger connection to the prototype: "But now beauty alone has this privilege, to be the most clearly visible and the most loved" (250d6–e1).

As with the *Phaedo*, a number of key requirements of a satisfactory cosmology are missing from the tale of the disembodied soul in the *Phaedrus*. Recall the four problems mentioned above with the *Phaedo* myth. Again, there is no serious account of the nature and structure of physical reality, in particular, no account of its relationship to the realm of Forms, despite the fact that they are more prominent here. Second, there is no account of what occurs when a soul is embodied, that is, of how exactly it becomes housed "in" a body and how the physical body is implicated in its various desires (so vividly described here with the erotic metaphor of the swelling wings). Third, the theory does not respond to the Parmenidean problem of change. And finally, teleology is again missing. Despite mention of Zeus here, there is no creation story. So once more, the central feature of an adequate cosmology, in Socrates' view at least, is absent: the explanation of the "why" or "purpose." There is perhaps a hint in the *Phaedrus* that the cosmic processes "aim at" a moral voyage of souls who are tested by embodiment, perhaps ultimately winning their way to a heavenly "reward" of sorts. But because of his mention of the gods and the higher reality of Forms, Plato cannot plausibly be taken to mean that we humans are "the" reason for creation of the physical cosmos. For a fuller and more complete cosmology that does answer all four of these questions, we will have to turn to the *Timaeus*.

Timaeus

The *Timaeus* is an unusually puzzling dialogue, for a number of reasons. It is part of a planned group of three dialogues, of which only it and the sketch of another exist. The *Timaeus* opens with a reference to a previous day's conversation which both does and does not sound like the dialogue of the *Republic*. Socrates had led it and produced a "feast" for his friends discussing the best state and its classes: workers and artisans, as well as guardians or rulers, who are to receive a philosophical education preparing them for harmonious and virtuous rule. Socrates now says that he remains dissatisfied with this picture of the state since it is like a beautiful painting of an animal which he wants to see animated – particularly so in situations of conflict. The first interlocutor, Critias, responds by sketching a story of the people of a mythical land, Atlantis, which was large and powerful but ultimately defeated by the ancestors of the Athenians. Critias' tale is told merely by way of a preview to a planned longer version which will follow up on the story of the birth of mankind, to be narrated by Timaeus, a distinguished visitor from Locri in Italy. We now possess only a part of the dialogue bearing Critias' name as title; and its planned sequel (a story of the alleged courageous and bold actions of the earliest Athenians) does not exist.

The *Timaeus* is mostly a monologue by the eminent astronomer Timaeus which lays out an entire, complex cosmology. He begins, after invoking the gods, by distinguishing between what comes to be and what always is, arguing that to each metaphysical category corresponds a relevant type of knowing. This sounds like familiar Platonic doctrine. So also is his next point, distinguishing types of human cognition in relation to their objects. There is Reason, which knows what is and must be, and which is also eternal; and sensation or opinion, which knows things that come to be, and is itself changing (27d5–28b2). What comes to be necessarily must have a cause, Timaeus argues. But what sort of cause? He hypothesizes that a beautiful world must have been made by a benevolent creator, and that it is manifestly true that our world is a fair and orderly one. "Let me tell you then why the creator made this world of generation. He was good, and one who is good can never become jealous of anything. And so, being free of jealousy, he wanted everything to become as much like himself as was possible" (29e1–3; translation modified).

The overall structure of the cosmology in the *Timaeus* resembles views we have found earlier in Plato. Again we see analogies between macrocosm and microcosm. However, this dialogue offers far more details about the movements of the heavenly bodies, as well as about the physical universe generally, and about human and animal embodiment in particular. Plato does much more here to integrate the Theory of Forms within a general physical theory. We can see in this work several important debts to pre-Socratic cosmologies, especially that of Pythagoras – not surprising, given Timaeus' origin in Locri, in Italy. Moreover, the beginning makes it crystal clear that this story will explain the purposive structure of the universe.

Another key development in the *Timaeus* cosmology is the much greater role played here by mathematics, in particular, geometry. Of course, there are many instances in earlier dialogues in which Socrates invokes geometry to describe order and balance, both of an individual person and of a larger whole. In *Grg.* 508A, Socrates' view is that the fact that the world order is a *kosmos* is taken by wise men to show that justice and proportionate equality have greater power than injustice and *pleonexia* (roughly, gaining more than one's share). In the *Republic* account of the philosophers' education, mathematics and geometry are included to develop a sense of order or *harmonia* and proportion (Johansen 2004).

Still, as noted above, the story Timaeus tells is hedged by being called only an "*eikos muthos*" or "*eikos logos.*" Here, "*eikos*" means likely or plausible. We are left to decide how seriously Plato meant the cosmology presented here, and whether it is truly his own view. On the former question, scholarly opinions differ. A. E. Taylor understands "myth" to be the contrasting term with "science," and maintains that it would be "a mistake to look in the *Timaeus* for any revelation of distinctively Platonic doctrines" (1928: 11). Taylor believes the dialogue advances views of its narrator, Timaeus, combining Italian biological views from Empedocles with aspects of Pythagorean physical theory. Gregory Vlastos, on the other hand, maintains that the *Timaeus* was meant seriously as indicating Plato's own views. "But," he says, "there remains an irreducible element of poetry, which refuses to be translated into the language of scientific prose" (1975: 32).

Many subtle issues can be raised about Timaeus' tale as a myth (Wright 2000; Rowe 2003). First, it is framed with a political story about Atlantis, which itself seems rather mythical. Perhaps given the ultimate moral-political goal of the planned trilogy, we ought to construe the story told here as an example of the kind of story that Socrates allows to be told to people in the *Republic*, i.e., the "Noble Lie" (Morgan 1998). However, Plato can also be seen here as creating a detailed picture or philosophical *ekphrasis*, or depiction in words, of the whole cosmos (Johansen 2004). I have argued that the sort of image developed by *Timaeus* represents bona fide Platonic knowledge that corresponds to the type of knowledge occupying the next to highest section in the famous analogy of the Divided Line in the *Republic*: a form of knowledge that uses images, like geometers do (Freeland 2004).

My exposition will assume that the *Timaeus* view, or something close to it, is a very serious one, and likely to be Plato's own, at least at the time of writing. A number of Plato's contemporaries and immediate successors, including Aristotle, regarded it as his view. Moreover, it solves the four problems listed earlier for both the *Phaedo* and *Phaedrus* views: it integrates Forms into the material world in a plausible way, provides a broad and cohesive account of teleology, explains many details about the soul's embodiment, and tackles the difficult problem of non-being posed by Parmenides in order to account for the reality of change.

Let's look, then, at the actual cosmology of this work. We can divide the cosmology of the *Timaeus* into the following topics for more complete discussion: (1) the Demiurge, heavenly creation and time; (2) the World-Soul and those of the gods; (3) the human soul and its initial placement in the head; (4) organization of the material world of the Receptacle, known as the Realm of Necessity; and (5) the cooperation of Reason and Necessity, which paves the way for a fuller account of human embodiment with all of its vicissitudes (including choices between a good life or vice, leading to subsequent reincarnation as either animals or higher beings).

First let us consider the creative actions of the Demiurge. Not much is said about this active agent, but clearly the Demiurge's work is not like that of the Judeo-Christian God who creates out of nothing or *ex nihilo*. The Demiurge begins within a framework already including both Forms and an unformed physical reality called the Receptacle. Intelligence is deemed obviously superior to what is devoid of soul. The Demiurge is a craftsman who operates through reason (*nous*) by looking toward a model of the Forms. This model must be eternal and good for the universe to be eternal and good (29A2–3).

To begin with, the Demiurge creates the most perfect body, which must be spherical and smooth. It is also alive, albeit without any organs of sensation or locomotion; but self-sufficient. It is capable of motion and moves in the most perfect pathway, spinning around itself (34A2–3). Obviously, apart from moving, this first god made by the Demiurge is a close analogue, if not a twin, of Parmenides' One Being. It is described with many similar adjectives and phrases: as one, unique, eternal, and complete in every way (30D1–31A1); spherical and homogenous (33B1–7); smooth and even, and a whole (34A8–B3).

What is this World-Soul like? We don't get much explanation. It sounds much like Aristotle's First Cause, since it is described both as a thinking being and a source of motion. But it has a spatial aspect too, since it is described as being seated at the center yet extended into the whole spherical body (34B4–5), spreading "from the center on out in every direction to the outermost limit of the universe [circumference of heaven]" (36E1–3). As with Aristotle, we might well ask how something allegedly immaterial can move or be spatially extended, but these questions are not answered.

How exactly does the Demiurge create the soul of the whole cosmos? This requires a complicated blend of the most important Forms: Being, Sameness, and Difference (the same Forms that are central in the *Sophist*'s discussion of the "blending" of Forms). Each one is mixed in a complex formula that involves separate blends of its own permanent and less permanent or divine versions, for example, "the indivisible kind of being with that portioned out in bodies." The three resulting mixtures are themselves blended together, and then divided up as one might divide a ball of dough into many specified parts according to mathematical intervals. These are in fact harmonic intervals involving proportions of 1, 2, 4, and 8; and, in a second sequence, also of 1, 3, 9, and 27 (Vlastos 1975). Each separate ball is rolled out flat and then made into a circle, with two big groups of circles angled at different points, and one group set inside the other. The two meet at a crossing in the shape of an "X." Plato is obviously thinking of the rings of this primeval "soul-stuff" as having *some* kind of material existence, since one is said to be inside the other. The way these circles work can be understood by recalling the armillary spheres that were constructed by ancient astronomers as models

207

of the universe. The outer sphere moves with the Motion of the Same, while the inner sphere, which is itself divided into seven circles, moves inside the circle of the Different.

The heavenly bodies mapped on this inner circle move in complex ways forming the paths of the sun, moon, and the planets Mercury, Venus, Saturn, Mars, and Jupiter. Earth is presumed to be and remain at the center. The planets move on the ecliptic. Their rates of movement are also hypothesized and explained according to complex geometrical formulas. The geometry of these cycles is not accurate in relation to the observed movements of the planets, even according to the knowledge available in Plato's own day. However, this work did launch further attempts to provide theoretically satisfying explanations that cohered with empirical observations.

The Demiurge does not create *in* time, since it actually creates time itself. That is, time does not exist until the Demiurge has created the heavenly bodies through which it is measured. "Time, then, came to be together with the universe so that just as they were begotten together, they might also be undone together, should there ever be an undoing of them" (38B6–7). It is only now that the Demiurge actually creates the sun, moon, and the stars that are assigned to each of the planets (treated as special "wandering" or *planetoi* stars), also placing them in their respective niches or pathways among the circles of the heaven.

In order to give as much eternity as possible to the world, the Demiurge makes it into a moving image of eternity. This means he must add more to creation after finishing the stars and planets, because too much of reality is unformed, not yet in any likeness of an eternal model. So the Demiurge now turns to the creation of living beings, human and animal souls, which require embodiment. There are four classes of living created beings: gods, birds, watery species, and pedestrian creatures.

As a perfect being, the Demiurge cannot create lower-level beings (41c2–3), since he will always impart immortality to his offspring; so he first creates lesser gods, and then instructs them to create more beings. He passes on to the lesser gods a mixture made of less pure versions of the very same elements that are mixed together to create the souls of higher beings, or heavenly bodies. In a hurried passage evoking the *Phaedrus* Socrates tells how each soul was assigned to a star and taken in a chariot to be shown higher things (41E1–3). The souls then begin the process of inhabiting or migrating into physical bodies.

This first stage of the creation of human soul and its embodiment is laid out in the part of the dialogue concerned almost entirely with the realm of reason and its purposes. Souls of humans need sensation and feelings or emotions, and accordingly, the lesser gods took the fundamental materials available and mixed them up, again following a recipe that uses complex geometrical proportions of the Same and the Different (43D2–E8). In the initial stage, all that is described is their embodiment in a human head. The head is both literally and figuratively the superior part of the body, since it emulates the perfect nature of the sphere. Also, it houses the "higher" and more refined senses: sight and hearing in particular. The head is created as a circular or spherical entity to emulate the spherical nature of the cosmos as a whole. Eyes are particularly valuable and receive the most detailed attention given to any physical or bodily part at this point of the dialogue. "Our sight has indeed proved to be a source of supreme benefit to us, in that none of our present statements about the universe could ever have been made if we had never seen any stars, sun, or heaven" (47A1–4). Sight is actually the sense that prompts us into the activity of philosophy, the best gift from gods to mortals (47A7–B2).

Timaeus now must switch to focus more on the material construction of the universe. As he puts it, he is shifting from an account of the realm governed by Reason or Intellect to that governed by, or at least activated also by, Necessity (47E3–5). For the universe to be tangible and visible, bodies were needed, especially fire. In fact, all of the four fundamental elements – earth, air, fire, and water – were necessary. Although these elements are given form by the Demiurge, Timaeus speaks of them, paradoxically, as existing in some fashion before the creation of heaven; this, strictly speaking, would mean before the start of time. He almost deliberately bumbles about in attempting to describe these elements, as Plato emphasizes the sheer difficulty or impossibility of talking about them in their pre-rationalized state as simply "powers" within the unformed Receptacle (Rowe 2003).

What is this Receptacle? In this very important addition to the metaphysics of the Theory of Forms, Timaeus says that the physical reality of the cosmos necessitates the existence of a space-like stuff, or womb, something in which the imitations of Forms can be realized (48E3–52D1). He calls this material realm the Receptacle or *chora*: a place (*topos*) and a seat (*hedra*) for everything that comes into being. It plays a role at the most primitive level of physical reality, since it must be cited to resolve the puzzle of how the four primary bodies can change into each other (in fact, Timaeus' theory does not fully resolve this problem, since earth is left out of the exchange process). Parts of Timaeus' discussion imply that the Receptacle itself is featureless, a mere "wax base" for ointments, or a material like gold that is formed into various objects. Other parts or metaphors suggest that the pre-cosmic Receptacle does have some qualities, since the four elements seem to occupy regions in it, and there is also a winnowing-basket metaphor which suggests the Receptacle is itself active or moving (52E5–53A2).

The Receptacle serves as the source of physical necessity in the realm of earthly beings. Timaeus links it to what he calls the "wandering cause." When Intellect persuades Necessity, by coordinating materials into something constructed to serve a purpose, then it is described as a "contributing cause" (*sunaitia*) (Strange 1985; Johansen 2004). A contributory cause is Necessity insofar as it has been persuaded by Intelligence to work for the good. Materials have their own natures, which dictate certain behaviors. These materials can be used to build more complex, purposive entities, in the way that wood is used to build a house, for example; but the resulting entities may be subject to forces of Necessity that work against purpose, as when a wooden house gets burned in a fire or blown away in a hurricane.

To understand the natures of materials, we need to turn to details of Plato's physical theory of the four elements, fire, air, water, and earth. He identified each of these elements with a regular solid, here apparently drawing upon geometrical achievements of his associate at the Academy, Theaetetus: fire was associated with the tetrahedron, air with the octahedron, water with the icosahedron, and earth with the cube. The construction of the "molecules" for each element involves the spatial/conceptual subdivision of each face of these solids into elementary triangles having two different natures or shapes, which he regarded as the basic units of matter. (The triangles themselves utilize or are organized around the "space" of the Receptacle.) Through rearrangement of these basic triangles, elemental transformations occur.

Water could be decomposed into fire and air when its icosahedron-shaped molecule is broken down into two octahedra and a tetrahedron. Plato's physical theory associates qualitative properties of materials in intuitive ways with their geometrical atomic shapes. For example, fire has the shape of a tetrahedron, which can cut into things (i.e., burn them), and earth that of the cube, since it is the most stable element, or moves less readily than others (Vlastos 1975).

After providing this account of the primary elements, Timaeus proceeds into a complex explanation of embodiment, offering accounts of a host of phenomena involving our human, mortal existence: pleasure and pain, sensation, eating, desire, temperance, flesh and bones, warmth, sinews and joints, breathing (respiration), nourishment, youth and health, disease and old age, inflammations, and other disorders. He adds to this a description of other mortal creatures, which exist not only since they are needed to fill out the order of creation, but also in order to serve as our food (77A–C). He sums up by telling how our body reflects the cosmos's divisions as a whole, since our top or highest part is also the best, with a divine power in the head; then comes the emotional part; and finally the nutritive/reproductive part (90A–D). These divisions, quite familiar to us from the three-fold division of the soul elsewhere in Plato, are refined here by the elaborate physical account of their association with parts of body. Furthermore, in this work, Plato has located the human soul and body within a vast cosmological theory that incorporates everything from the movements of their fundamental material elements (triangles) up to their relationship with vaster cosmic motions of the heavens.

But not everything is resolved in the *Timaeus*, nor is it always clear how to understand the claims of this work. Many questions can be raised about the metaphysics of the Receptacle. It is described by numerous metaphors, not all of which seem consistent; it is "space," which seems neutral, but it is also said to be active, full of disorderly motions (Rowe 2003; Johansen 2004). What is the exact nature of the kind of non-being Plato introduces here? Can an "empty space" manage to get past Parmenides' strictures, which would have included the void?

A further issue can be raised about whether the "molecular" geometrical theory of this dialogue successfully accounts for basic physical properties of matter. How is the geometrical structure of an element like fire related to the Forms that it would also appear to best exemplify, such as Hot and Bright? The work offers no explanation, nor can it successfully explain the interchanges of all the primitive elements, since earth, with its distinctive cubical construction, is explicitly left out (Vlastos 1975; Johansen 2004). Again, on the topic of teleology, although the dialogue includes a creation story and describes the motivation of the creator, we may ask whether Plato has really supplied an answer to Parmenides' challenging question of why a creator would act at one time rather than another. But the most fundamental question of all concerning the *Timaeus* is the status of our knowledge of the entire account, rendered questionable by its status as story, but at the same time propounded seriously as both likely and the best one we can come up with. It is, however, also possible that Plato made another stab at the project of physical theorizing in another late dialogue, the *Philebus*, which uses Eudoxus' number theory (referring to the Unlimited, Limit, and a Mixture) rather than geometrical theory to suggest an account of physical phenomena including health, music, and the seasons (*Phlb.* 24A–26A).

210

Plato accounts for the process and nature of the soul's embodiment within a context of reincarnation that allows for a possible final escape to a Nirvana-like pure, disembodied existence, when a virtuous soul is released from cycles of reincarnation and flies up to exist somehow on its original star (Robinson 1990; Mason 1994). Much as in his earlier myths, so here does a good, wise soul rise higher in subsequent lifetimes, while bad or corrupt souls fall each subsequent time into a lower animal life form, perhaps ultimately turning into snakes. This poses a problem similar to ones I have raised earlier: Does the universe offer an endless, or a finite, supply of souls? The material used for constructing souls appears finite, but if some souls escape reincarnation, then we should expect an end to living beings some day.

Integrated into the biology of the *Timaeus* is a moral/psychological story which works much like the teleological tales reviewed earlier from the *Phaedrus* and *Phaedo*. That is, the soul is at the center of cosmic creation and its journey is definitely one part of the rationale for creation. Still, I would not agree that this makes teleology and ethics the primary aim, with cosmology a mere backdrop or window-dressing. The physical theory offered here is so elaborate and carefully constructed that it seems evidence in itself of the seriousness of Plato's aim of offering a satisfactory physical theory that enlarges upon his metaphysical account of the relationship between realms of Being and Becoming.

Later Developments

The most obvious influence of the *Timaeus* is on the later Academy. Although it was not accepted as Plato's literal view by successors such as Speusippus and Xenocrates, they did emphasize its key components: the creator-god, World-Soul, and Forms. Of course, the *Timaeus* also had an impact on the thought of Aristotle, who regarded it as Plato's own view. He clearly owes much to it: his distinction between hypothetical and absolute necessity (particularly as these necessities play a role in the constitution of a human body); the role of form and matter in answering Parmenides' problem of change; the distinction between coming-to-be and alteration as fundamentally different types of change; and the circular motions of a conscious sort of god as central and prior to the other heavenly motions. Aristotle, of course, alters the cosmology in very significant ways, most notably by rejecting the creation story and thus dispensing with the Demiurge. Teleology is instead inbuilt into all natural substances, in his theory. Aristotle also roundly rejects Plato's geometrical account of the elements, but is perhaps prompted by this to develop his own "chemistry," which in turn makes possible a more elaborate biological theory (see 27: LEARNING ABOUT PLATO FROM ARISTOTLE).

Developments in astronomy were significant at the Academy after Plato's death (Goldstein and Bowen 1983). Eudoxus (390–337 BCE), who is often credited with turning astronomy into a science, was no doubt inspired by the views of both Pythagoras and Plato. A key contribution of the *Timaeus* to astronomy is its emphasis on giving orderly mathematical explanations of observed phenomena. This approach is applied not only to the analysis of physical elements but also to the heavenly movements and the composition of body parts and materials. But this influence was not always beneficial. The idea that the structure of observed heavenly bodies must live up to idealized geometrical shapes and figures would lead to a thousand years or more of astronomers supposing that the planets must follow paths meeting particular criteria, e.g., being circular rather than elliptical.

Beyond astronomy, probably the main influence of Plato's cosmology, both from the *Timaeus* and the earlier works, is the general theory of a teleologically structured cosmos which provides a moral framework for the activity and testing of human souls. The dialogue was translated into Arabic and referred to with some approval by al-Farabi, although Arab philosophers tended to associate the Demiurge with Aristotle's God as First Cause (d'Ancona 2003). Cicero's translation of it into Latin was used by Augustine, and its influence is clear in some of both men's reasoning on the existence of God and the problem of evil. This is particularly evident in Augustine's treatment of the matter, when he argues that God did not create evil, and that it is only an absence of the penetration of the goodness of God, just as darkness is an absence of light. Along with this association of divinity with goodness and the Receptacle with evil comes a set of conceptual links tying goodness and form with the male, and corruption and embodiment with the female (Dean-Jones 2000). There is an other-worldliness in much of Plato that is also quite evident here, and which has been the target of numerous attacks ranging from Derrida's critique of Plato's "Logocentrism" to feminist criticisms of Plato's misogyny (Derrida 1987; Freeland 2004).

There were literally dozens of ancient and medieval commentaries on the *Timaeus*, and it is the book held by Plato in Raphael's famous painting, *The School of Athens*. Marsilio Ficino (1433–99) also translated it into Latin and worked at some length to explore the dialogue's implications for scientific study of the physical world. Some scholars have argued that Ficino and other Platonists of the Renaissance paved the way for the Copernican revolution (Allen 2003). Kepler explicitly cited Plato, along with Pythagoras, as his true masters (Martens 2003). He described the *Timaeus* as a commentary on the first chapter of Genesis, converted into Pythagorean terms.

A crucial aspect of the *Timaeus*' teleology for subsequent western European philosophers and theologians was Plato's idea that because the creator was good, the resulting world of creation had to be in some important sense "complete." We find antecedents of a Principle of Plenitude in passages where the Demiurge tells the lower gods to create mortal creatures: "As long as they have not come to be, the universe will be incomplete, for it will still lack within it all the kinds of living things it must have if it is to be sufficiently complete" (41B7–c2). Plato's idea of the universe as a purposively constructed and beautifully arranged cosmos emerges repeatedly in later philosophers as different as the Stoics, Neoplatonists, Leibniz, Hegel, and Whitehead. This picture of the best universe as a "great chain of being" was famously explored in a book by that same title by Arthur O. Lovejoy, who wrote that "the fundamental conceptions of the *Timaeus* were to become axiomatic for most medieval and early modern philosophy" (Lovejoy 1974: 54).

Note

Translations of Plato are taken from J. M. Cooper (ed.) *Plato: Complete Works* (Indianapolis: Hackett, 1997).

References and further reading

Allen, M. J. B. (2003). The Ficinian *Timaeus* and Renaissance science. In G. J. Reydam-Schils (ed.) *Plato's* Timaeus *as Cultural Icon* (pp. 238–50). Notre Dame, Ind.: University of Notre Dame Press.

Ashbaugh, A. F. (1988). *Plato's Theory of Explanation: A Study of the Cosmological Account in the* Timaeus. Albany, NY: State University of New York Press.

Brisson, L. and Meyerstein, F. W. (1995). *Inventing the Universe: Plato's* Timaeus, *the Big Bang, and the Problem of Scientific Knowledge*. Albany, NY: State University of New York Press.

Cornford, F. M. (1975). *Plato's Cosmology*, translated with a running commentary. Indianapolis: Bobbs-Merrill (Library of Liberal Arts).

d'Ancona, C. (2003). The *Timaeus'* model for creation and providence: an example of continuity and adaptation in early Arabic philosophical literature. In G. J. Reydam-Schils (ed.) *Plato's* Timaeus *as Cultural Icon* (pp. 206–37). Notre Dame, Ind.: University of Notre Dame Press.

Dean-Jones, L. (2000). Aristotle's understanding of Plato's Receptacle and its significance for Aristotle's theory of familial resemblance. In M. R. Wright (ed.) *Reason and Necessity: Essays on Plato's* Timaeus (pp. 101–12). London: Duckworth and the Classical Press of Wales.

Derrida, J. (1987). Chora. In Poikila: *Études offertes à Jean-Pierre Vernant*. Paris: EHESS.

Finkelberg, A. (1998). On the history of the Greek KOSMOS. *Harvard Studies in Classical Philology* 98, pp. 103–36.

Freeland, C. (2004). Schemes and scenes of reading the *Timaeus*. In L. Alanen and C. Witt (eds.) *Feminist Reflections on the History of Philosophy* (The New Synthese Historical Library) (pp. 33–49). Boston: Kluwer.

Gill, M. L. (1987). Matter and flux in Plato's *Timaeus*. *Phronesis* 32, pp. 34–53.

Goldstein, B. R. and Bowen, A. C. (1983). A new view of Greek astronomy. *Isis* 74, pp. 330–40.

Johansen, T. K. (2004). *Plato's Natural Philosophy: A Study of the* Timaeus-Critias. Cambridge: Cambridge University Press.

Lovejoy, A. O. (1974) [1936]. *The Great Chain of Being: A Study of the History of an Idea*. Cambridge, Mass.: Harvard University Press.

Martens, R. (2003). A commentary on Genesis: Plato's *Timaeus* and Kepler's astronomy. In G. J. Reydam-Schils (ed.) *Plato's* Timaeus *as Cultural Icon* (pp. 251–66). Notre Dame, Ind.: University of Notre Dame Press.

Mason, A. S. (1994). Immortality in the *Timaeus*. *Phronesis* 39, pp. 90–7.

Mohr, R. (1985). *The Platonic Cosmology*. Leiden: Brill.

Morgan, K. A. (1998). Designer history: Plato's Atlantis story and fourth-century ideology. *Journal of Hellenic Studies* 118, pp. 101–19.

Robinson, J. V. (1990). The tripartite soul in the *Timaeus*. *Phronesis* 35, pp. 103–10.

Rowe, C. (2003). The status of the "myth" in Plato's *Timaeus*. In C. Natali and S. Maso (eds.) *Plato Physicus: Cosmologia e antropologia nel Timeo* (pp. 21–31). Amsterdam: Adolf Hakkert.

Sayre, K. (2003). The multilayered incoherence of *Timaeus'* Receptacle. In G. J. Reydam-Schils (ed.) *Plato's* Timaeus *as Cultural Icon* (pp. 60–79). Notre Dame, Ind.: University of Notre Dame Press.

Strange, S. K. (1985). The double explanation in the *Timaeus*. *Ancient Philosophy* 5, pp. 25–39.

Taylor, A. E. (1928). *A Commentary on Plato's* Timaeus. Oxford: Oxford University Press.

Vlastos, G. (1975). *Plato's Universe*. Seattle: University of Washington Press.

Wright, M. R. (2000). Myth, science and reason in the *Timaeus*. In M. R. Wright (ed.) *Reason and Necessity: Essays on Plato's* Timaeus (pp. 1–22). London: Duckworth and the Classical Press of Wales.

213

15

Plato on Language

DAVID SEDLEY

Language as the Medium of Thought

According to the principles of Plato's teleology as applied in his *Timaeus*, to understand the function of something you must start from the highest good that it helps bring about. Eyesight, for example, exists ultimately in order to enable us to study astronomy, a god-given route to philosophical understanding (*Ti.* 46E6–47c4). What, from this same point of view, is the function of language? The human mouth, we are told, has been created for two purposes, influx and efflux. The influx in question is one of mere necessities, namely food and drink, but the efflux, that of speech, is characterized as the "finest and best of all streams" (75E4–5). Why so? As the speaker Timaeus has explained earlier (47c4–7), both voice and hearing were created in us as principal means to philosophy, above all by the use of speech. He is undoubtedly referring to Plato's main philosophical method, dialectic, the systematic use of question and answer to eliminate falsehoods and arrive eventually at truths. Plato's worldview thus places an altogether pivotal importance on the gift of spoken language: as the basis of dialectic, it is a privileged means to philosophy, and thereby to the soul's salvation.

Dialectic familiarly features in Plato's dialogues as an interpersonal activity, usually between a principal interrogator and a more or less compliant respondent. But Plato sometimes refers to internal, unvoiced question and answer conducted by a single individual, Socrates (e.g., *Ap.* 21B2–7; *Chrm.* 166c7–D6), and in his later work he develops the idea that this process, which closely replicates the sequence of vocalized, interpersonal dialectic, is the structure of thought itself (*Tht.* 189E4–190A7; *Sph.* 263E3–264B5; *Phlb.* 38c2–E8). When we think, what we are doing is asking ourselves questions and answering them. Whatever answers we articulate to ourselves as silent internal statements are our beliefs. Nor is this a merely contingent feature of human psychology, for even god thinks in the same way: the divine world soul's unfailingly true beliefs about our world and its knowledge of eternal being take the form of silent "statements" (*logoi*) which it utters internally to itself (*Ti.* 37B3–c3). *What* language the World-Soul thinks in is not a question that Plato addresses.

We can thus begin to glimpse how fundamental language is to Plato's philosophy. Rather than being, for example, a convenient code in which to encapsulate and convey our thoughts to each other, it is the very stuff of those thoughts. This means, among other things, that the later philosophical problem of other minds' inaccessibility to us does not arise for Plato. If other people's thoughts are their internal utterances, these are fully open to inspection by us through external question and answer, and indeed Plato's dialogues depict a series of interrogators conducting just such inspections of their interlocutors' thoughts.

But what about thought at the very highest level? Doesn't this at least transcend language in Plato's eyes? So it has sometimes been held, but the hard evidence does not favor the idea. In the *Republic* the highest object of intellectual endeavor is the Form of the Good (see 24: PLATO'S CONCEPT OF GOODNESS). Yet even this ultimate object is understood only by those who can define it discursively and go on to defend their definition against all refutations that are forthcoming (534B3–D2). Thus even when Plato's speaker metaphorically describes a leap of understanding which sounds like direct intuition of truth, without reference to any mediation by discursive thought (e.g., *R.* 518B7–519A6, 532B6–D1; *Smp.* 210A4–212A7), it is safer to take this not as replacing or transcending the linguistic mode of thought, but as elucidating the kind of intellectual transformation this mode can itself achieve.

On the other hand, Plato certainly never meant to suggest that when you think you are *merely* uttering internal sentences. For example, as he puts it in the *Philebus* (38E9–39C6), if the sentences you utter to yourself are envisaged as the work of an internal scribe, then that scribe's writings are themselves accompanied by the work of an internal painter. That is, what you describe to yourself in words you also imagine. However, for the purposes of the present topic it must be on thought's linguistic core that we concentrate.

What are we doing when we think in sentences? Grammar was not a developed science in Plato's day, or indeed for two or more generations after. Nevertheless, Plato had a view on the rudiments of sentence structure, and his analysis was influential enough to become a basis for later grammatical theory. Throughout his writings (see *Ap.* 17B9–c2; *Smp.* 198B4–5, 199B4–5, 221D7–E4; *Cra.* 425A1–5, 431B3–c2; *R.* 601A5–6; *Tht.* 206c7–D5; *Sph.* 261E4–262D7), Plato treats complete linguistic discourse as compounded out of two main items: names (*onomata*) and descriptions (*rhēmata*). He also (*Cra.* 439D8–11) characterizes successful speech about anything by saying that first you must say that it is "that" (*ekeino*), then go on to say that it is "of such and such a kind" (*toiouto*). The essential point of such analyses either was or eventually became the following: to utter a complete statement (*logos*), you must first *name* your subject, then go on to *describe* it. This is formally set out in Plato's late dialogue the *Sophist*, and illustrated there with the specimen minimal statement "Man learns," prior to which Plato's speaker the Stranger from Elea has pointed out that stringing together a mere series of "descriptions," such as "Walks runs sleeps," or of "names," such as "Lion stag horse," is not yet to construct a statement (262A9–c7).

In these comments Plato is not far from the idea that a word is classifiable by its function within the sentence as a whole, a move in the general direction of grammatical analysis. Moreover, his terms here for "name" and "description" became in later usage (starting already with Aristotle in fact) semi-technical terms for, respectively, "noun" and "verb."

What is less clear, on the other hand, is that Plato's distinction between "names" and "descriptions" is meant to apply to single words only, and not to whole phrases too. Indeed, on the view (found at any rate in the *Cratylus* at 431B3−c2) that statements consist of *nothing but* names and descriptions, it is hard to avoid the latter extension beyond single words. That is no doubt one of the reasons why there has been a tendency among scholars to associate the two terms less with nouns and verbs than with *subjects and predicates*: to make a complete sentence, you must first identify a subject, then attach a predicate to it. On this view, Plato's foray is less into grammar than into the rudiments of logic. And one point that might tend to confirm the diagnosis is that he nowhere singles out anything that looks like a further grammatical category. In fact the one other type of word in which he shows an interest in this same context is the negation sign "not" (*Sph.* 257B1–258c6). Hardly surprisingly in a dialogue like the *Sophist*, whose central focus is the analysis of falsity, his interest is in the underlying logical structure of assertoric sentences.

So much for complete statements. Since truth and falsity are properties of these, we might expect Plato's linguistic interests to concentrate on them above all else. In reality, however, single words are much more frequently his focus. One reason is no doubt that from his earliest works Plato had depicted his main speaker, usually Socrates, in pursuit of definitions, always of single terms. The necessary preliminary to a philosophical inquiry about justice, temperance, or beauty is to find out precisely what it is that the word itself designates (see 6: PLATONIC DEFINITIONS AND FORMS).

Why so? Doesn't a preliminary procedure of this kind imply, questionably, that the name of the current definiendum is already, in existing Greek usage, so firmly tied to a single properly demarcated concept or entity that asking what the word signifies is a proper route to the discovery of that concept or entity itself? And that in turn raises further questions: How did the word enter our vocabulary in the first place, and on what authority was it attached to the concept it now names?

The *Cratylus*

Plato actually has fairly developed views on these questions, much more so than is generally recognized. One entire dialogue, the *Cratylus*, is devoted to the decoding of individual words, with a good deal of speculation about the mindset and assumptions that led these words' original inventors to construct and assign them as they did. There is enough similar speculation in other dialogues (as also in the works of Plato's foremost pupil Aristotle) to discount as improbable the almost universal modern assumption (not shared by readers in antiquity) that Plato is not serious in these etymological decodings, and that the *Cratylus* can be safely marginalized, at least so far as this kind of linguistic exegesis is concerned.

Plato's main views are as follows. (Much of what follows is based on my fuller exposition in Sedley 2003.) Whether words were first introduced by early members of the human race (the more favored view in the *Cratylus*), by a divine source (see, e.g., *Ti.* 73c6–D2), or by a mixture of the two, they were attempts to encapsulate the natures of the items they named. Their construction involved subtle compression of a whole message into just a few syllables, and the resultant difficulty of decoding them has been further complicated by misleading sound-shifts and other distortions during subsequent ages. Nevertheless, with sufficient expertise they can be decoded. With the help of such a technique, we can aspire to recover real insights by uncovering the hidden meanings of words.

All this reflects the fact that etymology was a flourishing activity in the time of Socrates and Plato, one in which many intellectuals professed expertise. Plato himself, even outside the *Cratylus*, twice manifests an interest in the etymology of *eudaimonia*, "happiness." Clearly the word comes from *eu*, "well," plus *daimōn*, a term for a lesser or intermediary divinity. Those who coined this word, then, were evidently privy to two Platonic insights: that personal happiness lies in having your resident divinity – the immortal rational faculty housed in your head – well ordered (*Ti.* 90B6–c6); and that political happiness depends on a political constitution in which laws take on the role of daimons, by acting as mediators of divine intelligence (*Lg.* 713D5–E3).

This double explanation of *eudaimonia* need not be viewed as embodying alternative and competing etymologies, because according to the *Cratylus* the best-constructed words achieve their impact precisely by combining a whole set of complementary messages. The word "sun" (*hēlios*) conflates no fewer than three distinct meanings (409A1–6): it is that which, by its rising, "assembles" (*halizein*) people, which "always rolls" (*aei eilein iōn*) around the earth, and which by its motion "variegates" (*aiollein*) the things that grow from the earth. Even when they lack this artful complexity, many of Plato's etymologies are liable to look implausible to readers informed by modern linguistic science. For instance, "man," *anthrōpos*, was according to Plato so named as being the creature that uniquely "reviews – i.e., reflects upon – what he has seen" (*anathrōn ha opōpe*: 399c1–6). But even examples like this are fully in keeping with ancient etymological practice, and there is no good reason to think Plato less than serious about them, as decodings of existing Greek words.

That is not of course to say that Plato is prepared to rely on the authority of the name-givers. He makes it clear, in fact, that although many of their coinages show real insight, especially about the nature of divinity, they are definitely not to be trusted with regard to the main Greek ethical vocabulary. The existing Greek nomenclature for this reveals systematic misunderstandings on the part of the name-givers, implicitly attributable to their reluctance to recognize the existence of *stable* values. It would, Socrates concludes, be a mistake to seek knowledge through this kind of etymological study, precisely because the opinions of the original name-makers, even though with sufficient skill they can be recovered, cannot necessarily be relied on. We should therefore study the things themselves directly, not via their names (*Cra.* 438D2–439B9). Importantly, this conclusion does *not* mean that philosophy should dispense with the use of language, just that it should not rely on the decoding of individual names as a guide to truth.

In the course of arriving at the above conclusion, Plato's Socrates reveals a good deal about how he believes language to work. A name (*onoma*, here Plato's nearest equivalent to "word," but almost exclusively illustrated with nouns and adjectives) is a tool with a double communicative function (388B13–c1): to provide "instruction," and to "separate being." The "instruction" in question might have been imagined as merely the mundane imparting of information, but that is not, at any rate, how Plato presents it. Rather, in keeping with the teleological principles with which I opened this chapter, he locates the function of a name in whatever is the highest good it aspires to bring about, and that good he implicitly identifies as the teaching of philosophical truths (hence, for example, at 390c–D the proper user of names is identified not as the ordinary language-speaker but as the dialectician). Even if few names actually achieve this elevated goal, it is nonetheless the ultimate purpose by reference to which any name's degree of success is best measured. We can therefore say that, in Plato's eyes, when names were devised as encapsulations of things' natures, the aim was all along to convey those things' essences. If, while falling short of this goal, names also serve handy labeling functions in daily discourse, that is not in the last analysis what they are for. Language, as we saw confirmed by the *Timaeus* at the outset, is ultimately for philosophy. Nevertheless, it is in keeping with the spirit of Plato's metaphysics for us to think of names' familiar use in mundane truth-attaining acts of communication as an approximation to this ideal, and therefore as best understood in terms of it.

As for a name's second and closely related function, "separating being," this too is in the last analysis philosophical in nature. A name separates "being" by so describing its object as to mark this off from all other things – that is, by distinguishing what the thing named *is*. But the notion of "being" (*ousia*) itself has a considerable semantic range in Plato. Marking off a thing's being may vary from merely indicating *what it is* that you are talking about all the way up to encapsulating the thing's *essence* in a definition. Hence the ideal function of a name as "separating being" is paradigmatically represented by the very top end of a certain spectrum, but all the way down that same spectrum names fulfill their function by means of a greater or lesser degree of approximation to the same ideal.

According to the *Cratylus* theory, any unified string of sound that (a) has been assigned to a thing and (b) descriptively picks that thing out qualifies as its name. There can therefore be two or more names for one and the same thing – as indeed, at least across languages, there undeniably are. What makes these all qualify as its names? Plato's first answer will be that they all participate in one and the same Form. This is, importantly, not the Form of the thing named, but the Form of its name. Some further explanation is called for here.

Any manufactured object with (let us say) a horizontal surface on which things can be placed above floor level is a table, regardless of what wood or other materials have been used and precisely how they are arranged. All such objects are linked by their shared participation in the Form of Table – in the *ideal function* of a table, as we might put it. Indeed, there is not just a single generic Form of Table, but no doubt a specific Form of Dining Table, another of Operating Table, and so on. (Plato makes this point about generic and specific artifact Forms only with regard to the Forms of Shuttle and Drill, at *Cra.* 389B–D, but the same must in principle apply to all artifact types, including Couch and Table, two artifact Forms introduced in a famous passage of *Republic*, X.596A10–597D2.)

What then if the manufacturer's aim is to make not an actual table, but a *name* for it? Plato assumes that names are themselves artifacts, and that whoever invents them and succeeds in bringing them into circulation is practicing a specific expertise, that of name-making. The same metaphysics as applies to the carpenter applies also, *mutatis mutandis*, to this name-making craftsman. Like the Form of Table, there is also a Form of Name, a Form to which the name-maker possesses specialized cognitive access. This Form finds its material embodiment, if at all, not in pieces of wood and the like, but in the material appropriate to names, which is in fact vocal sound. Each language uses a different sound system, just as carpenters may vary in the wood that they use.

Nevertheless, just as it is a minimum condition for a product's being a table that it to some extent fulfills the function that the Form of Table encapsulates, so too it is a minimum condition for a name's being a name that it to some extent fulfills the function that the Form of Name encapsulates. And that function is, as already noted, the double function of providing instruction and separating being. However, just as the generic Form of Table is analyzable into its various species, so too the generic Form of Name is analyzable into a huge number of these: the Form of the Name of Man, the Form of the Name of Horse, and so on, it seems, for every word in the lexicon (*Cra.* 389D4–390D8).

Ontologically extravagant as this proliferation of Forms may sound, we can make sense of it by observing that, just as all the world's tables are so characterized because they participate in a single Form, that of Table, so too all the world's words for table ("table," "Tisch," "tavolo," etc.) participate in a single Form. There is a single function they all discharge, namely to instruct us about Table by separating its being – telling us what it *is*. And it is not enough for the name-manufacturers to set about this act of naming by asking themselves what the generic function of a name is; the further pertinent question for them is, what specific kind of being is to be communicated by the name of *man*, the name of *horse*, etc.?

We have already seen that the Greek manufacturers of names chose a particular way of capturing the being of man: the one creature endowed with both eyesight and reason was given a name that encrypts "one who reflects on what he sees." Although Plato does not discuss foreign languages in any detail, he makes it clear that an item's being could be successfully captured by a name in more than one way, and it is entirely possible therefore that other languages' names for "man" might, in addition to using different sound systems as their vocal material, use those sound systems to indicate not rationality but upright posture, political capacities, or some other equally distinctive feature of the species. In Plato's terminology (394c1–9), all of these names would, in that case, have the same "power" (*dunamis*), and both "indicate" (*dēloun*) and "signify" (*sēmainein*) the same thing. All these locutions are his variant ways of conveying participation in the same specific Name-Form.

As for the means by which these and all other names succeed in signifying their objects, Plato has much to tell us. Names are vocal portraits, and achieve their power of signification primarily by means of a portrait-like resemblance to their objects. If we try analyzing a name downwards into its components, we find initially that this vocal portraiture operates by linguistic description, as not only in the preceding examples of *anthrōpos* ("man") and *eudaimonia* ("happiness"), but in innumerable others that Plato examines in the course of the dialogue. The name-makers' genius lay in compressing each description into a brief and catchy group of syllables, capable of achieving currency among users of the language. If we take the component words out of which the description is built, we find that each of *them* is likewise a compressed or otherwise encoded description. Thus for instance the *daimon* component of *eudaimonia* was chosen as meaning "knowing one," *daēmōn* (*Cra.* 398B5–c4). The analogue of this in visual portraiture will lie in analyzing a complex portrait into its component parts (hands, hat, eyes, etc.), and each of these into its own components (fingers, thumb, etc.; brim, crown, etc.; pupil, iris, etc.). But eventually, in the case of portraiture, the analysis will reach the level of the individual patches of color out of which the simplest parts are composed. And likewise in name analysis we will eventually reach the

219

DAVID SEDLEY

individual sounds out of which the simplest semantic units are composed. These, analogously to colors in a painting, will manifest a more direct kind of resemblance than
the semantic one that compressed descriptions have. As the colors are direct imitations
of the objects' primary visual qualities, so too the primary sounds in a language are vocal
imitations of primary properties like fluidity, stability, hardness, largeness, etc. Both in
painting and in language, imitation is maintained all the way down, but the nature of
the imitation changes at the lowest level to one of primitive, unmediated likeness.

A name, like a portrait, is a deliberate likeness. Whereas a portrait is a visible likeness aimed at capturing its object's visual properties, a name is an auditory likeness
aimed at capturing its object's *being*, i.e., at marking off what its object *is*. In both
cases, Plato is ready to allow that the resemblance will frequently be imperfect, but is
equally confident that the imitation remains an imitation of that particular object,
regardless of whether it is a complete and accurate likeness or a partial and even
misleading one. The minimum criteria for a sequence of sounds being something's
name seem to be: (a) that the name has been deliberately assigned to that specific
object by its creator (the verb for "assign," *tithesthai*, plays a vital role in the *Cratylus*
theory), and (b) that it possesses, if not a completely accurate likeness to the object to
which it has been assigned, at least a significant degree of resemblance. It is easy
enough to see how the portraiture model has led Plato to this view. If your passport
photograph, for example, is to be acknowledged as *your* picture, (a) it has to have been
created as a picture of *you*, and not merely picked out subsequently on the grounds of
resemblance; and (b) it may misrepresent your appearance in all kinds of ways –
perhaps it is monochrome, perhaps you have aged since it was taken, perhaps it exag-
gerates the size of your nose, and at all events unlike you it is only two-dimensional
– but there must be *some* salient resemblance that enables it to be recognized as
designating you in particular.

This resemblance thesis first enters the *Cratylus* discussion as the naturalist thesis –
there taken to fanatical lengths by one interlocutor, Plato's former teacher Cratylus –
that each thing's name belongs to it "by nature" (*phusei*). In Cratylus' eyes, this means
that the name must be a perfectly accurate encapsulation of the thing's nature or else
fail to be its name at all. At the start of the dialogue the other interlocutor, Hermogenes,
maintains on the contrary the commonsense view that nothing more than arbitrary
convention determines what name belongs to what thing; we could just as well have
called a man "horse" and a horse "man" (385A6–B1), if local convention so dictated.
Plato's spokesman Socrates opposes Hermogenes, arguing (partly for reasons expounded
above) that names are tools with a specific instructive function and therefore require
expert manufacture. However well or badly the name *anthrōpos*, "man," may turn out
to capture the distinctive being of the human race, once we understand what the
name-makers were trying to convey about human rationality by their choice of this
word we can no longer entertain Hermogenes' fancy that this same string of sounds
could equally appropriately have been assigned to a non-rational creature like the horse.

Right to the end of the dialogue, Socrates continues to resist Hermogenes' version of
linguistic conventionalism (especially 433E2–434A3). This is one reason for discount-
ing the statement in the Platonic *Seventh Letter*, 343B1–2, that "nothing prevents the
things that are now called 'round' being called 'straight' and vice versa," which seems
to be based on an easy misreading of the *Cratylus* as vindicating Hermogenes' original

position. The authenticity of this letter has often been doubted, on good grounds, which is why in the present chapter I shall be making no use of its often puzzling remarks about language. The *Cratylus* is in any case a far better guide.

By the end of the *Cratylus*, all that Socrates has conceded to Hermogenes is that, in view of the varying approximateness with which names may depict their objects, there is room for *some element* of convention to help in securing meaning. Readers of the *Cratylus* have frequently overestimated the scope of this concession. In only two specific cases is convention permitted a role. One is words that turn out to have an equal number of appropriately and inappropriately descriptive sounds: the chosen example (434B10–435B3) is *sklērotēs*, "hardness," which contains both one sound conveying hardness (K) and one conveying softness (L) – the remaining sounds being considered simply irrelevant for the purposes of the discussion. Here, Socrates concedes, nothing but convention can break the deadlock: just, one might say, as in cases where your portrait looks like you and unlike you in equal degrees, we might have to resolve our uncertainty by asking whether it is or is not, by virtue of its original assignment, *your* portrait, so too the signification of *sklērotēs* can be fixed and explained only by finding out which of the available items its manufacturer assigned it to. That this or any word might consist of predominantly inappropriate sounds, and therefore acquire its signification *purely* by convention – simply, that is, by having been assigned to the item in question – is a possibility never once conceded by Socrates.

The second case in which convention is granted a foothold is the names of numbers (435B3–c2). Here Socrates makes it clear convention is needed, not to replace resemblance, but precisely in order to allow resemblance to do its work. It is not too hard to see why. The number system is a remarkably good advertisement for the power of names to signify by description. From a limited stock of component names (one, two, three . . . , -teen, -ty . . . , hundred, etc.) an infinite number of further names can be constructed, every one of them descriptively individuating its object by analyzing it into its components. That those components themselves acquire their own significance by imitating their objects in some more direct way is neither affirmed nor denied by Socrates, but on his usual principles it is at least possible that they do. Where, then, does convention *unavoidably* enter the picture, as Socrates says it must? He apparently means that the names of larger numbers cannot, like the primary ones, *directly* imitate their objects, if for example the name for 1,000 might have to contain 1,000 sounds, and that it is the very fact that there are infinitely many numbers that guarantees that, along with the descriptive backbone of the number system, some set of *rules* must be in place to ensure the systematic mapping of names on to their objects. The nature of this minor concession confirms, rather than undermines, Plato's commitment to resemblance as the main basis of all signification, and the dominance in his semantic thinking of the portraiture model of word meaning.

Language and Dialectic

Plato then has at least the rudiments of a semantic theory: specifically, he has a developed theory as to how language achieves its power to signify things. What are its implications for the philosophical dialectic to which most of his dialogues are devoted?

221

We have already met one negative conclusion: words do not imitate their objects with a sufficient degree of reliability to provide a source of knowledge through the study of their etymology. But what about the nature of definitional inquiry itself? I return to my earlier question: How can a dialectician be confident that the word currently up for definition is already, in existing Greek usage, so firmly tied to a single properly demarcated concept that defining the word will lead to an understanding of the concept? (See 7: PLATO'S METHOD OF DIALECTIC.) Or, alternatively and more accurately, we may prefer to think of the *thing*, rather than the word, as what we are trying to define, comparing for example Plato's careful formulation at *Chrm.* 175B2–4 regarding his search for a definition of "moderation" (*sōphrosunē*):

> But as it is, we are defeated on all sides, and are unable to find what on earth the thing was to which the lawmaker [as Plato both here and in the *Cratylus* calls the original name-maker] assigned (*tithesthai*) this name, "moderation".

Even if we make this modification, however, the question remains: How can our discussion secure an intellectual focus on the thing if its name is our indispensable tool for doing so? For Plato, let us recall, considers thought itself to be linguistic in structure and content.

The first point to emphasize in answering this question is that Plato is *not* committed to the view that current conventional usage of the words at issue correctly captures either their meaning or their extension. For example "just," the definiendum of the *Republic*, is a term popularly applied to the enterprise of harming one's enemies, yet Socrates purports to show that harming could never in any circumstances be just (335B2–E1). Indeed, by the time Socrates has finished with it, this word turns out to have a very different meaning from that which conventional usage gives it (*Republic* IV), and to connote a kind of harmonious relation between the three parts either of a city or of a single soul. This outcome may lead one to wonder how Socrates can be confident that what he has picked out with his definition is the very same item that he was seeking when he started out on his quest for the definition of justice. That question is, indeed, a version of Meno's paradox (*Men.* 80D5–E5): if you don't already know the thing you are seeking, how will you recognize it when you find it? In the *Meno*, Socrates answers with the theory that you did in fact know it all along, namely through knowledge which your soul actively possessed before birth, subsequently forgot, and can aspire to recover or "recollect" in the course of learning (see 9: PLATO ON RECOLLECTION). However, it is worth pointing out that Plato's semantic theory was potentially the basis of an alternative or complementary answer. Words, like portraits, get their hold on the corresponding things by (a) being assigned to them in the first place, and (b) mimicking their properties to a significant extent. Neither condition requires that the word should be a completely accurate depiction of the object in order to acquire and retain its reference to it, and we are therefore not obliged to assume that either the original name-givers or those of us who use the word successfully have the full understanding of its object that would enable us to demarcate it with complete accuracy. The word's reference to its object is nevertheless secure, and can in principle lead us to its definition, much as an imperfect photograph of you might well be enough to lead a detective to your identification.

222

The question remains why the range of terms, such as "just," "brave," "moderate," "beautiful," and "good," found in an existing natural language like Greek, should provide even a preliminary sketch-map of the relevant terrain, as Plato's investigative practice regularly assumes it does. How do we know that ordinary language in any way at all maps reality? Alternatively, why should we assume that our well-placed confidence that, for example, the names of numbers map one-for-one onto the actual numbers is replicated when it comes to the much more controversial names of virtues? Plato's optimistic response to such questions will, it seems, be best served by the widely favored interpretation of his Theory of Recollection, according to which we all possess prenatally acquired knowledge of the Forms – not only of the Forms of numbers and the like, but also those of the virtues and related value-concepts – which we forgot at birth but are to some extent drawing on and recovering more or less throughout our incarnate lives, every time we impose on the world we perceive such concepts as large, small, equal, good, and just (see in particular *Phd.* 75B4–9). On this admittedly disputed reading not only are we born with a map of reality already buried in our souls, but our acquisition of a vocabulary is itself the beginning of that map's rediscovery. When, in his late works, Plato sets about the task of systematically charting certain sections of this same map by progressive division and subdivision of reality "at the natural joints" (*Phdr.* 265E1–3), he can be seen as taking much of his impetus from the Greek vocabulary, even if he finds it necessary in the interests of accuracy to expand and refine the available terminology.

Indeed, the foundational thesis of the *Cratylus*, that a name is a tool for separating being, attributes just such a function to words, however imperfectly Plato may consider existing languages to do the job. And the further thesis of the same dialogue that there are, quite independently of local culture and belief, objective Name-Forms which each language seeks to embody in sound both reflects and confirms Plato's conviction that our languages, far from representing our own probably misguided attempts to divide up reality, have an objectively determined structure which from the start is isomorphic with the structure of reality.

Synonymy and Equivocation

One obvious objection to this conviction lies in the evidence of the Greek language, whose vocabulary may seem to manifest too little one-to-one correspondence with things to make the divisions within the language a plausible guide to the divisions of reality itself. What about the numerous cases, said to have already been invoked by Democritus as proof of the arbitrary correlation of language to reality (B26 DK), where one thing has two or more names, or where two things share the same name?

The former case, that of alleged synonyms, seems not of great concern to Plato. He regularly presents it as the trademark interest of the sophist Prodicus, a professed specialist in "correctness of names." In Plato's dialogues, Prodicus can always be appealed to for a fine semantic distinction between two alleged synonyms. But the fact that this task is regularly delegated to a virtual lexicographer like Prodicus is itself a sign of its marginality in Plato's eyes.

For one thing, if two words really are synonymous, co-referential, or simply inter-changeable in a given context, the linguistic map of reality seems to suffer no great harm. No map is compromised if a place on it turns out to have two or more co-referential names, even if these names (e.g., "Holland" and "The Netherlands") are far from identical in sense. This may be sufficient justification of the palpable fact that Plato in his own writings makes little effort to retain a single term for any of his most cherished concepts, such as "Forms," "knowledge," and "wisdom," for each of which he regularly varies his nomenclature.

For another thing, the fine variations of meaning on whose detection Prodicus prides himself often mask the essential unity of the underlying concept. In the *Protagoras*, for example, Socrates defends, at least hypothetically, the thesis that all values are measurable on the scale of pleasure and pain; and here the likelihood that Prodicus will insist on semantic distinctions between "pleasant," "delightful," and "enjoyable" is brushed aside as irrelevant, with Prodicus' own amused agreement (358A5–B3). In the terminology of the *Cratylus*, Plato's view is probably that, even if not synonyms, these words all participate in the same specific Name-Form, and hence have the same "power": that is, there is a single item which they all, in their own respective ways, succeed in designating.

Where one would have expected Plato to show more concern is the converse case: a single word with two or more meanings. Aristotle, who was Plato's student for two decades, repeatedly in his works – including treatises widely held to have been written during that early period – shows himself sensitive to the multiple meanings of words, and to the need to distinguish between them in the interests of avoiding error (see 27: LEARNING ABOUT PLATO FROM ARISTOTLE). It is hard to imagine that this topic of the multivocality of words was never raised by the young Aristotle in class discussions at the Academy. Yet when we look in Plato's dialogues for any echoes of such conversations between the two of them, they prove extremely hard to detect. This is, I think, no accident. Plato has sometimes been thought deaf to equivocation, but it is fairer to say that he is ideologically opposed to it. (There are helpful discussions of this issue in Robinson 1969 and Blackson 1991.)

As mentioned above, Plato thinks of reality as divisible at its natural joints. Whatever bit of this reality you are analyzing, it will turn out to fit somewhere into a tree of genera, species, and subspecies. Any two coordinate species of a given genus, for example two kinds of madness, or two kinds of expertise, will be formally differentiated from each other by their definitions, and charting such interrelations is the very stuff of philosophical dialectic. But the fact that expertise, for example, is divisible into these and other species in no way makes the word "expertise" itself ambiguous, any more than the fact that there are different species of animal makes "animal" ambiguous.

This way of reclassifying apparent ambiguities is naturally favored by Plato's metaphysical leanings. In his early dialogues Socrates' requests for definitions regularly (e.g., *Euthphr.* 6D–E) ask for the *single* form common to all things that share the same name. And on this same basis, at *R.* 596A he enunciates the more overtly metaphysical one-over-many principle: any set of things that share a name falls under a single Form. This approach already seems to commit him to the univocality thesis: each name picks out a single reality at all its occurrences, even if that reality is a genus which contains specific differentiations.

Although Plato has plentiful opportunities to discriminate between two or more meanings of the same word, he systematically fails to do so. He may seem to come close to doing so near the beginning of the *Sophist*, where his main speaker, the stranger from Elea, says to his young interlocutor Theaetetus about their joint search for a definition of "sophist" (218c1–5):

> At present in this regard you and I have as common property only the name. As for the thing to which we each apply it, it may be that we each have that as a private possession. On every matter, it is the thing itself that ought to be agreed on, by means of discussion, rather than just the name, without discussion.

In this important methodological manifesto, Plato does arguably imply that different speakers may on occasion understand different things by the same word, but he stops far short of suggesting that the definiendum may turn out to carry two or more distinct lexical meanings. His main point is, rather, the need not just to share with each other a common language, but also, by the use of dialectic, to achieve a common understanding of the objects it designates.

On only one occasion in his entire corpus is it explicitly suggested that the solution to a problem might lie in disambiguating a word. This is in the *Euthydemus*, where young Clinias has been confronted by the sophists Euthydemus and Dionysodorus with a sophism based on the double meaning of *manthanein*: "learn," but also sometimes "understand." Socrates' advice to the boy includes the following (277E3–278A7):

> First, as Prodicus says, one must learn about correctness of names. These two visitors are showing you that you did not realize that people use the word "learning" (*manthanein*) for when someone starts out with no knowledge about something and then acquires it, but also call it by this same name when someone already has knowledge and uses it to consider this same object of action or speech. People call it "understanding" (*sunienai*) rather than "learning," but they do sometimes call it learning too. This, as they are showing you, is something that you didn't realise: that the same name is used for people in opposite conditions, the person who knows and the person who does not.

The uniqueness of this passage in the corpus should make us sit up and take note. In for once disambiguating a word, Socrates is doing something that falls right outside his characteristic methodology, and as if to emphasize that very alienness he effectively disowns the approach by attributing it to the peripheral figure Prodicus. Such verbal niceties are appropriately cited here only because the sophism that provoked the response is itself no more than a word game – as Socrates in fact goes on to make explicit (278B2–c5). In Plato's serious philosophical discourses the method of disambiguation never recurs. In saying this, I include even the *Sophist*, where attempts – unsuccessful in my view – have sometimes been made to find Plato distinguishing different senses of the verb "be" (valuable discussions in Bostock 1984; Brown 1986 and 1994). The assumption that Plato is, in this or that dialogue, seeking to draw our attention to some equivocation is a common source of misinterpretations.

One occasional Platonic strategy for responding to apparent equivocations is to insist that, of a pair of coexistent usages of a word, only one corresponds to its real meaning, the other being a misuse (*Smp.* 205B4–D9, *Lg.* 722D6–E4). But his more fundamental

225

approach, and the one which constitutes his reason for avoiding disambiguation wherever possible, lies, I suggest, in an assumption on his part that apparent cases of multiple meaning will on closer inspection turn out to reflect branching divisions within a genus-species tree: the two or more items that share a name are members of a single genus, and share their name generically, in the way that "mammal" is used of both cats and mice without thereby being ambiguous. Although Plato never actually argues for this genus-species mode of analysis as preferable to one in terms of simple equivocation, he is no doubt predisposed to it by the outlook we have already considered: that the structure of our language, however imperfectly, already mirrors the structure of reality.

Note

All translations are the author's.

References and further reading

Ackrill, J. L. (1997). Language and reality in Plato's *Cratylus*. In *Essays on Plato and Aristotle* (pp. 33–52). Oxford: Oxford University Press.

Barney, R. (2001). *Names and Nature in Plato's* Cratylus. New York and London: Routledge.

Baxter, T. M. S. (1992). *The* Cratylus: *Plato's Critique of Naming*. Leiden: Brill.

Blackson, T. A. (1991). Plato and the senses of words. *Journal of the History of Philosophy* 29, pp. 169–82.

Bostock, D. (1984). Plato on "is not." In *Oxford Studies in Ancient Philosophy*, vol. 2 (pp. 89–120). Oxford: Oxford University Press.

—— (1994). Plato on understanding language. In S. Everson (ed.) *Language* (pp. 10–27). Cambridge: Cambridge University Press.

Brown, L. (1986). Being in the *Sophist*: a syntactical enquiry. In *Oxford Studies in Ancient Philosophy*, vol. 4 (pp. 49–70). Oxford: Oxford University Press.

—— (1994). The verb "to be" in Greek philosophy: some remarks. In S. Everson (ed.) *Language* (pp. 212–36). Cambridge: Cambridge University Press.

Dalimier, C. (1998). *Platon,* Cratyle. Paris: Flammarion.

Denyer, N. (1991). *Language, Thought and Falsehood in Ancient Greek Philosophy*. London: Routledge.

Derbolav, J. (1972). *Platons Sprachphilosophie im* Kratylos *und in den späteren Schriften*. Darmstadt: Wissenschaftliche Buchgesellschaft.

Diels, H. and Kranz, W. (DK) (1985) *Die Fragmente der Vorsokratiker*. Zurich: Weidmann.

Fine, G. (1977). Plato on naming. *Philosophical Quarterly* 27, pp. 290–301. Repr. in *Plato on Knowledge and Forms* (pp. 117–31). Oxford: Clarendon Press.

Gaiser, K. (1974). *Name und Sache in Platons* Kratylos. Heidelberg: Winter.

Kahn, C. H. (1973). Language and ontology in the *Cratylus*. In E. N. Lee, A. P. D. Mourelatos, and R. M. Rorty (eds.) *Exegesis and Argument* (pp. 152–76). New York: Humanities Press.

Ketchum, R. J. (1979). Names, Forms and conventionalism: *Cratylus* 383–395. *Phronesis* 24, pp. 133–47.

Kretzmann, N. (1971). Plato on the correctness of names. *American Philosophical Quarterly* 8, pp. 126–38.

Reeve, C. D. C. (1998). *Plato,* Cratylus: *translated with introduction and notes.* Indianapolis and Cambridge: Hackett.

Robinson, R. (1969). Plato's consciousness of fallacy. In *Essays in Greek Philosophy* (pp. 16–38). Oxford: Clarendon Press.

Rosenmeyer, T. (1957). Plato and mass words. *Transactions of the American Philological Association* 88, pp. 88–102.

Schofield, M. (1982). The dénouement of the *Cratylus.* In M. Schofield and M. Nussbaum (eds.) *Language and Logos* (pp. 61–82). Cambridge: Cambridge University Press.

Sedley, D. (2003). *Plato's* Cratylus. Cambridge: Cambridge University Press.

Silverman, A. (2001). The end of the *Cratylus*: limning the world. *Ancient Philosophy* 21, pp. 1–18.

227

16

Plato and Mathematics

MICHAEL J. WHITE

Introduction: Mathematics and Philosophers – Plato, in Particular

"*Ageōmetrētos mēdeis eisitō*" ("Let no one who is ungeometrical enter"). According to legend, this was the inscription that Plato set up over the entrance to his school, the Academy (see Fowler 1999). Thus begins (or perhaps continues) a relationship between mathematics and philosophy that has often been close but not always easygoing. The figure of the philosopher with mathematical "pretensions" – the philosopher as amateur mathematician, the philosopher who wishes to instruct mathematicians about the proper foundations of their discipline, or even the philosopher as mathematician *manqué* – is not rare in the history of philosophy. To consider the notable example of Thomas Hobbes: Christiaan Huygens expressed the hope that the time he had spent on the refutation of Hobbes's geometrical paralogisms would not be wasted if Hobbes would but keep his promise to "abandon his extremely unsuccessful study of the whole of geometry" (Huygens, Letter 149, in Hobbes 1994, vol. 2: 538).

Of course, there have been philosophers of mathematical sophistication and competence much greater than that of Hobbes. However, the attitude toward mathematics on the part of those philosophers who might be described as enamored of mathematics has tended to be ambivalent. On the one hand, mathematical reasoning has presented a virtually unparalleled standard of intellectual rigor and exactitude. More particularly, the paradigm of mathematical exposition, the axiomatic-deductive system or *ordo geometricus* that was early (*ca.* 300 BCE) exemplified in Euclid's *Elements*, has had immense epistemological influence. On the other hand, a not uncommon conviction of those philosophers enamored of mathematics (who have *remained* philosophers) is that the intellectual outlook of the "dedicated mathematician," intense though it may be, is narrow and restricted. There are more things in heaven and earth, most (but not all) such philosophers have believed, than are dreamt of by the mathematicians in their mathematics.

Plato surely stands near the beginning of this tradition. Within Plato's circle were mathematicians such as Theodorus of Cyrene (born in the first half of the fifth century), who appears as a character in Plato's *Theaetetus* along with his pupil and contemporary of Plato, Theaetetus himself (*ca.* 414–369 BCE) (see 1: THE LIFE OF PLATO

OF ATHENS). Associated with Plato's Academy were other figures of mathematical significance. Perhaps the most important of these was Eudoxus of Cnidus, who was also a philosopher and important astronomer. The brothers Menaechmus and Dinostratus were also accomplished mathematicians connected with the Academy in the mid-fourth century. Plato seems always to have associated with mathematicians, and even the casual reader of Plato will be aware that mathematical references abound in the texts of his dialogues.

While it seems obvious from his texts that Plato holds that mathematics is a (perhaps necessary) preparation for philosophy and for gaining knowledge about "what is really real" (*to ontōs on*), other aspects of the relation between mathematics and Plato's thought are less certain. The degree to which Plato himself (or other ancient philosophers such as Zeno of Elea and Aristotle) influenced ancient mathematical theory and practice is a hotly contested issue. At the heart of what is probably the predominant position on this issue is the assumption that Plato's and other philosophers' enterprise of raising (and sometimes answering) "deep" foundational and conceptual issues must have had significant influence on the development and practice of Greek mathematics. In reaction, some distinguished historians of Greek mathematics, such as the late Wilbur Knorr, have argued that Greek "mathematical studies were autonomous, almost completely so, while the philosophical debates, developing within their own tradition, frequently drew support and clarification from mathematical work" (Knorr 1982: 112). However, one may doubt how effective this philosophical "support and clarification [drawn] from mathematical work" could have been if Knorr's impression of the mathematical competence of ancient philosophers is correct: "the philosophers of antiquity are, with no exception I know of . . . inept in the management of mathematical arguments" (p. 114).

I shall not, in the present chapter, enter further into this debate than I have already elsewhere done. My general belief is that the extant texts that we have suggest that Plato (as well as Aristotle) possessed some considerable knowledge of mathematical developments without establishing that either was what I have called a "creative practicing mathematician" (White 1992: 134–7). It is true that Plato (unlike Aristotle) was credited in later antiquity with some significant mathematical accomplishments. The most important of these is a solution of one of the famous geometrical problems of antiquity: given a cube a particular volume, to find the cube of twice that volume. According to tradition, Hippocrates of Chios had, in the fifth century BCE, "reduced" this problem of "duplicating" the cube to that of finding two mean proportionals in continued proportion between two straight lines. (With the aid of algebra, which the Greeks of course did not have, the relation is straightforward. The continued proportion $a : x = x : y = y : b$ yields the equations $y^2 = bx$ and $y = ab/x$ and, thus, $y^3 = b^2a$. Hence, if we let $a = 2b$, we obtain $y^3 = 2b^3$. So, the cube on the mean proportional y is twice the volume of the cube on the given line b.) The attribution of a solution of this problem to Plato is late, occurring in the commentary of Eutocius (first half of sixth century CE) on the second book of Archimedes' *On the Sphere and Cylinder* and in no extant earlier source. The consensus of modern scholars is that the attribution is false, not only because of the lack of extant earlier references to it but also for several other reasons. Among those reasons is the fact that the proof attributed to Plato uses a mechanical device (a sort of carpenter's square with a straight edge that slides along one side while remaining perpendicular to that side and parallel to the other side); and Plato is reported by Plutarch to have disapproved of the use of mechanical devices in geometry, maintaining that "the good of geometry is thereby lost and destroyed, as it is brought back to things of sense instead of being directed upward and grasping at eternal and incorporeal images" (Plutarch, *Quaestiones conviviales* 718E–F).

Whatever the exact extent of Plato's technical mathematical expertise, the primary importance of mathematics with respect to his thought lies in what might be termed his philosophy of mathematics. According to what certainly seems to be Plato's view, mathematics is propaedeutic to philosophy (dialectic). Why does he hold such a view? And how is mathematics supposed to fulfill this role? Does mathematics have any *intrinsic* value, according to Plato? Or is it merely of extrinsic value, providing a useful or necessary mental discipline?

These last questions lead to the issue of Plato's mathematical ontology. One very common view is that Plato was a mathematical Platonist in the contemporary sense of the phrase, holding that there is a realm of mathematical reality that is not constructed by but is discovered by mathematicians. Moreover, according to this interpretation of Plato, he holds that mathematical objects occupy an intermediate ontological status between the really real (*to ontōs on* or realm of the Forms) and sensible, physical reality – just as mathematical reasoning occupies an intermediate position between philosophical reasoning or dialectic, on the one hand, and reasoning about sensible, physical reality, on the other. However, alternative interpretations of Plato's mathematical ontology have a long history: from ancient "Pythagoreanizing" interpretations, which tend to conflate the objects of mathematics and the Forms (or even to mathematicize the Forms), to some contemporary interpretations, which question whether Plato actually did postulate a realm of mathematical objects ontologically "between" Forms and sensible, physical objects.

I do not propose, in the remainder of this chapter, to catalogue the mathematical references in Plato's text or to attempt to discuss all of the uses that Plato makes of mathematics. Nor shall I try to sort out the history of the relation between mathematics and Plato's Academy, during Plato's time or later. Rather, I shall briefly discuss two related but distinct issues in Plato's thought: (a) the relation between "doing mathematics" and "doing philosophy" and (b) the ontological place of the objects of mathematical investigation.

Mathematics and the Training of the Soul

In the *Republic* the character Socrates clearly sets forth what is usually taken to be Plato's short explanation for the pedagogical prominence accorded to mathematics in the ideal state: it is the study that "draws the soul from the realm of becoming to the realm of what is" (*R.* 521D3–4). Expanding upon the point, Socrates claims that

> it would be appropriate . . . to legislate this subject for those who are going to share in the highest offices in the city and to persuade them to turn to calculation [as well as other branches of mathematics subsequently discussed] and take it up, not as laymen do,

but staying with it until they reach the study of the natures of numbers by means of understanding itself, not like tradesmen and retailers, for the sake of buying and selling, but for the sake of war and for ease in turning the soul around, away from becoming and towards truth and being. (*R.* 525B9–c6)

In addition to "arithmetic and calculation" (*arithmētikē* and *logistikē*),[1] Socrates prescribes geometry, also for a reason other than its practical usefulness. Rather, the "greater and more advanced part of it tends to make it easier to see the form of the good" (*R.* 526D8–E1). Geometry, he says, is knowledge (*gnōsis*) of what always exists (*R.* 527B7–8); consequently it "draws the soul towards truth and produces philosophical thought (*philosophou dianoias*) by directing upwards what we now wrongly direct downwards" (*R.* 527B9–11).

Socrates adds three more mathematical disciplines to his mathematical curriculum: stereometry (solid geometry), astronomy, and harmonics. In keeping with the chronology of the *Republic*, Socrates complains of the difficulty and lack of theoretical development of stereometry, suggesting that its "researchers need a director [like Plato?], for, without one, they won't discover anything" (*R.* 528B7–8). There were certainly known "results" in stereometry in the late fifth and early fourth centuries BCE. Democritus, for example, is credited with discovering that the volume of a pyramid is one-third the volume of a prism of the same base and height. Plato's objection seems to be that stereometry is not being "consistently and vigorously pursued" (*R.* 528c2–4). He perhaps has in mind something like Theaetetus' subsequent theoretical construction of the five regular solids with the methods for inscribing them in a sphere, work that was to form the basis of the thirteenth book of Euclid's *Elements*.

Socrates' prescriptions concerning astronomy and harmonics have been a problem for most commentators, certainly for modern ones. Because of the history of western scientific developments, we cannot but help think of these disciplines as branches of physics or natural philosophy, where applied mathematics is used to "save" (explain) observed physical phenomena. However, it seems that, in the seventh book of the *Republic*, Socrates advocates a "pure astronomy" and a "pure harmonics." If it is correctly pursued, astronomy, characterized as the study of solid bodies in rotational motion (*en periphorai*) (*R.* 528A9), investigates things that "must be grasped by reason and thought, not by sight" (*R.* 529D4–5). If "we're to make the naturally intelligent part of the soul useful instead of useless," Socrates concludes, "let's study astronomy by means of problems, as we do geometry, and leave the things in the sky alone" (*R.* 530B6–c1). Similarly, Socrates criticizes current practitioners of harmonics because they "seek out the numbers that are to be found in these audible consonances, but they do not make the ascent to problems. They don't investigate, for example, which numbers are consonant and which aren't or what the explanation is of each" (*R.* 531c1–4). His ideal seems to be a "pure harmonics" in the sense of a number-theoretic specification and theory of consonance and dissonance, which is unrelated to auditory experience.

Plato's conception of a "pure" astronomy and harmonics (which apparently are not constrained by any physical data) no doubt is intimately related to a point that Plato himself repeatedly emphasizes. The study of mathematics *should* have the effect of turning the soul from the changeable realm of sensation (identified, in the best Platonic fashion, with "becoming") toward the unchangeable realm of thought (identified with "being"). The Greek arithmetic or number theory and the Greek geometry of Plato's day had progressed to a certain point of abstraction. A geometer proving the Pythagorean theorem did not think of himself as proving the theorem (only) for a particular diagram of a right triangle. And an arithmetician did not think of himself, when investigating the properties of "square" and "oblong" numbers, as investigating (only) certain sets of pebbles or other markers arranged in geometrically square or (non-square) rectangular configurations. The question is what Plato made of the "natural" tendency toward abstraction that he found in Greek mathematical practice.

The answer seems to be that he found a great deal that was suggested (but not, in his view, fully implemented or understood) by the sort of abstraction characterizing Greek mathematical practice. Speaking of his "pure harmonics," but perhaps implicitly referring as well to the other branches of mathematics, Socrates says that the discipline, *if properly pursued*, is "useful in the search for the beautiful and the good. But pursued for any other purpose, it's useless" (R. 531c6–7). He continues:

> if inquiry into all the subjects we've mentioned [i.e., the mathematical disciplines] brings out their association and relationship with one another and draws conclusions about their kinship, it does contribute something to our goal and isn't labor in vain, but . . . otherwise it is in vain. (R. 531c9–D4)

Somewhat later in the dialogue, Socrates legislates that at the age of 20 young men who are chosen to pursue the path toward becoming rulers will be taught in a more systematic (and advanced) way the "subjects that they learned in no particular order as children [and that] they must now bring together to form a unified vision of their kinship both with one another and with the nature of that which is" (R. 537c1–3). It is clear that the studies (*mathēmata*) to which Socrates is referring are the mathematical disciplines. Such advanced and synoptic mathematical instruction, Socrates claims, is the "greatest test of who is naturally dialectical and who isn't, for anyone who can achieve a unified vision (is *sunoptikos*) is dialectical, and anyone who can't isn't" (R. 537c6–7).

It is far from obvious exactly what Plato means by the "synoptic view" of mathematics. He may, in part, be pointing to the relation between his "pure astronomy" and stereometry, and the relation between his "pure harmonics" and arithmetic. He may also be alluding to the proper order of study of the five mathematical disciplines. Perhaps he means no more than the systematization of a mathematical discipline imposed by an axiomatic-deductive formulation of the sort we find in Euclid. I believe that it would be rash to hypothesize that Plato anticipated the sort of unification of and cross-fertilization of branches of mathematics that has been such a fruitful element of modern and contemporary mathematics. However, a recent commentator on mathematics in Plato, M. F. Burnyeat, finds something deeper in Plato's advocacy of the synoptic view: "mathematics provides the lowest-level articulation of objective value"; and "mathematics is the route to knowledge of the Good because it is a constitutive part of ethical understanding" (Burnyeat 2000: 45, 73).

232

To Pythagoreanize or Not To Pythagoreanize

I term such an interpretation of Plato "Pythagoreanizing" and will soon attempt to explain more clearly what I mean by that characterization. There is, I believe, the basis for such a view such as Burnyeat's in Plato's texts. Plato does, after all, envisage that his ruler-candidates should spend ten years studying advanced mathematics (between the ages of 20 and 30) before undertaking five years of study of dialectic (*R.* 539D–E). This is followed by a fifteen-year "descent into the cave" of administrative and military service; and then, at age 50, the worthy ones "must be compelled to lift up the radiant light of their souls to what itself provides light for everything. And once they've seen the good itself, they must each in turn put the city, its citizens, and themselves in order, using it as their model" (*R.* 540A7–B1). Now, it scarcely seems that ten years of training in higher mathematics would be necessary were the purpose of this training merely to provide the mental discipline for sharpening the intellect for dialectic, or accustoming the soul to turn away from the concrete and sensual toward the universal and abstract. A "purely instrumentalist" view of the value of mathematics would locate that value in what Burnyeat calls "mind-training"; it is a view that "implies that the *content* of the mathematical curriculum is irrelevant to its goal" (Burnyeat 2000: 3).

As Burnyeat notes, there were certainly ancient representatives of such a view who were contemporaneous with Plato. Perhaps most notable was the fourth-century BCE rhetorician Isocrates. He maintains that, through the study of geometry and astronomy (along with "eristic" argument),

> we gain the power . . . of grasping and learning more easily and more quickly those subjects which are of more importance and of greater value. I do not, however, think it proper to apply the term "philosophy" to a training which is no help to us in the present either in our speech or in our actions, but rather I would call it a gymnastic of the mind and a preparation for philosophy. (*Antidosis* 265–6, in Isocrates 1956: 333)

In what appears to be a remark aimed at "professional mathematicians," Isocrates observes that

> some of those who have become so thoroughly versed in these studies as to instruct others in them fail to use opportunely the knowledge which they possess, while in the other activities of life they are less cultivated than their students – I hesitate to say less cultivated than their servants. (*Panathenaicus* 28–9, in Isocrates 1956: 391)

Isocrates is more tolerant of mathematic tutelage than the sophists Protagoras and Aristippus of Cyrene. The former is portrayed by Plato as avoiding giving instruction in arithmetic, astronomy, geometry, and harmonics so that he can "cut to the chase" and instruct his students in "sound deliberation, both in domestic matters . . . and public affairs – how to realize one's maximum potential for success in political debate and action" (Plato, *Prt.* 318E–319A2). Aristippus is reported by Aristotle to have dismissed the mathematical disciplines because "they produce no account (*logon*) concerning goods and evils" (Aristotle, *Metaph.* III.2.996a35–b1). In fact, this report occurs in a passage in which Aristotle himself claims that in mathematics "nothing is demonstrated through this kind of account [i.e., in terms of an end or what is good]; nor is there any demonstration (*apodeixis*) because of what is better or what is worse" (*Metaph.* 996a29–31).

But what is Plato's view? Burnyeat notes that "the goal of the mathematical curriculum is repeatedly said [by Plato] to be knowledge of the Good (526D–E, 530E, 531C, 532C)" (Burnyeat 2000: 5). Indeed. But the question is whether mathematics itself supplies (some) knowledge of the Good: whether, to use Burnyeat's words, "the content of mathematics is a constitutive part of ethical understanding" (p. 6). To interpret Plato as holding that the content of mathematics, properly pursued, is to some degree constitutive of "ethical understanding" (or, more broadly, constitutive of the understanding of what is "really real," *in toto*) is, in my sense, to Pythagoreanize. As I previously suggested, I do not think that Pythagoreanizing interpretations of Plato are without foundation. Not only do we have the long, deep, and advanced tutelage in mathematics that Plato envisions for potential rulers. We also have clear indication that what, in particular, impresses Plato about mathematics is that it is capable of providing a virtually unparalleled instance of unshakeable and unambiguous conviction of truth. With respect to Socrates' eliciting from the slave-boy in the *Meno* (82B–85C) a construction for the "duplication of a square" (that is, a proof that the area of the square constructed on the diagonal of a given square is twice the area of that square), Ian Hacking comments,

> what impressed Plato, and what impresses me, is that by talk, gesticulation, and reflection, we can find something out, and see why what we have found out is true. . . .
>
> The fact that we can see not only that the theorem is true, but also why it must be true, is one of the core phenomena of *some* proofs, the sheer feeling of having "got it." That feeling, we well know, can be illusory. Every would-be proof-inventor has had many a false "Aha!" experience. Plato was not ignorant of this. Firm reflection and ability to recapitulate the argument insightfully were essential ingredients in grasping the proof. (Hacking 2000: 94–5)

It is easy enough to conclude that Plato recognizes that in some instances of mathematical proof we encounter a genuine but *conditional* "Aha!" experience, which could be transformed into an *unconditional*, "absolute" "Aha!" experience if the unshakeable conviction and understanding that the proof gives us, *relative to its premises*, could be extended to the premises as well. That is, mathematical proof can serve as a nonpareil instance of unshakeable understanding/conviction of truth if only that understanding and conviction pertains to its premises as well as what is deduced from those premises.

And it is easy enough to conclude that this recognition is what underlies the distinction in *Republic* VI within the "highest," intelligible section of the Divided Line. The lower part of the intelligible section represents the "Aha!" sort of mathematical understanding (*dianoia*) that makes use of assumptions or hypotheses, which they "don't think it necessary to give any account of . . . either to themselves or to others, as if they were clear to everyone" (*R.* 510c6–D1). But the higher part of the intelligible section represents the "Aha!" sort of *unconditioned* understanding (*noēsis*) yielded by dialectic, when it "does not consider these hypotheses as first principles (*archas*) but truly as hypotheses – but as stepping stones to take off from, enabling it to reach the unhypothetical first principle (*archēn*) of everything" (*R.* 511B5–7).

Dialectic, then, represents the sort of comprehensive understanding in which nothing remains that has not been subjected to and passed the "Aha!" test (see 7: PLATO'S METHOD OF DIALECTIC). Such a characterization obviously does not settle the identity of that ultimate *archē*, which (deductively?) grounds all other knowledge and is itself not in need of any further grounding. As an historical matter, "the Good" has been the most common candidate for this ultimate *archē* (see 24: PLATO'S CONCEPT OF GOODNESS. However, the eminent logician-mathematician W. W. Tait has argued that Plato is here simply looking for an axiomatic foundation for mathematics (representing the "exact sciences"), a set of "*primary truths*, as represented by the Common Notions and Postulates of Euclid's *Elements*" (Tait 2002: 26). The problem with the hypotheses at the lower, *dianoia*-stage, then, is that they are "drawn from consideration of empirical examples" (p. 25), and thus fail to satisfy the "Aha!" test. Tait suggests that, at least in the case of geometry, the first principles of Euclid's *Elements* eventually (largely) satisfied the bill.[2]

The problem with Tait's view is that, despite the fact that it interprets dialectic as a matter of attempting to establish unshakeable foundations for the exact (mathematical) sciences, it perhaps does not Pythagoreanize enough. Considerations of value, including ethical value, appear to have disappeared in Tait's account. And Plato – with all his talk of the Good, etc. – certainly seems to believe that considerations of value are fundamental to the highest, unified sort of understanding, *noēsis*, which is to be obtained by philosophy or dialectic.

Unlike Tait, Burnyeat Pythagoreanizes: "the content of mathematics [is] a constitutive part of ethical understanding" and "mathematics provides the lowest-level articulation of the world as it is objectively speaking" (2000: 6, 22). I do not have space to do justice to Burnyeat's ingenious account of this phenomenon. But, in brief, it begins with the observation that for Plato mathematical concepts such as "concord, attunement, proportion, order, and unity . . . [are] important values" (p. 76) and, thus, are central to the ethical dimension of reality. He then argues that the person who has studied mathematics deeply and correctly (and for a long time) has thus become assimilated to "objective value" and that "someone whose soul has become assimilated to objective being can take it as a model for reorganizing the social world" (p. 72). Burnyeat denies that Plato holds that the relationship between these concepts in their mathematical and in their ethical contexts is equivocal or simply metaphorical. Indeed, their ethical sense is fixed by their mathematical sense.

Different forms of Pythagoreanizing were probably present in the Academy from its beginning. Xenocrates (*ca.* 396–314 BCE), its third head, may have been the referent of Aristotle's remark that "some say that Forms and numbers have the same nature" (Aristotle, *Metaph.* VII.2.1028b25–6). A later resurgence of Pythagoreanizing Platonism, beginning with Numenius and Nicomachus of Gerasa in the second century CE, has been chronicled by Dominic O'Meara. In the *Theologoumena arithmeticae* of Nicomachus (which survives only in a paraphrasis produced by the ninth-century Byzantine patriarch Photius), the Platonic Forms become "properties or 'characters' (*idiōmata*) of numbers" (O'Meara 1989: 17). Along the way, deities get assimilated to (the first ten) numbers as well, yielding Nicomachus' "arithmetical theology." With respect to Nicomachus' contemporary Numenius, O'Meara asks whether his Pythagoreanizing brought

> him so far as to soften the distinctions Plato makes here between mathematics and its objects, on the one hand, and the "highest study" (called "dialectic") and its objects (pure being, or the Forms, and the source of the Forms, the Good), on the other. Did his Pythagorean programme prompt him to identify mathematics with dialectic, numbers with Forms? (O'Meara 1989: 14)

I submit that Pythagoreanizing typically manifests these tendencies. As a modern scholar, Burnyeat seeks to understand and interpret Plato's intentions. It is thus difficult for him to accept the radical Pythagoreanized Platonism of some Neoplatonists, who were more interested in what they regarded as the *truth* of Platonism than in Plato's intentions. A modern scholar such as Burnyeat simply cannot ignore a passage such as the following:

> don't you know that all these [mathematical] subjects are merely preludes to the song (*tou nomou*) itself that must also be learned? Surely you don't think that people who are clever in these matters are dialecticians.
>
> No, by god, I don't. Although I have met a few exceptions. (*R.* 531D7–E3)

Such passages suggest that there is more to dialectic than mathematics, and that knowledge of *to ontōs on*, the Forms and the Good, is different from and superior to mathematical knowledge. One solution to those moderns who wish to Pythagoreanize is to cast dialectic as a sort of value-laden meta-mathematics. And, indeed, we find Burnyeat characterizing the studies that "lead potential philosophers to knowledge of the Good" as "mathematics and meta-mathematical dialectic" (Burnyeat 2000: 77) and asserting that "dialectic is described in terms that we might call a meta-mathematical inquiry" (p. 46).

It may seem improbably strange to us moderns to think that a "meta-mathematical inquiry," in the sense of investigation into the "foundations" of mathematics and mathematical epistemology and ontology, could have any relevance to ethical matters, or, indeed, relevance to anything beyond what we take mathematics to encompass. But there certainly are ancient precedents for such a view. In his *Commentary on the First Book of Euclid's Elements*, Proclus (412–85 CE) interprets Plato as constructing the soul out of mathematical forms and takes the function of what he calls "general mathematics" (*hē holē mathēmatikē*) to be dianoetic intellection (*In pr. Eucl.* 16.22ff. and 18.10–11, in Proclus 1967). General mathematics is a "single science encompassing all the kinds of mathematical knowledge." Its principles apply to numbers, magnitudes, and motions alike and, says Proclus, pertain especially to proportions, ratios, and the general theorems dealing with equality and inequality. But, in addition to dealing with the methods of synthesis (deduction) and analysis, it also is concerned with beauty and order (*to kallos kai hē taxis*) (*In pr. Eucl.* 7–8). The dianoetic intellection of mathematics consists of two sorts of power, according to Proclus' interpretation of Plato. Its "lower" powers form the basis not only of the branches of mathematical science as

Plato distinguishes them (arithmetic or number theory, geometry and stereometry, astronomy, and harmonics) but also applied mathematics. With respect to its higher powers, Proclus Pythagoreanizes:

> The range of this thinking extends from on high all the way down to conclusions in the sense world, where it touches on nature and cooperates with natural science (*phusiologia*) in establishing many of its propositions, just as it rises up from below and nearly joins intellectual knowledge in laying hold of the first principles of contemplation (*theōria*). (*In pr. Eucl.* 19.20–4; trans. altered from that of Morrow in Proclus 1970: 16–17)

He adds that the "beauty and order of mathematical discourse, and the abiding and steadfast character of this *theōria*, bring us into contact with the intelligible world itself" (*In pr. Eucl.* 20.27–21.2, in Proclus 1970: 17). Thus mathematical science, "directed upward," makes contributions of the greatest importance to philosophy and theology; in the realm of human value, it benefits political philosophy and "perfects us with respect to moral philosophy (*ēthikēn philosophian*) by instilling order and harmonious living into our characters" (*In pr. Eucl.* 21.25ff., 23.12ff., and 24.4–6, respectively).

Proclus, like Burnyeat, manifests a salient feature of much Pythagoreanizing Platonism: Mathematics "directed upward," or meta-mathematics in Proclus' Pythagoreanized sense, provides a seamless transition to noetic comprehension of the totality of *to ontōs on*, what is really real, with the Good at its apex. Such upward-directed meta-mathematics thus supplies the essential objective basis for all forms of value, including human moral and political value. On the other hand, if one "anti-Pythagoreanizes" it seems difficult to avoid the Isocratic conception of mathematics as a "gymnastic of the mind and preparation for philosophy," where philosophy not only is something distinct from what the "professional mathematician" does but also has a *content* that is not essentially mathematical.

Pythagoreanized Meta-Mathematics and Ancient Mathematical Practice

It seems that the specialization and compartmentalization of mathematics was a phenomenon that began to be manifest as early as the fourth century BCE. If one anti-Pythagoreanizes, it is possible to make room, so to speak, for such mathematical specialization. *Some* mathematical training (the amount may be disputable) provides one with the "transferable skills" (Burnyeat 2000: 19) necessary for moving on to the practice of dialectic and achieving understanding of value-laden reality, *to ontōs on*. But the goal of such training is not "professional" mathematical competence, or an exclusive preoccupation with mathematics that might or might not be interpreted as a case of arrested development. However, if one Pythagoreanizes, it is rather more difficult to know what to make of increasingly professionalized, technical mathematical practice.

Pythagoreanized, upward-directed mathematics or meta-mathematics takes us into the rarefied realm of (value-laden) static, necessary, universal being. But, as a number of modern commentators have noted, the Platonic realm of Forms-ordered-by-the-Good seems to be a singularly unsuitable domain for the developing practice of technical ancient mathematics. Ancient mathematics is intimately wedded to actions, constructions, and processes. Even Socrates, in the seventh book of the *Republic*, is made to complain of the opposition between the science of geometry and the "words spoken by those practicing it":

> They give ridiculous accounts of it, though they can't help it, for they speak like practical men, and all their accounts refer to doing things. They talk of "squaring," "applying," "adding," and the like, whereas the entire subject is pursued for the sake of knowledge ... knowing what always is, not what comes into being and passes away. (*R.* 527A6–B6)

Plato is surely correct in claiming that geometers who use such terminology do so "necessarily" (*anangkaiōs*). As Euclid's proof of the "Pythagorean theorem" (I. 47) demonstrates, appeal to a supposed Form of squareness or the-square-in-itself, the-triangle-itself, etc. is not much help. Rather, we are given a right triangle *ABC*, asked to construct squares on the hypotenuse *BC* and on the sides *BA* and *AC*, to draw a line through the vertex of the right angle and parallel to either of the sides of the square constructed on the hypotenuse *BC*, etc. *Problēmata* (constructions to be made) are just as essential to Euclidean geometry as *theōrēmata* (propositions to be "seen" or understood).

Even in the supposedly Eudoxian proportion theory of Euclid V and the number theory of Euclid VII, idealized but still quasi-physical processes of manipulation figure centrally. The concept of one magnitude (*megethos*) or number (*arithmos*) "measuring" (*katametrein*) another magnitude/number figures largely in these books. The idea is that of taking the smaller magnitude/number and reiterating or "repeatedly laying it down" until it comes to "cover" (equal-without-remainder) the larger magnitude/number. And in the Euclidean algorithm for finding the greatest common measure (aliquot part) of two numbers that are not relatively prime (Euclid VII. 2), there is a process of repeated reciprocal "taking away" of lesser from greater numbers (represented by line segments) until "some number will be left which will measure the one before it." As Paul Pritchard emphasizes, a Greek number (*arithmos*) must be some definite (non-infinite) plurality of units (*monades*), where the unit is either some (kind of) physical object or an "abstract" unit; and, indeed, even lowly calculation (addition, subtraction) depends on treating numbers as collections of units (Pritchard 1995: 65, 123). If (as Plato may suggest at *Phaedo* 101Bff.), the cause of a group of five things being five in number and a group of three things being three in number is the participation of the groups in the non-composite, eternal, unchanging Forms of the-three-in-itself and the-five-in-itself, respectively, these Forms are not going to be much use in arithmetic calculation (or in ancient number theory, for that matter).

Although the import of Aristotle's critical discussion (beginning in the sixth chapter of Book XIII of the *Metaphysics*) of *asumblētoi arithmoi* (non-comparable numbers) is controversial, he seems to be making the point that "mathematical numbers" (i.e., the numbers actually used by mathematicians) must be constituted from comparable units or monads. But with respect to the numbers posited by those who "say that numbers are separate substances and the first causes of things" (*Metaph*. XIII.6.1080a13–14), "after 1, [there is] a distinct 2 which does not include the first 1, and a 3 which does not include the 2, and the other numbers similarly" (1080a33–5). There is thus a kind of discontinuity – a "disconnect," if you will – between these "higher" (Form?) numbers and the numbers encountered in actual mathematical practice.

The evidence suggests that Pythagoreanizing, upward-directed meta-mathematics was largely detachable from actual, technical mathematical practice and had little effect on it. When we consider the ancient mathematics that found its way into the western "mathematical canon" – that of Eudoxus, Menaechmus, and Euclid, of Archimedes and Eratosthenes, of Apollonius of Perge, of Diophantus and Pappus – any Pythgoreanizing features do not seem to be essential to their technical mathematical accomplishments. One of Menaechmus' methods for determining two mean proportionals in continued proportion between lines *a* and *b* certainly depends on the properties deriving from the essence of "parabola-hood"; but it also depends on constructing *two* parabolas with *latera recta a* and *b*, arranged so that their axes are perpendicular and that they share a common vertex. Devising the proof clearly requires the possession of a large share of what seems to be strictly *mathematical* intelligence, particularly spatial imagination. It does not require, in any apparent way, recognition of the beauty or nobility of parabolas relative to other conic sections. It does not require that one recognizes any political or moral applications of the mean proportionals determined by the construction or, indeed, that one understands the place of mathematics with respect to what is really real, *to ontōs on*. In summary, the only part of Pythagoreanizing, upward-directed mathematics that seems germane to ancient mathematical practice is that concerned with methodology (for example, the methods of synthesis and analysis) – if such methodological issues are included in upward-directed mathematics, as Proclus seems to suggest.

Mathematical Ontology

It is curious that Aristotle is the source of what is perhaps the most direct, early evidence for the existence of mathematical Platonism, in the contemporary sense (hereafter, just "Platonism"). This is the doctrine that the practice of mathematics lies in the *discovery* (not the stipulation or construction) of properties and relations of mathematical objects – objects that have a timeless and necessary existence that is independent of the physical, material world. To begin with, Aristotle countenances a sort of methodological or operational Platonism: "each thing," he says, "is best understood if one posits what is not separable as separate, as the arithmetician and geometer do" (*Metaph*. XIII.3.1078a21–3). It seems that Aristotle has here discerned a common feature of mathematical practice, of "the way mathematicians think." But he claims that Plato transforms operational Platonism into an ontological doctrine:

> Further, besides sensible things and Forms he says there are the objects of mathematics (*ta mathēmatika*), which occupy an intermediate position, differing from sensible things in being eternal and unchangeable, from Forms in that there are many alike, while the Form itself is in each case unique. (*Metaph*. I.5.987b14–18, trans. W. D. Ross)

I think that we must accept the conclusion of Julia Annas that, although there *may* be references to the *ta mathēmatika* as *ta metaxu* (ontological "intermediates" between Forms and sensible objects) in various places in Plato's extant corpus, "Plato nowhere explicitly uses the argument for them that Aristotle treats as standard" (Annas 1975: 147). That argument is really an argument from mathematical practice encapsulated in the above quotation from the fifth chapter of *Metaphysics* I: Mathematicians do not make their constructions and prove their theorems about (collections of) physical objects but use idealized "eternal and unchangeable" circles, triangles, parabolas, units and collections of units in their constructions and proofs. And they do not make their constructions and prove their theorems about Forms (which are "unique" and *sui generis*) but, typically, use *multiple* entities of the same kind – circles, triangles, parabolas, units, collections of units – which are thought of as being manipulated in various ways in the constructions and proofs.

Aristotle, of course, rejects the inference from operational to metaphysical Platonism. Although some of the details of Aristotle's own doctrine are less than pellucid, he seems to have held some sort of constructive-abstractionist doctrine of the objects of the mathematical sciences. Some scholars believe that the evidence that Plato himself made such an inference is so weak that they refuse to attribute a doctrine of mathematical ontological "intermediates" to him. Not surprisingly, the result is often a very Aristotelian interpretation of Plato on mathematics: For example, in Pritchard's estimation,

> neither Plato nor Aristotle is committed to an ontology of separately existing mathematical objects. The difference between them seems rather to be that Aristotle is able to give a more detailed account [with the aid of the *"qua*-operator"] of the nature of the imagination and of mathematical abstraction. (Pritchard 1995: 111)

There is also, I believe, some tension between mathematical Platonism and a Pythagoreanizing interpretation of Plato. The postulation of a realm of ontological mathematical "intermediates" simply to accommodate mathematical practice would seem to introduce a level of ontology that has been stripped of value and, in that sense, is discontinuous with the value-laden realm of Forms, organized by the Good. Such an ontological discontinuity makes it even more mysterious how technical mathematical practice could substantively contribute to value-laden, Pythagoreanizing upward-directed mathematics. Proclus presents a Neoplatonist attempt to finesse the ontological problem. Mathematical reasoning is the constructive activity of imagination (*phantasia*), which is constrained not by abstraction from sense experience but by Forms apprehended by *nous*:

> For the understanding (*dianoia*) contains the ideas (*tous logous*) but, being unable to see them when they are wrapped up, unfolds and exposes them and presents them to the imagination, or with its aid, it explicates its knowledge of them, happy in their separation from sensible things and finding in the matter of imagination [so-called "intelligible matter"] a medium apt for receiving its forms (*tōn heautēs eidōn*).
>
>   Thus thinking (*noēsis*) in geometry occurs with the aid of the imagination. Its syntheses and divisions of the figures are imaginary, and its knowing, though on the way to understanding being, still does not reach it. (*In pr. Eucl.* 54.27–55.10, in Proclus 1970: 44)

Somewhat later, Proclus approves the view of the "followers of Menaechmus" that "the discovery of theorems does not occur without recourse to matter [literally, "*proodou*– Neoplatonic 'procession' – into matter"], that is, intelligible matter: in going forth into this matter and shaping it, our ideas are plausibly said to resemble acts of production; for the movement of our thought in projecting its own ideas is a production, we have said, of the figures in our imagination and of their properties" (*In pr. Eucl.* 78.17–22, in Proclus 1970: 64). Proclus proceeds to invoke actual mathematical practice:

> But it is in our imagination that the constructions, sectionings, superpositions, comparisons, additions, and subtractions take place, whereas the contents of our understanding all stand fixed, without any generation or change. (*In pr. Eucl.* 78.25–79.2, in Proclus 1970: 64)

It is clear that Proclus is attempting to accommodate a plausible account of mathematical practice to a *continuous* Neoplatonic ontology, in which the "levels" are bound together by "procession" (*proodos*). But it is interesting that he connects this attempt with Menaechmus, an associate of the Academy and a contemporary or near-contemporary of Plato.

Conclusion

In our age of intellectual specialization and compartmentalization, there is pervasive skepticism whether "technical" knowledge, however deep and systematic, has much to do with Wisdom. Mathematics began to be developed as a technical and specialized intellectual discipline by the Greeks by at least the fourth century BCE. There is thus some irony in the fact that Plato, at this same time, appears to be committed to the belief that there *is* a profound connection between mathematical knowledge and Wisdom. Pythagoreanizing Platonism evidently early became, and remains, a program for securing and explaining that connection.

Is it a plausible program? My own view is that the historical development of mathematics suggests that it is not. There certainly is an aesthetic dimension to the way many mathematicians, particularly those who work in certain areas of "pure mathematics," conceptualize their discipline. However, I am inclined to think that the aesthetic value that they discern is very much discipline-specific. It may well be true that there is a sense in which a mathematician such as John Nash has "a beautiful mind." But does it follow that his mind is therefore *kalos kai agathos*, "noble and good," either in the Platonic or some other, more common sense? Pythagoreanizing Platonism must confront the negative answer that I – and, I think, most of us – are inclined to give.

Notes

Translations of Plato are taken from J. M. Cooper (ed.) *Plato: Complete Works* (Indianapolis: Hackett, 1997). Translations of Aristotle are the author's unless otherwise noted, in which case they come from J. Barnes (ed.) *Complete Works of Aristotle* (Princeton, NJ: Princeton University Press, 1984). Other translations are the author's unless otherwise noted.

241

1 Proclus gives an account of the distinction between *logistikē* ("calculation") and *arithmētikē* that became common in later Greek thought: *logistikē* pertains to "applied" counting and arithmetic calculations (dealing with sensible objects), while *arithmētikē* is more theoretical number theory (*In pr. Eucl.* 40.2–9, in Proclus 1967). However, as (Klein 1968: ch. 3) argues, references to the two sciences that we find in Plato (e.g., *Grg.* 451A–C, *Chrm.* 165E–166B, *Tht.* 198A–B, *R.* 525C–D) do not seem to fit this later account very well. Klein maintains that, for Plato, *arithmētikē* is not "number theory" but "first and foremost the art of correct counting" (p. 19). *Logistikē* pertains more to the operations on the numbers, the "mulifarious relations which exist between different numbers" (p. 20). Both sciences can be pursued at a more applied and a more theoretical level.

2 Proclus maintains that "it is necessary that geometrical first principles [*archai*: definitions, postulates, axioms, however they are distinguished] differ from their consequences in being simple, indemonstrable, and evident in themselves" (*In pr. Eucl.*, 179.12–14). In Proclus' estimation, Euclid's famous fifth ("parallel") postulate doesn't satisfy these conditions and "ought to be excluded from the postulates altogether" (191.21–2).

References and further reading

Annas, J. (1975). On the "intermediates." *Archiv für Geschichte der Philosophie* 57, pp. 146–66.
—— (1976). *Aristotle's* Metaphysics: *Books M and N*. Oxford: Clarendon Press.
Burnyeat, M. F. (2000). Plato on why mathematics is good for the soul. In T. Smiley (ed.) *Mathematics and Necessity: Essays in the History of Philosophy* (pp. 1–81). Oxford: Oxford University Press.
Fowler, D. (1999). *The Mathematics of Plato's Academy: A New Reconstruction*, 2nd edn. Oxford: Clarendon Press.
Hacking, I. (2000). What mathematics has done to some and only some philosophers. In T. Smiley (ed.) *Mathematics and Necessity: Essays in the History of Philosophy* (pp. 83–138). Oxford: Oxford University Press.
Heath, T. (1981) [1921]. *A History of Greek Mathematics*, vol. 1: *From Thales to Euclid*. New York: Dover Publications.
Hobbes, T. (1994). *The Correspondence of Thomas Hobbes* (2 vols.), ed. N. Malcolm. Oxford: Clarendon Press.
Isocrates (1956) [1929]. *Isocrates*, trans. G. Norlin. Loeb Classical Library, vol. II. Cambridge, Mass. and London: Harvard University Press and William Heinemann.
Klein, J. (1968) [1934–6]. *Greek Mathematical Thought and the Origin of Algebra*, trans. E. Brann. Cambridge, Mass. and London: MIT Press.
Knorr, W. K. (1982). Infinity and continuity: the interaction of mathematics and philosophy in antiquity. In N. Kretzmann (ed.) *Infinity and Continuity in Ancient and Medieval Thought* (pp. 112–45). Ithaca, NY and London: Cornell University Press.
Mueller, I. (1992). Mathematical method and philosophical truth. In R. Kraut (ed.) *The Cambridge Companion to Plato* (pp. 170–99). Cambridge: Cambridge University Press.
O'Meara, D. J. (1989). *Pythagoras Revived: Mathematics and Philosophy in Late Antiquity*. Oxford: Clarendon Press.
Pritchard, P. (1995). *Plato's Philosophy of Mathematics*. Sankt Augustin: Academia.
Proclus (1967) [1873]. *Procli Diadochi in primum Euclidis elementorum librum commentarii*, ed. G. Friedlein. Hildesheim: Georg Olms Verlagsbuchhandlung.
—— (1970). *A Commentary on the First Book of Euclid's Elements*, trans. G. R. Morrow. Princeton, NJ: Princeton University Press.

Tait, W. W. (2002). *Noēsis*: Plato on exact science. In D. B. Malament (ed.) *Reading Natural Philosophy: Essays in the History and Philosophy of Science and Mathematics* (pp. 11–30). Chicago and La Salle, Ill.: Open Court.

Tarán, L. (1978). Aristotle's classification of number in *Metaphysics* M 6, 1080a15–35. *Greek, Roman and Byzantine Studies* 19, pp. 83–90.

—— (1981). *Speusippus of Athens: A Critical Study with a Collection of the Related Texts and Commentary*. Leiden: Brill.

Theon of Smyrna (1987) [1878]. *Philosophi Platonici: expositio rerum mathematicarum ad legendum Platonem utilium*, ed. E. Hiller. New York and London: Garland Publishing.

Wedberg, A. (1955). *Plato's Philosophy of Mathematics*. Stockholm: Almqvist and Wiksell.

White, M. J. (1992). *The Continuous and the Discrete: Ancient Physical Theories from a Contemporary Perspective*. Oxford: Clarendon Press.

243

17

Platonic Religion

MARK L. MCPHERRAN

The dialogues of Plato – like the things of Thales – are full of gods; for in them Plato consistently invokes the realm of divinity by using the religious vocabulary of his own time and place. Sometimes these allusions are merely figures of speech (e.g., *R.* 578E), but typically Plato has his characters speak of the divine in an unmistakably serious and positive fashion, referring to features of mainstream religion and esoteric cults in order to make points that are simultaneously philosophical and religious in nature. So prominent is this feature of Plato's work – and so clear his theism – that the ancient world took it for granted that the chief goal of those who follow the Platonic line was to "become as much like god as is possible" (Sedley 1999: 309). Although this aspect of Plato's thought has been underplayed in modern scholarship, it should not surprise us: Plato was born into a culture that took the existence of divinities for granted. More importantly, he was a discerning student of Socrates, a thinker who was himself not only a rational philosopher of the first rank but a profoundly religious figure as well, someone who understood his religious commitments to be integral to and informed by the philosophical mission he conducted on behalf of Delphic Apollo (*Ap.* 20D–23c). These commitments were, however, not those of a small-town polytheist but of a sophisticated religious reformer (see Beckman 1979; McPherran 1996). Plato should be understood, then, to have followed the path laid down by his teacher by appropriating, reshaping, and extending – but not entirely rejecting – the religious conventions of his own time in the service of establishing the new enterprise of philosophy. The results – in particular, Plato's conception of a singular God who is the source of order and goodness in the cosmos – were far-reaching, impacting his intellectual heirs (e.g., Aristotle and Plotinus), and with them, Jewish, Christian, and Islamic thought. (See 27: LEARNING ABOUT PLATO FROM ARISTOTLE; 28: PLATO AND HELLENISTIC PHILOSOPHY; 29: PLATO'S INFLUENCE ON JEWISH, CHRISTIAN, AND ISLAMIC PHILOSOPHY.) Within the space available, I shall trace out here the main threads of the religious dimension of Plato's philosophy.

Popular, Socratic, and Platonic Piety

It is reasonable to distinguish between Plato's early, Socratic dialogues and those typically deemed to be middle and late, and to assume that in his early works Plato is philosophizing in the manner of Socrates (see 2: INTERPRETING PLATO). In his middle and late work Plato then reveals distinctive views of his own. This approach is justified by the evidence for the view that Plato developed a metaphysics and epistemology that went far beyond those claims that can be reasonably attributed to his teacher (a teacher who was much more a moral philosopher than anything else; Aristotle, *Metaph.* XIII.1078b9–32); it also accounts for the important differences between the way the notion of piety is treated in Socratic dialogues such as the *Euthyphro* as opposed to more explicitly theory-laden, constructive works such as the *Republic*, *Phaedrus*, *Timaeus*, and *Laws* (see Vlastos 1991: 49). In this section I will briefly spell out these differences and their relation to traditional, popular Greek piety.

The distinct phenomena we designate by using terms such as "religion" and "the sacred" were, for Plato and his contemporaries, seamlessly integrated into everyday life: every facet of existence had what we would call a religious dimension (thus there is no Greek term for religion; the root "*religio*" is Latin). Moreover, no ancient text such as Homer's *Iliad* had the status of a Bible or Koran, and there was no organized church, trained clergy, or systematic set of doctrines enforced by them. What marked out a fifth-century BCE Greek city or individual as pious (*hosios*; *eusebēs*) – that is, as being in accord with the norms governing the relations of humans and gods – was thus not primarily a matter of belief, but rather, correct observance of ancestral tradition. The most central of these activities consisted in the timely performance of prayers and sacrifices (see, e.g., *Il.* 1.446–58), with sacrifices ranging from an individual's libation of wine to the great civic sacrifices of cattle held on the occasion of a religious festival, culminating in a communal banquet that renewed the ties of the citizenry with their city-protecting deities through the mechanism of a shared meal (see, e.g., *Od.* 3.418–72).

Even though ancient conceptions of divinity were not elaborated or enforced by an official theological body, religious education was not left to chance. The compositions attributed to Homer and Hesiod were a part of everyone's education, and both authors were recognized as having established for the Greeks a canon of tales about the great Powers that rule over us. Here, of course, we find a notion of divinity rather different from modern traditions: for in the works of Homer and Hesiod we find gods who did not create the cosmos, who often gained their power through duplicity and violence, who are neither omniscient nor omnipotent, and who regularly intervene in human affairs for good or ill (inflicting, for example, famine, war, and plague; see Zaidman and Pantel 1992: ch. 13). Later writers then drew from this poetic repertory, "while simultaneously endowing [these] traditional myths with a new function and meaning" (ibid.: 144). Thus, for example, the dramas of Aeschylus and Sophocles juxtapose some present situation against the events represented in Homer's texts, extending that mythology while also calling into critical question some facet of the human condition and contemporary society's response to it. By the time of Socrates, some of this probing of the traditional stories was influenced by the speculations and skepticism of those thinkers working within the new intellectualist traditions of nature philosophy (e.g., Xenophanes) and sophistry (e.g., Protagoras). As a result, in the work of authors such as Euripides and Thucydides even the fundamental tenets of popular religion concerning the gods and the efficacy of sacrifice and prayer became targets of criticism. Socrates should be placed within this movement.

One key text for determining the religious dimension of Socratic philosophy is Plato's dialogue on piety, the *Euthyphro*. There we find Socrates suggesting that the traditional connection between justice and piety ought to be interpreted in such a way that piety is understood to be that part of justice that is a service of humans to gods, assisting the gods – as assistants to shipwrights help shipwrights – in their primary task to produce their most beautiful product (12E–14A) (McPherran 1996: ch. 2.2). Since Socrates rejects the poetic tradition of quarreling, rationally imperfect gods, and affirms instead that the gods are entirely good (because they are wise; e.g., *Hp.Ma.* 289B) and that the only true good is virtue/wisdom (e.g., *Euthd.* 281D–E), he then likely thinks that the only or most important component of the gods' chief product is virtue/wisdom (see 22: THE UNITY OF THE VIRTUES). Thus, since piety as a virtue must be a craft-knowledge of how to produce goodness (e.g., *La.* 194E–196E), our primary service to the gods would appear to be to help them produce goodness in the universe via the improvement of the human soul (*Ap.* 29D–30B). Because philosophical self-examination is for Socrates the key activity that helps to achieve this goal by reducing the inconsistency of our moral beliefs and by deflating our presumptions to divine wisdom (e.g., *Ap.* 22D–23B), philosophizing is a pre-eminently pious activity. Indeed, Socrates took himself to be philosophizing in accord with the mandate of Delphic Apollo (*Ap.* 20E–23B): the god is using him as a *paradigm* to deliver the virtue-inducing message that the person is wisest, who – like Socrates – becomes most cognizant through philosophizing of how little genuine wisdom he or she possesses (*Ap.* 23B) (see 8: SOCRATIC IGNORANCE). This result, together with Socrates' insistence on the perfect goodness of the gods, however, has the threatening consequence of making burned sacrifice and petitionary prayer much less central to the lived piety of one's life (see McPherran 1996: ch. 3).

Socrates, then, should be understood to have appropriated the principles of traditional Apollonian religion that emphasized the gap separating the human from the divine in terms of wisdom and power by connecting those principles with the new enterprise of philosophical self-examination (see, e.g., *Il.* 5.440–2). As the *Apology* portrays the matter, Socrates' relentless use of that question-and-answer method we call "the *elenchus*" had revealed the human capacity for achieving real wisdom to be exceedingly limited (see 5: THE SOCRATIC *ELENCHUS*), and hence, as providing one reaffirmation of the Apollonian insistence on the fact of human fragility and ignorance in the face of the divine. So although some partial measure of moral knowledge is made possible by maintaining a continual philosophical vigilance via elenctic examination of oneself and others, the prospects for human perfection – especially in comparison to divine perfection and happiness – appear quite bleak. To "know thyself" on this account is, as it always was for Socrates' fellow Greeks, to know how ignorant and far from the divine one really is.

Plato, however, proved much more philosophically ambitious and optimistic about our natural capacities for knowledge and wisdom. Plato's philosophical theology was influenced on the one hand by Socrates' new intellectualist conception of piety as elenctic "caring of the soul" (*Ap.* 29D–30B) and the success of the methods of the mathematicians of his day that he took to overcome the limitations of Socrates' elenctic method (Vlastos 1991: ch. 4) (see 16: PLATO AND MATHEMATICS), and on the other by the aim at human-initiated divine status (especially immortality) as expressed by some of the newer, post-Hesiodic religious forms that had entered into Greece. Consequently, his philosophical theology offered the un-Socratic hope of an afterlife of intimate Form-contemplation in the realm of divinity (*Phd.* 79c–84B; *R.* 490A–B; *Phdr.* 247D–E). Self-knowledge on Plato's scheme leads not so much to an appreciation of limits, then, as to the realization that we are ourselves divinities: immortal intellects that already have within them, if we can but recollect it, all the knowledge there is to be had (*Men.* 81c–D; *Phd.* 72E–77E; *Smp.* 210A–211B). In such a scheme there is little room for Socratic piety, since now the central task of human existence becomes less a matter of assisting gods and more a matter of becoming as much like them as one can (e.g., *Tht.* 172B–177c). This fact, plus the more complex psychology Plato develops in Book IV of his *Republic*, may explain Plato's decision in that book to no longer count piety as a cardinal virtue (427E–428A) (see 19: THE PLATONIC SOUL). For it seems that there Plato came to the view that there is little *internal* difference between the knowledge of how to do what is just toward gods and the knowledge of how to do what is just toward mortals; as a result, piety as a form of psychic virtue seems to be nothing other than justice *simpliciter*. So although, as we will see below, Plato continues to speak of pious actions in the *Republic* and after, piety as a virtue is subsumed under the virtue of justice (and wisdom) as a whole (McPherran 2000b).

Plato's *Polis* Religion

Plato's most explicit statement of the way in which he intends to both retain and transform traditional religious forms is to be found in his *Republic* and *Laws* (I shall focus on the *Republic*). The *Republic* contains over a hundred references to "god" or "gods," with most occurring within the outline of the educational reforms advanced in Books II and III. The traditional gods are first brought into the conversation in their guise as enforcers of morality by Glaucon and his brother Adeimantus (357A–367E). These gods are rumored to repay injustice with frightful post-mortem punishments, but, according to Adeimantus, ambitious people can create a façade of illusory virtue that will allow them to lead profitable lives here and in the afterlife (364B–365A; cf. *Lg.* 909A–B). For we need not fear the gods' punishments if (a) the gods do not exist or (b) they are indifferent to human misconduct. (c) Even if they are concerned with us, given "all we know about them from the laws and poets" (365E2–3) they can be persuaded to give us not penalties but goods (365c–366B, 399B; cf. *Lg.* 885B). No wonder, then, that in the view of the many "no one is just willingly" but only through some infirmity (366D) (see 18: THE SOCRATIC PARADOXES). As a result, the challenge that Socrates must now meet by constructing the perfectly just state Kallipolis is to demonstrate the superiority of justice to injustice independently of any external consequences (366D–369B) (see 23: PLATO ON JUSTICE). Then, when at last Kallipolis is established, he must outline the educational system necessary for producing the character traits its rulers will require (374D–376c).

Socrates asserts that it would be hard to find a system of education better than the traditional one of offering training for the body and music and poetry for the soul, but he quickly finds fault with its substance. We expose the young to music and poetry that employ two kinds of mythic narrative, the true and the fictional (*pseudeis logoi*);

247

and of these two, it is best to begin with entertaining fictions of the kind provided by Homer and Hesiod (376E–377B). This form of education molds the character of the young by using myths to shape the form of their aspirations and desires in ways conformable to the development of their rational intelligence. However, although such stories are false, some approximate the truth better than others and some are more conducive to the development of good character than others (377A, 377D–E, 382C–D). Plato assumes that the most accurate representations of the gods and heroes will also be the most beneficial (e.g., by providing good role models), but the converse is also true, and – famously – this means that there will have to be strict supervision of the poets and storytellers of Kallipolis. Moreover, much of the old literature will have to be cast aside because of its lack of verisimilitude and its debilitating effects on character-formation (see 26: PLATO AND THE ARTS).

First on the chopping block is Hesiod's *Theogony*, with its false, harmful tale of Cronos castrating Ouranos at the urgings of his vengeful mother Gaia, then unjustly swallowing his own children to prevent his overthrow by Zeus (377E–378B). Poetic lies of this sort, which suggest that gods or heroes are unjust or retaliate against each other, must be suppressed. To specify with precision which myths are to be counted false in their essentials, Socrates offers the educators of Kallipolis an "outline of theology" (*tupoi theologias*; 379A5–6) in two parts, establishing a pair of laws that will ensure a sufficiently accurate depiction of divinity (379A7–9) (L1, L2a, L2b below):

1   All gods are [entirely] good beings (379B1–2).
2   No [entirely] good beings are harmful (379B3–4).
3   All non-harmful things do no harm (379B5–8).
4   Things that do no harm do no evil, and so are not the causes of evil (379B9–10).
5   Good beings benefit other things, and so are the causes of good (379B11–14).
6   Thus, good beings are not the causes of all things, but only of good things and not evil things (379B15–379C1).
7   Therefore, the gods are not the causes of everything – as most people believe – but their actions produce the few good things and never the many bad things there are (379C2–8; 380B6–C3).

LI: God is not the cause (*aitia*) of all things, but only of the good things; whatever it is that causes bad things, that cause is not divine (380C6–10; 391E1-2; see *Lg.* 636C, 672B, 899B, 900D, 941B).

The argument for conclusion 7 is a reasonably cogent inference, but we are bound to ask how Plato can simply presuppose the truth of the non-Homeric premise 1 which, once granted, drives the rest of the argument (premise 2 is also questionable). He can do so, I think, because of his inheritance of Socratic piety: the gods are good because they are wise (see also *Lg.* 900D, 897B), and they are wise because of their very nature. That said, however, we are left wondering how the new poetry is to depict the causes of evil, what those causes might be, and how they could coexist within a cosmos ruled by omni-benevolent gods. On that score, Socrates appears to have been silent, whereas the traditional stories of the poets were able to give cathartic shape to the fears of their audiences (e.g., *Od.* 1.32–79; Hesiod, *Op.* 58–128). Plato himself addresses this issue in his other, later work (see below). Here, at any rate, the practical upshot of L1 is clear: stories of the gods' injustices like those at *Il.* 4.73–126 and 24.527–32 must be purged. If the poets insist, they may continue to speak of the gods' punishments, but only so long as they make it clear – as Plato himself does in Book X (614B–621D) – that these are either merited or therapeutic (380A–B; see also *Grg.* 525B–C).

Next up for elimination are those tales that portray the gods as changing shape or otherwise deceiving us. By means of two further arguments Socrates establishes a law with two parts that (L2a): No gods change (381E8–9) and (L2b): The gods do not try to mislead us with falsehoods (383A2–6). This second law will allow Kallipolis to purge traditional literature of all variety of mythological themes, ranging from the shape-shifting antics of Proteus (381C–E) to the deceptive dreams sent by Zeus (e.g., *Il.* 2.1–34) (383A–B). Book III continues with further applications of Laws 1 and 2 to popular poetry, and by its end – and without overtly signaling the fact – the gods of that poetry have been demoted to the status of harmful fabrications (see also the *Laws*; e.g., 636C, 672B, 941B). Although the revisionary theology that results puts Plato at striking variance with the attitudes of many of his fellow Athenians, there is nothing in it that directly undermines the three axioms of Greek religion: the gods exist, they concern themselves with human affairs, and there is reciprocity of some kind between humans and gods. Moreover, it would have been no great shock for Plato's audience to find his Socrates denying the poets' tales of divine capriciousness, enmity, immorality, and response to ill-motivated sacrifice. As mentioned earlier, they had long been exposed to such criticisms by thinkers such as Xenophanes and Euripides, and Hesiod himself had admitted that poets tell lies (*Th.* 26–8). Moreover, others such as Pindar could speak plainly of "Homer's lies" (*N.* 7.23) without incurring legal sanctions. In any case, the providential gods left for use in the educational literature of Kallipolis can still be called by their proper civic names and must be continuous with those referred to in its religious rituals.

Although Plato, like Socrates, vigorously rejects the idea that gods can be magic-ally influenced to benefit us (*R.* 363E–367A; cf. *Lg.* 885B–E, 888A–D, 905D–907B, 948B–C), it is clear that he retains a role for traditional-appearing religious practices (McPherran 2000a). There will still be sacrifices (419A) and hymns to the gods (607A), along with a form of civic religion that features temples, prayers, festivals, priests, and so on (427B–C). Plato also expects the children of Kallipolis to be shaped "by the rites and prayers which the priestesses and priests and the whole community pray at each wedding festival" (461A6–8). The *Republic* is lamentably terse on the details of all this, but that is because its Socrates is unwilling to entrust the authority of establishing these institutions to his guardians or to speculative reason (427B8–9). Rather, the founda-tional laws governing these matters will be introduced and maintained by "the ancestral guide on these matters for all people" (427C3–4): Delphic Apollo (see 427A–C). Plato assigns the same function to Delphi in his *Laws* (738B–D, 759A–E, 828A) and pays better attention there to the details (e.g., 759A–760A, 771A–772D, 778C–D, 799A–803B, 828A–829E). These details are rather conventional, something we should expect, given that Plato's Stranger insists that his Cretan city will absorb and preserve unchanged the rites of the Magnesians (848D). It is, though, puzzling that after declar-ing these educational elements to be the most important, Plato assigns their formula-tion not to the semi-divine philosophers of Kallipolis but to the obscure dispensations of an oracle. This choice reflects Plato's desire to build on the respect his contemporaries had for the Delphic oracle, one clearly shared by Plato (see Dodds 1951: 222–3; Morrow 1960: 402–11). All this, then, suggests that the ritual life of Kallipolis – with the exception of its cult for deceased philosopher-kings (540B–C) – will be very hard to distinguish from that of Plato's Athens. Confirmation of this occurs when we are told that the citizens of Kallipolis will "join all other Greeks in their common holy rites" (470E10–11; see also *Lg.* 848D).

Plato holds that worship is a form of education that should begin in childhood where it can take root in the feelings; thus, he finds charming tales, impressive festivals, seeing one's parents at prayer and so on to be effective ways of impressing upon the affective parts of the soul a habit of mind whose rational confirmation can only be arrived at in maturity (401D–402B; see also *Lg.* 887D–888A). Most citizens of Kallipolis, however, will be non-philosophers who are unable to achieve such confirmation, but who will still profit from the habitual practice of these rites insofar as they promote the retention of their own sort of psychic justice. For philosophers, however, such pious activity is quite secondary to the inwardly-directed activity that it supports; this is their quest for wisdom – for direct apprehension of the Forms – an activity that focuses directly on making oneself "as much like a god as a human can" (613A–B) (see 11: KNOWLEDGE AND THE FORMS IN PLATO). The education given to these future philosopher-kings of Kallipolis will thus take them far beyond the limitations imposed by the anti-hubristic tenets of Socratic piety. For by coming to know the ultimate Form, the Good-itself, they will no longer be regarded as servile assistants of the gods, but will serve Kallipolis as the gods' local representatives (540A–B).

Plato's Philosophical Religion: Gods and Forms

It should be clear by this point that the inner religious life of Plato's philosophers will be vastly different from that of the ordinary citizens of Kallipolis. Thus we might reasonably expect to learn more about the purified gods of *Republic* Books II and III in the later metaphysical books' account of their heavenly abode: the realm of Forms (Books V, VI, VII). However, despite this section's discussion of these immaterial and divine objects of knowledge, the gods hardly appear at all. This fact, in concert with Plato's confessions of the difficulty of conceiving of god/gods (e.g., *Phdr.* 246c), can create the impression that although Plato is willing to retain morally uplifting talk of all-good gods for the children and non-philosophers of his Kallipolis, when he turns to the serious business of educating his philosophers he finds that the only true divinities are the Forms. (Plato's ascription of agency and mental states to his gods, e.g., 560B, 612E–613A, make it clear that the Forms are not gods.) Nevertheless, justice-enforcing gods are redeployed as real features of the cosmos in Book X (612E; see also *Lg.* 901A). Secondly, Plato frequently alludes to genuine gods in dialogues contemporaneous with, and later than, the *Republic* (e.g., *Phaedrus, Parmenides, Laws*).

Probably the clearest expression of the relationship between the middle-dialogue Forms and gods occurs in the second half of the Greatest *Aporia* of the *Parmenides* (133A–134E), where we find an argument purporting to establish the impossibility that the gods could either know or rule over sensible particulars such as ourselves (see

McPherran 1999). This argument is founded on the account of sensibles and Forms we find in the *Phaedo* and *Republic*, with the clear implication being that the Form-realm is also the heavenly home of gods who govern us as masters govern slaves and who apprehend all of the Forms, including Knowledge-itself (as opposed to the instances of knowledge we possess, 134A–E). This brief glimpse of gods and Forms corresponds with the account of the gods offered first in the *Phaedo*, and then in the more complex portrait of the *Phaedrus*. In the course of the *Phaedo*'s Affinity Argument for the soul's immortality (78B–84B), for example, we are told that our souls are most like the divine – hence, the gods – in being deathless, intelligible, and invisible beings that are inclined to govern mortal subjects (e.g., our bodies). When the philosophically-purified soul leaves its body, then, it joins good and wise gods – our masters – and the Forms (80D–81A). The sorts of activities they carry on together are left unclear, but since this section and others parallel the *Parmenides*' attribution of mastery to the gods (62C–63C, 84E–85E), we can expect that these gods are likewise able to rule wisely because of their apprehension of the Forms.

The *Phaedrus* also features souls and gods who know Forms and who have the capacity to rule, and by detailing their relations in his outline of "the life of the gods" (248A1) Plato gives us a partial solution to the identity of the gods of the *Republic* and other middle dialogues. As part of his palinode (*Phdr.* 242B–257B), Socrates first offers a proof that the self-moving souls of both gods and humans are immortal (245C–E), and then turns to a description of their natures (246A–248A). It is, he says, too lengthy a task to describe accurately the soul's structure in a literal fashion; a god could do it, but not a mortal, but we can at least say what the soul resembles (246A3–6; see also 247C3–6). Dismissing the common conception of the Olympian deities as composites of soul and body (246C5–D5), Socrates offers his famous simile, comparing every soul to the natural union of a team of two winged horses and their charioteer (246A6–7), whose ruling part is Reason and whose horses correspond to the spirited and appetitive parts of the soul described in the *Republic* (Book IV).[1] Unlike the mixed team with which mortal drivers must contend, however, the souls of gods and *daimōns* have horses and charioteer-rulers that are entirely good. The most important of these gods are to be identified with the twelve traditional Olympians; their "great commander" is Zeus, who is then trailed by Hera, Poseidon, Demeter, Apollo, Artemis, Ares, Aphrodite, Hermes, Athena, and Hephaestus, while Hestia remains at home. Being entirely good, these gods roam the roads of heaven, guiding souls, and then travel up to heaven's highest rim (247A–E). From these heights each driver – each god's Intelligence – is nourished and made happy by gazing upon the invisible, fully real objects of knowledge to which he or she is akin: Forms such as Justice and Beauty themselves. Even Knowledge-itself is here, "not the knowledge that is close to change and that becomes different as it knows the different things that we consider real down here," but "the knowledge of what really is what it is" (247D7–E2). This account should recall both the *Parmenides*' characterization of the two kinds of knowledge there are – the Knowledge-itself that ruling gods possess and the knowledge-among-us that we possess (see *Tht.* 146E) – and the *Republic*'s declaration in L1 that the gods are the causes of only good. Moreover, this *Phaedrus* myth parallels the epistemology of the *Republic* insofar as the latter alludes to the knowledge possessed by those guardians who are able to rule by virtue of the wisdom they have come to possess (428C–D) and whose intellects are nourished and made happy by their intercourse with the Forms (490A–B). (Both texts also possess parallel psychologies and eschatological myths that contain Olympian post-mortem rewards and punishments (*Phdr.* 256A–C; *R.* 621C–D) and reincarnation into a variety of lives (*Phdr.* 247C–249D; *R.* 614B–621D).)

In view of such parallels, it is reasonable to suppose that the deities sanctioned by the *Phaedrus* (or similar ones) would also be those of the *Republic*, and this seems especially true when we consider the conservative streak Plato displayed by putting Delphic Apollo in charge of the establishment of temples and sacrifices; hence, the installment of the specific deities the city will honor, at *Republic* 427B–C. Thus, when Socrates acknowledges the Apollo of Delphi at 427A–B and Zeus at 583B and 391C, and defends the reputations of Hera, Ares, Aphrodite, Hephaestus, and Poseidon at 390c and 391c, he is affirming the existence of distinct deities with distinct functions who may still be credited with distinctive personalities, each one resembling the kind of human soul he or she will lead up to the nourishment of the Form realm (248A–E). The series of cosmological etymologies concerning the names of the gods, including the Olympians, provided by the *Philebus* (395E–410E) reinforces this account (see Sedley 2003: 39–41, 89–112). Here, for example, we learn that the name "Zeus" actually signifies "the cause of life always to all things," his father "Cronos" signifies "pure intellect," and "Hades" decodes as "he who knows all fine things" (395E–404B). In almost every case, the pantheon is accorded "a nomenclature which recognizes that god is the intelligent cause of good in the world" (Sedley 2003: 95). Plato's strategy here seems plain: he will grant that the poets correctly differentiated and named the gods – although what they call themselves is beyond our knowledge (*Cra.* 400D) – but will then insist that they are accurately referred to only when references to their alleged deceits, enmities, ignorance, and responses to justice-indifferent cult are omitted and they are understood to be intellects who, knowing the Forms, guide souls and help govern the universe (some, perhaps, by serving as judges in the afterlife; e.g., *R.* 614c–615c).

What, then, is the relation of that superordinate Form, the Good-itself (*R.* 504D–534D), to these gods? It was a commonplace in antiquity that the Good is God (e.g., Sextus, *M.* 11.70), a view that still finds some favor. If that were right, we could then postulate that the image of the Great Commander Zeus is one of Plato's ways of conceptualizing the Good in order to make it a subject of honorific ritual. In fact, we are encouraged to think of the Good as a god in several ways: the Good is said to be (a) the *archē* – the cause of the being – of the Forms (509B6–8) and everything else (511B, 517B–C); (b) a ruler over the intelligible world in the way the sun, a god, rules over the visible realm (509B–D); and (c) analogous to the maker (*dēmiourgos*) of our senses (507c7), the sun, one of the gods of heaven (508A–C (and an offspring of the Good, 508B; 506E–507A)). This identification can then (d) explain Book X's odd and unique claim that the Form of Bed is created by a craftsman god, who is, in a sense, the creator of all things (596A–598c). Finally, if the Good were not a god, then (i) the gods of the *Republic* would apparently be the offspring of a non-God (the Good), or (ii) the Good would be subordinate to these gods, or (iii) the gods would exist in independence from the Good; but none of these possibilities seem to make sense in light of (a) through (d). Despite all this, however, the characterization of the Good as being beyond all being in dignity and power (509B8–10) means that it cannot be a mind, a *nous*, that knows anything; rather, it is that which makes knowledge possible (508B–509B). Thus, since for Plato a necessary condition for something's being a god is that it be a mind/soul possessing intelligence, the Good cannot be a god.

One way to resolve this problem is to suppose that Plato's foremost concern in the *Republic* is ethical, where Plato intends for the Good to function as both a formal and final cause of all beings. Given that emphasis, he is willing to talk as though the Good might be a God that we could call Great Commander Zeus (e.g., at 596A–598C), but without working out the problems of ascribing mental states to a being beyond being or explaining how the gods as knowers of Forms are the efficient causes of good events and things. But when in the late dialogues his concerns turn from ethics to cosmology, he then realizes that he requires the existence of a creator-deity who can serve as an ultimate efficient cause; and this is what we find in the Maker-god of the *Timaeus* (27A–92C) and *Philebus* (26E–30E) (see *Plt.* 269C–274E; *Lg.* 893A–907B, 967B; *Cra.* 399D–401A; Benitez 1995).

Plato's Maker-god, the Demiurge, marks another of Plato's debts to his teacher (see 3: THE SOCRATIC PROBLEM). For in Xenophon's *Memorabilia* we find Socrates arguing that since individual beings in the universe are either the product of intelligent design or mere dumb luck, and since human beings are clearly the products of intelligent design, we ought to be persuaded that there exists a vastly knowledgeable god, a god who is moreover, "a wise and loving Maker (*dēmiourgos*)" (1.4.2–7; see also 4.3.1–18; McPherran 1996: ch. 5.2). Plato's mature expression of this idea in the *Timaeus* and elsewhere goes well beyond this Socratic inheritance by incorporating his Theory of Forms in a conscious attempt to rebut materialists who deny the priority of soul over body (27D–29B; see also *Phlb.* 30C–D; *Lg.* 889B–C, 891E–899D). The "likely account" (29B–D) Plato puts forward there is, in brief, that:

1   The cosmos is an ordered, perceptible thing.
2   All ordered perceptibles are things that come to be.
3   Thus, the cosmos is not eternal but came to be.
4   Every ordered thing that comes to be has a craftsman as the cause of its coming to be.
5   Thus, the cosmos has a Craftsman as the cause of its coming to be.
6   The Craftsman-cause of the cosmos patterned the cosmos after one of two kinds of model: (a) a changeless model grasped by reasoned understanding or (b) a changing model grasped by opinion involving sense perception.
7   If the cosmos is beautiful and its craftsman is good, then its craftsman used (a) a changeless model grasped by reasoned understanding.
8   The cosmos is beautiful and its Craftsman is good.
9   Thus the cosmos "is a work of craft, modeled after that which is changeless and is grasped by a rational account, that is, by wisdom" (29A6–B1).

The claim that the Craftsman is good in premise (8) appears to come out of thin air, but is perhaps to be inferred from the evident beauty and order of the Cosmos, and its providential, human-serving design (see Xenophon, *Mem.* 1.4.10–19; see also 4.3.2–14). In any event, from that goodness it is then supposed to follow that the Demiurge was free of jealousy prior to the creation, and hence, he desired that everything that exists be as much like himself as possible, and thus, as good as possible. This desire then led the Demiurge to bring order to the recalcitrant, disorderly motion of visible material by making it as intelligent as possible (it cannot be made perfectly good, because its natural disorder is immune to even the vast – though not omnipotent – power of this god (see n. 3)). This required that he put intelligence into a World-Soul, placing that soul into the body of the Cosmos, thereby making it a living being "endowed with soul and intelligence" (30B6–c1), modeling it after the generic Form of Living Thing (29D–31A), a Form that contains at least all the Forms of living things, if not all Forms.

In Plato's middle-dialogue account of physical change in the *Phaedo* (99c–107B), the Forms are treated as having the ability to act as both the formal and efficient causes of a subject's possession of properties, somehow radiating instances of themselves into sensible individuals (so that, say, Simmias comes to be tall by coming to possess an immanent character instance of Tallness-itself, *Phd.* 100B–105c; cf. *Prm.* 130B, 133A–134E). The *Timaeus* retains this same ontology of immanent characters and Forms, though without making mention of the *Republic*'s Good-itself, and appears to give the job of implanting immanent characters to God (*Ti.* 48D–53c). Then, in place of the plural sensible subjects of participation, Plato posits a single particular subject that is the Receptacle, Nurse, and Mother of all becoming (49B, 50D); like a plastic substance such as gold (50A–c), it provides a place or Space (52A–B) for Form-instances to manifest themselves in those various locations that we call by individual subject names.

Apart from the Demiurge, the created cosmos, and the stars, there is little mention of the activities of other, more traditional gods. Although these gods seem to be invoked generically at the outset of the creation story (*Ti.* 27c–D), and the Muses receive a mention (47D–E), the only other significant mention of gods appears to undermine their having any genuine existence in this scheme. For when it comes time to account for the origin of the gods other than the star-gods, we are told that

> it is beyond our task to know and speak of how they came to be. We should accept on faith the assertions of those figures of the past who claimed to be the offspring of the gods. They must surely have been well informed about their own ancestors. So we cannot avoid believing the children of the gods, even though their accounts lack plausible or compelling proofs. Rather, we should follow custom and believe them . . . Accordingly, let us accept their account of how these gods came to be and state what it is. (*Ti.* 40D6–E4; see also *Lg.* 948B)

It appears that the past figures referred to are such legendary and quasi-divine authors as Orpheus and Musaeus. But the account Plato ascribes to them with this odd argument seems to take in other storytellers such as Hesiod, for it has Earth and Heaven giving birth to Oceanus and Tethys, who then give birth to Phorcys, Cronus, and Rhea, and "all the gods in that generation" (40E6–41A1), with Cronus and Rhea then giving birth to Zeus, Hera, and the other Olympians (40E–41A). In any case, the reasoning here is so specious and the denial of rational warrant so emphatic that it appears Plato is recommending merely lukewarm acceptance of and not actual belief in the existence of beings bearing the names of the Olympians (see *Phdr.* 229c–230A).

Here it is hard to resist the impression that the old gods have become little more than noble lies that philosophers offer to children and non-philosophers in order to train and keep in check their unruly souls.

Nevertheless, gods bearing the names of the Olympians make a prominent appearance in the *Laws* from its outset, as its discussants make their way from Cnossus to Zeus' birthplace and shrine on Mount Ida (625B). There are, for example, close to two hundred references to god or gods (Zeus, Hera, Apollo, and Dionysus are frequently referred to by name), and even Zeus Xenios is cited in his traditional role as protector of foreigners (729E–730A). Moreover, when he addresses the inhabitants of his new Cretan city, the Athenian Stranger tells them that they must "resolve to belong to those who follow in the company of god" (716B8–9) and so model themselves after god. The most effective way to do this, he tells them, is to pray and sacrifice to the gods, and this means the gods of the underworld, the Olympians, the patron deities of the state, and *daimōns* and heroes (716B–717B; see Burkert 1985, chs. 3.3.5 and 4). Later, as he mounts his case against atheism, the Stranger makes it clear that he and his companions' memories of seeing their parents addressing the Olympian gods with an assured belief in their actual existence are not to be undermined by skepticism (887C–888A; see also 904E). Finally, the argument for there being a Craftsman-god of the cosmos refers to the existence of lesser gods spoken of in the plural (893B–907B): this Maker or Supervisor of the universe has established these gods as rulers over various parts of the universe (903B–C). We found similar gods in the *Phaedrus*, and such beings appear elsewhere (*Plt.* 271D, 272E; *Ti.* 41A–D, 42D–E), and thus it seems that Plato consistently understood his Maker-god to be a supreme deity who may be called Zeus (e.g., *Phlb.* 30D; *Phdr.* 246E) overseeing a community of lesser deities (Morrow 1966: 131) who may still be called by the names of the Olympians (see 14: THE ROLE OF COSMOLOGY IN PLATO'S PHILOSOPHY).

Plato's Philosophical Religion: Immortality and Postmortem Judgment

At the end of the *Apology* Socrates expresses confidence that death is a good thing, but it is an ambivalent confidence grounded on his dilemma that death is either like being nothing or is like a journey from here to another place, where our souls will have the supreme happiness of philosophizing with great judges, poets, and heroes (40c–41c) (McPherran 1996: ch. 5.1). Plato, however, solves the dilemma in favor of this second optimistic horn by advancing a variety of arguments for the immortality of the soul; we find four in the *Phaedo* (the Cyclical Argument, 69E–72E; the Recollection Argument, 72E–77E; the Affinity Argument, 78B–82B; and the Final Argument, 102A–107B), a different one in the *Republic* (608D–611C), and another in the *Phaedrus* (245C–246A). There is not sufficient space here to assess these arguments; but it is useful to observe how Plato appropriates the language of traditional myth and religious mystery cults (e.g., the Eleusinian Mysteries) to link our natural human hope for post-mortem happiness with the new intellectual enterprise of philosophy that sees the philosopher as driven by an erotic desire or a kind of madness for union with the Forms (e.g., *R.* 490A–B; *Phdr.* 249c–253c; Eleusinian references to purification (*katharsis*), initiation, and sudden revelation (*epopteia*) include *R.* 378A, 560E; references to the Bacchic Mysteries include *Smp.* 218B, *Lg.* 672B, *Phdr.* 250B–C, 265B; Corybantic references include *Cri.* 54D and *Euthd.* 277D. Eleusinian Mystery motifs also contribute to the Myth of the Cave in *Republic* Book VII, the *Symposium*'s Ladder of Love (209E–212C), and the Myth of the Soul in the *Phaedrus* (244A–257B). See Morgan 1990: chs. 3–6 and 20: PLATO ON EROS AND FRIENDSHIP).

Consider, for example, the *Phaedo*'s Affinity Argument (78B–82B). Here, Socrates contends that since (1) there are two classes of things: (i) invisible, unchanging, incomposite, pure things not subject to dissolution, in particular, Forms such as Beauty-itself, and (ii) visible, changing, composite things subject to dissolution, in particular, sensible particulars; and since (2) human beings are part visible body and part invisible mind/soul (115C) – where it is the soul in distinction from the body that apprehends Forms – we must agree that (3) the soul is more like the Forms than sensible particular things, and so must be placed in the class of invisible things. Thus, (4) the soul is unchanging, incomposite, and is therefore not liable to dissolution: it travels on to Hades. However, throughout this argument Plato emphasizes the requirement that coming to know the Forms in Hades involves the soul in becoming more like them in terms of their purity, that is, their lack of sensible characteristics. Hence, for the soul this means freedom from attachment to the impure body and its desires for pleasure. To obtain such freedom requires that the soul be purified not by traditional religious methods but by philosophical training of one's reason, which – as an heroic "practice for death" (81A1, 89B–C, 94D–E, 95B) – releases it from the chains of bodily desire; without this, the soul will be reimprisoned in another body (81A–E; cf. 66D–67A, 67D). Sometimes this purification is characterized as the turning around of the soul (e.g., *R.* 518B–521C) or similar to what the initiates in the Mysteries undergo (e.g., *Phd.* 81A) or as the soul's attempt to become as much like god as possible in respect of justice and wisdom (*Smp.* 207C–209E; *Phdr.* 248A, 252C–253C; *R.* 613A–B; *Tht.* 172B–177C; *Ti.* 90A–D; *Lg.* 716C; Sedley 1999). Here and elsewhere Plato also assimilates the less mainstream Pythagorean, possibly Orphic, view that the body is a kind of prison for the soul which must undergo many trials of intellectual purification (*katharsis*) and initiation (*teletē*) for it to achieve liberation, a homecoming whose rewards include a final revelatory vision (*Phd.* 62A–B, 69B–D, 79D, 82D; *R.* 533C; *Phlb.* 400B–C; Dodds 1951: ch. 7; Edmonds 2004: 175–9). In the *Symposium* this vision is presented as though it was the unveiling (*epopteia*) of those Mysteries revealed to the initiates of Eleusis, but what is seen by those initiated into the mysteries of philosophy are not the sacred objects of Demeter, but the most perfect and sacred objects of all: Beauty-itself and all the other Forms (210A–212B) (Morgan 1990: ch. 4).

In a number of places Plato attempts to characterize the soul's immortality in terms of post-mortem rewards and punishments, followed by reincarnation (*Phd.* 107C–115A, cf. 63E–64A; *R.* 612C–621D; *Phdr.* 246A–257B; *Ti.* 91D–92C; see also *Grg.* 522B–527E). These accounts are cast in the traditionally authoritative language of poetry, and incorporate many of the motifs of various traditional myths of descent (*katabasis*), death, and judgment (e.g., *Il.* 23.65–107; Hesiod, *Op.* 178–94; Pindar, *O.* 2.57–60, 63–73). The idea of reincarnation is itself called an "old legend" by Socrates (*Phd.* 70C5–6); it turns up before Plato in the works of Pindar and Empedocles, and was allegedly introduced into Greece by Pythagoras (Porphyry, *VP* 19). We are also led to believe that these myths are approximations of the truth (*Phd.* 114D; *R.* 618B–D, 621B–D; see also *Grg.* 523A), although we are given little help in determining which of their elements come closer to the truth than others (see Edmonds 2004: ch. 1).

The *Republic*, for example, ends with a consideration of the previously dismissed question of the rewards of justice by first proving the soul's immortality (608C–612A) and then arguing for the superiority of the just life in consequentialistic terms. Plato first affirms Adeimantus' earlier story (362D–363E) that the gods reward the just person and punish the unjust during the course of their lives (612A–614A), but then offers the Myth of Er to show how they also do the same in the afterlife (614A–621A). This story is similar to Plato's other main eschatological myths that display a willingness to use the prospects of pain and pleasure as inducements to virtuous behavior for those of us as yet unready to pursue virtue for its own sake.[2] Nevertheless, its complex portrait of the long-term rewards for striving after justice is often found to be depressing, not reassuring (e.g., Annas 1981: 350–3). For although there are ten-fold rewards for the just and ten-fold punishments for the unjust, there are also non-redeeming, everlasting tortures for those who have become morally incurable (615C–616B; see also *Grg.* 525B–526B). Moreover, unlike the eschatologies of the *Phaedo* and *Phaedrus*, Plato rules out there being any final liberation from the cycle of incarnations (Annas 1982: 136). True to L1, however, Plato explicitly relieves the gods of all responsibility for the suffering we will experience in our next incarnation, by means of a lottery (617E, 619C). As he constructs it, a soul's choice of a happy life of justice will depend both on the random fall of the lots and that soul's ability to choose wisely. But it is unclear whether the lottery is rigged by Necessity, and a soul's degree of practical wisdom is constrained by its prior experiences, experiences that were in turn the result of prior ignorant choices. This means that those who have lived lives of justice, through habit and without philosophy, and so arrive at the lottery after experiencing the rewards of heaven will, by having forgotten their earlier sufferings, make bad choices and suffer further (617D–621B). Finally, aside from the chancy work of the lottery, Plato has never adumbrated the many sources of evil mentioned in Book II, against which even the gods are powerless.[3] So although the last lines of the *Republic* encourage us to race after justice so that we may collect our Olympian rewards (621B–D), given their uncertainty and lack of finality, some will find Thrasymachean shortcuts a better gamble.

There is no sure way to determine how Plato meant for us to read this and other such myths: perhaps modern readers are right to find its details of colored whorls and lotteries to be only entertaining bits of window-dressing, not to be taken as contributing to a philosophically coherent eschatology (see Annas 1981: 351–3). This is poetry, after all, and it is composed within the framework of a dialogue that consistently disdains poetry. On the other hand, it is possible to read Er's tale of reincarnation as alluding to the beneficial initiations of Eleusis, but now connected to the true initiation and conversion of the soul provided by philosophical dialectic (Morgan 1990: 150). There are also reasons to suppose that the display of whorls, Sirens, and Necessity are symbolic of the metaphysical elements of the *Republic's* middle books, and are thus meant to impress on each soul prior to its next choice of life and its drink from the River of Unheeding (620E–621C) the message of those books: that the happiest life is the life of Justice and the Good, and so ought to be chosen for that reason alone (Johnson 1999).

257

The message that does come through in all of Plato's eschatological myths, however, is that no god or *daimōn* can be blamed for whatever fix we may happen to find ourselves in when we put down Plato's texts. Moreover, the many complications of these stories and the way in which they put our future judgment in the hands of gods and fate seem intended to undermine our using that future state as a source of motivation and choice-making in the here and now. Perhaps we are being encouraged to dismiss the cheap motivations of carrot and stick that drive the vulgar many so that we might recall the truly pious aspirations of philosophy developed in the preceding main body of Plato's text (see *Phd.* 114D–115A; Annas 1982). At the same time, however, Plato appears to be using "traditional mythic material . . . to ground his advocacy of the philosophical life in the authority of the [mythic] tradition" (Edmonds 2004: 161), giving that life motivational substance by persuasively picturing the unseen noetic realm that is the goal of every true philosopher. These myths, then, can be read as returning us to both the stern Socrates of *Republic* Book I (and elsewhere; e.g., *Cri.* 48A–49E), who urges us to choose the path of justice *simpliciter*, and the hopeful Socrates of the *Phaedo* who foresees a return to the friendly divinities and Formal delights of heaven (*Phd.* 63c, 81A; *Phdr.* 247c). Through all this and more, Plato laid the groundwork for the flowering of western theology and mysticism.

Notes

Translations of Plato are taken from J. M. Cooper (ed.) *Plato: Complete Works* (Indianapolis: Hackett, 1997).

1 Plato's appropriation of the immortal horses of the gods (*Il.* 5.352–69) is typical of his entire approach to the myths of Greek religion: he retains the traditional ambrosia and nectar as food and drink for the lower, horsy parts of the soul (247E), but has the philosophical Intellect feed on the new, true ambrosia of the immortal Forms.

2 Although it is hard to know how to view this particular fiction in light of Plato's earlier categorical denigration of all mimetic writing (*R.* 595A–608B). See Morrison 1955, for discussion of the myth. Morgan (1990: 152), notes that although the precise sources of the myth "are beyond our grasp. There are doubtless Orphic, Pythagorean, and traditional elements." See Edmonds 2004: ch. 4, and Kingsley 1995: chs. 6–12, for discussion of the *Phaedo*'s myth.

3 The role of chance here, though, suggests that Plato may have had his later *Timaeus* view of the causes of evil in mind, causes that he locates in the disorderly motions of matter (see Cherniss 1971; see also *Phdr.* 248c–D; *Plt.* 273c–E). The *Republic* does at least make clear that human evil is a consequence of our having souls that are maimed by their association "with the body and other evils" (611c1–2; see also 611B–D, 353E; *Phd.* 78B–84B; *Tht.* 176A–B; *Lg.* 896c–897c); e.g., not even the *Republic*'s rulers are infallible in their judgments of particulars, and so Kallipolis will fail owing to the inability of the guardians to make infallibly good marriages (given their need to use perception; *R.* 546B–c). Such imperfection is, however, a necessary condition of human beings having been created in the first place, a creation that Plato clearly thought was a good thing, all things considered.

References and further reading

Annas, J. (1981). *An Introduction to Plato's* Republic. Oxford: Oxford University Press.

—— (1982). Plato's myths of judgment. *Phronesis* 27, pp. 119–43.

Beckman, J. (1979). *The Religious Dimension of Socrates' Thought.* Waterloo: Wilfrid Laurier University Press.

Benitez, E. E. (1995). The good or the demiurge: causation and the unity of good in Plato. *Apeiron* 28, pp. 113–40.

Burkert, W. (1985). *Greek Religion.* Cambridge, Mass.: Harvard University Press.

Cherniss, H. (1971). The sources of evil according to Plato. In G. Vlastos (ed.) *Plato,* vol. 2 (pp. 244–58). Garden City, NY: Anchor Books.

Dodds, E. R. (1951). *The Greeks and the Irrational.* Berkeley: University of California Press.

Edmonds, R. G. (2004). *Myths of the Underworld Journey: Plato, Aristophanes, and the "Orphic" Gold Tablets.* Cambridge: Cambridge University Press.

Johnson, R. R. (1999). Does Plato's myth of Er contribute to the argument of the *Republic? Philosophy and Rhetoric* 32, pp. 1–13.

Kingsley, P. (1995). *Ancient Philosophy, Mystery, and Magic: Empedocles and the Pythagorean Tradition.* Oxford: Oxford University Press.

McPherran, M. L. (1996). *The Religion of Socrates.* University Park, Pa.: Pennsylvania State University Press. Pbk. edn. 1999.

—— (1999). An argument "too strange": *Parmenides* 134c4–E8. In M. L. McPherran (ed.) *Recognition, Remembrance, and Reality: New Essays on Plato's Epistemology and Metaphysics. Apeiron,* supplementary volume 32.4, pp. 55–71.

—— (2000a). Does piety pay? Socrates and Plato on prayer and sacrifice. In N. D. Smith and P. Woodruff (eds.) *Reason and Religion in Socratic Philosophy* (pp. 89–114). Oxford: Oxford University Press.

—— (2000b). Piety, justice, and the unity of virtue. *Journal of the History of Philosophy* 38, pp. 299–328.

Morgan, M. L. (1990). *Platonic Piety.* New Haven, Conn.: Yale University Press.

—— (1992). Plato and Greek religion. In R. Kraut (ed.) *The Cambridge Companion to Plato* (pp. 227–47). Cambridge: Cambridge University Press.

Morrison, J. S. (1955). Parmenides and Er. *Journal of Hellenic Studies* 75, pp. 59–68.

Morrow, G. R. (1960). *Plato's Cretan City.* Princeton, NJ: Princeton University Press. Repr. 1993.

—— (1966). Plato's gods. In K. Kolenda (ed.) *Insight and Vision: Essays in Honor of Radoslav Andrea Tsanoff* (pp. 121–34). San Antonio, Tex.: Principia Press of Trinity University.

Sedley, D. (1999). The ideal of godlikeness. In G. Fine (ed.) *Plato 2: Ethics, Politics, Religion, and the Soul* (pp. 309–28). Oxford: Oxford University Press.

—— (2003). *Plato's* Cratylus. Cambridge: Cambridge University Press.

Vlastos, G. (1991). *Socrates: Ironist and Moral Philosopher.* Ithaca, NY: Cornell University Press; Cambridge: Cambridge University Press.

Zaidman, L. B. and Pantel, P. S. (1992). *Religion in the Ancient Greek City,* trans. P. Cartledge. Cambridge: Cambridge University Press.

Part IV

PLATONIC PSYCHOLOGY

18

The Socratic Paradoxes

THOMAS C. BRICKHOUSE AND NICHOLAS D. SMITH

Of the many paradoxical positions attributed to Socrates in Plato's early dialogues, two are perhaps most closely associated with the philosopher. Adopting the labels used by Santas (1979: 183–94), let's call the first the "prudential paradox," which states that no one ever acts contrary to his knowledge of what is best for him, and the second the "moral paradox," according to which no one voluntarily does what is unjust. Seeing why Socrates would have held these positions in spite of their obvious conflict with common sense will allow us to understand better a number of issues at the heart of the moral epistemology and psychology we find in Plato's early dialogues and to deepen our understanding of the philosophy Plato gave to Socrates generally (and, we suspect, for a time accepted himself). (For simplicity's sake, we will henceforth refer simply to the positions as those of "Socrates," leaving aside all question of their connections either to the historical person of that name or to Plato, who presented these positions to us by putting them into the mouth of a character named Socrates in the early dialogues.) Because the moral paradox depends crucially on the prudential paradox and because the moral paradox assumes issues discussed in detail elsewhere in this volume, we shall discuss the prudential paradox first and at greater length.

The Prudential Paradox

The best-known attribution of the prudential paradox to Socrates outside the pages of Plato can be found in Aristotle's *Nicomachean Ethics*, 1145b23–7. According to Aristotle, Socrates thought:

> it would be strange when knowledge is present for something else to rule and to drag it around just as if it were a slave. For Socrates vigorously fought against this claim, since there is no such thing as weakness (*akrasia*). For no one acts contrary to what is best while grasping that he is doing so. Rather, he does so on account of ignorance.

Aristotle is often understood to be saying that Socrates rejects the notion that someone could know what is best for him and not do it because his *belief* about what is best for him is sufficient to produce action in accordance with that belief, and if belief is sufficient for the corresponding action, then knowledge, which implies belief, must also be sufficient for the corresponding action. Let's call this characterization of Socrates' position, following Penner (Penner 1996: 199–229; and 1997: 117–47) the rejection of "belief-*akrasia*" (or BA). It follows that anyone who fails to do what is best for him must be ignorant in the sense that at the time he acts he fails to see what is truly in his interest.

It may be helpful to pursue Socrates' endorsement of the prudential paradox by asking how well Aristotle's understanding of Socrates' position fits with what we find in the pages of Plato. Scholars often claim that Plato's Socrates sets forth reasons against the possibility of *akrasia* in two passages: *Men.* 77B6–78c2 and *Prt.* 352B1– 358D4. Let's take up the shorter and less complicated *Meno* passage first.

The *Meno* Argument

After twice failing to define "virtue," Meno makes a third effort: "Virtue," he says, "is the desire for noble things (*epithumounta tōn kalōn*) and the power to acquire them" (77B4–5). After Socrates gets the initial clarification that "noble things" are "good things," he immediately begins to question Meno's assertion that there are people who do not desire good things. Among these people, Meno claims, we can find some who actually desire bad things, mistaking them for good things, while others desire (*epithumousin*) bad things, knowing they are bad things (*gignōskontes hoti kaka estin*, 77c3–7). Scholars are virtually unanimous that Meno's claim that people sometimes knowingly choose bad things is the proposition Socrates targets for rejection.

Socrates' first piece of business is to make sure that Meno really wants to say that there are those who desire bad things even though they know that bad things harm their possessor (77D1–4). Meno concedes that if those who knowingly pursue bad things also know they are harmed by them, they know they are made miserable (*athlious*) to the extent they are harmed (78A1–3). And if they are miserable, they are unhappy (*kakodaimonas*, A3). What Meno cannot accept, however, is that there can be anyone who wishes (*bouletai*) to make himself miserable (A4–5), and so Meno admits, "it is likely that no one wishes (*boulesthai*) for bad things" (78A9–B2).

So what seals Meno's defeat is his admission that no one wishes to be miserable and unhappy. But why is Meno so quick to concede this point? Unfortunately, Plato does not spell out the answer for us. Many scholars (e.g., Irwin 1977: 78, 1995: 75–6; Nehamas 1999: 27–58; Penner 2000: 164) believe that Socrates accepts only one kind of motivation, rational desire, that is, a desire for what we take to be good for us. If so, since we always desire our own happiness as the ultimate good, anything else we desire we desire as a good that we believe will in some way – either constitutively or instrumentally – promote our happiness. This is sometimes known as Socrates' commitment to intellectualism with respect to motivation. If he is indeed an intellectualist of this sort and if Meno and Socrates are assuming this theory of motivation in this argument, it is not difficult to see why Meno is defeated. The fact that no one desires what he recognizes to be a bad thing follows directly from the sort of intellectualism about motivation most scholars say that Socrates endorses. According to this way of construing the argument, it appears that Aristotle is right about Socrates' denial of *akrasia*, at least as we find it in the *Meno*. Socrates denies that one can act contrary to one's knowledge of what is best, because his theory of motivation rules out the possibility of BA, and since knowledge implies belief, action contrary to what one knows to be the best course must also be impossible. According to this reading, Socrates rejects what Penner (Penner 1996, 1997: 117–49) terms "knowledge-*akrasia*," or KA, because he rejects the possibility of BA.

We might wonder, though, if this is really the correct way to understand the argument. In the first place, even if Socrates is an intellectualist about motivation, why should Meno be? Many people would say that such intellectualism is utterly counterintuitive and that it is only commonsensical to think that some desires are nonrational in the sense that they aim at pleasure and the absence of pain independently of how they are thought to bear on our conceptions of the good. Moreover, Meno's initial position, that some people want bad things, knowing they are bad, seems to assume the falsity of an intellectualistic account of motivation. Why would Meno admit defeat if all that has been shown is that his view conflicts with a theory of motivation he does not accept?

Perhaps, though, Socrates is relying on a different point. It is interesting to note that when Socrates initially asks whether people desire bad things, he uses the verb "*epithumein*." But when he inquires about whether people want to be miserable and unhappy, he switches to the verb "*boulesthai*." Now ordinary Greek would allow Socrates to use the two verbs interchangeably. But as Devereux points out (see Devereux 1995: 396–403), Socrates may be using the verbs in the technical senses we find elsewhere in Plato and in Aristotle and thus may be using them to refer to different kinds of desires. If so, when he uses "*epithumein*" he is asking whether anyone ever forms a nonrational desire for what he knows to be a bad thing, and when he employs "*boulesthai*" he is asking whether anyone ever forms a rational desire to be miserable and unhappy. We don't have to suppose that Meno manages to understand the distinction Socrates introduces in this way. Socrates is seeking to gain Meno's agreement that no one forms a rational desire to be miserable and hence to gain his agreement that no one forms a *rational desire* for bad things, that is, for things that contribute to misery. This would be a sensible thing for Socrates to do, inasmuch as it then follows, as Socrates points out, that *everyone* has a rational desire to be happy and, accordingly, *everyone* has a rational desire for good things. This would be telling because Meno, recall, claimed that virtue is, by definition, the desire for fine things and the ability to attain them. In this view, precisely because Meno himself has not yet managed to make the distinction between rational and nonrational desires, and how the objects of desires are represented in those different kinds of desire, the outcome of this argument is that his attempted definition of virtue now seems to him to be wholly indefensible. At the conclusion of the argument we have been examining, Meno is forced to concede that everyone is the same with respect to their desire for fine things (78B4–6). Yet plainly not everyone is the same with respect to virtue. The first conjunct in Meno's proposed definition, then, will have been shown to be otiose.

According to this second way of construing the argument, the target proposition is not, contrary to what scholars usually say, Meno's claim that some people knowingly desire bad things. Rather, because "*epithumia*" could be used in a general sense to refer to any desire or to refer to a specific kind of desire, nonrational desire, Socrates wants to know which one Meno has in mind. Indeed, Socrates is prepared to concede, at least for the purposes of this argument, that one can know that something is bad and have a *nonrational* desire for it. What Socrates is after is Meno's concession that no one ever has a *rational* desire for what is bad, for it is then a short step to a compelling criticism of the first part of Meno's proposed definition of virtue. This is significant because is shows that this passage in the *Meno* fails to provide evidence one way or the other for Socrates' denial of BA, since at least in this passage Socrates is not really concerned with the possibility of acting contrary to the agent's beliefs about what is best.

If this second way of reading the *Meno* passage is correct, we lose the *Meno* as evidence for Aristotle's way of understanding Socrates' denial of *akrasia*. Unfortunately, the passage in the *Meno* that has attracted so much attention is quite brief, making it difficult to say with confidence whether the challenge to the traditional reading is successful. Any compelling case for Aristotle's understanding of Socrates' position, accordingly, will have to rest on the evidence drawn from the *Protagoras.*

Socrates' Argument against "The Many" in the *Protagoras*

At *Prt.* 351B3 Socrates abruptly interrupts his investigation of the relationship between wisdom and courage to conduct another inquiry. Now he imagines himself questioning "the many" (*hoi polloi*) about their view that sometimes a person voluntarily does what is bad for him even though he knows it is bad for him. The many, according to Socrates, maintain that knowledge (*epistēmē*)

> is neither a strong, nor a leading, nor a ruling element . . . but that often when knowledge is present in a person, it does not rule him at all, but something else does, sometimes anger, sometimes pleasure, sometimes pain, sometimes love, and often fear, thinking simply that knowledge is dragged about by all these things just as if it were a slave. (*Prt.* 352B4–c1)

The failure of knowledge always to direct its possessor, we learn a few lines later, owes to the fact that it can be "overcome by pleasure or pain" (352E6–353A1).

Two points are worth making at the outset. First, the reference to knowledge being "dragged about like a slave" strongly suggests that Aristotle is thinking about this very passage when he attributes to Socrates the denial of BA. But, second, the many initially state their position in terms of the insufficiency of *knowledge* to resist pleasure. The many begin by characterizing their position in terms of what we are calling "knowledge-*akrasia*," or KA. They maintain that KA sometimes occurs. We can now state Socrates' initial characterization of the many's position somewhat more formally as follows:

(KA) Sometimes a person, *P*, does *X*, which he knows to be bad for him, because *P* is overcome by pleasure.

Socrates' initial move is to clarify just what it is about being "overcome by pleasure" that makes the many say that being overcome is a bad thing for the agent. Bad things are bad not because they provide pleasure, Socrates states on behalf of the many, "but because of what happens later, diseases and such like" (353E1). Being overcome by pleasure, therefore, is not bad because the agent gains *some* pleasure from his action, but because the pleasure he gains is not worth the bad consequences of the choice. Being overcome by pleasure, we might say, is on balance a bad thing for the person who is overcome.

The same applies, *mutatis mutandis*, to good things. Although such things as athletics, military training, and surgery are painful, we nonetheless judge them to be good "because at a later time they bring about such things as health and the good condition of bodies and the preservation of their cities and power over others and wealth" (354B2–5). Moreover, the many deem these things good because they result in pleasure (and relief from pain) that is worth the cost of the pain that must be endured initially.

Socrates sums up the many's view of the relationship between both the good and pleasure and evil and pain as follows:

> Accordingly, you think that pain is bad and pleasure is good, since you call bad whatever deprives one of greater pleasures or brings about greater pains than the pleasures that are in it . . . and again you call what is painful good whenever it exchanges greater pains for those in it or provides greater pleasures than the pains that are in it. (354C5–D7)

So Socrates takes the many to be hedonists of the sort that allows for the unqualified substitution of "pleasure" with "good" and "pain" with "bad" (354C3–5, 355A1–5). Whether Socrates himself endorses the many's view of the good is controversial. Irwin and Dodds, for example, maintain that he does (see Dodds 1959: 21–2; Irwin 1995: 81–3, 1997: 102–14). Others argue that Socrates nowhere endorses hedonism (see, e.g., Sullivan 1961: 10–28; Vlastos 1969: 71–88; Zeyl 1980: 250–69).

At this point Socrates announces, somewhat cryptically, that it is the many's adherence to hedonism that will eventually sink KA (355A1–B1). To see the problem, he suggests we need only substitute "good" for "pleasure" and "bad" for "pain" in KA (355A3–B1), yielding KA′:

(KA′) Sometimes *P* does *X*, which he knows to be bad, because he is "overcome by good."

KA′, however, is "absurd" (*geloion*, 355C8–D6), according to Socrates. But why?

It is perhaps tempting to think that KA′ is absurd because it is self-contradictory. This is the way Vlastos first understood the problem with KA′ (Vlastos 1956: xxxix). According to this interpretation, when we substitute "good" for "pleasure" in the many's explanation of why *P* fails to do what he knows is best for him, we get "*P* is overcome by a desire for what is best for him." But it is nonsense to say, "*P* knowingly fails to do what is best for him, i.e., *P* knowingly chooses what is worse for him, because he wants what is best for him."

Unfortunately, this reading badly distorts the many's position. As 355A6–B3 shows, the many's claim is that *P* is overcome, not by a desire for what is best for himself overall, but by a desire for some *immediate* pleasure, a pleasure he can gain by not doing what he knows to be best for himself overall. In choosing *X*, the many would say, P knows perfectly well that he is not doing what is best for him overall, but his desire for the pleasure at hand, that is, the good at hand, defeats him and "drags his knowledge about like a slave." If KA' is absurd, it is not because it is self-contradictory.

If the many are to hold on to their position, they must be prepared to say that when P acts akratically he knowingly foregoes a greater package of goods because there is something about a good that is immediately available that makes his desire for it stronger than his knowledge of what is best. Not surprisingly, Socrates' next move is to argue that such is not really possible. He first points out that there is nothing about an immediate pleasure, considered as a pleasure, that makes it differ from a remote pleasure except its quantity (356A7–B3). He then remarks that "if you weigh pleasures against pleasures you have to take (*lēptea*) the greater and the more, and if you weigh pains against pains, you must take the less and the smaller" (356B3–5).

Now in what sense "must" we choose the greater pleasures and avoid the greater pains? Some scholars (e.g., Taylor 1991: 189–90) have argued that Socrates is here imputing to the many what we might call "evaluative hedonism," according to which "one must choose" the greater pleasures and avoid the greater pains if one is to achieve what is best. On this interpretation, Socrates is pointing out what the many must think constitutes the correct choice so that he can later provide his own account of how the incorrect choice is made by P, namely because of P's ignorance. But if this is what Socrates has in mind, there is no reason for the many to concede defeat, since they can happily point out that there is no contradiction in claiming, as they do, that P has knowledge and P makes a mistake. It is not contradictory because, the many can say, there is no conflict in saying that, on the one hand, P knows what is best and how to obtain what is best and, on the other, that P errs because he was precluded from acting in accordance with his knowledge.

Another view (see, e.g., Gallop 1964: 125–9; Santas 1971: 278–84, esp. pp. 280–1 n. 21; Irwin 1995: 83–4) holds that when Socrates says "one must choose" the greater pleasure and the less pain he is attributing "psychological hedonism" to the many. If so, Socrates thinks that the many believe that as a matter of psychological necessity we always act for the sake of what we either believe or know will provide us with the greatest overall pleasure and the least overall pain. Socrates has reason to make this attribution because psychological hedonism is a consequence of the many's concession that the immediacy of a pleasure gives it no special status as the object of desire. When they make this concession, the many lose whatever ground they may have for claiming that a desire for an immediate pleasure can conflict (synchronously) with a desire for what we judge to be best. As a result, the many must admit that all pleasures are pursued as a result of a decision, that is, as a result of "weighing" one pleasure against the other and choosing the one that appears to "weigh" more.

Now the question is how to account for the phenomenon the many call *akrasia* if one desire cannot conflict with another. The explanation, Socrates says, derives from the fact that pleasures and pains, like the objects of sense-perception, have the power to appear larger (or smaller) than they in fact are (356c4–8). Thus whenever P chooses X, which is on balance bad for him, X must have at the time of its selection appeared to P to "weigh" more than its alternative. Fortunately, we are not necessarily doomed to succumb to the power of pleasure and pain to appear larger (or smaller) than they in fact are.

> If our doing well depended on this, namely in engaging in and taking larger things and avoiding and not engaging in the smaller ones, what would be our salvation in life: the craft of measurement (*hē metrētikē technē*) or the power of appearance (*tou phainomenou dunamis*)? Doesn't the latter often make us wander all around and regret what we do in our actions and choices of the great and the small? The craft of measurement, on the other hand, would make the appearances lose their power by showing us the truth, and would give us peace of mind that abides in the truth, and would save our lives. (356c9–E2)

Socrates is now in a position to explain what really happens when the many say that P is "overcome by pleasure." "Being overcome" is really being guided by the power of appearance, for had P the craft of measurement P could have judged the pleasures involved in the decision correctly. Since the craft of measurement is moral knowledge, being overcome is lack of knowledge (357D2–7). Being overcome is really ignorance (357B6–E2).

Knowledge and Belief

So Socrates believes that if P knows what is best for him he will do what is best for him, because he weighs the competing pleasures and pains correctly. There remains a crucial point to clarify, however. Is Socrates only suggesting that no one acts contrarily to his knowledge of what is best *at the time he acts*, or is he suggesting something stronger, namely that if P possesses moral knowledge P can never be deceived about pleasure and pain? The former leaves open the possibility that P can know at time t_1 that X is bad and yet do X at a later time, t_2, P's assessment of X having changed through a subsequent failure to cognize X correctly at some point between t_1 and t_2. If Socrates holds the latter, he thinks that it is not possible for P to know at t_1 that X is bad and yet do X at t_2, his knowledge that X is bad having been replaced by a false belief that X is good. Let's call the former thesis, borrowing the terminology of Penner (1996, 1997: 217–49) the denial of "synchronic *akrasia*," and the latter thesis the denial of "diachronic *akrasia*." According to both views, Socrates thinks that *at the time* an action is performed knowledge cannot be overcome. But if he accepts "diachronic *akrasia*," he thinks that there is a sense that knowledge can succumb to the power of appearance over time, whereas if he rejects diachronic *akrasia* he denies that knowledge can ever be defeated by changing appearances.

As Aristotle understands Socrates' denial of *akrasia*, Socrates denies only "synchronic *akrasia*," and on this point modern interpreters have followed Aristotle's lead (e.g., Vlastos 1956: xxxviii; Santas 1964, Taylor 1991: 201–4). Let's call this "the sufficiency of knowledge or belief view." In this view, action always reflects the agent's present beliefs (whether those beliefs are instances of knowledge or are "mere" beliefs). To support their case, those who take this line point to the text. Immediately after noting that the many are committed to equating being overcome by pleasure with ignorance, Socrates makes the following remark:

> If pleasure is the good . . . no one who knows or believes (*eidōs oute oiomenos*) that something is better than what he is doing, something possible, that is, keeps doing what he is

THOMAS C. BRICKHOUSE AND NICHOLAS D. SMITH

doing, when it is possible to do what is better. Nor is "being overcome" anything other than ignorance, nor is controlling oneself anything other than wisdom. (358B6–c3; see also 358c3–D4, 358E2–359A1, and 360A4–6)

But if Socrates only wishes to deny synchronic *akrasia*, why does he begin his discussion with the many by emphasizing that it is *knowledge* that cannot be overcome? Why would he not say that *either* knowledge *or* belief about what is good cannot be overcome at the time one acts? Those who maintain that Socrates is merely denying synchronic *akrasia* have a ready answer: since knowledge implies belief, then if one can never do what one *believes* is bad, one can never act contrarily to what one *knows* is bad.

In a number of important papers, Penner argues that the sufficiency of knowledge or belief view is a mistake (1991: 147–202, 1996: 199–229; 1997: 217–49). According to Penner, Socrates is arguing against the possibility of diachronic *akrasia* for anyone who possesses knowledge. Let's call Penner's position, the "stability of knowledge" view. If Penner is right, when Socrates says that being overcome is really just ignorance, Socrates means by "ignorance" "not *knowingly* recognizing" that what one is set on doing is bad. If so, Socrates never wishes to challenge the possibility that at t_1 P could believe that X is bad and yet be overcome in the sense that at t_2 P changes his mind about X's value. What Socrates denies is that it is possible for P at t_1 to *know* that X is bad and yet at t_2 to have come to believe that X is good. As evidence Penner points to the fact that when Socrates begins his discussion with the many he clearly believes that knowledge should be praised for its *strength*. Indeed, he even endorses Protagoras' claim that "knowledge and wisdom . . . are the strongest of all elements in human activities" (*kratiston . . . einai tōn anthropeiōn pragmatōn*, 352D1–3). But if Socrates merely rejects synchronic *akrasia*, it is hard to see why knowledge's strength would be of any significance. Belief alone is also sufficient protection against doing what is bad at the time the action is performed.

Not only does the stability of knowledge view explain Socrates' references to the strength of knowledge in a way that the sufficiency of knowledge or belief view cannot, the stability of knowledge view also attributes to Socrates a far more interesting moral epistemology, one that would explain why Socrates would claim that knowledge "saves our life" (356E2). According to the sufficiency of knowledge or belief view, P can know at t_1 that X is bad for him and then at t_2 succumb to the power of the appearance, abandoning his knowledge in favor of a false, perhaps even disastrously false, belief. But this is hardly a view of knowledge as a power that "saves our life." The stability of knowledge view, then, allows us to see why knowledge makes the soul, as Socrates says, "abide in the truth."

But if Socrates is denying the possibility that knowledge but not belief can be overcome diachronically, how are we to understand Socrates' assertion at 358B6–c1 that knowledge *and* belief are always sufficient for doing what one takes to be best for one? In making this claim, Socrates is talking about the agent's state of mind at the time of action, and there is nothing about the stability of knowledge view that conflicts with Socrates' conviction that all action is motivated by rational desire. The stability of knowledge view only maintains that if P has moral knowledge, he will not be swayed over time about what is good and bad for him. If, however, P possesses mere belief, P is

270

liable to change his mind as various different circumstances arise in which X appears more pleasant than in fact it is. Socrates' assertion that knowledge saves us from the appearances, then, seems to favor the stability of knowledge view.

What Endows an Object with the Power of Appearance?

Under what conditions does an object acquire the power of appearance and just how is it that knowledge but not belief thwarts that power once it is acquired by an object? Rather than tackling these questions head-on, perhaps we would do well first to return to the received view of Socrates' view of motivation. There is no debate about the claim that Socrates thinks all actions are motivated by rational desire. Most scholars would endorse the additional point that, for Socrates, rational desires are not only the sole motivational forces behind actions, they are the only sort of psychic condition that has causal consequences (see, e.g., Irwin 1977: 78, 1995: 51–3, 75–6; Penner 1991, 1996, 1997: 117–49; Vlastos 1991: 148–54; Reshotko 1992: 145–70; Brickhouse and Smith 1994: 91–101; Nehamas 1999: 27–58). So according to the received view of desire in Socratic philosophy, if something appears good to us it does so only because we already have a rational desire for things of that sort and we form the belief that the particular object appearing good to us is of that sort.

If we now ask why some objects acquire the power of appearance, proponents of the traditional view can only answer that it is *always* rational to desire what provides the most pleasure and least pain on balance. Of course we will change our minds and form a contrary rational desire if we come to believe that an object Y will not provide more pleasure than X. According to the stability of knowledge view, Socrates values the craft of measurement so highly because it always provides its possessor the right reason regarding whether an object that appears pleasant ought to be pursued.

Still, how does an object acquire the power of appearance, according to the traditional view? Assuming that Socrates holds the stability of knowledge view, consider again how Socrates wants to handle "being overcome." At t_1, P believes that X is bad for him. At t_2, P believes that X is good for him and pursues X. At t_3, P regrets having pursued X (*Prt.* 356D6–7). Plainly, at t_2 X possesses the power of appearance and, at t_1 and t_3, it lacks that power. We need some way of explaining X's acquisition of the power of appearance at t_2. Specifically, what proponents of the traditional account must provide is an explanation of why P comes to believe that X is good at t_2.

Traditionalists might argue that Socrates explains the change of mind between t_1 and t_2 in terms of P's changing his perspective on X. Unless P has the craft of measurement, which guarantees correct judgment about the objects of pursuit, as P moves closer to X, for example, X will appear larger than it is. As a result, P judges X to be better than it is. This is why Socrates asks the many, "Do things of the same size appear larger when near at hand and smaller when seen at a distance, or not?" (356c5–6). Because P's desire to pursue X at t_2 is, according to this reading, always the product of P's changed perspective, what motivates P's pursuit at t_2 is a rational desire.

A little reflection, however, shows us that this cannot very well be what Socrates has in mind. Surely the most common case of the phenomenon Socrates is trying to explain occurs when X is ready to hand and so can be enjoyed either immediately or

271

later. When X is ready to hand at t_1 and P judges it to be on balance bad, what accounts for P's change of mind at t_2 – *when P's perspective on X has not changed* – when P pursues X? Let's imagine a person trying to lose weight because he believes it would be good for him and who has a piece of chocolate cake placed directly in front of him. At one point he declines the offer to eat it, citing his belief that it would be bad for him. Later, with the cake still in front of him, he proceeds to eat it. When he has had his fill, he says that he regrets having eaten the cake. Plainly perspective, temporal or spatial, has nothing to do with the agent's change of assessment.

In our discussion of the *Meno*, we mentioned that Socrates uses the term "*epithumia*," the favored term of both Plato and Aristotle for nonrational desire, that is, desire that aims at some non-good end. We might of course think that Socrates is just using the term in a loose sense, whereas Plato and Aristotle are using it in a strict sense. But as Devereux points out (1995: 400–1), there is at least one passage, *Chrm.* 167E1–5, in which Socrates quite explicitly distinguishes between "wish" (*boulēsis*), which he says aims at some good, and *epithumia*, which he says aims at pleasure. We cannot very well dismiss this as a slip on Socrates' part, for even in the *Apology* he clearly thinks that the passions have a role to play in explaining some actions. We see this, for example, in Socrates' claim that he does nothing but exhort people to pursue virtue and to shame them if they do not (29E3–30A3). His discussion of how he has remained at his god-assigned post in spite of the hostility he has faced clearly implies that he thinks that, in some sense, fear has a role to play in how others are motivated to do shameful things (32B1–D4).

But do not these considerations just show that Socrates' theory of motivation is incoherent? Does not the admission of nonrational desires into his moral psychology conflict with his view, expressed in the *Protagoras*, that all actions are guided by some cognition – either knowledge or belief – of what is best for us (*Prt.* 358B6–c1)? In the paper just cited and to which our own view is deeply indebted, Devereux explains that Socrates' views are consistent if he thinks that nonrational desires can cause, not actions, but changes in belief about whether the objects to which they are attracted are good (1995: 381–408). A nonrational desire for an object can come upon us and cause us to believe that the object that we previously judged not to be good for us really is good for us after all. Devereux argues that the craft of measurement is compatible with strong nonrational desire and that what is important about knowledge for Socrates is that knowledge is always stronger than any desire.

If this is how Socrates' view of nonrational desire operates, it is fair to call his theory of motivation "intellectualism," for he remains committed to the notion that one never acts contrary to what one knows or believes is best for oneself at the time of action. It is a modified version of intellectualism, however, because Socrates recognizes the causal power of nonrational desires and thinks that they can overcome belief but not knowledge.

Does Socrates have the *Metrētikē Technē?*

At this point an interesting question arises concerning whether Socrates himself possesses the craft of measurement (*metrētikē technē*). In the *Apology* (37A5–6) Socrates declares that he "is convinced that [he] has not done wrong to anyone," including presumably himself. It follows that no object ever possessed the *dunamis tou phainomenou* over him, at least not to the extent that it caused him to believe some object was good when it was not and then to act on his false belief. It is tempting to conclude that, in spite of his many professions to the contrary, Socrates must possess moral knowledge after all, since in the *Protagoras* he strongly suggests that only the craft of measurement can "save us" from the power of appearance. And yet in the *Apology* he also insists to his jurors, as he does so often with his interlocutors in the dialogues, that he lacks any such wisdom beyond the recognition of his own ignorance (see 8: SOCRATIC IGNORANCE).

There are, we believe, good reasons to be wary of attributing moral wisdom to Socrates (Brickhouse and Smith 1994: 30–55). So before we accept the implication that Socrates would mislead the jury about such an important issue, let us briefly pursue another possibility. Recall that if Socrates' moral psychology allows for nonrational desires, their power is to be found in their effect on our beliefs about the goodness of the objects of those desires. In the *Gorgias* Socrates implies that some nonrational desires are more powerful than others and that a particular nonrational desire can grow stronger or weaker over time. This seems to be what is behind Socrates' remark to Callicles in the *Gorgias* when he tells him that if a person is to avoid engaging in the worst sort of activities, "he should not let his appetites (*epithumias*) become uncontrolled and try to fill themselves up" (507E1–3). Those which are not allowed to "fill themselves up," it seems, remain relatively weak. Socrates would advise us to keep our appetites weak if he thinks that strong appetites are dangerous because they prevent reason from doing its work as the craft of measurement by inhibiting deliberation about what the best course available to us is (see Brickhouse and Smith 2002: 23–35). Although this way of understanding Socrates' position presents an important departure from Devereux's, which argues that the craft of measurement is compatible with strong nonrational desire (Devereux 1995: 38–89), it allows us to see why Socrates has managed over the course of his life never to succumb to the power of appearance. If Socrates has scrupulously managed to avoid allowing his appetites "to fill themselves up," he has kept them from interfering with his deliberations about what is best.

If this is right, we can reconcile Socrates' denial that he is in any morally important sense wise and his assertion that he has never treated anyone wrongly. Socrates has reason to think that although the craft of measurement is the most reliable way to defeat the power of appearance, it is not the only way. One can defeat such a formidable power through careful deliberation, the very sort of thing Socrates says he always engages in (*Cri.* 46B4–6). If so, and if he has been able to keep his nonrational desires weak and compliant and thus insufficient to cause him to believe something that appears pleasant is on balance good, he has been able to guide his life by reason, free of the power of appearance. Socrates still has reason to think that only the craft of measurement saves us, because only the craft of measurement *guarantees* that its possessor reaches correct judgments about what is and is not to be pursued. Even if his weak nonrational desires do not pre-empt his power to deliberate and decide, lacking knowledge Socrates cannot be sure that the outcome of his deliberation is correct (Brickhouse and Smith 2000: 149–53). Socrates may think, then, that even the objects of weak appetite appear good. What they lack is the power to compel belief that they are good. The power to compel belief is the province of strong appetite, in which case the absence of strong appetite is a necessary condition of moral knowledge.

There is yet another reason for thinking that the craft of measurement requires weak nonrational appetites. Recall that in the *Protagoras* Socrates says that the craft of measurement "gives us peace of mind" (*hēsuchian epoiēsen echein tēn psuchēn*; 356E1). Although Socrates does not spell out exactly what he means by "peace of mind," he tells Callicles quite explicitly in the *Gorgias* that happiness requires that our appetites be "orderly" and that orderly appetites are those that do not incline us to act contrarily to a judgment about what is to be pursued (507B4–6). If, as seems reasonable, the "peace of mind" to which Socrates refers in the *Protagoras* implies that the soul is not pulled in different directions at the same time, then it is hard to see how moral knowledge could be compatible with appetites that strongly oppose its judgments about what is best.

The Moral Paradox

In the *Gorgias* Socrates argues first against Polus and then against Callicles that the tyrant, the most immoral of all people, is not really powerful. The outline of Socrates' argument for this astounding claim is not hard to discern. The tyrant has the ability to harm others unjustly, but his ability to do so is not really power if we think that power is a good thing (468D1–E5). If Socrates is right, doing injustice is never a good thing, since it inevitably yields the very opposite of the tyrant's ultimate goal, happiness. Injustice is, as Socrates tells Callicles, "the very worst thing for the person who commits it" (509B1–5). The reason of course is that by acting unjustly the tyrant is actually doing great damage to his own soul, his most precious possession.

In an important sense Socrates sees the tyrant and all who engage in immorality as acting involuntarily because they are acting from factual ignorance about what they are doing. To be sure, the tyrant who destroys an entire village in an act of vengeance knows that he will be hated for what he has done, that he must always watch his own back, that his children will be in danger, and so forth. But he judges that the good he gains for himself is worth the potential danger he puts himself and his loved ones in. The tyrant's error, which renders his unjust actions involuntary, is the factual mistake of not grasping that no matter what harm he does to others he does greater damage to himself. Given the thesis basic to the prudential paradox that every bad action is the result of false belief, it follows that if every immoral action is harmful to the agent, every immoral action must be the product of false belief. Thus not only is action that ends up harming the agent himself the product of ignorance, but so is every action that harms another.

The *Gorgias* is not the only Socratic dialogue in which Socrates claims that immoral action harms the soul. In the *Crito* he says he has long believed that one must follow the opinion of the one who has knowledge in moral matters lest one "corrupt and destroy that which becomes better by what is just but is destroyed by what is unjust" (47D3–5). Surprisingly, nowhere does Socrates explicitly tell us why this claim is true. We can begin to put together a plausible answer if we briefly review several basic

Socratic claims about the soul and what its good condition is. In the *Apology*, Socrates tells the jury that he has done nothing else with his life than to go around exhorting his fellow citizens to care about "wisdom, truth, and the best condition of their souls" (29ε1–2). This "best condition of the soul" he subsequently identifies as virtue, *aretē* (30β2–4). Now there are a number of passages that strongly suggest that Socrates believes that the virtue he is seeking is nothing less than knowledge (see 22: THE UNITY OF THE VIRTUES). But in *Republic* I, Socrates explicitly states that the characteristic function of the soul is "taking care of things, ruling, deliberating, and all such things" (*R.* 353D4–6). Since *aretē* is that condition of anything that has a function that enables it to perform its function well, Socrates draws the conclusion that the power "to take care of things, to rule, and to deliberate" well is the virtue of the soul (353ε4–5).

So how does unjust action destroy the soul? Socrates may think that unjust action, in some way, destroys the power of the soul to perform its function. To see how this could be, let's return to Socrates' remarks in the *Gorgias* about the importance of appetites being orderly and disciplined if we are to be happy. There Socrates said that it is necessary for us to prevent our appetites from "filling themselves up" because in so doing they become increasingly less disciplined. As we argued in the last section, we can make good sense of this if Socrates means that strong appetites cause a person to believe that an object of appetite is in fact good when it is not. Since pleasurable objects always *appear* good, if we are to find what is actually good among the appearances, it is necessary that we be able to deliberate well about our choices. But if strong appetite is actually sufficient for belief that the object of that appetite is good, plainly strong appetite is incompatible with any sort of effective deliberation about our good (see 24: PLATO'S CONCEPT OF GOODNESS). This allows us, we maintain, to see why Socrates says that the commission of unjust action is the worst thing we can do for ourselves, for insofar as it strengthens our appetites, it destroys our most precious possession, which is the soul's capacity to engage in the activity that gives us a distinctly human life (Brickhouse and Smith 2002: 26–31). Although the notion that no one does injustice voluntarily is deeply paradoxical, acceptance of these views about the growth of appetite, the commission of injustice, and the destruction of our ability to deliberate, convince Socrates that no one who understands what he is doing to himself through injustice does what is unjust voluntarily.

Socrates, Plato, and Aristotle

Plato and Aristotle agree with Socrates that knowledge is sufficient for doing what is good. But because Socrates believes that our actions are always undertaken in the pursuit of what we take to be good, his moral psychology is nonetheless importantly different from that of either Plato or Aristotle. Most scholars maintain that Socrates differs from Plato and Aristotle on this point because, as we have seen, most scholars believe that Socrates rejects the notion that there are any nonrational desires. We have argued, however, following Devereux, that there is good reason to think that Socrates agrees with Plato and Aristotle that there are nonrational desires that have real causal powers.

But even if the three major figures in Greek philosophy agree that there are nonrational desires and that knowledge is always invulnerable to any inclination to act other than as it directs, Socrates nonetheless disagrees with Plato and Aristotle about how nonrational desire operates in the soul. According to Plato and Aristotle, we can feel the urge to move towards a pleasure even after we have deliberated and decided that what we desire is not good for us. Moreover, if that urge is sufficiently strong it can motivate contrarily to what we believe is good. For some people, Plato and Aristotle agree, the motivational urge to act contrarily to their judgment about what is good is not sufficient to make them do what they think they ought not. For others, Plato and Aristotle hold, that urge is sufficiently strong. In contrast, Socrates, so we argue, sees nonrational desire as operating not as an independent motivation to act, but as a cause of belief about what is good.

We have also argued that the strength of nonrational desire explains its power to alter belief about what is good. If nonrational desire is strong enough, it prevents our soul from performing its natural function of deliberating about our good and that causes us to see the pleasurable object as a good (contra Devereux 1995: 404–8).

Doubtless, Plato and Aristotle later disagreed with Socrates, at least in part, because Socrates' view of desire leads to the very paradoxes we have been exploring. For Plato and Aristotle, a paradox is something for philosophy to dispel; Socrates views paradox as something philosophy can embrace and explain. On this point concerning the very nature of the philosophical enterprise, we can only here note how far apart Socrates stood from his most famous successors in Athens and, indeed, from most thinkers in the western philosophical tradition.

Note

All translations are the authors'.

References and further reading

Benson, H. (2000). *Socratic Wisdom: The Model of Knowledge in Plato's Early Dialogues*. Oxford and New York: Oxford University Press.
Brickhouse, T. C. and Smith, N. D. (1994). *Plato's Socrates*. New York: Oxford University Press.
—— and —— (2000). *The Philosophy of Socrates*. Boulder, Colo.: Westview Press.
—— and —— (2002). Incurable souls in Socratic psychology. *Ancient Philosophy* 22, pp. 1–16.
Devereux, D. T. (1995). Socrates' Kantian conception of virtue. *Journal of the History of Philosophy* 33, pp. 381–408.
Dodds, E. R. (1959). *Plato: Gorgias*. Oxford: Clarendon Press.
Frede, M. (1991). Introduction. In *Plato*: Protagoras (pp. vii–xxxiv). Indianapolis: Hackett.
Gosling, J. and Taylor, C. C. W. (1982). *The Greeks on Pleasure*. Oxford: Clarendon Press.
Hackforth, R. (1928). Hedonism in Plato's *Protagoras*. *Classical Quarterly* 22, pp. 39–42.
Irwin, T. (1977). *Plato's Moral Theory*. Oxford: Clarendon Press.
—— (1995). *Plato's Ethics*. Oxford and New York: Oxford University Press.

McTighe, K. (1992). Socrates on desire for the good and the involuntariness of wrongdoing: *Gorgias* 446a–468e. In H. Benson (ed.) *Essays on the Philosophy of Socrates* (pp. 263–97). New York and Oxford: Oxford University Press.

Nehamas, A. (1999). Socratic intellectualism. In A. Nehamas (ed.) *Virtues of Authenticity: Essays on Plato and Socrates* (pp. 27–58). Princeton, NJ: Princeton University Press.

O'Brien, M. J. (1967). *The Socratic Paradoxes and the Greek Mind.* Chapel Hill: University of North Carolina Press.

Penner, T. (1990). Plato and Davidson: parts of the soul and weakness of will. In D. Copp (ed.) *Canadian Philosophers: Celebrating Twenty Years of the* Canadian Journal of Philosophy, supplementary volume 16 of the *Canadian Journal of Philosophy,* pp. 35–72.

—— (1991). Desire and powers in Socrates: the argument of *Gorgias* 466A–468E that orators and tyrants have no power in the city. *Apeiron* 24, pp. 147–202.

—— (1996). Knowledge vs. true belief in the Socratic philosophy of action. *Apeiron* 29, pp. 199–229.

—— (1997). Socrates on the strength of knowledge in the *Protagoras* 351B–357E. *Archiv für Geschichte der Philosophie* 79, pp. 117–211.

—— (2000). Socrates. In C. J. Rowe and M. Schofield (eds.) *The Cambridge History of Greek and Roman Political Thought* (pp. 164–189). Cambridge: Cambridge University Press.

—— (2001). Desire, action and self-interest in Socratic philosophy. Symposium paper given at the American Philosophical Association, Pacific Division, San Francisco.

Penner, T. and Rowe. C. (1994). The desire for the Good: Is the *Meno* inconsistent with the *Gorgias? Phronesis* 39, pp. 1–25.

Reshotko, N. (1992). The Socratic theory of motivation. *Apeiron* 25, pp. 145–70.

Rudebusch, G. (1999). *Socrates, Pleasure and Value.* New York and Oxford: Oxford University Press.

Santas, G. (1964). The Socratic paradoxes. *Philosophical Review* 73, pp. 147–64.

—— (1971). Plato's *Protagoras* and the explanation of weakness of will. In G. Vlastos (ed.) *The Philosophy of Socrates* (pp. 264–98). Garden City, NY: Doubleday.

—— (1979). *Socrates: Philosophy in Plato's Early Dialogues.* London and Boston: Routledge and Kegan Paul.

Sullivan, J. P. (1961). The hedonism of Plato's *Protagoras. Phronesis* 6, pp. 10–28.

Taylor, C. C. W. (1991). *Plato*: Protagoras. Oxford: Clarendon Press.

Vlastos, G. (1956). Introduction. In *Plato's* Protagoras (pp. vii–lviii). Indianapolis: Bobbs-Merrill.

—— (1969). Socrates on akrasia. *Phoenix* 23, pp. 235–63.

—— (1991). *Socrates: Ironist and Moral Philosopher.* Ithaca, NY: Cornell University Press.

Zeyl, D. (1980). Socrates and hedonism: *Protagoras* 351–358D. *Phronesis* 25, pp. 250–69.

19

The Platonic Soul

FRED D. MILLER, JR.

Introduction

At his trial Socrates professed to never cease practicing philosophy. "I go around doing nothing but persuading both young and old among you not to care for your body or your wealth in preference to or as strongly as for the best possible state of your soul" (*Ap.* 30A7–B2). The care for the soul was thus central to Socrates' philosophical mission. Not surprisingly the soul continues to play a leading role throughout Plato's dialogues.

Plato's term *psuchē*, usually translated "soul," often corresponds closely to the modern term "mind," and his dialogues tackle issues like those discussed by modern philosophers of mind. One set of issues concerns how the soul is related to the body. Plato argues that the body and the soul are distinct entities with different natures, material and immaterial. This view is often called "Platonic dualism." The dualist faces another issue involving causation: how does the soul interact with the body? Plato seems to agree with the modern dualist, René Descartes (1596–1650), who argues that the mind is not merely dependent on the body but is able to act on its own and even cause changes in the body. (Broadie 2001, however, points out important differences between Plato and Descartes.) Another issue is whether the soul is simple or if it has parts and, if so, what sort of parts it has. In the *Republic* Plato argues that the soul has three parts: reason, spirit, and appetite. This tripartite soul looks like an obvious precursor to the tripartite personality defended by Sigmund Freud (1856–1939) who also distinguished between the id, the ego, and the superego (see Kenny 1969). There is also the perennial issue of whether it might be possible for the soul to survive the destruction of the body and, if so, what sort of existence it might lead in a disembodied state.

Plato's treatment of the soul differs from modern philosophy of mind, however, in important ways. First, his vocabulary presents problems for modern translators. The word "mind" does not correspond exactly to Plato's *psuchē*, since every living thing, even a plant, has a *psuchē* (see *Ti.* 77A–B). Admittedly, "soul" is also inexact, but it is less misleading if only because it has fallen out of favor as a philosophical term. Likewise, "intelligence," "reason," "spirit," "appetite," and so on are only rough translations of Platonic terms such as *nous, logos, thumos, epithumia*, and so forth which lack strict modern parallels. Plato's vocabulary offers in effect an alternative mapping of the psychological landscape (see 2: INTERPRETING PLATO).

Further, the paradoxical psychological doctrines attributed to Socrates often provide the backdrop for Plato's arguments: that everyone always seeks what is good for themselves and that virtue is what is best for oneself, so that vice is always involuntary and incontinence (*akrasia*, knowingly choosing evil over good) is impossible (see 18: THE SOCRATIC PARADOXES). Agents are virtuous, according to Socrates, if and only if they possess moral knowledge. This "Socratic intellectualism" is very different from the view of David Hume (1711–76) that "reason is and ought to be the slave of the passions."

Moreover, while modern philosophers are especially interested in the relation of consciousness to entities discovered by modern science (for example, neurons and synapses in the brain), Plato is concerned with other sorts of metaphysical issues such as the relation between Forms and particulars.

Finally, Plato frequently refers to the religious belief in the postmortem transmigration of souls into other bodies, nonhuman as well as human bodies (see 17: PLATONIC RELIGION). He presents colorful myths describing the fate of humans before birth and after death in *Gorgias*, *Phaedo*, *Republic*, and *Phaedrus*, and alludes to such stories elsewhere. The myths sometimes complement philosophical arguments for the immortality of the soul, and are typically introduced with guarded language. Although the myths differ on various details, they agree that virtuous souls are rewarded and vicious ones punished after death and that philosophy is indispensable for postmortem blessedness. (Partenie 2004 is a useful selection.)

The interpretive difficulties common to Plato's texts are especially acute where the soul is concerned. Plato sometimes seems to take pains to create "distance" between himself and his dialogues about the soul (see 3: THE SOCRATIC PROBLEM). For example, the *Phaedo* presents a conversation with Socrates, as recounted by Phaedo, who mentions Plato's absence as being due to illness. Important psychological texts are also attributed to other persons. Socrates in the *Phaedrus* purportedly recites a speech by Stesichorus, a lyric poet of the early sixth century. Timaeus in the dialogue named for him tells a "likely story" about the creation of the cosmos, a cosmos including the soul. An unnamed Athenian Stranger also discusses souls as divine agencies in the *Laws*. This presents a problem as to whether Plato's various characters are speaking for themselves (as in a Greek drama) or he has an identifiable spokesperson. On the former view, "the Platonic soul" is a misnomer, since the dialogues present positions of Plato's characters that are incompatible.

If, on the other hand, Plato is advancing his own views through his characters, as many, if not most, commentators believe, one should still exercise caution in attributing to Plato any doctrine expressed in his text, especially as his considered judgment. This becomes apparent when one tries to reconcile incompatible claims made in the various dialogues. For example, is the soul a simple unity (as in the *Phaedo*) or composed of parts (as in the *Republic*, *Phaedrus*, and *Timaeus*)? And are all three parts immortal (as in the *Phaedrus*) or only the rational part (as in the *Timaeus*)? There are three main lines of interpretation. The particularist approach is to interpret the dialogues separately. This of course leaves open the question whether a coherent psychology is expressed in Plato's corpus. On the unitarian approach, the different passages agree on a fundamental level; alleged inconsistencies are merely apparent or superficial. On the developmental approach, the inconsistencies are real, because Plato's theories gradually evolved as he wrote successive dialogues. This assumes that we can determine the order in which Plato wrote the dialogues. Although this is controversial, it is generally held that the most important dialogues dealing with the soul are, from earliest to latest, *Phaedo, Republic, Phaedrus, Timaeus, Laws*.

So Plato's dialogues deal with many questions concerning the soul in a variety of ways. But he often appeals to the Socratic dictum that we should try to understand what a thing is before trying to know whether it has some attribute: for example, we can know whether virtue can be taught only if we know what virtue is (*Men.* 71B3–4). In general, to understand what *X* is we must find the definition which states its essence (*ousia*), that is, the form (*eidos, idea*) common to every *X* (*Euthphr.* 5D1–5, 11A; *Men.* 72B1–2, c7–8; *Hp.Ma.* 300A9–B2) (see 6: PLATONIC DEFINITIONS AND FORMS; 8: SOCRATIC IGNORANCE). Assuming that this principle applies to the soul, Plato would advise that we begin by attempting to come to know what the soul is. Plato's dialogues contain three main theories concerning the nature of the soul: that the soul is an animating principle, that it has three parts, and that it is able to move itself. These doctrines emerge within various arguments concerning the nature and destiny of the soul. Many arguments seem to build on or modify other arguments. Hence, the rest of this chapter will discuss these three theories within the context of Plato's arguments.

Soul as Animating Principle

Plato's *Phaedo* (or *On the Soul*) describes the final day in the life of Socrates. Before drinking the hemlock, Socrates converses with Simmias and Cebes and defends his view that those who practice philosophy in the right way are best prepared for death. He offers a series of arguments for the immortality of the soul and concludes with a myth concerning the existence of souls after death.

In his opening argument Socrates maintains that a philosopher is best prepared for death along two lines: from knowledge (64c–67B) and from purification (67c–69D). First he explicates death as follows: "the body comes to be separated by itself apart from the soul, and the soul comes to be separated by itself apart from the body" (64c5–8). The crux is that the philosopher more than anyone else frees his soul from his body because his body is of no help, and is even an obstacle, in his quest for knowledge. The main point is that knowledge is of the Forms – for example, the Just-itself, the Beautiful-itself, and the Good-itself – and this knowledge is acquired most purely not through sense-perception, but through thought (*dianoia*) alone and separately from our sense organs as far as possible (see 11: KNOWLEDGE AND THE FORMS IN PLATO; 12: THE FORMS AND THE SCIENCES IN SOCRATES AND PLATO). The body only confuses the soul because the senses are not clear and precise (65A–66A). Further, the desires of the body distract us and make us too busy to practice philosophy (66B–D). Thus we can attain pure knowledge only insofar as we keep our souls independent of our bodies. Therefore, while we are alive we come closest to knowledge if, as philosophers, we have as little to do with the body as possible and do not infect ourselves with its nature, but remain pure from it; and we shall thereby best prepare ourselves for grasping all that is pure – that is, the truth – after death (66D–67B).

This serves as a transition to the argument from purification (67c–69D). Socrates explicates purification (*katharsis*) as follows: "to separate the soul as far as possible from the body and accustom it . . . to dwell by itself as far as it can be freed, as it were, from the bonds of the body" (67c5–D2). Socrates identifies purity with moral virtue, which is misunderstood by the unenlightened many. They think that courage, for example, is the disposition to risk bodily pain in order to avoid greater evil, which they mistakenly equate with more pain. But we have genuine virtue only if we have wisdom and know that only states of the soul are truly valuable. Hence, moderation and courage and justice are a "purging" away of all bodily concerns, and wisdom is a kind of "purification" (69B–c). Socrates compares the practice of philosophy to the initiation in popular mystery rituals that allegedly enables initiates to dwell with the gods after death (see 81A–B). Only philosophy purifies the soul and prepares its practitioner for death (69D).

This opening is rather programmatic, adumbrating tendentious assumptions including the Theory of Forms and the Socratic identification of virtue with knowledge. The definitions of death and purification both assume that each person has a soul as well as a body, each of which comes to be separated itself by itself from the other. If Socrates' interlocutors had challenged these assumptions it would have been hard to get the argument off the ground (see 13: PROBLEMS FOR FORMS). It is also noteworthy that the soul and body are here treated on a par with each other, a claim later qualified. Since the expression "itself by itself" (*auto kath' hauto*) is applied to both the soul and body here, Socrates implies that they have distinct identities or natures. The argument is also unclear about the nature of the soul. It associates desires, pleasures, and pains with the body yet indicates that the souls are often in an impure condition after death, that is, bound up with desires, pleasures, and pains. This implies that the soul has a complex nature involving conative in addition to cognitive capacities.

Cebes objects that even if the soul is separable from the body, it may perish as soon as it leaves the body. This provides the impetus for a series of arguments by Socrates that the soul is immortal and indestructible.

In his cyclical argument (*Phd.* 70D–72E) Socrates recalls an "ancient story" involving reincarnation: souls of the deceased go to the underworld and then return here to be reborn. (For other references to reincarnation see *Phd.* 107c–108A; *Men.* 81B; *R.* X.615A–619E; *Grg.* 493A; *Phdr.* 248B–E, 250B–c; *Ti.* 44c, 89E–90D.) The cyclical argument offered in support of this religious dogma may be reconstructed as follows:

1.1 If there is a process from O_1 to O_2 there is also a process from O_2 to O_1 (where O_1 and O_2 are opposites). For example, heating is the process from cold to hot, and cooling is the process from hot to cold (71A12–B4).

1.2 If things came to be O_2 from being O_1 but not O_1 from being O_2, everything would end up having the same form; for example everything would end up hot (72A11–B5).

1.3 [Everything will not end up having the same form.] (Tacit premise)

1.4 Therefore, if things come to be O_2 from being O_1, they also come to be O_1 from being O_2.

281

1.5 Life and death are opposites (71c1–5).
1.6 Souls come to be dead from being alive (71D10–11).
1.7 Therefore, souls come to be alive from being dead (71D14–15).

This argument suffers from serious difficulties. First, it is invalid unless we add (1.3) as a tacit premise. But it is not obvious that (1.3) is true. Is it impossible for the universe to become completely hot or completely cold? According to the second law of thermodynamics, whenever two systems come into contact, caloric energy is always transferred from the system with the higher temperature to that with the lower temperature. It seems possible that such a law could apply to the universe as a whole. Also, (1.4) is ambiguous, with at least two readings:

(a) If things go from O_1 to O_2, some things go from O_2 to O_1.
(b) If things go from O_1 to O_2, the *same* things go from O_2 to O_1.

Only (a), the weaker reading, follows from the previous premises. But the stronger (b) is needed in order to establish that the same souls return to life that previously departed from life. In any case the argument as it stands seems to conflict with the closing myth which implies that one can escape the cycle of rebirth: "those who have purified themselves sufficiently by philosophy live in the future altogether without a body" (114c2–4).

The next argument from recollection (72E–77D) assumes that our awareness of Forms is a consequence of recollection (*anamnēsis*) based on sense-experience. For example, we recollect the Form of Equality when we perceive equal sticks and stones (see 9: PLATO ON RECOLLECTION). On the basis of this theory Socrates argues that the soul exists before birth (76A–c):

2.1 Since we recollect the Forms when we see particulars, then either we were born with knowledge of them or we acquired it since birth or we obtained it in a previous existence and lost it at birth.
2.2 We did not acquire knowledge of the Forms at birth or after that, because we cannot give an account (*logos*) of them.
2.3 Therefore, we acquired knowledge of the Forms in a previous existence and lost it at birth.

The theory of recollection on which this argument is based involves an idea which some philosophers still find appealing. When we recognize certain truths about perceptible particulars we often display a peculiar kind of knowledge; it is abstract or conceptual knowledge, yet implicit or tacit, since we are not then able to back it up by means of an account, that is, by a fully satisfactory demonstration or definition. This knowledge is innate according to Plato, but it can be converted into explicit knowledge by means of rational reflection (see *Men.* 86A). The process is similar to recollection, for example, when you vaguely recognize an old acquaintance at a school reunion but it takes considerable mental effort to match the face with a name and other details. One problem with this argument, however, is that (2.1) assumes that our implicit knowledge now is the result of explicit knowledge which we had of the Forms before birth. Even if we now possess innate implicit knowledge (for example, of mathematics, logic, or syntactical structures), it doesn't follow that we obtained it by contemplating the Forms before birth. It might, for example, have been "hard wired" into us through some sort of evolutionary process.

Socrates' Affinity Argument (77ᴇ–84ʙ) involves the idea that the soul is most like, and the body least like, the Forms. There are two main premises:

3.1   Because like is known by like and the soul knows Forms by itself, the soul most resembles the Forms, which are pure, immortal, and unchanging.
3.2   Because the divine rules the mortal and the soul naturally rules the body, the soul most resembles the Forms, which are divine.
3.3   Thus because the soul is most like the Forms which are divine, immortal, intelligible, and uniform, the soul, unlike the body, is altogether indissoluble or nearly so.

Premise (3.1) relies on the principle that like is known by like, which was widely held by Plato's predecessors, although some, like Anaxagoras, rejected it (see Aristotle *de An.* III.4.429b22–4). Premise (3.2) depends on the principle that the divine is a natural ruler over the mortal. Socrates does not explain here how the Forms could be said to "rule" over anything, although he will later discuss their role as causes. The claim that the soul rules over the body will also be explained soon. The conclusion (3.3) seems a departure from Socrates' opening argument, which treated the soul and body as on a par. But (3.3) only claims that the soul is *like* the Forms, not that it *is* a Form, and Socrates adds that the soul will reach the divine realm after death only if it is purified or purged of "confusion, ignorance, fear, violent desires and the other human ills" (81ᴀ6–8).

Simmias objects (85ᴇ–86ᴇ) that even if the soul is invisible, incorporeal, and divine, it might be like the attunement or harmony of a musical instrument, e.g., a lyre. An attunement supervenes on the instrument when its parts are arranged finely and in due measure. Similarly, the soul supervenes on a body when its parts are combined the right way. Of Socrates' three replies the following (92ᴇ–95ᴀ) is especially interesting:

4.1   The soul rules over the body by opposing its desires, for example when one is thirsty the soul drags one the opposite way not to drink (94ʙ7–c1).
4.2   An attunement cannot act or be acted on otherwise than on the parts of its instrument; nor can it oppose the parts in any way (94c3–7).
4.3   Therefore, the soul cannot be an attunement (94c8–95c1).

Simmias' attunement theory of soul resembles an influential modern theory, namely that mental states differ from but supervene on physical states. On the attunement view, whether a lyre is in tune depends on whether its strings are stretched the right way, and likewise whether the body has a soul depends on whether its parts are arranged appropriately. Similarly, on the modern supervenience theory, mental events depend on underlying physical causes, for example events in brain cells. Socrates attacks the attunement by appealing to the aforementioned claim (3.2) that the soul is the body's natural ruler. For example, the soul restrains the body when it is thirsty and hungry. Thus, according to Socrates, the soul is not a mere byproduct of the body; it exercises a kind of "top-down" causation (see Taylor 1983 and Wagner 2000).

Cebes raises a further objection (87A–88B): even if the soul may survive the death of the body, this does not show it is immortal. The soul might stand to the body like a weaver to a cloak, who wears out many cloaks but eventually perishes himself. To meet this objection Socrates must prove that the soul is necessarily immortal and indestructible. This "requires a thorough investigation of the cause of generation and destruction" (95E9–96A1).

Socrates' final argument for immortality (95E–106E) is complicated and difficult to interpret. It presupposes that any adequate causal explanation must refer to the Forms. Socrates starts by criticizing previous philosophers for treating "air, ether, water, and many other strange things" as causes of natural phenomena. They mistakenly supposed that one could explain a natural phenomenon by pointing to some material object that allegedly caused it. Socrates offers an example: why is Socrates now sitting in prison? A pre-Socratic philosopher might try to explain that Socrates' body contains bones and sinews, which have the sort of physical characteristics that enable him to remain sitting with his limbs bent. Socrates objects that it is absurd to view his bones and sinews as the cause of his being there, since he could have chosen to escape and been elsewhere, bones, sinews, and all. The bones and sinews are not a real cause but "that without which the cause would not be able to act as a cause" (they are what is now called a "necessary condition"). Socrates' point is that a real cause must *guarantee* that the effect comes about (it must be what is now called a "sufficient condition") and that such a cause must involve the Forms. He accordingly lays down two hypotheses: first, the Forms exist, e.g., the Beautiful-itself, and second, other things are F because they share in the Forms, e.g., beautiful things are beautiful because they share in the Beautiful-itself (see 100B3–E3). For example, if Helen of Troy partakes of the Form of Beauty, this guarantees that she is beautiful. This deceptively simple theory presents various difficulties (see 7: PLATO'S METHOD OF DIALECTIC).

The first problem is that Simmias can be taller than Socrates but shorter than Phaedo, so that Simmias is both tall and short at the same time. But how can opposite Forms coexist in the same particular? To solve this problem Socrates distinguishes between two types of Forms: *transcendent* Forms (e.g., "the tallness in nature") and *immanent* Forms (e.g., "the tallness in us"). (See 102D6–7, 103B5; the labels "transcendent" and "immanent" are due to commentators.) In general, if a particular partakes of a transcendent Form it must also have an immanent Form in it. The first problem is solved because Simmias' immanent Form of Tallness-in-relation-to-Socrates is compatible with Simmias' immanent Form of Shortness-in-relation-to-Phaedo. However, the immanent Form of Tallness-in-relation-to-Socrates could not coexist with the immanent Form of Shortness-in-relation-to-Socrates. If Socrates undergoes a sudden growing spurt so that he becomes taller than Simmias, then Simmias' immanent Form of Tallness-in-relation-to-Socrates "retreats or is destroyed" (102E1–2). This solution also enables Socrates to clarify the meaning of step (1.4) of the earlier cyclical argument. When he said, "if things come to be O_2 from being O_1, they also come to be O_1 from being O_2," he was talking about particulars like Simmias, who go from being short to being tall (103B2–c2).

284

The second problem is that Socrates' proposed causal explanations seem uninformative if not vacuous. He wards off this difficulty by distinguishing two types of causal explanation. The "safe and ignorant" account is, for example, that something is hot because it is occupied by heat. The "sophisticated" account is that it is hot because it is entered by something else, namely, fire, that makes it hot (105B5–c7). In addition to the Form "there is something else that is not the Form but has its character whenever it exists," and it "brings along" the opposite (e.g., heat) to whatever it occupies (103E2–5, 104E10). For convenience, let this "something else" be dubbed a *special bearer* of the Form.

Drawing on this theory, Socrates sets forth his final proof:

5.1   A special bearer of O_1-ness is O_1 and it brings O_1-ness to whatever it occupies. E.g., fire is hot and it brings heat to whatever it occupies (104E10).
5.2   What brings O_1-ness to whatever it occupies will never admit its opposite, O_2-ness. E.g., what brings heat to whatever it occupies will itself never admit coldness (105A1–5).
5.3   The soul is a special bearer of Life (105D3–4).
5.4   Life and Death are opposites (105D6–9). (Compare (1.5) above.)
5.5   Therefore, the soul will not admit Death (105E4–5).
5.6   Therefore, the soul is deathless (*athanatos*) (105E6).
5.7   What is deathless is imperishable (106B2).
5.8   Therefore, the soul is imperishable (106B2–3).

In order to interpret and evaluate this argument, it is necessary to clarify the difficult notion which we are labeling a "special bearer." There is some evidence that the special bearer has a distinctive Form. Socrates refers to "the Form of Three," which is the special bearer of Oddness, and he says that three has "its own Form" as well as "the Form of the Opposite," i.e., Oddness (104D1–7). This suggests that the special bearer has *two* Forms: e.g., fire has the Forms of Fire and Heat. In what Socrates calls a "sophisticated" causal explanation, then, because the special bearer fire brings one Form (i.e., Fire) it necessarily brings the other Form (i.e., Heat).

But where does this mysterious special bearer – and in particular the soul – fit into Plato's ontology? There are three possibilities: transcendent Form, immanent Form, or particular. It is clearly not the first, or else Socrates and Phaedo would have identical souls. Commentators disagree over whether the soul is more like an immanent Form or more like a particular. Socrates describes the soul in similar terms to an immanent Form which "retreats or is destroyed" at the approach of an opposite Form, although the soul is indestructible because the opposite Form in its case is Death (106A3–c7, cf. 102E1–2). If the soul is like an immanent Form, however, the inference from (5.5) to (5.6) looks fallacious. To say that the soul does "not admit" death is to assert a relation of incompatibility between the Forms of Soul and Death. From the fact that the presence of soul (understood as an immanent Form) entails the absence of death (understood as an immanent Form), it does not follow that the soul itself partakes of life in the sense of being a "living" thing like a plant or animal. The inference to (5.8) introduces a further fallacy of equivocation. Even if the soul were "deathless" in the sense of being "living," it would not follow that it is deathless in the sense of being "immortal," as required by (5.8). (See Keyt 1963 for interpretation along these lines.)

Alternatively, other commentators view the special bearer as a particular of a special sort. It obviously cannot be a particular like a body that can partake successively of both the Forms of Heat and Cold. Instead, on this interpretation, the special bearer is like what Aristotle calls a "substance" (*ousia*), that is, a particular with an essence. An essence is a basic property which defines what a thing is and necessitates its other properties. Just as fire is necessarily hot and snow is necessarily cold, soul is necessarily living. Each special bearer brings its necessary properties to whatever it occupies, and it excludes the opposite properties. This interpretation requires that we attribute a concept of essence to Plato (see Silverman 2003) as well as a concept of substance anticipating Aristotle (see 27: LEARNING ABOUT PLATO FROM ARISTOTLE). But it has the advantage of avoiding the logical fallacy mentioned above. Still, the final step remains problematic. Even if the soul is necessarily living (5.6), this only means that the soul is alive as long as it exists. It doesn't follow that the soul *always* exists and is living (5.8). (See Frede 1978 and Weller 1995 for interpretation along these lines.)

The final argument leaves another question unanswered: What is the basis for (5.3), the crucial claim that the soul is the animating principle? And how is this related to other indications in the *Phaedo* that the soul is above all a rational principle? For answers it is necessary to turn to other dialogues.

The Tripartite Soul

The theory that the soul has three parts comes to the fore in the *Republic, Phaedrus,* and *Timaeus*. The theory is defended most systematically in the *Republic* in support of Socrates' argument that a just person is better off than an unjust person. In order to explain the nature of justice Socrates develops an elaborate analogy between the soul and the city-state, both of which have three parts. Justice obtains when each part carries out its proper function, and when the part that is natural ruler is obeyed by the other parts. In the case of a just soul, the rational part (*logis tikon*) is the natural ruler and is obeyed by the spirit (*thumoeides*) and appetite (*epithumētikon*) (see 23: PLATO ON JUSTICE).

In his argument for the tripartite soul in *Republic* IV, Socrates distinguishes the parts of the soul by appealing to familiar cases of mental conflict. Reason differs from appetite because a person who desires to drink can be stopped by reasoning (presumably about health) (439c5–d2). Appetite differs from spirit because Leontius' desire to look at corpses overcame his sense of shame (439e6–440a3). Spirit differs from reason because the angry Odysseus wanted to kill his disloyal servants but controlled himself after reasoning that it would be bad to commit such a self-destructive act (441b2–c2). It is interesting that the drinking case and the Odysseus example are both used in the *Phaedo* to support premise (4.2) to refute the attunement theory of soul. In the *Phaedo,* however, the monadic soul is opposed to the body and its desires. In the *Republic* the example is used to illustrate conflict *within* the soul. The logical structure of the argument is illustrated in the case of reason and appetite:

6.1   The same thing cannot do or undergo opposite things in the same respect toward the same object at the same time (436b8–9).

6.2   Hence, if there are opposing actions in *X*, the actions must be due to different parts of *X* (436b9–c1).

6.3   Desiring to *A* and being unwilling to *A* are opposite actions (437b1–c6).

6.4   Some persons want to drink but are also unwilling to drink (439c2–3).

6.5   Therefore, the part in them (i.e., appetite) that wants to drink is different from the part (i.e., reason) that wants not to drink (439d4–8).

(6.1), which may be called "the principle of non-opposition," is a logical truism, a corollary of the principle of non-contradiction. (Proof: If O_1 and O_2 are opposites, then a thing is O_1 only if is not O_2. But a thing cannot be both O_2 and not O_2 (non-contradiction). Hence, a thing can't be both O_1 and O_2). Socrates illustrates (6.2) with a person who is moving and standing still at the same time, because his hands are moving while his feet are not (436c8–d2). An apparent problem for the argument is that (6.3) is false: wanting to drink and being unwilling to drink are not opposites in the sense required by the argument. This reasoning seems to confuse two distinct principles: a person cannot both have and not have a pro-attitude to the same thing; and a person cannot have both a pro-attitude and a con-attitude to the same thing. The former is a logical truism, the latter a disputable empirical claim. Why can't a dieter have both a pro-attitude and con-attitude toward a sweet? However, Plato may have thought that (6.3) is true, because he compared desires and aversions with physical movements such as pushing and pulling (see 437b1–c6). If volitions can be understood along these lines, it is more plausible to view desire and aversion as genuine opposites (see Stalley 1975 and Miller 1995).

Having distinguished the parts of the soul, Socrates lays down a normative principle, the rule of reason: "is it not appropriate for the rational part to rule, since it is really wise and exercises foresight on behalf of the whole soul?" (441e4–5). Reason aims at the common good in that each part of the soul has its own desires and values. The appetitive part desires food, drink, sex, and above all money, which can be used to satisfy other appetites; the spirited part values honor and victory; and the rational part learning and truth (IX.581a3–b10, 586d–587a). Plato compares the human soul to a teeming menagerie containing a "human being within the human being": a "many-headed beast," with some gentle heads and some savage; and a lion, the human's natural ally (588e3–589b6). Commentators disagree about how deep the divisions run within the tripartite soul. (Bobonich 1994 and Shields 2001 offer contrasting interpretations.)

Proceeding from the idea that virtue involves the harmony of the soul's parts, Socrates offers a proof of immortality from natural evil in *R*. X.608c–611a:

7.1   Everything has its own natural good and evil.

7.2   A thing cannot be destroyed except by its own natural evil.

7.3   The natural evil of the soul is injustice and vice.

7.4   The soul cannot be destroyed by injustice and vice.

7.5   Therefore, the soul is indestructible and hence immortal.

Premise (7.1) presupposes that everything has a natural function or end in terms of which its natural good and evil can be defined. But even if this is true, why suppose that (7.2) is true? It would seem that a thing could be destroyed by agents other than its natural evil. For example, a tree can be destroyed not only by rot but also by fire, insects, lumberjacks, and so forth. Many commentators regard this as one of Plato's weaker arguments (but see Brown 1997 for a defense).

It might also be objected that the claim that the soul is immortal is incompatible with the claim that it has a tripartite structure. Socrates himself cautions that "it isn't easy for anything composed of many parts to be immortal if it isn't put together in the finest way, yet this is how the soul now appeared to us" (611B5–7). The problem is that if a thing has parts, what prevents it from breaking up?

There may be a way, however, of reconciling the argument that the soul has parts in *Republic* IV with the argument that the soul is immortal in *Republic* X. It depends on what it means to say that the soul has "parts." There are different senses in which one thing may be a part of another: an aggregative part (as a brick is part of a brick wall) is different from a conceptual part (as an arc is part of a circle). In contrast with an aggregative part, a conceptual part is dependent on the whole for its identity conditions, and the whole is not dissoluble into conceptual parts. Significantly, one of Socrates' own examples involves conceptual parts: a spinning top is moving with respect to its circumference and stationary with respect to its axis (436D4–E6). If the three parts of the soul are merely conceptual parts, the tripartite soul may be immortal in the sense argued in *Republic* X. (Shields 2001 defends this interpretation.)

Socrates suggests that the tripartite soul may reflect what the soul is like when it is "maimed by association with the body" and not how it is "in truth" and in its "pure state." He offers the simile of the sea-god Glaucus whose primary nature can no longer be discerned, since parts of his body have broken off or been maimed and he is encrusted with shells, seaweeds, and stones (611B9–D8). The *Republic* leaves unresolved the true nature of the soul, "whether it has many parts or just one and whether or in what manner it is put together" (612A3–5).

This issue is hard to resolve even when one looks to other dialogues that mention the tripartite soul. In the *Phaedrus* the immortal soul seems to be essentially tripartite, when it is compared to the natural union of winged horses and their charioteer. The gods also have charioteers and horses, but the gods' horses are both good, whereas humans have one noble horse (the spirit) and one that is the opposite (appetite) (246A6–B4). Human souls are originally able to grasp Reality (i.e., the Forms), but by some accident they take on a burden of forgetfulness and wrongdoing, lose their wings, and fall to earth where they attach to bodies and form living things (248c5–8, cf. 246B7–c6). In the *Phaedrus* myth the soul is tripartite *before* it falls from heaven and enters the body. To be sure, the chariot simile is preceded by a caveat: "To describe what the soul actually is would require a very long account, altogether a task for a god in every way; but to say what it is like is humanly possible and takes less time" (246A4–6). The simile thus requires careful interpretation, but the point seems to be that "what the soul is like" is in some way tripartite.

The *Timaeus* in contrast distinguishes between an immortal part of the soul, reason, which is located in the head, and two mortal souls, spirit and appetite, which are located in the chest and abdomen respectively (69A–70B). The appetitive part is totally devoid of reason although it shares in sensation, pleasure, pain, and desires (77B5–6). The rational part is singled out as divine. "To the extent that human nature can partake of immortality, [one] can in no way fail to achieve this: constantly caring for his divine part as he does, keeping well-ordered the guiding spirit that lives within him, he must be supremely happy" (90c2–6). The implication seems to be that the immortal soul is monadic and the mortal parts are accretions resulting from the embodiment of reason. This raises questions: Can the account of the soul in the *Timaeus* be reconciled with that of the *Phaedrus*? If not, is either of these accounts more defensible or more likely to be favored by Plato? (see Guthrie 1957 for discussion).

The Soul as Self-Moving Principle

The conception of the soul as self-moving emerges in the *Phaedrus* and is an important theme in later dialogues such as the *Timaeus* and *Laws*. The soul is characterized as both self-moving and tripartite in the *Phaedrus* and *Timaeus*, but in the *Laws* the tripartite soul seems played down, if not suppressed altogether. The *Timaeus* and *Laws* also introduce the notion of a self-moving World-Soul as playing a central role in their cosmological theories.

Socrates recites an argument from self-motion in the *Phaedrus*. Here "what moves itself" is asserted to be the essence (*ousia*), definition (*logos*), and nature (*phusis*) of soul. This definition appears at the end of a compact but difficult proof (245c5–246A2) that the soul is immortal. (The following reconstruction is indebted to Robinson 1971 and Bett 1986.)

8.1   Whatever is always in motion is immortal.
8.2   Only what moves itself never ceases from moving, since it does not leave off being itself.
8.3   A self-mover is the source of motion in everything else.
8.4   Therefore, a self-moving source is ungenerated.
8.5   Since a self-mover is ungenerated, it cannot be destroyed.
8.6   Therefore, a self-mover is indestructible.
8.7   Whatever moves itself is essentially a soul.
8.8   Therefore, a soul is necessarily ungenerated and immortal.

The interim conclusion (8.6) is evidently based on two distinct sub-arguments. The first sub-argument, using (8.1) and (8.2) as premises, involves the idea that because a self-mover is essentially in motion it can never stop moving; hence, it moves forever. This seems vulnerable to an objection like that against the *Phaedo*'s final argument. If a thing is essentially self-moving then it necessarily follows that it is "always moving" only in the sense that it is moving *whenever* it exists, not in the sense that it *always* exists. The second sub-argument relies on (8.3) through (8.5). The crucial premise (8.5) is a lemma for which a separate proof (245D3–E2) is supplied:

8.51   Everything gets started from a source.
8.52   If a self-mover were destroyed, nothing could start it up again [since it isn't generated by anything else].

289

8.53   If this self-mover couldn't start up again, the universe would stop moving and never start up again.

8.54   [The universe won't stop moving and fail to start up again.] (tacit premise)

8.5   Therefore, since a self-mover is ungenerated, it cannot be destroyed.

Note the similarity between (8.54) and (1.3), the tacit premise of the cyclical argument in the *Phaedo*. (8.54) is an undefended empirical claim that the cosmos as a whole will never come to a standstill. Another problem is that (8.53) would be false if another self-mover was available to keep things moving. One way to avoid this difficulty would be to deny that the conclusion is that every single self-mover is indestructible. This is a possible interpretation because the argument is preceded by a pronouncement, "All soul is immortal" (245c5), which has no definite article before *psuchē* in the Greek, permitting at least two readings: "All soul (collective sense) is immortal" and "Every soul (distributive sense) is immortal." However, the former reading would make the ultimate conclusion (8.8) less exciting. It would not establish that each individual soul (e.g., Socrates') is immortal but only that soul in a collective sense is immortal.

In spite of the problems with the proof, the definition of soul as self-mover is a significant contribution (see Skemp 1967 and Demos 1978). A living thing is a combination of a body and a soul. It is due to the latter that the animal seems to move itself. The presence of the soul as a self-moving power explains how living things differ from nonliving bodies (246c4–6). The *Phaedrus* thus sheds valuable light on the *Phaedo*'s enigmatic special bearer of life.

The *Laws* also contains an argument that soul is prior to body. The Athenian Stranger undertakes to refute irreligious persons who undermine law and morality by contending that the gods don't exist, or, if they do, they are unconcerned with human beings or easily influenced by sacrifices and rituals. He advances the following argument for the existence of the gods who are identified with souls that control the cosmos.

9.1   Some things move, others are motionless (893c1).

9.2   One kind of motion has the ability to move other things but not itself, and another kind the ability to move both itself and other things (894B8–c1).

9.3   In a series where one thing moves another, which moves another, and so forth, the entire series must have a source which can only be self-generated motion (894E4–895A3).

9.4   If somehow the whole universe came to a standstill, self-motion is the only kind of motion that could arise first in it (895A6–B3).

9.5   Therefore, self-generating motion is the original source of all other motions (895B3–7).

9.6   An object that moves itself is alive (895c7–8).

9.7   An object with a soul is alive (895c11–12).

9.8   Soul is defined as "motion capable of moving itself" (896A3–4).

9.9   Therefore, soul is the original source of the generation and motion of all past, present, and future things and their contraries (896A5–8).

9.10   Therefore, soul is prior (causally) to body; i.e., soul is the natural ruler and body the natural subject (896B10–c3).

The Athenian Stranger goes on to assert that the soul rules everything, including the heavens, by means of its own motions, which are "wish, reflection, diligence, counsel, true and false opinion, joy and grief, cheerfulness and fear, love and hate" (896E8–897A3). Using these and the secondary motions of bodies, the soul is able to ally itself with divine intelligence (*nous*) and produce a successful outcome, or with ignorance (*anoia*) and produce the opposite. Whether the motion is orderly (i.e., circular) or disorderly depends on whether a rational or irrational soul is in charge (897A–898C). The Athenian Stranger does not provide much of an argument for these final claims. He seems to take it for granted that cosmic souls will perform the same sorts of actions and have the same sorts of attributes as human souls.

Regarding the proof that the soul is prior to the body, steps (9.6)–(9.8) make explicit the *Phaedrus'* suggestion that what makes the soul a special bearer of life is its capacity for self-motion. The point of (9.8) is that (9.7) *explains* (9.6). Premises (9.3) and (9.4) offer separate reasons for (9.5), that a self-mover is the first cause of all motion. (9.3) argues that every sequence of motions has a first cause, namely, a self-mover. An obvious objection is that there might be *no* first motion; each motion in the series is caused by a preceding motion *ad infinitum*. The argument assumes that there cannot be an infinite causal regress, an assumption that needs to be proven. And even if an infinite regress is ruled out, why does the first cause have to be a self-mover? Premise (9.2) mentions only two options, with self-motion as the only reasonable choice. But there might be other possibilities, for example, an *unmoved* mover, as Aristotle later argued. Similar objections arise for (9.4). If we accept the thought-experiment that the universe might somehow grind to a halt, is a self-moved mover the only thing that could start it up again? Could an unmoved mover do the trick, or might things just begin moving again spontaneously?

The *Timaeus* argues along similar lines. Timaeus relates a "likely story" about how the cosmos was created by an intelligent god, the Demiurge, who used the Forms as a model (*paradeigma*) (see 14: THE ROLE OF COSMOLOGY IN PLATO'S PHILOSOPHY). He also created a World-Soul because "in the realm of things naturally visible no unintelligent thing could as a whole be better than anything which does possess intelligence as a whole," and "it is impossible for anything to possess intelligence apart from soul. Guided by this reasoning, he put intelligence in soul, and soul in body, and so he constructed the universe" (30B1–5; cf. 34B3–4). Timaeus also describes the soul as a self-mover (37B5, 46D5–E2, 89A1–3). The *Timaeus* yields interesting details about human souls, their operations, and their relation to the body, and it also offers an ingenious if perplexing attempt to explain the rational capacity in terms of self-motion (36C–37D).

But the *Timaeus* also contains some puzzling claims which are difficult to reconcile with other dialogues. Especially problematic is the statement that souls were made by the Demiurge, which conflicts with the claim of the *Phaedo* and *Phaedrus* that the soul is ungenerated. The Demiurge of the *Timaeus* fashions the World-Soul and other souls as a mixture of divisible and indivisible Being, Sameness, and Difference (34c–37c). The different parts of human souls are even due to different makers: the rational part alone made by the Demiurge and the two nonrational parts left to lesser gods (41c–D). This seems at odds with the *Phaedrus* description of the soul as tripartite before it falls to earth and is embodied. Also difficult is the statement in the *Timaeus* that the Demiurge "took over all that was visible – not at rest but in discordant and disorderly motion – and brought it from a state of disorder to one of order" (30A3–5, cf. 47E–53C). This indication that disorderly motion existed before the soul-like Demiurge entered the scene seems to conflict with the arguments of the *Laws* and *Phaedrus* that all motion is due to the soul. One way of avoiding this problem would be to blame disorderly motion or evil on an irrational soul in opposition to the rational Demiurge. There does not seem to be any evidence for this interpretation in the *Timaeus*, however, and little elsewhere. It is hard to reconcile the *Timaeus* with other dialogues on this point. (See Mohr 1980 for further discussion.) These difficulties are bound up with a more general problem of how to interpret the *Timaeus*: should the "likely story" about the generation of the cosmos be understood literally or metaphorically? The *Timaeus* seems to contradict the other dialogues more flagrantly if its claims are intended to be literally true.

Conclusion

The contours of the Platonic soul are coming into view. But many important questions remain. Can the various strands in the different dialogues be woven together into a coherent psychology? Can Plato's arguments concerning the nature and immortality of the soul be defended against the sort of objections mentioned above? How reliable are the various Platonic myths, especially when they intimate personal survival of death and reincarnation? Is myth an indispensable supplement to philosophy or can the stories be supplanted by rational arguments? What is Plato's final answer concerning the nature and structure of the soul? The self-moving soul is an important theoretical breakthrough, but is it the last word? Granting that self-motion is a capacity of the soul, what *kind* of entity is it that has this capacity? Some of Plato's followers thought they had found the answer – the soul is a self-moving *number* – but Aristotle complained that this theory is incoherent (*de An.* I.4.408b32–3). If this is not Plato's final answer, what is?

Note

Translations of Plato are taken from J. M. Cooper (ed.) *Plato: Complete Works* (Indianapolis: Hackett, 1997).

References and further reading

Bett, R. (1986). The argument for immortality in Plato's *Phaedrus*. *Phronesis* 31, pp. 1–26. Repr. in E. Wagner (ed.) (2001) *Essays on Plato's Psychology* (pp. 335–62). Lanham, Md.: Lexington.
Bobonich, C. (1994). Akrasia and agency in Plato's *Laws* and *Republic*. *Archiv für Geschichte der Philosophie* 76, pp. 3–36. Repr. in E. Wagner (ed.) (2001) *Essays on Plato's Psychology* (pp. 203–37). Lanham, Md.: Lexington.
Broadie, S. (2001). Soul and body in Plato and Descartes. *Proceedings of the Aristotelian Society* 101, pp. 295–308.

Brown, E. A. (1997). A defense of Plato's argument for the immortality of the soul at *Republic* X.608c–611A. *Apeiron* 30, pp. 211–38. Repr. in E. Wagner (ed.) (2001) *Essays on Plato's Psychology* (pp. 297–322). Lanham, Md.: Lexington.

Cooper, J. M. (1984). Plato's theory of human motivation. *History of Philosophy Quarterly* 1, pp. 3–24. Repr. in E. Wagner (ed.) (2001) *Essays on Plato's Psychology* (pp. 91–114). Lanham, Md.: Lexington.

Demos, R. (1978). Plato's doctrine of the psyche as a self-moving motion. *Journal of the History of Philosophy* 6, pp. 133–45.

Frede, D. (1978). The final proof of the immortality of the soul in Plato's *Phaedo* 102A–107A. *Phronesis* 23, pp. 27–41. Repr. in E. Wagner (ed.) (2001) *Essays on Plato's Psychology* (pp. 281–96). Lanham, Md.: Lexington.

Gallop, D. (1982). Plato's "cyclical" argument recycled. *Phronesis* 27, pp. 207–22. Repr. in E. Wagner (ed.) (2001) *Essays on Plato's Psychology* (pp. 263–80). Lanham, Md.: Lexington.

Guthrie, W. K. C. (1957). Plato's views on the nature of the soul. In *Recherches sur la Tradition Platonicienne, Entretiens*, tome 3 (pp. 3–22). Vandoeuvres-Genève: Fondation Hardt. Repr. in G. Vlastos (ed.) *Plato II* (pp. 230–41). New York: Anchor Books.

Kenny, A. (1969). Mental health in Plato's *Republic*. *Proceedings of the British Academy* 60, pp. 229–53.

Keyt, D. (1963). The fallacies in *Phaedo* 102A–107B. *Phronesis* 8, pp. 167–72.

Miller, F. D. (1995). Plato on the parts of the soul. In J. M. Van Ophuijsen (ed.) *Plato and Platonism* (pp. 84–101). Washington, DC: Catholic University of America Press.

Mohr, R. (1980). The sources of evil problem and the principle of motion doctrine. *Apeiron* 14, pp. 41–56.

O'Brien, D. (1967, 1968). The last argument of Plato's *Phaedo*. *Classical Quarterly* 17, pp. 198–231; 18, pp. 95–106.

Partenie, C. (2004). *Plato: Selected Myths*. Oxford: Oxford University Press.

Robinson, T. M. (1971). The argument for immortality in Plato's *Phaedrus*. In J. P. Anton and G. L. Kustas (eds.) *Essays in Ancient Greek Philosophy* (pp. 345–53). Albany, NY: State University of New York Press. Repr. in E. Wagner (ed.) (2001) *Essays on Plato's Psychology* (pp. 223–33). Lanham, Md.: Lexington.

—— (1995). *Plato's Psychology*, 2nd edn. Toronto: Toronto University Press.

Shields, C. (2001). Simple souls. In E. Wagner (ed.) (2001) *Essays on Plato's Psychology* (pp. 137–56). Lanham, Md.: Lexington.

Silverman, A. (2003). Plato: psychology. In C. Shields (ed.) *The Blackwell Guide to Ancient Philosophy* (pp. 130–44). Oxford: Blackwell.

Skemp, J. B. (1967). *The Theory of Motion in Plato's Later Dialogues*. Amsterdam: Hakkert.

Stalley, R. F. (1975). Plato's argument for the division of the reasoning and the appetitive elements within the soul. *Phronesis* 20, pp. 110–28.

Taylor, C. C. W. (1983). The arguments in the *Phaedo* concerning the thesis that the soul is a *Harmonia*. In J. P. Anton and A. Preus (eds.) *Essays in Ancient Greek Philosophy*, vol. 2 (pp. 217–32). Albany, NY: State University of New York Press. Repr. in E. Wagner (ed.) (2001) *Essays on Plato's Psychology* (pp. 51–67). Lanham, Md.: Lexington.

Wagner, E. (2000). Supervenience and the thesis that the soul is a *Harmonia*. *Southwest Philosophy Review* 16, pp. 1–20. Repr. in E. Wagner (ed.) (2001) *Essays on Plato's Psychology* (pp. 69–88). Lanham, Md.: Lexington.

Weller, C. (1995). Fallacies in the *Phaedo* again. *Archiv für Geschichte der Philosophie* 77, pp. 121–34. Repr. in E. Wagner (ed.) (2001) *Essays on Plato's Psychology* (pp. 35–49). Lanham, Md.: Lexington.

20

Plato on Eros and Friendship

C. D. C. REEVE

Plato discusses love (*erōs*) and friendship (*philia*) primarily in two dialogues, the *Lysis* and the *Symposium*, though the *Phaedrus* also adds significantly to his views. In each work, Socrates as the quintessential philosopher is in two ways center stage, first, as a lover of wisdom (*sophia*) and discussion (*logos*), and, second, as himself an inverter or disturber of erotic norms. Plato's views on love are a meditation on Socrates and the power his philosophical conversations have to mesmerize, obsess, and educate.

This chapter consists of six sections: Socrates and the Art of Love; Socrates and Athenian *Paiderastia*; Loving Socrates; Love and the Ascent to the Beautiful; The Art and Psychology of Love Explained; Writing about Love.

The first section deals with the *Lysis* and *Symposium*, and the next three primarily with the *Symposium* alone. The fifth section deals with the *Phaedrus*, and the last with the closing section of the *Symposium* and with parts of the *Ion*, *Protagoras*, and *Laws*. Sections are not self-contained, however, and are intended to be read sequentially. Most scholars agree that the order of composition of the "erotic" dialogues is *Lysis*, *Symposium*, *Phaedrus*, though some put the *Phaedrus* earlier than the *Symposium*.

Socrates and the Art of Love

"The only thing I say I know," Socrates tells us in the *Symposium*, "is the art of love (*ta erōtika*) (177D7–8). Taken literally, it is an incredible claim. Are we really to believe that the man who affirms when on trial for his life that he knows himself to be wise "in neither a great nor a small way" (*Ap.* 21B4–5) knows the art of love? (see 8: SOCRATIC IGNORANCE). In fact, the claim is a non-trivial play on words facilitated by the fact that the noun *erōs* ("love") and the verb *erōtan* ("to ask questions") sound as if they are etymologically connected, a connection explicitly exploited in the *Cratylus* (398c5–E5). Socrates knows about the art of love in that – but just insofar as – he knows how to ask questions, how to converse elenctically (see 5: THE SOCRATIC ELENCHUS).

Just how far that is, we discover in the *Lysis*, where Socrates makes a similar claim. Hippothales, like Socrates, loves beautiful boys and philosophical discussions (203B6– 204A3). But he does not know the art of love and so does not know how to talk to

Lysis, the boy with whom he is in love. What Hippothales does is sing eulogies to Lysis, and *that*, Socrates argues, no skilled lover would ever do. For if your suit succeeds "everything you've said and sung turns out to eulogize yourself as victor in having won such a boyfriend," but if it fails, then "the greater your praise of his beauty and goodness, the more you will seem to have lost and the more you will be ridiculed." Consequently, someone "who is wise in the art of love (*ta erōtika*) doesn't praise his beloved until he has him: he fears how the future may turn out" (205E2–206A2). Convinced, Hippothales asks Socrates to tell him "what someone should say or do to get his prospective boyfriend to love him" (206c1–3). As in the *Symposium*, Socrates is uncharacteristically forthcoming: "if you're willing to have him talk with me, I might be able to give you a demonstration of how to carry on a discussion with him" (c4–6, adapted from Lombardo trans.). What follows is an elenctic examination of Lysis. Socrates' lessons in love, we may infer, are elenctic lessons: lessons in how to ask and answer questions.

At the end of the examination, Socrates characterizes what he has accomplished: "This is how you should talk to your boyfriends, Hippothales, making them humble and drawing in their sails, instead of swelling them up and spoiling them, as you do" (210E2–5). It sounds simply chastening put like that. But in the overall context of the *Lysis*, where love is a desire and desire is an emptiness, it is much more. It is a step in the creation of the canonical lover: the philosopher:

> Those who are already wise no longer love wisdom (*philosophein*), whether they are gods or men. Neither do those who are so ignorant that they are bad, for no bad and stupid person loves wisdom. There remains only those who have this bad thing, ignorance, but have not yet been made ignorant and stupid by it. They are conscious of not knowing what they don't know. (218A2–B1, adapted from Lombardo trans.)

So by showing Lysis that he isn't already wise, by getting him to recognize that he doesn't know, Socrates sets him on the road to philosophy (cf. *Sph.* 231B3–8).

The *elenchus* is important to love, then, because it creates a hunger for wisdom, a hunger which it cannot itself assuage. So even though Lysis is already something of a philosopher when he meets Socrates and receives a rare accolade from him – "I was pleased with his love of wisdom (*philosophia*)" (213D6) – he, too, is left in puzzlement (*aporia*). He is made aware of his desire by Socrates but the desire itself remains unsatisfied. Socrates may be the master of foreplay, of arousing desire, and may to that extent be a master of the art of love, but when it comes to satisfying desire, he is a failure. In the *Clitophon* – perhaps spurious, but arguably by Plato – this criticism is raised to Socrates' face and receives no answer. If we aren't already persuaded to pursue virtue, Clitophon claims, Socrates "will wake us up from our sleep" (408c3–4). But if we are, and now want to know what virtue is and what benefit it, in particular, brings to its possessor, he "is pretty much a stumbling block for reaching complete virtue and becoming happy" (410E7–8).

The connection, amounting to an identification, between the art of discussion and the art of loving boys explored in the *Lysis* allows us to see why Plato's own explorations of love invariably involve an exploration of discussion too: love-talk in the *Lysis*, symposiastic speech-making and drama in the *Symposium*, oratory and rhetoric in the

Phaedrus. Loving boys correctly, after all, is – in part at least – just a matter of knowing how to talk to them, of how to persuade them to love you back.

Socrates and Athenian *Paiderastia*

As a man who loves boys in an idiosyncratic, because elenctic, way, Socrates is placed in potential conflict with the norms of a peculiar Athenian social institution, that of *paiderastia*: the socially regulated intercourse between an older Athenian male (*erastēs*) and a teenage boy (*erōmenos, pais*), through which the latter was supposed to learn virtue. And this potential, as we know, was realized with tragic consequences. In 399 BCE Socrates was found guilty of corrupting the young men of Athens and condemned to death (see 1: THE LIFE OF PLATO OF ATHENS). The effect on Plato is palpable in his works, turning very many of them into defenses – not always uncritical – of Socrates, and of what he represented for the young men he encountered. His account in the *Symposium* of one such relationship, that with the brilliant and beautiful Alcibiades, is an illuminating case in point.

Alcibiades was so in love with Socrates – "it was obvious," the *Symposium* (222c1–3) tells us – that when asked to speak of love, he speaks of his beloved. No general theories of love for him, just the vividly remembered story of the times he spent with a man so extraordinary there has never been anyone like him: a man so powerfully erotic he turned the conventional world of love upside down by "seeming to be a lover (*erastēs*) while really establishing himself as a beloved boy (*pais*) instead" (222B3–4).

The stories of all the other symposiasts, too, are stories of their particular loves masquerading as stories of love itself, stories about what *they find* beautiful masquerading *as* stories about what *is* beautiful. For Phaedrus and Pausanius, the canonical image of true love – the quintessential love story – features the right sort of older male lover and the right sort of beloved boy. For Eryximachus the image of true love is painted in the languages of his own beloved medicine and of all the other crafts and sciences; for Aristophanes it is painted in the language of comedy; for Agathon, in the loftier tones of tragedy. In ways that these men are unaware of, then, but that Plato knows, their love stories are themselves manifestations of their loves and of the inversions or perversions expressed in them. They think their stories are the truth about love, but they are really love's delusions, "images," as Diotima will later call them. As such, however, they are essential parts of that truth. For the power of love to engender delusive images of the beautiful is as much a part of the truth about it as its power to lead to the Beautiful-itself. Later, we shall learn why.

Love stories, however inadequate as theories of love, are nonetheless stories, *logoi*, items that admit of analysis. But because they are manifestations of our loves, not mere cool bits of theorizing, we – our deepest feelings – are invested in them. They are therefore tailor-made, in one way at least, to satisfy the Socratic sincerity condition, the demand that you say what you believe (*Cri.* 49c11–D2; *Prt.* 331c4–D1). Under the cool gaze of the elenctic eye, they are tested for consistency with other beliefs that lie just outside love's controlling and often distorting ambit. Under such testing, a lover may be forced to say with Agathon, "I didn't know what I was talking about in that story" (201B11–12). The love that expressed itself in his love story meets then another love: his rational desire for consistency and intelligibility; his desire to be able to tell and live a coherent story; his desire, to put it the other way around, not to be endlessly frustrated and conflicted, because he is repetitively trying to live out an incoherent love story.

In Alcibiades' love story, in particular, these two desires are self-consciously in play: "Socrates is the only man in the world who has made me feel shame . . . I know perfectly well that I can't prove he's wrong when he tells me what I should do: yet, the moment I leave his side, I go back to my old ways: I cave in to my desire to please the crowd" (216c8–b5, trans. Nehamas and Woodruff). Even such awareness of conflict as is manifested here, however, is no guarantee of a satisfactory resolution. For the new love – the one that seems to offer coherence, satisfaction, and release from shame – may turn out to be just the old frustrating one in disguise.

Alcibiades' famous failed attempt to seduce Socrates shows that this is so in his case too (218b8–e5). For Alcibiades doesn't try to win Socrates' love by undertaking the difficult task of self-transformation that is required to become a more virtuous, and so more truly beautiful and lovable, person. Instead, he takes the easy, familiar path of offering the physical attractions he already has, the ones that have earned him the approval of the crowd. When these fail him, it is to the crowd (in the form of the Bacchic revelers we meet at the end of the *Symposium*) he will regressively return, having never really succeeded in turning away.

That he has never turned away is made yet more vivid in one of the most intriguing passages in the *Symposium*. Socrates, Alcibiades says, is

> ironical (*eirōneuomenos*) and spends his whole life playing with people. Yet, I don't know whether anyone else has seen the figures within (*ta entos agalmata*) when he is serious and opened up, but I saw them once, and I thought that they were so divine and golden, so marvelously beautiful, that I just had to do whatever Socrates told me. (216e4–217a2)

For those who think Socrates a profoundly ironic figure, it is an amazing moment, in which Socrates is seen without his mask of mock modesty. Alas, as is so often the case with love, it is fantasy we are dealing with. What Alcibiades thinks he sees in Socrates are embryonic virtues, which – like spermatozoa in the embryology the *Symposium* implicitly embraces when it speaks of *the lover* as pregnant and as seeking a beautiful boy in which to beget an offspring – need only be ejaculated into the right receptacle in order to grow into their mature forms (209a5–c2). Sex can lead to virtue, in other words, without the need for hard work. As soon as the illusion is enjoyed, therefore, it gives birth not to a realistic attempt to acquire virtue, but to the sexual seduction fantasy mentioned earlier.

The origins of this fantasy – though, no doubt, partly personal – are predominantly social. It is the complex ideology of Athenian *paiderasteia* that has shaped Alcibiades' own desires. For, according to it, love is really "two things": good Uranian love, whose object is the soul, and whose aim is to instill virtue in the younger male; and bad Pandemotic love, whose object is the body and whose aim is sexual pleasure for the older lover (180c3–e3). What causes the split is the need Pandemotic love has to mask itself as Uranian love in order to preserve the illusion that the young man's participation in it is compatible with his status as a future male citizen. The young man cannot, then, be motivated by a reprehensible desire to adopt a passive, slavish, female pleasure-seeking role. Instead, another motive must be invented for him: a willingness to accept "slavery for the sake of virtue" (184c2–3).

A major cost of preserving this split, however, is that the older male's body-focused, sexual intercourse must itself be masked as intercourse of a more respectable sort. Alcibiades' later re-description of Socrates' inner figures shows Alcibiades succumbing to the double-vision that inevitably results:

> If you were to listen to his arguments, at first they'd strike you as totally ridiculous; they're clothed in words as coarse as the hides worn by the most vulgar satyrs. He's always going on about pack asses, or blacksmiths, or cobblers, or tanners . . . But if the arguments are opened and one sees them from the inside, he will find first that they are the only arguments with any sense in them, and next that they contain within themselves utterly divine and multitudinous figures of virtue (*agalmat' aretēs*). (221E1– 222A4, partially adapted from Nehamas and Woodruff trans.)

For Alcibiades, then, Socrates' body is identical to his words; the virtues that are in him are in them; talking philosophy is having sexual intercourse, and vice versa.

Loving Socrates

At the beginning of the *Symposium*, an unidentified man wants to hear what was said about love by Socrates and the others at Agathon's house. He has heard a garbled account. Now he wants Apollodorus to tell him what was really said. But Apollodorus wasn't there either. He got his account of the proceedings second-hand from Aristodemus. All these men who ought to be chasing boys are presented as so besotted with Socrates and his conversations that one of them – Apollodorus – makes it his business to know exactly what Socrates does and says each day (172c4–6), while another – Aristodemus – is so far gone in his passion for Socrates that he walks barefoot like his beloved (173B1–4). One reason for this complex set-up is to let us see the inverting impact of Socrates, and so of philosophy, on Athenian paiderastic norms. Another is more subtle. Alcibiades' love for Socrates focuses on the beautiful figures of virtue which he thinks he sees lying beneath those "words as coarse as the hides worn by the most vulgar satyrs," which are the analog for him of Socrates' ugly, satyr-like body (215B3–4). Aristodemus' love for Socrates, by contrast, seems to focus on his coarse exterior, so that Aristodemus himself is a sort of inverted Alcibiades, whose very name associates him with Pausanias' body-centered goddess of love, *Pandēmos*. Loving Socrates, we may infer, is a complex business, since just what someone loves in loving him is tied to that person's peculiar desires, and the limits they impose on how like Socrates he can become.

In the dialogue's next few scenes, this point is driven home. When Aristodemus meets him, Socrates has just bathed and put on his fancy sandals, "both very unusual events" (174A3–4). Aristodemus remarks on this because he is naturally sensitive to those aspects of Socrates which he himself, perhaps because of his own size and appearance (173B2), has chosen to emulate. The reason for the departure from his usual habits, Socrates explains, is that he is going to Agathon's party and wants "beauty to go to beauty" (174A9). Oddly, this doesn't stop him from bringing Aristodemus – un-bathed, un-sandaled, un-beautiful – along. But what is odd from the point of view of *Socrates'* self-ascribed motivations is not at all odd from that of *Plato's*. He has now made the complexity of Socrates – his beautiful insides and ugly outsides or vice versa – as dramatically present to our eyes as to those of Agathon and his other guests.

Socrates is invited to Agathon's (Goodman's: "Agathon" means good in Greek). He thinks, wrongly as it happens, that Aristodemus isn't invited, but offers to take him along anyway. Aristodemus' reply – "I'll do whatever you say" (174B2) – again connects him to Alcibiades: "I just had to do whatever he told me" (217A1–2). "Come with me then," Socrates responds, "and we shall prove the proverb wrong; the truth is, 'Good men go uninvited to Goodman's feast'" (174B4–5, trans. Nehamas and Woodruff).[1] Aristodemus is not convinced. "Socrates, I'm afraid . . . mine is the case of an inferior arriving uninvited at the table of a wise man" (174c5–7). The familiar Socratic tri-unity – good, beautiful, wise – are all now in play.

Despite his reservations, Aristodemus agrees to accompany Socrates, but with an important proviso: "See what defense you're going to make (*apologēse(i)*) for bringing me along, because I won't admit I came uninvited, I'll say you brought me!" (174c7–D1). It is this proviso that initiates the next mystifying episode. It begins when Socrates replies by under-quoting Homer: "We'll take counsel about what to say 'when two go together along the way'" (174D2–3). What he leaves out is what happens when two *do* go together, namely, "one of them knows before the other" (*Il.* X.24). The elision of this phrase is matched by an elision of Plato's own. For what happened on the road to Agathon's is that "Socrates began to think about something, lost himself in thought, and kept lagging behind" (174D4–7, trans. Nehamas and Woodruff). Yet we are never told what he thought about: what it was that one knew before the other.

That the match between these two elisions is significant is evidenced by the close parallels between the preamble to Socrates' speech in praise of *Erōs* and that to his speech of defense in the *Apology*. There he is "amazed (*ethaumasa*)" by what his accusers say (*Ap.* 17A4–5); here Agathon's speech is "amazing (*thaumasta*)" (*Smp.* 198B4). There he isn't a clever (*deinos*) speaker, unless cleverness consists in speaking the truth (*Ap.* 17A4–B6). Here he isn't clever in the art of love unless encomia to *Erōs* involve telling the truth about it (*Smp.* 198c5–199A6). There "what the jurors will hear will be spoken extemporaneously (*epituchousin*) in whatever words come to mind" (*Ap.* 17c1–2); here the symposiasts will "hear the truth spoken about *Erōs* in such words and arrangements as occur to me extemporaneously (*tuchē(i) epelthousa*)" (*Smp.* 199B3–5). Whatever occupies Socrates on the road to Agathon's, we may infer, ends not in the knowledge Homer is so confident either he or Aristodemus will have, but in the aporetic awareness of the absence of knowledge that distinguishes Socrates' "human wisdom" from the "more than human wisdom" claimed by the sophists (*Ap.* 20c4–E8).

The result of Socrates losing his way in thought and ending up stymied in Agathon's neighbor's porch is that Aristodemus, like a proper Socratic paraclete, arrives at Agathon's quite a bit before Socrates. When Socrates finally does arrive in *propria persona*, Agathon says: "Socrates, come lie down next to me. Who knows, if I touch you, I may catch a bit of the wisdom that came to you under my neighbor's porch" (175c7–D1, trans. Nehamas and Woodruff). Socrates replies with an obviously sexual simile, which acknowledges, so as later once again to invert, paiderastic norms: "If only wisdom were like water which always flows from a full cup into an empty one when we connect them with a piece of yarn. If wisdom were that way too, I value the place beside you very much indeed; for I think I will be filled from you with wisdom of great beauty" (175D4–E2, partially adapted from Nehamas and Woodruff trans.). What actually happens, however, is the very reverse. Socrates responds to Agathon's fancy speech about love with an *elenchus*, so that his emptiness, his lack of knowledge, flows into Agathon, destroying the wisdom of great beauty that had won his tragedy a first prize the day before (175E4–7).

Love and the Ascent to the Beautiful

Socrates is adept at some parts of the art of love but cannot take his beloveds all the way. So he is clearly in need of further instruction in the art of love. In the *Symposium*, this is provided to him by Diotima, whom he describes as "the one who taught me the art of love" (201D5). And what she teaches him, in a nutshell, is Platonism. What the *elenchus* needs if it is to satisfy rather than frustrate love, in other words, is the theory of Platonic Forms. What Socrates needs, and so ought to love, is Plato! The story of Platonic love is, one might say, the story of the Platonizing of Socrates.

If what Socrates learned from Diotima was about all love, however, it would be refuted by the very fact of Alcibiades, whose love for Socrates has not led him to love the Beautiful-itself. It would be equally refuted, indeed, by all the other symposiasts, none of whom has been led there by his love. But Diotima's love story is not so general. It is self-advertised as a story about "loving boys correctly (*to orthōs paiderastein*)" (211B5–6): as a lesson in "the correct way to go or to be led by another to the art of love" (211B7–c1). To be sure, it doesn't itself explicitly provide us with a story about how *Erōs* can act as a force which retards development. But that isn't because Plato thought *Erōs* could not act as such a force – consider Alcibiades. Rather, it is because Diotima's story is a story about successful or correct love.

The credibility of Diotima's love story is another matter, of course. To many, it has seemed both incredible and distasteful, because it seems to say that beautiful individuals have only instrumental value. When one has climbed the ladder, of which they are merely the first rung, one should kick it – and them – away. But is this message really Diotima's?

What we all love, according to Diotima, is the good; that is to say, we want good things to be ours forever (see 21: PLATO ON PLEASURE AS THE HUMAN GOOD; 24: PLATO'S CONCEPT OF GOODNESS). But because we are mortal, the closest we can come to satisfying this desire is to initiate an endless cycle of reproduction in which each new generation has good things. We achieve this, in a famous phrase, by "giving birth in beauty (*tokos en kalō(i)*)" (206B7–8, E5). What does this mean? Like Athenian *paiderasteia*, Diotima recognizes two fundamentally different kinds of love, two fundamentally different varieties of the desire to give birth in beauty. In the case of heterosexual lovers, who are "pregnant in body," such giving birth consists in producing children who resemble, and so share in the beauty of their parents (208E1–3). Homosexual lovers, however, are a different story. What they give birth to is "wisdom and the rest of virtue" (209A3–4). When a man who is pregnant in soul finds a beautiful boy, Diotima says, it "makes him instantly teem with accounts of virtue" (209B8), or "beautiful accounts" (210A8). Giving birth to virtue and giving birth to accounts of it are obviously different. But some of the other phrases Diotima uses show us how to lessen the difference. For what homosexual lovers want is to give birth to accounts of virtue of a particular sort, ones that can be used in "the proper ordering of cities and households" (209A6–7), and so can "make young men better" (210c1–3).

If the lover's accounts are to achieve this goal, however, they mustn't be the product of distorting fantasy, as Nietzsche thinks so many of our moral concepts are and as some feminists think our concept of romantic love itself is. What is intended to ensure that they will not is their openness to reality, an openness guaranteed by the fact that in the course of his ascent the lover must study the beauty of ways of life and laws (210c3–5) and the beauty of the sciences (c6–7). What he gains from these studies are the conceptual resources needed to see the world, including the human world, aright – to gain knowledge of it. This is not the project an analysand takes up in psychoanalysis. Nor is it the one that we less formally undertake when we reflect on our own love stories in hopes of understanding them (often a project provoked, alas, by an unhappy ending). It is instead the project of philosophy, as Plato conceives of it. That is why it culminates in "the birth of many gloriously beautiful accounts and theories in unstinting love of wisdom (*philosophia*)" (210D5–6). Yet the grander project intersects with the analysand's project and with ours in an interesting way. The terms or concepts we use to tell our love stories must themselves be coherent if the stories we use them to tell are to be coherently livable.

In Plato's view, this means that they must be the concepts the true lover uses once he has seen the Beautiful-itself: the concepts whose ontological correlates are Forms. If they are not, they will be incoherent and the lover who employs them will find himself embroiled in a love story he does not understand, a love story whose incoherence the *elenchus*, or psychoanalysis, or just plain critical scrutiny will reveal. It is this incoherence, indeed, encountered at lower stages in the ascent, that leads the correct lover, under pressure from his rational desire for truth and consistency, and the pain of inconsistency, to climb to the next stage.

We can see Diotima, then, not only as revealing the other more abstract loves that a true lover of boys must have, but also as exploring the conditions that concepts must meet if they are to figure in genuinely coherent love stories. Her story isn't about a lover who abandons the individual boys he loves, but about someone who comes to love boys successfully by coming to love something else as well.

Like Diotima herself, we have been concentrating on what other things a lover is led to love by his love for his beloved boy. We have said nothing about the changes that explorations in this enlarged erotic field effect in the desires and feelings of the lover himself. But these, too, help us to see what happens to his love for his boy in the course of his explorations. What hooks the lover to begin with is love for a particular body: "First, if the Leader leads aright, he should love one body and beget beautiful accounts there" (210A6–8). At this stage, what the boy engages in the lover is his sexual desire for physical beauty, albeit one which, in firm keeping with the norms of Athenian *paiderastia*, is supposedly aim-inhibited: instead of sexual intercourse, it leads to discussions about beauty and to accounts of it. Here the beauty at issue is, in the first instance, the boy *who represents Beauty-itself to the lover.* That is why, when the lover finally comes to see the Beautiful-itself, "beauty will no longer seem to you to be measured by gold or raiment or beautiful boys or youths, which now you look upon dumbstruck" (211D3–5). One effect of generating *accounts* of this beauty, however, is that the lover comes to see his beloved's beautiful body as one among many: if it is beautiful, so are any other bodies the accounts fit. And this initially cognitive discovery leads to a conative change: "Realizing this he is established as a lover of all beautiful bodies and relaxes this excessive preoccupation with one, thinking less of it and believing it to be a small matter" (210B4–6).

It is important in reading Diotima's description of this change that we see it as comparative and contrastive: the lover used to *overvalue* his beloved (211D5–8); now he *values him appropriately.* But valuing appropriately is still valuing. The boy is still included in the class of beautiful bodies the lover now loves. It is also important to notice that cognitive and conative changes are going hand-in-hand. To recognize that his beloved is one among many, the lover's love for him has to change. And that means that psychological resources within the lover, beyond his sexual responsiveness to physical beauty, are coming into play. More of the lover is now involved in his love. Hence what his beloved might be thought to lose in exclusivity he gains in richness, and no doubt in endurance and reliability, of response. When his physical bloom fades, he will now still be loved.

But love that is to escape frustration cannot stop with bodies. The attempt to formulate an account of love free from puzzles and immune to elenctic refutation must lead on from beautiful bodies to beautiful souls, and so to the beautiful laws and practices that will improve souls and make young men better. Again this cognitive achievement is matched by a conative one. When the lover sees that all these beautiful things are somehow akin in the beauty, he comes to think that "bodily beauty is a small thing" (210C5–6), and so, as before, becomes less obsessed with it.

At the top of the *scala amoris* lies the Beautiful-itself, the first loved object that – like the "primary object of love" (*prōton philon*) in the *Lysis* (219D2–E4) – is not in any way gone beyond. Here, it seems, the lover at last finds something worthy of the obsessive attention he once lavished on his beloved boy (211D8–212A7). Nonetheless, obsession is out of place even here. For the Beautiful-itself can no more satisfy the lover's desires to eat and drink than his beloved can. Here, as there, what he would do if it were possible must not be confused with what he can and does do. After all, the lover himself cannot become immortal except by giving birth in the beauty he has at last found. He does that, however, precisely by arranging for his beloved to grow up, become truly virtuous, and be with him in the contemplation of – and, to the extent that it is possible, the possession of – true beauty.

The Art and Psychology of Love Explained

In the *Phaedrus* we find a more detailed account of the psychology and art of love than in the *Symposium.* This account will be our exclusive focus. The soul, whether divine or human, Socrates claims, is like "the natural union of a team of winged horses and their charioteer" (246A6–7). But whereas in a divine soul all three elements are "good and come from good stock," in a human soul the white horse (familiar from *Republic* IV as the honor-loving spirited element) is "beautiful and good, and of similar stock," while the black one (the *Republic*'s appetitive element) is "the opposite and of the opposite stock," so that "the driving in our case is necessarily difficult and trouble-some" (A7–B4). When spirit together with the charioteer (the *Republic*'s rational element, there too identified with what is truly human rather than bestial in us (588B10–589A4)) "leads us towards what is best and is in control," we possess moderation (*sōphrosunē*) (237E2–3). But when "appetite drags us irrationally towards pleasures and rules in us, its rule is called excess (*hubris*)" (238A1–2). Of this excess, gluttony is one species, but erotic love another (238B7–c4). This is the bad kind of love – Pandemotic in the *Symposium* – that Lysias rightly disparages in the speech Phaedrus admires and reads to Socrates (230E6–234c5).

In Socrates' view, however, there is also another kind of love, namely, "the madness of a man who, on seeing beauty here on earth, and being reminded of true beauty, becomes winged, and fluttering with eagerness to fly upwards, but unable to leave the ground, looks upwards like a bird, and takes no heed of things below – and that is what causes him to be regarded as mad" (249D5–E1). This madman is the philosopher of the *Symposium*, who when he falls in love with a boy is led by his love to ascend by stages to the Form of the Beautiful. What makes his madness a divine gift, however, is that the ascent is now revealed as involving recollection of a prior prenatal ascent taken in the company of a god (see 9: PLATO ON RECOLLECTION).

From the rich literary account of this ascent, we need to take away just one idea: souls have different psychological structures depending on which god they followed, and this sets an upper limit on how much of the Forms they see, and so on how much they can subsequently recollect. Since gaining access to Forms nourishes and strengthens the rational element in the soul (248B5–c2), this also helps deter-mine its motivational structure: the stronger its reason is, the more likely it will be to succeed in controlling the other elements in the soul.

Followers of Zeus, for example, choose someone to love whose soul resembles their patron god. So they seek someone who is "naturally disposed to philosophy and leadership, and when they have found him and fall in love they do everything to make him philosophical" (252E1–5). Nonetheless, the falling itself involves a huge psycho-logical upheaval. The black horse of appetite immediately urges towards sexual inter-course. The white horse, "constrained then as always by shame" (254A2), holds itself back. Eventually, however, the black horse forces both the charioteer and the white horse "to move towards the beloved and mention to him the delights of sex" (A5–7). Again they balk, "indignant at being forced to do terrible and improper things" (B1). But finally, "when there is no limit to their plight, they follow its lead, giving in and agreeing to do what it tells them" (B2–3). As they come close to the beloved, however, to initiate intercourse, the flashing face of the beloved reminds the charioteer of the Beautiful-itself, so that his memory "again sees it standing together with temperance on a holy pedestal" (B5–7). He becomes frightened and "in sudden reverence falls on his back, and is forced at the same time to pull back the reins so violently as to bring the horses down on their haunches, the one willingly, because of its lack of resistance to him, but the unruly horse much against its will" (B7–c3). Eventually, "when the same thing happens to the evil horse many times, it allows the charioteer with his

303

foresight to lead" (E5–7). If this control of appetite by reason and spirit continues – even when the boy has accepted his lover and embraces, kisses, and lies down with him – and draws them to "a well-ordered life and to philosophy," they are blessedly happy here on earth, and, if they live such a life for three successive incarnations, they re-grow their wings and re-join the entourage of their god (255E2–256B7).

When followers of Ares fall in love, on the other hand, they "adopt a lower way of living, not philosophical, but honor-loving" (256B7–c1). When they are drinking together, for example, or are careless in some other way, "the licentious horses in the two of them catch their souls off guard," and since the man's recollection of beauty is dimmer and is not rekindled by philosophical conversation, they end up having sex together – something "the masses regard as the happiest choice of all" (c1–5). Nonetheless, they don't have sex very often, because "what they are doing has not been approved by their whole mind" (c6–7). So while the degree of their love and happiness is less than that of the philosophical pair and, on their death, "they leave the body without wings," still they have an impulse, coming from love, to try to gain them. Hence they aren't punished in the next life, but helped on the way to future happiness together (c7–E2).

The love that is divine madness is a good thing, therefore, especially when, "accompanied by philosophical discussions (erōta meta philosophōn logōn)" (257B6), it leads to the Beautiful-itself and the other Forms, which are what we – identified most of all with the rational element in our souls – truly love and crave. The question is, What makes a discussion philosophical? What makes it of the sort to be included in the true art of love that the philosopher who loves the Beautiful-itself practices? The answer now proposed is that it must be a technē or craft, and so must have the defining characteristics of one. As applied to love itself, for example, it must begin with a definition of love, and reach its conclusions by ordering its discussion in relation to it (263D5–E3). And this definition, in turn, must be established by what Socrates refers to as collection and division (266B3–4).

Collection is a process of "perceiving together and bringing into one form items that are scattered in many places" (265D3–4). It is a process that we, unlike other animals, are able to engage in, because our souls include a rational element that has prior acquaintance with Forms: "a soul that never [prenatally] saw what is true cannot take a human shape, since a human being must understand what is said by relation to a form that is reached from many sense-perceptions being collected into one by reasoning" (249B5–c1) (see 12: THE FORMS AND THE SCIENCES IN SOCRATES AND PLATO; 27: LEARNING ABOUT PLATO FROM ARISTOTLE). (It is useful to compare this description with the one given in Aristotle, APo. II.19.)

Once a Form has been reached in this way, division begins. This is a matter of "cutting the form up again, by relation to [sub-]forms, by relation to its natural joints" (265E1–2). As an example, Socrates cites the case of love itself:

> just as a single body naturally has its parts in pairs, with both members of each pair having the same name, and labeled respectively left and right, so the two speeches regarded madness as naturally a single form in us. The one [Socrates' reorganized version of Lysias' attack on love] cut off the part on the left side, then cutting it again, and not giving up until it had found among the parts a love which is, as we say, "left-handed,"

and abused it with full justice, while the other speech [Socrates' own defense of love] led us to the parts of madness on the right-hand side, and discovering and exhibiting a love which shares the same name as the other, but is divine, it praised it as a cause of our greatest goods. (265E4–266B1)

Thus, while each speech tells only half the story, the two together show how correct division should proceed. The goal, however, isn't just truth or correctness, but explanatory adequacy. Thus if the Form in question "is simple, we should consider . . . what natural capacity it has for acting and on what, or for being acted upon and by what," and if it is complex, we should count its sub-Forms, and consider the same things about them as about the simple ones (270D3–7). That Socrates, the archetypal searcher for explanatory definitions (*Euthphr.* 6D9–E6), should pronounce himself "a lover of these divisions and collections" is no surprise, therefore (266B3–4).

Philosophy aims at true definitions and true stories based on them (see 6: PLATONIC DEFINITIONS AND FORMS). But it also aims at persuasion, since the philosophical lover wants to persuade his boy to follow him on the path to the Forms. Philosophy and rhetoric must thus go together, which means that rhetoric, too, must be developed as a *technē*. It must, first, distinguish and give definitions of the various kinds of souls and kinds of speeches, revealing their respective capacities and susceptibilities, and, second, "coordinate each kind of soul with the kind of speech appropriate to it, explaining why one kind of soul is necessarily convinced by one kind of speech, while another is not" (271B1–5). Mastery of such a science, however, requires one further thing: "the student must observe these things as they are in real life, and actually being put into practice, and be able to follow them with keen perception" (D8–E1). It isn't enough, in other words, to know what kinds of speeches affect what kinds of soul, the philosophical rhetorician must also know that this man in front of him is of such and such a kind, and be able to talk in the kind of way that will prove convincing to him (E2–272B2).

Writing about Love

At the end of the *Symposium*, Alcibiades has gone off, presumably with the throng of Bacchic revelers, who burst into his life as representatives of his overpowering love for the approval and flattery of the crowd. Socrates, Aristophanes, and Agathon are left behind discussing tragedy and comedy: "the main point was that Socrates was trying to prove to them that the same man knows (*epistasthai*) how to write both comedy and tragedy, that someone who is by craft (*technē*) a tragic poet is a comic poet too" (223D2–6).

The key words here, as we learn in the *Ion*, are *epistasthai* and *technē*. Ordinary poets cannot write both comedy and tragedy, because they do not write out of knowledge and craft (*technē*) but out of divine inspiration (*Ion* 534C5–6). If they did write out of craft and knowledge, if they were *craftsmen poets*, they would be able to write both comedy and tragedy, because opposites are always studied by the same craft. Thus the comedic craft and the tragic craft would have to be one and the same, just as one and the same craft, medicine, deals with both sickness and health.

305

Socrates tells us what a craftsman poet would *be able to* write, he does not tell us what he *would* write. Other Platonic spokesmen are somewhat more forthcoming. "We ourselves are poets," the Athenian Stranger tells us in the *Laws*, "who have to the best of our ability created a tragedy that is the finest and the best; at any rate, our entire constitution is constructed as an imitation of the finest and best way of life – the very thing which we claim is the truest tragedy" (817B1–5). Earlier in the same discussion, the Stranger is equally explicit that this same constitution, though not a comedy, does nonetheless embody comedic knowledge:

> Someone who is going to gain practical wisdom can't learn serious matters without learning ridiculous ones, or anything else, for that matter, without its opposite. But if we intend to acquire virtue, even on a small scale, we can't be serious and comic too, and this is precisely why we must learn to recognize what is ridiculous, to avoid being trapped by our ignorance of it into doing or saying something ridiculous, when we don't have to. (816D5–E5)

The *Laws* is a tragedy, then, because it is "an imitation of the finest and best way of life." The *Symposium* is a tragedy for an analogous reason: it contains an imitation of one part of such a life, namely, what the *Protagoras* terms a "symposium of beautiful and good men" who "test each other's mettle in mutual argument" by asking and answering questions (347D3–348A9). This is how Socrates responds to Agathon's speech. It is how Diotima converses with Socrates. It is the type of symposium Socrates tries to re-establish when Alcibiades' "satyr-play" is finished, and the throng of Bacchic revelers has left.

Unlike the *Laws*, however, the *Symposium* is a comedy too, since it also contains an imitation of the second best kind of symposium described in the *Protagoras*. This is one in which poets figure as authorities, either by being present themselves (as Aristophanes is), or by being quoted by the participants, without being there to be questioned (as Homer and Hesiod are by Phaedrus), and where the participants "argue over points that can't be established with any certainty" (347E1–7).

Finally, Alcibiades arrives with – significantly enough – a flute-girl (212c5–E3; cf. 176E6–7). And though she does not play, her arrival inaugurates the further decline of the symposium into something even more like the kind of symposium reviled in the *Protagoras* as "a symposium of common, vulgar fellows . . . who, unable to entertain one another with their own conversation, put up the price of flute-girls, and pay large sums to hear the sound of the flute instead of their own talk" (347c4–D2). This is the element of satyr-play in the *Symposium*; satyr imagery is frequent in Alcibiades' speech.[2]

The idea is the one mentioned earlier. Some love stories – the good ones – are tragedies (in the special sense of the term introduced in the *Laws*): they involve the kind of love found in the best kind of life, a life that comes as close as possible to the divine, one in which we achieve happiness by making good things become ours forever (205D1–206A12). Other love stories are comedies: they involve a lesser kind of love. Others still are satyr plays: genital farces. But the true story of love, the story that is Plato's *Symposium* itself, is the story of all these stories. In the *Symposium*, it takes the form appropriate to its genre and audience. But in the *Phaedrus*, we learn of the longer, more technical road it might take in the future, when armed with a scientific psychology and rhetoric it becomes a matter for experts.

Notes

All translations are the author's unless otherwise noted.

1 The proverb is that "good men go uninvited to an inferior man's feast" (Eupolis fr. 289).
2 The relevance of the *Protagoras* to the *Symposium* was drawn to my attention by Manuela Teçusan, *Logos Sympotikos*, in Oswyn Murray (ed.) *Sympotica* (Oxford: Clarendon Press, 1990).

References and further reading

Allen, R. E. (1966). The elenchus of Agathon: *Symposium* 199c–201c. *The Monist* 50, pp. 460–3.
—— (1991). *Plato's* Symposium. New Haven, Conn.: Yale University Press.
Bury, R. G. (1973). *The* Symposium *of Plato*, 2nd edn. Warminster: Aris and Phillips.
Davidson, J. (1998). *Courtesans and Fishcakes: The Consuming Passions of Classical Athens*. London: St Martin's Press.
Dover, K. J. (1978). *Greek Homosexuality*. Cambridge, Mass.: Harvard University Press.
—— (1980). *Plato's* Symposium. Cambridge: Cambridge University Press.
Edelstein, L. (1971). The role of Eryximachus in Plato's *Symposium*. In *Ancient Medicine: Selected Papers of Ludwig Edelstein* (pp. 153–71). Baltimore: Johns Hopkins University Press.
Ferrari, G. (1987). *Listening to the Cicadas: A Study of Plato's* Phaedrus. Cambridge: Cambridge University Press.
—— (1992). Platonic love. In R. Kraut (ed.) *The Cambridge Companion to Plato* (pp. 248–76). Cambridge: Cambridge University Press.
Gould, T. (1973). *Platonic Love*. London: Routledge and Kegan Paul.
Griswold, C. L. (1986). *Self-Knowledge in Plato's* Phaedrus. New Haven, Conn.: Yale University Press.
Hackforth, R. (1952). *Plato's* Phaedrus. Cambridge: Cambridge University Press.
Halperin, D. (1990). Why is Diotima a woman? In *One Hundred Years of Homosexuality* (pp. 113–51). New York: Routledge.
Irwin, T. (1995). *Plato's Ethics*. New York: Oxford University Press.
Lear, J. (2000). *Happiness, Death, and the Remainder of Life* (see esp. pp. 106–65). Cambridge, Mass.: Harvard University Press.
Lesher, J., Nails, D., and Sheffield, F. (2005). *Plato's* Symposium: *Issues in Interpretation and Reception*. Cambridge, Mass.: Harvard University Press.
Moravcsik, J. M. E. (1972). Reason and eros in the ascent passage of the *Symposium*. In J. P. Anton and G. L. Kustas (eds.) *Essays in Ancient Greek Philosophy* (pp. 285–302). Albany, NY: State University of New York Press.
Nussbaum, M. C. (1986). *The Fragility of Goodness*. Cambridge: Cambridge University Press.
Price, A. (1989). *Love and Friendship in Plato and Aristotle*. Oxford: Clarendon Press.
Reeve, C. D. C. (1992). Telling the truth about love: Plato's *Symposium*. *The Boston Area Colloquium in Ancient Philosophy* VIII, pp. 89–114.
Rowe, C. J. (trans.) (1986). *Plato:* Phaedrus. Warminster: Aris and Phillips.
Sheffield, F. (2005). *Plato's* Symposium: *The Ethics of Desire*. Oxford: Clarendon Press.
Vlastos, G. (1981). The individual as the object of love in Plato. In *Platonic Studies*, 2nd edn. (pp. 3–42). Princeton, NJ: Princeton University Press.

21

Plato on Pleasure as the Human Good

GERASIMOS SANTAS

Plato's views on the nature of pleasure and his attitude toward pleasure have been subjects of lively debates for a long time. Since the mid-twentieth century some main issues have been whether his Socrates or Plato himself was a hedonist some of the time; and if not, whether Plato succeeds in evaluating and ranking pleasures non-hedonistically. And there have been distinguished scholars on all sides: Gosling and Taylor (1982), Irwin (1995), Rudebusch (1999), for example, in the affirmative on the first issue, Vlastos (1991), Zeyl (1980), on the negative, and D. Frede (1992, 1993) in the affirmative on the second issue.

These debates have not settled the questions. But they have served to clarify Plato's view on the nature of pleasure, to understand better the major arguments we find in Plato's dialogues for and against the hypothesis that pleasure is the human good, and to see more clearly the subtler view of the value of pleasure Plato eventually works out when he disagrees with hedonism.

In this article I am not concerned so much with whether Plato or his Socrates was ever a hedonist. But I shall try to take advantage of the benefits of the debates on this issue as I take up what is our main focus: the theoretical and practical advantages Plato saw in the hypothesis that pleasure is the human good, his objections to that view, and his efforts to account non-hedonistically for the value of pleasure. I place Plato's discussions of pleasure within the context of his main ethical question, how we should live, and suppose that his main interest in hedonism was as an answer to this question.

The Attractions of Hedonism

In the *Euthyphro* (7B6–D11) Plato has Socrates observe that when we disagree about the number, size, or weight of things, we can resort to the arts of arithmetic, geometry, and weighing to settle the dispute; such disagreements do not make us angry and enemies of each other. But when we disagree about the just and the unjust, the beautiful and the shameful, the good and the bad, we do become angry and enemies, being unable to reach agreement similarly; even the gods cannot do it, according to popular belief. This presupposes that the sciences of number, measurement, and weight have no application to the good, the beautiful, and the just.

308

But in the *Protagoras* (356B1–57A3) Plato's Socrates says that if the good and the bad are identical with pleasure and pain, then we can resolve disputes about the good and the bad, the just and the unjust, the beautiful and the shameful, apparently because the arts of number, measurement, and weighing can be applied to pleasure and pain.

> Weighing is a good analogy; you put the pleasures together and the pains together, both the near and the remote, on the balance scale, and then say which of the two is more. For if you weigh pleasant things against pleasant, the greater and the more must always be taken; if painful against painful, the fewer and the smaller . . . If, then, our well-being depended upon this, doing and choosing larger things, avoiding and not doing the small ones, what would we see as our salvation in life? Would it be the art of measurement, or the power of appearance? . . . What then would save our lives? Surely nothing other than knowledge, specifically some kind of measurement. (*Prt.* 356B1–357A3, trans. Lombardo and Bell)

In these passages we see Plato presenting an important problem in ethics and a bold dream of a solution. The problem is how to resolve disputes and disagreements about the good, the just, and the beautiful without going to war, in view of the apparent fact that the mathematical sciences, which do enable us to resolve disagreements rationally, do not seem to apply to such ethical concepts and entities. The bold dream is that on a given hypothesis, we can bring ethics not only within the province of reason's arguments, as Plato has Socrates try to do in the *Crito* and indeed in the rest of the *Euthyphro*, but within the province of that part of reason that has created mathematics and the arts of counting, measuring, and weighing. The hypothesis is hedonism, the idea that the good and the pleasant are identical and the painful and the bad are identical (*Prt.* 355B5–9); we have several terms but only two things. Apparently, it is taken for granted that pleasure and pain are susceptible to the arts of number, measurement, and weighing. If so, good and bad can be counted, measured, and weighed; and if so, the just and the unjust, the beautiful and the shameful, being dependent on the good and the bad, are also brought within the scope of the arts of measurement. (See Rudebusch 1999: ch. 7, for the clearly stated alternative view that Plato is using measurement as a metaphor; it is only comparability that is in question, and the scales in question are not interval scales but ordinal scales which do not require units; against this, see Taylor 1991: 190–200; for other hedonistic views, see Bentham 1789: ch. 4; Sidgwick 1981: 123–50.)

A bold dream it was indeed, as can be seen in discussions some twenty-four centuries later in Mirrlees (1982), and John Broome (1996); the first author maintains that Hedonism has failed the test of measurement and the second tries to weigh goods without the assumption of hedonism and in less ambitious ways.

For Plato the dream must have held enormous theoretical and practical attraction: to turn ethics into a science and to be able to settle disputes about the good, the just, and the beautiful, not in the way of the *Protagoras* (in which things appear to us as they really are), nor by the sword of the strong (the way of Thrasymachus), but in the ways we can settle disputes about the size of Athens, the length of the road to the Piraeus, or the weight of the statue of Athena. The glory of reason would rise even above the Socratic method, a method of reasoning in ethics which does not use the arts of measurement, and be complete.

No doubt Plato found other attractions in hedonism. If pleasures and pains are commensurable, and if pleasure is identical with the good and pain with the bad, then all goods and bads are commensurable; and they can be ranked, not only ordinally and intuitively, but by measuring them and deducing the rankings from their cardinal values. Hedonism seems to make possible a universally applicable, unified, and complete theory of the good as the fundamental choice-guiding concept. Pleasure is the common value coin, as it were, by which all good can be measured. Just as wealth can be defined as anything that can be measured by money, so the good can be defined as anything that can be measured by pleasure. And if the just and the beautiful can be derived from the good, then all of ethics can be based on a universally applicable, unified, and complete theory of choice. Theoretically, we would be able to place whole life options on the scales, weigh them, and make a rational choice, i.e., choose the life that gives us the greatest net balance of pleasures over pains.

Further, if pleasure and the good are the same, and if pleasures and pains can be counted, measured, and weighed, the Socratic supremacy of knowledge can be vindicated, on an assumption few if any would dispute: that the arts of measurement are branches of human knowledge. On these premises, the knowledge that these arts would supply when applied to pleasures and pains would be clearly necessary for making rational choices, choices of the greater good or the lesser bad. More than that, as the *Protagoras* passage clearly shows, Plato thought that it might now be possible to show that such knowledge is also sufficient for choosing the greater good or the lesser evil – to show that there is no such thing as knowing the better and doing the worse, at least when one can do the better. For on this issue ethical hedonism has a great ally, psychological hedonism: that generally and above all men desire pleasure and seek to avoid pain. This general psychological fact seems to provide the motivation needed for the knowledge of the measurements of pleasures and pains to be sufficient reason or cause for doing the better and avoiding the worse. The hypothesis of hedonism, the assumptions of measurability and co-measurability of pleasures and pains, the distinction between apparent and real sizes of pleasures and pains, and psychological hedonism – all these conspire to turn pleasure from a temptress for bad to a motivator for good. And if the just and the fine can be brought within the scope of the science of measurement, by supposing that they derive from the good, then indeed the knowledge of pleasures and pains, together with their connections to the just and the fine, would be sufficient for virtue. Knowledge of pleasure and pain would be necessary and sufficient for virtue.

Finally, hedonism seems to be a more determinate choice-guiding theory than eudaimonism; either psychological eudaimonism, (the idea that we all desire happiness as the ultimate end of all our choices) or ethical eudaimonism (the idea that happiness is the ultimate human good and anything else good is good as a constituent of or means to happiness). But happiness and *eudaimonia* in Greek seem to be equivocal concepts. Men may agree that the ultimate human good is happiness, but, as Aristotle remarks, this is a purely verbal agreement, since different men understand happiness to be different things, i.e., pleasure, knowledge, virtue, even health when they are sick, or wealth when poor (*EN* I.5). One can imagine how different the choices would be when such diverse conceptions of happiness are taken as the ultimate end or ultimate good. But even though people may take pleasure in different things, there seems to be no similar ambiguity in pleasure itself. That all men desire pleasure seems as evident as that all men desire happiness, but pleasure seems a much more determinate, specific, and clearer guide to choice.

To sum up, the main attractions Plato saw in pleasure as the good are the possibility of measuring value and turning ethics into a science, the possibility of bringing all goods and all the virtues within a unified theory of the good as a choice-guiding concept, a basis for the vindication of the Socratic supremacy of knowledge in human conduct, and the motivational and choice-guiding powers of pleasure and pain.

It is fair to say, though, that Plato did not work out the first and most fundamental of these attractions, and he left behind more questions than answers. To begin with, how are pleasures and pains to be measured? In what dimensions, in what scales, and by what instruments? Bentham, who worked up the hedonistic calculus some twenty centuries later, was clear that the primary measurable dimensions of pleasures and pains are duration and intensity, although there are other properties, such as certainty and proximity, that need also be taken into account. Pleasures and pains are spread out in time, so duration is an obvious dimension for measurement, and anything that measures time can be used to measure pleasure, even the ancient crude devices of sun clocks and hourglasses. Plato often speaks of the great intensities of bodily desires and pleasures, and presumably his Socrates in the *Protagoras* would agree that this is another dimension that is in principle measurable. Aristotle mentions both dimensions and worries about their interplay in ranking pleasures (*EN* 1169a17–26).

But how is intensity to be measured? Even now, with all our sciences and technology, we would be hard put to point out how we might measure pleasures and pains (see Savage 1972 and Sidgwick 1981: 176–95). Further, Plato does not tell us how intensity is to be balanced against duration, something we need to know, since clearly we can have choices between more intense but shorter and longer but less intense pleasures (see Rawls 1971: 554–60). Nor does Plato tell us how pleasures are commensurable with pains, to make it possible to add up pleasures and add up pains and subtract the lesser from the greater sum of either, in order to determine the net balance of pleasure over pain or pain over pleasure.

In the *Protagoras* (356A5–E3) Plato does discuss an important problem in hedonistic choice that measurement is supposed to solve. He makes two fundamental points. First, Socrates points out that the size or magnitude (presumably of the duration or intensity or both?) of pleasures (and pains) appears different to us at different (presumably temporal) distances, even though their actual magnitude is the same; in a similar way the size of visible objects (even of sounds, we might add) appears different at different spacial distances, even though their actual size remains the same. Thus we can speak of apparent and real magnitudes of pleasures (and pains), as we speak of apparent and real sizes of visible objects (e.g., the apparent and real size of the sun). Second, the discrepancy between apparent and real magnitudes is the reason why we need the science of measurement, since presumably we want to make hedonistic choices on the basis of real and true magnitudes of prospective pleasures (and pains), rather than on the basis of apparent and false ones. Pleasure can be not only a seductive temptress but also an arch deceiver. The art of measurement can unmask its deception and reduce the temptation.

In the discussion of apparent and real magnitudes of pleasures, Plato has Socrates claim that the art of measurement would disregard the proximity of pleasures and pains, their variable distances from the choosing agent. The near and remote pleasures, he claims, differ only in whether they are more or less; we would put the pleasures themselves on scales that disregard differences in distance and decide only which pleasure is greater. Since the apparent magnitudes of pleasures differ with distance, disregarding the proximity is in effect disregarding the appearance. Bentham apparently does not agree, since he claims that proximity, as well as certainty, should be taken into account by the choosing agent (Bentham 1789: ch. 4). Sidgwick (1981: 124, n. 1) apparently agrees partly with Plato, partly with Bentham:

> A . . . proximity is a property which it is reasonable to disregard except in so far as it diminishes uncertainty. For my feelings a year hence should be just as important to me as my feelings next minute, if only I could make an equally sure forecast of them.

Modern decision theory takes into account certainty or probability, which Plato ignores in the *Protagoras*; and through the back door, as it were, probability brings in proximity.

Finally, it is doubtful that the hypothesis of hedonism enables Socrates to succeed in showing the supremacy of knowledge. The very distinction between apparent and real magnitudes tends to undermine his efforts. Even if we disregard proximity in the calculations for rational hedonistic choices, it is conceded that proximity affects the apparent magnitudes of pleasures and pains, and these appearances can causally affect the desires for pleasures. And if they do, Socrates cannot take it for granted that the causal efficacy of appearances will correlate perfectly with the rational decision made on the basis of true measurements and correct logic. I may judge correctly that a distant pleasure is greater than an immediate one, but the differences in the way these two pleasures appear to me may cause me to give up the distant pleasure in favor of the one right now. I may know or correctly believe that the distant pleasure is greater than the immediate, but I may still have a more intense desire for the nearer pleasure because of the causal efficacy of appearances.

Plato's Objections to Hedonism

There are two related objections to hedonism, which Plato makes in several dialogues: that some pleasant things are bad, or that some pleasures themselves are bad.

The first is voiced by Protagoras when Socrates tries to promote the hypothesis of hedonism: "So, then, to live pleasantly is good, and unpleasantly, bad? Yes, so long as he lived taking pleasure in honorable things." Socrates tries to win him over, by asking: "Isn't a pleasant thing good just in so far as it is pleasant?" But again Protagoras protests: "There are pleasurable things which are not good . . . there are painful things which are not bad . . . and a third class which are neutral – neither bad nor good." Socrates tries again, clarifying his question: "You call pleasant things those which partake of pleasure or produce pleasure? Certainly," he said. "So my question is this: Just in so far as things are pleasurable are they good? I am asking whether pleasure itself is not a good" (*Prt.* 351c1–e7, trans. Lombardo and Bell). But Protagoras is still cautious, saying that they should examine the matter to see whether or not pleasure and the good are the same.

So far Socrates has treated a pleasant action as something complex, distinguished its pleasure from its other elements (e.g., the pleasure of eating sweets from the causes of the pleasure or the later results of the action), and asked whether the pleasure itself is not a good thing. Even though an affirmative reply would have committed Protagoras to no more than the general view that pleasure itself is one of the things that are good, Plato has him instead raise the issue whether the pleasant and the good are the same. Socrates changes the subject to the issue of the supremacy of knowledge, but soon returns to the hypothesis of hedonism, though with a dramatic shift which has Socrates and Protagoras answering questions on behalf of the many, the very same many who claim that one can know the better but do the worse because one is overcome by pleasure.

Having distinguished between the pleasure of a pleasant but bad action and its other elements, Socrates asks whether the many would say that the action is bad because of the pleasure itself present in it or because of bad things which would result from it later, such as disease or poverty. On affirming the latter on behalf of the many, he asks in turn whether the many would not agree that these bad things which come later are bad for no other reason than that they end up in pains or deprive us of other pleasure (*Prt.* 353d1–354c9). The many would agree, Socrates claims, and secures analogous answers for actions that are both painful and good (physical training, military service, and medical treatment), and now he thinks he has all the data necessary to answer the objections to hedonism that Protagoras or he himself has brought up (pleasant but bad or shameful actions, and painful but good or noble actions), and to be free to use the hypothesis of hedonism.

In sum, pleasant but bad actions are bad not because of the pleasure but because they result in later pains that exceed the pleasure or deprive us from later but greater pleasures; analogously for painful but good actions. The good and the pleasant are the same; there are four names but really only two things, and we can substitute the name "pleasant" for the name "good" or the reverse, and we can substitute the name "bad" for "pain" or the reverse. These substitutions then enable Socrates to argue that the explanation of the many, that a man can know the better and do the worse because he was overcome by pleasure, is absurd (*Prt.* 354b4–356c3).

It should be observed that while Socrates ends up with an equation of the pleasant and the good (and the painful and the bad), it is pleasure that has explanatory primacy in his argument: the badness of pleasant actions that are bad is explained by the resulting later pains or later deprivations of greater pleasures; and the goodness of painful but good actions is explained by later resulting pleasures or later avoidance of greater pains. Thus the good is explained by pleasure, not vice versa, and the bad is explained by pain, not vice versa. And this of course is what would enable ethics, the discipline of the good and the bad, the just and the unjust, the shameful and the noble, to become a science through measurement; it is the pleasures and the pains that are measurable; and it is pleasure and pain that account totally for good and bad. We have four names and two things; the two things are pleasure and pain.

In sum, in the *Protagoras* Plato has Protagoras bring up a main objection to hedonism – that there are pleasant but bad things and painful but good things – and has Socrates answer the objection as a hedonist would, and apparently to the satisfaction of both Protagoras and Socrates.

But in the *Gorgias* (495A2–7) Plato has Callicles expound what appears to be the hedonism of the *Protagoras* (the same language is used to state the view in both dialogues: "the good and the pleasant are the same," Gosling and Taylor 1982: 69–70), and then Plato has Socrates attack and try to refute Callicles' hedonism. Interpreters who think that Socrates is Plato's spokesman and believe that the Socrates of the early dialogues has a unified ethical view try to avoid this apparent contradiction by distinguishing different kinds of hedonism: long-term hedonism in the *Protagoras* (Gosling and Taylor 1982) and Callicles' hedonism confined to short-term bodily pleasures; or a hedonism of real magnitudes of pleasures (and pains), and a hedonism of apparent magnitudes of pleasures (Rudebusch 1999: ch. 3). These authors claim that once we make one of these distinctions the apparent conflict between these two dialogues disappears; they think that long-term hedonism or the hedonism of real magnitudes of pleasures is the better theory; and both think that Socrates was a true believer of the hedonism he expounds and uses in the *Protagoras*: that he was a long-term hedonist (Gosling and Taylor) or a modal hedonist (Rudebusch).

But the *Gorgias* presents a second challenge to this interpretation. In the *Protagoras* Plato explains well how a hedonist would answer the objection that some pleasant things are bad, but avoids dealing with the objection that some pleasures themselves are bad or shameful. But in the *Gorgias* Plato has Callicles admit, after two rather inconclusive arguments by Socrates, that some pleasures are bad, and Socrates treats this admission as showing that Callicles has given up his hedonism (*Grg.* 499B1–D2, 500D8–10).

The *Republic* confirms that Plato regarded the objection that some pleasures themselves are bad, not merely that some pleasant things are bad, as decisive:

> What about those who define the good as pleasure? Are they any less full of confusion than the others? Aren't even they forced to admit that there are bad pleasures? Most definitely. So, I think, they have to agree that the same things are both good and bad. Isn't that true? Of course. (*R.* 505c5–D2, trans. Grube and Reeve)

In sum, at the very least, and consistently with all three dialogues, we can say that Plato believed that while the existence of pleasant but bad complexes can be accounted for by a hedonist, the existence of some pleasures themselves bad could not be.

It remains an open question, however, whether Plato succeeds in giving clear and convincing examples of pleasures themselves that are bad, as distinct from examples of shameful pleasures, and as distinct from complexes that are both pleasant and bad. The controversial nature of this premise is conceded in the *Philebus* (13B–C), when Socrates implies that there are bad as well as good pleasures and Protarchus replies: "What do you mean, Socrates? Do you suppose that anyone who asserts that the good is pleasure will concede, or will endure to hear you say, that some pleasures are good and some are bad?"

Socrates has no direct answer to this challenge, and indeed it is only after Socrates makes another objection to hedonism and Protarchus gives up hedonism, that Plato proceeds to distinguish between good and bad pleasures. The new objection is an isolation preference test which Sidgwick and Moore revived, Sidgwick to defend hedonism indirectly (1981: 398–9), Moore to attack it directly as Plato did (1903: 88–96).

After some discussion (whether there are different kinds of pleasures and whether some pleasures are contrary to other pleasures), in which Socrates fails to convince Protarchus that some pleasures are bad (*Phlb.* 13B5–20B9), he tries to decide in a new way whether "pleasure is the good, or wisdom, or some other third thing" (14B4–6, 20B8–10); these are the two candidates for the good refuted differently in *R.* 505B6–D2.

The new way is a thought-experiment: "Let us put the life of pleasure and the life of knowledge on trial, and reach some verdict by looking at them separately . . . Let there be neither any knowledge in the life of pleasure, nor any pleasure in that of knowledge." And Protarchus, representing hedonism, is invited to judge whether he would find it acceptable to live his "whole life in enjoyment of the greatest pleasures" [but without any knowledge] (*Phlb.* 20E1–21A8, trans. Frede).

Before considering Protarchus' first whole-hearted reply in the affirmative and his sudden reversal at the end of Socrates' argument, we note that just before the thought-experiment Socrates proposes, and Protarchus agrees, that the good – whatever its content, pleasure, wisdom, or something else – has three properties, which may be called formal properties of the good, given their independence from content. The good is complete (or perfect), it is sufficient, and every being who knows it pursues and desires it and "has no interest in anything in which the good is not included." Though these properties are not explained, it is clear that completeness or sufficiency are taken to imply that "if either of them [pleasure or wisdom] is the good, it cannot have need of anything else, and if either is found to need anything, we can no longer regard it as our real good" (*Phlb.* 20E6–8). This in turn prompts Socrates to ask Protarchus whether he thought he would need anything further, if he lived his whole life "in the enjoyment of the greatest pleasures." Nothing at all, Protarchus replies. For a third time Socrates asks him, now more specifically, whether he would not have "some need for wisdom and mind and the power to calculate and similar things." "Why should I? If I have enjoyment, I have everything," Protarchus replies (21B3–4).

Socrates now points out to him that if he did not have "memory, knowledge, or true opinion, you would not know whether or not you were enjoying . . . you could not remember that you ever did enjoy . . . you could not think that you were enjoying when you were enjoying . . . and you could not calculate that you would enjoy in the future . . . your life would not be that of a man, but of a mollusk or some other shellfish . . . is such a life choice worthy?" Protarchus' reversal is stunning: "This argument, Socrates, has made me utterly speechless for the present" (*Phlb.* 21D5–6).

In a very brief sequel they readily agree that a life of wisdom and mind and knowledge and memory but with "no share of pleasure, small or great" would not be choiceworthy. Further, they agree that everyone would prefer a life of a mixture of wisdom and pleasure to either one in separation from the other.

In Protarchus' speechlessness Plato may be indicating the originality and startling nature of Socrates' thought-experiment. It is doubtful indeed that any hedonist, anyone who made pleasure the ultimate end of his life and chose everything else for the sake of it, thought that he was thereby committed to a preference or choice of a life of enjoyment without any cognition whatsoever, past, present, or future, of that enjoyment. When the argument apparently reveals this commitment, Protarchus recoils with a start – he never thought of that! The result of the separation of pleasure from wisdom is so radical that Socrates has to come up with the life of a mollusk as an example of what the hedonist would be choosing! Not only a bad choice, but an unreal choice, an impossible choice.

In the *Philebus* the test is regarded as decisive against hedonism, since the rest of the dialogue assumes that hedonism has been hereby defeated and the remaining question is whether knowledge or pleasure takes second place in the mixed life, with pleasure ending up defeated into second, third, and even fourth place.

Commentators record that readers have indeed objected that Socrates' test is unreal (Hackforth 1972: 32) or unfair (Frede 1993: xxxii) or both. The locus for both objections is the same: Socrates' abstraction or separation of all knowledge, of memory, of belief, and of calculation about future pleasures – even bare awareness of pleasures – from the life of enjoyment.

The test is unreal not only in being a thought-experiment, but in being an experiment which could never be run in reality, even with the most advanced technology imaginable, even a technology that makes a brain in a vat possible. How would the experimenters know that the subject was enjoying the greatest pleasures, when even the subject himself was not aware of them?

Plato may have thought that hedonism, the view that the good is identical with pleasure, commits the hedonist to the idea that he would be satisfied if he had the greatest pleasures, even if he had nothing else. Protarchus' second reply to the question whether he would need some wisdom or mind or the power to calculate seems to suggest that idea: "Why should I? If I have [the greatest] enjoyment[s], I have everything." And indeed this is a plausible reply, if he is not counting the separation of pleasure from the awareness of pleasure. If he is enjoying the greatest pleasures, an idea that usually goes together with the awareness that he is enjoying the greatest pleasures, why would he need the powers of calculation, for example? That power is only a means to getting future pleasures, but if he has all the pleasures – by hypothesis – then the lack of power does not deprive him of any pleasures. So a hedonist responding to the thought-experiment might indeed be satisfied if he had all the pleasures without the causal means to them, if these means can be separated from the pleasures. But not even being aware or conscious of the pleasures is too much for Protarchus to accept; this separation stuns him and leaves him speechless.

But can the possibility of such separation be taken for granted? Can I be enjoying myself without being aware than I am enjoying myself? Moore thought this might actually be common, though he still felt the need to argue that a hedonist is committed to the possibility of this separation (1903: 89). But can I feel pleasure without being aware or conscious that I feel pleasure? This seems to be a harder question. And the possibility of a whole lifetime of feeling pleasures without ever being conscious or aware of such pleasures is in danger of being a life indistinguishable from one of zero pleasures. In any case, if Plato supposed that the hedonist is so committed, we can understand why he treated the argument as decisive in the dialogue.

In the *Philebus* Plato is trying to discover first what goodness is in the whole cosmos, not just in human life; and after that he tries to discover what goodness is relative to human beings, the human good. The thought-experiment serves to reveal that a life of pleasures without any cognition might be the good of a lower animal, but not of a human being, while the life of knowledge without joy or grief would be the good of a god, not a human being. For a human being, a mixture of knowledge and pleasure would be the good. And in the rest of the dialogue, by trying to discover which would take first, second, third, and so on, place in the mixed life, Plato is trying to work up a theory of the human good which will be choice-guiding about options within a human life.

Plato's Own View of the Value of Pleasure

All the hedonists in Plato's dialogues, the many of the *Protagoras*, Callicles in the *Gorgias*, and Protarchus in the *Philebus*, share some assumptions. They all of course hold that pleasure itself is the only thing that is good by itself (or good as an ultimate end); all other things that are good are good as a means or sources of pleasure; and apparently they suppose some possible separation between the pleasures themselves and these other things. They do not admit that any pleasures themselves are bad. They evaluate and rank pleasures on the basis of magnitude alone. And they all suppose that a person who feels pleasure knows or is the ultimate judge whether she feels pleasure. Plato is not a hedonist; his evaluations and rankings of pleasures in Book IX of the *Republic* presuppose his earlier proof in that work that the good is not identical with pleasure; and as we saw, in the *Philebus* he explicitly refutes in a new way the hypothesis that pleasure is the good, before he proceeds to his own evaluations of pleasures. But neither does he think that no pleasure of any kind has value for human life. He thinks that some pleasures are better than others and that some lives are better off or happier than others insofar as they contain the better pleasures. This is what he argues in the ninth book of the *Republic*, apparently as part of his whole argument that the just man is happier than the unjust: the life of the just man who is ruled by reason and who pursues knowledge as his ultimate end is happier than the life of the unjust man who is ruled by spirit and pursues honor; and the latter is in turn happier than the life of the more unjust man who is ruled by appetite and who pursues wealth as the ultimate end of his life. And this is partly because the first life contains more valuable pleasures (the pleasures of gaining knowledge) than the the second, whose pleasures of victory and honors are in turn more valuable than those of wealth or appetite satisfaction (*R*. 580D2–587c4).

This presupposes that pleasures have some value and that some pleasures have more value than others. But Plato evaluates and ranks pleasures differently from the hedonist. He disagrees that the value of pleasures depends entirely on their magnitude, as the hedonists of the *Protagoras* suppose; and he disagrees that a man who thinks he feels pleasure can make no mistake about that, as all hedonists suppose; though they can concede that a man can make a mistake about the magnitude of prospective imagined pleasures or the magnitude of remembered pleasures (*Protagoras, Philebus*). It is Plato's task then to explain what other bases there are for evaluating pleasures and how a man can be deceived in thinking that he feels pleasure. Here I shall consider how he carries out this project, mostly in the *Republic*; though I shall refer to the *Philebus*, the evaluation of pleasures there is far more complex, and we refer the reader to D. Frede's (1992) excellent discussion.

In the *Republic* (583c2–587c4) Plato proposes two criteria for evaluating and ranking pleasures: purity of a pleasure or its non-admixture with pain; and truth or reality of a pleasure as distinct from falsehood or appearance of a pleasure. He also discusses the nature of pleasure, or what he thinks pleasure is – something which for him is necessary to do before we can rank or evaluate pleasures. His argument then attempts to show that the life of the man of knowledge is the most pleasant by showing that the pleasures of eating, drinking, and having sex (the main pleasures of the appetitive part of the soul and of the man of wealth) and the pleasures of victory and honors (the pleasures of the spirited part of the soul) are neither pure nor true (real), whereas the pleasures of the man of knowledge are true and pure as far as is humanly possible.

Now purity might be thought compatible with the hedonist's basis for evaluating and ranking pleasures. Indeed, Bentham counts it, although he points out that purity is not strictly speaking a property of a pleasure itself, but rather of the act which produces pleasure; all pleasures themselves are pure, but some may be produced in such a way that there is "a chance" that the pleasure may followed by pain and these are the impure pleasures (Bentham 1789: ch. 4). Moreover, a hedonist would rank pure and impure pleasures by magnitude alone, the net balance of pleasure over pain. Thus an impure pleasure might be more valuable or rank higher than a pure pleasure if the net balance of pleasure over pain in the mixed pleasure was greater than the pure pleasure.

Plato, however, does not seem to be thinking of purity in the hedonist's way. First, he has a theory of what some pleasures are, from which it follows that these pleasures are always mixed; or at least that the pains are necessary conditions of the pleasures, not just a probable effect of the acts that produce them. And second, he seems to think that pure pleasures are always more valuable than mixed pleasures, apparently no matter what the quantitative relations are between them; indeed, he explicitly tells us so in the *Philebus* (53B10–c3): "any pleasure, however small or infrequent, if uncontaminated with pain, is pleasanter and more beautiful than a great or often repeated pleasure without purity." Not only more beautiful; but even "pleasanter," though apparently here pleasanter does not mean that it is of greater intensity or duration or frequency!

In the *Gorgias* (491E5–494D1) we already have a picture of what a large class of impure pleasures are. Callicles thinks of pleasure as the satisfaction of bodily appetite, admits that appetite itself is painful, and thinks that the intensity of a pleasure is directly proportional to the intensity of the appetite it satisfies. He thinks primarily of bodily appetites and pleasures and seems to accept a physiological model of appetite and pleasure: appetite occurs when the body is depleted or deficient of something (e.g., one is thirsty or hungry) and pleasure occurs when the body is replenished and the desire (e.g., for drink or food) satisfied – a model that seems to fit well with hunger and thirst and perhaps even some sexual longing. It would seem then that all Calliclean pleasures are mixed or impure.

In the *Republic* (585D8–586c7) Socrates himself proposes a similar model of desire and pleasure, but he modifies it in two significant ways. First, he applies the depletion-replenishment model not only to desires and pleasures that arise in the soul through the body but also to some of the soul's own desires and pleasures: "And is not ignorance and folly in turn a kind of emptiness in the condition of the soul? It is indeed. And he who partakes of nourishment and wisdom fills the void and is filled?" (*R*. 585B3–7). If the ignorance and folly are felt as painful and a desire arises for filling this emptiness with wisdom, then the gaining of wisdom will be pleasant and this pleasure will not be pure. But perhaps, unlike hunger and thirst and sexual longing, folly and ignorance are not always felt as painful, if for no other reason than that the person may not be aware of his ignorance or folly, as is often demonstrated in Plato's early dialogues.

Second, Plato does not think that all pleasures that arise in the soul through the body are to be understood on the empty/filling model. He explicitly mentions pleasures of smell as pure pleasures that can be very intense (*R*. 584B6–9); and in the *Philebus* (51D7–10) he adds pleasures of hearing (say, listening to music) and sight (e.g., watching a sunset or a looking at a beautiful painting) – indeed all the "aesthetic" pleasures, literally the pleasures of sense-perception – might be of this kind. These are not preceded by any deficiency in the body or soul, even though in a very general sense we sometimes lack them (or simply, do not have them) and so can desire them.

In the *Philebus* the model is extended beyond its initial remedial or restorative dimension (perhaps by comparison to the gods, a comparison we have already seen earlier in Socrates' thought-experiment). We can think of the human body in health or illness; some bodily pleasures then occur when health is restored or deficiency remedied. Similarly, we can think of the soul as having health or soundness of the soul, such as virtue and knowledge, or as being corrupted by vice or ignorance; and in such cases, once more, we can think of pleasure as occurring when virtue is restored or knowledge gained. But we can also think of human beings not as being deficient as human beings, but as being imperfect beings relative to gods. There are things we do not have, even though these lacks are not deficiencies: coming to know an elegant mathematical proof, the appreciation of the peaceful scene at the banks of the Cephisus, the smelling of a gardenia, the listening of Mozart's fortieth symphony – all these one might not have and might enjoy partly because one did not already have them, though they are not restorations to health or the remedying of any psychic deficiency.

Now why should pure pleasures always be ranked above mixed pleasures, as Plato claims in the *Philebus*, no matter what the quantities of these pleasures and pains are? He might have thought, perhaps, that a life of pleasures and no pains – a life of pure pleasures only – is rationally preferable to a life of some pleasures and some pains, even if the net balance of pleasure over pain in the life of mixed pleasures exceeds the sum total of pleasures in the life of pure pleasures. One's aversion to pain might be considerable, or one's tolerance of pain might be near zero; and in such circumstances the choice of a life of pure pleasures over a life of mixed pleasures might well be rational for such a person, assuming it is possible. But there is no evidence in our texts that Plato thought of the matter in this way.

Rather, he seems to want to evaluate pleasures on the basis of things other than the pleasures themselves or their intrinsic properties, in the way in which we normally

319

evaluate another psychic phenomenon, desires: we usually evaluate and rank our desires by evaluating and ranking the objects of our desires. We evaluate the desire for a certain food or drink, for example, by finding out whether that food or drink is good for us; if it is, the desire is a good desire, if not, it is not. And this is how Plato evaluates desires generally, as he does, for example, in his distinction between necessary and unnecessary appetites (R. 558D5–559D2). Now what makes it possible to evaluate desires in this way is that desires come, ready-made as it were, with a certain structure: a desire must be a desire for something, it must have an object. Indeed, it is standard Platonic theory (e.g., Smp. 199E6–200B5) that desire is always for something. This structure gives us a handle for evaluating our desires. But pleasure does not seem to have any such structure. It may have causes and conditions under which it arises, but it does not seem to have, as part of its nature, an object; at any rate not as evidently as desire does. Plato's essential thought, in the Republic and the Philebus, is that pleasure does really have an object, and it should be evaluated by evaluating that object. It is no more appropriate to evaluate and rank pleasures by their intensities, as the hedonist does, than it is to evaluate desires by their intensities, or to evaluate both by their intensities, as indeed Callicles does in the Gorgias. Purity is indeed a basis for evaluating a pleasure, but the purity of a pleasure is due to the purity of its object; it is because the object of a pure pleasure is better than the object of an impure pleasure that pure pleasures should be ranked above impure pleasures.

To determine what are better and worse objects Plato relies on his metaphysics: Forms are better than their sensible participants, which are in turn better than the images of sensible participants – the metaphysics (and epistemology) of the Divided Line in the Republic. Thus the pleasure of learning or knowing Platonic Forms is pure because Platonic Forms are pure, flawless specimens of their kind, whereas their sensible participants are flawed in some way or other; thus the pleasures of knowing the Forms will rank above even the pure aesthetic pleasures whose objects are, say, colors or sounds – the pleasures of viewing beautiful paintings or listening to music.

Even for the mixed pleasures Socrates finds a basis for evaluation and ranking that comes from outside the pleasures themselves (that is, other than their intrinsic properties of intensity and duration), but this time it is not reliance on heavy Platonic metaphysics, but on the medicine of the day and its psychic analogues. Using the depletion/replenishment or restorative physiological model of pleasure, Socrates points out that the replenishment of a depletion may be appropriate or not for the depletion, good or bad for the person filling the emptiness. This is certainly true of foods and drinks; they can be good or bad for our health, excessive or defective in amounts, too frequent or not frequent enough, and so on. The medicine of the day routinely evaluated the physical pleasures on the basis of health and disease; enjoying the foods and drinks that are good for us makes for good enjoyment; enjoying harmful foods and drinks makes for bad enjoyment. And something similar, Socrates teaches, may be true of filling the emptiness of ignorance and folly; ignorance can be filled with false opinion, for example, and even though a person might enjoy the false belief, he is in a fool's paradise (R. 585E, 586E). Presumably, then, it is on the basis of the goodness or badness of the object that fills the emptiness that the pleasure is to be evaluated, and Plato might have thought that here he is evaluating the pleasure not hedonistically, but by something other than the pleasure itself – for example, health. The hedonist might reply, to echo a line from the *Protagoras*, that the value of health in turn depends on the pleasures it enables us to enjoy or the pains to avoid; so that this is not ultimately evaluating pleasures non-hedonistically. But Plato may be relying here on his arguments against the identity of good and pleasure, which, if successful, open up some space for other things besides pleasure to be good in themselves.

The other property on which Plato relies to evaluate pleasures in the *Republic* (and the *Philebus*) is truth or reality. This unusual, difficult, and obscure view has been discussed most extensively in the secondary literature (see, e.g., Taylor 1991; Frede 1992, 1993), and we can take it up only briefly here. There are at least two different issues.

First, Plato claims that sometimes we mistake relief from pain for pleasure. He thinks that besides the two states of pleasure and pain there is a psychological state in the middle which is neither pleasant nor painful: a neutral or zero hedonic point as it were. When our body becomes depleted – let us say dehydrated – we may feel the depletion as pain; this is like a movement downward from zero and this is real or true pain; when our body gets replenished we are moving from pain back to zero, but because of the contrast to the pain that is leaving us we mistake this relief from pain for pleasure. It is like a case where we do not know our whereabouts in a building, say, and we mistake the movement from the basement to ground zero level as a movement from the street level to the top of the building. But this relief from pains is not pleasure but only a phantom of true pleasures, he says (*R*. 586b7–9); apparently he thinks that relief from pain is similar to pleasure, as a phantom is similar to its object, and we mistake this similarity for identity. Real or true pleasure is felt when there is a movement upwards from zero, as when we are in neither pleasure or pain and then enjoy the smell of a rose, the exhibit of an elegant mathematical proof, or the beholding of Beauty-itself. These are real or true pleasures, Plato claims, and they should always be ranked above apparent or false pleasures, which are relief from pain.

A second issue is Plato's apparent application of truth and falsity to pleasure and pain. Especially since Hume, the moderns think that truth and falsity can be applied to psychic states that represent something, such as beliefs, expectations, and memories; these can be true or false by comparison to the realities they represent. But, they say, pleasure and pain are not representational psychic entities; they do not represent anything by comparison to which they can be true or false. The Humean and the hedonist might concede of course that an expectation of pleasure may be false; and a memory of pleasure can be false too, but that is a different matter. Such cases do not show that pleasures themselves can be false, but only that these pleasures did not in fact obtain.

It is not clear how strictly we can take Plato's application of the Greek terms for truth and falsity to pleasure; sometimes the same words can mean real and apparent; and though one might still dispute that the distinction between real and apparent can be applied to pleasures, it is a different kind of dispute, and not necessarily a confusion or even category mistake. In any case this dispute, whether truth and falsity can be applied to pleasures, may not affect Plato's view that sometimes we can mistake relief from pain for pleasure. Even if pleasure and pain are not representational psychic entities, as they do not seem to be, still we could mistake relief from one as being the other. Plato speaks of such mistakes in the *Republic* and the *Theaetetus*: we can mistake a beautiful sound or color for Beauty-itself, on account of their similarity; we mistake similarity for identity.

There remains perhaps an air of paradox about Plato's evaluation and ranking of pleasures by purity and truth. We saw that he does not use purity in the way the hedonist does, by taking it into account in the calculations of the net balance of pleasure over pain. Nor does he conceive it in the way a hedonist does, by whether or not a pleasure is preceded or followed by pain. Rather he claims that the purity of a pleasure depends on the purity of its object. And despite his perhaps more moderate view of false pleasures in the *Philebus*, the air of paradox persists there too. In any case, it is clear enough that purity and truth of pleasures are not for Plato quantitative criteria; so that not only is he not a hedonist, but even in evaluating pleasure as one of the good things of life, he wants to do it qualitatively rather than by magnitude and number. He has come a long way from the Hedonism of the *Protagoras*.

Note

All translations are the author's unless otherwise noted.

References and further reading

Bentham, J. (1789). *The Principles of Morals and Legislation*. London.

Broome, J. (1996). *Weighing Goods*. Oxford: Oxford University Press.

Frede, D. (1992). Disintegration and restoration: pleasure and pain in Plato's *Philebus*. In R. Kraut (ed.) *The Cambridge Companion to Plato* (ch. 14). Cambridge: Cambridge University Press.

—— (trans.) (1993). *Philebus*. Indianapolis: Hackett.

Gosling, G. C. B. and Taylor, C. C. W. (1982). *The Greeks on Pleasure*. Oxford: Clarendon Press.

Hackforth, R. (1972). *Plato's* Philebus. Cambridge: Cambridge University Press.

Irwin, T. (1995). *Plato's Ethics*. Oxford: Oxford University Press.

Mirrlees, J. (1982). The economic uses of Utilitarianism. In A. Sen and B. Williams (eds.) *Utilitarianism and Beyond* (pp. 63–84). Cambridge: Cambridge University Press.

Moore, G. E. (1903). *Principia Ethica*. Cambridge: Cambridge University Press.

Penner, T. (1971). False anticipatory pleasures: *Philebus*, 36A3–41A6. *Phronesis* 15, pp. 166–78.

Rawls, J. (1971). *A Theory of Justice*. Cambridge, Mass.: Harvard University Press.

Rudebusch, G. (1999). *Socrates, Pleasure, and Value*. Oxford: Oxford University Press.

Savage, C. W. (1972). *The Measurement of Sensation*. Berkeley: University of California Press.

Sidgwick, H. (1981). *The Methods of Ethics*, 7th edn. Indianapolis: Hackett.

Taylor, C. C. W. (1991). *Plato:* Protagoras, rev. edn. Oxford: Oxford University Press.

Vlastos, G. (1991). *Socrates: Ironist and Moral Philosopher*. Cambridge: Cambridge University Press.

Zeyl, D. (1980). Socrates and hedonism: *Protagoras* 351B–358D. *Phronesis* 25, pp. 250–69.

Part V

PLATONIC ETHICS, POLITICS, AND AESTHETICS

22

The Unity of the Virtues

DANIEL DEVEREUX

The doctrine of the unity of the virtues was championed in one form or another by most of the ancient philosophers, but it is chiefly associated with its originator, Socrates. Socrates claimed that all of the virtues are somehow one, and he connected this with his view that the virtues consist in a kind of knowledge. But exactly what he meant by the claim that "the virtues are one" has puzzled scholars for generations. Our primary sources for Socrates' views about this topic are a couple of Plato's short, "Socratic" dialogues, the *Protagoras* and *Laches*, and unfortunately these dialogues do not give us a clear, unambiguous account of how the virtues are supposed to form a unity. The virtues Socrates discusses in these dialogues are justice, courage, temperance, piety, and wisdom. He clearly holds that these virtues form a unity in the sense that one cannot have one of them without having all the rest, but whether he intends to make the stronger claim that the virtues are *identical* with each other is not clear. Some passages seem to commit him to the view that there is really just one virtue with five different names, while others point to a view according to which each virtue has its own distinct essence and definition. We might for convenience call the stronger view (that there is just one virtue with five names) the Identity View, and the weaker view (that the virtues are distinct in their essence and definition but are inseparably linked to each other) the Inseparability View.

Both of these views are paradoxical in the sense that they fly in the face of our ordinary conceptions of the virtues. It is a common belief that some people who are courageous are not very wise or prudent, and that, for example, a dishonest person might be quite prudent and temperate in carrying out his deceptions. Socrates' contemporaries also regarded his views as paradoxical; Protagoras expresses the common view when he says "many are courageous but unjust, and many again are just but not wise" (*Prt.* 329E5–6). Protagoras also asserts, at Socrates' prodding, that the virtues are distinct parts of a whole and that they are unlike each other in the way that the parts of a face are unlike each other (329c2–330B6). In response to these claims, Socrates does not defend his own view of the unity of the virtues; he doesn't even give a clear statement of his position. Instead, in good "Socratic" fashion, he attempts to refute Protagoras' position by examining the relationships among the particular virtues. Thus one reason for the lack of clarity of Socrates' position is that his aim is not so much to explain and defend his own view, but to refute the view of his interlocutor.

Nevertheless, his arguments give us *some* indications of where he stands, and scholars generally believe that we can piece together a clear picture of his position on the basis of these arguments (see 5: THE SOCRATIC *ELENCHUS*). In the following discussion, I will explore and assess the different interpretations of Socrates' position on the unity of the virtues, and also try to understand what might have led him to his paradoxical view. Towards the end, I will briefly discuss relevant portions of the *Republic* and *Statesman* in order to see how Plato's views on the unity of the virtues might have differed from Socrates'.

Unity as Identity

Most scholars today understand Socrates' unity doctrine as the claim that the virtues are identical with each other. Our first reaction to this claim is likely to be astonishment. What could the proponent of identity *mean* by the claim that there is no difference between, for example, being just and being courageous? These virtues are obviously not identical with each other (or with the other virtues). It is important to note, however, that Socrates distinguishes between a virtue such as justice and the actions or behavior associated with it. The virtue of justice is an internal state of the soul which is expressed or "exercised" in just actions. Socrates' interlocutors, when asked to give a definition of a virtue, often give an account in terms of a certain kind of behavior, such as, "justice is telling the truth and paying one's debts" (*R.* 331B1–c2); Socrates then, typically, steers them towards an account which focuses on the source within the soul of such behavior (see, e.g., *La.* 191E9–192c1; cf. *Chrm.* 160D5–E5). The virtue is the state of the soul, not the behavior that derives from and expresses that state. Thus what Socrates would mean by the claim that justice is identical with courage is that the state of the soul that gives rise to just actions is identical with the state that gives rise to courageous actions. And, according to the Identity View, Socrates holds that there is a single form of knowledge ("knowledge of good and evil") which is the key to just, courageous, and virtuous action in general. This knowledge guarantees both that one's judgment about how to act will be correct, and that one will act accordingly, since one's desire will be properly directed towards what is good. So even though being courageous in the sense of acting courageously is obviously not the same as being just in the sense of acting justly, it might still be true that the virtue of justice is identical with the virtue of courage: i.e., the source of both just and courageous action might be one and the same state: "knowledge of good and evil."

The next question we need to consider, then, is whether Socrates holds that there is a single source of just, courageous, etc. action: whether the virtues are identical with each other. Several of Socrates' arguments in the *Protagoras* seem to support the Identity View. For instance, in the argument for the unity of temperance and wisdom, he first gets Protagoras to agree that folly is the opposite of both temperance and wisdom, and that a single thing has only one opposite; he then draws the following conclusion.

> [P1] Then which of these propositions should we abandon, Protagoras? The proposition that for one thing there is only one opposite, or the one stating that wisdom is different from temperance and that each is a part of virtue . . . ? Which should we abandon? The

two statements are dissonant; they are not in harmony with one another. How could they be, if there is one and only one opposite for each single thing, while folly, which is a single thing, evidently has two opposites, wisdom and temperance? Isn't this how it stands, Protagoras?

He assented, although very grudgingly, and I continued:

Wouldn't that make wisdom and temperance one thing? (333A1–B5)

Here in [P1] Socrates concludes that wisdom and temperance are one and the same thing. (Note for future reference that Socrates takes the conclusion, "temperance and wisdom are one thing," to be incompatible with the claim that each is a part of virtue.) Whatever we might think of his argument, it seems clear that *he* thinks he has established the identity of temperance and wisdom.

Another passage that supports the Identity View is the following:

[P2] So right now I want you to remind me of some of the questions I first asked, starting from the beginning. Then I want to proceed together to take a good hard look at some other questions. I believe the first question was this: (a) Wisdom, temperance, courage, justice, and piety – are these five names for the same thing, or (b) is there underlying each of these names a unique thing, a thing with its own power or function, each one unlike any of the others? You said that they are not names for the same thing, but that each of these names refers to a unique thing, and that all these are parts of virtue, not like the parts of gold, which are similar to each other and to the whole of which they are parts, but like the parts of a face, dissimilar to the whole of which they are parts and to each other, and each having its own unique power or function. If this is still your view, say so; if it's changed in any way, make your new position clear. (349A6–c7)

Socrates distinguishes two positions, (a) and (b), and then points out that Protagoras originally rejected (a) and opted for (b). Since Socrates argues against (b), it seems that he must accept (a); and (a) is clearly the view that there is just one virtue with five different names, i.e., the Identity View (see also 349E1–350c5, esp. 350c4–5).

Thus there are several passages in the *Protagoras* that provide strong support for the Identity View. However, at least one of Socrates' arguments poses a problem for the view. Recall that the Identity View holds that the several virtues are all identical to a single form of knowledge, a general knowledge of value or "knowledge of good and evil." Now in the final argument of the dialogue courage is identified, not with a general knowledge of value, but with "knowledge of what is and is not *to be feared*" (360D4–5). This definition seems clearly tailored to fit courage: consider how odd it would be to propose "knowledge of what is and is not to be feared" as a definition of justice or temperance. And yet, if courage is identical with justice and temperance, the same definition must apply to them as well. This argument thus seems to treat courage as different in nature from the other virtues.

Proponents of the Identity View have a reply: they claim that Socrates identifies knowledge of what is and is not to be feared with knowledge of good and evil, and as evidence they cite the final argument of the *Laches* (see, e.g., Penner 1999: 98–100). In this argument, Socrates *seems* to reject Nicias' proposed definition of courage as knowledge of what is and is not to be feared (the same definition that he himself argues for in the *Protagoras*!). It will be helpful to give an outline sketch of the argument (which is found at 197E10–199E11).

1   Courage is a part of virtue.
2   Courage = knowledge of what is and is not to be feared (definition proposed by Nicias).
3   Things to be feared and not to be feared are future evils and future goods.
4   Therefore courage = knowledge of future goods and evils.
5   Knowledge of future goods and evils = knowledge of all goods and evils.
6   Hence courage = knowledge of all goods and evils.
7   Knowledge of all goods and evils = "virtue as a whole."
8   Courage is therefore not a part of virtue; it is the whole of virtue.
9   But it was initially agreed that (1) courage is [only] a part of virtue.
10 Thus it seems that the definition of courage in (2) cannot be right.

As the identity proponent points out, Socrates does seem to argue that knowledge of what is and is not to be feared is identical with "knowledge of all goods and evils." We might therefore conclude that the definition of courage given in the *Protagoras* is misleading in that it seems to imply that courage is not identical with the general knowledge of all goods and evils. The *Laches* provides clarification by showing that knowledge of what is and is not to be feared is really the same thing as knowledge of all goods and evils. And since this knowledge is the basis not only of courageous action, but of wise, temperate, just, and pious action as well (199D4–E1), it is the single entity to which the various virtues are identical. The final argument of the *Laches* thus supplements and clarifies the final argument of the *Protagoras*.

One thing that might give us pause about this way of understanding the purpose of the final argument of the *Laches* is the conclusion that Socrates draws. He seems to reject the identification of courage with knowledge of good and evil since it conflicts with the initial assumption (1) that courage is [only] a part of virtue. Identity proponents argue that Socrates is actually presenting us with a choice between (1) and (2): we must either give up the view that courage is a part of virtue, or give up the definition of courage as knowledge of what is and is not to be feared. And it is clear that Socrates wants us to give up (1) rather than (2), since he argues in favor of (2) in the *Protagoras*, and, as we have seen in [P1], he also seems to reject (1).

If this is a plausible way of understanding the upshot of the final argument of the *Laches*, it appears that the Identity View gives a satisfactory account of all of Socrates' arguments for the unity of the virtues in the *Protagoras*. Although there appears to be a glaring contradiction between the two dialogues – the definition of courage that Socrates argues for in the *Protagoras* seems to be rejected in the *Laches* – the Identity View provides a nice way of harmonizing them. The argument of the *Laches* does not reject the *Protagoras*' definition of courage, but shows that it is equivalent to "knowledge of good and evil," and this formula can serve as the definition of each of the other virtues as well.

Problems with the Identity View

According to the Identity View, the final argument of the *Laches* is designed to show that courage is not a part of virtue, but rather is identical to the "whole of virtue."

However, the conclusion of the argument is hard to square with this view: Socrates says that since courage is a part and not the whole of virtue, we must reject the definition proposed by Nicias (199E3–11). It does not seem that we are given a choice between (1) and (2), as the Identity View suggests; Socrates clearly indicates that (2) must be rejected because it conflicts with (1). Moreover, he seems to emphasize his commitment to (1) in the passage leading up to the final argument.

[L1] And you, Nicias, tell me again from the beginning – you know that when we were investigating courage at the beginning of the argument, we were investigating it as a part of virtue?
Yes, we were.
And didn't you give your answer supposing that it was a part, and, as such, one among a number of other parts, all of which taken together were called virtue?
Yes, why not?
And do you also speak of the same parts that I do? In addition to courage, I call temperance and justice and everything else of this kind parts of virtue. Don't you?
Yes indeed.
Stop there. We are in agreement on these points. (197E10–198B2)

Socrates wants to make sure at the outset that he and Nicias are in agreement about courage being a part of virtue. He clearly indicates his commitment to the view when he says "I call temperance and justice [and courage] . . . parts of virtue." Let us call this the Parts Doctrine. In the *Laches* Socrates commits himself to the Parts Doctrine, and what he means by this is that each virtue is definitionally distinct from the whole of virtue and from the other parts. According to the argument of the *Laches*, then, the virtues are not identical with each other. Are they inseparable, or can one have one of the virtues without having the others? Socrates suggests that they *are* inseparable when he says that knowledge of all goods and evils guarantees possession of all the parts of virtue (see 199D4–E1).

We have seen that the *Protagoras* provides strong evidence for the Identity View, while the *Laches* seems to be committed to the Inseparability View, i.e., the view that the virtues have distinct definitions but are inseparably linked to each other. Further, if the definition proposed by Nicias in the *Laches* is rejected because it conflicts with the Parts Doctrine, then we are faced with a glaring contradiction between the final argument of the *Laches* and the final argument of the *Protagoras*, in which Socrates endorses this very definition.

Unity as Inseparability

One way of resolving the discrepancies between the *Laches* and *Protagoras* was suggested by Gregory Vlastos in an influential paper published in the 1970s. Vlastos holds that it is "standard Socratic doctrine" that the virtues are distinct parts of a whole, and cites both the *Laches* and *Meno* for support. He thus rejects the Identity View and argues for the Inseparability View. What, then, does he make of the passages in the *Protagoras* that seem to provide clear support for the Identity View, e.g., the argument for the claim that "temperance and wisdom are one"? In order to see how Vlastos

329

interprets these passages, it will be helpful to consider Socrates' first argument for unity in the *Protagoras* (330B7–331B8). In this argument, which immediately follows Protagoras' claim that none of the virtues is like any of the others, Socrates focuses on the relationship between justice and piety. His aim is clearly to refute Protagoras' claim in the case of these two virtues, i.e., to show that these two virtues "are very similar to each other" (see 330E3–331A5). But his argument is puzzling in a couple of respects. He begins by getting Protagoras to agree to the following statements, (1) "justice is just" and (2) "justice is pious," and (3) "piety is pious" and (4) "piety is just," and then concludes that since justice and piety share two properties (the properties of being just and pious) they must be "very similar" to each other. Protagoras reasonably objects that being similar in a couple of respects does not mean that they are "very similar" (331D1–E4). But what is most puzzling about the argument is the premises. What exactly does Socrates mean by the claim, for example, that justice is just? We speak of actions as just, and also laws and individuals, but how could a property like justice be just (or pious)?

Vlastos suggests that we take these premises as "Pauline" predications (Vlastos 1981: 252–9). That is, instead of understanding "justice is just" as an ordinary predication in which we attribute the property of being just to itself, he suggests that we understand it along the lines of St Paul's statement that "charity is long-suffering and kind"; what St Paul clearly meant is that those who are charitable are also long-suffering and kind. On a Pauline reading, the statements "justice is just" and "justice is pious" would mean that justice is such that *all of its instances* are just and pious. Taking this a step further, if the Pauline predications "justice is pious" and "piety is just" are both true, this may be expressed in the Pauline way as "justice *is* piety" or "justice and piety are *one.*" Understood in this way, the statements do not imply that the virtues are identical with each other, but only that (a) justice is such that all of its instances (all just individuals) are pious, and (b) piety is such that all of its instances are just; i.e., these two virtues are inseparable.

Vlastos's suggestion not only supports the Inseparability View, but has the added advantage of making sense of Socrates' puzzling statements (1)–(4). According to his interpretation, the arguments of the *Protagoras* are not at odds with Socrates' commitment to the Parts Doctrine in the *Laches*. In the *Protagoras*, too, each virtue is taken to have its own distinct essence and definition (e.g., courage = knowledge of what is and is not to be feared); Socrates' claim that "temperance and wisdom are one" does not deny that they have distinct definitions: it affirms that all those who are wise are temperate and all those who are temperate are wise, i.e., it affirms the inseparability of temperance and wisdom.

Problems with the Inseparability View

While it is true that Vlastos's suggested readings make good sense of Socrates' puzzling statements and provide a way of harmonizing the arguments of the *Protagoras* with those of the *Laches*, there are some strong reasons against understanding (1)–(4) as Pauline predications. As we have just noticed, on Vlastos's Pauline reading, if justice is pious and piety is just, it follows immediately that justice *is* piety (or that justice and piety are *one*). But once Protagoras agrees that justice is pious and piety is just, Socrates does not conclude that justice *is* piety (or that justice and piety are *one*); he draws the weaker conclusion that they are very similar (331B5–6). And at the end of his argument for the unity of temperance and wisdom, he says that these two virtues "are one," while it was shown earlier that justice and piety are *"almost* the same" (333B5–6). If Socrates understands these statements as Pauline predications, there would be no reason for him to distinguish the conclusions of the two arguments in the way he does, and no reason to stop short of the conclusion that justice *is* piety.

Another difficulty for the Pauline reading has to do with the range of instances of justice, piety, and the other virtues. According to Vlastos's account, we should understand the statement "justice is pious" as equivalent to: "justice is such that, necessarily, all of its instances are pious." If we take the instances of justice to be restricted to persons, the claim is that all just individuals are pious – a claim that Socrates would accept. But of course the class of instances of justice includes actions (and laws and institutions) as well as persons. Strictly speaking, then, "justice is pious" should be understood as the claim that all just individuals and all just actions are pious, and there is good reason to doubt that Socrates would accept this claim. In the discussion of piety in the *Euthyphro*, Socrates suggests that "the pious" is a part or subclass of "the just;" in other words, everything that is pious is just, but not everything that is just is pious (11E4–12D4). Although he does not specify which things are just but not pious, he is presumably thinking of actions; the claim that some just persons are not pious would conflict with Socrates' view that possession of one virtue entails possession of all the others. So it seems clear that Socrates would not accept the claim that justice is pious if this is understood as a Pauline predication. (For another way of understanding these predications see Devereux 2003: 78–9.)

Finally, we should recall that in [P1] Socrates takes the conclusion that "temperance and wisdom are one" to be incompatible with the claim that the virtues are parts of a whole; thus, appealing to the notion of Pauline predication to make this conclusion compatible with the Parts Doctrine is misguided from the start. It seems that in this and other arguments in the *Protagoras* Socrates is defending a position that he takes to be incompatible with the virtues being parts of a whole.[1]

Unity through Wisdom in the *Laches*

The results of our investigation so far may be summarized as follows:

1   Most of Socrates' arguments in the *Protagoras* support the Identity View, but the final argument seems more in line with the Inseparability View. The *Protagoras* thus gives us "mixed signals" regarding Socrates' position on the unity of the virtues.
2   In the *Laches*, on the other hand, Socrates' position seems clear and consistent: he is committed to the Parts Doctrine, and his arguments support the Inseparability View.
3   While Socrates regards the virtues as parts of "the whole of virtue" in the *Laches*, he apparently does not see them as species or subdivisions of a general knowledge of good and evil.

The final argument of the *Laches* presents us with a couple of puzzles. (a) As we have seen, Socrates affirms that courage is a distinct part of virtue, and he refers to knowledge of good and evil as the "whole of virtue." We have also noticed that what distinguishes courage from the other virtues is not that it is a particular species or subdivision of knowledge of good and evil. The knowledge that seemed to be distinctive of courage – knowledge of what is and is not to be feared – turns out to be identical with the general knowledge of good and evil. What is it, then, that distinguishes courage from the other virtues? (b) A second puzzle has to do with Socrates' claim that knowledge of good and evil is the "whole of virtue." If this knowledge is a "whole" and courage is one of its parts, it might seem obvious that courage must consist in a species or subdivision of the general knowledge of good and evil. Yet Socrates seems to deny this. How, then, can courage be a "part" of knowledge of good and evil without being a subdivision of it?

Let us approach these puzzles by first noting an interesting difference between the *Laches* and *Protagoras* in their treatments of "wisdom." In the *Protagoras*, when Socrates speaks of the view that virtue is a whole made up of parts, he counts wisdom as one of the parts, along with temperance, justice, piety, and courage (see 349B1–c5, 359A4–7). In the *Laches*, however, wisdom does not seem to be treated as a part of virtue; in the final argument, knowledge of good and evil is characterized as the "whole of virtue," and there is general agreement among scholars that Socrates identifies knowledge of good and evil with wisdom. This identification seems to be implied by his explanation of how knowledge of good and evil is the "whole of virtue"; he claims that the courageous person, who by assumption possesses this knowledge, "would not lack" any of the parts of virtue, for he would necessarily possess temperance, justice, and piety (199D4–E1). Wisdom is not mentioned. Further, wisdom is absent from the list of parts of virtue at the beginning of the final argument (see [L1] above, and *Men.* 78D7–79A5). In the *Laches* at least, Socrates apparently takes wisdom to be identical with knowledge of good and evil, i.e., with the whole of virtue (cf. *Men.* 87D2–89A3 with *Chrm.* 174A10–175A8).

If wisdom is the whole of virtue, and the other virtues are its parts, how exactly are we to understand this part–whole relationship? As we noted earlier, Socrates' final argument apparently rules out the possibility that courage is a species or subdivision of wisdom. The argument suggests that wisdom, understood as knowledge of good and evil, is an indivisible unity: it cannot be split up into parts corresponding to the different virtues. The knowledge that is essential to each of these parts of virtue is one and the same, and its name is *wisdom*. If courage and the other virtues require knowledge, and if the knowledge involved in each of these virtues is knowledge of good and evil, it seems clear that the definitions of courage and of the other virtues must include a reference to this knowledge. And since these virtues are distinct parts of a whole, each must have some distinctive aspect that differentiates it from the others as well as from the whole. Since the knowledge involved in each of the virtues is the same, the aspect which distinguishes each virtue from the others must be something different from the knowledge involved. We should consider, then, whether the *Laches* provides evidence of another factor essential to courage which is distinct from the knowledge involved.

A number of scholars have pointed out that there are indications in Socrates' discussion with Laches that he favors including the quality of *endurance* in the definition of courage. For instance, in his response to Laches' definition of courage as endurance, Socrates first points out that endurance is too broad. Since courage is assumed to be admirable and beneficial, it cannot be identical with a quality that may or may not be admirable and beneficial; and, as Socrates notes, there is such a thing as foolish or stupid endurance which is neither admirable nor beneficial. He therefore suggests amending the definition to "courage is *wise* endurance" (192c2–D11).[2] The next step is to clarify "in what sorts of things" the courageous man is wise (192E1). Socrates implies that they will have a satisfactory account of courage if they can specify the sort of wisdom involved. However, the investigation founders when Socrates presents Laches with a series of examples designed to clarify the kind of knowledge that is characteristic of courage, but Laches is unable to see the point of the examples (192E2–193D9). At the end of the discussion with Laches, Socrates does not reject the definition of courage as wise endurance. His treatment of the definition suggests that it may turn out to be correct if a clear account of the courageous person's wisdom can be given. And his final comment to Laches indicates his approval of including endurance in their account of courage.

> [L2] But are you willing that we should agree with our statement to a certain extent?
> To what extent and with what statement?
> With the one that commands us to endure. If you are willing, let us hold our ground in the search and let us endure, so that courage itself won't make fun of us for not searching for it courageously – if endurance should perhaps be courage after all. (193E8–194A5)

This comment emphasizes Socrates' view of the importance of endurance for an understanding of the nature of courage (see also 191D6–E2; for fuller discussion, see Devereux 1995). Socrates has also made it clear that he thinks that a certain kind of knowledge is essential to courage. Thus the correct account of courage must include mention of two factors, endurance and wisdom. What is lacking at the end of the discussion with Laches is a positive account of the courageous person's wisdom. The next stage of the discussion goes some way towards filling this lack when Nicias argues persuasively that the knowledge involved in courage is not knowledge of what is likely to happen in the future or knowledge of particular skills, but rather a general knowledge of what is good and evil for human beings (195B2–197c1). But Nicias ignores Socrates' advice about not leaving endurance out of their account. If he had included endurance, his definition would have been: "courage is endurance combined with knowledge of what is and is not to be feared." Then Socrates' final argument that knowledge of what is and is not to be feared is the same thing as knowledge of good and evil would have led to the result that: "courage is endurance combined with knowledge of good and evil." And this definition would not be open to the objection that courage turns out to be not a part but the whole of virtue; for the inclusion of endurance provides a way of distinguishing courage from the other parts as well as from the whole of virtue.

These indications in the discussion with Laches show that Socrates regards endurance as an essential component of courage that should be included in its definition. The definition would then include two factors: endurance and knowledge of good and evil; the knowledge factor unites it with the other virtues, while endurance sets it apart from them. The parts of virtue are different from each other, not because each is a species or subdivision of knowledge of good and evil, but because each is characterized by a distinctive aspect separate from knowledge of good and evil.[3]

But how are we to understand the claim that courage is a "part" of knowledge of good and evil if it is not a subdivision of it? In the final argument, Socrates explains how knowledge of good and evil is the whole of virtue by pointing out that someone who possesses such knowledge would "not be lacking" in temperance, justice, piety, or courage (199D4–E1). In other words, wisdom is the "whole of virtue" in that its possession guarantees possession of all of its parts (as in the case of any whole). However, on this view it seems that possession of courage would also guarantee possession of the other virtues: if courage requires wisdom, and wisdom guarantees possession of the other virtues, then courage also guarantees possession of the other virtues. But Socrates' explanation implies that it is *through* wisdom that the other virtues are possessed: the courageous person must be just because courage requires wisdom and one who is wise cannot fail to possess justice and the other virtues (we do not explain how wisdom entails justice by appeal to some *other* virtue). The other virtues are inseparably linked to each other *through* wisdom. Furthermore, only wisdom seems to be manifested in all virtuous actions. Some actions might be both just and courageous, but most courageous actions will not be instances of justice and many just actions will not be instances of courage. However, all virtuous actions will be wise insofar as they are based on knowledge of good and evil. To sum up: there are two reasons for Socrates' claim that wisdom, understood as knowledge of good and evil, is the whole of virtue: (a) like other wholes in relation to their parts, the possession of wisdom guarantees possession of the other virtues; (b) while the other virtues are manifested in some but not all virtuous actions, wisdom is manifested in all virtuous actions.

Unity in the *Protagoras* and *Laches*

Our discussion so far has brought to light several striking inconsistencies between the *Protagoras* and *Laches*. (1) We noticed that in the *Laches* Socrates regards all of the virtues except wisdom as distinct parts of a whole; he characterizes wisdom, or knowledge of good and evil, as the "whole of virtue" because it guarantees possession of the other virtues. Wisdom is the key to the unity of the virtues, for it is through wisdom that the other virtues are inseparably linked to each other. This rather complex view of the unity of the virtues *through wisdom* has no parallel in the *Protagoras*. As we have seen, most of Socrates' arguments in the *Protagoras* are aimed at establishing the identity of the virtues, which is clearly at odds with the *Laches'* view that the virtues are distinct from each other. (2) Also, when Socrates spells out the view that the virtues are distinct parts of a whole in the *Protagoras*, he includes wisdom as one of the parts, along with justice, piety, temperance, and courage; there is no suggestion in the *Protagoras* that wisdom is the whole of virtue. (3) We noticed further that the *Protagoras* gives "mixed signals" regarding Socrates' view of the unity of the virtues. While most of the arguments are designed to show the identity of the virtues, the final argument seeks to establish that courage is identical with knowledge of what is and is not to be feared, and this suggests that Socrates regards courage as definitionally distinct from the other virtues (since the definition seems designed to fit courage but not the other virtues). The arguments in the *Laches*, on the other hand, give a consistent view of the unity of the virtues: virtue is a whole made up of parts, and each part is definitionally distinct from the other parts and from the whole; all arguments point to the Inseparability View. (4) Finally, the most striking inconsistency between the two dialogues is seen in their final arguments: in the *Protagoras* Socrates argues that courage should be defined as knowledge of what is and is not to be feared, but in the *Laches* he argues against this very definition when it is proposed by Nicias.

How are we to understand the inconsistencies between the *Protagoras* and *Laches*? Why would Plato, for example, have Socrates argue for conflicting accounts of courage – and its relationship to knowledge – in two dialogues which are generally agreed to have been written in the same period? Although we have seen that both the Inseparability and Identity Views have difficulties accounting for parts of each dialogue, proponents of these views might contend that we have overestimated the difficulties. And since it would be puzzling if Plato defended inconsistent views of the unity of the virtues in works written in the same period, there is good reason to look again at both dialogues in order to see if there is a way of reconciling their apparently divergent views.

But there is perhaps another way of explaining the inconsistencies. Our other main sources for Socrates' views, Xenophon and Aristotle, both attribute to him the view of courage which is endorsed in the final argument of the *Protagoras*: "knowledge of what is and is not to be feared" (see, e.g., Xenophon, *Mem.* IV.6.1–11; Aristotle, *EE* III.1, 1229a12–16, and *EN* III.8, 1116b3–15). There is no trace in Xenophon and Aristotle of the *Laches*' view that the knowledge of the courageous person is actually "knowledge of all goods and evils." We also find in Xenophon the same "mixed signals" about the unity of the virtues that we noticed in the *Protagoras*: in some passages the virtues are claimed to be identical, but in others they are given distinct definitions (see, e.g., *Mem.* III.9.4–6, IV.6.1–6, and IV.6.11. Unfortunately, Aristotle has nothing to say about Socrates' view of the unity of the virtues). Here again, Xenophon's Socrates is close to the Socrates of the *Protagoras*, and contrasts with the Socrates of the *Laches*.

Xenophon's and Aristotle's reports suggest that the views and arguments ascribed to Socrates in the *Protagoras* derive from the historical Socrates (see 3: THE SOCRATIC PROBLEM). If so, then the *Laches*' different position on the unity of the virtues, and the final argument refuting the (Socratic) definition of courage argued for in the *Protagoras*, would seem to be Platonic innovations. Xenophon's and Aristotle's reports thus suggest the following explanation of the inconsistencies between the two dialogues. In writing the *Protagoras*, Plato set himself the task of formulating the various claims and arguments of the historical Socrates concerning the interrelations among the virtues. As it happens, there were unresolved tensions in Socrates' views, and these are preserved in Plato's depiction of the great debate between his mentor and Protagoras. Then, in the *Laches*, Plato resolves these tensions and articulates a more consistent doctrine; on the one hand, he drops the claim that the virtues are identical, and on the other, he develops and refines the idea that the virtues are distinct parts of a whole and that wisdom is the key to their unity. His aim is not to overthrow Socrates' view of the unity of the virtues, but to strengthen it by making it more consistent and defensible.

This is at least a possible explanation of the inconsistencies between the *Protagoras* and the *Laches*. But it is also reasonable, as mentioned before, to search for an interpretation of the two dialogues that resolves their inconsistencies rather than leaving them in place.

Unity in the *Republic* and Later Dialogues

In the *Republic*, Plato discusses in detail the nature of courage, temperance, justice and wisdom, but he does not directly address the question of their unity. Nevertheless, it seems clear that he does not subscribe to either the Identity or the Inseparability View. Since the virtues have different definitions, they cannot be identical (see 6: PLATONIC DEFINITIONS AND FORMS). And in the case of courage, and perhaps temperance and justice as well, Plato seems to hold that it (they) can exist apart from wisdom. An important, new factor in his discussion of the virtues is a distinction between knowledge and true opinion. In the *Protagoras* and *Laches*, Socrates holds that the virtues require (if they are not identical with) a certain kind of knowledge or wisdom. In the *Meno*, however, he distinguishes between knowledge and true opinion, and suggests that some people may be virtuous without possessing wisdom or knowledge. Their virtue, i.e., their courage, temperance, justice, and piety, would be based on true opinion rather than knowledge (96E1–100A7). However, Socrates also claims that true opinion, in contrast with knowledge, is inherently unstable (97c4–98A8), and thus it is unclear how it could serve as a basis for consistent virtuous action. If one could "stabilize" true opinion about what is good and evil, then it would seem possible to possess one or more of the virtues without being wise.

According to the *Republic*'s account of the education of the guardians, one of the aims of "music" and "gymnastic" is to instill *stable*, true beliefs about values and how one should live (stability is emphasized in, e.g., 429c7–430B9) (see 26: PLATO AND THE ARTS). Those who are selected to become rulers receive a "higher" education, which involves acquiring knowledge of the Form of the Good, the foundation and source of all value. They possess wisdom as well as courage, temperance, and justice. The guardians who do not become rulers – who become the soldiers and defenders of the city – do not possess wisdom. But they do apparently possess courage, since it is their courage and not the rulers' that is responsible for the city being courageous. Just as the city is wise because of the wisdom of its rulers, so the city is brave because of the courage of its soldiers (cf. 428E7–9 with 429A8–B3; 429B5–c3 clearly implies that the soldiers are courageous).

It might be argued that since the "courage" of the soldiers is characterized as "political" courage, it does not count as genuine or full-fledged courage. But let us note that this section of Book IV (429A8–430c2) provides an account of the courage of the city; later in the book Socrates gives a brief description of courage in individuals (442B5–c3). Since it is the courage of the soldiers that is responsible for the courage of the city, it is their courage that is described in the earlier section. This description specifies that courage is the preservation of true opinions about what is to be feared – opinions inculcated by the laws – in the face of fears, pains, pleasures, and desires. The courage of the rulers does not fit this description since it is based on knowledge rather than true opinion. Socrates' description of courage in the individual is neutral as between true opinion and knowledge (442b11–c3), which suggests that he does not hold that only courage based on knowledge counts as true courage. The reference to "political" courage (at 430c3–4) serves to indicate that the courage described is that of the city, not the individual; it is *not* meant to suggest that the courage of the soldiers is less than genuine courage.

In the *Republic*, then, Plato abandons Socrates' view that the virtues are inseparable: at least one of the virtues, courage, can be possessed without being wise. He does not, however, adopt the common view, expressed by Protagoras, that one might be courageous and at the same time unjust, intemperate, and foolish (cf. *Prt.* 349d2–8). He retains the notion that the courageous person will make correct judgments about what is worth risking for the sake of what, and will reliably act on these judgments. While it is unclear from Plato's account in the *Republic* whether courage entails possession of temperance and justice, it is clear that it is incompatible with intemperance, injustice, and folly.

The *Republic* also retains the *Laches*' view that possession of wisdom guarantees possession of the other virtues, for Plato seems to hold that one must first acquire the habits and dispositions of the ethical virtues before one can achieve knowledge of the Form of the Good, the capstone of the rulers' wisdom (518c4–519b5). According to the *Republic*, then, at least some of the other virtues are separable from wisdom, but wisdom is not separable from them; that is, individuals may possess some virtues without possessing wisdom, but anyone who is wise will necessarily possess the other virtues.

In two of Plato's later dialogues, the *Statesman* and *Laws*, we notice a further loosening of the unity of the virtues. In the *Statesman* Plato claims not only that courage and temperance can exist apart from each other (and from wisdom) but that they are naturally opposed to each other: those who are courageous but not temperate tend to be hostile towards those who are temperate, and vice versa (307d6–308b8; cf. 306a8–c5). The two virtues are united in a few fortunate individuals (311a4–5); as for those who are either courageous or temperate but not both, the wise ruler will try to bring about harmony and agreement between them by instilling shared beliefs about what is noble and just and good (309c1–310a5). The most important part of the statesman's art is to "weave together" these two character types and bring about their cooperation in conducting the city's affairs for the good of the whole community (311a4–c7). There is no suggestion that "true" courage or "true" temperance requires possession of the other virtues. (This is disputed by some scholars; see, e.g., Cooper 1999a and Bobonich 2002: 117–18, 413–16.)

In the *Laws*, Plato's last work, courage is regarded as a quality that even animals may possess, and thus it does not seem to require either knowledge or true opinion (963e; the contrast between this passage and *Laches* 197a6–c1 is quite striking). The *Laws* also treats courage as compatible with injustice and intemperance (661d6–662a3). Of course, Plato may be "speaking with the vulgar" in saying these things, but it is interesting that he does not "correct" this view elsewhere in the dialogue. He may still hold that a certain kind of knowledge is sufficient for possession of the other virtues, but he seems in old age to have come around to the commonly held view, expressed by Protagoras, that the other virtues can exist apart from wisdom, and that courage, at least, can exist apart from any of the other virtues (*Prt.* 349d6–8).

Plato's move away from the Socratic view of the inseparability (if not identity) of the virtues raises questions about the unity of the *concept* of virtue. If courage or temperance can be possessed by individuals who are unwise or unjust, and if these qualities enable such people to be more successful in their endeavors (see *Euthd.* 281B4–E1), then we can no longer say that the virtues are necessarily beneficial (*Men.* 88c4–5); and we might well wonder what courage, temperance, justice, and wisdom have in common. What underlies the fact that they are all called "virtues"? We might distinguish, as Aristotle does, between courage and temperance as "virtues in the strict sense" on the one hand, and as natural propensities towards courageous and temperate behavior on the other; the former presuppose the possession of wisdom and are always beneficial, but the latter may be harmful through lack of sound judgment (*EN* VI.13, 1144b1–1145a2). But Plato does not seem to take this route. And thus it is a real puzzle for him, as perhaps for us, to explain the unity within the concept of virtue. It is this puzzle that he points to in an interesting passage near the end of the *Laws*. Plato's spokesman, the Athenian Stranger, reminds his interlocutors that the single aim of their legislation is *virtue*, and then points out that since there are four virtues – courage, temperance, justice, and wisdom – it will be necessary to identify the single thread that unites them. It is easy, he says, to explain how they are distinct from each other; the real problem is to explain what unites them (963D4–7). To illustrate what he has in mind, he selects two virtues, courage and wisdom.

> Here's the question for you to put to me: "Why is it that after calling both by the single term 'virtue', in the next breath we speak of them as two, courage and wisdom?" I'll tell you why. One of them, courage, copes with fear, and is found in wild animals as well as human beings . . . The soul, you see, can become courageous by a purely natural process, without the aid of reason, but in the absence of reason a wise and sensible soul has never yet come to be nor will come to be – these being distinct things.
>   That's true.
>   So there's your explanation of how these differ and why they are two. Now it's for you to explain to me how they are one and the same. Your task, you understand, is to tell me why the four of them nevertheless form a unity. (963E1–964A4, translation slightly modified; cf. 965c9–E4)

Not surprisingly, this task is not accomplished in the *Laws*. Given the Athenian Stranger's conception of courage, it is unclear why it should count as a virtue rather than as a morally neutral power, like cleverness, which may be used for good or bad ends. It seems that Plato, even at the end of his life, was still puzzled about the nature of virtue because of what he saw as the lack of unity and heterogeneity of the individual virtues.

Notes

Translations of Plato are taken from J. M. Cooper (ed.) *Plato: Complete Works* (Indianapolis: Hackett, 1997).

1   Some have tried to find a middle ground between the Identity and Inseparability Views, a view according to which the virtues can be parts of a whole and at the same time identical

with each other; see, e.g., Ferejohn 1982, and Brickhouse and Smith 2000: 169–73. However, as we have seen in [P1] and [P2], Socrates takes the claim that the virtues are parts to be inconsistent with the claim that they are identical; see *La.* 199E3–9.

2   This part of Socrates' argument indicates one reason for his attraction to the unity doctrine. For he clearly thought that any quality that deserved to be called a virtue had to be admirable and beneficial (to its possessor as well as to others; see *Men.* 87c11–E4). Someone might have great endurance, or be very daring, but if these qualities are not "guided" by wisdom, they will sometimes result in actions that are harmful and not admirable. Thus the virtue of courage must be grounded in wisdom; and the same reasoning can be applied to the other virtues as well: justice, temperance, and piety must also be grounded in wisdom. But if one possesses wisdom, one will see the value of each of the other virtues and will make every effort to gain full possession of them. Thus one can't have a virtue without possessing wisdom, and if one possesses wisdom one will have the other virtues as well (see *La.* 199D4–E1).

3   The identity theorist might object that since Socrates claims wisdom, or knowledge of good and evil, is necessary for courage, and also sufficient (see 199D4–E1), there is no need to include endurance in the definition. However, wisdom is the source of *all* virtuous actions, not just courageous actions. If there is another quality of the soul such that the combination of wisdom and this quality is manifested in all *and only* courageous actions, this would allow us to distinguish courage from the other parts of virtue and from the whole (and such a distinction is called for by Socrates' affirmation that courage is a part of virtue). Endurance seems to fill the bill. And if endurance is a necessary concomitant of wisdom, then there is no conflict between the claims (a) that wisdom is both necessary and sufficient for courage, and (b) that endurance is an essential and distinctive characteristic of courage (see Devereux 1992).

References and further reading

Bobonich, C. (2002). *Plato's Utopia Recast: His Later Ethics and Politics.* Oxford: Clarendon Press.

Brickhouse, T. C. and Smith, N. D. (2000). *The Philosophy of Socrates* (see pp. 158–73 on the unity of virtues). Boulder, Colo.: Westview Press.

Cooper, J. M. (1999a). Plato's *Statesman* and politics. In J. M. Cooper (ed.) *Reason and Emotion: Essays on Ancient Moral Psychology and Ethical Theory* (pp. 165–91). Princeton, NJ: Princeton University Press.

—— (1999b). The unity of virtue. In J. M. Cooper (ed.) *Reason and Emotion: Essays on Ancient Moral Psychology and Ethical Theory* (pp. 76–117). Princeton, NJ: Princeton University Press.

Devereux, D. (1992). The unity of the virtues in Plato's *Protagoras* and *Laches*. *Philosophical Review* 101, pp. 765–89.

—— (1995). Socrates' Kantian conception of virtue. *Journal of the History of Philosophy* 33, pp. 381–408.

—— (2003). Plato: metaphysics. In C. Shields (ed.) *The Blackwell Guide to Ancient Philosophy* (pp. 75–99). Oxford: Blackwell.

Ferejohn, M. (1982). The unity of virtue and the objects of Socratic inquiry. *Journal of the History of Philosophy* 20, pp. 1–21.

—— (1984). Socratic thought-experiments and the unity of virtue paradox. *Phronesis* 29, pp. 105–22.

Irwin, T. (1995). *Plato's Ethics* (see pp. 79–85, 223–39 on the unity of virtues). Oxford: Oxford University Press.

Penner, T. (1992). What Laches and Nicias miss – and whether Socrates thinks courage is merely a part of virtue. *Ancient Philosophy* 12, pp. 1–27.

—— (1999). The unity of virtue. In G. Fine (ed.) *Plato 2: Ethics, Politics, Religion, and the Soul* (pp. 78–104). Oxford: Oxford University Press.

Vlastos, G. (1981). *Platonic Studies* (see pp. 221–69, 418–23 on the unity of the virtues). Princeton, NJ: Princeton University Press.

23

Plato on Justice

DAVID KEYT

Introduction

Justice is one of the most ubiquitous topics in Plato's dialogues, second in importance only to reason. It is discussed to some degree in almost every major dialogue including even the *Parmenides* (130B7–9, 130E5–131A2, 135c8–D1) and the *Timaeus* (41c6–8, 42B21–2), but it is only in the *Republic* that the concept is defined and the definition argued for. Consequently, any account of Plato's theory of justice must concentrate on that dialogue.

The search for a definition of "justice" is part of the larger project of the *Republic* to respond to the challenge of Glaucon and Adeimantus. Speaking as devil's advocate, Glaucon classes justice among the goods chosen, not for their own sake, but for the things that come from them. People, he claims, want no shackle on their natural desire for more and more of everything, and only agree to act justly towards others in order to avoid being treated unjustly themselves. That no one is just willingly is shown, he says, by the story of Gyges' ring, a ring that bestows invisibility upon its possessor; no one who possessed such a ring could resist the temptation to become "like a god among men" by using it to satisfy his natural desires unrestrained by justice (*R.* II.357A1–360D7). Socrates sets out to show that, contrary to this impressive chal-lenge, justice is good both in itself and for what comes from it and that injustice, even if it goes undetected, is injurious to the unjust person. The first step in meeting the challenge, a large one, is to understand what justice is. Only when we understand this, Socrates reasonably claims (*R.* I.354c1–3), will we be able to determine whether justice is good in itself or good only because of what comes from it. This chapter is devoted entirely to this first step, Plato's definition of justice, and does not discuss the sort of good it is or the link Plato endeavors to forge between justice and happiness (see 24: PLATO'S CONCEPT OF GOODNESS).

The burden on anyone expounding Plato's theory of justice is to fill the numerous gaps in his argument, to supply the missing premises. The further afield an interpreter must go to find appropriate premises the less credible their attribution to Plato will be. In this paper I never look beyond Plato's dialogues themselves, and only at one or two crucial junctures beyond the *Republic* itself. I never appeal to other ancient Greek philosophers or to the philosophical imagination itself. This does not mean that mine is the only way, or the best way, to fill out Plato's argument (see 2: INTERPRETING PLATO). There are alternatives (e.g., Dahl 1991; for the interpretative strategy followed in this paper and its ramifications see Cohen and Keyt 1992).

I assume that Socrates is Plato's spokesman in the *Republic* and that the Eleatic and Athenian Strangers speak for Plato in the *Statesman* and the *Laws* respectively.

Phusis and Nomos

In the *Laws* the Athenian Stranger considers two connected ideas about justice that are advanced by some poets and prose-writers identified only as certain "modern wise men" (*Lg.* X.886D2–3). These ideas are that justice is an unstable artifact of human contrivance, and that might makes right. According to the modern wise men:

> [T]he just things are not at all by nature (*phusei*) but people are continually disputing with one another about them and are forever changing them, and whatever changes they make at any time are each at that time authoritative, having come into existence by art (*technē(i)*) and by the laws (*nomois*) but not in any way by nature. All these things . . . are the theme of men considered wise by young people – prose-writers and poets – who maintain that what is most just is what a person can win by force. (*Lg.* X.889E6–890A5)

The claim of the modern wise men that the just things exist by art (*technē(i)*) and by the laws (*nomois*) but not in any way by nature (*phusei*) exploits a favorite antithesis of fifth- and fourth-century Greek philosophy, that between *nomos* (law or convention) and *phusis* (nature) (for which see *Prt.* 337c6–D3 and *Grg.* 482E2–484c3, 488D5–489B6). In this antithesis *nomos* is associated with artificiality, diversity, and variability, *phusis* with truth, sameness, and invariability (see in particular Aristotle, *SE* 12.173a7–18 and *EN* I.3.1094b14–16). To claim that the distinction between what is just and what is unjust exists by *nomos* only and not in any way by *phusis* is to claim that it has no firmer basis in reality than that between, say, Greek and barbarian (for which see *Plt.* 262c10–D6).

This claim leads in Plato's view to Protagorean moral relativism. If the just is simply the lawful and laws are always being changed, then what is just is relative not only to each *polis*, but to each point in time in each *polis*. In the *Theaetetus* Socrates imagines Protagoras saying that "whatever things *seem* just and fine to each *polis* *are* so for it as long as it holds by them" (*Tht.* 167c4–5; see also 172A1–5) and claims that "with regard to things just and unjust, pious and impious [the followers of Protagoras] are ready to insist that none of them has by nature (*phusei*) a being (*ousian*) of its own, but rather that what seems to people in common to be so is true, at the time when it seems so and for as long as it seems so" (*Tht.* 172B2–6).

As the Athenian Stranger indicates, the doctrine that the just is the lawful carries in its train the unsavory doctrine that might makes right. To connect the two all that is needed is the plausible assumption that a *polis*'s laws are in the hands of the stronger. If (1) the just in a *polis* is what is lawful in it and if (2) those who make and enforce a *polis*'s laws – the *polis*'s rulers – are those who monopolize the coercive force in the *polis*, then, as the modern wise men claim, (3) what is just and what is won by force are the same. This conditional, it is worth noting, expresses a major part of Thrasymachus' argument that the just is the advantage of the stronger (*R.* I.338D7–339A4). The second conjunct of its antecedent, proposition (2), is difficult to deny since this comes close to being a definition of a ruler; thus, anyone who has a reason for rejecting its consequent, proposition (3), has a reason for rejecting the first conjunct of its antecedent, proposition (1). But anyone who thinks that the forced is not *ipso facto* just has just such a reason.

If the just is not the same as the lawful – if "just law" is not a pleonasm nor "unjust law" an oxymoron – we need a standard of justice beyond law. Plato finds this standard, of course, in his realm of Forms. In the *Parmenides* Socrates is confident that there is a Form of Justice "itself by itself" whether or not there are Forms of such things as man, fire, water, hair, mud, and dirt (*Prm.* 130B7–D9); in the great myth in the *Phaedrus* the discarnate soul beholds Justice-itself in the place beyond heaven (*Phdr.* 247C3–D6); and in the *Republic* the Form of Justice is one of Socrates' first examples of a Form (*R.* 476A4–5) and the only Form, aside from the Form of the Good, mentioned specifically in the Allegory of the Cave (*R.* 517E1–2). Plato envisages the Forms as incorporeal entities (*Phd.* 65D4–66A10; *Sph.* 246B8), without color, shape, or solidity (*Phdr.* 247C6–7), existing beyond time and space (*Ti.* 37C6–38C3, 51E6–52B2). Having the features of truth, sameness, and invariability (*R.* V.476A4–7, 478E7–479A5, 479E7–8), they fall on the *phusis* side of the *phusis/nomos* antithesis. Plato is thus able to refer to the Form of justice as "the just by nature" (*to phusei dikaion*, *R.* VI.501B2) and, in general, to identify his world of Forms with the realm of nature (*Phd.* 103B5; *R.* X.597B5–7, c2, 598A1–3; *Prm.* 132D2). In so doing he provides an avenue, for anyone who can countenance Forms, for an appeal beyond law to nature. Some laws will be just by nature, and some will not. (For just and unjust laws see *Lg.* IV.715B2–6 and VII.807C4; and for Plato's concept of nature see Morrow 1948.)

The issue shifts now to the content of the Form of Justice. What does one who apprehends the Form of Justice apprehend? Plato begins his complex answer to this question by analyzing the justice of a *polis*: political justice.

Political Justice

Plato's ultimate goal in Books II through IV of the *Republic* is to discover what justice is in an individual soul, or psyche (*psuchē*), rather than what it is in a city, or *polis*. The definition of political justice is ostensibly only a way-station on the road to the definition of psychic justice, though in the overall structure of the dialogue the way-station threatens to overshadow the ultimate terminal. Socrates claims that the justice in a *polis* should be the easier to apprehend because, a *polis* being larger than an individual, justice should be more prominent (*pleiōn*) in it (*R.* II.368E). Plato cannot mean that political justice is easier *to perceive* than psychic justice, as large letters are easier to see than small; for justice, unlike beauty, is not a sensible property (*Phdr.* 250B1–E1). What he must mean is that political justice is easier *to comprehend* than psychic. This does turn out to be the case for justice as Plato conceives it; for the tripartite division of a *polis* that underlies his definition of political justice is much easier to understand than the corresponding division of the psyche underlying his definition of psychic justice (*R.* IV.435B4–D9).

In searching for a definition of political justice Plato focuses on what Socrates describes as "the beautiful *polis*" (*hē kallipolis: R.* VII.527c2), which we shall call "Kallipolis." Socrates hopes to find justice in Kallipolis because Kallipolis is completely good (*teleōs agathē*): "I think our *polis*, if indeed it has been correctly founded, is completely good . . . Clearly, then, it is wise, brave, temperate, and just" (*R.* IV.427E6–11). Wisdom, bravery, temperance, and justice are virtues, or excellences (*aretai*). Socrates is inferring that Kallipolis has certain *aretai* because it is *agathē*. Verbally the step is a small one, from adjective (*agathē*) to corresponding noun (*aretē*): Kallipolis, being "excellent," has certain "excellences." Philosophically the step is larger and more problematic, for Socrates does not say how the virtues, or excellences, of a *polis* – its wisdom, bravery, temperance, and justice – are connected to its goodness.

But he does provide a clue in the function argument at *R.* I.352D8–354A12. The importance of this passage for understanding the larger argument of *Republic* II–IV has been demonstrated by Gerasimos Santas (Santas 1985 and 2001). The function argument in the passage cited is one application of what Santas calls "the functional theory of the good." This theory consists of three definitions. (1) The *function*, or *ergon*, of each thing that has a function is (a) what it alone can do or (b) what it can do better than anything else (*R.* I.353A10–11). The function of the eyes is to see; the function of a knife is to cut. Santas calls a function of type (a) an "exclusive" function and a function of type (b) an "optimal" one. Eyes are defined by their exclusive function since an animal can see with no other organ; a pruning knife, on the other hand, is defined by its optimal function since other kinds of knives can be used, though not so efficiently, for pruning. (2) A thing that has a function is *good*, or *agathos*, if it performs its function well (see *R.* I.353E4–5). Good eyes see well; good knives cut well. (3) The *virtue*, or *aretē*, of anything that has a function is that by means of which it performs its function well (*R.* I.353c5–7; see also X.601D4–6). The virtues of a knife blade are the qualities that enable it to cut well, such as sharpness and hardness. The functional theory of the good allows us, then, to bridge the gap between a city's goodness and its virtues. To apply the theory we need to answer three questions: (1) what is the function of a *polis*? (2) What is it for a *polis* to function well? (3) What qualities allow it to function well?

The first step, then, is to determine the function of a *polis*. What is it that only a *polis* can do or can do better than anything else? Plato never addresses this question directly. This no doubt is what gives rise to the general disagreement among scholars about what the goodness of Plato's ideal *polis* consists in. Julia Annas attributes its goodness to its organization (Annas 1981: 110); David Reeve claims that it is completely good because its citizens are maximally happy (Reeve 1988: 84); and Nicholas White, vehemently denying that either the happiness or the goodness of its citizens has anything to do with the matter, finds its goodness in its cohesiveness and resistance to destruction (White 1979: 39, 114).

We may be able to resolve this dispute by going beyond the *Republic* and considering some of Plato's remarks about statesmanship (*politikē technē*). We find a list of the functions of statesmanship in the *Euthydemus*:

Then the other functions (*erga*), which someone might say belong to statesmanship – these perhaps would be many, such as making the citizens wealthy and free and without faction – all these appeared neither bad nor good; but [statesmanship] had to make [the citizens] wise and give them a share of knowledge, if this was to be the [art] that benefited them and made them happy. (*Euthd.* 292B4–c1)

According to this passage the function of a statesman is to promote the wealth, freedom, domestic tranquility, wisdom, and happiness of the citizens of his city, and to save them from poverty, slavery, faction (*stasis*), folly, and wretchedness. It seems plausible to assume that the function of a true statesman (*politikos*) is to foster the well-functioning of his state (*polis*). Combining this idea with Socrates' claim that *poleis* are created by human needs (*chreia*) (*R.* II.369c9–10), it would seem to follow that the function of a *polis* is to meet the needs of its citizens for the five specified goods and to save them from the five corresponding evils.

That we are on the right track – that this is, indeed, Plato's implicit notion of the function of a *polis* – is borne out by his description of his ideal *polis*; for the social, economic, and political institutions of Kallipolis address exactly these needs. Wise leadership is provided by its rulers; the city's freedom is protected by its warriors; and the need for food, shelter, and other material goods is met by its workers. The community of wives and children and the absence of private property among the rulers and warriors are designed to prevent faction, or *stasis* (*R.* IV.422E3–423D6, 461E5–465c7). The one need that is not addressed directly is the need for happiness. But Plato does not seem to conceive of happiness as a distinct good over and above the other goods but rather as a natural product of them. One of Socrates' remarks can, at any rate, be so interpreted. In response to the objection that in depriving the warriors and rulers of Kallipolis of gold and silver and private property he is also depriving them of happiness, Socrates replies that they along with the other citizens must be persuaded and compelled to "be the best possible craftsmen at their own work" and that "in this way, as our whole *polis* grows and is well governed, one must let nature (*hē phusis*) allot each group its share of happiness" (*R.* VI.421B3–c6).

The ground has now been prepared for question (2), concerning the well-functioning of a *polis*. In Plato's view Kallipolis functions well because it is organized on the basis of a principle of efficiency and quality, dubbed (by Nicholas White) the principle of "the natural division of labor": "more and finer things are produced more easily when each man does one thing for which he is suited by nature, at the right time, being free from other pursuits" (*R.* II.370c3–5). This principle matches careers and vocations with natural talent and ability appropriately trained or educated. Plato thinks there is a natural hierarchy of such talent and ability symbolized in the myth of the metals by gold, silver, iron, and bronze (*R.* III.415A1–7). When applied to this natural hierarchy the principle produces the tripartite social and political structure of Kallipolis in which every citizen has a place from which he is not to stray. Golden souls rule; silver souls defend; iron and bronze souls work; and the adage that a cobbler should stick to his last is heeded:

But we prevented a shoemaker from trying to be a farmer, weaver, or builder at the same time, and bade him remain a shoemaker, in order that the work of shoemaking would be well done; and similarly we assigned to each one of the others one occupation, for which he was naturally fitted and at which, being free from other pursuits, he was to work all his life, not letting slip the right moments for doing the work well. (*R.* II.374B6–c2)

The principle of the natural division of labor, it should be noted, is the root of Plato's rejection of the two defining aspects of (modern and Athenian) democracy: freedom and equality (*R.* VIII.557A4, B4, 562B9–c2, 563B8). The freedom treasured by the democrat, as Plato recognizes, is the freedom to live as one wishes (*R.* VIII.557B4–10). But such freedom would be empty if human nature were as rigid as the Platonic principle implies, if each human being had the potential for just one vocation, just one way of life, rather than for a wide variety. Democratic freedom presupposes, contrary to the principle of the natural division of labor, that human nature is sufficiently plastic to allow for real choices among different lives. This assumption of human plasticity also lies behind the happy versatility in which Athenian citizens took pride (Thucydides II.41.1), their ability to turn with ease from one occupation to another, from farming to bearing arms to ruling. The founders of Kallipolis, on the other hand, are so convinced that such doing of many things (*polupragmosunē*, *R.* IV.434B7, 9) precludes expertise – "Jack of all trades, master of none" – that they are prepared to back their principle of specialization by force, as the passage quoted above – "We *prevented* a shoemaker from trying to be a farmer" – makes plain (see in this regard Annas 1981: 79). As for the moral and political equality treasured by democracy, we see that the principle of the natural division of labor in conjunction with the myth of the metals denies both. The moral equality of human beings is at variance with the implication of the myth that some souls are worth more than others just as gold is worth more than silver, and silver more than bronze or iron. Political equality and the notion that goes along with it, that average citizens have sufficient intelligence to discuss and to decide public policy (*Prt.* 319B3–D7), are at variance with the idea, entailed by the Platonic principle in conjunction with the myth, that ruling is an art requiring specialized knowledge attainable only by a few individuals naturally endowed with exceptional intellects. Socrates affirms both aspects of Platonic inequality at one stroke when he asserts that in Kallipolis "the better rules the worse (*to ameinon tou cheipronos archei*)" (*R.* IV.431B6–7). Democracy, he complains, "distributes a sort of equality to both equals and unequals alike" (*R.* VIII.558c5–6). The total breakdown of the principle of the natural division of labor in a democracy produces in Plato's view a kind of anarchy (*R.* VIII.562E3–5) superior only to the slavery of tyranny (*R.* VIII.564A6–8).

We come now to question (3), concerning the virtues of a *polis*. On the reconstruction of Plato's argument that I have been offering, the virtues of a *polis*, the qualities that allow it to function well, correspond to its various sub-functions. It is this matching of virtue to subordinate function that explains what is otherwise a mystery: why Plato assumes, without argument, that there are exactly the four virtues of wisdom, bravery, temperance, and justice. The function of a *polis*, it will be recalled, is to answer the needs of its citizens for wisdom, freedom, domestic tranquility, and wealth – happiness flowing naturally from the satisfaction of these needs. Plato thinks that Kallipolis functions well (is completely good) because he thinks these needs are fully and efficiently met by the cultivated and channeled natural endowments of its citizens. Its wisdom, residing in its rulers, provides wise policy; its bravery, residing in its warriors, preserves its freedom; its temperance – its "like-mindedness" (*homonoia*) or "concord" (*sumphōnia*) of naturally worse and better as to which of the two ought to rule (*R.* IV.432A6–9) – prevents faction, or *stasis* (see *Rep.* IV.442c10–D1; and for *stasis* as the opposite of *homonoia* see I.352A7 and VIII.545D2); and its justice – each citizen doing his own – ensures, among other things, that the workers by sticking to their jobs and not meddling in war or politics create the wealth a city needs.

"Doing one's own," as Socrates notes, is just another expression of the principle of the natural division of labor (*R.* IV.432B2–433B4). It should not be surprising that this principle, being the main condition of the well-functioning of Kallipolis, should turn up as one of its virtues. What is problematic is that this virtue should be identified with justice. Socrates is alive to this problem and offers four arguments in support of the identification. The first, the argument from residue, is that doing one's own is the virtue that allows wisdom, bravery, and temperance to take root in a city, from which it follows that it must be a distinct virtue and hence identical with the only one left over, namely, justice (*R.* IV.433B7–c3). The second, or comparability argument, is that doing one's own rivals wisdom, bravery, and temperance in its contribution to the virtue of a city, and no virtue aside from justice does that (*R.* IV.433c4–E2). The third, or juristic argument, claims that the jurors in a law court, in aiming at justice, aim "that neither litigant should have what is another's or be deprived of his own" and links such having one's own with doing one's own (*R.* IV.433E3–434A2). The fourth is an argument from opposites: the meddling and exchange between the three classes, being the greatest evil that can befall a *polis*, is injustice; so doing one's own, the opposite of such meddling and exchange, is identical with the opposite of injustice (*R.* IV.434A3–D1).

The prime question about these arguments is whether they establish that doing one's own is anything that is recognizable by us or by Plato's contemporaries as justice. The second and fourth arguments are of little help in this regard since they make no conceptual connection between doing one's own and justice. The juristic argument is better, appealing as it does to the use of "justice" in a legal system, thus connecting doing one's own to corrective or to penal justice. It has been objected that no ancient Greek juror would link having one's own with doing one's own or attempt to ensure the former by requiring the latter (Santas 2001: 91). But the juristic argument, like the other three arguments, applies not to historical Greek jurors but to jurors in Kallipolis (*R.* III.408c5–410A10); and, as Julia Annas reminds us, in Kallipolis having one's own and doing one's own do go together: "all have their own (that is, position, wealth, and honor are fairly and securely distributed) just because all do their own (that is, the basis of his society is one that reflects natural differences of endowment)" (Annas 1981: 120; see also Vlastos 1973: 119–21 and 1995: 70–8).

As the juristic argument provides a reason from the standpoint of legal justice for identifying doing one's own with justice, the argument from residue provides a reason from the standpoint of distributive justice, a reason moreover that would be readily accepted by Plato's younger contemporary Aristotle. According to the argument from residue, doing one's own allows wisdom, bravery, and temperance to take root in a city. The way it does this is by assigning the tasks of ruling and bearing arms to those most qualified to perform them. From an Aristotelian perspective it distributes the most valuable of the goods that can be apportioned, political office, among the citizens of Kallipolis according to the standard of wisdom. (Other standards are wealth and free status.) But if this is what doing one's own amounts to, then by Aristotle's theory of justice "doing one's own" is the expression of one conception (among others) of distributive justice: the aristocratic (*EN* V.3; *Pol.* IV.8.1294a9–11; Keyt 1991). One virtue of this interpretation of the argument is that it explains why Plato finds it natural to call Kallipolis an "aristocracy" (*R.* IV.445D6; VIII.544E7, 545c9, 547c6).

Whether the Platonic, or aristocratic, conception of distributive justice is a correct one is a separate matter, dependent upon the correctness of the Platonic conception of a good *polis*; and this, of course, will be contested by both Athenian and modern democrats, who value freedom and equality and reject the principle of the natural division of labor upon which Kallipolis is based.

Psychic Justice

Plato now moves from *polis* to psyche and argues that the formula that defines justice in a *polis* also defines justice in a psyche: a psyche, like a *polis*, is just when each of its parts does its own (see 19: THE PLATONIC SOUL). The passage justifying the transfer of the formula from one sphere to another has been variously interpreted, so it will be well to quote it in full:

> Well, then, I said, [1] when one calls a larger and a smaller thing the same, are they unlike in that respect in which they are called the same, or like? Alike, he said. [2] And a just man will differ in no way from a just *polis* with respect to the form itself of justice, but will be like it. Like it, he said. [3] But a *polis* was deemed to be just when each of the three natural kinds (*genē*) within it did its own, and to be temperate, brave, and wise on account of certain other affections and states (*pathē te kai hexeis*) of these same kinds (*genōn*). True, he said. [4] And consequently, my friend, the one who has these same forms (*eidē*) in his psyche [5] we shall thus expect, on account of affections (*pathē*) the same as those, to rightly deserve the same names as the *polis*. Necessarily, he said. (*R.* IV.435A5–c3)

Focusing one's attention on (1) and (2) above, one might think that Plato subscribes to some principle of univocality, that he believes that a formula that defines a term in one application defines it in all applications (see 27: LEARNING ABOUT PLATO FROM ARISTOTLE). The problem with reading the passage this way is that Plato provides a counterexample to such a principle a few pages later, in *Republic* IV itself. By his theory the formula that defines "just" when the term is applied to *poleis* and psyches does not define "just" when the term is applied to actions. A just action is characterized as an action that *produces and preserves*, in the agent, a psyche in which each part does its own (*R.* IV.443E5–6, 444c10–D1). By this characterization the formula defining a just psyche is a proper part of, and hence distinct from, the formula defining a just action.

The remainder of the passage above and the subsequent argument in *Republic* IV suggest a more subtle principle. Plato does not argue directly from the use of the same term to the applicability of the same formula; only after he has shown that *polis* and psyche have the same kind and number of parts does he define a just psyche as one in which each part does its own. His procedure indicates that he is assuming, not a principle of univocality, but a principle of similarity, or more precisely a principle of isomorphism: if a formula defines a term in one application, it defines it in all *relevantly similar* applications, similarity being understood as sameness of structure.

We can extract the general principle upon which his argument turns from (3), (4), and (5) above once we understand what Socrates means when he says that a psyche contains the same natural kinds (*genē*) or forms (*eidē*) as a *polis*. Kinds or forms are presumably different from parts (*merē*) since *polis* and psyche do not share their parts. (For the language of parts see *R.* IV.428E7; 429B2, 8; 442B11, C5.) What Socrates must mean when he speaks of the same natural kinds being in both *polis* and psyche is that *polis* and psyche have the same kinds of parts. Using the language of parts and kinds, we have two three-part systems, and three different kinds. One part of each system belongs to each kind. Thus, each part of one system has a counterpart in the other, part and counterpart being the parts that share the same kind. The general principle upon which Plato relies can now be expressed as follows: if (a) two systems have the same number of parts, if (b) the parts of the one system can be paired one to one with the parts of the other on the basis of the kinds to which the parts belong, if (c) these kinds of parts are the seat of certain affections (*pathē*), and if (d) the one system has a quality in virtue of its parts having such an affection, then (e) the other system has the same quality if its parts have the same affection. An affection, or *pathos*, in the context of the argument is apparently a property, attribute, or characteristic (for this use of the word see *Prm.* 158E6–159A7).

This principle of isomorphism is used every day in epigraphy. Suppose that an epigrapher transcribes a Greek inscription letter by letter from a stone tablet on to a sheet of paper, and suppose that he transcribes the unbroken string of capitals of the original by an unbroken string of lower case Greek letters. Since each letter of the Greek alphabet can be written as either upper or lower case, the corresponding characters of the inscription and transcription belong to the same kind: both A and α are alphas, both B and β are betas, both Γ and γ are gammas, and so forth. Many things will be true of the transcription that are not true of the inscription: it is written on paper rather than inscribed on stone, it was written recently rather than long ago, it is written in lower rather than upper case letters, and so forth. However, any sequence of letters that forms a word in the transcription forms the same word in the inscription; so a translation into English of the transcription will also be a translation of the inscription. This is an important fact if, as we may suppose, the transcription is more readily available and easier to read than the original.

The isomorphism of *polis* and psyche is supposed to resemble that of inscription and transcription (see *R.* II.368D1–7). Since it is far from obvious that a psyche has any parts at all, let alone the same number and kinds of parts as a *polis*, Plato mounts a long and elaborate argument to show "that there are the same [natural] kinds (*genē*), equal in number, in the *polis* and in the psyche of each individual" (*R.* IV.435C4–441C7). These natural kinds shared by *polis* and psyche, sometimes called "forms and characteristics" (*eidē te kai ēthē*) (*R.* IV.435E2; see also VIII.544D6–E2), are three kinds of love: love of learning (*to philomathes*), love of honor (*to philotimon*), and love of money (*to philochrēmaton*) (*R.* IV.435E1–436A3 together with VIII.553C1). Within the psyche reason naturally loves learning, spirit honor, and appetite money (*R.* IX.580C9–581B11). Within the *polis* those who naturally love learning, honor, or money are

DAVID KEYT

respectively incipient rulers, warriors, or workers (R. II.374D8–376c6). When they
are organized into three classes and properly trained and educated, the *polis* they
constitute is just in virtue of each doing his own. The application of the principle of
isomorphism is now straightforward: (a) *polis* and psyche each have three parts (b) of
the same three kinds, which (c) provide the basis for doing one's own, and (d) a *polis* is
just in virtue of each part doing its own; hence, (e) a psyche is just if each of its parts
does its own.

The problem with this argument is not the principle of isomorphism upon which it
rests but the problematic psychological theory that Plato must adopt if the principle is
to be applied. The wisdom lovers, honor lovers, and money lovers, who compose the
parts of a *polis*, are agents with cognitive powers. If a psyche must have parts of the
same kinds, they too must be agents with cognitive powers. Thus, Plato's argument
seems to demand that he anthropomorphize the parts of a psyche, that he conceive of
reason, spirit, and appetite as three little men, or homunculi. This anthropomorphism
is explicit in Plato's two great similes of the soul, the composite creature (R. IX.588B10–
E2) and the charioteer driving two horses (Phdr. 246A3–B4, 253c7–255A1), in each
of which the psyche is depicted as consisting of multiple centers of consciousness; and
it is implicit in Plato's definitions of justice and the other virtues. A *polis* and a psyche
are just when each part of the *polis* or of the psyche does (*prattei*) its own (R. IV.441D5–
E2). But to do its own a thing must act (*prattei*) and not simply move (*kinei*), which is to
say that it must be an agent and not simply a faculty; and to act an agent must have
cognition. The anthropomorphism of the two great similes is not simply metaphor.

It is important to bear in mind that, for the principle of isomorphism to apply,
Plato's definitions of justice and of the other virtues must carry over word for word from
polis to psyche. Political and psychic justice are not for Plato two species, or kinds, of
justice but two applications of the very same concept: they are related as tall and short
man, not as warm-blooded and cold-blooded animal. Plato's definition of temperance
makes the general point crystal clear: "we should rightly say that this like-mindedness,
this concord between the naturally worse and the naturally better as to which of the
two is to rule *both in a polis and in each individual*, is temperance" (R. IV.432A6–9). This
means that anything presupposed by a definition of a virtue when the definition is
applied to a *polis* is also presupposed when the definition is applied to a psyche. Since
like-mindedness (*homonoia*) and concord (*sumphōnia*) imply the sharing of a belief among
the parts of a *polis*, the parts of a psyche must also have this capacity. And, indeed,
when Plato, in discussing the virtues in a psyche, returns to the concept of temperance, he makes this implication explicit: "Isn't he temperate," Socrates asks, "because
of the friendship and concord of these same elements, when the one that rules and the
two that are ruled *believe in common* (*homodoxōsi*) that the rational element ought to
rule and do not engage in faction against it?" (R. IV.442c10–D1). But if the parts of
the psyche share beliefs, they must have cognitive powers. Plato's definition of bravery
has the same implication. The bravery of a *polis* is the ability (*dunamis*) residing in one
part of a *polis* to preserve a correct belief (*orthē doxa*) about what is to be feared (R.
IV.429B7–c2, 430B2–5); the bravery of an individual is the same ability residing in
the spirited element of the psyche (R. IV.442B11–c3). Thus the spirited element of the
psyche has beliefs. Admittedly Socrates' definition of bravery in the individual, unlike
his definition of bravery in the *polis*, does not mention belief explicitly; but, as we have

350

just noted, this is not significant since the principle of isomorphism demands that the definitions be identical.

Of the many problems facing the sort of psychology that Plato is forced into by his use of the principle of isomorphism the most notable (and ironic) for a philosopher who stresses the importance of political unity is the problem of the unity of consciousness. The psyche as Plato conceives it has no center of consciousness; it is an harmonious or disharmonious committee of three. It is in need of an element that synoptically cognizes the actions and cognitions of its three parts, brings them to a focus, and acts for the psyche as a whole. Reason cannot perform this role since in the Platonic psyche reason is not always in the ascendant.

Plato implicitly recognizes the need for such an element when he describes the inner turmoil created by unjust action. He suggests that an embodied soul resembles a composite creature (man, lion, and many-headed beast) wearing a costume shaped like a man, and then continues as follows:

> Let us say to one who asserts that it profits this man to act unjustly, but does not benefit him to do just things, that he asserts nothing other than that it profits him [1] to make the multifarious beast strong by feasting it, and also the lion and the things connected with the lion, [2] to starve the [inner] man and to make him weak, so that he is dragged wherever either of the other two leads, and [3] not at all to accustom one [creature] to another or make them friends, but rather to allow them to bite and fight and devour one another. (R. IX.588E3–589A4)

The "man" referred to at the beginning of the sentence is the composite creature dressed in its costume (the image of a soul dwelling in a human body). What is noteworthy is that the agency of this costumed creature is not reducible to the agency of its three inner parts: feasting the lion and the many-headed beast and starving the inner man are not actions of the lion, the beast, or the inner man. Nor is this agency due to the creature's costume, the symbol of the human body. On Platonic principles bodies are totally inert and thus incapable of initiating action. All motion, and *a fortiori* all action, originates, according to Plato, in a soul (*Phdr.* 245c5–246A2, *Lg.* X.894B8–896B8). Plato's description tacitly posits a zoo-keeper who tends the menagerie of man, lion, and many-headed beast. The analogue of the zoo-keeper must be a psychic element distinct from reason, spirit, and appetite. I suggest that this element is the synoptic cognizer, or center of consciousness, that Plato's psychology seems to demand on theoretical grounds.

My conclusion, then, is that Plato's argument for his definition of psychic justice succeeds only at the price of a disjointed psychology of homunculi.

Just Action

Socrates says that justice resembles the principle of the natural division of labor, "though not in regard to the external doing of one's own, but in regard to what is inside, to what is truly oneself and one's own" (R. IV.443c9–D1). This idea, that justice is an inner state rather than a mode of action, is Plato's climactic and revolutionary idea about what it is for an individual to be just. It is climactic in being the conclusion of a long argument extending over three books of the *Republic*; it is revolutionary in overturning an idea that seemed commonsensical then and still seems so today about the conceptual, or definitional, priority of *just action* and *just man*. The commonsensical idea, tacitly assumed by Polemarchus in his conversation with Socrates in *Republic* I, is that *just act* is conceptually prior to *just man*. Polemarchus claims that justice is giving to each his due (*R.* I.331E3–4), and Socrates takes this claim to imply that the just man is the man who gives to each his due (*R.* I.335E1–4). As this interchange makes plain, Polemarchus is tacitly assuming that "just act" is defined first and that a "just man" is a doer of just acts. Socrates thinks the conceptual, or definitional, priority runs in the other direction; he defines a "just man" as a man whose reason, spirit, and appetite each do their own and then defines a "just act" as an act that produces or preserves, in the doer of the action, this inner state (*R.* IV.441D12–E2, 443E4–444A2, 444c10–D1). An unjust act, on his theory, is one that destroys this inner state.

Since Plato is defining words of ordinary language, his definitions cannot depart too far from ordinary usage and still be regarded as correct definitions. Thus it is important for him to test his definitions against the commonplace, or ordinary (*ta phortika, R.* IV.442E1). He must show that a man who is just, as he defines "justice," will act, for the most part, as a just man would ordinarily be expected to act. He needs to show, in particular, that a Platonically just man will not do things that are ordinarily regarded as unjust. Consequently, just as he previously attempted to connect each citizen's doing his own with the ordinary notion of political justice, he now attempts to dispel doubts about the transference of this formula from *polis* to individual by claiming that an individual each element of whose psyche does its own will act as a just person would ordinarily be expected to act: he will not embezzle a deposit of gold or silver, rob a temple, steal, betray his friends or his *polis*, break an oath or other agreement, commit adultery, disrespect his parents, or neglect the gods (*R.* IV.442D10–443B3).

That a person with the inner state of justice will not do such things is, however, just a bald assertion on Socrates' part (*R.* IV.443E2–444A2) with nothing, in the immediately surrounding text at least, to back it up; and it is far from clear how the actions that Socrates enumerates fit his definition of "unjust act," how stealing, betraying friends, committing adultery, and so forth destroy the inner state of justice in the soul of the doer. It has sometimes been thought that Socrates leaves the connection between action and inner state unexplained because no explanation is available, that there is a gap in his argument that cannot be bridged (Sachs 1963). Why, it is asked, must my conduct toward others affect the inner state of my soul? What prevents a person in whose psyche reason rules and the other psychic elements keep to their proper place from being a thief or an adulterer? Can no thief or adulterer be psychically healthy? (For injustice as a psychic disease see *R.* IV.445A5–B4.)

A charitable interpreter must seek answers to these questions and try to fill the gap in Plato's argument. The distance he must travel to do this will determine the plausibility of attributing the filling to Plato rather than to the free imagination of the interpreter. Fortunately, in the present case the interpreter need not go beyond Plato's dialogues. Most of the answer can be found in the *Republic* itself.

We can begin with Plato's idea that the source of most evildoing is *pleonexia*, the desire for more and more, especially more and more money and more and more power. The nature and scope of *pleonexia* can be gleaned from Thrasymachus' encomium of the pleonectic tyrant (*R.* I.343E7–344C8), Glaucon's story of Gyges' unrestrained *pleonexia* (*R.* II.359B6–360B2), and Socrates' castigation of the pleonectic and bovine life of the many (*R.* IX.586A1–B6). In Plato's view the state of the psyche of someone in the grip of *pleonexia* is like the state of the composite creature described in the passage quoted at the end of the last section; by feasting the lion and the many-headed beast while starving the inner man the zoo-keeper creates insatiable desires in the creature's subhuman parts. The analogue of a just psyche is a composite creature in which the inner man is the strongest part; he (the inner man) fosters the tame heads of the many-headed beast while curbing its wild heads, and enlists the lion as his ally (*R.* IX.589A6–B6). Similarly, in a just psyche reason is the strongest part; with spirit as its ally it fosters the necessary appetites and curbs the unnecessary ones, thereby purging the soul of *pleonexia* and removing the usual motive for theft, adultery, and other such crimes. (For the distinction between necessary and unnecessary appetites see *R.* VIII.558D8–559D3.)

This psychological analysis is only the beginning of a solution to the problem; it does not fully bridge the gap between a just psyche and forbearance from the acts on Socrates' list. Consider adultery. A man can be an adulterer without being licentious (*akolastos*): he can have a temperate sexual appetite for the wrong woman. What prevents a Platonically just man from being a temperate adulterer? Furthermore, adultery involves harm to others, to those who are betrayed. Surely, this consideration should play some role in the Platonically just man's forbearance from adultery. Finally, adultery (*moicheia*) is a legal concept and one that is defined differently in different legal systems. Adultery in Kallipolis where wives are held in common (*R.* V.457C7–461E9) is different from adultery in ancient Athens where a wife had a single husband and was required to be sexually faithful to him (MacDowell 1978: 88, 124–5). Psychic justice must be moored somehow to positive law, law as actually laid down in a particular *polis*, if a Platonically just Athenian is even to be able to recognize what counts as adultery.

The issue is complex because in Plato's view positive law is often unjust (*Lg.* IV.715B2–6). Only ideal law, law that is correct (*orthos*) according to the standard of nature (*Lg.* I.627D3–4), is completely just. In the *Laws* the Athenian Stranger appeals to such a standard in passing judgment on the legal systems of the ancient world. Correct law, he claims, differs from faulty law in two respects: it aims at the common good rather than simply the maintenance in power of the established constitution; and it aims at the inculcation of all the virtues, not just one (*Lg.* IV.705D3–706A4, 714B3–715B6). The laws of Sparta and Crete fall short of the ideal in aiming at victory in war and the bravery upon which victory depends while ignoring the other virtues (*Lg.* I.625C9–626C5, 631A3–8; II.666D11–667A7); democracy, oligarchy, and tyranny are deficient in neglecting the virtues entirely and focusing only on maintaining the power of their rulers (*Lg.* VIII.832B10–C7). The aforementioned constitutions can be ranked according to the degree of correctness (*orthotēs*) or faultiness (*hamartia*) of their laws; and indeed the constitutional decline depicted in *Republic* VIII reflects such increasing faultiness. Timocracy, identified with the Spartan constitution (*R.* VIII.545A2–3), comes first after the ideal constitution; oligarchy precedes democracy because the miserliness of its rulers enforces a deviant sort of temperance, whereas even this caricature of virtue is missing from democracy (*R*. VIII.554B3–E6, 560c5–561A5); and tyranny comes last because of the tyrant's disrespect for law (*R*. IX.574D1–575A7).

There are two points about Plato's conception of correct law that bear on the Platonically just man's observance of the law concerning adultery. The first is that correct law, in aiming at the inculcation of all the virtues, is in Plato's view a form of moral education (*R*. IX.590c2–591A3, especially 590E1–2; *Lg*. IX.857E4–5). Thus obedience to correct law both produces and preserves psychic justice. But any action that does this is in Plato's view just (*R*. IV.443E4–444A2, 444c10–D1; see 25: PLATO ON THE LAW).

The second point is that correct law is an expression of reason. The connection of law and reason is a major theme of the *Statesman* and the *Laws*. In the latter dialogue the Athenian Stranger bids us obey the immortal element within us "giving the distribution of reason (*nous*) the name of law" (*Lg*. IV.714A1–2), and in the former the Eleatic Stranger claims that laws are better or worse imitations (*mimēmata*) of the truth (*Plt*. 300B1–301A5). Though the theme is not so prominent in the *Republic*, it is there nonetheless. Socrates speaks of the tyrant fleeing law and reason (*logos*) (*R*. IX.587c2), declares that reason and law counsel a person to resist the pain of loss (*R*. X.604A10–B1), warns that pleasure and pain will be kings instead of law and reason if the pleasure-giving Muse of lyric or epic poetry is admitted to Kallipolis (*R*. X.607A5–8), and claims that what is furthest from reason is furthest from law and order (*R*. IX.587A10–11).

The connection of reason with law is understandable. Humans are embodied souls. That is why the psyche has its two lower parts, spirit and appetite (*Ti*. 69c3–72D8). As embodied souls humans are not self-sufficient, and their natural needs drive them to cooperate and to form *poleis* (*R*. II.369B5–7). Thus, if reason is to exercise foresight on behalf of the whole soul (*R*. IV.441E4–5), it must deal with these natural needs – the soul's carnal appetitive desires – within a social and political framework. Recognizing the role of law and the common (*to koinon*) in binding a *polis* together (*Lg*. IX.874E7–875B1; see also *Grg*. 507E6–508A4), reason wishes the soul of which it is a part to live in a *polis* in which law is respected and where there is friendship (*philia*) and a sense of community (*koinōnia*) rather than faction (*Lg*. III.695D2–3, 697c9–D1). Thus, if the law is correct and promotes the common, the person in whom reason rules has a strong motive to uphold it; and since he has no pleonectic motive to violate the law, he has no motive to be (like Gyges) a free rider and benefit from the observance of the law by others while secretly breaking it himself.

But Athenian law is faulty. Does a Platonically just man have a motive to obey *it*? Here it is important to distinguish among the individual laws, and notice that the criminal actions that Socrates claims a psychically just man will not do would be proscribed by any legal code (Santas 2001: 61) and hence by the ideal code. (For the law on adultery in Magnesia, the imaginary *polis* of the *Laws*, see *Lg*. VI.784E1–7.) In refraining from adultery one is obeying correct law, whatever sort of constitution one lives under. The gap in Plato's argument can be bridged. The Platonically just Athenian will not be a thief, traitor, or adulterer.

A problem remains: will the Platonically just person obey faulty laws, particularly when his obedience will cause someone else to be treated unjustly? For example, will a

Platonically just person, acting in an official capacity, enforce an unjust law or enforce an unjust application of a just law? Consider Socrates' jailer. Socrates' sentence, we may agree, is unjust (*Cri.* 54B8–c1). Would a Platonically just jailer administer the hemlock? This problem of the just executioner is a serious one for Plato because he appears to subscribe to three principles that are potentially conflicting: (1) that some laws are unjust (*Lg.* IV.715B2–6), (2) that law should be strictly obeyed (*Plt.* 297D10–E2, 300E11–301A3), and (3) that one should never do anything that is unjust (*Cri.* 49A4–E3). He deals with a related problem in the *Crito*, whether a just person should attempt to evade an unjust verdict of a legally constituted law court. But that problem is easier, from a philosophic standpoint at least, in that Socrates can avoid doing anything unjust by accepting his sentence of death. The harder problem is what leads Socrates to say that a person of reason (*ho noun echōn*) will not participate in politics in any except the ideal city (*R.* IX.591c1, 592A5–B1; see also *Ap.* 31c4–32E1).

Notes

All translations are the author's.

I am grateful to Hugh Benson, Gerasimos Santas, and my wife, Christine Keyt for helpful comments on earlier drafts of this paper.

References and further reading

Annas, J. (1981). *An Introduction to Plato's* Republic. Oxford: Clarendon Press.

Cohen, S. M. and Keyt, D. (1992). Analysing Plato's arguments: Plato and Platonism. In J. C. Klagge and N. D. Smith (eds.) *Methods of Interpreting Plato and his Dialogues* (pp. 173–200). *Oxford Studies in Ancient Philosophy*, supplementary volume. Oxford: Clarendon Press.

Dahl, N. O. (1991). Plato's defense of justice. *Philosophy and Phenomenological Research* 51, pp. 809–34.

Keyt, D. (1991). Aristotle's theory of distributive justice. In D. Keyt and F. D. Miller, Jr. (eds.) *A Companion to Aristotle's* Politics (pp. 238–78). Oxford: Blackwell.

MacDowell, D. (1978). *The Law in Classical Athens*. Ithaca, NY: Cornell University Press.

Morrow, G. R. (1948). Plato and the law of nature. In M. R. Konvitz and A. E. Murphy (eds.) *Essays in Political Theory* (pp. 17–44). Ithaca, NY: Cornell University Press.

Reeve, C. D. C. (1988). *Philosopher Kings: The Argument of Plato's Republic*. Princeton, NJ: Princeton University Press.

Sachs, D. (1963). A fallacy in Plato's *Republic*. *Philosophical Review* 72, pp. 141–58.

Santas, G. (1985). Two theories of good in Plato's *Republic*. *Archiv für Geschichte der Philosophie* 67, pp. 223–45.

—— (2001). *Goodness and Justice: Plato, Aristotle, and the Moderns*. Oxford: Blackwell.

Vlastos, G. (1973). Justice and happiness in the *Republic*. In *Platonic Studies* (pp. 111–39). Princeton, NJ: Princeton University Press.

—— (1995). The theory of social justice in the *polis* in Plato's *Republic*. In *Studies in Greek Philosophy*, vol. II: *Socrates, Plato, and their Tradition* (pp. 69–103). Princeton, NJ: Princeton University Press.

White, N. P. (1979). *A Companion to Plato's* Republic. Indianapolis: Hackett.

24

Plato's Concept of Goodness

NICHOLAS WHITE

A treatment of Plato's views about goodness has to start with the *Republic*. That work contains Plato's most explicit and emphatic exposition of the relation of goodness to other concepts and properties, and of the essential and central role of goodness in human knowledge.

Nevertheless the beginning of the *Republic* presents the work as a treatment of justice. (Plato's word is *dikaion*, which can also be translated by "right" or "righteous.") Only later on, by the end of Book VII, is the reader made aware that in the philosophical scheme that the work expounds, the central concept isn't justice at all, but goodness. In Plato's view, it's only by understanding goodness that we, and also the philosopher-rulers in his ideal city-state (*polis*), are able to understand justice, and indeed all other concepts and properties (these two being, for Plato, much the same) (see 23: PLATO ON JUSTICE).

Plato's treatments of the two concepts are intertwined throughout, just as goodness (and its close relative, *to kalon* or "beauty") is linked closely with other virtues in other Platonic works. Justice can't be understood without grasping goodness, Plato says, but equally his thoughts about goodness, in the *Republic* especially, are presented as parts of an elucidation of justice. The two can't be discussed separately.

We can ask, however, "Why does Plato stress goodness so strongly in this particular work?" Most of what he says about it is oblique. If we're going to read the *Republic* intelligently, it makes sense to link its hints about goodness to the philosophical ideas that are actually used in the work. So since justice is the occasion for discussing goodness in the first place, we should ask this question: What points does the *Republic* make about justice that actually require, or at least strongly recommend, taking up the issues about goodness that Plato actually treats? On that I think we can make some headway.

There's a clear difference between what the rulers are supposed to know about goodness and what we're told about it. Plato says explicitly that the philosopher-rulers complete their education only when they fully grasp the concept of good. (Since I am concerned with the views of Plato throughout, I will be using "Plato" for convenience, when literal accuracy would require "Socrates.") The philosopher-rulers do this by having an account (*logos*) of it:

> to define the Form of the Good (*tēn tou agathou idean*) by an account (*diorisasthai tō(i) logō(i)*), separating it from all other things, and making it through all tests (*dia pantōn elenchōn*) . . . without being tripped up at any point . . . (534B8–c3)

Only then do they know why justice is good. Subsequently they can use their knowledge of the Form of the Good (not simply the Form of the Just) to govern the city and to make it just (540A–B). We, Plato's readers, however, aren't given the account (*logos*) of the Good that Plato says that a ruler will have – or indeed any other account.

The account that the rulers will have has the features that Plato standardly attaches to a definition. It's called a *logos* or "account" (usually translated in many contexts also by "definition") and it's the result of *diorizesthai*, defining (see 6: PLATONIC DEFINITIONS AND FORMS). It has to be defended against *elenchoi* or "refutations," just like the candidate definitions in "Socratic" works like the *Euthyphro* and *Charmides* (see 5: THE SOCRATIC *ELENCHUS*). It also serves to distinguish goodness from other things with which it might be confused.

This fact seems to me to provide a decisive reason to deny (what some interpreters have claimed) that according to Plato goodness can't be defined. The fact that he doesn't actually give a definition doesn't mean that he's holding anything back. And there's no good reason for thinking that he is.

It will be clear in a moment that his argument employs important premises about which kinds of things are good, without basing these premises on a definition. The most reasonable assumption is that he isn't himself sure exactly how to define goodness. He simply takes for granted – and asks us to take for granted in the work – assumptions about it that seem to him plausible. They're required for us to follow his identification of justice and to see what supports some of his claims about it. Those assumptions will be the main focus here.

Our main task is to see how Plato thinks that a grasp of goodness is necessary for understanding and supporting his main views about justice. To see that we'll need at the same time to comprehend his way of investigating concepts in general.

In particular, we have to deal with the fact that according to Plato, the correct account of a concept can depart quite substantially from the ordinary or everyday understanding of it. I'll fill out this claim later, but it needs to be brought into view at the start. The elucidation of a concept isn't, to Plato's way of thinking, simply a way of explaining or rationalizing ordinary usage. Therefore he doesn't believe that he's obliged to adhere to ordinary or pre-reflective judgments that that or any other standing usage enshrines.

This point arises because of a long-standing objection that critics make to Plato's argument. The objection is based on the following well-known facts.

In Book I, Plato's character Socrates gets into a wrangle with the character Thrasymachus over whether a just person benefits from being just. Socrates says yes;

Thrasymachus says no. Thrasymachus has in mind that a person who commits what are ordinarily called "wrongs" or "injustices" could escape punishment by being "completely unjust," that is, going on to commit even more wrongs, such as lying about what he did, and thus end up benefiting overall.

In Book IX, on the other hand – where Plato claims finally to demonstrate that justice is beneficial to the person who has it – the justice in question seems quite distant from the ordinary notion. Plato tells us here that a person benefits from having a personality that's in "harmony," in the sense that its various aims aren't in conflict. That's what Book IV had declared justice to be: a harmony among either the components of the personality or soul (both words can translate Plato's word *psuchē*) (see 19: THE PLATONIC SOUL), or among the groups in a city-state (*polis*) or constitution (*politeia*). Under that harmony each part obeys the Principle of the Assignment of Natural Functions (we may call it): each part should perform its function within the entity in question.

Prima facie, therefore, Plato has indeed shifted the sense of the word "justice" in the middle of his argument, and so hasn't really argued against what Thrasymachus had claimed (see Grote 1988: 99–106; see also Sachs 1963).

Although some discussions of this kind of objection to Plato have focused on the word "justice," the same criticism can be made of his treatment of other terms as well, notably the term "good." There's ample reason to ask whether Plato doesn't also, and even more violently, shift his use of the term "good" in the course of his argument. We should keep this question in view while we examine his idea that a grasp of goodness is needed to help us understand justice.

Plato seems fully aware of the line of criticism just described, and provides the materials for an answer to it. He openly acknowledges that his account of justice will seem unexpected. Contrary to some interpreters, he never tries to show a substantial equivalence between his notion and an ordinary one. Moreover, on his view of how we understand concepts, that wouldn't make sense. In addition, he doesn't regard the failure of the account to fit ordinary conceptions closely as a sign of weakness. Rather, he thinks that only a loose connection is required, and that to expect more would be misguided. This holds for his accounts of justice, goodness, and any other concept.

A Greek saying had it that justice is tending to that which is "one's own" (*ta hautou prattein*, 443c–e, 496d, etc.). Plato agrees with that much. He thinks, though, that it has to be construed in a special way if it's to be correct. According to him, ordinary thinking wrongly treats justice as a matter of tending to "external" things of one's own, whereas he believes that it has to do with tending to what's "most truly one's own," namely, to order among the constituents of one's personality. Plato stresses that in saying this he's intentionally looking at things in an unusual way (443c). But he still claims to be showing what justice really is.

In particular, he's well aware that someone who adopts his view of justice will actually apply the word "just" to other things and actions than will someone who uses the word in the ordinary way. He thinks that ordinary beliefs are simply wrong about which things are just. But this discrepancy between ordinary applications – which Thrasymachus accepts as standard – and Plato's own causes him no dismay.

To be sure, there's some overlap between the two kinds of applications. For instance, both uses call temple-robbing and embezzlement unjust. But there are also plenty of discrepancies. For example, Plato asserts that just rulers in his just city-state will do things that aren't regarded as by any means right, such as holding wives and children in common and abolishing private property. That certainly isn't tending to one's own in an ordinary sense. Moreover, it's one of the features of Plato's social scheme that shocks his interlocutors (449A–450c).

How much of a divergence, though, can Plato sustain – without, that is, simply making up his own arbitrary meanings to attach to words? If he doesn't argue that his notions of justice and goodness are equivalent to more ordinary ones, how are the former tethered to the latter? Is there a principled way for him to support this deviation from ordinary conceptualization? Can he justify his claim that his own account captures what "justice" or any other word "really" signifies?

———

However, what takes place from Book I through Book IV is less significantly a shift from one notion to another than it is a general change of *approach* to *what it is to grasp a concept*. The concept of the good is central to this shift.

In Book I Plato's interlocutors attempt to define justice as a property of *actions*: individual actions specified either individually or by the types under which they fall that are given by our normal vocabulary. Candidate definitions are: telling the truth, repaying what one owes, helping one's friends and harming one's enemies, and doing what's in the interest of the stronger or of the rulers. All of these candidates fall to objections.

In this respect these candidates are like all the candidate definitions offered in Plato's early "Socratic" dialogues for other ethical concepts. These include piety (*Euthyphro*), courage (*Laches*), and temperance (*Charmides*). In each such work a definition is in part to be a specification that will allow us to pick out the actions that we're to perform, by specifying which actions are covered by a term designating a virtue. All of these attempts fail too. We should think of *Republic* I as reproducing the failure of the Socratic dialogues in such a way as to set the stage for a more successful way of understanding concepts and how to apply them. Whether those dialogues reflect the view of the historical Socrates is a separate issue (see 3: THE SOCRATIC PROBLEM).

The Socratic attempts all fail. The main reason is that each proposed definition is subject to counterexamples. These are actions or classes of actions that are agreed to fall under the concept to be defined but don't fall under the definition, or else that fall under the definition but are agreed not to fall under the concept. This happens in *Republic* I, for instance: returning what you owe isn't just when one owes a weapon to a madman (331c–D). Such concepts, as applied to actions, resist definition by such specifications.

They don't, however, resist every specification completely. Plato gives one in *Republic* IV: we should call just actions, he says, those that *preserve* or help to *produce* the just condition of soul, and unjust actions those that *dissolve* it (443E–444A). This is a *causal* (in a broad sense) specification of just and unjust actions. Just actions are picked out by which condition they "bring about or maintain" (443E), namely, the just condition of personality and constitution. That condition of a personality is just in the *primary* way. The word as applied to action is thus being granted a secondary, *derivative* use.

Notice now that this division of applications of "justice" – into primary and secondary, with the secondary use applying to things that lead causally to things to which the primary use apply – resembles what Plato says about goodness at the beginning of Book II (357B–358A). There Plato distinguishes between things that are good for themselves, things that aren't good for themselves but are good for their consequences, and things that are good both for themselves and for their consequences. The treatment of goodness in Book II prepares the way for the closely similar treatment of justice in Book IV.

This procedure shows us how Plato views the business of understanding certain concepts, in particular goodness and justice. We have central cases, and we also have applications to things that bring about the central cases. Just actions fall into the latter class, of causes of things belonging to the central class. However, the attempt in Book I directly to define just actions fails. We can't specify certain ordinary types of actions – keeping promises, returning what you owe, helping your friends, etc. – and say that those are the actions that are just. Such definitions are all susceptible to exceptions that generate counterexamples.

So if we can't specify justice by giving ordinary types of actions, how can we specify it? The answer of Book IV is that we must give a different kind of specification. Here's the point at which the account of justice becomes explicitly dependent on the notion of goodness.

The central cases of justice in Book IV are of course a *just personality* and a *just constitution*. As I'll explain in a moment, these are also a *good personality* and a *good constitution*. Just actions, to repeat, are those actions that bring about or maintain justice in the individual's soul (or, Plato implies, in the city too, when it's already in a good condition).

As Plato treats them, good and just personalities and constitutions are, in contrast to actions, quite definite sorts of things. They're structures. Goodness and justice, moreover, are both structural properties. A just city, for instance, is a city each of whose parts that has a function performs it well and doesn't encroach on the functions of the other parts (432B–434C). The justice of such a structure is an aspect of its goodness.

Moreover – and this point is especially important – it's through the ascription of goodness to a well-ordered structure that Plato arrives in Book IV at his identification of justice both for city and for soul. These two ascriptions of goodness are entirely explicit, and are premises in the argument leading to the identifications of justice. Plato elicits agreement that the city that he's described is a good city (427E–428A; cf. 433A, 434D–E, 449A), and that the people whom he proposes to put in charge of it are also good (434D–E, 444B, 449A).

He then asks what makes them good. Four factors – the four standard virtues – are mentioned (427E). For the city these are wisdom (428E–429A), courage (429A–430C), temperance (430c–432A), and finally justice (432B–434c), and likewise for the individual personality (all described analogously at 441c–442D).

In the cases of both city and soul, the ascription of goodness to their structure is an indispensable component of Plato's reasoning, and leads to the identification of the justice of the structure as the feature just mentioned, namely, the fact that each part performs its own proper function and no other.

To put it briefly, Plato cites in each case stability (443E; cf. 412E–414B, 423D–425B), coherence and unity (422E–423D; cf. 461E–462E), and the capacity to work to fulfill the needs of the city and of the soul itself (369B–D, 373D–374E). These structural features of a compound entity counteract the tendency to decay and internal strife, which are the deleterious factors that he mentions (462A9–B2):

> Is there any greater evil for a city-state than what pulls it apart and makes it many instead of one, or a greater good than what binds it together and makes it one?

These features, then, are the basis for calling such structures good.

Justice is a constituent or aspect of this sort of goodness. When a compound thing of a certain sort is stable and free from internal conflict, that can only be, Plato thinks, because *inter alia* its components all perform their functions.

Though the putatively good-making features of stability and consistency are mentioned emphatically, they're not regimented into any systematic argument for the ascription of goodness to the city and its rulers. The status of the ascriptions as premises isn't highlighted. No definition of goodness has been given and, as noted, none will be. The philosopher-rulers, who as we've seen do supposedly have a definition, would presumably be in a position to support the ascriptions of goodness more systematically. We readers have less to go on: simply these features that Plato mentions – especially stability and freedom from strife – to commend the city and the soul that he calls good.

If his line of argument is to have any force, Plato must have thought that we have enough grasp of what goodness consists in to be in a position reasonably to accept these ascriptions, and to base upon them the identification of justice and the other three virtues.

Notice how restricted the notions of goodness and justice are that are in play here. Justice is explained only as applied to two sorts of structures, constitutions and personalities, not as applied to anything else. That's why Plato doesn't say here that he's giving a "definition" of justice; the language of *logos* and the rest that's stressed in the passage about the rulers quoted earlier from Book VII is absent here. Moreover Plato doesn't do more than hint how to extend our grasp of goodness beyond those two cases. The capacity to go on to generalize these notions simply isn't either delivered or presupposed by the line of reasoning that Plato presents.

Plato's way of dealing with goodness is a part of his overall metaphysical view of conceptual understanding and knowledge which is best labeled "paradeigmatism." This view includes theses about what it is to grasp a concept, what a concept is (and how it's linked to a corresponding property), and how concepts are applied to particular things. There is space here only to give the bare outlines of Plato's view. But expounding even simply the basic facts about Plato's notion of goodness requires giving those outlines.

The traditional account of Plato's so-called Theory of Forms says that Forms (*eidē* or *ideai*) are paradigms or patterns (*paradeigmata*) or ideals of which particular sensible objects are in some way copies or approximations (*mimēmata*) which participate (*metechein*) in them or imitate them (see 11: KNOWLEDGE AND THE FORMS IN PLATO; 12: THE FORMS AND THE SCIENCES IN SOCRATES AND PLATO; 13: PROBLEMS FOR FORMS). I prefer to rely mainly on the language of ideal and approximation, largely because it suggests both the geometrical picture that was so influential in Plato's thinking, and the more general notion of structure that he developed out of it. The task of rulers in Plato's city, he says, is "to grasp the good and use it as a paradigm (*paradeigma*) for the right ordering of the state and the citizens and themselves" (540A9–B1).

It's clear that in Plato's view this business of "ordering" involves matters of degree. Actual cities – he makes this point especially clear in the descriptions of constitutions in Books VIII–IX – can approximate a paradigm closely or only very distantly. It's up to the philosopher-rulers to keep their city approximating the good, and accordingly justice and the other virtues, as closely as they can. Plato doesn't try to conceal the fact that these notions of participation and approximation are problematic. (That's also clear in, e.g., *Phd.* 100D and *Prm.* 130A–136A.) Nevertheless, he thinks they are clear enough for him to operate with.

According to Plato's view about what it is to grasp concepts (issues about their metaphysical status aside), the understanding of a concept consists in the grasp of what it is for a thing to exemplify that concept *ideally*. Geometrical examples, as Plato recognized, are especially apt for conveying the point. To understand what "circle" signifies is to understand what it is for something to be ideally circular, not, as sensible circles are, lumpy or otherwise deformed. We use roughly this notion when we say that a circle in the geometrical sense is an "idealization."

The capacity, then, to *apply* the concept of a circle to a particular thing is a matter of being able to determine the degree to which it (taken together with its context and relations) approximates that idea. This is essentially the idea of the account of Forms that Plato expounds in *Phaedo* and *Symposium*. He employs it throughout the *Republic* – without trying to address by any means all of the difficulties that it raises.

The application of concepts to particular things is hampered by various factors. For example, saying whether a figure is circular can be hard because it might tend toward the elliptical, or be seen in bad light, or be observed from an oblique angle, or because one can't tell just what angle one's seeing it from, and so on. Plato tends sometimes to lump together all of these sources of difficulty of application, as being all products of the fact that particulars are embedded in a sensible manifold. (In the *Parmenides* and other later works, however, he tries to cope with the fact that something analogous is true of the Forms themselves.)

One particular difficulty affecting the application of concepts to particulars arises from the way in which Plato thinks causation operates in the physical world. Throughout his works, Plato holds that although causation is associated with regularity – roughly, a principle of "same cause, same effect" (*Phd.* 100D–101c) – the regularities that are instantiated by physical things always have exceptions. That makes it hard to predict events reliably. As Plato emphatically asserts, the rulers' efforts to keep the city well ordered will inevitably founder on the impossibility of making the predictions on which his eugenic scheme depends (546A–D).

This fact raises an obvious difficulty for Plato's account of justice as applied to actions. If a just action is an action that "preserves or helps to produce the just condition of soul" (443E), and if the rulers can fulfill their function only by determining to do actions that have these effects, their job is made problematic – just as Plato says – by the failure of the physical world to be predictable. It's simply not going to be possible to say just which actions, or which types of actions will in fact turn out to be just.

All that the rulers can do is to arrive at the best judgments that can be made about approximations. That is, by knowing the regularities that would obtain if the relations between Forms held perfectly in the physical world (Plato thinks this is a priori), the philosopher-rulers make the best conjectures available about future events. He thinks that the rulers' education has to be trusted to enable them to make these conjectures as well as they can. The guiding idea, which he takes as evident, is that the more clearly they understand the ideal cases, the better they'll be able to judge and so manage their approximations.

Now consider the role that goodness plays in Plato's paradeigmatism. He presents the basis of his way of thinking in a somewhat more systematic (though still rather skeletal) way in the *Timaeus*, likewise making use of goodness. Not only are particular physical things individually approximations of certain Forms. The physical world as a whole is an approximate copy of the global structure of Forms, and this whole is good (30A–D). The so-called Demiurge who shapes the physical world, is trying to make it as good as possible, and therefore tries to make it as much as possible like the global structure of Forms (see 14: THE ROLE OF COSMOLOGY IN PLATO'S PHILOSOPHY).

In order to see why Plato thinks that by understanding this whole structure the philosopher-rulers will be able best to organize a physical – and therefore changeable – city and prevent its decay, it's necessary to be aware of how much the structure of Forms itself involves.

It's not a static structure; Plato doesn't stick as close to the geometrical model as that. Rather, the model is dynamic. That's shown by, for instance, the description in *Republic* 529c–530c of the ideal astronomy and kinematics that Plato prescribes as part of the rulers' education. Motions, in other words, exhibit ideal patterns just as much as static figures do, and the rulers must grasp the concepts required for describing them.

Furthermore since these dynamic patterns involving Forms exhibit regularity (*Phd.* 103c–105c), they must (as just now noted) exhibit what Plato thinks of as causation. What makes the rulers better governors than anyone else could be, i.e., better at figuring out what to do so as actually to *cause* the city to conform to the paradigm of goodness, is neither a knack nor some information processed out of empirical observation. That's why the rulers are fully ready to govern the city just as soon as they finish their time philosophizing (519D, 539E), without any period of *practice* at putting their definitional knowledge of the Good into effect.

As *Phaedo* is generally taken to show (96A–99D), Plato doesn't think of causality as empirically discovered, but rather as a priori. So causal connections – dynamic patterns holding among *changes* – are integral to the structure of Forms and the concepts that they correspond to. That means that the ideally good structure, after which the *Timaeus* says the Demiurge forms the physical world, includes dynamic causal connections. Grasping the goodness of this ideal a priori comprehensible structure therefore includes grasping causal connections. (This means that what's grasped a priori is in Plato's view all set up, so to speak, to be instantiated in a physical world.)

To reiterate, these regularities aren't exemplified by physical things with complete accuracy or, therefore, reliability. Plato stresses the fact that they fail unpredictably. In that sense the physical world is, in whole and in part, deficient in comparison to – and in that sense less good than – the ideal structure of the Forms. Still, in Plato's view it's the rulers' understanding of the ideal regularities – about what leads to what – that allows them to govern as well as could be done, that is, to determine how to educate future rulers and engage in administrative activities. Thus the better one understands geometry, the better one will be able to engage in the physical mensuration of the surveyor or the military commander (521E–522D). That's the model from which Plato works (expanded, of course, to include dynamic patterns).

As I've already hinted, the picture presented in the *Timaeus* provides one way of understanding Plato's claim in the *Republic* which has deeply puzzled many commentators, that knowledge of the Good is necessary and also, it seems, sufficient for understanding all other Forms (509D–511E, 514A–517C).

The relevant points from the *Timaeus* are that the global structure of the Forms is *good*, and that the physical world approximates it. These can be taken to imply that in each sufficiently well-organized structure, a part is good contributively. What's good about each part is that it contributes to the goodness of the whole structure by holding its place within it. To understand the goodness of each such part would then arguably be necessary to understand the goodness of the whole structure.

Moreover a grasp of the Good might be held also to be sufficient for the understanding of each part of such a structure. Assume, in accordance with paradeigmatism, that grasping the concept of goodness amounts to grasping what it is for a thing to exemplify goodness ideally. Then a grasp of the Good would be a grasp of the structure of the physical cosmos insofar as the latter is paradigmatically structured. But that grasp of the overall structure, it might be argued, would include its articulation into its parts, and therefore would include, it might be argued, a grasp of the parts too.

There's an additional way (as Hare shows) of explaining this same Platonic thesis, that a grasp of the Good is necessary and sufficient for the understanding of other concepts. Consider again the view that to understand the concept of being such-and-such is to understand what it is for a thing to be paradigmatically or ideally such-and-such. Notice, too, that Plato shows signs of assimilating the concept of goodness with the notion expressed here by "ideally." It seems to follow that the understanding of any concept requires the understanding of goodness. Moreover it might be held also to follow that a grasp of goodness is sufficient for understanding all other concepts, given the supposition that the grasping of the Good consists simply in the grasping of the way in which that concept operates, in the case of each concept "such-and-such," to yield the idealization of it.

It's not clear that these two interpretations are mutually exclusive. They might be combinable. Certainly other ideas, too, may also play a role in generating Plato's proposal that goodness must be taken to be the central concept for the understanding of all others. But in any case we shouldn't assume that when Plato wrote the *Republic*, he had a complete story with which to support it. Philosophers very often work with a sense of the best general approach, knowing that they'll have to work it out more fully if it's to hold up.

One question about Plato's thinking that many interpreters have had a strong motivation to answer, but to which the *Republic* betrays no response, is whether we should think of the opposite of goodness, badness (*kakia*) as so to speak a "positive" state or, as one interpretative tradition has it, merely a "deficiency" or "lack of goodness." Some of what I've said thus far might seem to fit in with the latter construal. If physical things are less good than paradigms by virtue of only being approximations of them, one might suppose that badness itself is a kind of deficiency that consists in imperfect approximation.

On the other side, it's often pointed out that Plato seems to name "the bad" as a Form alongside, and as far as one can tell on a par with, the good (479A–B), and that might appear to point to the former way of taking him (see Vlastos). It doesn't seem to me that in the *Republic* Plato openly espouses the one view or the other.

The motivations that many interpreters have had for adopting the latter view, however, aren't in play in Plato's thought. Christian thinkers like Augustine and Leibniz have defended the idea of an omnipotent and wholly benevolent god. They've felt (whether justifiably or not) that it would be easier to explain the seeming presence of badness in the world if they could say that it was only a lack of goodness. That has led people to interpret Plato in the same way. But no such theological motivations drive him. The Demiurge in the *Timaeus*, though he wants to make the physical world as good as possible, isn't pictured as either omnipotent or wholly benevolent.

In fact the *Republic* isn't committed to either position on this question. It isn't committed to any clear view about the precise relation of opposite concepts to each other. It mentions such pairs (479A–B), but it doesn't spell out whether one of them is positive and the other "merely" negative. The *Sophist* doesn't take a stand on the issue either, thought it treats negation, falsehood, and contrariety; which could have occasioned a treatment of the question but doesn't. Plato doesn't need to tackle the issue, and doesn't.

365

The stated purpose of introducing goodness is to elucidate justice (see first section). The point of doing this is to convince people to be just: to convince, that is, Plato's readers and also to indicate, in a more fully articulated way, how the philosopher-rulers are to be convinced.

In both cases conviction is to be produced (at least through Book IX) by rational argument. For Plato that statement isn't trivial. He thinks that aside from the desire for the Good, non-rational motivations – including simple cravings – also exist. These don't involve thinking of something as good, and don't deploy that concept at all (437B–439B). He doesn't accept the view that everything that's aimed at is aimed at *sub specie boni*, i.e., as being good. If he thought there were a craving for justice that didn't involve thinking of it as good (a kind of *ressentiment*, perhaps along Nietzschean lines, which could be quieted only by fairness), he might have used that non-good-directed desire as a spur to people to be just. As it is, however, he thinks that convincing people to be just requires showing that it's good. The question is, though, "Good in what way?"

One aspect of Plato's effort here is to argue that justice is "objective" in a way that his opponents claim that it isn't. Most of his interlocutors in *Republic* I–II cleave to the idea that the norms of justice are arbitrary, established by conventions or the power of rulers. Plato denies that. So he tries to show that those norms have a kind of non-arbitrary status.

The argument of Books II–IV uses the notion of goodness in two ways. First, cities don't arise arbitrarily. They arise because individuals aren't self-sufficient, and cities have the function of providing for their needs, and also of making it possible to live well. Together these features are held to yield the conclusion that Plato's city is good (427E, 433E–434E). Plato also says that a personality with the analogous structure is good (434D–E, 444B, 449A). The chief factor responsible for the cities' being good in this way is its justice, i.e., its conformity to the Principle of the Assignment of Natural Functions.

Therefore Plato takes this structural feature – being guided by the Principle – as a sufficient ground for calling something good. So we know this much about his conception of goodness: goodness in a city is implied by a city's having this structural feature. This isn't a *definition* of goodness, to be sure; it applies only to two kinds of things, and it doesn't purport to give either a necessary condition of goodness or a complete set of sufficient conditions. But it certainly tells us something – something that Plato's argument can't do without.

Moreover, Plato thinks that this structural condition of a constitution or personality is good in a non-arbitrary, and in that sense objective, way. Two considerations seem to support this idea.

First, Plato thinks that ordinary people unreflectively regard goodness – unlike justice and some other things – as objective. He says,

> [I]n the case of the just and the beautiful (*kala*) many would prefer to do or possess or believe the appearance without the reality. Yet when it comes to the good it's not enough for anyone to possess the appearance, but everyone seeks the reality, and mere opinion doesn't satisfy anyone here. (505D5–9)

This is a surprising thing to many nowadays, who tend to believe that the objectivity of goodness is just as suspect as that of other evaluative notions. Nevertheless that Plato takes this view is confirmed by a passage in the *Theaetetus*, where he uses a statement about objective goodness to construct one of his arguments against the relativism of Protagoras (172A–177E).

Second, Plato takes mathematical considerations to show that the presence, to a certain degree, of structural conditions can be an objective matter of fact. A physical figure may be only approximately a circle, but it's a matter of fact both that that figure is so, and also that to be circular is to satisfy a certain condition non-approximately.

Given these facts, it can be seen that Plato in effect tries to base his argument for the objective justice of the city on his belief in the objectivity of goodness. Given that the city is objectively good, and that justice is an aspect of this goodness, he takes it to follow that the city is just objectively too. That, he hopes (vainly, as is shown by more than two millennia of history of philosophy since), should put to rest the idea that norms of justice are merely arbitrary.

———

Plato appeals to the concept of goodness to convince people by rational argument to be just. Understanding the *Republic* requires understanding that appeal.

It's commonly thought that Plato bases this appeal entirely on arguing that being just is good *for* the just person, i.e., that people who are just, and only they, are happy or possess well-being. Unquestionably it's part of Plato's argument that this is so. He believes that the just are far happier than the unjust. He also believes that that's a good reason for being just. He has none of Kant's belief (in the *Groundwork of the Metaphysics of Morals*, at any rate) that doing a right act for the sake of one's own happiness is a corrupt motive.

However, Plato also has a further way of deploying the notion of goodness in his argument for being just. This involves thinking of justice as good in a way that's not tied to one's own well-being, but in a way that is both graspable and has motivating force independently of one's own well-being. This line of thought is constructed from the idea that the instantiation of justice in the world, and in one's own personality, is good for its own sake. This idea doesn't include consideration of one's own happiness. Moreover, these two considerations are separate in a way that makes it possible, under special conditions exemplified by the philosopher-rulers, that these two reasons for being just come into conflict. This can happen precisely because of the rulers' full grasp of the concept of goodness.

The rulers' situation and thinking are revealed in Book VII, when they finish the last, philosophical stage of their education, and are obliged to "return to the cave" in order to govern the city which has educated them. Plato says that they'll certainly go to govern "as to something that must (*dei*) be done" (521B4). (See also *katabateon* at 520c1 and *anagkaseis* at 521B7). The "must" here is connected explicitly with justice: "we shall be giving just orders to just men [the architects of the ideal city-state]" (520E1). It's also contrasted with what's good or best for them: we're "making them live a *worse* life when they could live a *better* one" (519D8–9), since they know ". . . a better life than the political" (521B1–2). By "better" here Plato means "better for them."

That's shown by his insistence that his whole arrangement for the city depends on there being "a way of life which is better than governing *for the prospective governors*" (520E4–521A2, *ameinō tou archein tois mellousin arxein*).

These passages show that Plato draws a distinction between what's "best for the rulers" and, on the other hand, what's "just" and what the rulers therefore "must" do. Since an understanding of what's just is vouchsafed by a grasp of the good, we have a conceptual distinction between what "must" be done because it's "just," and accordingly "good" in a non-self-regarding way, and what's "good for" oneself.

Moreover the philosopher-rulers make their choice recognizing what it is. They *know* . . . a better life than the political (521B8–10), which is a life that's "better than governing *for* the prospective governors" (520E4–521A1). Moreover the rulers have gained this knowledge from their philosophical education, so Plato can't be suggesting that this "knowledge" is anything but accurate and conceptually correct.

The decisive consideration for the rulers' choice isn't what's good for them, but rather what's good for the city. Their aiming at the good of the city is in turn the result of their taking the Good-itself as their model (540A–B). Philosophically informed deliberation about what to do therefore doesn't consist, Plato believes, simply in thinking about what's good for oneself. Rather it also includes consideration of what's good in a way that doesn't consist simply in some kind of contribution to one's own happiness. If it consisted only in that, the rulers could under favorable circumstances choose to philosophize, and try to be like those philosophers who in actual cities withdraw from public life (496A–497A, 520B).

The rulers are accordingly swayed by both the consideration of good or happiness for themselves, and also by the consideration of what's good for the city. When the two conflict, the latter is overriding. The broader good is the more extensive instantiating of the structure that is the paradigmatic good (see 604B–C).

Some interpreters suggest that according to Plato, the rulers pursue the good of the city because that good is "included in" their happiness, or because pursuing the good of the city is a worthwhile "part" of their own future, or is a good or value that they're trying to "create" or "propagate," or involves standing in some proper relationship to the Forms which are themselves good (see Kraut 1993: 328–30 and Irwin 1995: 192–3, 311–13). In that way, it's said, Plato is depicting the rulers' reason for ruling as arising fundamentally out of the consideration for their own happiness.

Two facts seem to me to militate decisively against this suggestion. First, this line of argument and the language that goes with it don't appear in Plato's discussion of the rulers' reasons for governing the city rather than philosophizing. It seems to me rather a product of the interpreter's art (see 2: INTERPRETING PLATO). Second, such an argument doesn't in fact depict the rulers' reason for governing as based fundamentally in their own happiness. For one thing, according to such interpretations the good of the city is held to be valuable or worthwhile or good in a way that's independent of the fact that it's (putatively) part of the rulers' happiness.

For another thing, even more crucially, the judgment that the philosophers' governing of the city is a "part" of the rulers' happiness seems plainly – according to all such interpretations that have been offered – to be *based on* the claim that that governing and its results are good. Moreover the rulers are surely supposed to see this. They wouldn't reason thus: "The condition of a city that I would govern is part of my happiness; therefore it's good." On the contrary, they'd reason thus: "The condition of a city as I would govern it is good; therefore it's a part of my happiness."

In fact, however, the passages cited above show that according to Plato, the rulers simply argue that their ruling is good *for the city*. That it's conducive to their happiness isn't brought in as a reason for them to rule. On the contrary, to the extent that consideration of what's best *for the rulers* is raised, it weighs on the other side, in favor of philosophizing rather than governing.

Another reason for saying that the rulers' willingness to govern must be based on their own well-being is sometimes thought to arise from the danger, if they don't govern, that the city will collapse and their own chances to philosophize would be jeopardized or ruined. A different reason is that if they do an unjust action, they would thereby disrupt the harmony of their personality and hence make themselves less happy.

It weighs substantially against this interpretation that in Book VII Plato nowhere mentions these self-relational arguments. But they would obviously have been helpful to his case and easy to formulate, if he'd wished.

An even more significant count against the interpretation comes into view when we ask why a ruler's decision not to rule would disrupt the harmony of his or her soul. It would be a failure to repay a debt, Plato says, which the ruler has incurred by being educated by the city (520B–C). It can't, however, be the mere fact of not repaying a debt that engenders the injustice. In Book I (331C–D) Plato decisively refutes the claim that it's always unjust to do such an action. What shows that a ruler's decision to philosophize would be unjust is this: it would be disruptive to the order and so the justice of the city. But to explain *why* that would be a decisive reason against doing it, and would be regarded by the ruler as being so, there's nothing else to appeal to but the fact that the good of the city is valuable, and that the ruler takes it to be so. Once again the ultimate basis of the rulers' choice is the good of the city, not their own happiness.

As the foregoing line of thought demonstrates, the rulers' function within the ideal city is a double one. It's made up jointly of philosophizing and governing. No other group within the city has such a double function. That's because Plato thinks that the two functions are yoked together in a way in which no two other functions are. For that reason the case of the rulers' conformity to the Principle of the Assignment of Natural Functions has to be more complex than any other case.

The rulers have the function of governing and so preserving the city. To perform it, they need to understand justice and the good. To do that, Plato thinks, they must have the function of philosophizing, and they must philosophize before they govern. But in philosophizing they discover two things. First, philosophizing is the most pleasant activity – far more so than governing – and would make them happier. Second, despite that, making the city instantiate the Good obligates them to rule, partly to repay the debt that they've incurred because the city has educated them so as to be able to philosophize (520A–C). So if they're to rule they must philosophize, and if they philosophize they must realize that they must break off philosophizing and rule, even though philosophizing is better for them than ruling. There's the conflict.

Thus the conflict that the rulers must negotiate is brought about directly by Plato's understanding of the goodness of the city itself, construed as that conformity to the Principle of the Assignment of Natural Functions that gives the city its paradigmatic structure. There seems to be no getting around the fact that the consideration of what's good for the city can have its own weight, separable from considerations of what's good for oneself.

This line of thought doesn't appear out of the blue in Book VII. It's in play throughout the work. The way is prepared for it in Books I and IV, which thereby provide an additional example of the way in which Plato employs the concept of goodness, even before it's stressed in Books VI and VII. The theme appears first in Book I, at 347A–E and 345E–346A:

> In a city of good men, if there were such, they would probably compete with each other not to rule and not, as now, to rule. There it would be very clear that the *nature of the true ruler* is *not to seek his own benefit but that of his subjects*, and everyone, knowing this, would prefer to receive benefits rather than take the trouble to benefit others. (347D2–8, my emphasis)

It reappears again in Book IV at 420B–C and 421B–C:

> · We should investigate, then, with this in mind, whether our aim in establishing our guardians is that they should have the greatest happiness, or whether our aims concern *the whole city*, and how *its greatest happiness* can be secured. We must compel and persuade the auxiliaries and the guardians to be excellent performers of their own task, and so with all the others. So as the whole city grows and is well governed, we must leave it to nature to give each group its share of happiness. (421B3–C6, my emphasis)

Thus Plato is operating with the same conceptual distinction as the one that he ascribes to his rulers in Book VII.

Book VII reveals, however, that guiding one's deliberations by what's good for the city, as distinguished from the notion of what's good for oneself, is essential to Plato's political scheme. There, picking up the theme just cited from Book I, Plato says, "For in fact if you can discover a way of life that's *better than* ruling *for* those who are to rule, a well arranged city becomes possible; for only in such a city . . ." (520E3–521A2).

Not only do the rulers make the distinction between the life that's better for them and what's best for the city; in addition, their making this distinction is required for a city to be well governed. Plato contradicts the idea, which some ascribe to him (on the basis of 412D–E), that the rulers actually identify themselves and their good with the city and its good. Rather, the essential thing for a good society is that its rulers be capable of distinguishing what's good for them from what's good for the city, and that they deliberate on the basis of the latter consideration.

In another way, too, the concept of a good that's not simply good *for oneself* is essential to Plato's argument. As noted above, the reasoning that leads to Plato's identification of justice in Book IV depends on ascribing goodness to his ideal city and to its rulers. The notion of goodness that's used here isn't a notion of good for oneself or for some particular person, just or not. The goodness of the city, in particular, arises out of its serving the needs of the inhabitants and doing so in a harmonious way. One can see an analogy here with the aim of the Demiurge in the *Timaeus*. He tries to make the physical cosmos good. The aim is not what's good for himself nor *for* anyone, nor is it derivative from such a notion.

From this use of goodness by Plato another point follows, which doesn't fully square with a common and tempting picture of his thinking.

Plato assigns the concept of goodness the central place in his scheme. People often assert that by contrast, modern ethics accords this same centrality not to goodness but to obligation or duty. This assertion leads easily to the thought that whereas modern ethics is dominated by the thought of commands (including those issued by God) and duties, ancient ethics is characterized instead by an idea of what's attractive or beautiful. On this picture, the notion of duty would be foreign to the main content and also the *mood* of ancient ethics. This thought would in turn fit with the idea that in ancient ethics, including Plato, one's aim is always one's own happiness, and that no aims exist that could rationally ever be in conflict with it.

However, if justice is an aspect of goodness, and if doing what's just can in any situation lead away from one's own happiness – as it does when the rulers must govern rather than continue to philosophize – this picture has to be revised. In effect, we have to admit that Plato has a notion of goodness that (in Sidgwick's terminology) isn't purely "attractive" but is, rather, partly "imperative." To call something good can, in Plato's thinking, indicate, not that it exerts simply an attraction on the person who pursues it, but, in this case involving the rulers, a sense of being obligated to do something that's not optimal for one's own condition.

This sense can also attach to the English word "good." For instance, "is good" can be equivalent to "*ought* to exist," where "ought" has some of its customary imperative flavor, suggesting a violation of a norm if something good doesn't exist. Plato's concept of good thus covers both what one rationally welcomes unreservedly, as part of one's well-being, and also what's obligatory in spite of working to some extent against that well-being.

Note

All translations are the author's.

References and further reading

Bambrough, R. (ed.) (1965). *Studies in Plato's Metaphysics*. New York: Humanities Press.

Grote, G. (1988). *Plato and the Other Companions of Socrates*, vol. IV, new edn. London: Wes, Richard.

Hare, R. M. (1965). Plato and the mathematicians. In R. Bambrough (ed.) *Studies in Plato's Metaphysics* (pp. 21–38). New York: Humanities Press.

Irwin, T. (1995). *Plato's Ethics*. Oxford: Oxford University Press.

Kraut, R. (1993). The defense of justice in Plato's *Republic*. In R. Kraut (ed.) *The Cambridge Companion to Plato* (pp. 311–37). Cambridge: Cambridge Press.

Sachs, D. (1963). A fallacy in Plato's *Republic. Philosophical Review* 72, pp. 141–58.

Shorey, P. (trans.) (1935, 1937). Plato's *Republic* (2 vols.), rev. edn. with commentary. London: Heinemann.

Sidgwick, H. (1907). *The Methods of Ethics*, 7th edn. London: Macmillan.

Vlastos, G. (1965). Degrees of reality in Plato. In R. Bambrough (ed.) *Studies in Plato's Metaphysics* (pp. 1–20). New York: Humanities Press.

White, N. (1979). *A Companion to Plato's* Republic. Indianapolis: Hackett.

—— (2002). *Individual and Conflict in Greek Ethics*. Oxford: Oxford University Press.

25

Plato on the Law

SUSAN SAUVÉ MEYER

Our topic is Plato on the law. "Law" in this context translates the plural noun "*nomoi*" (laws). The *nomoi* of concern to us are the products of legislation intended to govern the life of a *polis*. Rule by law is distinguished from rule by a person (*Plt.* 294A). Laws are distinguished from kindred regulatory mechanisms such as custom (*nomima*), usage (*ēthē, epitēdeumata*), or ancestral "law" (*patroious nomous*) (*Lg.* 680A, 681B–C; 793A–D; 808A; *Plt.* 298E; *R.* 425A–B). Although the latter are sometimes referred to as "*nomoi*" (*Lg.* 681B7), the crucial feature that distinguishes them from the laws of concern to this study is that the latter are the results of legislation (681C–D; 683C). Hence an inquiry into the origin of laws is an inquiry into the beginnings of legislation (680A). Typically, laws are written down, which again distinguishes them from mere custom and usage (*Lg.* 680A, 793B–C; *Plt.* 292A; 293A, 298E, 300B–C). Indeed, they are often referred to in Plato's dialogues simply as "what is written" (*ta gegrammena*, e.g., *Plt.* 293B4, 297D6, 300A3–5).

Plato's last and longest work, the *Laws*, is an inquiry into the goals and proper methods of legislation. The interlocutors discourse upon the merits of different kinds of political constitutions, and embark upon the project of detailing the constitutional and statutory legislation for a soon-to-be-founded Cretan colony. The *Republic* too contains a large and detailed legislative project, in which Socrates outlines the *nomoi* that will structure the ideal city (425E, 452C). He and his interlocutors regularly refer to themselves as engaging in the project of legislation (e.g., 425B, 427A–B, 456C, 457A) and refer to the philosopher-rulers as "guardians of the laws" (421A; cf. 484B–C, 504C), a term used for the most important political office in the *Laws* (752D–E). Since, however, the law is not an explicit topic of reflection in the *Republic*, we will not discuss that dialogue directly (see 23: PLATO ON JUSTICE; 24: PLATO'S CONCEPT OF GOODNESS; 26: PLATO AND THE ARTS).

The earliest dialogue to focus on the law is the *Crito*, in which the personified Laws of Athens argue that Socrates has an absolute duty of obedience to them. The much later dialogue, *Statesman*, includes a long and detailed discussion of the role of law in correct and incorrect constitutions, and makes what is arguably an even stronger claim than the one made by the Laws in the *Crito*: that even where the laws of a *polis* are thoroughly bad and have been arrived at by the worst means, it is still imperative that citizens obey them (298A–300A). The understanding of law in the *Statesman* has much in common with that in the *Laws*, although there are crucial differences between the two dialogues. Working through these differences will allow us not only to grasp the full force of the reasons that support the thesis in the *Crito*, but also to appreciate Plato's conception of the proper principles of legislative practice.

The *Crito*

As Socrates sits in prison waiting to be executed, Crito exhorts him to escape. Crito's position, in a nutshell, is that the verdict of the court was unjust. Socrates was wrongfully convicted and sentenced to death, and if executed will have been executed unjustly. It is the business of his friends to help him escape this injustice (44B–C, 45E–46A) and indeed, he owes it to himself (45C–D). Socrates does not contest Crito's claim that he has been unjustly condemned to death; indeed he all but endorses the claim more than once (49B–C, 50C, 51E–52A; cf. 54B–C). Nor does he contest Crito's assumption that one should help one's friends escape from injustice. Nonetheless, he refuses to cooperate in the escape that Crito has planned and financed, on the grounds that it would itself be an injustice. What Crito conceives of as at worst a victimless crime would, on the contrary, constitute a grave injustice to the city of Athens and its laws (51E).

The remainder of the dialogue is devoted to Socrates' argument that it would be an injustice for him to escape from prison (50A–54D). He presents this argument as a speech by the personified Laws of Athens because they are the party he would be wronging if he escaped. Socrates is not appealing to the simple notion that the laws define justice, and hence that breaking the law is unjust. Rather, he thinks it requires an argument (*logos*, 46B–47A) to show that flouting the law would be unjust. Hence his invocation of the injured party.

The Laws address Socrates as if he was intending to escape. Their claim of injury is quite straightforward:

> Do you not by this action you are attempting intend to destroy us, the laws, and indeed the whole city, as far as you are concerned? Or do you think it is possible for a city not to be destroyed if the verdicts of its courts have no force but are nullified and set at naught by private individuals? (*Cri.* 50A9–B5; cf. 50D1, trans. Grube)

Note that the Laws are not making the highly implausible claim that Socrates' escape would single-handedly undermine the laws and destroy the city. Such dire consequences would result only if flouting the law became a general practice among the population, as the second sentence claims (cf. *R.* 557E, 558A, 563D–E; *Lg.* 701A–D). Rather, the Laws' claim of injury, in the first sentence, is properly qualified by the adverbial accusative: "as far as you are concerned" (*to son meros*, 50B2). That is, Socrates would be doing his part to overthrow the city. This is not to charge Socrates with conspiracy, or to predict bad consequences from his escape. It is not the consequences of Socrates' action, but the attitude it expresses, to which the Laws object. To escape would be an affront to the Laws, even if it does not actually damage them.

374

The Laws give two sets of reasons why it would be wrong for Socrates to "do his part" to harm them. First of all, they claim, Socrates stands in a filial relation to them. Since they governed his parents' marriage and his own education, they claim to have "begotten" and "raised" Socrates, and given him all good things (50D–E; repeated at 51C–D). Thus he is their offspring and servant (*doulos*, 50E; cf. *Lg.* 919D–E), a notion made much of in the *Laws*: 698B, 700A, 715D, 762E. A son is not on "equal footing" with his father, and thus may not try to injure his father even if the father has wronged him (*Cri.* 50E–51C; cf. *Lg.* 717D). Therefore Socrates may not seek to destroy the laws, even if they are trying to destroy him.

Second, the Laws argue, Socrates has made an implicit agreement to obey them (51D–52D). In contrast with a filial relation to biological parents, one's filial relation to the laws is revocable. It is open to the citizen of a *polis*, upon reaching adulthood, to leave the city and escape the jurisdiction of its laws. There is no penalty assessed for leaving, and no pressure of time to make the decision; all of his adult life it is open to him to leave (52E). To remain is to agree to abide by the laws and institutions of the city "warts and all." This includes the decisions of its courts, however unjust they may be (50C).

An important claim in the Laws' argument is the assumption that Socrates' implicit agreement with them is just (49E–50A). The Laws' point is *not* that because Socrates agreed to obey them, it is unjust for him to renege on his agreement. Rather, they argue that since this was a *just* agreement to obey, he is obligated to obey. What makes the agreement a just agreement? In addition to being unforced and free from pressure of time, the agreement must involve a fair exchange of goods. A significant exchange of benefits must underlie the hypothetical social contract. What benefit does Socrates get from the laws?

The Laws in their harangue are not specific about the benefit, but they make it clear that Socrates is aware of it (52B–C, 53A) and that it is considerable. No law-abiding city will welcome him if he escapes, they warn (53B–C). As a fugitive, he will have to live in a lawless community or in no community at all – which he clearly understands to be a great cost. Life will not be worth living in such circumstances (53C–D).

The benefits conferred upon citizens by the laws are not further elaborated upon in the *Crito*. The *Statesman* and the *Laws* give a fuller account of that benefit.

The *Statesman*

The *Statesman* inquires into the nature of political expertise (*politikē epistēmē*), which is the knowledge characteristic of the *politikos* or "statesman" of the dialogue's title (258B). Among other things, it seeks to distinguish the true statesman from the sophist (whose nature is the subject of inquiry in the companion dialogue, *Sophist*). A sophist is a teacher, like Protagoras, who offers to teach, for a fee, all that an ambitious young person needs to learn in order to become an accomplished and respected participant in the political life of his city (*Prt.* 319A). That is, a sophist offers to train someone to be a *politikos*. In the picture painted in Plato's dialogues, the sophist, however, is only a pretender to knowledge (*Sph.* 233C–236D). What one learns from a sophist, or his close cousin the orator, is how to flatter and manipulate the citizens rather than to rule them with justice (*Grg.* 464B–465E).

When the discussion in the *Statesman* turns to consider the merits of the sophist's claim to the title *politikos* (291A–303D), Plato's dominant speaker, the unnamed Eleatic Stranger (henceforth "ES"), puts special emphasis on the point that statesmanship is a kind of knowledge (292B–C). In a nutshell, he argues that the sophist, who only pretends to this knowledge but does not have it, is not a *politikos*. Indeed, ES argues, anyone who participates in politics with only the qualifications of a sophist is the very opposite of a *politikos*: a *stasiastikos* or "expert in faction" (*Plt.* 303c). It is in the tortuous chain of argument between this premise and conclusion that ES raises the issue of the role of legislation in expert rule.

ES begins by invoking what was at the time a standard classification of political constitutions (*politeiai*), according to whether the rulers are one, few or many, rich or poor, rule according to laws or not, or have willing subjects or not (291D–292A). In opposition to the practice of defining the best *politeia* with reference to these criteria, ES insists on a single criterion for the correctness of a *politeia*: that the rulers have knowledge. If this criterion is satisfied, it makes no difference whether the rulers are wealthy or poor, whether they govern willing subjects or not, or even whether they rule according to laws or not (*Plt.* 292A, 293A–E; cf. 296C–297B).

This last point elicits a sharp reaction from ES's usually compliant interlocutor, who is shocked to hear him deny that the rule of law is a feature of the best constitution (293E). Specifically, the issue concerns whether rulers should be bound by laws. ES has flouted the conviction, widespread among his audience (297D–E), that rule by laws is superior to rule by men (294A). Thus Plato introduces a major theme of the dialogue, worked out elaborately if not neatly in 294A–303D, of the relation of expertise to law.

In defense of the thesis that the best constitution is ruled by an expert who is not bound by laws (294A), ES explains that since laws are general principles or rules, they are at best only approximations to the knowledge of the expert statesman. The statesman's knowledge concerns what is just and beneficial to the citizens (297B), but:

> law could never accurately embrace what is best and most just for all at the same time, and so prescribe what is best. For the dissimilarities between human beings and their actions, and the fact that practically nothing in human affairs ever remains stable, prevent any sort of expertise whatsoever from making any simple decision in any sphere that covers all cases and will last for all time. (294A10–B6, trans. Rowe)

This feature is common to all crafts, ES here says, echoing a prevalent fourth-century view, which is famously endorsed by Aristotle in the *Nicomachean Ethics* (1094b14–22; see Hutchinson 1988).

Given the imprecision of general rules in practical matters, to follow such rules rigidly is inevitably to make some mistakes. Whether one's enterprise is shoemaking or politics, one will fall short of acting in a fully expert manner. In circumstances where his expertise tells him that the rules do not give the right, or best, directions, the expert quite properly will make exceptions to, suspend, or adjust the rules. Thus, ES explains, in practical matters the principle of the rule of law is incompatible with the practice of expertise.

This is not to say, however, that the expert statesman (or other craftsperson) will not make use of laws or rules. Indeed, he must do so as a practical necessity. This is because it is impossible for him to apply his expertise directly to every action of every person:

> For how would anyone ever be capable, Socrates, of sitting beside each individual perpetually throughout his life and accurately prescribing what is appropriate to him? (*Plt.* 295A9–B5, trans. Rowe)

Thus laws are necessary even in the only correct constitution (cf. *Lg.* 713E2). What distinguishes the correct constitution from all the others, whose rulers lack expertise, is that the ruler is not bound by the laws.

For these reasons, the ES explains, the Principle of the Rule of Law does not apply to a *politeia* with expert rulers. The principle applies, rather, only in the second-best scenario where there is no expert ruler. In the absence of an expert ruler (which is to be expected, 301D–E), the best way to imitate the correct constitution is to subordinate the rulers to the law (293E, 297D–E).

The principle applies not only when the laws that make up the *politeia* are as good as the ones the political expert would have devised (*Plt.* 297D). Rulers must be subject to the laws even when the laws are vastly inferior to those of the best *politeia*. Such is the case in the democratic constitution that ES proceeds immediately to discuss (298A–299E). The democratic process of legislation does not recognize the existence of political expertise (299C–D). Anyone's opinion is as good as anyone else's, and laws are to be adopted only if a majority of people finds them agreeable (298C–E, 300B). ES drives home the message that such a method for establishing rules is antithetical to expertise. The laws one can expect to emerge from such a process will be vastly inferior to those that would be written by the expert statesman. Indeed it amounts to legislation from ignorance rather than from knowledge or expertise (299E, 302A). However ignorant such laws, and however inferior to those that would be employed by an expert ruler, ES still insists it would be "many times worse" if the rulers were not bound by the laws (300A–B). Thus ES endorses the rule of law for any constitution without expertise:

> For these reasons, then, the second-best method of proceeding, for those who establish laws and written rules about anything whatever, is to allow neither individual nor mass ever to do anything contrary to these – anything whatever. (*Plt.* 300B8–C2, trans. Rowe; cf. 300E11–301A3)

The principle is articulated here to apply not only to rulers but also to private citizens (such as Socrates in the *Crito*). For a constitution to "not allow" a private person to do anything contrary to the laws is simply to enforce a penalty for lawbreaking. It is because escaping from prison would subvert this corrective process that Socrates takes it to have such grave political implications in the *Crito* (cf. *R.* 558A). Such is not the case with the civil disobedience he promises to commit in the *Apology* if the jury orders him to desist from philosophy on pain of death (29C–D). He promises there to disobey any such injunction, not to flout the penalty for disobedience. (Thus we have here a means to resolving the long-standing controversy about whether Socrates' promise to disobey in the *Apology* is consistent with his argument against escaping in the *Crito*. As long as he is willing to accept the legal penalty for the disobedience he promises in the former dialogue he is not there rejecting the principle of the rule of law, and thus his position there is consistent with his argument against escaping in the *Crito*.)

Regardless of the principle's implications for the conduct of individual citizens, in those rare cases where an individual citizen has the power to avoid the penalties for breaking the law, its primary message is to insist that those who exercise political authority in a polity must be bound by the laws. Life, which is already "difficult to bear" in any non-expert constitution (302B; cf. 299E–300A), will be even worse without the rule of law. More precisely, ES ranks the non-expert constitutions from best to worst as follows (302B–303B):

1   monarchy (single ruler bound by laws)
2   aristocracy (few rulers bound by laws)
3   law-abiding democracy (many rulers, bound by laws)
4   "lawless" democracy (many rulers, not bound by laws)
5   oligarchy (few rulers, not bound by laws)
6   tyranny (single ruler, not bound by laws)

According to this ranking, the law-abiding constitutions are all better than their counterparts where the rule of law is absent. Within the law-abiding constitutions, the one with a single ruler is the best and the one ruled by the many is worst. ES offers no explanation in the immediate context of this ranking within the law-abiding constitutions. (Perhaps he is relying on an epistemological principle akin to his repeated claim in the preceding context that expertise is a property of the very few, never of the many (292E, 297B–C; cf. 302E10–12). That is, he may be assuming that the more people are involved in an inquiry, the less expert will be the result. On such a line of reasoning, democracy, which has the most legislators, would have the worst laws. This would explain why ES ranks democracy as the worst of the law-abiding constitutions.) In any case, the important feature of the ranking, for our present purposes, is that all of the law-disregarding constitutions rank below the law-abiding ones.

Recall that the argument in the *Crito* assumes that there is a substantial benefit to living under laws, even bad ones. We will understand (at least part of) what this benefit is supposed to be if we can identify the reason for ranking the law-abiding democracy (3) above its "lawless" counterpart (4). ES explains:

> [Rule by] the mass (*plēthos*), in its turn, we may suppose to be weak in all respects and capable of nothing of any importance either for good or for bad as judged in relation to the others, because under it offices are distributed in small portions among many people. (303A3–6, trans. Rowe)

Why does ES think democracy is capable of producing nothing good or evil of any significance? Its inability to do good presumably relates to its incapacity for intelligent legislation. As we have seen, he thinks that the more people are involved in a deliberation, the less expert the result will be (292E, 297B–C). This is why democratic laws are the worst of the three. But in what does democracy's inability to do evil consist? Our passage explains that the wide distribution of offices also dilutes maximally the capacity of the democratic rulers to do evil when they rule unconstrained by laws.

The unstated assumption here is made explicit when ES first describes the non-law-abiding version of democracy. The ruler or office-holder who fails to adhere to the laws is a scoundrel out for his own gain, or for the interest of his faction. Such a person takes "no notice of what is written down, in order either to profit in some way or to do some personal favor" (300A6–7, trans. Rowe). Thus ES is endorsing (at least in the context of non-expert rulers) the popular rationale for the Principle of the Rule of Law. Those who insist on the rule of law typically do so because "they think a person in such a position always mutilates, kills, and generally maltreats whichever of us he wishes" (301D2–4, trans. Rowe; cf. 298A–B; cf. *Lg.* 714A, 716A–B).

So the assumption behind the claim that lawbreaking constitutions are far inferior to their lawful counterparts is that those who exercise political power unconstrained by laws are scoundrels who will use it for their own ends. The dubious distinction of the non-law-abiding democracy is that so many people have a share in political power that the evil effects of their unscrupulousness tend to cancel each other out. As the number of office-holders or rulers decreases, as in the case of oligarchy and tyranny, their capacity to harm their subjects increases.

We must keep this explanation in mind in order to understand ES's final claim when he rounds off his discussion of the sophist's claim to the title "*politikos*":

> Those who participate in all these constitutions, except for the one based on knowledge, [are not] statesmen, but experts in faction (*stasiastikous*); we must say that, as presiding over insubstantial images, on the largest scale, they are themselves of the same sort, and . . . they turn out to be the greatest sophists among sophists. (303B9–c5, trans. Rowe)

By "those who participate" in the non-expert constitutions, ES is unlikely to mean those who hold office in law-abiding constitutions. In other contexts, he uses terms such as "*stasiastikous*" (faction-mongers) to refer to those who exercise political authority in their own narrow interest, rather than for the common good (*Lg.* 715A–B, 832c). Here he is using the term to refer to sophists, that is, pretenders to political expertise. Such pretenders, he has just said, try to ape the political expert's prerogative of giving directives unconstrained by the laws (301B–c). Thus ES is talking about people who participate in the political life of non-law-abiding constitutions. He is reiterating his warning against allowing non-experts to make exceptions to, revoke, or emend the laws.

ES's argument, however, raises the following dilemma. Non-experts are barred from engaging in legislation (on the grounds that they are scoundrels), but political experts are not forthcoming (301D–E). Thus there is no prospect of relief from the sorry condition of those who live under bad laws. It is a wonder, ES exclaims, that cities have managed to survive (302A). This bleak result demands that we reconsider the dilemma that gives rise to it. The first horn in particular invites skepticism. Is it not possible that someone might fall short of the full expertise of the expert *politikos* without being a scoundrel? Plato seems to be inviting his readers to consider the prospect of there being legislators who, while not fully expert, are still capable of improving upon existing legislation. If this is possible, then those who live under bad laws may yet be able to improve them. This is precisely the possibility explored and developed in the *Laws*.

The *Laws*

The *Laws* agrees with the *Statesman* on the importance of the rule of law (713B–714B, 856B, 874E–875D; cf. 684A–B, 762E), the inferiority of law to expertise (875C–D), and the doubtful prospects for expertise ever coming to be in a human polity (657A–B, 968E–969C). In marked contrast with the *Statesman*, however, the *Laws* allows for the possibility of improving laws even in the absence of political expertise. In doing so it also provides a fuller picture than we find in the *Statesman* of the benefits, assumed in the *Crito*, of living under laws.

The project of the dialogue's three interlocutors is twofold. First of all, they inquire "about constitutions and laws" (625A6–7, trans. Saunders), with a focus on the principles of proper legislative practice (630E–631A). This theoretical project occupies Books I–IV. Their second task is practical: to devise the body of legislation that will govern a soon-to-be-founded city. As we find out at the end of Book III, a number of Cretan cities are in the process of founding a colony, and a committee of nine citizens from the city of Cnossus has been charged with writing the legislation for the new city, to be called Magnesia (702B–D). The other interlocutors, a Spartan named Megillus and an unnamed Athenian (the dominant speaker of the dialogue), agree to undertake this project of legislation as an intellectual exercise (702D–E). After completing their methodological discussions in Book IV, they devote the remaining eight books to detailing legislation for the new colony.

Legislating without Expertise

The Athenian makes it abundantly clear that neither he nor his two partners in legislation possess expert political knowledge (632D, 859C). Indeed, he suggests that only a god would possess such knowledge (657A–B) – which is presumably the moral of the myth in the *Statesman* (296C–274E; cf. *Lg.* 713C–714A). Nonetheless, he does not think that they are unqualified for the job of legislators. Indeed, he claims that it is inevitable for the work of legislators to be imperfect, and to require correction by subsequent legislators. Legislation is expected to be an ongoing process in the history of any state. In Book VI, he compares a body of legislation to a statue or other work of art that is exposed to the elements (769C–770A).

A painter who hopes to paint "the most beautiful picture in the world, which would never deteriorate but always improve at his hands as the years went by" (769C1–3, trans. Saunders) knows that his work will need regular maintenance to repair the ravages of time and make up for his own deficiencies in skill (769C3–8). Similarly, the legislator must "realize that his code has many inevitable deficiencies which must be put right by a successor, if the state he's founded is to enjoy a continuous improvement in its order (*kosmos*) and administration, rather than suffer a decline" (769D6–E2, trans. Saunders). Legislators, like painters, are not immortal; therefore they will need successors to improve upon and repair deficiencies in the original legislation (769C–770A).

Not even these later legislators can be expected to have the precise knowledge of the expert statesman or philosopher ruler. In Book VI, the Athenian proposes to select the next generation of legislators from the state officials previously described as "guardians of the laws" (770A). These law-guardians are among the most important officials in the state (752D–E), and serve as the pool for many administrative and judicial bodies. The procedures for their selection, detailed earlier in Book VI, aim at identifying citizens who have achieved the highest standards of virtue, as identified by citizens who themselves are most law-abiding in the judgment of their fellow citizens (753A–D; cf. 751C–D). These high standards of character, however, do not amount to or entail a requirement that the guardians will have expert knowledge, for the Athenian makes a point of saying that at least some of the law-guardians will have only true belief (632C). Indeed 653A suggests that stable true belief amounts to wisdom for human beings (688B; cf. *Plt.* 309C).

This is not to say that there are no epistemological credentials for these legislators. In addition to being of good character, the Athenian notes that they must also understand the goals and principles of legislation – which he then proceeds to outline (770C–E). Anyone who engages in legislation should have in mind "that a person should become as good as possible and have the virtue appropriate to a human being" (770C7–D2). Any misfortune, even the destruction or enslavement of the state itself, is preferable to a change in the laws that will make the citizens worse (770E).

The content of this instruction, which the Athenian delivers to a hypothetical audience of future legislators, does not amount to political expertise. The original three legislators, whom we know do not themselves possess such knowledge, are simply relaying to their successors no more than what they themselves already agree on (770C1–3: cf. 631B–632D). His expectations of what the later legislators can learn on this subject from their predecessors are also explicitly quite low. The point is to find some device, "whether argument (*logos*) or example (*ergon*)" to make the successive legislators "have some understanding (*ennoia*), more or less, of how to keep the laws in good repair" (769E5–8).

We can see how far this instruction falls short of imparting political expertise by contrasting it with the much higher epistemological goals articulated in Book XII for the Nocturnal Council (so dubbed because its mandated meeting time is before dawn, 951D, 961B). Here, at the end of the *Laws*, the Athenian returns to the question of the future repair and maintenance of the body of laws of Magnesia, which as in Book VI, he conceives will be an ongoing project over the life of the polity (960E–969D). The members of the Nocturnal Council will be the future legislators.

The Council, first referred to at 951D–952A and described again at 961A–C, is to consist of the most experienced of the law-guardians along with the minister of education (whose character credentials are even higher than theirs, 756D–766B). In these respects, the council members' qualifications are no different from the credentials for legislators articulated in Book VI. However, the Athenian soon makes it clear that if the council members are to succeed in securing immortality for their "work of art," they will need expert knowledge (961E–962C), specifically, that of the *politikos* (936B). In addition to knowing that virtue is the proper goal of legislation (the content of the instruction to legislators in Book VI), they must also understand "what virtue is" and how the various virtues are related to each other (963C–964B, 965B–966B). That is, they must be able to answer a question which Socrates, in dialogues such as *Euthyphro*, *Laches*, *Charmides*, and *Republic* Book I, is never able to answer (see 6: PLATONIC DEFINITIONS AND FORMS).

Knowing the answer to this question does not consist simply in being able to discriminate between virtuous and vicious alternatives in particular circumstances. Rather, this is esoteric knowledge that goes beyond such practical competence. It involves understanding the *logos* (account) of virtue (964A–B; cf. 966B) as well as of the good (*agathon*) and the fine (*kalon*) (962B–963A). This will in turn require the mastery of esoteric subjects such as theological astronomy (966C–968A). Once equipped with this knowledge, the Council's legislative decisions will always be correct, and as a result the Magnesian constitution will be secure against the potential for decline and ruin (960D–E, 961C–962C; 965A, 968A).

The Athenian, however, raises doubts about whether the council members will ever actually succeed in achieving this esoteric knowledge (see 965E–966A). They must "make every effort" to achieve it (963C). The hope that they will succeed is a gamble on which the long-term survival of the state depends (968E–969B). It is important to note however, that even if the council members never achieve this philosophic knowledge, through the further studies that will be assigned to them (968D), they will still engage in the business of legislative repair and maintenance (951E–952C; cf. 961A). Their credentials for doing this are thus no different from those outlined for the future legislators in Book VI. Let us turn therefore to examining those credentials, along with the further observations about proper legislative practice outlined by the Athenian. We shall see that even if they lack the esoteric knowledge that will guarantee their infallibility, the deliberations of such human legislators are epistemologically quite respectable.

We have seen that while credentials for legislators articulated in the *Laws* do not include political expertise, they do include good character. Thus the Athenian in the *Laws* locates the properly qualified human legislator in the region between the two extremes considered in the *Statesman*: the political expert and the ignorant scoundrel. While the Athenian agrees with ES that an individual person who exercises political authority without being bound by the laws will be corrupted, owing to the frailty of human nature (692A–C, 713C–E, 875B–C), he has an institutional solution to the problem. The constitution of Magnesia will be a hybrid of monarchy and democracy (693B–E, 756E; cf. 691B–692C). No individual person will have unchecked political authority. Accordingly, no one guardian of the laws (or member of the Nocturnal Council) operates in isolation from the others, and there are plenty of mechanisms for scrutinizing the conduct of office-holders, as well as checks to the authority of any single person. Indeed, the institutional mechanisms adopted by the Athenian for the scrutiny of the conduct of the Magnesian public officials coincide almost exactly with those articulated for the law-abiding democracy in the *Statesman* (298E–299A).

Thus the subsequent legislators in Magnesia, even though they have the authority to change the law, are still bound by the laws. Unlike the false pretenders to political expertise in *Statesman*, they do not operate "above the law." Indeed, the character credential for law-guardians, and hence for legislators, picks out another important way in which the legislators will be bound by laws. For laws, as we will see below, are internalized in the characters of those who are raised under them. Proper legislative practice, in the view articulated by the Athenian, takes place in the context of existing norms and is conducted by those who are shaped by those norms.

The account in *Laws* III of the origins of legislation makes this clear (676B–681D). It begins at a point where human societies already exist in rudimentary form, in pre-political forms of organization. A flood or other catastrophe has wiped out all forms of political life, as well as all memories of it (678A). Humans live in small isolated pockets high on hills and mountains without any means of communicating between groups (678C–E). The unit of social organization is the family or clan, ruled by its elder and following its own practices, rituals, and customs, which have been passed down from generation to generation (681A–B). These unwritten norms inform the life, practices, and dispositions of the community members.

The impetus for writing legislation comes when such homogenous ancestral groups join together to form a larger community, a move which is itself prompted by the need for security from wild animals and the benefits of cooperation in agriculture (680E–681A). The problem for which legislation is the solution arises from the fact that the ancestral customs of the various ancestral groups that seek to join forces are very different from, and in certain respects antithetical to, each other (681B).

Those who first bear the title "lawmaker" (*nomothetēs*) are representatives from the different groups that have come together to form a community (681C). They review the rules and customs of the original groups, and propose to the leaders those that "particularly recommend themselves for common use" (681C7–D1, trans. Saunders). The leaders of the clans who subsequently share rule in accordance with those laws instantiate a rudimentary form of aristocracy (681D). This is how a genuine *politeia* develops out of the earlier pre-political *dunasteia* (681D4–5). The crucial change is marked by the emergence of legislation.

Legislation, on this account, arises from a deliberative process in the light of existing norms and rules. The Athenian notes that legislators from the different groups will inevitably be inclined to find their own *nomima* most congenial (681C). This implies that they have been well raised under these institutions and thus satisfy the character credentials for legislators discussed above. Insofar as they are of good character, so understood, these legislators are not operating outside the scope of those norms – in marked contrast with the scoundrel legislators of *Statesman*.

To be sure, the deliberative process engaged in by these legislators in the original legislative moment requires the legislative representatives to take a more detached perspective on their own rules than the one cultivated by their experience as a product of the community's institutions. One might worry that they will be unable to rise above their cultivated partiality. However, two features of this original legislative moment augur well for the success of their deliberations. First of all, each of the candidate norms is "represented" by a legislator who, in virtue of having been shaped by it, is in a good position to appreciate its merits. Second, all parties to the deliberation have a strong interest in coming to a shared understanding of the relative merits of their respective norms. Otherwise the project of the *polis*, undertaken for the benefit of the members of all groups, will fail. These procedural and practical constraints in the original legislative moment make it epistemologically respectable.

Deliberations in the original legislative moment, since they concern the relative merits of different sets of norms, are in effect exercises in comparative politics. Such comparisons feature in every legislative moment described or enacted in the text of the *Laws*. The Nocturnal Council will conduct systematic research into the laws of foreign states, and their track records (951A–952C, 961A–B). The nine legislators for Magnesia are charged with composing "a legal code on the basis of such local laws as we find satisfactory, and to use foreign laws as well – the fact that they are not Cretan must not count against them, provided their quality seems superior" (702C5–8, trans. Saunders).

One epistemological disadvantage of the latter legislative body relative to the original legislative moment is that the nine legislators for Magnesia are from a single city, Cnossus. Thus they lack the epistemological resource of having co-deliberators with a deep appreciation for the "foreign laws" that they are supposed to consider. This defect is remedied in the triumvirate of legislators in the dialogue *Laws* itself, where the Cnossan Cleinias is joined by the Spartan Megillus and the unnamed Athenian.

The conversation between these three interlocutors replicates very closely the deliberations in the original legislative moment. Their discussion is a sustained inquiry into the relative merits of different systems of legislation, undertaken by representatives from societies that cultivate the same "opposing" dispositions as occur in the original legislative moment: the restrained (*kosmios*) and aggressive (*andreios*) dispositions (681B). The aggressive or warlike disposition is promoted by the institutions typical of Dorian societies (625C–626C, 633A–C), while the restrained or temperate (*sōphrōn*) disposition is promoted by characteristically Athenian institutions (635E–642A; cf. 666E–667A). These are the two basic natural character tendencies, ES claims, out of which the statesman has to "weave" the *polis* (*Plt.* 306A–309C), and according to the Athenian, both dispositions must be cultivated in order to achieve genuine virtue (*Lg.* 649B–C). The Dorian and Athenian institutions emphasizing these tendencies are subject to considerable criticism in Books I–IV of the *Laws*, with the resulting legislation for Magnesia incorporating the best from each.

This exercise in comparative politics draws heavily on the lessons of history. Book III continues its history of legislation past the original legislative moment to analyze the historical development of Dorian and Athenian, as well as Persian constitutions. Which constitutions survived, which perished, and for what reasons (693A–B)? Reflections on such empirical, historical, and causal questions are all accessible to practitioners in the ongoing legislative project of human polities. Plato thus shows the readers of the *Laws* that the comparison of alternative laws in the light of history is well within the epistemic scope of the legislators who lack the esoteric knowledge of the political expert.

Law and Reason

Even though legislators don't need esoteric knowledge to legislate properly, the Athenian insists that the laws they produce exemplify excellence of reason. Since wisdom (*phronēsis* or *nous*) informs all the virtues (631C–D), the legislator who is supposed to make the citizens virtuous must inculcate in them some sort of wisdom

(687D–688D, 701D). Even though he explicitly allows that the "wisdom" thereby inculcated falls short of the standards of philosophical wisdom (and may amount simply to stable true opinion about what actions or pursuits are good and bad, 688B, cf. 653A; *Plt.* 309C), the Athenian still insists on characterizing it as an excellence of reason. This is because, in his view, law in its very essence is an expression of reason.

Even though laws are only imperfect approximations of political expertise (857E), to live according to laws is to live "in obedience to what little spark of immortality lies in us" (*Lg.* 713E8, trans. Saunders; cf. 762E). This "spark of immortality" is reason or intelligence (*nous*), which we "dignify with the name of law (*nomos*)" (714A1–2, trans. Saunders; cf. 957C). Laws, in this view, are expressions (albeit imperfect ones) of divine reason. They are also expressions of human reason: the ability to discriminate between better and worse objects of pursuit (644D), which, "when it becomes the common dogma of the city, is called law (*nomos*)" (644D2–3). It is for this reason that the Athenian proposes that a human being is a "puppet (*thauma*) of the gods" (644D6–7, cf. 803C–804B). Insofar as we conduct ourselves wisely, we are following the divine element in ourselves (cf. *R.* 590E–591A).

The very respect in which law falls short of political expertise serves to explain why even laws that fall far short of the best ones still count as expressions of reason. The exceptionless regularity of law embodies order (*taxis* – 673E4, 688A2, 875D4 – a point obscured by Saunders' translation). And order is the defining characteristic of the ultimate intelligible reality that, in Plato's view, governs the cosmos (*Lg.* 966E–967C; *Ti.* 30A–B, 47B–C). This intelligence is expressed in the regular motions of the heavenly spheres, also called *thaumata* or "wonders" at 967A8–10 (see Laks 2000). Any restraint of desire by law (*nomos*) introduces a similar order (*taxis*) in a person's soul (*Lg.* 653E, 783A; cf. *Ti.* 47D; *Grg.* 503E, 504D, 506D–E). To make the soul orderly thus assimilates it to the divine (cf. *Lg.* 716C–D), that is, to reason.

We here have identified a second benefit one receives from living under laws, additional to the protection it affords one against the wrongdoing of rulers. Presumably this is the more important benefit Socrates has in mind in the *Crito* when he assumes that the benefits he receives from living in a law-governed society make his implicit contract to obey the laws a just agreement.

Preludes and Persuasion

In the light of his view that laws are reason "writ large," the Athenian advocates a change to legislative practice. The distinctive feature of reason's influence, he claims, is that it is "gentle not violent" (645A6). Accordingly, laws should employ persuasion (720A). In the actual practice of legislators, however, laws are simply coercive. They issue commands to the citizens, and outline the penalties for non-compliance (722D–E). Legislation of this sort is like the medical care administered by slave doctors to slave patients (720A–C). In such "slave medicine" the practitioner has no understanding himself of the underlying nature of the body or the causes of disease, and simply prescribes remedies to a patient without entering into any dialogue with him to convince him of the appropriateness of the remedy to his malady (720C), or even giving him enough information to apply the directive himself (cf. 719E).

The proper legislator, by contrast, fashions laws in the manner of a "free doctor" administering medicine to a free patient (720D–E; cf. 822D–823A). The doctor, who knows about the body and its maladies, and has some understanding of when various treatments are appropriate and how they work, is able to enter into a dialogue with the patient to persuade him to take the medicine that he prescribes. The proper legislator is supposed to be similarly "gentle" (720A) in his prescriptions for the citizens. In addition to giving simple directives backed up by coercive sanctions (the coercive aspect of the law, which the Athenian recognizes as essential) his legislation must also include explanatory or hortatory preludes. These preludes will address the citizens themselves and seek to persuade them to accept these directives (720D–E).

The *Laws* contains a considerable number of preludes. These vary considerably in form and content. Some are fairly theoretical and didactic in tone, as in the case of the long prelude at the beginning of Book V, which seeks to convince the citizens to value virtue of character more than any other good (726A–730A). The prelude has much in common with the theory of goods endorsed by the legislator in Book I (631B–D), which legislators are supposed to explain to the citizens (631D). Other preludes, however, are largely rhetorical and hortatory, as, for example, the prelude to the marriage law which is offered as a paradigmatic prelude (721B–D).

Rhetorical status, however, is perfectly consistent with the preludes' project of persuasion. Rhetoric, after all, is the art of persuasion (*Grg.* 456B–D), and is to be used for proper purposes in a well-governed polity (*Plt.* 304C–D). The Athenian's stated expectations of the prelude's effects are, furthermore, perfectly consistent with rhetorical methods of persuasion. The preludes are to provide *paramuthia*: encouragement (720A1). Legislators should be satisfied if they make citizens "easy to persuade (*eupeithestatous*) along the paths of virtue" (718C8–9, trans. Saunders). Even if the prelude has "no great effect but only makes his listener more favorably inclined (*eumenesteron*), and so that much easier to teach (*eumathesteron*), the legislator should be well pleased" (718D4–7, trans. Saunders; cf. 723A, 730B).

This way of characterizing the goals of legislative preludes is strongly reminiscent of the goals of *paideia* (cultural education) outlined in Books I–II. By means of stories, poetry, music, singing, and dancing, along with more serious literature, *paideia* cultivates a person's "feelings of pleasure and affection, pain and hatred" (653B2–3, trans. Saunders) so that they are "channeled in the right courses, before he can understand the reason why (*logos*)" (ibid.). This preliminary cultivation of his sentiments, which "makes us hate what we ought to hate from first to last, and love what we ought to love" (653B6–C3, trans. Saunders) is *paideia*.

The proper objects of love and hate inculcated by *paideia* are on the one hand, the fine (*kalon*) and the good, and on the other hand, the shameful (*aischron*) and the bad (654C–D, 655D–656A). In like manner the legislator, in his preludes, is supposed to "give advice about what is fine and good and just" (858D7, cf. 858E, 822E–823A). Given the Athenian's later comment that to legislate using preludes is in fact to engage in *paideia* (857E), we should not be surprised to find the preludes appealing to the citizens in rhetorical as well as intellectual terms.

The Athenian likens legislation without preludes to the directives of a tyrant or despot (720C, 722E), even when the directives they contain are good for the citizens. This is because we often desire things that are not good for us and a proper law will

386

not allow us to satisfy such desires (687E). So unless the legislator cultivates the citizens' desires and emotions so as to align them with his directives, citizens who obey will do so unwillingly. They will respond to the coercive incentive of the penalty without appreciating the wisdom of the rule. Such laws therefore fall short of achieving the legislator's goal of producing citizens who are "willing (*hekontes*) servants of the laws" (700A4–5, cf. 698B, 832C). It is a mark of a true *politeia*, the Athenian remarks in Book VIII, that those who are subject to the laws should follow them willingly (*hekontes*, 832C).

This claim by the Athenian is in superficial contradiction with ES's claim in the *Statesman* that the willingness of subjects is irrelevant to the correctness of a constitution (293A–D, 296A–D, cf. 276E). But ES is operating with a different interpretation of the criterion of willingness than the Athenian is using in these contexts. ES rejects the criterion in the context of his rejection of the democratic constraint that all changes to the laws must be approved by the citizens (*Plt.* 296A). On this democratic view, which the Athenian too rejects (*Lg.* 684C), laws must appeal to the pre-existing desires and sensibilities of the people whom they are to govern. On the interpretation that the Athenian accepts, by contrast, it is not the laws that are to be shaped by the people, but the people who are to be shaped by the laws.

Note

Translations are the author's, or, if otherwise noted, are from J. M. Cooper (ed.) *Plato: Complete Works* (Indianapolis: Hackett, 1997).

References and further reading

Barker, E. (1960). *Greek Political Theory: Plato and his Predecessors*. London: Methuen.

Bobonich, C. (2002). *Plato's Utopia Recast*. Oxford: Oxford University Press.

Hutchinson, D. S. (1988). Doctrines of the mean and the debate concerning skills in fourth-century medicine, rhetoric and ethics. *Apeiron* 21, pp. 17–52.

Kraut, R. (1984). *Socrates and the State*. Princeton, NJ: Princeton University Press.

Laks, A. (2000). The *Laws*. In C. Rowe and M. Schofield (eds.) *The Cambridge History of Greek and Roman Political Thought* (pp. 258–92). Cambridge: Cambridge University Press.

Lane, M. (1998). *Method and Politics in Plato's* Statesman. Cambridge: Cambridge University Press.

Menn, S. (forthcoming). On Plato's *Politeia*. In J. J. Cleary and G. Gurtler (eds.) *Proceedings of the Boston Area Colloquium in Ancient Philosophy*, vol. 21. Leiden: Brill.

Morrow, G. (1960). *Plato's Cretan City*. Princeton, NJ: Princeton University Press.

Rowe, C. (1995a). *Plato:* Statesman, edited with an Introduction, translation and commentary. Warminster: Aris and Phillips.

—— (1995b). *Reading the* Statesman: *Proceedings of the Third International Symposium Platonicum*. Sankt Augustin: Academia.

Stalley, R. F. (1983). *An Introduction to Plato's* Laws. Indianapolis: Hackett.

Saunders, T. and Brisson, L. (2000). *Bibliography on Plato's* Laws, by T. Saunders. Revised and completed with an additional *Bibliography on the* Epinomis by L. Brisson. *International Plato Studies*, vol. 12. Sankt Augustin: Academia.

26

Plato and the Arts

CHRISTOPHER JANAWAY

From a modern point of view it is striking that Plato refuses to grant autonomous value to what we call art. For him there is a metaphysical and ethical order to the world which it is philosophy's task to discover by means of rational thought, and the arts can have true worth only if they correctly represent this order or help in aligning us with it. So although Plato will praise some art works for their beauty, he will not allow their giving pleasure per se to be a defense of their worth in human life. Poets who compose with an inspired invention that leads to fine works we cannot help admiring should not be trusted to set standards of value. Plato's endeavor is to establish philosophy in opposition to the prevailing culture that prizes the arts uncritically or adopts certain ill-thought-out theoretical views concerning their value. It is a culture of sophists, rhetoricians, artistic performers, and connoisseurs who advocate the educational value of poetry, but who lack a genuine conception of knowledge, a proper understanding of beauty, and any grasp on the distinction between what is genuinely good or beneficial and what is fine because it brings pleasure. Without the rigor of philosophical thinking, this culture lacks the critical distance required to assess the true value of the arts.

Yet Plato's response is not merely that of head-on dialectical confrontation. He realizes that the art-loving, pleasure-seeking soul in all of us must be charmed and enticed towards the philosophical life. In the *Republic* (608A4) he speaks of his argument as an "incantation" which will counter our deeply ingrained but "childish" love for poetry. But his enterprise of persuading the reader of the primacy of rational argument does not rely solely on the use of rational argument. To supplant tragedy and Homer he uses rhetoric, myth, wordplay, poetic metaphor, and dramatic characterization. Socrates in the dialogues is an image or invention of Plato's, who enacts for us the life and style of the ideal philosophical thinker. If Plato is "of all philosophers the most poetical" (Sidney 1973: 107) he is so in the service of leading us, by poetry's means of persuasion, to philosophy proper, a place from which we may begin to understand and evaluate poetry and all the arts. The enduring interest of Plato throughout the history of the philosophy of art is owed in some measure to the fact that the famous "quarrel between philosophy and poetry" plays itself out within Plato's works themselves (*R.* X.607B6–7). There have been numerous attempts to answer Plato on his own ground by claiming that art puts us in touch with the eternal and the absolute, or that it provides a privileged form of knowledge. Others have sought to reject Plato's criteria of evaluation as misguided, and have looked to aesthetic responses of various kinds to secure an autonomous value for art. Some have even combined both approaches (Schopenhauer 1969: 169–267). But Plato's writings themselves offer none of these resolutions and for that reason continue to be a unique stimulus to profound questioning about art, philosophy, and the relations between them.

The Arts and Education in *Republic* II and III

Plato's most prominent, and most pointedly critical, treatments of the arts occur in the *Republic*, where we can see especially clearly the criteria of value he uses. He first considers the role of the arts in education. The young guardians who will be responsible for the city's well-being must receive an education that properly forms their characters. In Plato's view the young soul is impressionable and capable of being molded by any material that comes its way. Hence practitioners of the productive arts and crafts in his ideal city will have to be regulated so that they pursue

> what is fine and graceful in their work, so that our young people will live in a healthy place and be benefited on all sides, and so that something of those fine works will strike their eyes and ears like a breeze that brings health from a good place, leading them unwittingly, from childhood on, to resemblance, friendship, and harmony with the beauty of reason. (*R.* III.401c4–d2)

This emphasis on harmony and well-formed-ness (*euschēmosunē*) gives the arts a noble and exalted role and provides the basis for a kind of positive Platonic aesthetic. However, the arts can fulfill their educative role only after a thorough overhaul of both content and form, and even the imposition of detailed regulations concerning which instruments and musical modes may be performed. Unregulated, the arts cannot be trusted to impress the right form upon the soul or to be in harmony with reason and the good.

Much of Books II and III concerns the scenes and characters poetry contains. Plato assumes that fictional tales and poetic representations will play a dominant role in education – a conventional assumption, as we see from remarks in the *Protagoras*:

> they are given the works of good poets to read at their desks and have to learn them by heart, works that contain numerous exhortations, many passages describing in glowing terms good men of old, so that the child is inspired to imitate them and become like them. (*Prt.* 325e5–326a3)

But for Plato it is not sufficient that the young read the works of "good poets." The *Protagoras'* later discussion of interpretations of Simonides' lines about the hardness of being good might be taken to illustrate one difficulty involved in relying on poetry for one's moral education. Any few lines of poetry can be ambiguous and contradict other utterances of the poet, leading to endless unresolved debate about their meaning (*Prt.* 339a1–347a4).

A similar source of unease – perhaps less remarked than it might be by commentators – is suggested by the case against injustice constructed by Glaucon and Adeimantus in the earlier part of *Republic* II. They make their case by recounting an imaginative narrative myth about the ring of Gyges, and by citing Homer and Hesiod to the effect that justice is an arduous and unrewarding thing. Adeimantus asks

> When all such sayings about the attitudes of gods and humans to virtue and vice are so often repeated, Socrates, what effect do you suppose they have on the souls of young people? I mean those who are clever and are able to flit from one of these sayings to another, so to speak, and gather from them an impression of what sort of person he should be and of how best to travel the road of life. He would surely ask himself Pindar's question, "Should I by justice or by crooked deceit scale this high wall . . . ?" And he'll answer: "The various sayings suggest that there is no advantage in my being just if I'm not also thought just, while the troubles and penalties of being just are apparent. (II.365A4–B6)

The image of bee-like flitting parallels that in the *Ion* (discussed below), and the sweetness of honey is an appropriate metaphor, since for Plato the collecting of poetic imagery is an intensely pleasure-giving activity for the talented – hence his concern especially with the best poetry, whose value seems vouchsafed by the criterion of pleasure, even as it inculcates false, ambiguous, or contradictory opinions about the virtues.

Plato still assumes that a great part of the education of his young guardians will consist of *mousikē*, which embraces not only music but poetry, drama, and storytelling more widely. However, fiction, imaginative enactment, and music will be useful to the ends of the city only if they are subjected to rigorous standards of value that come from outside these activities themselves. Thus while Plato consistently praises Homer as a fine poet, in the *Republic* he proposes ruthless censorship of Homer's works on the grounds that certain kinds of content are corrupting to the young mind. Gods and heroes must not be represented as cowardly, despairing, deceitful, and ruled by their appetites, or committing crimes; hence the excision of many well-known scenes from the *Iliad* and *Odyssey*. A good fiction is one which (though false or invented) correctly represents reality and impresses a good character on its audience. There is a potential difficulty here, by which Plato seems characteristically untroubled. Might not an accurate representation of the way human beings behave in battle or in love fail to impress what Plato regards as the best character on its recipients? If so, is truthful representation or ethical effect the higher criterion of what is acceptable and what must be suppressed? For all his championing of truthfulness, Plato at one point suggests it is the latter: some violent mythical tales, such as the castration of Ouranos, are not true, and should not be told to the young *even if they were* (II.378A1–3). On the other hand, the representation that he is seeking is one true to an ideal: that of the noble, virtuous individual governed by reason. To show Achilles overcome with grief may be to portray one kind of truth, but Plato is seeking truthful representation only of the paradigmatic character-type required in his guardians-to-be.

The other main topic for discussion in *Republic* II and III is the appropriate mode of discourse (*lexis*) for poetry in its educative role. Plato is concerned in particular with *mimēsis*, which here should be taken as impersonation or dramatic characterization, one species of "mak[ing] oneself like someone else in voice or appearance" (III.393c4–5). There are two modes of poetic discourse: one where the poet speaks in his own voice, the other (*mimēsis*) where he hides himself and makes his language as like as possible to that of whatever person he has told us is about to speak, and – at the beginning of the *Iliad* – "tries . . . to make us think that the speaker isn't Homer, but the priest himself – an old man" (393a9–b1). Plato presents this division between straight narration (*diēgēsis*) and *mimēsis* in the manner of a new theoretical discovery, and points out that poetry can be categorized as wholly narrative, wholly mimetic, or a mixture of the two modes of discourse, as in the case of the Homeric poems. "Hiding oneself" behind a make-believe character is implicitly deceitful and dubious. But Plato's objection to *mimēsis* is more sophisticated. He claims that to enact a dramatic part by making oneself resemble some character causes one to become like such a person in real life. From this and a prior argument that all members of the ideal community, and a fortiori its guardians, should be specialists who exercise only one role, it follows that the city will produce better guardians if it restricts the extent to which they indulge in dramatic enactment. The guardians should use *mimēsis* as little as possible, and be restricted to enacting the parts of noble, self-controlled, and virtuous individuals, a practice which will assist in assimilating them to the kind of human being the state requires them to become.

Those artists whose dominant aim is the production of *mimēsis* are ingenious and versatile individuals, whom Plato can even call "holy, wonderful, and pleasing" (III.398a4–5), but the ideal state will not tolerate them. Plato gives us here his first image of banishing poets. But who exactly is Plato banishing, and what style of poetry is he retaining? When Socrates asks Adeimantus to choose between three styles of poetry, commentators have sometimes thought that Plato means the same technical threefold distinction that he made earlier between *mimēsis*, *diēgēsis*, and a style that uses both – or that he confuses his new distinction with that earlier one (Annas 1981: 99). But Plato is clear that his guardians will be permitted to enact *mimēsis* of the actions of the good individual; his concern is rather with the fundamental motivations or evaluative criteria assumed by different kinds of poetic enterprise. For someone who aims to produce the greatest possible quantity and diversity, *mimēsis* is governed by what thrills the audience. Someone whose concern is for the good can include *mimēsis*, but only of the right models. A "mixed" style, on this reading, would be that of a poet who vacillated between the two criteria of evaluation; this, as Plato says, would make for a style higher on immediate attraction, but lacking in integrity.

One objection to Plato is that he is paternalistic in extending his strictures on consumption of the arts to his adult population, treating them as if they were no different from the children whose souls he initially sets out to protect. But Plato will have an answer to this challenge once he has argued, later in the *Republic*, for the complexity of the human soul, and for the claim that poetry appeals to an emotional, desiring, and genuinely childish part within each individual. However rationally governed and however much in command of the distinction between reality and artistic make-believe (as children are not), a part of each of us still craves emotional expression and likes to indulge itself in a welter of powerful images.

The Case against Mimetic Poetry in *Republic* X

Republic X contains Plato's most vehement and most discussed criticisms of the arts. *Mimēsis* is the central topic, but now we must understand this term in a different sense, as image-making: making something that is not a real thing, but merely an image of a thing of a certain kind. Both poets and visual artists are practitioners of *mimēsis* in this sense, and it is tempting to see this passage, uniting different art forms under a single concept, as offering at least the beginnings of a general "theory of art." Modern writers in aesthetics sometimes attribute such a theory to Plato, though it would be anachronistic to translate any of Plato's terms using the distinctively modern term "art," or even to find an evaluative stance towards art as such in his writings. The aim of the discussion in *Republic* X is to justify the banishment of mimetic poetry from the ideal city. Plato never speaks of banishing painters or anyone else who might count as a mimetic artist. The grounds for banishing mimetic poetry are that it is far removed from truth, though easy to mistake for the work of someone with knowledge, and that it appeals to an inferior part of the soul and thereby helps to subvert the rule of intellect and reason. In other words, poetry is doubly deleterious: while falsely promising cognitive gain, it delivers only psychological and ethical damage to individual and community.

Plato starts by asking after the nature of *mimēsis* as such, using the illustrative example of painting. Judging by this example, *mimēsis* occurs when someone makes an image of the way some kind of thing appears, rather than making a real thing. A painting of a bed is *mimēsis* in that what is made is not a real bed, but an image of a bed, and one which attempts to show a way in which a bed might happen to appear. Plato attempts to locate this rather simple view about artistic representation within his metaphysical Theory of Forms, producing a hierarchy of three kinds of object, the Form of Bed, a bed, and a painting of a bed, and, to go with it, a hierarchy of three makers and kinds of making, a god who makes Forms, a carpenter who makes beds, and a painter who "in a certain way" (X.596E10) makes something. But the point is that what the painter makes is no real thing at all, only an image.

The use of the Theory of Forms here is in some respects anomalous. Plato has a god bring Forms into existence, though elsewhere they exist eternally and no one creates them. Forms are often thought to be paradigms existing in nature, which perhaps makes it puzzling how there could be Forms of man-made objects such as a bed (as opposed to the Forms of Justice, Beauty, Largeness, Equality, and suchlike mentioned in other passages). Finally, the Forms in the main body of the *Republic* provide the objects of knowledge for philosophers, which appears to be a different role from that of providing patterns from which craftsmen can construct objects like beds (see 12: THE FORMS AND THE SCIENCES IN SOCRATES AND PLATO; 13: PROBLEMS FOR FORMS). For someone seeking a coherent interpretation of Plato's philosophy, this passage from Book X may raise more puzzles than it solves, though arguably the chief points that Plato wants to make about the cognitive deficiency of poetry and poets are relatively unaffected by these difficulties. As Stephen Halliwell has put it, it is enough for Plato "if the argument communicates the idea that there are criteria for truth which transcend the material world . . . and if mimetic art is convicted of being limited . . . to this lower world" (1988: 110). Similarly the hierarchy of three makers and kinds of making seems primarily designed to add weight to the insinuation that mimetic activity is an unusual and unworthy kind of making.

Two further points are worth mentioning here concerning Forms and *mimēsis*. First, we should not assume that the relation of painting to bed is the same as that of bed to Form. The latter is the vexed relation of participation, instantiation, or whatever exactly it should be called; the former is simply the contrast between an image of a thing of a certain kind and a real thing of that kind. And Plato never says that a painting is an "imitation of an imitation" (Nehamas 1982: 60). Secondly, we should resist an optimistic reading that was once popular: that Plato thinks only "bad art" is a *mimēsis* of appearances, implicitly leaving open a space for a "good art" that imitates the true paradigms of the Forms (Tate 1928). There is no evidence that Plato wants this contrast to be understood here, and, besides, his most trenchant criticisms are of the best poetry he is aware of, Homer and the tragedians. He never tires of praising Homer's greatness, and thinks it all the more important for that reason to understand how distant from truth and knowledge Homer is.

Plato disparages *mimēsis* in the visual arts by comparing it with holding up a mirror in which the world mechanically reproduces itself. With a mirror "you can quickly make the sun, the things in the heavens, the earth, yourself, the other animals, manufactured items, plants, and everything else" (X.596E1–3). The point of the comparison is arguably just that the painter makes no real thing, only an image. Plato need not be saddled with the crudity of thinking that all painting is mindless, mechanical duplication of some particular material object. There need be no particular bed copied in order to make a picture of a bed. Plato's point is that the painter's product is an image, which, when compared with a real bed and with the Form of Bed, is at two moves from reality, and that to make such an image requires no genuine knowledge: no knowledge of the real things of which one makes an image. Plato is heading for the crucial conclusion that a poet makes only images and is distant from knowledge: "all poetic imitators, beginning with Homer, imitate images of virtue and all the other things they write about and have no grasp of the truth" (X.600E4–6). They produce only images of human life, and to do so requires no knowledge of the truth about what is good and bad in life. The analogy by which Plato makes the transition from painter to poet is slightly strained and has sometimes baffled readers. He imagines a painter who

can paint a cobbler, a carpenter, or other craftsman, though he knows nothing of these crafts. Nevertheless, if he is a good painter and displays his painting of a carpenter at a distance, he can deceive children and foolish people into believing that it is truly a carpenter. (X.598B9–c4, trans. modified)

The point of this extremely non-standard imaginary painter is that one can make an image of *someone knowledgeable about X* without oneself being knowledgeable about *X*. (The "painter of a bed" example made the slightly different point that one can make an image of *X* without oneself knowing how to make an *X*.) So the real target of this passage is the poet's lack of knowledge of what his characters appear to know – ethical truths.

To see the motivation for this analogy, we should ask why it matters that poetic image-making entails no genuine knowledge. To Plato it matters because there are those who hold the opposite view:

> We hear some people say that poets know all crafts, all human affairs concerned with virtue and vice, and all about the gods as well. For they say that if a good poet produces fine poetry, he must have knowledge of the things he writes about, or else he wouldn't be able to produce it at all. (X.598E1–4)

Plato aims to refute these claims. Fine poetry is a species of image-making – it "imitates" human beings acting in all kinds of ways, faring well or badly and experiencing either pleasure or pain (603c5–6) – and its being of this nature is compatible with the poet's ignorance of truths about what is real. This represents Plato's chief challenge to poetry, and suggests many difficult questions for philosophers of art: What are the criteria for something's being a fine poem? Do we judge a poem's quality on the basis of truths that it conveys? Can a work of art succeed in presenting a convincing, pleasing image of human life with its goods and ills without its producer having any special or distinctive knowledge? At 599A–600E Plato attempts to reinforce his case by saying that there is no evidence of any good poet's manifesting ethical or political competence, but these seem especially weak stretches of argument. To argue that nobody would want to write poetry, or be allowed by their community to write poetry, if they also had genuine expertise in a useful field of knowledge, assumes that everyone agrees writing poetry to be an activity of low value, but that is precisely to beg the question at issue.

Plato also undertakes to show (from 602c) which part of the human psyche mimetic poetry appeals to. He refers back to the division of the soul made in *Republic* IV, where it was argued that the soul often contains conflicting attitudes towards the same objects, which must be explained by assigning the attitudes to distinct "parts" within the soul (*R*. 603D and 439cff.) (see 19: THE PLATONIC SOUL). In Book X Plato does not stick to the clear tripartite division of Book IV, though he retains the idea of the higher part of the soul that uses reasoning and considers what is for the overall good, and the idea of its being opposed by other parts. The images of mimetic poetry, he now argues, are gratifying to an "inferior" part of us, which is childish, unruly, and emotional, and reacts in an unmeasured fashion to events in real life and in fiction. For example, when someone close to us dies, part of us considers what is for the best and desires restraint in feeling and outward behavior. At the same time another part tends towards indulgence in unbounded lamentation. There is a conflict of attitudes towards the same object, analogous to the phenomenon of visual illusion, where part of the mind calculates that a stick in water is straight, while another part persists in seeing it as bent. Poetry affects us emotionally below the level of rational desire and judgment. The kinds of events that provide the most successful content for mimetic poetry (and for tragedy especially) involve extreme emotions and actions driven by emotion. So mimetic poetry naturally addresses and gratifies the inferior, lamenting part of us and fosters it at the expense of the rational and good-seeking part that should rule in a healthy soul.

Plato's "most serious charge" against mimetic poetry (605c4) also concerns its effects on the psyche. It is that "with a few rare exceptions it is able to corrupt even decent people." Even the individual who attains the Platonic ideal and is governed by the noble, rational, good-seeking part of the soul, is powerfully affected by the experience of hearing

394

Homer or some other tragedian imitating one of the heroes sorrowing and making a long lamenting speech or singing and beating his breast . . . we enjoy it, give ourselves up to following it, sympathize with the hero, take his sufferings seriously, and praise as a good poet the one who affects us most in this way. (605c9–D3)

The distancing provided by the artistic context insidiously lulls us into a positive evaluation of responses which we should avoid in real life. We relax our guard and allow the rule of the rational part of ourselves to lapse:

only a few are able to figure out that enjoyment of other people's sufferings is necessarily transferred to our own and that the pitying part, if it is nourished and strengthened on the sufferings of others, won't be easily held in check when we ourselves suffer. (606B5–9)

The positive evaluation of our sympathetic feelings for the hero's sufferings rests on the fact that to see them brings us pleasure. So instead of regarding as valuable that which we judge to be best, we begin to value responses that happen to please us, and, Plato argues, this habit can corrode our attachment to the rational and the good in real life.

Plato makes many assumptions here, but perhaps most notable is one that has featured in recent debates about the psychological effects of television and films: that if we enjoy seeing the image of something enacted in a dramatic narrative, this causes in us an increased disposition to act or react similarly in real life. It is as if *mimēsis* is transparent in a particular way: to enjoy or approve of a poetic image of X is not really different from enjoying or approving of X itself. This is an assumption worth questioning. Aristotle already remarks in the *Poetics* that the enjoyment of *mimēsis* is natural for human beings as a way of learning (Aristotle 1987: 34). We may say that Aristotle trusts the human mind's inbuilt disposition to handle the distinction between reality and representation, and to benefit from it, in a way that Plato does not. Plato's campaign to show up mimetic activities as bizarre and dubious receives an important corrective here. Yet Plato seems more alive to the forceful subrational pull exerted on us by *mimēsis*, and is arguably right to leave open the question whether this is always healthy for the soul.

As the culmination of his argument in *Republic* X Plato banishes poetry from his ideal city, on the grounds that it falsely masquerades as knowledge and is detrimental to the human mind. We may wonder how much of poetry this affects. At the beginning of the discussion "poetry that is mimetic" is to be excluded, but by the end it appears that all poetry is meant, and the intervening argument seems to tell us that all poetry is indeed mimetic, although Homer and the tragic poets (seen as a single tradition) provide the most focused target. Plato proposes to retain some poetry, namely "hymns to the gods and eulogies to good people" (607A3). Given the earlier comments about beauty and grace, these works need by no means be conceived as dull and worthy, but clearly Plato prefers them because they will present a correct ethical view of the world and be a means of instilling the right character in the citizens.

In his concluding remarks Plato mentions the "ancient quarrel between poetry and philosophy" (607B4). Poetry (of the kind excluded) aims at pleasure and *mimēsis*, but

395

if it can satisfy philosophy by producing an argument that is beneficial to the community and to human life, then it can reclaim its place. If philosophers hear no such justification, they will use the argument of *Republic* Book X "like an incantation so as to preserve ourselves from slipping back into that childish passion for poetry" (608A2–3). It is like keeping oneself away from a person one is in love with but with whom an association is not beneficial. This image and the accompanying invitation to poetry to defend itself reveal Plato as less authoritarian than he often appears in the *Republic*. He recognizes the power of poetry over the human soul and intimates that he has full appreciation of its pleasures. It is not through insensitivity that Plato rejects pursuit of the pleasures of poetic image-making. It is because he has a reasoned case that shows we should resist these pleasures unless poetry or its lovers perform on philosophy's home ground and present a good counter-argument.

Inspiration and Beauty

Two sources of complication in the modern reception of Plato's views about the arts are his scattered remarks about inspiration and his more pervasive concern with beauty or *to kalon*. Modern readers have not always seen that for Plato inspiration is not a source of over-riding value for poetry and that for him beauty does not attach primarily or distinctively to the arts. In the short early dialogue *Ion*, Plato has Socrates say that poets are divinely inspired to produce their fine works. The character Ion is a rhapsode, a professional reciter of poetry and a would-be critic or expert on Homer. Socrates undertakes a demolition of Ion's claim that he succeeds as performer and critic because he has knowledge. An important concept in this dialogue is *technē*: "craft," "skill," or "expert knowledge." Plato regards doctors, generals, and mathematicians as possessing a *technē*, meaning that they are knowledgeable about a specific subject matter, can transmit their knowledge in teaching, understand general principles or rules that apply across all instances within their field, and can give a rational account of why their practice succeeds. Further criteria of *technē*, offered in the *Gorgias*, are that it both aims at the good and has a basis in knowledge of the good (*Grg.* 463A–465A).

An older translation for *technē* is "art" (via the Latin *ars*) but examination of this concept will not yield Plato's "philosophy of art," chiefly because practices we regard as "artistic" tend to be denied the status of *technē* (Janaway 1992). In the *Gorgias* Plato argues that persuasive rhetoric, tragedy, and musical performances by choruses or instrumentalists fail to be cases of *technē*, on the grounds that their aim is not to make their audiences better, but to gratify them. He argues that there are no principles concerning what pleases a mass audience, and that it is by guesswork that these practices succeed, rather than by rational principle or knowledge. The *Ion* takes a similar line: the rhapsode discerns what is fine and pleasing in Homer's poetry, but in so doing (a) he works to no generalizable principles, as evidenced by his inability to discourse convincingly on any other poets; and (b) there is no specific subject matter on which he is an expert solely in virtue of being a rhapsode and being familiar with Homer's fine work. Ion's preposterous claim to be an expert on "everything," because Homer writes finely of everything, prefigures the superficially more plausible claim, rejected in the *Republic*, about the supposed capacious knowledge of poets themselves.

How is it then, Socrates asks, that Ion succeeds in discerning the fineness in Homer's poetry and performing it so brilliantly as to delight his audiences? His answer is itself poetic, or perhaps mock-poetic:

> poets tell us that they gather songs at honey-flowing springs, from glades and gardens of the Muses, and that they bear songs to us as bees carry honey, flying like bees. And what they say is true. For a poet is an airy thing, winged and holy, and he is not able to make poetry until he becomes inspired and goes out of his mind and his intellect is no longer in him. (*Ion* 534B1–6)

The power of poetry is divine: the Muse attracts the poet, who is then a mouthpiece through which the divine speaks. The performer succumbs to the same attraction and transmits it to the audience. But at no stage does rational thought or expert competence account for the success of the proceedings. There seems to be a mixed message here: Ion is praised as admirable and even (if ironically) "divine" for the fineness of his performances. But he deserves no credit for his artistic success, because he is "out of his mind." Not only can he give no rational account of why he succeeds; he is also, Plato assumes, irrational in responding emotionally to the dramatic scene he performs, despite his awareness of that scene's unreality. Although the *Ion* locates features regarded in the modern era as characterizing the "artistic" – Shelley, for example, translated the dialogue and in his own defense of poetry echoes its opposition between what is truly artistic and the productions of self-possessed rational thought – it nevertheless rates these features disparagingly, or at best equivocally. We should therefore resist the temptation to use the *Ion*'s picture of inspiration to attribute to Plato any decidedly positive account of art.

The later work *Phaedrus*, itself a literary masterpiece which explores the nature of rhetoric, writing, love, beauty, Forms, and the philosophical life, promises a more openly positive account of the inspiration of poets. Here Socrates praises "madness," explicitly including the state of mind in which good poets compose, "a Bacchic frenzy" without which there is no true poetry:

> If anyone comes to the gates of poetry and expects to become an adequate poet by acquiring expert knowledge (*technē*) . . . he will fail, and his self-controlled verses will be eclipsed by poetry of men who have been driven out of their minds. (*Phdr.* 245A4–7)

It has been claimed that the *Phaedrus* marks Plato's recantation of the hard-line condemnation of poetry in the *Republic* (Nussbaum 1986: 200–33). However, other passages in the dialogue point to greater continuity with the *Republic*'s position. Part of the extravagant myth Socrates enunciates in the *Phaedrus* concerns the fate of reincarnated souls, who are placed in rank order. The highest, most worthy soul is that of "a lover of wisdom or of beauty . . . cultivated in the arts (*mousikos*) and prone to erotic love" (248D3–4). Sixth in rank, lower than generals, statesmen, gymnasts, doctors, and prophets, is a poet or some other form of life among those concerned with *mimēsis* (248E2–3). The contrast again challenges the modern reader's intuitions. Surely the

397

prime rank must go to the genuine artist, while some poor uninspired dabbler is relegated to the sixth? Yet there is no word for "art" here, as Alexander Nehamas reminds us: "the 'musical' . . . is not the artist, but the gentleman who patronizes the artists and knows what to take from them" (1982: 60). The first-ranking soul is rather that of the cultured philosopher and lover, with whom poets, all mimetic poets, including the great Homer, cannot compete. The comparative evaluation of the *Republic* is echoed in a very different tone of voice, but it is not reversed.

Some commentators on Plato have thought that a positive philosophy of art is implicit in his evocative passages on the love of beauty as an absolute value. But Iris Murdoch is nearer the mark when she writes that "Plato wants to cut art off from beauty, because he regards beauty as too serious a matter to be commandeered by art" (1977: 17). Plato's concept of beauty is arguably quite different from the modern aesthetic concept, whatever exactly that is. We translate Plato's word *kalon* as "beautiful," but a preferable translation in many contexts is "fine." Definitions and examples from the *Hippias Major* illuminate the broad application of *kalon*: a fine girl is fine, so is anything made of gold, so is living a rich and healthy life and giving your parents a decent burial. Here even the first two may not be cases of beauty in what we might call a purely aesthetic sense; desirability and exchange value play a part in their fineness. Another aspect of fineness is "what is pleasing through hearing and sight":

> Men, when they're fine anyway – and everything decorative, pictures and sculptures – these all delight us when we see them, if they're fine. Fine sounds and music altogether, and speeches and storytelling have the same effect. (*Hp.Ma.* 298A1–3)

This indeed looks like a rudimentary definition of the aesthetically pleasing in art. In the dialogue this definition fails to define *to kalon* as a whole because of a logical technicality. In addition it neither embraces the whole range of *kalon* nor lends the arts a value that rescues them from the critique of the *Republic*, since Plato never there disputed the fineness and pleasure-giving qualities of the works he was proposing to censor and banish.

Plato portrays non-philosophers such as the sophist Hippias as unable to grasp that there is a single unvarying Form of Beauty. Hippias equates beauty with a beautiful girl and then with the property of being made of gold. But a girl is beautiful in one relation (to other girls), not in another (to goddesses), and being made of gold makes some things beautiful, but not others; the eyes of a statue, for instance, would be repulsive if fashioned from gold. So it looks to Plato as if no object or property accessible to the senses can be what constitutes beauty as such. A similar distinction occurs in the *Republic*, where Plato disparages "lovers of sights and sounds" (475D–476B) who eagerly attend arts festivals, and think there are "many beautiful things" but no single Form of the Beautiful that the philosopher recognizes.

Beauty finds its most significant treatment in the *Symposium*, in the speech by Socrates, which he presents as the teaching of the wise woman, Diotima. Despite this double-nesting of narrators, the speech is usually seen as revealing Plato's own philosophical views. The whole dialogue concerns the nature of love, whose highest object is beauty. To grasp this, we must distinguish, on the one hand, the beauty of things and properties as they occur in the sensible world and, on the other, the Beautiful-itself (*auto to kalon*), the eternal, unchanging, and divine Form of Beauty, accessible not to the senses, but only to the intellect (*Smp.* 211D1). Instances of beauty in the sensible world exhibit variability or relativity: something is beautiful at one time, not at another; in one respect or relation, not in another; to one observer, not to another. The Beautiful itself lacks all such variability, it "always *is* and neither comes to be nor passes away, neither waxes nor wanes" (211A1–2). This passage may be taken to imply that the Form of Beauty is itself beautiful. That reading seems to make sense of Beauty's being an object of love on a continuum with other such objects; but scholarly debate has made it unsafe to assume that Plato thinks of Beauty as "being beautiful" in the same way as a boy or girl is beautiful (Vlastos 1981; Meinwald 1992).

In the *Symposium* the ideal lover is portrayed as ascending through a hierarchy of love-objects – first the beautiful body of a particular human beloved, then all beautiful bodies equally, then the beauty of souls, then that of laws, customs, and ideas – and ending as a lover of wisdom or philosopher. At the culmination of his progress the philosophical lover will "catch sight of something wonderfully beautiful in nature . . . the reason for all his earlier labors" (210E8–9), namely the Form of Beauty itself. ("Fineness" here will hardly convey the requisite fervor.) All love desires some kind of offspring. The highest kind of love catches hold of a superior object and produces a superior offspring:

> if someone got to see the Beautiful-itself, absolute, pure, unmixed, not polluted by human flesh or colors or any other great nonsense of mortality . . . only then will it become possible for him to give birth not to images of virtue (because he's in touch with no images), but to true virtue (because he is in touch with the true Beauty). (211E1–212A7)

If we recall that in the *Republic* Plato applies the phrase "images of virtue" to poets, a particular contrast suggests itself. While the poet makes only images, and understands only images, the philosopher, who strives for and encounters the eternal unchanging Beauty, can bring genuine goods into the world because he understands what virtue is. This contrast can be hard to accept for the modern reader, because Plato's own literary genius is fully manifest in this extraordinary and moving passage, and because we imagine that he must find something like art a place in his hierarchy of beauties, or at least think that art enables its author to produce something immortal and universal. "Strangely enough," one noted historian of aesthetics has written, "Diotima and Socrates do not assign a role to the arts in this process of reawakening to Beauty, though it takes but a short step to do so" (Beardsley 1966: 41). But this is another anachronistic reaction. If anything comprises Plato's "next step," it is the arguments of the *Republic*, probably written shortly afterwards, in which, as we have seen, the admitted fineness of artistic productions does not save them from criticism on the basis of standards which for him must always be higher.

Note

Translations of Plato are taken from J. M. Cooper (ed.) *Plato: Complete Works* (Indianapolis: Hackett, 1997).

References and further reading

Annas, J. (1981). *An Introduction to Plato's* Republic. Oxford: Clarendon Press.

Aristotle (1987). *Poetics*, translation and commentary by S. Halliwell. Chapel Hill: University of North Carolina Press.

Asmus, E. (1992). Plato on poetic creativity. In R. Kraut (ed.) *The Cambridge Companion to Plato* (pp. 338–64). Cambridge: Cambridge University Press.

Beardsley, M. C. (1966). *Aesthetics from Classical Greece to the Present: A Short History.* New York: Macmillan.

Belfiore, E. (1982). Plato's greatest accusation against poetry. *Canadian Journal of Philosophy*, supplementary volume 9, pp. 39–62.

Ferrari, G. R. F. (1989). Plato and poetry. In G. A. Kennedy (ed.) *The Cambridge History of Literary Criticism*, vol. 1: *Classical Criticism* (pp. 92–148). Cambridge: Cambridge University Press.

Halliwell, S. (1988). *Plato: Republic 10.* Warminster: Aris and Phillips.

—— (1991). The importance of Plato and Aristotle for aesthetics. *Proceedings of the Boston Area Colloquium on Ancient Philosophy* 5, pp. 321–48.

Havelock, E. A. (1963). *Preface to Plato.* Cambridge, Mass.: Harvard University Press.

Janaway, C. (1992). Arts and crafts in Plato and Collingwood. *Journal of Aesthetics and Art Criticism* 50, pp. 45–54.

—— (1995). *Images of Excellence: Plato's Critique of the Arts.* Oxford: Clarendon Press.

Keuls, E. (1978). *Plato and Greek Painting.* Leiden: Brill.

Meinwald, C. (1992). Goodbye to the third man. In R. Kraut (ed.) *The Cambridge Companion to Plato* (pp. 365–96). Cambridge: Cambridge University Press.

Moravcsik, J. (1986). On correcting the poets. In *Oxford Studies in Ancient Philosophy*, vol. 4 (pp. 35–47). Oxford: Oxford University Press.

Moravcsik, J. and Temko, P. (eds.) (1982). *Plato on Beauty, Wisdom, and the Arts.* Totowa, NJ: Rowman and Littlefield.

Murdoch, I. (1977). *The Fire and the Sun: Why Plato Banished the Artists.* Oxford: Oxford University Press.

Nadaff, R. A. (2003). *Exiling the Poets: the Production of Censorship in Plato's "Republic."* Chicago: University of Chicago Press.

Nehamas, A. (1982). Plato on imitation and poetry in *Republic* 10. In J. Moravcsik and P. Temko (eds.) *Plato on Beauty, Wisdom, and the Arts* (pp. 47–78). Totowa, NJ: Rowman and Littlefield.

—— (1988). Plato and the mass media. *The Monist* 71, pp. 214–33.

Nussbaum, M. C. (1986). *The Fragility of Goodness: Luck and Ethics in Greek Tragedy and Philosophy.* Cambridge: Cambridge University Press.

Schaper, E. (1968). *Prelude to Aesthetics.* London: George Allen and Unwin.

Schopenhauer, A. (1969). *The World as Will and Representation*, vol. 1, trans. E. F. J. Payne. New York: Dover Publications.

Sidney, Sir P. (1973). A defense of poetry. In K. Duncan-Jones and J. van Dorsten (eds.) *Miscellaneous Prose of Sir Philip Sidney* (pp. 73–121). Oxford: Clarendon Press.

Tate, J. (1928). Imitation in Plato's *Republic. Classical Quarterly* 22, pp. 16–23.

Tigerstedt, E. N. (1970). Furor poeticus: poetic inspiration in Greek literature before Democritus and Plato. *Journal of the History of Ideas* 31, pp. 163–78.

Vlastos, G. (1981). Degrees of reality in Plato. In G. Vlastos (ed.) *Platonic Studies* (pp. 58–75). Princeton, NJ: Princeton University Press.

Woodruff, P. (1982). What could go wrong with inspiration? Why Plato's poets fail. In J. Moravcsik and P. Temko (eds.) *Plato on Beauty, Wisdom, and the Arts* (pp. 137–50). Totowa, NJ: Rowman and Littlefield.

Part VI

PLATONIC LEGACY

27

Learning about Plato from Aristotle

CHRISTOPHER SHIELDS

As a boy of about 17, Aristotle came to Athens in order to study at Plato's Academy. Evidently, he was impressed with what he found once he arrived: he joined the Academy and remained there for twenty years, first as a student and then as a co-researcher into all matters philosophical, not leaving, in fact, until Plato's death. Accordingly, when we find Aristotle criticizing Plato, sometimes rather caustically, we should recall the evident affection he expresses when he commends him as "a man whom the wicked have no place to praise: he alone, unsurpassed among mortals, has shown clearly by his own life and by the pursuits of his writings that a man becomes happy and good simultaneously" (fr. 650 R^3, fr. 673 R^3, Olympiadorus, *Commentarius in Gorgiam* 41.9). Aristotle praises Plato not simply for his intellectual prowess, nor yet solely for his human goodness. Instead, he honors Plato for his perfect concord of mind and life: Plato, he contends, shows uniquely, or at any rate to a degree unmatched by any other mortal, that human flourishing resides in the goodness of intellectual attainment.

Still, we do find Aristotle criticizing Plato, sometimes in ways so strident as to occasion derision from his ancient detractors, who were inclined to cast him in the role of an ingrate, a pupil who having been received into the Platonic Academy and showered with the benefits of its membership preferred to sneer at the convictions of its principal like an immature schoolboy too self-smitten to appreciate all the master had done for him. For example, the ancient biographer Diogenes Laertius reports a story, surely apocryphal, that Plato once referred to Aristotle as "the foal who kicked its mother" (*DL* v 2). Nor are such criticisms of Aristotle restricted to antiquity. On the contrary, they extend down to the present time. Thus, one eminent Platonic scholar sums up Aristotle's level of understanding contentiously: "In the first place it is certain that he never understood the teaching of the head of the Academy" (Burnet 1928: 56). Although such contentions are unhelpfully monodimensional, Aristotle's detractors do pose some irresistible questions concerning the interaction of Plato and Aristotle in the Academy. Although he remained in the Academy for two decades, Aristotle indicates in several passages that he is completely out of sympathy with some of Plato's most central and philosophically distinctive claims. How, then, does he fault him? And why?

We may also wonder how, if at all, Aristotle's criticisms affected and shaped Plato's philosophy. Can we, for example, detect the sorts of anti-Platonic criticisms advanced in Aristotle's works reflected in Plato's dialogues? Should we, more speculatively, understand the evident shifts in Plato's thinking, especially about the Forms, as reactions to the sorts of criticisms we find articulated in Aristotle's writings?

Such questions are delicate and difficult, though well worth pursuing. As propaedeutic to addressing them in their full complexity, it will be useful to recount and assess some of Aristotle's most vocal criticisms of Plato. We will focus on two sets of issues clustering around: (a) the Theory of Forms; and (b) the nature of goodness. A third set of telling issues concerns the divergent attitudes of Plato and Aristotle regarding the authority of the state, which are to some extent, though only to some extent, to be explained by the prior disagreements concerning the nature of goodness. Careful attention to his treatment of Plato in these areas reveals that however acerbic their rhetoric, Aristotle's criticisms are not so obviously compelling as they are sometimes assumed to be. Moreover, and perhaps more importantly, this same attention reveals that teacher and student are not so diametrically opposed as the tradition has often wanted to portray them. That said, however we may come to regard the directions of mutual influence or dialectical superiority between these two thinkers, our own eventual appraisal of Plato's primary philosophical positions will be richly informed by considering the critical reactions of his first highly astute opponent, Aristotle.

Aristotle's Treatment of Plato's Theory of Forms: A Characteristic Exchange

Suppose we are tempted to believe that there are Forms (see 12: THE FORMS AND THE SCIENCES IN SOCRATES AND PLATO). Then we are evidently tempted to believe – although the matter is disputed – that there exist abstract mind- and language-independent entities which are perfect and unchanging, purely what they are, never subject to flux, and are thus ideally suited to be the objects of knowledge. We also believe, it seems, that as perfect, these Forms may serve as paradigms, first for the divine craftsman who looked to them as models when creating the universe, and second, and in another sense, as the paradigm instances of F-ness after which non-paradigm instances are named. On this latter score, if we think that two sticks are equal, then we might think that neither of them is completely or purely equal, or equal in an unalloyed or perfect respect: they might be equal in weight but not in length or color, and even then, they might be equal in length only to an approximation. That is, although when weighing them we find that each weighs 0.6 kilos, but that upon closer inspection, one weighs 0.61 kilos and the other 0.62; or if each weighs 0.61 kilos, when we subject them to more delicate tests, we see that the first weights 0.611 and the other 0.612 kilos and so on. So, we might say that even in respect of weight they are and are not equal, depending upon the context of our assessment. In that case, we will think of them as other than *perfectly equal* and as therefore other than Equality-itself, which will never turn up, in any context, as unequal. These characterizations draw upon passages scattered throughout the corpus, including *Phd.* 76D–E, 100A; *Phdr.* 247C; *R.* 477A–480E, 523A–E, 597D; *Smp.* 210E–211E; *Ti.* 27D–28A, 52A–B; *Prm.* 126A–135D.

Because Plato seems to offer different sorts of considerations for believing in Forms in these different contexts, and even suggests different and incompatible ranges of

Forms in different dialogues, it is salutary for our present purpose to ask how Aristotle construes Plato's dominant motivation. One of his clearest and most direct representations of Plato's motivation occurs early in his *Metaphysics*, in I.6.987a29–987b24, where he is concerned to recapitulate the approaches of his predecessors as preliminary to offering his own views. Here he ascribes a thoroughly *epistemological* motivation to Plato. He contends that Plato was heavily influenced by Heraclitus, that having been made familiar with his conception of *flux* as a young man, Plato continued to embrace his views even into old age, though with one central difference. Plato, reports Aristotle, restricted Heraclitus' view to the sensible world, arguing that there could be no knowledge if there were only sensible entities forever in flux. As Aristotle suggests in a similar context elsewhere, trying to know what is forever changing is like pursuing flying game (*Metaph.* 1009b38–1010a1). Thus, if we assume that there is some knowledge – for example, that we know that 2 + 2 = 4 – then there must be non-sensible objects of knowledge, objects which are perfectly stable and never varying. These are Forms. Taken together then, Aristotle's argument on behalf of Platonic Forms is: (1) objects of perception are forever in flux; (2) what is in flux cannot be known; so, (3) objects of perception cannot be the objects of knowledge – if there are any; (4) there are objects of knowledge, since we do after all know some things; hence, (5) the objects of our knowledge must be non-sensible and never in flux. Call such objects Forms.

Now, there are a number of points at which one might want to query this argument. Neither Plato nor Aristotle, however, has much sympathy for the thought that (4) is false, since its denial would require a global skepticism incompatible with our knowing even the must humble necessary truths. That seems extreme. It is accordingly interesting to ask which of (1) or (2) Aristotle himself rejects. For he must reject one or the other, given his repeated pronouncements about the untenability of Plato's Theory of Forms. We find such scattered throughout Aristotle's writings, though often given without the benefit of the full arguments which lay behind them. His complaints vary. Aristotle contends, for example: (1) that Forms are causally inert and so cannot explain change or generation (*Metaph.* 991a8, 1033b26–8); (2) that postulating Forms offends theoretical economy (*Ph.* 259a8); (3) that Forms, if ever they existed, would be epistemologically otiose (*Metaph.* 991a12–14); (4) that introducing Forms as paradigms is empty metaphor (*Metaph.* 991a20–3); (5) that Forms cannot be essences if they are separated, since essences are intrinsic features of things (*Metaph.* 991b1); (6) that in general, Forms, once separated, contribute nothing to particulars; and (7) at his most caustic, Aristotle recommends a "farewell to the Forms," since "they are tra-la-las and even if they do exist they are wholly irrelevant" (*APo.* 83a32–4). Some of these claims are provided with support, though in some instances severely truncated, while others arrive without any backing at all. Consequently, with respect to at least some of his criticisms, any attempt to reconstruct Aristotle's motivating arguments is a highly conjectural business.

For this reason it is fortunate that the Aristotelian commentator Alexander of Aphrodisias, who lived some five centuries after Aristotle, had available to him a manuscript of a short treatise entitled *On Forms*. The work, quoted or paraphrased closely at length by Alexander in his commentary on Aristotle's *Metaphysics*, appears to have been written by Aristotle, perhaps at a time approaching the end of his stay in the

Academy. *On Forms* recounts a series of arguments intended to refute the Theory of Forms. Some of its arguments have counterparts in Aristotle's extant writings, especially in *Metaph.* X.9; and some of them are continuous with the sorts of arguments considered by Plato himself in the *Parmenides* (see 13: PROBLEMS FOR FORMS). It accordingly seems likely that the arguments advanced in *On Forms* reflect to a considerable degree the sorts of criticisms current in the Academy at the time of its composition.

In order to determine whether Aristotle's criticisms are justified – that is, whether we should ourselves join him in rejecting Platonic Forms – we will need first to understand the criticisms, and then to decide whether Plato is vulnerable to them, and finally to ascertain whether, if so, minor improvements might yet resurrect a Platonic theory which escapes the sorts of criticisms Aristotle finds compelling. Each of these tasks is demanding. The second, in particular, is complicated by the fact that there is no reason to suppose that Plato's theory arrived full-blown and remained unchanged for the duration of his long and rich career (see 2: INTERPRETING PLATO). So, in order to determine the question of vulnerability, it is necessary also to determine which of Plato's shifting characterizations of Forms Aristotle might have in view in a given criticism. Still, we might without undue violence to Plato simply ask how the author of *On Forms* seems to be conceiving the Forms he rejects, while leaving in abeyance the more complicated question of whether the Theory of Forms he rejects answers to any reasonably clear expression in an extant Platonic dialogue. We might, when proceeding this way, come to learn something about the theories bandied about in the Academy, whether or not these theories eventually found their way into Plato's published dialogues.

Among the many arguments advanced, one seems both especially engaging and ideally suited to consideration because of its touching the nerve of a deeply ingrained Platonic impulse. It is an argument which has come to be called the "One Over Many."

In the One Over Many Argument, we find Aristotle faulting Plato for believing that there corresponds a Form to every general term. As a first approximation, suppose that there are fifty-five olive trees in a grove on the side of a mountain. Though they will invariably differ in countless ways from one another, the trees will also be in some ways exactly the same; to begin, each and every one of them *is a tree*. So, we might say, speaking only a little oddly, that each of them has an attribute in common, namely *being a tree*. Although some are smaller and some larger, and some more fruitful and some less, the attribute *being a tree* belongs to them all, and to no one more or less than any other. One might then be tempted to say, as Aristotle reports that Plato was in fact disposed to say, that all these trees have some one trait in common, a trait which is distinct from any individual tree, something which might even be thought to remain if all of the specific trees on the hillside were destroyed by fire. After all, there would even then remain the *possibility* of there being many trees, perhaps fifty-five, on that very hillside. So, we might be inclined to conclude that *being a tree* names an attribute, an attribute distinct from any particular group of actual or even possible trees. This attribute could then play various roles. It could be the meaning of our word "tree," and it could be a meaning which would exist even if there were no trees at present. In addition, it could be that very attribute, *being a tree*, which all and only trees have in common. Finally, that attribute could then underwrite the possibility of trees when no trees existed. That alone would make true the sentence "There could be trees on that hillside" when there were none, because of their having been destroyed by fire. We would not have to appeal to anything so outlandish as possibly-but-non-actually-existing trees. Rather, we would simply be saying that the attribute, *being a tree*, might come to be exemplified on that hillside once again.

Accordingly, the supposition that there is one attribute set over many trees proves both economical and explanatorily rich. This attribute would be an instance of a One Over Many. Generalizing, then, for any group of *F* things, there would be an attribute *F*-ness which all and only *F* things have in common. One thing, *F*-ness, is set over many *F* things. Taken slightly more rigorously, then, we see Aristotle ascribing to Plato an argument of the following sort:

1 Whenever many things are *F*, they are *F* in virtue of exhibiting some one common attribute, *F*-ness.
2 It is not possible to suppose that this attribute is itself identical with either (a) any one of the *F* things, or even (b) the entire class of *F* things.
3 So, this attribute, *F*-ness, must be distinct from the *F* things and set over them.
4 Further, this *F*-ness, which is distinct from the class of *F* things and set over them, underwrites the permanent possibility of there being *F* things.
5 If (4), then *F*-ness: (a) cannot depend upon the *F* things for its existence and so must be capable of existing without them, and (b) must be everlasting.
6 So, *F*-ness must be capable of existing without the *F* things and be everlasting.

It is striking how quickly, on the basis of just the simple assumption of there being one trait over many particulars, this argument brings us close to a Platonic conception of Forms. (6) implies that there are entities distinct from any material particulars, capable of existing everlastingly without the slightest reliance on them for their continuing to be. We may call such entities "Forms."

Although in some ways plainly critical of this argument, Aristotle proves himself to be in some other ways surprisingly sympathetic. Let us consider first his criticisms. In *On Forms*, Aristotle first faults this argument for proving too much if it proves anything at all. If sound, he suggests, the One Over Many Argument would generate Forms unwanted even by the Platonists, Forms corresponding to negations and to things which do not exist at all. Focusing on negations, Aristotle contends, we can see that just as we can predicate *being a man* of any random group of men, so that there will be a one over many, so too can we predicate *not being a man* over any randomly selected group of things which are not men, say a tree, a horse, and a little girl's elbow. Shall we say then that there is something, *not being a man*, or worse, *being not a man*, set over all of these many things which are not men? Surely that would be absurd. To begin, there would be countless numbers of negative Forms. Moreover, these Forms would be set over bewildering collections of particulars having nothing in common with one another save that they are *not* something or other, e.g., *not a man*. This second criticism seems especially pointed if we had been assuming at the very beginning of the argument, in premise (1), that we needed to posit an attribute of some sort or other to explain the commonalities we observe in the world. Now it turns out, if this criticism is justified, that we need to posit Forms for precisely the opposite reason: we

need to set Forms over disparate and random collections of objects with nothing positive in common at all.

In reflecting on this argument, we might wonder whether it is compelling even in
its own terms; and we might also inquire into the tangled matter of whether Aristotle
is justified in attempting to saddle Plato with its presuppositions. In assessing the
justifiability of Aristotle's ascriptions, we are sorely limited in our resources. On the
one hand, Aristotle alludes, though only once, to Plato's "unwritten doctrines" (*Ph.*
209b14), evidently, however, only in connection with some issues pertaining to the
relationship between matter and space rather than to the Forms as such. Still, the
allusion makes vivid something which cannot sensibly be denied, though it *has* indeed
been denied in modern times by Cherniss (1944: 72), namely that Aristotle had regular interaction with Plato over the two decades he spent with him and that he no
doubt relied upon that interaction when coming to recount and recast Plato's views
for appraisal. (Some evidence from the Aristotelian corpus where we seem to see him
alluding to such reliance can be found at *Metaph.* 992a20–22, 1019a1, 1070a18,
1083a32; *EN* 1095a32; *GC* 330b13.)

So, there is a legitimate question as to whether, when we find Aristotle ascribing a
view not otherwise attested in Plato's own extant writings, we should simply suppose
that it corresponds to something Plato actually held, something Aristotle would naturally know he held on the basis of their personal interactions. While it is reasonable
to suppose that such a practice is perfectly sensible, two factors militate against our
treating it as easily or uncontroversially practicable. First, sometimes Aristotle ascribes
a view to Plato which is patently problematic; so, if we are being charitable to Plato,
we should pause to wonder whether the view in question is authentically Plato's, or,
more neutrally, whether the view reported is formulated in terms Plato would find
congenial. Second, if we find something objectionable in a view ascribed to Plato by
Aristotle, we might well ask a still more nuanced question regarding whether Plato
himself, having appreciated its problematic consequences, might not have revised or
amended it in one way or another. That is, if we are prepared to draw data about
Plato's doctrines from Aristotle's otherwise unattested reports concerning them, then
we should equally be prepared, heading in the other direction, to assume that Plato
might have offered rejoinders to Aristotle left unreported in Aristotle's representations.

For these and other like reasons, we should tread lightly upon Aristotle's unattested
reports, focusing instead, so far as we are able, on the evidence we do find present in
Plato's surviving writings. In the matter currently under investigation, the One Over
Many Argument, we do indeed find some awareness of its key premises reflected in
Plato's dialogues, though it is an awareness which is at times itself rather wary. On
the one hand, Plato once says in the *Republic*: "We are everywhere accustomed to
positing some one Form for each of the many things to which we apply the same
name" (596A6–7). This seems, on its surface to embrace the driving assumption of the
One Over Many Argument in an especially telling way. For we may view (1), the
premise that whenever many things are *F*, they are *F* in virtue of exhibiting some one
common attribute, *F*-ness, in one of two not necessarily exclusive ways: (a) *metaphysically*, so that any time we find many things which are *F* we are constrained to set some
one attribute *F*-ness over them; or (b) *semantically*, so that any time we use the predicate "*F*-ness" in the same sense of a range of different subjects, we think there is a

meaning, *F*-ness, which is expressed by the predicate "being-*F*." The idea behind the metaphysical understanding of Plato's remark is that whether or not anyone cares to notice or say so, when many things are *F*, they share a common attribute, *F*-ness; on the semantic understanding, the attribute in question is meaning, something expressed by our linguistic utterances when we say that something or other is *F*. Although these views may be discrete, they need not be, as is sometimes supposed, because Plato may be assuming that what we express, the meaning of our term, simply is the attribute shared by all the *F* things. In effect, this is what I assumed in my initial presentation of the One Over Many Argument, when praising it as an impressively economical hypothesis. In any event, on its surface, Plato's remark at *R*. 596A6–7 seems at least to have a semantic purport, if not also a metaphysical one.

That said, it would be injudicious at best to rely upon just this one passage in attempting to determine whether Plato endorsed some form of One Over Many Assumption (cf. also, in any case, *R*. 523–5 and *Plt*. 262A–E; and also, more tentatively, *Euthphr*. 5D1–5; *Men*. 72C7; *Chrm*. 158E7, 159A1–2). To begin, even if he had, he might well nonetheless have changed his mind over the long course of his development. More importantly, the One Over Many Assumption indisputably makes an appearance in Plato, though in a highly charged passage in which Plato recounts, in *propria persona* or not, a series of stingingly critical arguments, at least some of which bear a strong family resemblance to the arguments of Aristotle's *On Forms*. In the *Parmenides*, Plato in fact uses a One Over Many Assumption to criticize the theory, by suggesting that it, together with several other assumptions, lands the Theory of Forms in an unhappy regress which shows it to be untenable (see esp. *Prm*. 132A1–4).

For these reasons, we should be chary of any easy endorsement of the unchecked suggestion to the effect that Plato relies – or relies unreflectively, or relies for the duration of his career – on some form of One Over Many Assumption, understood either metaphysically or semantically. Still, we can proceed by bracketing the question of the legitimacy of Aristotle's ascription and engage a purely philosophical question, one we can answer ourselves: does the One Over Many Assumption have the untoward consequences Aristotle drops on its doorstep? The answer will depend in part upon why we should think that the argument as stated entails that there are Forms for negations. Taken one unsympathetic way, it seems, it might. If we think that the notion of a "common attribute" in (1) embraces any true thing that we can say of any disparate group of objects, including even that none of them is *F*, that they are not-*F*, surely the implication would follow. Still, it is altogether appropriate for Plato or anyone else to respond that there are any number of more restricted conceptions of commonality to which the argument might reasonably appeal, beginning with the thought that the objects in question must have some *positive* attribute or that the attribute held in common must be in one way or another *natural*. While any such retort places an onus on the respondent to specify what is meant by "positive" or "natural" in this connection, it seems reasonable to suppose that anyone embracing any form of a One Over Many Assumption will be thinking along these lines. That is, the respondent can be expected to say whether, e.g., *being mortal* is positive or negative, or whether, e.g., *being a country*, as opposed to *having a positive charge*, is, in the required sense, natural. Even so, there is no reason to suppose up front that no such account could be provided. More to the point, there is nothing in Aristotle's objection to the One Over Many Argument which suggests that no such accounts could be forthcoming.

In view of these sorts of reactions, which are after all not difficult to fathom as arising from Plato himself (since, indeed, something approaching them is already suggested in the *Politicus*, at 262A–E), the force of Aristotle's argument is conditional at best. We cannot regard his complaint as devastating to the Theory of Forms; but neither is it idle. It raises an issue which Plato, or a Platonist, needs to address. That allowed, the One Over Many Argument itself provides no grounds for supposing that its own contentions are irreproachable. If that is right, then the argument is neither devastating nor ill-advised. It is, instead, a fruitful objection in an ongoing dialectical disputation. This is just how one could readily imagine life in the Academy.

Indeed, if we pay close attention to the presentation of Aristotle's argument given by Alexander of Aphrodisias, we learn something still more striking: Aristotle does not himself think that the argument destroys all aspects of the Theory of Forms. According to Alexander (*On Forms*, 81.8–11), at any rate, Aristotle does think that the argument establishes the existence of something distinct from particulars, if not the existence of Forms. It is supposed to show that there are "common things" or "commonalities" (*koina*) which exist and which, while not capable of independent or everlasting existence, are nevertheless distinct from particulars. Now, if that is correct, then we find something quite interesting about the argument, that Aristotle himself is sympathetic to at least its first three steps, since it is only thereafter that Plato is represented as arguing that Forms can exist eternally and independently of particular things. Any such sympathy would immediately complicate our attitude towards Aristotle's criticism: the contention that the argument invites Forms for negations seems to enter the argument immediately, in the first premise, which contains the One Over Many Assumption. That ought to be regarded as surprising, since if the argument really does generate Forms unwanted by Plato, Forms corresponding to negations, then so too should it generate unwanted common things, since if it is true for Plato that horses, trees, and a little girl's elbow are in common *not men*, then so too is it true for Aristotle. More pointedly, if the argument commends the existence of common things at all, then the common things it countenances must be common for both Plato and Aristotle. Thus, Aristotle can restrict the range of the common things covered by the first premise if – and only if – Plato can.

It turns out, then, that the dialectical interaction captured by the One Over Many Argument is less transparent than it might otherwise seem. Accordingly, we should not expect Plato to bow down before such an objection, especially when the objection, if compelling, seems equally to cut against its author. In this instance, if Plato has something to learn from Aristotle, then Aristotle likewise has something to learn from Plato.

The Good and the Goods

An equally complex and engaging exchange between Plato and Aristotle pertains to the nature of the Good. In a memorable passage of the *Nicomachean Ethics*, we find Aristotle speaking rather tenderly of Plato, if not by name then by implication. In the midst of providing his own positive account of the human good, Aristotle pauses and notes:

> We had probably better examine the universal good and run through the puzzles concerning what is meant by it, even if this sort of inquiry is unwelcome to us because of the fact that those who introduced the Forms are our friends. Even so, it is better, and indeed our duty, to destroy even what is close to us for the purpose of preserving the truth, especially if we are philosophers. For though we love them both, piety requires us to honor the truth above our friends. (*EN* 1096a11–17)

In the *Republic*, Plato had, famously in view of its pre-eminence relative to other Forms, given pride of place to the Form of the Good (*R*. 504E7–509c4) (see 24: PLATO'S CONCEPT OF GOODNESS). Aristotle has some suspicions about Plato's conception of the Good which induce him to destroy – or to attempt to destroy – a central feature of that Form, even though his doing so puts him at variance with one of the deepest teachings of someone he holds dear. So much, he reflects, is the duty of the philosopher. So much is indeed the duty of the philosopher – of any lover of wisdom, as the name "philosopher" signifies. If a brilliant physicist comes to detect a flaw in his dissertation director's most celebrated theoretical result, his duty, however affectionate he may feel towards his teacher, is to expose the flaw to the light of day.

The dominant flaw Aristotle claims to detect in Plato's conception of the universal good concerns a *univocity assumption*. To understand what is meant by this complaint, let us return to a passage from Plato already discussed, that "We are everywhere accustomed to positing some one Form for each of the many things to which we apply the same name" (*R*. 596A6–7). So far we have focused on the questions of whether this thesis is best understood semantically or metaphysically (or both), and of whether, however it is taken, it implicates Plato in an unwelcome One Over Many Assumption. Now, though, we may focus on another feature of Plato's suggestion: he seems to assume that there is *one*, and only one, Form associated with every general term, including, then, with each key philosophical general term. The idea is that if we begin to analyze a given philosophical notion – say, justice or piety or knowledge or causation or consciousness – we can safely proceed on the assumption that there is just one thing we are seeking to analyze. We can suppose, that is, that if we analyze, e.g., justice successfully, at the end of the day we will have arrived at an essence-displaying definition which captures the nature of justice such that the definition is *single* and *non-disjunctive* (see 6: PLATONIC DEFINITIONS AND FORMS). The successful definition will be single in the sense that it will display just one essence; and it will be non-disjunctive in that it will need no recourse to disjunctions to be complete. To illustrate, suppose we consider as a definition of what it is to be a *successful person* the following:

X is a successful person =$_{df}$ (a) *x* has made a lot of money, or (b) *x* is happy.

In some sense, we have a single definition before us. In another sense, however, it is plain that two very different things are being said: to begin, many people who have made a lot of money are unhappy and many more people who are happy have not made a lot of money. So, even if the definition were otherwise acceptable, it would not have captured any single trait which all and only successful people have in common. For this reason, disjunctive definitions may be assumed to violate a univocity assumption.

Aristotle's complaint about his friends' conception of the Good is, then, that they have, without warrant, adopted a univocity assumption, an assumption to the effect that there is some one property held in common by all and only good things, and that the nature of goodness can be grasped as something simple and non-disjunctive.

The interest of this complaint resides partly in the fact that when we turn from trifling illustrations to philosophically interesting cases, it is often difficult to determine whether univocity is or is not reasonably assumed. Two simple examples show this. First, suppose we want to provide an account of *consciousness*. As we proceed, we may or may not be justified in assuming that there is some one common property had by all and only conscious beings insofar as they are conscious beings. Some philosophers contend that what makes a being conscious is not some one feature at all; it is, rather, a cluster of closely related features, the presence of some subset of which suffices for being conscious. Others counter that those claiming to have isolated discrete traits of consciousness are simply unfinished: when the analysis is complete, they contend, it will be unified. Second, for an example somewhat closer to the dialectical relationship of Plato and Aristotle, consider *friendship*. We speak of friendship as obtaining between children and between adults, between political allies and between business associates, and even between persons and abstract classes: "He has always been a true friend to the working man." Is there some one relationship, friendship, which all of these parties bear to one another? There may be; but this is not obviously so. Even upon a cursory inspection, we discover that in some cases the relation appears symmetrical and in others not. Philosophers concerning themselves which such inquiries can and should reflect on the prospects for univocity in their final account.

Aristotle criticizes Plato for failing to reflect adequately on the prospects for univocity in the case of *goodness*. In fact, Aristotle thinks he can show that goodness is positively *non-univocal*, so that any talk of *a* Form of the Good, of a single Form for all Good things, is already misguided. Now, Plato does surely sometimes talk this way, as when he speaks of "the Idea [= Form] of the Good, from which everything that is good and right receives its value for us" (R. 505A2–4). Aristotle's counter is direct: "the good cannot be something universal, common [to all good things] and single" (EN 1096a28).

If we are inclined to suppose that Forms are meanings, as semantic values for general terms, then we may also be immediately inclined to accept Aristotle's complaint. We call a vast array of distinct sorts of things *good*: moral agents, opera performances, desserts, economic systems, ripostes, artificial hearts, and periods of time. Surely when we say that capitalism is good we mean something other than when we say that a joke is good? If someone says that capitalism is good, presumably she means *inter alia* that it is *an efficient and just sociopolitical system*; by contrast, when we say a joke is good, we mean that it is *funny*. Obviously, being funny is not the same as being an efficient and just sociopolitical system. Because these paraphrases of "good" are clearly different in meaning, we may infer that what is meant by "good" in these distinct applications must also differ in meaning. Given that these sorts of examples could easily be multiplied, goodness is not only, one might conclude, non-univocal, but wildly so.

412

Plato should not be so easily dissuaded from his univocity assumption regarding goodness. To begin, we are already assuming something he need not, even if he does intend his Forms to be semantic values of general terms, namely that corresponding to each general term is a single Form which answers to every *shallow* or *lexical* meaning. Plainly, Plato does not think that. When, for example, Meno reports at the back end of a Socratic *elenchus* that he cannot say at all what *virtue* is, even though he has, in his own estimation, given many fine speeches on that very topic, he gives no indication that he never knew the meaning of the word adequate to the purpose of speechifying (*Men.* 80A9–B4). Rather, as he says, he cannot say *what it is* (80B4). What Meno means, and what Plato understands him to mean, is that he cannot specify the essence of virtue (see 8: SOCRATIC IGNORANCE). Every time he dips below the surface, Meno ends up contradicting himself. This does not disqualify him from using the word "virtue" in his daily business; but it does reveal him as someone without any appreciation of the *deep meaning*, or essence, of the words whose shallow meaning he has grasped. It is for this reason open to Plato to resist any easy objection to the effect that he had wrongly assumed the univocity of goodness. Plato, like Aristotle, practices philosophy and not lexicography. Even if the shallow meanings of "good" diverge across a range of applications, it remains possible that there is yet a single, non-disjunctive essence of goodness underlying all correct shallow meanings the term may have acquired in daily discourse. Indeed, one might even suggest that there must be such an underlying notion which implicitly controls the acceptable range of applications as somehow normative for its extension.

Aristotle's objection to Plato's univocity assumption therefore grows interesting only when it emerges that he has a purely non-lexical objection, rooted not in ordinary language but in some putative facts about Aristotle's own theory of *categories*. In fact, Aristotle aligns the non-univocity of goodness with a highly technical thesis of his own, that *being* is non-univocal. He contends that goodness is univocal if and only if being is univocal; but since, he maintains, being is non-univocal, neither is goodness. He argues:

> Since the good is spoken of in as many ways as being is – for it is spoken of in the category of substance, for example god and mind; in quality, the virtues; in quantity, a suitable amount; in relative, the useful; in time, the propitious; in place, a location; and in other categories other such things – it is clear that the good cannot be something universal, common to all good things and single. For if it were, it would not be spoken of in all the categories, but in one only. (*EN* 1096a23–9)

Whatever we are to make of the ultimate success or failure of Aristotle's objection, it should be immediately clear that he does not suppose that he can refute Plato's univocity assumption merely by pointing to disjointed lexical meanings. On the contrary, Aristotle thinks that he must advert to some highly technical apparatus of his own in an effort to make his case.

That apparatus is the theory of categories. Aristotle contends that there are irreducibly distinct sorts of beings, including substances (e.g., Socrates or his horse), qualities (e.g., being pale or being swift), quantities (e.g., weighing 170 pounds or being

16 hands). Crucially, Aristotle maintains that what it is for each of these irreducibly distinct categories to exist is also distinct. That is, not only is it the case that *what it is to be a quantity* differs from *what it is to be a quality*, for that is uncontroversial, but also, and what is by contrast surely controversial, that what it is *for a quality to exist* differs from what it is *for a quantity to exist*. Presumably, Aristotle is contending that if we analyze the notion of existence as it attaches to the various categories, we will turn up different properties or attributes, not some one feature that all and only existing things share. Aristotle sometimes seeks to shore up this contention by maintaining that being is not a genus (e.g., *APo.* 92b14; *Top.* 121a16–19, b7–9; *Metaph.* 998b17–28). Whatever else we think about this suggestion, we should agree that Aristotle does not proceed by assuming that we can simply see, on the basis of our linguistic competence, that either being or goodness is non-univocal. Accordingly, once again, we should not expect Plato to be at all moved away from his univocity assumption by any such shallow linguistic data. (For a fuller introduction to Aristotle's theory of categories, see Shields 2003: 111–16.)

Instead, if there is to be a telling objection against Plato's univocity assumption, it will have to derive from deeper theoretical concerns deriving from Aristotle's theory of categories (see 11: KNOWLEDGE AND THE FORMS IN PLATO). Although the role the categories play in Aristotle's anti-Platonic argument has been disputed, the basic structure seems clear:

1   Goodness is univocal if, and only if, being is univocal.
2   If the theory of categories is correct, being is non-univocal.
3   The theory of categories is correct.
4   Hence, being is non-univocal.
5   Hence, goodness is non-univocal.

Now it turns out that Aristotle's objection to Plato is highly theoretical, because it requires for its eventual appraisal the acceptance of at least some of the rudimentary features of Aristotle's category theory. It is also, to this degree, less general in scope and also less immediately damaging than some of Plato's detractors might assume.

In any event, in arguing as he does, Aristotle opens to Plato at least two courses of response. First, he might query the coupling of being and goodness: why accept (1)? Second, even granting (1), Plato might attack (2) and (3) in conjunction with one another.

Thinking first about (1), Plato might reasonably wonder why goodness must be univocal if and only if being is. We have seen that Aristotle draws the comparison by suggesting that being and goodness march in step insofar as each of them can be used across the divergent categories. So, to develop only a partial example, we are supposed to appreciate, according to Aristotle, the following pairings:

	Being	*Goodness*
Substance:	Socrates exists.	Socrates is good.
Quality:	Virtue exists.	Virtue is good.
Quantity:	A suitable amount exists.	A suitable amount is good.

And so on for the remaining categories. Moving beyond lexical meaning, we are meant to appreciate that just as what it is for Socrates to exist differs from what it is for virtue to exist and so again for a suitable amount, so too is there a directly analogous difference between what it is for Socrates to be good, for virtue to be good, and for a suitable amount to be good. In each case, evidently, it is the analyzed, or theoretically motivated account which is in question.

Minimally, if that is so, we are not in a position to agree with either Plato or Aristotle until we have the analyzed notions set before us. Accordingly, if we are inclined at least provisionally to accept a univocity assumption for goodness, we need not despair of our prospects for ultimate success any time before our final analyses are complete. In this respect, Aristotle's assaults on Platonic univocity, while they may resonate with contemporary readers enamored of Wittgenstein-inspired talk of family resemblances, are in the end only as cogent as the analyses Plato or Aristotle (or their contemporary supporters) might eventually produce. For this reason, now perhaps unsurprisingly, we learn that Aristotle's assaults on Platonic univocity are simultaneously more complex and less immediately compelling than they may at first appear. For the beginning of Aristotle's argument, (1), that goodness is univocal if, and only if, being is univocal, is the beginning of a conversation rather than an established conclusion. (For more on the possible ways to develop Aristotle's argument against the univocity of goodness, see Shields 1999: 194–216.)

Indeed, someone might well attempt at this juncture to turn Aristotle's (1) against him, not by objecting to it but rather by accepting it and then going on to reject the combination of (2) and (3). Suppose, that is, that we grant (1) but then insist that to the degree that Aristotle's category scheme is defensible it is so only because all of the ultimate kinds he identifies are precisely kinds of existing things, so that being is after all itself spoken of univocally. There would be some point in this sort of contention. Suppose, e.g., that Plato argues that a given Form exists and that it is a certain sort of quality, one which is mind- and language-independent and which exists without being instantiated. Aristotle, we imagine, denies the existence of this sort of quality. Still, Plato and Aristotle both agree, let us say, that Socrates exists. Plato, or a Platonist, might now insist that what Aristotle grants to Socrates, he withholds from Platonic Forms, namely existence. If it were something other than the very same attribute that Socrates manifests, then Aristotle would presumably need also to allow that the sentence "Socrates exists but Forms do not," is actually equivocal, heading in the direction, though perhaps not so overt, as "The king carried a sack of grain and the hopes of a nation on his shoulders," or "Lady Elizabeth's aspirations were shattered; so was her best crystal." Again, it may be that Aristotle will prove vindicated in arguing for a covert non-univocity in existence; but it is by no means obvious that he will prevail. On the contrary, the Platonist has a point in insisting that all talk of different senses or kinds of existence will prove too tenuous to discern, and will be established, if at all, only on the basis of theories which will themselves prove open to independent objection. (For more on the prospects of establishing the non-univocity of being, see Shields 1999: 217–66.)

Now, according to this line of response, if being really is, as (1) asserts, in precisely the same situation as goodness regarding its univocity, then it will turn out, against Aristotle, and for Plato, that goodness too is univocal. Here too, then, we have not a refutation of Plato, nor even a stalemate between Plato and Aristotle, but rather the beginning of a deep and decidedly difficult ongoing inquiry into the natures of being and goodness and the relationship, if any, between them. It is fair to say that Aristotle mounts an important challenge to a central Platonic thesis regarding the nature of goodness; but it is equally fair to observe that Plato need not be crushed by the challenge. Instead, as one might well imagine, their opposing viewpoints on this topic prove resistant to facile first rebuttals.

Conclusions

Plato and Aristotle spent two decades, off and on, in each other's company. They were, of course, not the only members of the Academy, and any full history of that school which focused exclusively on the two of its members favored by posterity would be woefully incomplete, however plausible history's judgment of their pre-eminence may be. It is nonetheless clear from their surviving writings that interactions between Plato and Aristotle are especially consequential for them both. Their criticisms are not only far-reaching, but also doubtless mutually edifying. When we consider just two sources of disagreement – Plato's One Over Many and Univocity Assumptions – we see directly that Aristotle has put his finger on the pulse of something deep and animating in Platonic metaphysics; and we see at the same time that Plato need not merely cede Aristotle's objections to him. On the contrary, Aristotle's criticisms, although at times trenchant, prove less immediately decisive than some have supposed, even while they do pose deep and probing challenges to some of Plato's most distinctive and cherished theses. Consequently, if those who follow Plato will have difficulty meeting all of Aristotle's objections, those who find Aristotle's often keen observations immediately decisive will be unpleasantly surprised if they fail to give Plato his due.

We learn a fair bit about Plato from Aristotle and a fair bit about Aristotle from Plato. From them both, individually and then again in common, we learn how philosophy may be practiced at its most lively dialectical zenith.

Note

All translations are the author's.

References and further reading

Burnet, J. (1928). *Platonism.* Berkeley: University of California Press.

Cherniss, H. (1944). *Aristotle's Criticisms of Plato and the Academy.* Baltimore: Johns Hopkins University Press.

Düring, I. (1957). *Aristotle in the Ancient Biographical Tradition.* Stockholm: Amqvist and Wiksell.

Düring, I. and Owen, G. E. L. (1960). *Aristotle and Plato in the Mid-Fourth Century.* Stockholm: Almqvist and Wiksell.

Fine, G. (1980). The one over many. *Philosophical Review* 89, pp. 197–240.

—— (1993). *On Ideas: Aristotle's Criticisms of Plato's Theory of Forms.* Oxford: Oxford University Press.

—— (2003). Plato and Aristotle on form and substance. In G. Fine (ed.) *Plato on Knowledge and Forms* (pp. 397–425). Oxford: Oxford University Press.

Guthrie, W. K. C. (1981). Aristotle: an encounter. In *A History of Greek Philosophy*, vol. 6 (pp. 4–26). Cambridge: Cambridge University Press.

Owen, G. E. L. (1968). Dialectic and eristic in the treatment of the forms. In G. E. L. Owen (ed.) *Aristotle on Dialectic: The* Topics (pp. 103–25). Oxford: Oxford University Press.

Shields, C. (1999). *Order in Multiplicity: Homonymy in the Philosophy of Aristotle.* Oxford: Oxford University Press.

—— (2003). *Classical Philosophy: A Contemporary Introduction* (see chs. 2 and 3). New York: Routledge.

28

Plato and Hellenistic Philosophy

A. A. LONG

Orientation

How was Plato interpreted and utilized by philosophers in the Hellenistic epoch, meaning the period of Greek culture that runs from about 322 to 31 BCE? Who were his admirers and detractors during these three centuries? Which of his voluminous works were most closely studied, and which of his methodologies and theories had the strongest afterlife throughout this time? In order to take up these large questions, we need to begin with a sketch of the internal history of the post-Platonic Academy and its relation to the new developments in philosophy constituted by Early Pyrrhonism, Epicureanism, and Stoicism.

At the time of his death in the year 347 Plato's philosophical legacy consisted of most of the dialogues that have been transmitted under his name; and it also included the oral teaching he had conducted with his associates in the Academy. The fertility of this legacy was enormous, but it did not yet provide a clear and systematic synopsis of anything sufficiently unified to be called Platonism. Plato had not identified his own opinions in his dialogues, and his oral teaching was probably more speculative than firmly doctrinal. Up to about 274 BCE his successors in the Academy mainly devoted themselves to codifying a set of positions that they took to be Platonic or Platonizing doctrines, a project we can also observe Aristotle conducting from within his own school (see 27: LEARNING ABOUT PLATO FROM ARISTOTLE). The principal subjects of this exegetical interest were metaphysics and cosmology, and the Platonic work that received most attention, unsurprisingly, was the *Timaeus*; for here, if anywhere, Plato's students seemed to have a comprehensive account of the world's structure and the human condition from their master's pen. The *Timaeus* was the subject of a commentary by the Academic philosopher Crantor, writing at the end of the fourth century (see Dillon 2003). And throughout the Hellenistic epoch, the discourse Plato puts into the voice of the (probably fictional) astronomer Timaeus, notwithstanding its difficulty and disclaimer to exactitude, would prove to be the main source for summary accounts of Plato's own thought.

The early Academic codification of Plato's philosophy, principally executed by Speusippus and Xenocrates, was probably available in book form to all Hellenistic philosophers. Yet, rather than instigating a continuous development of doctrinal

Platonism, it was interrupted within the Academy itself by that school's dramatic turn, under the headship of Arcesilaus, to interpreting Plato's philosophical message as one of entirely exploratory dialectic, from which no substantive doctrines are ascertainable. For the next two centuries Academic philosophers would be characterized as "those who suspend judgment about everything" or, in modern parlance, as skeptics.

The reasons why this remarkable shift took place will concern us later. What needs to be emphasized now is that Academic skepticism, in spite of its ostensible allegiance to Plato, was a new development in philosophy rather than a continuation of the Academic exegesis that had begun before the period we moderns call Hellenistic.

In the main, the questions with which I began this chapter are about how Plato was viewed by members of the four philosophical movements that are often referred to collectively as Hellenistic philosophy: Early Pyrrhonism, Epicureanism, Stoicism, and the skeptical Academy. All these movements owed their origin to charismatic and near contemporary teachers: Pyrrho, Epicurus, Zeno the founder of Stoicism, and Arcesilaus. Only the last of the four claimed affinity with Plato; but, while Early Pyrrhonism and Epicureanism are markedly anti-Platonic in their respective outlooks and methodologies, Zeno, though hostile to Plato's metaphysics, made Stoicism a philosophy that captured enough of Plato's legacy, as the years went by, to make Antiochus, a prominent Academic at the time of Cicero, claim that the main differences between the Academy and the Stoa were terminological rather than substantive (see Cicero, *De legibus* I.54–5). By his time the rigorously skeptical phase of the Academy had largely run out of steam. Henceforth, as the Hellenistic epoch was succeeded by the Roman Imperial period, most Platonists reverted to a study of Plato that concentrated on identifying systematic doctrine from within the dialogues, ushering in the movements that we call Middle Platonism and Neoplatonism.

My focus in this chapter, then, is largely restricted to a period when Plato was not being studied by philosophers systematically, not even within the Academy itself. Plato is a significant presence in Hellenistic philosophy, but one that casts a large shadow rather than being visible in full frontal identity. His relative obscurity – which is not the same thing as his never questioned renown – is due not only to the dominance of the new Hellenistic philosophies but also to the extremely fragmentary state of our evidence (see 2: INTERPRETING PLATO). We can infer positive or negative recourse to Platonic concepts and contexts more often than we are able to attach explicit acknowledgements of them; and the leading Academic skeptics (Arcesilaus and Carneades) refrained from publication, probably in imitation of Socrates. What all philosophers in this period did with Plato is not unlike the way we ourselves make use of a seminal thinker of the past. Although the Academic skeptics were doubtless sincere in claiming to be Plato's true heirs, they had their own complex agenda. As for the other schools, they criticized or drew on Plato as and when he had something to say that was relevant to issues germane to their own thought rather than out of any interest in interpreting him for his own sake.

The status of Plato in Hellenistic philosophy is also complicated by the positions the new schools adopted with reference to Socrates. Along with Xenophon, but to a much greater extent, Plato was the principal source for the life and philosophy of Socrates. Stoicism throughout its history deemed itself to be "Socratic" as distinct from being avowedly Platonic, but Socrates, in his professed identity as one who knew nothing and devoted himself to a critical examination of other people's opinions, was also the principal inspiration of the Academic skeptics. In fact, these philosophers, starting with Arcesilaus, took the Stoics as their main targets. Their motivation for doing so clearly included a strong desire to wrest the great figure of Socrates away from the Stoics and situate him exclusively in the Academy. In Epicureanism, on the other hand, Socrates was the target of unremitting criticism, and Pyrrho's publicist, Timon, mocked him in his satirical verses, conforming to his project of undercutting every philosopher other than Pyrrho himself.

Although the Hellenistic philosophers drew most of their reflections on Socrates from Plato, they chiefly identified his thought and methodology, as Aristotle had already done, by reference to the Socrates that Plato portrays in the dialogues we take to precede the *Republic* and other works where Plato seems to use Socrates to present full-blooded theories of his own. Because the Hellenistic philosophers largely separated Socrates from Plato, I shall follow suit, but in doing so I do not wish to imply that this procedure has strong backing as far as the historical Socrates is concerned; for I strongly doubt whether anything that Plato attributes to Socrates can be fully detached from Plato's authorship and philosophical intentions.

There was, of course, more to Plato's presence in Hellenistic culture than can be gleaned just from studying the fragmentary record of that period's philosophers. The man himself was an obvious subject for biographers, and his dialogues seem to have acquired classic status instantly (see 1: THE LIFE OF PLATO OF ATHENS). The corpus of them that we possess was presumably available in the book trade from an early date. By about 300 BCE it probably already included many of the spurious works that ancient editors have transmitted under Plato's name, most of which were probably written within the Academy, perhaps as student exercises. The present division of the dialogues into tetralogies was the work of Thrasyllus, writing in the early Roman Empire, but Aristophanes of Byzantium had already classified them, for the famous Alexandrian Library, into fifteen trilogies (Diogenes Laertius [*DL*] 3.62). Members of the Academy may well have made still earlier classifications. The *Life of Arcesilaus* composed by Diogenes Laertius goes out of its way to report that Arcesilaus "was in possession of Plato's books" (*DL* 4.33), which might mean not simply that he owned a complete copy of Plato but that he had acquired Plato's personal library, something that would be entirely in keeping with his status as a head of the Academy.

Plato in Stoicism

When the Cypriot Zeno arrived in Athens in about 310 BCE, he was initially drawn to the Cynics, who looked back to Socrates and his follower Antisthenes as well as Diogenes in their asceticism and contempt for purely conventional values. Diogenes and Plato, according to our sources, shared a mutual antipathy, which helps to explain the fact that Zeno's most famous and probably earliest work, *Republic*, appears to have been a Cynicizing and radically utopian retort to Plato's work of that name.

We have only a sketchy outline of the content of Zeno's *Republic*, but what survives of it is sufficient to show the work's critical relationship to the Platonic original (see Long and Sedley 1987: ch. 67). Zeno endorsed Plato's goal of a completely concordant community, but he went much further than Plato in his proposals for achieving civic unification. He eliminated Plato's tripartite class structure, envisioning a male and female citizenship that would be completely wise and virtuous, require no legal statutes, and be cemented by both homoerotic and heterosexual love. He extended Plato's abolition of the nuclear family and use of coinage to everyone in the state, and advocated unisex clothing combined with partial nudity. The rationale behind Zeno's *Republic* was that moral knowledge is sufficient to equalize all other differences between persons and provide them with all that they need in order to flourish as individuals and as communities.

The two *Republics*, with their implicit approval of many Spartan practices, are not sufficiently divergent to make Zeno's work a comprehensive attack on Plato. Yet Zeno and the Stoic tradition he initiated marked their differences from Plato in many other significant ways. They reduced Platonic Forms to mere conceptions, they denied the existence of anything incorporeal, and they rejected the immortality of the soul, while allowing that virtuous souls have a limited post-mortem duration. If we take Platonism to represent a view of the physical world as the imperfect copy of an ideal original, a world of *seeming* rather than fully *being*, opinable rather than knowable, with a transcendently divine author, Stoicism presents itself as a firmly physicalist and this-worldly philosophy. These are certainly deep differences, but they are not sufficient to exclude from Stoicism other areas of strong indebtedness and affinity to Plato. In order to identify these creative borrowings, we need to begin by reviewing the formative influences the Stoics derived from their reflections on Plato's Socratic dialogues.

It was probably Zeno's allegiance to Socrates that led him to enroll as a student with Polemo, head of the Academy from about 314 to 276. The little that we know about Polemo suggests that his principal interests were ethical theory and practice rather than metaphysics, though his predecessor Xenocrates had not neglected ethics. If, as seems likely, Polemo was distinctive among early Academics in beginning to emphasize the Socratic elements in Plato's dialogues, Arcesilaus' rigorous adoption of that stance would lose some of its abrupt breach with the immediately preceding work of the Academy.

Much of Stoic ethics is a creative formalization of positions for which Plato's Socrates argues in such dialogues as *Apology*, *Gorgias*, *Protagoras*, and especially *Euthydemus*. This is not to say that Zeno and his followers drew the Socratic tenor of their ethics solely from Plato and Polemo (on Polemo's probable influence see Dillon 2003: ch. 4). What we know of Antisthenes, exiguous though it is, strikingly foreshadows Stoic doctrine, especially in its focus on the complete self-sufficiency and impregnability that virtue and wisdom generate (*DL* 6.10–13). But, although Antisthenes was a forerunner whom the Stoics also honored, Plato's Socratic dialogues exhibit Socrates arguing for identical propositions to much that is attributed to Antisthenes, including, above all, the thesis that virtue is sufficient for happiness. Consequently, there is every reason to think that the Platonic dialogues I have just mentioned were central to Stoic philosophy in its formative years.

The most fundamental doctrines of Stoic ethics were (1) the unqualified restriction of goodness to ethical excellence; (2), as a corollary to (1), the indifference to happiness of all bodily and external advantages or disadvantages (conventionally deemed good or bad respectively); (3) the necessity and sufficiency of ethical excellence for happiness; and (4) the conception of ethical excellence as a kind of knowledge or craft. There can be no doubt that, in defending these doctrines, the Stoics took themselves to be authentically Socratic, and little doubt that, in doing so, they drew especially on Socrates' main argument in Plato's *Euthd.* 278E–281E (see Long 1996: 23–32 and Striker 1996).

There Socrates attempts to convince his interlocutor that the foundation of happiness is simply and exclusively knowledge or wisdom. All other so-called goods, such as wealth, health, and honor are beneficial and superior to their opposites if and only if they are correctly, i.e., wisely and knowledgeably, used (see 18: THE SOCRATIC PARADOXES). Otherwise they are more harmful than their opposites. Neither do wealth and the like, just by themselves, have any positive value, nor do poverty and the like, just by themselves, have any negative value. Socrates concludes:

> Of the other things [i.e., everything except wisdom and ignorance], none is either good or bad, but of these two things, one – wisdom – is good, and the other – ignorance – is bad. (*Euthd.* 281E3–5)

This argument provided Zeno not only with Socratic authority for the doctrines I outlined above. More specifically, it offered him support for his essential concept of "intermediate" or "indifferent" things, neither good nor bad in themselves, but materials for wisdom or ethical knowledge to use well. Moreover, it is highly probable that a crucial ambiguity or equivocation in the argument helped to feed a great disagreement between Zeno and his leading disciple Aristo.

According to Zeno, although only ethical excellence is strictly good and constitutive of happiness, and only ethical failings are strictly bad and constitutive of misery, such indifferent things as health and wealth have positive value and their opposites corresponding disvalue. Aristo disagreed. He rejected Zeno's categories of "preferred" and "dispreferred" indifferent things, holding that the grounds for selecting one of these over the other was nothing intrinsic to the value of the items themselves, but solely a wise or knowledgeable decision. Aristo's position was heterodox (as was his restriction of Stoic philosophy to ethics, in imitation of Socrates). However, he could say that it was exactly true to the letter of Socrates' argument in the *Euthydemus*, where no intrinsic value is attributed to things like wealth and no intrinsic disvalue to things like poverty. Zeno, on the other hand, could say that, notwithstanding Socrates' statement to that effect, Socrates had also argued that wisely used wealth and the like were greater *goods* than their opposites (see 24: PLATO'S CONCEPT OF GOODNESS). As formulated, Socrates' argument equivocates between the position that health and the like have no intrinsic value (Aristo's doctrine) and the position that they are greater goods than their opposites if they are well used. Zeno's solution to the equivocation was to deny that they are ever good, but to credit them with "preferential value."

There are other Socratic contexts in Plato that the Stoics probably drew upon in elaborating their own ethics and moral psychology (see Sedley 1993; Striker 1996; and Vander Waerdt 1994). For the sake of brevity, I offer this one example, choosing it because it shows that they were creative as well as imitative in their appropriation of Plato's Socrates.

The *Timaeus*, as I have mentioned, was Plato's most salient work for his Academic successors. It also furnished the Stoics, though not exclusively or perhaps directly, with many of their principal ideas in cosmology and theology. By way of access to this complex subject, I can do no better than quote the following report:

> The Stoics say that fire is the element of existing things, just as Heraclitus does, and its principles are matter and god, as Plato says. But Zeno says that both of these are bodies, both that which acts and that which is acted upon, whereas Plato says that the primary active cause is incorporeal. (Aristocles, quoted by Eusebius, *Praeparatio Evangelica* 15, 816D = *Stoicorum Veterum Fragmenta* 1.98, ed. von Arnim)

The Stoics' recourse to Heraclitus as a precursor of their cosmology is well attested and standard history, but it is only recently that scholars have adequately recognized Stoic indebtedness to the *Timaeus*, or, to be more precise, to ways in which that text was being expounded in the early Hellenistic period (see Reydams-Schils 1999: ch. 1). Plato, of course, does not literally say that the world consists of active and passive principles, named god and matter respectively. That is an exact description of the Stoics' position. However, in a probably Hellenistic summary of Plato's doctrines, god and matter are named as his principles, with the latter characterized, as in Stoicism, as "formless," and the former as "mind" and "cause" (*DL* 3.69). Is this a projection of Stoicism onto Plato? Hardly, because Theophrastus, Zeno's older contemporary at the Peripatos, had already given a virtually identical paraphrase of the *Timaeus* and also said that Plato attaches the active causal principle to "the power of god and of the good" (see Theophrastus fr. 230, in Fortenbaugh et al. 1992). As Sedley remarks,

> It is hard to believe that this highly revisionist interpretation is one that Theophrastus had arrived at simply by his own reading of the *Timaeus*. He surely must be echoing a way in which that text was currently being expounded in Plato's school – a hypothesis which would also comfortably explain how the matter–god doctrine passed in due course into the Stoicism of Polemo's pupil Zeno. (1998: 349)

Plato's interpreters of the *Timaeus* were faced with many problems. The cosmology Timaeus elaborates includes a triad of principles: (1) the divine and benevolent Demiurge; (2) the Form of Living Being, which the Demiurge takes as his ideal model for creating the World-Soul and the World-Body; and (3) the mysterious Receptacle in which the Demiurge constructs Elements with geometrical shape out of the physical traces present before the cosmos was created. Was the divine act of creation to be understood literally or only metaphorically? What was the relation of the Demiurge to the Form of the Good or to the cosmic Mind and World-Soul Plato writes about in other late dialogues? How was the mysterious Receptacle to be conceptualized? (see 14: THE ROLE OF COSMOLOGY IN PLATO'S PHILOSOPHY).

We cannot say how Plato would have reacted to the reduction of this complex scheme to the twin principles, god and matter, but as an exegetical exercise it was a brilliant move. It allowed the Demiurge to be identified with the Form of the Good, the World-Soul, and cosmic Mind or Cause, while the Receptacle could be more tractably interpreted as the purely plastic matter that divine causality acts upon. As for the

Forms that the Demiurge takes as his model, some Platonists interpreted them as the thoughts of god, and that interpretation may go right back to the time of Polemo (see Dillon 1977: 95).

What we have in Stoic cosmology and theology (setting aside their notions of periodic world conflagration and everlasting recurrence) is a very close adaptation of this scheme, modified to accommodate the basic Stoic postulate that only bodies can engage in causal interaction. Taking their cue from Heraclitus, the Stoics identified their divine causal principle with what they called "designing fire." By acting upon matter, this principle generates the four elements and functions within the cosmos as the World-Soul. As such, it distributes itself throughout all the world's matter, organizing everything according to what the Stoics called "seminal principles" (*spermatikoi logoi*). (For the basic evidence, see Long and Sedley 1987: chs. 44–7.) Here we see how the Stoics have incorporated Plato's Forms, under the interpretation god's thoughts, into their cosmology.

It was a basic Stoic datum that the divine causal principle is completely providential, organizing the world as a cosmic city for the benefit of its divine and human inhabitants (Arius Didymus, quoted by Eusebius, *Praeparatio Evangelica* 15.15.3–5 = Long and Sedley 1987: 67 L). Plato in the *Timaeus* (30A) had attributed unrestricted benevolence to the Demiurge, and the rational World-Soul he postulates in the *Laws* (X.897B) organizes everything for the best. However, Plato is not as explicit as the Stoics in the anthropocentric motivations with which he endows his divine principle. The Stoics' most obvious precursor here was Xenophon (*Mem.* 4.3), who credits Socrates with an unqualifiedly anthropocentric theology. As evidence for this, Socrates cites the organization of the seasons, the earth's resources, human intelligence and language, and the provision of animals entirely for human use. There is no question that Xenophon's text was of primary importance to the Stoics (see Sextus Empiricus, *M.* 9.92–103). It also helps to explain how they could retain their professed allegiance to Socrates while also drawing so heavily on Plato's *Timaeus*. They knew that Socrates had disclaimed any interest in cosmological speculation on his own account, but they could justify their recourse to the Platonic cosmology by observing that Socrates himself is a listener to Timaeus' discourse, and indeed thoroughly approves the preamble of his speech and urges him to continue it (*Ti.* 29D).

From Zeno onward, as we have seen, the Stoics drew critically and constructively on certain works of Plato: the *Republic*, the *Euthydemus* and other Socratic dialogues, the *Timaeus*, and the cosmology expounded in Book X of the *Laws*. In fact, however, that tally gives only a selective impression of the attention they paid to the Platonic corpus. There is good reason to think that Zeno closely studied the *Theaetetus* in developing his celebrated theory of the *kataleptic* impression, the cognitive state that guarantees a completely accurate representation of its object (see Long 2002). Socrates in the dialogue had advanced the model of the mind as a wax tablet, which retains memory imprints of its perceptual objects. Zeno took over that model and adapted it to his own theory of impressions that accurately imprint their source object on the mind.

Another Platonic dialogue we can be confident the Stoics studied is the *Cratylus*. They were intensely interested in the origins and structure of language, including, as they proposed, its etymological roots in a mimetic relationship between sounds and significations. Some of the etymologies they canvassed are identical to ones that

Socrates advances in this dialogue, and, if I am right, they also took themselves to be improving upon the theories of meaning that the *Cratylus* explores (see Long 2005).

Even more central to the general thrust of Stoic philosophy was the critical reaction Chrysippus adopted to Plato's tripartite model of the soul. Rather than dividing the soul into a rational mind and the two irrational faculties ambition and appetite, as Plato does in the *Republic*, *Phaedrus*, and *Timaeus*, Chrysippus argued that a mature human soul is rational through and through; by which he meant that every action and emotion is motivated by a value judgment (see Long and Sedley 1987: ch. 65). He did not deny that human beings can be conflicted in their minds or that they can act irrationally or be overcome by passions. In such cases, what happens, according to Chrysippus, is not a struggle for dominance by distinct parts of the soul, as Plato had proposed. Rather, the mind, though it is a unity, is capable of making errors of judgment; in which case, though rational, it acts contrary to normative reason and hence irrationally as a whole.

This revisionist psychology is another telling example of Plato's afterlife in Hellenistic philosophy. Just as the Stoics in general knew and rejected the theory of Forms, so Chrysippus not only knew Plato's tripartite model of the soul; he also did with it what good philosophers at all times do with a worthy predecessor's controversial theory: he studied it, and having found it wanting, came up with his own highly creative alternative as a backhanded compliment to his target. Nor did the issue rest there. The Stoic Posidonius, Cicero's elder contemporary, criticized Chrysippus for failing to account adequately, with his unitary psychology, for irrational behavior. Accordingly, Posidonius advanced a tripartition of the soul's faculties, clearly modeled on Plato's accounts. For later Stoics Chrysippus' theory held sway. The point that matters for the subject of this essay is that virtually all of Plato's dialogues were texts that Stoics recognized they had to study and come to terms with.

In the early days of the Stoa, their recourse to Plato was probably more piecemeal and polemical, setting aside their keen appropriation of his portrayal of Socrates. For Panaetius and Posidonius, and for the Roman Stoics Seneca, Epictetus, and Marcus Aurelius, Plato as well as Socrates has become a virtual Stoic authority.

Plato in Academic Scepticism

While much of doctrinal Platonism found a welcome home in Stoic circles, the Hellenistic Academy, as we have already seen, attached its startling skeptical credentials to Plato himself. Cicero, speaking as an Academic, outlines Arcesilaus' position as follows:

> Arcesilaus, the pupil of Polemo, was the first to derive this principal point from various of Plato's books and from Socratic discourses – that there is nothing that the senses or the mind can grasp . . . He is said to have belittled every criterion of mind and sense, and begun the practice – though it was absolutely Socratic – not of indicating his own opinion, but of speaking against what anyone stated as his [i.e., the speaker's] opinion. (*De oratore* 3.67)

Rather than looking to Plato's dialogues as a source of substantive philosophy, the Hellenistic Academy focused on those works' representation of the critical dialectic which Socrates employs in questioning and refuting his opinionated interlocutors. As for Plato himself, they defended his skeptical posture by claiming that "in his books nothing is asserted and there is much argument pro and contra, everything is investigated and nothing is stated as certain" (Cicero, *Academica* 1.46).

Before considering what to make of this reading of Plato, we need to review the philosophical context in which Arcesilaus found himself as head of the Academy. This was Athens' premier school of philosophy, but, by the beginning of the third century BCE, its status as such was under considerable challenge. The Aristotelian Peripatos, under the direction of Theophrastus, was its oldest rival, but philosophy students now had many further options, including especially the Epicurean Garden and the Zenonian Stoa. They could also become disciples of Pyrrho or enroll with Cynics, Cyrenaics, or Dialecticians such as Diodorus Cronus. What was at stake here was not simply or mainly competition for pupils, but rather a plethora of conflicting philosophies, each with its own claims to allegiance and its own recipes for living a well-reasoned life. How was Arcesilaus as a Platonist to position himself and his long-standing school?

One of the best-attested facts about Arcesilaus is his controversy with Zeno, his older contemporary, concerning the Stoic's claims to have identified an infallible criterion of truth. Zeno, as we have seen, was far from being a card-carrying Platonist; but, like Arcesilaus, he had studied with Polemo and incorporated into his Stoic system not only the main tenor of Plato's Socratic ethics but also a cosmology strongly redolent of the *Timaeus*. As Dillon (2003: 236) trenchantly puts it, "Everything Polemonian Platonism could do, it would seem, Zeno could do better." Arcesilaus' response was to assume the dialectical mantel of the Platonic Socrates. His doing so, however, should not be judged a mere ploy. The objections he launched against Zeno's epistemology are immensely telling. Everything we know about Arcesilaus indicates not only dialectical virtuosity but also philosophical integrity. We have to assume that his advocacy of suspending judgment was grounded in sincere convictions that, thus far, all claims to philosophical certainty (especially those advanced by the Stoics) were unwarranted. According to our sources, he drew major support for this position not only from Socrates' profession of ignorance and refutative style of argument but also by invoking Democritus and other early philosophers who had supposedly denied the possibility of knowledge (Cicero, *Academica* 1.44).

The philosophical identity that Arcesilaus adopted and bequeathed to his successors, most notably Carneades, was skeptical in the original Greek sense of the word, meaning exploratory or investigative. The Academics did not call themselves skeptics – that self-description pertains to the later Pyrrhonists – and it would strain the limits of this essay to explore the extent to which they committed themselves to the thesis that nothing can be securely known. My own view is that their advocacy of suspended judgment was not intended as a dogmatic stance, but as the only rational response to philosophical positions which can be opposed with arguments as strong as those employed in their defense.

Ancients and moderns alike have frequently asked whether Arcesilaus was justified in claiming a Socratic and Platonic lineage for his skepticism (see Annas 1994 and Cooper 2004). We have noted Cicero's references, on Arcesilaus' behalf, to Socrates' dialectical practice (probing his interlocutors' opinions and withholding his own) and to the inconclusive results that Plato's dialogues achieve. If the question is taken to be about the interpretative accuracy of making Socrates or Plato an exact precursor of Academic skepticism, the answer is plainly negative. The Platonic dialogues do not foreshadow Academic *pro* and *contra* argumentation with a view to inculcating suspension of judgment. Nor does Plato's Socrates consistently mask his own opinions or cast doubt on the general possibility of knowledge. Neither Socrates nor Plato was a skeptic. But it is a mistake to suppose that Arcesilaus made precisely that claim. What we need, instead, is an interpretation of his position that steers a middle course, neither misattributing to Socrates and Plato a fully-fledged skeptical identity, nor foisting on them an inauthentic relation to his own methods and outlook.

In Plato's Socratic dialogues Socrates frequently engages in *ad hominem* argument, subjects his interlocutors' opinions to examination, and finds them inadequate as responses to his "What is *X*?" questions (see 5: THE SOCRATIC *ELENCHUS*). Such dialogues as the *Euthyphro* or *Laches* conclude that Socrates' interlocutors do not know what they have claimed to know. Arcesilaus was clearly justified in taking such material to exhibit a Socrates who could stand as a model for his own dialectical engagement with doctrinal philosophers; and he was almost certainly innovative in making Socrates' profession of ignorance a basic feature of Socratic philosophy, as presented by Plato – a feature with which any interpreter of that figure must come to terms (see Long 1996: 11–16).

We should assume that Arcesilaus regarded the *Theaetetus* as both a prime exhibit of Socrates' know-nothing stance and exploratory dialectic, and also as a firm indication of Plato's own epistemic reticence. This dialogue's repeated failures to reach a satisfactory definition of knowledge will always be a challenge to Plato's interpreters. If, as I think, Zeno was drawing positive doctrine from the *Theaetetus*, Arcesilaus will have had further reason for reading the dialogue as a purely aporetic exercise.

It is not difficult to identify other Platonic dialogues that could support Arcesilaus' assessments of Plato's quasi-skeptical procedures and outlook. These include the *Parmenides* with its remorseless criticism of the Theory of Forms and its concluding antinomies that continue to puzzle Plato's readers. Quite probably too he adverted to the *Phaedo* and the *Republic*, where the fallibility of the senses is powerfully emphasized. He would have had good reason, as a Platonist, to dwell upon such passages as a weapon against Epicureans and Stoics with their respective doctrines of a perceptual criterion of truth.

We cannot say how he would have responded to the obvious objection that Plato, through his leading spokesmen, frequently voices ideas that are too substantial and mutually consistent to be regarded as talking points from which their author is completely detached. In the end, Arcesilaus' profession to be a genuine Platonist must be judged a selective and one-sided reading of the dialogues. That judgment, however, is hardly less accurate a representation of Plato's philosophy than its reduction to a codified body of doctrine. Arcesilaus was described in antiquity as "being the first to *disturb* the discourse transmitted by Plato and, by means of question and answer, to make it more disputatious" (*DL* 4.28). There is a much more charitable and useful way to make that point: Arcesilaus was the first thinker fully to appreciate Plato's supreme achievement as the author of works that display the practice of engaging in philosophical discussion at the highest level. By focusing on the Platonic dialogues as demonstrations of how to ask and respond to philosophical questions, Arcesilaus shows himself to have been a genuine pioneer of modern philosophizing; and it is this, rather than his skepticism, that earns him the status of being an authentic Platonist.

Plato in early Pyrrhonism

Ancient tradition made Pyrrho, not Arcesilaus, the originator of Greek skepticism. I turn to Pyrrho only now because his relevance to this essay is much less central to Hellenistic philosophy's reception of Plato. Like Socrates and Arcesilaus, Pyrrho did not produce any published account of his own thought. What we know about it comes most directly from the fragmentary work of Timon, his leading follower (see Long 1978). There is no way to tell whether Pyrrho himself discussed Plato. Timon, however, gave prominence to Plato and Arcesilaus in his satirical *Silloi* (squint-eyed verses). The purpose of this remarkable poetry was to eulogize Pyrrho, give half-hearted praise to the few philosophers who had already showed skeptical leanings, and debunk all the rest.

The exact thrust of Pyrrho's thought is a contentious subject we need not consider here. From Timon's perspective, Pyrrho had achieved a way of life that was unique in its tranquillity and liberation from what he calls "passions, opinion, and futile legislation" (fr. 9).[1] Pyrrho, it seems, had completely abandoned "inquiry" (the traditional goal of ancient philosophy), out of a conviction that the objective nature of things is completely indeterminable. We can infer that any interest he took in Plato, whether as a source of doctrine or as an encouragement to speculation, was entirely negative.

As Pyrrho's publicist, Timon used satire and parody to highlight the pretentiousness and futility of doctrinaire philosophers. The four passages that specifically mention Plato are interesting for what they reveal by way of highly literate and intelligent chitchat. Timon represents Plato as "a big fish" (punning on his name), the leader of the Academy, with a sweet voice and a manner of writing that imitates the cicadas (fr. 30). This assessment of Plato's style is a subtle allusion to the *Phaedrus* (258E–259D), where Socrates invokes a chorus of cicadas to supervise the dialogue's discussion of good speaking and writing. In a further line that puns on Plato's name (fr. 19), Timon charges Plato with fashioning "wondrous fabrications" (*peplasmena*). One of the sources for this line cites it to support the report that Gorgias and Phaedo, on reading their eponymous dialogues, denied that they had said or heard any of what Plato attibutes to them. As for Plato's Socrates, that figure, according to Timon (fr. 62), is a fictional embellishment because the historical Socrates confined his interests to ethics, whereas Plato represents him as also discoursing on topics in logic and physics.

We should not suppose that Timon was original in fastening upon Plato's dialogical methodology and the historicity of his spokespersons. His observations give us a window on the interests and perceptions of some of Plato's readers in the early Hellenistic period. That is equally evident in his fourth mention of Plato: "You had such a passion for learning that you bought a little book for a lot of money, and starting from it, you taught yourself to 'write a *Timaeus*'" (fr. 54).

As we have seen, the *Timaeus* was Plato's most thoroughly conned dialogue. Here, Timon draws on scurrilous stories that Plato filched the ideas of the *Timaeus* from Pythagorean sources or from a Pythagorean work composed by Timaeus.

In some of the surviving *Silloi* Timon mocks philosophers in ways that satirically allude to substantive features of their thought. He may have done so in the case of Plato too, but we lack the evidence to say whether he did. His portrait of Socrates (fr. 25) seems to depend largely on Plato, emphasizing, as it does, "sharply pointed assertions, sneering, and irony." He does not call either Socrates or Arcesilaus a skeptic, for that status in the *Silloi* pertains exclusively to Pyrrho, but Timon was sufficiently aware of Arcesilaus' skeptical stance to have him say: "I shall swim" (presumably as an Academic fish) "to Pyrrho or to crooked Diodorus" (fr. 32).[2]

What seems to emerge from Timon's tantalizing material is his recognition that Plato's dialogues, in his day, had a wide and critical readership over and above their contributions to technical philosophy. As a brilliant writer himself, Timon evidently appreciated Plato's literary virtuosity, and he may have been content to focus his satire on Plato the author rather than attempt an explicit denunciation of Plato the philosopher.

Plato in Epicureanism

If Plato's philosophy and Platonism were not the primary targets of Early Pyrrhonism, they clearly occupied that position in the Epicurean tradition. The evidence for this fact is both direct and indirect. Epicurus explicitly criticized the theory of atomic elements advanced in the *Timaeus*, probably as part of a sustained attack on Platonic theology and cosmology (see Clay 1983: 156–8). The first generation of his followers wrote books against some of Plato's Socratic dialogues (see Long 1996: 9–11). Although their motivations for doing may have been more anti-Socratic than specifically directed at Plato, the Epicurean Colotes also attacked the Myth of Er in Book X of Plato's *Republic*, doubtless because it endorses the soul's postmortem existence (see Einarson and De Lacy 1967: 154–5).

The indirect evidence for Epicurean hostility to Plato takes us much further. As Sedley (1976: 133) rightly says: "Few of his [Epicurus'] mature doctrines could not be explained in some sense as reactions against Platonism." These include such basic Epicurean claims as the following: pleasure is the only intrinsic good, the value of virtue to a happy life is entirely instrumental, justice has no reality independent of a society's contingent norms, all perceptions are true, the primary existing things are body and void, and the soul is a perishable compound of atoms (see 21: PLATO ON PLEASURE AS THE HUMAN GOOD). Epicurean hedonism, physicalism, and empiricism, are completely antithetical to the ethics, metaphysics, epistemology, and psychology that Plato appears to approve in those dialogues that apparently contain his most mature philosophy.

The fact that Epicurus disagreed fundamentally with Plato does not imply, of course, that he did not study the dialogues carefully and learn from them. His treatment of pleasure, for instance, betrays the influence of the *Philebus*, and his theory of justice implies his considered rejection of the Platonic conception of an objectively existing and ideal Form. Through the teaching of Pamphilus, a Platonic philosopher (Cicero, *De natura deorum* 1.72), Epicurus was exposed to Platonism at an early age. He rejected it, but it provided him with the stimulus to develop a philosophy that, for the rest of antiquity, would present itself as a radical alternative not only to Platonism but also to the mind-directed and divinely purposed world-picture advanced by Aristotle and the Stoics. From a general perspective, these two schools as well as Platonism were often perceived (and quite reasonably) as providing a united front against the hedonistic materialism of the Epicureans.

While Epicurus' opposition to Plato is implicit in nearly all parts of his philosophy, I shall restrict myself here to the stance he adopted in relation to the cosmology and theology of the *Timaeus*; for Epicureanism most conspicuously diverges from Platonism in its insistence that human beings inhabit a purely mechanistic universe that has nothing to do with intelligent design and divine providence. Thanks to Lucretius, we can infer that Epicurus himself launched a wholesale attack on the *Timaeus*, and thereby supplement his attested criticism of Plato's geometrical atomism (which is all that remains of his focus on Plato in the surviving fragments of his great series of books *On Nature*).

Lucretius never refers to Plato, but the cosmological errors he seeks to expose in his *De rerum natura* chime so exactly with doctrines of the *Timaeus* that his polemic was almost certainly directed against "a currently fashionable way of reading it," if not directly against Plato's text as such (see Sedley 1998: 349). Since Lucretius is a remarkably faithful and precise expositor of Epicureanism, we have good reason to suppose that he is an accurate spokesman for Epicurus himself.

As Sedley (1998) has shown, the topics Lucretius tackles in his treatment of Epicurean cosmology are closely modeled on Epicurus' own procedure, which in turn may be plausibly interpreted as a powerful rejoinder to the foundations Timaeus lays down for his cosmological story. According to that account, the world is the excellent product of a divine and benevolent creator, a living being endowed with a soul, modeled on the ideal Living Being (referring to Plato's Forms), and destined to last forever, thanks to its creator's goodness. By contrast, Lucretius argues at length that (1) the world is neither divine nor everlasting; (2) the gods had no motivation or model for creating it; and (3) it is too intractable and inhospitable to have been benevolently fabricated for human benefit. Although, as I remarked earlier, Plato himself does not explicitly state the converse to Lucretius' third rejoinder, this anthropocentric reading of the *Timaeus* may well have been familiar to Epicurus and hence passed down to Lucretius.

Conclusion

It will be evident from this survey that Plato's role in Hellenistic philosophy was completely implicated in the positions and methodologies that the competing schools adopted in response to one another. At the beginning of this period, philosophers within the Academy continued the process of identifying a positive set of Platonic or supposedly Platonic doctrines, but that approach was soon superseded by Arcesilaus, whose skepticism included both pro-Socratic and anti-Stoic elements.

Systematic commentary on the dialogues was probably not undertaken by anyone after Crantor, at least in published form or before about 100 BCE; but it is highly probable that Arcesilaus and his followers frequently referred to Plato's dialogues in their oral teaching. As the Academy's hard-line skepticism abated, with Philo and Antiochus disputing the correct interpretation of Plato's doctrinal commitments, fresh impetus must have been given to studying Plato's dialogues for their own sake, as we can observe the Academic Cicero doing at the end of the Hellenistic epoch.

Outside the Academy, Plato (including the Platonic Socrates) remained a presence whose influence and importance, whether it was construed positively or negatively, remained paramount. His strongest critics were the early Pyrrhonists and, much more prominently and persistently, the Epicureans, whose anti-teleological cosmology was directly opposed to the Platonist model of a world that conforms to intelligent design. In Stoicism assessments of Plato were more complex and subject to modification as time went by. From Zeno down to and including Chrysippus, the Stoics tended to emphasize their differences from Plato; but they drew heavily on his Socratic dialogues for their appropriation of Socrates and incorporated much else that looks Platonic in their cosmology and theology. By the middle of the second century BCE, Antipater, as head of the Stoa, was claiming that Plato and the Stoics agree on most things (*Stoicorum Veterum Fragmenta* III Antipater 56), and the later Stoics Panaetius and Posidonius seem to have been unconcerned about any charges of being crypto-Platonists. The final demise of the skeptical Academy is probably in large part attributable to the fact that Plato, taking the dialogues as a whole, had begun to seem more at home in the Stoa than he was in the Academy.

I began this essay by asking about Plato's Hellenistic admirers and detractors, the afterlife of his methodologies and theories, and the dialogues that were taken to be his principal legacy. Enough has been said in response to the first question. As to the third, though the *Timaeus* clearly occupied center-stage, we have observed sufficient references to other dialogues to think that little or none of Plato's corpus was completely ignored during this period. A fully adequate response to my second question would require a much lengthier study. I have highlighted the Academic skeptics' interest in Plato's dialectical methodology, and I have called attention to positive and negative responses to Platonic cosmology and to the Stoics' recourse to such dialogues as the *Republic*, *Euthydemus*, *Cratylus*, and *Theaetetus*, which show the vitality of Plato's contributions to social theory, ethics, linguistics, epistemology, and psychology. That, however, is only a selective tally. For reasons of space, I have passed over the *Sophist*, which probably helped to shape Stoic thinking on active and passive cosmological principles, metaphysics, and semiotics (see Brunschwig 1994: ch. 6). Further research is needed on other possible marks of Plato's legacy to the early Stoics.

What can be said with finality is that the metaphysical and mystical Plato adopted by the Neoplatonists was not alive in the Hellenistic period. The earliest Academic exegesis, with its interests in numerology, hierarchical gradations of reality, and an ultimate One, helped to prepare for the late Platonists' Plato. There is no sign that either the Academic skeptics or the Stoics were at all sympathetic to this way of interpreting Plato's philosophy.

Notes

All translations are the author's unless otherwise noted.
I would like to thank David Sedley for his valuable comments on an earlier draft.

1 My references to Timon draw on the 1989 edition of di Marco.
2 Timon clearly drew on the Stoic Aristo's famous quip about Arcesilaus, which parodies Homer's description of the monstrous chimaera: "Plato in front, Pyrrho behind, Diodorus in the middle" (*DL* 4.33).

References and further reading

Annas, J. (1994). Plato the skeptic. In P. Vander Waerdt (ed.) *The Socratic Movement* (pp. 309–40). Ithaca, NY: Cornell University Press.

Brunschwig, J. (1994). *Papers in Hellenistic Philosophy*. Cambridge: Cambridge University Press.

Clay, D. (1983). *Lucretius and Epicurus*. Ithaca, NY: Cornell University Press.

Cooper, J. M. (2004). Arcesilaus: Socratic and sceptic. In *Knowledge, Nature and the Good: Essays in Ancient Philosophy* (pp. 81–106). Princeton, NJ: Princeton University Press.

Dillon, J. (1977). *The Middle Platonists*. Ithaca, NY: Cornell University Press.

—— (2003). *The Heirs of Plato: A Study of the Old Academy (347–274 BC)*. Oxford: Oxford University Press.

di Marco, M. (ed.) (1989). *Timone di Fliunte: Silli*. Rome: Edizioni dell'Ateneo.

Einarson, B. and De Lacy, P. (1967). *Plutarch's* Moralia XIV. Cambridge: Cambridge University Press.

Fortenbaugh, W., Huby, P. M., and Sharples, R. W. (1992). *Theophrastus of Eresus*. Leiden and New York: Brill.

Hankinson, R. J. (1995). *The Sceptics*. London: Routledge.

Long, A. A. (1978). Timon of Phlius: Pyrrhonist and satirist. *Proceedings of the Cambridge Philological Society* 204, pp. 68–91.

—— (1996). *Stoic Studies*. Cambridge: Cambridge University Press.

—— (2002). Zeno's epistemology and Plato's *Theaetetus*. In T. Scaltsas and A. Mason (eds.) *Zeno and his Legacy* (pp. 113–32). Larnaka: Pierides Foundation.

—— (2005). Stoic linguistics, Plato's *Cratylus*, and Augustine's *De dialectica*. In D. Frede and B. Inwood (eds.) *Language and Learning: Philosophy of Language in the Hellenistic Age* (pp. 36–55). Cambridge: Cambridge University Press.

Long, A. A. and Sedley, D. N. (1987). *The Hellenistic Philosophers*. Cambridge: Cambridge University Press.

Reydams-Schils, G. (1999). *Demiurge and Providence: Stoic and Platonist Readings of Plato's* Timaeus. Turnhout, Belgium: Brepols.

Sedley, D. (1976). Epicurus and his professional rivals. In J. Bollack and A. Laks (eds.) *Études sur l'épicurisme antique* (pp. 121–59). Lille: Cahiers de Philologie.

—— (1993). Chrysippus on psychophysical causality. In J. Brunschwig and M. Nussbaum (eds.) *Passions and Perceptions: Studies in Hellenistic Philosophy of Mind* (pp. 313–31). Cambridge: Cambridge University Press.

—— (1998). Theophrastus and Epicurean physics. In J. van Ophuijsen and M. van Raalte (eds.) *Theophrastus: Reappraising the Sources* (pp. 331–54). New Brunswick, NJ: Rutgers University Press.

—— (2002). The origins of Stoic God. In M. Frede and A. Laks (eds.) *Traditions of Theology: Studies in Hellenistic Theology, its Background and Aftermath* (pp. 41–83). Leiden and New York: Brill.

Striker, G. (1996). Plato's Socrates and the Stoics. In *Essays in Hellenistic Epistemology and Ethics* (pp. 316–24). Cambridge: Cambridge University Press.

Vander Waerdt, P. (1994). Zeno's *Republic* and the origins of natural law. In P. Vander Waerdt (ed.) *The Socratic Movement* (pp. 272–308). Ithaca, NY: Cornell University Press.

29

Plato's Influence on Jewish, Christian, and Islamic Philosophy

SARA AHBEL-RAPPE

Introduction: Plato in Late Antiquity

In order to understand the influence of Plato on the formation of Jewish, Christian, and Islamic philosophy, it is useful to distinguish between Plato and Platonisms. Philosophers such as Philo of Alexandria or al-Farabi read the dialogues through the dual lenses of exegetical traditions (i.e., Pythagorean or Neoplatonist) already established, as well as through the religious contexts in which they performed their own, newer exegeses. For the purposes of this essay, it will be of only minor relevance that our notions of Plato and his philosophy may or may not coincide with those of ancient Christian, Jewish, and Islamic readers of the dialogues. For example, the Platonists of late antiquity did not read the dialogues as adumbrating purely theoretical positions, or as a series of intellectual puzzles. For them, the dialogues contained decidedly positive doctrines that served to guide the reader in pursuing the life of philosophy (see 2: INTERPRETING PLATO; 4: FORM AND THE PLATONIC DIALOGUES). But while reason and rationality were centrally important to this life, they did not in and of themselves provide the philosopher with the tools he needed to practice his discipline successfully. The end of ancient Platonism was the contemplative life itself; this life, involving as it did union with the divine, could not have been the fruit of reason alone. Instead, many Jewish, Christian, and Islamic thinkers understood Platonism as underwriting a mysticism adumbrated in the dialogues, but necessarily escaping direct or explicit description.

This mysticism goes hand in hand with the assumption shared by late antique Platonisms, that at the root of what Plato himself referred to as the realm of becoming (*Ti.* 28A) is a transcendent unity that functions both as cause of all lesser forms of reality, and as the *telos* (end) toward which all human wisdom must ultimately aspire. Now this first principle or original One can be associated with the Unwritten doctrines, the Pythagorean teachings that Plato evidently espoused and that were developed by his immediate heirs, Speusippus and Xenocrates (Dillon 2002: 107–29). For Platonists who practiced within the monotheistic traditions, however, the relationship between the One conceived as absolute or non-dual, and the multiplicity of which it is the cause, became problematic. The impulse toward absolute unity dominated Platonisms both polytheist (so-called Middle Platonism and Neoplatonism) and monotheist

(Christian, Jewish, Islamic), but this impulse met with frequent resistance in the religions associated with monotheistic revelations; there, the strictly maintained distinction between creator and created, God and the Soul, had to be negotiated by thinkers who were nevertheless committed to its implications. In addition to this mystical orientation, the principal themes of Platonism, whether polytheist, Christian, Jewish, or Islamic, were the distinction between the corporeal and intelligible worlds, the assimilation of the human soul to the divine, the ideas or Forms as aspects of God, and utopian or theocratic conceptions of human society, as related to the Platonic notion of the Good (O'Meara 2003).

Middle Platonisms

Our story begins with Philo Judaeus, the first century CE Alexandrian philosopher and statesman who undertook a vast defense of Jewish religion (48 works survive, the majority in Greek, but a significant group only survives in Armenian); it is in the form of a sprawling commentary on the Five Books of Moses. Philo belonged to the elite of Alexandrian Jewish society. His nephew became the Prefect of Alexandria, and we know that it was the very prominent social status of Philo that allowed him to form part of the embassy to Gaius Caesar in 38, the unsatisfactory results of which Philo reports in his own *Legatio ad Gaium*. Philo wrote this political essay in the aftermath of a pogrom-like event that resulted in the massacre of countless Jews living in Alexandria (Gruen 2002: 60–5).

We can better approach Philo if we keep in mind that he believes that Moses literally composed the entire Pentateuch, the first five books of the Jewish Scripture. According to Philo, Moses, like Philo himself, received a thoroughly "Greek" education in both science and philosophy, in Egypt at the court of Pharaoh. This education in the Greek curriculum was possible because it was Pythagoras (certain strains of Platonism actually trace their lineage back to Pythagoras) who brought the Hellenic tradition to Egypt during his travels. Thus the two traditions, Jewish and Hellenic, are really branches of the same primordial stream of wisdom. We shall have to explore this Pythagorean aspect of Platonism more carefully, below.

His *De opificio mundi*, actually a commentary on Genesis, echoes other Platonist interpretations of the *Timaeus*, according to which two constituent principles, an active or divine cause, and a passive or material substrate, are completely fused and present in each other throughout the whole of nature (cf. Cicero, *Academica* 1. 24, with Sedley 2002: 48–50). To see how closely Philo reflects the contemporaneous Platonism of Antiochus, the last head of the so-called New Academy, we can compare the following excerpts from Philo's *De opificio mundi* and from the summary of Antiochean physics found in Cicero's *Academica*, his history of the Academy during the reigns of Philo of Larissa and later, Antiochus of Ascalon:

> When it came to nature . . . they spoke in such a way as to divide it into two things, so that one was active, the other at this one's disposal, as it were, and acted upon by it in some way. In the active one they held that there was a power, in the one which was acted upon just a kind of matter. (*Academica* 1. 24, 1–5, trans. Sedley)

But Moses, who had early reached the very summits of philosophy and who had learnt from the Oracles of God the most numerous and important of the principles of nature, was well aware that it is indispensable that in all existing things there must be an active cause, and a passive subject; and that the active cause is the intellect . . . (*De opificio mundi* 8.1–5, trans. Younge)

Philo takes the Stoic aspect of this interpretation, which posits a pantheist or imman-ent account of deity *vis-à-vis* the world and inserts it into a Judeo-Middle Platonist retelling of the Demiurge's tale. The Forms supply a blueprint for the creative aspect of God, our divine architect, who uses the blueprint to provide a model for the temporal world:

As therefore the city, when previously shadowed out in the mind of the man of architectural skill had no external place, but was stamped solely in the mind of the workman, so in the same manner neither can the world which existed in ideas have had any other local position except the divine reason which made them. (*De opificio mundi* 8.20, trans. Younge)

Here Plato's Forms have become the thoughts of the divinity, a feature that is absent from Plato's text, but which generally characterizes Middle Platonist readings of the *Timaeus*. Jewish, Christian, and Islamic interpreters tend to understand the Forms, not only (as we have them here) as the content of divine thought, but actually as aspects of the highest deity and as names or veils of God. Philo's work on the Forms in this passage anticipates a long tradition of relocating them within the domain of a spiritual world.

For Philo, God brings the intelligible order, the blueprint, into being on day one of creation. Hence, although it is intelligible and should be in strictly Platonic terms an aspect of eternal being, in fact Philo finds that Moses understands that the blueprint (i.e., the Forms), actually occupies a space in genesis, the world of becoming (see 13: PROBLEMS FOR FORMS). This example shows us that Philo uses Platonic conceptions in order to penetrate beneath the surface of the Mosaic text and uncover a theological doctrine that suggests that God is at once the creator of the universe but also utterly transcends any created nature. Moreover, God's activity as creator is only one aspect of the deity, one of the seven powers, as Philo calls them, that communicate but do not exhaust the divine substance (Runia 2002: 304–6).

In Philo's *De opificio mundi*, we witness a typically Middle Platonist transformation of Plato's Demiurge and World-Soul to two functions of deity: one trans-cosmic, the self nature of God that does not manifest and does not change; the other, cosmic, manifest-ing the divine nature in the properties of the universe, which is eternal.

In order to read the Mosaic text as a Middle Platonist cento, Philo relies on a transformation of the meaning of Platonism, which for Philo, Numenius, and other contemporaries, was best understood as an offshoot of the Pythagorean tradition. In fact, Platonists such as Numenius and Moderatus thought that anything of value in Plato had already been taught by Pythagoras. Insofar as Plato was an original philosopher, he could only be approached as a renegade Pythagorean. Far better to consider Plato as unoriginal and as a follower of a more ancient path. The Middle Platonist/Pythagorean Numenius wrote a history of the Academy that emphasized its Pythagorean roots:

436

Socrates asserted the existence of three gods, and philosophized about them in expressions suited to each single auditor . . .

Plato, who followed Pythagoras, knew that Socrates had derived his teachings from no other source [than Pythagoras]. But Plato did not [teach] in the ordinary way nor did he [reveal his Pythagorean doctrines] openly. (Numenius, *On the divergence of the Academy from Plato*, fr. 24. 53–60, trans. des Places, with omissions)

Of course it seems odd to talk about the three gods of Socrates; we know that Numenius here makes Socrates the author of Platonic doctrine as it appears, for example, in the *Philebus* (16c ff.), where Plato hints of an ancient tradition that espoused three principles at the root of all things: limit, unlimited, and the mixture of these two. Pythagorean interpreters elaborated these root principles in various ways, not all of which are easy to trace because of the fragmentary nature of the evidence. If the late antique philosopher, Proclus, is to be trusted, then Numenius' three gods, "Father, Creator, and Creation," where the first transcends the creative activity of the others, are indeed strikingly like Philo's account of creation in *De opificio mundi*. Both Philo and Numenius somehow interpret the Demiurge/Creator as including a dynamic aspect that infuses matter with form, and a more passive aspect that is immanent within matter.

To return to Philo, we see that his work on the *Timaeus* proves to be conventional within the milieu of Middle Platonism, and yet his project of, as Jaap Mansfeld has called it, "philosophy in service of scripture" (1988), laid the foundations for a Christian exegetical tradition that elaborated the *Logos* theology we see operative in Philo; for Philo, the immanent deity responsible for communicating being to the manifest world is exactly the *Logos*. But equally important for the development for Philo's Platonism is his mystical interpretation of the Pentateuch as allegory for the flight of the soul from this lower, material order, to divine knowledge. Philo's exegetical work begins the tradition of reading the biblical stories in terms of a specifically Platonist mysticism, which emphasizes the kind of dualistic approach one encounters in the *Phaedo*, for example, with its insistence on separating the soul from the body (see 19: THE PLATONIC SOUL). Philo's *On the Migration of Abraham* employs this theme as a way of illustrating the various stages of the soul's ascent to the Good which, for Philo and for the subsequent Platonist tradition, consists in knowledge of, or assimilation to God. Philo opens this treatise quoting Genesis 12: 1, "Depart from thy land," interpreting the verse as God's exhortation to the soul, to "quit the region of the body," and as the awakening of an impulse toward enlightenment. Abraham's original country is all that pertains to his lower self, body, mind, senses, and speech, all of which should be subject to the highest principle within the human person, the intellect, the only aspect of the human being that enjoys an innate affinity with the Good.

One place that we see a development of Philo's methods of reading the Bible is in the work of Origen, the third-century Alexandrian exegete and older contemporary of Plotinus, and a man deeply influenced by Philo's allegorical interpretations of the Pentateuch. Born in 185, Origen was a teenager in Alexandria when the persecution of the early third century erupted. Origen's father was arrested and martyred while the imperial government confiscated all of the family property, forcing Origen to go to work as a teacher. He taught successfully for several years, but at some point decided to return to the study of philosophy.

Origen's relationship to Platonism is a controversial topic, and has been since at least the fifth century, when Epiphanius' massive *Panarion*, a treatise designed to expose the origins of all heresy as native to the thought of ancient Greece, heaped ire on Origen for his purportedly pagan teachings (*Panarion* 64.65.5–6, 64.72.8). Origen was excommunicated in 553 in a council convened by the Emperor Justinian; he is thus distinguished as the first person to be tried after his own death (in 254) for holding heretical beliefs. The Council listed 15 propositions, several of which have a decidedly Platonist ring, though whether or not Origen actually held them was hotly disputed by the sixth-century Latin translator of Origen, Rufinus. It is his Latin translation of the *Peri Archon* (the original Greek was destroyed by Justinian (Edwards 2002: 4–9)) that gives us an understanding of how Origen applied Platonic ideas to biblical narrative. From the fragments of the original Greek text, it seems that Origen's discussion of the differences between the first and second persons of the Trinity involved the Pythagorean terminology: the Father is *autoagathon* (Good in itself); the Son is the *dunamis* (power or manifestation) of the father, and is also the image of the indefinite divine nature (fr. 34–6 from the *De principis*, Gögemanns and Karpp). For Origen, God in himself is a monad whereas the Son or *Logos* is the principle that introduces diversity, functioning like the dyad of Pythagorean speculation.

Above we saw Philo using Plato's *Timaeus* in his commentary on Genesis but transforming what was, after all, a Platonic myth, via a Jewish interpretation of the Stoic *logos*, in his *Peri Archon*. We can see Origen using what was perhaps a Gnostic variant of the *Phaedrus* myth in order to explain the diverse kinds of embodiment enjoyed by rational beings. Origen's topic in *Peri Archon* I.6 is the resolution of all diversity in the unity of God. This analysis of reality into two aspects, unity and multiplicity, already puts us in mind of the Pythagorean Platonist traditions. Indeed it is precisely this tendency to elide the distance between divinity and creature that is denounced in the edict of 553 (Article 14: if anyone shall say that all reasonable beings will one day be united in one . . . let him be anathema (quoted in Edwards 2002: 9)).

The story of how each soul receives its appropriate body echoes the myth that Plato recounts at *Phdr.* 248c. There, souls failing in their vision of the Forms owing to motivational conflict fall to earth, where each is ranked according to its recollection of the Forms, from the highest ranking souls, philosophers, down to lowly sophists. In Origen's narrative, souls neglect and feel aversion to their participation in the divine, and through their own fault, experience differing degrees of distance from their original station in the divine, and so become, respectively, angels, principalities, virtues, and the diverse array of rational beings, both human and nonhuman. The condition of separation is only temporary, at least in the case of the human soul, to whom it remains open to become restored to the original condition of perfection after a period of remedial learning that constitutes embodied life: "it is not an absolute separation, but it remains possible for the soul to return to its origin and to be reestablished in its original condition" (*Peri Archon* I.3.8). Below we shall look more closely at the relationship between the soul and God, according to Origen.

I mentioned how controversial it has been to assign the label of Platonist to Origen. The tensions between the two tendencies are ancient, stretching back to Origen's own *Contra Celsum*, a massive refutation of the Platonist philosopher, Celsus, who had penned an anti-Christian polemic some seventy years before (Frede 1997). Celsus' Platonism objects to key Christian conceptions such as the incarnation of the divine *Logos* and the doctrine of bodily resurrection. In his reply Origen makes use of another Middle Platonist development of the *Phaedrus*, the doctrine of the vehicle of the soul. The ethereal body, or light body, takes on considerable importance in the ritual development of Neoplatonism fostered by Iamblichus (a third-century Syrian philosopher and student of Porphyry). For Iamblichus and those whose tradition he follows, the ethereal body is a psychic envelope that is formed from the accretions of the material world as the soul receives embodiment. This covering condition of the human soul is the object of ritual purification within the Neoplatonist rites known as theurgy (see below), but is always attached to the individual soul as a kind of reward body that specifically marks the soul's place within the cosmic order. Origen too seems to share in this idea of the soul's vehicle, one that helps the human soul in particular to negotiate its status as a member of the spiritual order and as an embodied being. It is this body and not the material body of ordinary life that Origen alludes to when responding to Celsus' attack on the Christian idea of resurrection (see also *Peri Archon* II.10–11).

Neoplatonism

Before leaving Origen and continuing our story, it will be necessary to situate his work within the world of third-century Platonism. It was Plotinus (204–70 CE) as recorded in the *Enneads*, edited and published by Plotinus' disciple Porphyry, who inspired and provided the foundations for the work of later Neoplatonists such as Iamblichus (active 245 CE) and Proclus (412–85). In *Ennead* V.1 Plotinus uses the three initial hypotheses in the second half of Plato's *Parmenides* in order to sketch his own metaphysical doctrine, according to which reality has three primary different hypostases or orders: the One, Intellect, and Soul. Plotinus refers the first hypothesis ("if the one is," *Parmenides* 137c4) to the One beyond being, the transcendent source of all. The second hypothesis refers to a subsequent stage of reality that arises when the wisdom inherent within the One turns back on the One, giving rise to Being/Intellect, the intelligible world that consists of intellects each contemplating all the other intellects, rather like a hall of mirrors. This order of reality represents Plotinus' transformation of the Platonic Forms via an Aristotelian conception of divine thought eternally contemplating itself. Transitory being originates in the third hypostasis, at the level of Soul, which is present both on a cosmic level as caretaker of all that is soulless, and as the embodied individual whose destiny is to return to his origin by recovering his lost unity with the One.

There is also a dynamic aspect of the philosophy that is best understood as a spiritual circuit. In *Ennead* V.1 Plotinus uses the physical similes of perfume, snow, and sunlight to describe the eternal process of emanation, the radiation of all beings from the One. The cosmic respiration or universal pulse that constantly sends forth beings from the One into a state of manifestation derives from the self-giving nature of reality. Nevertheless the soul can begin to recover from its apparent separation and only discovers its native fullness when it undertakes its cosmic mission of returning the multiplicity back into the source. Once again we see in the spiritual circuit a crucial aspect of late antique Platonism, the assimilation of the soul to God. This is also central to Origen's narrative.

We can now compare Origen's discussion of the soul, the *logos*, and the godhead to these basic Neoplatonic principles. Above we saw that rational souls undergo embodiment when they fail in their ardor for the divine nature. Origen likens this failure to someone who has a skill or knowledge but slowly neglects to cultivate it and to keep up his practice (*Peri Archon* I.3). Plotinus alludes to this falling away from the One in *Enneads* V.1.1, when he refers to the reason for the soul's separation from the unity of the One as a desire to be independent, even as "rashness." But he also insists that the soul is never actually separate from the divine nature of the Intellect and that it does not descend entirely, but remains part of the intelligible universe (IV.8.8). In a similar way, Origen teaches both that all human souls are initially united to the divine through participation through love and knowledge in the godhead, and that each soul participates in the Word of God, which is directly present as the soul's intelligible aspect (*Peri Archon* I.3, 5). Moreover, the nature of the soul that belongs to Christ is exactly the same nature as that of all other rational souls: *Naturam quidem animae illius hanc fuisse, quae est omnium animarum, non potest dubitari.* (For it cannot be doubted that the nature of his [Christ's] soul is the nature of all souls) (II.6, 5). Finally the soul becomes identified with its most perfect aspect, i.e., becomes spirit (or intellect, to use Platonist language), when it returns to its original condition.

This aspect of Origen's teaching, later called "isochrist" or equating the human soul with the *Logos*, engendered within the Church as a series of doctrinal disputes known as the "Origenist Controversy" (Clark 1992). In Origen's discussion of the *Logos*, he uses a series of descriptors, *epinoiai*, to portray the relationship of the second person to the first person of the Trinity. As we have seen, his language, especially when he calls the *Logos* the "image" of God, suggests that there is a subordination, rather than an equation, between the first two members of the Trinity. This language is perfectly natural within a Middle Platonist context, where the second mind is an active principle, rather like an active cause, responsible for the temporal changes that take place within the world of particulars in a way that the highest aspect of deity never could be. Yet again, we know that as a result of the fourth, fifth, and sixth centuries' reevaluation of his orthodoxy in light of the Council of Nicea, Origen became associated with forms of Arianism (the heresy that maintained the subordination of Christ or the *Logos* to the godhead or Father). The Council of Nicea, convened by Constantine in 325, used a formula designed to dismiss any idea of subordination among the three persons.

But here we must cease at last our comparisons and embark on a series of contrasts. Origen plays down the creaturely aspect of soul, as we saw, just because all of the souls are contained in the fullness of the divine *plērōma*, or spiritual world that became, in Origen's work, another interpretation of Plato's Forms. Yet for other Christian thinkers, there is a much sharper divide between the world that God created out of nothing (and the contingent nothingness of all such creatures, including human souls), and the Creator, or God as Trinity. The evolution of a specifically Christian metaphysics arrived on the foundations of Origen's work, but emphasized the divide, actually present in earlier forms of Platonism, between the spiritual and material worlds. The nothing of Christian creation replaces the matter of dualists such as Plutarch or Albinus (Dillon 1997). Yet the nothing of the creature in himself opens the door to the question of the human being's status as the image of God. Plotinus is always at pains to make clear, as he does very decisively in *Ennead* IV.8.8, that the soul is never actually separate from the divine nature of the Intellect and that it does not descend entirely, but remains part of the intelligible universe. How then does Christianity negotiate the soul's restoration to God and in what ways is this return aligned with Platonism?

To look for traces of Plotinian mysticism in the early Church fathers, it is usual to turn to the mystical writings of St Augustine, particularly to *Confessions* 7.10.16, 7.17.23 (with 7.18 and 7.20), which recount the post-Platonic but pre-Christian mystical experiences that took place in his garden in Milan. A long-standing scholarly discussion revolves around whether Augustine's Platonism was informed by Marius Victorinus' Latin translations of Porphyry or indeed by translations of Plotinus himself (Courcelle 1950). Augustine discusses these experiences just after he relates that he managed to obtain certain books of the Platonists: *procurasti . . . quosdam platonicorum libros ex graeca lingua in latinam versos, et ibi legi* (I obtained some books of the Platonists translated from the Greek tongue into Latin, and there I read). *Confessions* 7.10.16 and 10.7.17 are built around two moments of what ancient Platonists would have understood as spiritual ascent: "with the eye of my soul (such as it was) I saw above the same eye of my soul, above my mind, the Unchangeable Light." Here Augustine navigates between the hypostases of soul and Intellect. Courcelle cites *Ennead* I.6.9 in connection with this chapter in the *Confessions*:

> when you are self-gathered in the purity of your being, nothing now remaining that can shatter that inner unity, nothing from without clinging to the authentic man, when you find yourself wholly true to your essential nature, wholly that only veritable Light which is not measured by space. (*Ennead* I.6.9.15–20, trans. Mackenna)

However, Augustine's orientation is markedly different from that of Plotinus, insofar as the latter suggests one fundamentally is identical to the light of the intellect, and not, after all, actually a soul, whereas throughout chapter 10, Augustine insists rather on his difference from the intellect. This is how we ought interpret Augustine's phrase, *et nondum me esse qui viderem* or "I was not such as to be one who could see" (7.10.16), that is, in an ontological sense, indicating Augustine's conviction that the human soul is by nature and even generically a different kind of being, not a member of the intelligible world (Finan 1991: 83). This difference confirms what we saw in the case of Origen's detractors, that the doctrinal emphasis on unity or assimilation between soul and God, so characteristic of Platonism, met with resistance when translated into certain Christian contexts. At any rate, we can be certain that Augustine's various encounters with Platonism mark his intellectual development in this period of his life (indeed some have suggested that Book VII marks Augustine's conversion experience as more Platonist than Christian), just as in his youth he had been seduced by the arguments of the Academicians to the effect that no certainty was possible (*Contra academicos*).

This brief discussion of Augustine's Platonism in the *Confessions* should be complemented by another important text where Augustine reveals his affinity for Porphyry. In the *City of God*, Augustine devotes a book to the examination of Porphyry's *Philosophy from Oracles*. In Porphyry he recognizes a great philosopher who had sought and proclaimed the possibility of a universal path for liberation (*DCD* X). In this sense, Augustine appropriates for Christianity a long-standing Platonist tradition, found already in Celsus' *On the True Doctrine*, where apparently Celsus adapted certain Stoic doctrines concerning the natural revelation afforded by reason, to suggest that there was one primordial and universal wisdom tradition. This true doctrine is attested among the highest and most ancient civilizations, including Egypt, Assyria, Persia, India, and various other tribes (*Contra Celsum* I.6). Augustine also approves of Porphyry's rejection of ritualism in favor of the purification that comes to the soul by way of knowledge alone, that is, knowledge of the highest principles:

> You say, indeed, that ignorance, and the numberless vices resulting from it, cannot be removed by any mysteries, but only by the *Patrikos Nous,* that is, the Father's mind or intellect conscious of the Father's will. But that Christ is this mind you do not believe. (*DCD* X.26)

In order to appreciate Porphyry's denunciation of what Augustine here calls "mysteries," it will be necessary to say a few words about the main subject of attack in Book X of the *De civitate dei,* which is theurgy: The word "theurgy" literally means "activity associated with the gods," and refers to the use of ritual in conjunction with the soul's effort to free itself from bondage to the world of birth and death. The Syrian Neoplatonist philosopher, Iamblichus, discusses theurgy in his work *On the Mysteries of the Egyptians.* Iamblichus adopts the persona of an Egyptian prophet who will attempt to answer Porphyry's objections concerning the ritual efficacy of certain symbols for the purpose of uniting the individual soul with the gods. Iamblichus insists that knowledge does not deliver the soul from the constraints of embodiment. To complete its cosmic task, the soul must win over the whole chain of being that links our ordinary world with the ultimate principles of reality. "Thinking does not connect theurgists with divine beings . . . Rather . . . it is the power of ineffable symbols comprehended by the gods alone, that establishes theurgical union" (*DM* 96). Offerings can be made to higher or lower gods; the higher gods can be worshipped only by "intellectual" gifts. For this kind of worship, wisdom is the true sacrifice or offering. In *Abst.* ii, 34, Porphyry distinguishes different levels of sacrifice. At the highest order, Porphyry says, "the sacred sacrifice" consisting of wisdom is made. One who reads through Book X of the *City of God* will come to have some appreciation of how Porphyry's own conception of wisdom as a sacred offering influenced Augustine. The latter's formulation of the way to liberation consists in the knowledge of God, although for him this knowledge is granted only by the grace of God. One might wonder how different Augustine's conception of grace is from the Neoplatonist reliance on the power of the gods to elevate the soul beyond its own boundaries (see 17: PLATONIC RELIGION).

Late Athenian Neoplatonism

Our last chapter of Neoplatonism returns to Athens, where the Athenian Academy under the direction of Proclus and then Damascius flowered again, only to close its doors in 529 under Justinian. Proclus Diadochus is best known for his *Elements of*

Theology, an aphoristic work that sets out the basic principles of Neoplatonic meta-physics in a systematic presentation modeled on Euclid's *Elements* (see 16: PLATO AND MATHEMATICS). Proclus elaborates what by comparison is Plotinus' austere view of the unseen world (One, Intellect, Soul) into a complex and intricate series of triads. They are characterized in various ways, principal among which are the intelligible triad: limit, unlimited, and mixed (with the mixed, or Being, itself the head of a triad that consists in Being, Life, and Intellect), and also the dynamic triad of procession, remaining, and reversion. The three kinds of realities that inhabit this world, which devolves from the One or Good, are henads or gods, intelligences, and souls. In a sense, Proclus reinvests in the cultural aspect of paganism, translating the Iamblichean valorization of pagan ritual into a spiritual vortex of endless possibility. And yet at the heart of what may fairly be described as the Proclean system, rests the One in its function as cause and source, to which all lower forms of reality are destined to return. This One grounds the metaphysics of Proclus in what pagans and Christians alike understood as a way of negation, of reaching God by denying any attributes or any qualities. This way of negation, or apophatic theology, resonates strongly throughout late antique philosophy, showing up in Christian writers such as Gregory of Nyssa and Evagrius Ponticus. For Proclus, any name applied to the One is already a limitation and presents the One according to a certain power or aspect. Because activities manifest their causes, they at once delimit the nature of their causes, and at the same time they distort or compromise them. Therefore the names, "The One" and "The Good" veil the first god under two different aspects, that of unity and that of creation. Damascius, the last Platonic scholar, went so far as to suggest that the highest principle could only be referred to as "the Ineffable," and it was entirely outside the scope of any metaphysics or theology to determine its nature (*Peri Archon* I.1).

Having glimpsed at developments in Athenian Neoplatonism, we are in a position to appreciate the achievement of Pseudo-Dionysius. This most influential of Platonizing theologians owes his success in part to his appropriation of the identity of Dionysius the Areopagite, who is mentioned in Acts 17: 34. In this passage, Dionysius, a member of the Areopagus, the judicial council in Athens, encounters St Paul and is instantly converted. Although he wrote in around 520 (a date deduced from the first mention of his work by Severus of Antioch), his quasi-apostolic status afforded his teaching some protection from the politics of the *regula fidei*. So, despite his rampant Platonism, as we shall see, he offered a deeply philosophical understanding of Orthodox ritual that remained important for the Eastern Church, while his negative theology inspired centuries of mystical thinkers, including Eriugena. His editor, John of Scythopolis, to some extent participated in perpetuating the authenticity of his writings, claiming in his scholia to the Dionysian corpus (composed *ca.* 530) that pagan writers (John calls them "external" or "outsiders") "especially Proclus, frequently employ the doctrines of Blessed Dionysius, and [plagiarize] his words literally" (Scholia I, *Patrologia Graece*, vol. 4, col. 21D–24; Saffrey 1990: 240).

The Dionysian world consists of three triads: the thearchy, or Trinity, followed by the celestial hierarchy, the order of intelligent beings, and the ecclesiastical hierarchy, the ideal form of the Church as vehicle of enlightenment, functioning within the human order. Each of these structures is bestowed by the highest good to promote *homoiosis theō(i)* or "assimilation to God" (*Tht.* 164D3; *CH* III.1). For Dionysius, the

443

entire order of reality reflects the three moments we have seen operating in Neoplatonism, as "each procession of the light spreads itself generously toward us, and, in its power to unity, it stirs us by lifting us up. It returns us back to the oneness and deifying simplicity of the father" (CH I.1). Dionysius' *Divine Names*, a work that most resembles Proclus' own *Platonic Theology* (which attempted to isolate the characteristics of the highest Good in each of Plato's dialogues), is actually a sketch of the entire cycle of procession and reversion, which progresses through a series of names that belong to the Word of God under its aspect of differentiation or Unity. Readers of Proclus again will be reminded of the Neoplatonic principles, limit and unlimited, or the monad and the dyad, which govern the entire order of manifestation.

Dionysius is most famous for his *Mystical Theology*, a contemplative work that inspired such Christian mystics as St John of the Cross and Nicholas of Cusa (author of *De docta ignorantia*), among many other authors. Dionysius' work follows upon the *Divine Names* in the sense that while the former worked within the framework of Proclus' strictures in the *Elements of Theology*, affirming as we have seen that everything derived from a single cause, the *Mystical Theology* emphasizes much more the Ineffable side of the One, eschewing metaphysics in favor of contemplative *askēsis* (exercise, practice). In the case of this work, we are reminded very strongly of a roughly contemporary Neoplatonist, Damascius; he outlines an approach to the One that rests precisely on the same practice of unknowing, that is, of abandoning all conditioned states of mind and of being, letting go of all conceptual thinking and even abandoning the content of one's most compelling intuitions. Let us compare this brief excursus on the method of knowing the One in Damascius' *On First Prinicples* with the first paragraph from Dionysius' *Mystical Theology*:

First Damascius (Section 10.10 Ruelle):

> Knowledge demands separation, as I said above, but separateness as it approaches the One collapses into unity, so that knowledge disappears into unknowing. Perhaps this is what Plato intends by his analogy. We attempt to look at the sun for the first time and we succeed because we are far away. But the closer we approach the less we see. And at last we see neither [sun] nor other things, since we have completely become the light itself, instead of an enlightened eye.

Now Dionysus (*MT* I.3; 1001A, trans. Luibheid):

> But then he [Moses] breaks free of them, away from what sees and is seen, and he plunges into the truly mysterious darkness of unknowing. Here, renouncing all that the mind may conceive, wrapped entirely in the intangible and the invisible, he belongs entirely to him who is beyond everything. Here, being neither oneself nor someone else, one is supremely united by a completely unknowing inactivity of all knowledge and knows beyond the mind by knowing nothing.

Of course both Damascius and Dionysius are able to ground their methodologies in what they took to be standard Platonic doctrine, particularly as they discovered it in Letter VII (Damascius quotes 342A7–343C6 just before this passage). But here we have to acknowledge that at this time, apophaticism and the *via negativa* had reached the height of their influence within Platonizing schools, and that it was this zenith of contemplative negative theology that fueled the burst of mysticism in the Middle Ages and later. Some of this mysticism was equally and ardently Platonizing (Eriugena, Nicholas of Cusa). Here we must end our survey, brief though it has been, of Christian Platonism in late antiquity. We now turn to survey the development of Islamic Platonism.

The Harmony of Plato and Aristotle

Already we have seen that it is difficult to separate the expressions of Platonism that operate within religious traditions from infra-Platonist developments. In particular, we saw above that the place of ritual within late antique Platonism resonated with Christian thinkers, while the fifth-century Academy's radical embrace of apophaticism helped fuel an explosion of Christian mystical thought. One aspect of Platonism that is central for the last part of our story, Islamic Platonism, in fact is rather a development within Aristotelian philosophy: the rise of the Commentator tradition together with its central dogma, the harmony of Aristotle and Plato. This doctrine can be traced back to two lost works of Porphyry, *On the School of Plato and Aristotle Being One* and *On the Difference Between Plato and Aristotle*, and is moreover evidenced by the fact that Porphyry himself wrote at least six commentaries on Aristotelian works, including his famous *Isagoge*, or *Introduction to the Categories.* Thus, while Neoplatonism was the dominant intellectual school of the Roman empire, perhaps the greatest literary output of this late antique Neoplatonism takes the form of Commentaries on Aristotelian treatises (*Commentaria in Aristotelem Graeca*). The Commentator tradition, beginning with Alexander of Aphrodisias in the second century, extends to Porphyry (232–309); his pupil, Iamblichus (*ca.* 240–*ca.* 325); Plutarch of Athens (died 423); his students Syrianus (died 437) and Hierocles; Ammonius (534–17), student of Proclus and teacher in his turn of Simplicius and Philoponus; and includes many other philosophers as well. As Sorabji (1990: 3) summarizes, Porphyry solved the conflict between Aristotelian categorical theory and Platonism by means of a compromise that – roughly speaking – saw Aristotle as yielding valid results for the sensible world and Platonism as relevant for understanding the intelligible world. Later Commentators forged an even more sympathetic alliance between the two classical philosophers. Ammonius' views are particularly important for the Arab world, as he was able to synthesize an Aristotelian cosmology that saw God as the efficient cause of the world through the instrumentality of ideas in the divine mind. Ammonius' views are reflected in al-Farabi's work, *The Harmony of Plato and Aristotle*. It is to al-Farabi, the first Islamic Neoplatonist, that we now turn.

A brief look at the translation movement of the ninth century CE will help us to understand how this doctrine of harmony underlies the development of Islamic Platonism. This school of thought truly fused the philosophies of Plato and Aristotle into a syncretic vision of reality that borrowed equally from Aristotle's divine mind and Plotinus' emanationism; it lasted until the twelfth century and the advent of al-Suhrawardi, the founder of the Illuminationist or Ishraqi school. The early 'Abbasid ruler, al-Ma'mun and his successor, al-Mu'tasim (ruled 833–42) sponsored several translation complexes (Gutas 1998), which involved the rendering of Greek philosophical texts into Arabic. Of primary importance was the translation of the entire Aristotelian *Organon*, including the Porphyrean *Isagoge*, as well as works completed by the philosopher and translator al-Kindi and his circle. This remarkable corpus of translations directly from the Greek included Aristotle's *Metaphysics*, the *De caelo*, paraphrases of certain Platonic dialogues, a work known as the *Theology of Aristotle* (actually a paraphrase of *Enneads* IV–VI), and a treatise entitled *The Pure Good* (a collection of Propositions extracted from Proclus' *Elements of Theology*). These latter works, circulating widely within philosophical circles, vouchsafed the harmonizing tendencies of al-Farabi, Ibn Sina, Ibn Rushd, and later, of the Jewish philosopher Maimonides.

Al-Farabi is perhaps best known for his *Principles of the Views of the People of the Best State* (Mabadi' ara' ahl al-madina al-fadila), a work that, like Plato's *Republic*, is a political treatise grounded in a metaphysical framework (see 23: PLATO ON JUSTICE; 24: PLATO'S CONCEPT OF GOODNESS). The treatise begins with a discussion of the first principle as a unique and necessary being, cause of all other beings. This One fits into a causal scheme that appears indebted to Proclus, but at the same time functions like Aristotle's First Mover, insofar as it is an intellect that engages in self-awareness. A brief quote from chapter 1.1 of the *Madina*, as I shall refer to it, will recall the first Proposition of Proclus' *Elements of Theology*:

> The First Existent is the First Cause of the existence of all the other existents. It is free of every kind of deficiency, whereas there must be in everything else some kind of deficiency, either one or more than one; but the first is free of all their deficiencies. Thus its existence is the most excellent and precedes every other existence. No existence can be more excellent than or prior to, its existence. (trans. Walzer)

The activity of self-contemplation on the part of the first existent/mind then gives rise to a second intellect and so the flow of existence all the way down the series of intellects marks off the ranks of various stations of intelligent life. Angels populate the intermediate realms, with the human soul stationed in the sublunar world, but capable of achieving a kind of self-transcendence, known as actualization, whereby the human intellect becomes in fact one with the divine intellect, or first principle (*Madina*, sect. V, ch. 13). Readers of the *Enneads* will immediately see that al-Farabi is far less troubled than Plotinus by the implications of multiplicity within the first principle to the degree that this principle is active, or actualizes itself through its own self-knowledge. Indeed the transcendent and causal aspects of the One were already in conflict by the time of Plotinus and were severed in the work of Damascius, as we saw. In later Islamic Neoplatonism the tensions between the transcendence of the One versus its causal activity continued to exercise Ibn Sina, the brilliant successor to al-Farabi. Wisnovsky has argued (2003) that the Neoplatonist understanding of the One or God as efficient cause of the universe, the source of procession and seat of emanation into the world of becoming, coupled with the Neoplatonist understanding of God or the One as the final cause of the Universe, the transcendent goal into which all of the multiplicity finally resolves, presented Islamic theologians with an unacceptable dualism. Ibn Sina took up this problem with his original metaphysical distinction between existence and essence. Ultimately Ibn Sina's definition of God is slightly different from that of his predecessor. He arrives finally at the definition of a being whose existence is uncaused and necessary in itself, without relation or reference to its successive effects (Wisnovsky 2003: 13).

To return to the *Madina*: for our purposes, it is especially important to see how this basic structure undergirds the treatise as an exercise in political science. Of course, like Plato's philosopher-kings, the ruler of the *Madina* will have a vision of the Good, and in terms of al-Farabi's theory of knowledge, will have actualized his intellect or have acquired the supreme intellect that enters the mind from outside (Greek: *nous epiktētos*, Arabic: *al-'aql al mustafad*), so that he in effect understands the causes of the universe as a whole and the nature of human flourishing in particular. Only the city founded by such a legislator, to whom al-Farabi refers with the Arabic word, *ra'is* (something like "president") as well as with the Arabic word "Imam" (V, 11 and 12), is capable of guiding the city through the use of religion as a cornerstone of his political edifice. This perfect man, the ruler who has actualized his intellect but is also supported by vision-ary or prophetic gifts, will make efforts to establish a polity in which the ordinary person, one whose intellect cannot be actualized, will nevertheless be able to enjoy the benefits of living in a just society, in which the virtues that are practiced make possible the contemplative life for those who are able. Moreover, the state as a whole will imitate the workings of the cosmos itself, above all cooperating with the ruler in con-forming to the divine pattern (V, 15, 4). Hence, above all he will need to acknowledge the authority of the legislator, while the legislator in turn will have to mold the will of the ordinary citizen into compliance. The instrument for this conditioning will be rhetoric and the vehicle for its dissemination will be religion. The masters of rhetoric (*khutaba'*; V, 15, 6) will use their gifts to convince non-philosophical minds of a lesser form of truth (religion, as opposed to pure philosophy which rests principally on reason) (al-Farabi: 438).

Al-Farabi Redivivus: Leo Strauss

Outside of Islam proper, the impact of Islamic Platonism on Jewish medieval philo-sophy is enormous. One such philosopher is the founder of Jewish Neoplatonism in Spain, Solomon ben Judah ibn Gabirol, whose philosophical treatise, written in Arabic, the *Fons Vitae*, has come down to us under the name Avicebron. Ibn Gabirol struggled, as Philo had done before him, to express the relationship between the absolute godhead and creation through a mediating principle, the Divine Will. Just as Christian exegetes found themselves drawn to Philo's conception of the *Logos*, so Gabirol's Will could be adapted to Trinitarian schemes. Ultimately his work attracted a Christian rather than a Jewish readership.

A modern postscript to the Arabic Platonist, al-Farabi concerns his direct bearing on the contemporary interpretation of Plato associated with Leo Strauss. Not only is it of interest that al-Farabi presents a purely secular argument for the Imam, the leader of the community of the just, but it is interesting that he sees religion as subordinate to philosophy. This struggle to advance the cause of reason above the claims of revela-tion and to subordinate the state-sanctioned religion to the rational conclusions of the philosopher not only reflects al-Farabi's doctrinal disagreement with the *Mutakallimun*, but it also has historical reverberations throughout the Islamic world, as the struggle between philosophy and faith played out in a series of attacks and counterattacks.

Most famous of the attacks on philosophy in the Muslim world is the *Tahafut al-falasifah* of the eleventh-century philosopher, al-Ghazali. Al-Ghazali focused on three doctrines that appeared in Islamic Neoplatonism and initiated a dispute that continued to resonate in the Islamic world, as we shall see. He criticized as heretical Ibn Sina's thesis that God does not know particulars, the Aristotelian thesis that the world is eternal, and the generally Platonist position that the soul does not undergo a bodily resurrection (al-Ghazali 1928: 6-7). Indeed, for al-Ghazali the whole paradigm of emanation, insofar as it proceeds, comes not from the fiat of a divine will, but is rather without volition, because it is the very nature of things to be in conflict with Qur'anic revelation. Now the objections of the *Tahafut* were treated to a masterful reply in the treatise of Ibn Rushd, the *Tahafut al-tahafut*, or *Incoherence of the Incoherence*. And this book, along with the works of al-Farabi, provided the basis for the work of the Jewish philosopher of the twelfth to thirteenth centuries, Moses Maimonides. In his *Guide for the Perplexed*, he also attempts to reconcile biblical accounts of creation with the rational philosophy bequeathed to him by the Muslim Neoplatonists. It is usual to consider Maimonides as the pinnacle of the Jewish Aristotelian movement, but he is relevant to our topic because of his influence on the twentieth-century philosopher, Leo Strauss. Maimonides declares his adherence to the Farabian distinction between the two kinds of audience, those who are able to engage rationally with truth, and those who must use their imaginations in order to comprehend an image of it. Thus, Maimonides' final positions concerning the creation of the world lie buried within the treatise, while his mannerisms of obscure writing, deliberate inconsistency, and authorial misdirection are motivated by his own self-imposed distinction between esoteric and exoteric writing, i.e., work intended for audiences capable of rational inquiry, and for audiences whose imaginations had to be affected through the rhetoric of religion. In his *City and the Man*, *Platonic Political Philosophy*, and the *Argument of Plato's Laws*, Strauss, whether correctly or incorrectly, reads these same techniques into the work of Plato. He thus discovers a Farabian/Maimonidean wariness lurking within Plato's political provisions, the wariness of the philosopher in the face of the state religion. In the *Structure of the Guide for the Perplexed* Strauss writes:

> The God whose being is proved on the assumption of eternity is the Unmoved Mover, thought that thinks only itself and that as such is the form or the life of the world. The God whose being is proved on the assumption of creation is the biblical God who is characterized by Will and whose knowledge has only the name in common with our knowledge. (1952: 180)

Strauss bequeaths to the modern world, in his turn, a sophisticated and subtle reading of the dialogues; they presuppose the philosopher's reluctance to speak freely before those who are not qualified by philosophical disposition and training to accept the demonstrations of reason, but instead have to be conditioned by rhetoric to accept lesser versions of the truth. In this sense he enlarges on the differences posited by al-Farabi and Maimonides between esoteric and exoteric teaching and develops an entire methodology of reading Plato's dialogues on the basis of this distinction. As readers of Plato, we do well to appreciate the etiology of the Straussian reading, namely, that it is rooted in the conflict between reason and revelation, between *falasafah* and *Mutakallimun*, that roiled throughout the entire duration of the Arabic Platonist movement.

This brief mention of Strauss's Plato brings to mind the central theme of this chapter, which has been to demonstrate the role that the Platonisms of late antiquity played in the intellectual lives of Jewish, Christian, and Muslim thinkers. Within the complex of Platonism that emerged as Straussian, the interwoven paths of Platonist developments within the first five centuries CE bend back toward the modern reader. Strauss's God of the philosophers is an Aristotelian First Mover; his philosopher-king lives in a theocratic state where religion is a political discourse that masks the insights of the contemplative life, the only authentic source of knowledge and guide for human happiness. Meanwhile, the world itself emanates eternally from the self-contemplation of this First Mover.

Epilogue: al-Suhrawardi's Return to Plato

Islamic philosophy did not stagnate or crystallize with the Farabian synthesis of Aristotle and Plato. Even within Islam, the fortunes of Aristotle waxed and waned variously. One of the most severe critics of Aristotelian essentialism was the twelfth-century founder of the Ishraqi (or Illuminationist) school of philosophy, al-Suhrawardi. His great Arabic work, *The Philosophy of Illumination*, recommends a visionary approach to the question of knowledge, much as we saw in the case of Plotinus or Augustine, an approach that al-Suhrawardi distinguishes sharply from the Aristotelian notion of definition, and rather associates with what he understands as the Pythagorean strain in Plato. As al-Suhrawardi says in the Introduction "who ever wishes to learn only discursive philosophy, let him follow the method of the Peripatetics" (1999: 4). The first part of the treatise includes a critique of Aristotelian definition *per genus et differentiam*: if the hearer knows these, he knows the definition already, whereas if he does not know them, the definition will fail to convey the essence of the thing (1999: 10). Al-Suhrawardi's visionary philosophy is based on the immediacy of consciousness and on the ability of the immaterial nature to apprehend its own essence through the self-evident fact of self-illumination. As he says, "You are never unconscious of your essence or your apprehension of your essence" (1999: 80). This theory of knowledge by way of self-evidence is closely related to the Neoplatonist ideas of the soul's reversion on itself, as we find it in Proclus. In al-Suhrawardi, however, we return to the radical Platonic insistence that everything, including the human soul itself, must resolve in the absolute, the first principle that constitutes the original nature of every intelligent being. For al-Suhrawardi this first principle simply is incorporeal light. And so he concludes his section on self-knowledge by affirming the non-separation of the first principle and the human soul. "It [one's own awareness] is simply the evident itself – nothing more. Therefore it is light in itself, and it is thus pure light" (1999: 81). Perhaps there could be no better summary of the message of Platonism in antiquity than Suhrwardi's doctrine as it is expressed here: that the light of intelligence is the essential nature of the human self as well as the highest principle

449

of reality. Readers of Plato will have to judge for themselves whether they can find any such doctrine in the dialogues of Plato.

Note

All translations are the author's unless otherwise noted.

References and further reading

al-Ghazali, Abu Hamid (1928). *Tahafut al-falasifah*, ed. M. Bouyges. Beirut.

Clark, E. (1992). *The Origenist Controversy*. Princeton, NJ: Princeton University Press.

Courcelle, P. P. (1950). *Recherches sur les "Confessions" de saint Augustin*. Paris: Éditions de Boccard.

Damascius (2002). *Traité des premiers principes*, texte établi par Leendert Gerrit Westerink et traduit par Joseph Combès. Paris: Les Belles Lettres.

Daniélou, J. (1948). *Origène*. Paris: La Table Rond.

Dillon, J. (1997). Logos and Trinity: patterns of Platonist influence on early Christianity. In J. Dillon (ed.) *The Great Tradition*, Variorum Collected Studies Series. Aldershot: Ashgate.

—— (2002). *The Heirs of Plato: A Study of the Old Academy, 347–274 BC*. Oxford: Oxford University Press.

Edwards, M. J. (2002). *Origen Against Plato*. Aldershot: Ashgate.

al-Farabi (1985). *Al-Farabi on the Perfect State*: Abu Nasr al-Farabi's Mabadi ara ahl al-madina al-fadila, a revised text with introduction, translation, and commentary by R. Walzer. Oxford: Oxford University Press.

Finan, T. (1991). A mystic in Milan: Reverberasti revisited. In F. X. Martin and J. A. Richmond (eds.) *From Augustine to Eriugena* (pp. 77–91). Washington, DC: Catholic University of American Press.

Frede, M. (1997). Celsus' attack on the Christians. In J. Barnes and M. Griffin (eds.) *Philosophia Togata* II (pp. 218–40). Oxford: Oxford University Press.

Gruen, E. (2002). *Diaspora*. Berkeley: University of California Press.

Gutas, D. (1998). *Greek Thought, Arabic Culture*. New York: Routledge.

Iamblichus (2003). *De mysteriis Aegyptorum*: Les mystères d'Égypte. Jamblique: text établi et traduit par Édouard des Places. Paris: Les Belles Lettres.

Lloyd, A. C. (1998). *Anatomy of Neoplatonism*. Oxford: Oxford University Press.

Mansfield, J. (1988). Philosophy in the service of scripture. In J. Dillon and A. Long (eds.) *The Question of Eclecticism* (pp. 70–102). Berkeley and Los Angeles: University of California Press.

Nasr, S. H. (1964). *Three Muslim Sages*. Cambridge, Mass.: Harvard University Press.

Nasr, S. H., Nasr, S. F., and Leaman, O. (eds.) (1996). *History of Islamic Philosophy*. New York: Routledge.

O'Meara, D. (1993). *Plotinus: An Introduction to the* Enneads. Oxford: Oxford University Press.

—— (2003). *Platonopolis: Platonic Political Philosophy in Late Antiquity*. New York: Oxford University Press.

Origen (1978). *Traité des premiers principes*. Introduction, texte, critique de la version de Rufin, traduction par Henri Crouzel et Manlio Simonetti. Paris: Éditions du CERF.

—— (1986). Contra Celsum. In M. Markovich (ed.) *Origen Contra Celsum*. Berlin: de Gruyter.

Runia, D. T. (1990). Philo, Alexandrian and Jew. In *Exegesis and Philosophy: Studies on Philo of Alexandria* (pp. 1–18). Aldershot: Variorum.

—— (2002). The beginnings of the end: Philo of Alexandria and Hellenistic theology. In M. Frede and A. Laks (eds.) *Traditions of Theology: Studies in Hellenistic Theology, its Background and Aftermath* (pp. 281–316). Leiden and New York: Brill.

Saffrey, H. D. (1990). *Recherches sur le néoplatonisme après Plotin.* Paris: J. Vrin.

Sedley, D. (2002). The origins of the Stoic God. In M. Frede and A. Laks (eds.) *Traditions of Theology: Studies in Hellenistic Theology, its Background and Aftermath* (pp. 41–85). Leiden and New York: Brill.

Shaw, G. (1995). *Theurgy and the Soul: The Neoplatonism of Iamblichus.* University Park, Pa.: Pennsylvania State University Press.

Sorabji, R. (1990). *Aristotle Transformed: The Ancient Commentators and their Influence.* London: Duckworth.

Strauss, L. (1952). The literary character of the *Guide for the Perplexed.* In *Persecution and the Art of Writing* (pp. 38–94). Glencoe: The Free Press.

al-Suhrawardi (1999). *The Philosophy of Illumination,* trans. J. Walbridge and H. Ziai. Provo, Ut.: Brigham Young University Press.

Wallis, R. T. (1972). *Neoplatonism.* London: Duckworth. Reissued by Hackett, Indianapolis, 1995.

Wisnovsky, R. (2003). *Avicenna's Metaphysics in Context.* Ithaca, NY: Cornell University Press.

451

Index

astronomy, 136, 211–12, 214, 231–2, 363
Athena, 251
Athenian Council (*boule*), 3
Athenian Stranger (*Laws*), 255, 279, 290–1, 306, 338, 342–3, 353, 354, 380, 382
Athenian Stranger (*Sophist*), 57
Athens, 1, 2, 3, 354
Atlantis, 205
attributes, 168, 178–9
attunement theory, soul, 283–4
Augustine, St, 180, 212, 365, 441, 442
Axiothea of Phlius, 11

Bacchic Mysteries, 256
bad, the, 314, 365
Beardsley, M. C., 399
beautiful
  and Beautiful, 71, 72–3, 89, 184
  good, 178, 310
  Hippias Major, 72–3, 77, 78–9, 82, 107–8, 111
  inspiration, 396–9
  lovers of, 136, 137, 144
  Phaedo, 194
Beautiful, the
  and beautiful, 71, 72–3, 89, 184
  Diotima, 83, 296, 398
  Good, 178–9, 180
  lovers, 301–2
  lovers of, 136, 137, 144
  Parmenides, 196
  Phaedo, 201, 251
  Republic, 144
  Socrates, 89–90, 155, 194
  Symposium, 130, 204, 398–9
belief
  eyewitnesses, 134
  justified true belief, 112
  knowledge, 47, 112, 151, 153, 160, 269–71
  perception, 144–5
  soul, 90
belief-*akrasia*, 264, 266
Benson, H., 107, 114–15, 116
Bentham, J., 311, 312, 318
body
  appetite, 318
  desire, 311
  pleasure, 319, 320–1

soul, 134–5, 138–9, 142, 143, 210, 256, 278, 280–1, 283
Bradley, F. H., 197
bravery: *see* courage
Brickhouse, T. C., 115, 116–17
Broome, J., 309
Burnet, J., 28, 403
Burnyeat, M. F., 232, 233, 234, 235

Callias of Alopece, 5
Callicles (*Gorgias*), 47, 56–7, 273, 274, 314, 317, 320
Carneades, 35, 419, 426
categories doctrine, 168, 413–15
catharsis, 248, 256, 281
causality
  evil, 248
  formal, 151–2
  god, 423–4
  knowledge, 122
  logic, 150
  perception, 141
  Phaedo, 66, 364
  safe/sophisticated, 285
  simple/subtle, 154–8 (*see also* aitia)
Causality, Transmission Theory of, 77–8
Cave Allegory, *Republic*, 130, 153, 172, 256
Cebes (*Phaedo*), 32, 156, 280–1, 284
Celsus, 438–9, 442
censorship, 390
Cephalus, 42
Certification Program, 147–8, 150–1
Chaerephon, 43, 103
chance, 258 n. 3
Charmides, 4
Charmides, 3, 40
  aporia, 44
  cheating, 62–3, 64–5
  education, 2
  elenchus, 65
  irony, 48
  moderation, 222
  temperance, 61, 62–3, 65, 66, 78, 105–6, 133, 359
  wish/desire, 272
cheating, 62–3, 64–5
Cherniss, H., 408
Christian philosophy, 434, 438, 440–1, 443
Chrysippus, 425, 431
Cicero, 425–6, 431

circles, 362
citizenship, 345–6, 347–8, 421
city: *see polis*
civil disobedience, 377–8
Clitophon, 295
cognition
  action theory, 272
  faculties, 143
  Forms, 126
  knowledge, 128
  noetic, 128
  ontology, 124
  prenatal, 126–7
  a priori, 129
  Republic, 135–7
  sense/intellect, 123
Collection and Division, Method of, 71, 87,
    97, 159–60, 304–5
color, 138, 140, 143
Colotes, 429
commensurability, 309, 310
  see also measurement
consciousness, 351, 412
consequentialism, 202, 257
Constantine, 440
constitutions, 376, 377, 378, 382
Cooper, J. M., xiii
Copernican revolution, 212
Cornford, F. M., 159
Corybantic references, 256
cosmogony, 199
cosmology
  ancient, 199–200, 418
  Aristotle, 211
  Demiurge, 207–8
  etymology, 199, 252
  Laws, 424
  order, 385
  Phaedo, 200–3, 204
  Receptacle, 207
  Stoicism, 424
  Timaeus, 205–11, 418, 423, 430
  World-Soul, 207
courage
  endurance, 333–4, 339 n. 3
  knowledge, 327–8
  Laches, 64, 66–7, 72, 75, 327–8, 332–3,
    359
  Laws, 337
  political, 336–7

Protagoras, 334–5
Republic, 336, 360–1
of rulers, 336–7
Socrates, 29, 106–7
soul, 350–1
temperance, 337
virtues, 334–5
wisdom, 336, 346–7
Courcelle, P. P., 441
craft analogy, 148, 166–7, 177
craftsmen, 43, 58–60, 95, 103–4, 114,
    166–7
Crantor, 418, 431
Cratylus, 5, 17, 39, 216–21, 294, 424–5
creation myth, 137–9, 254, 279, 291,
    292
creator-god, 211, 252–4, 255
  see also Demiurge
Crete, 353, 380
Critias, 29, 30
Critias, 15, 39, 205
Critias (*Charmides*), 3–4, 105–6
Critias (*Timaeus*), 205
Crito
  certification, 148
  historical context, 4, 39
  immoral action, 274–5
  laws, 355, 373, 374–5, 377–8, 385
  moral action theory, 27
  reason, 309
  Socrates, 56
Crito (*Euthydemus*), 41–2
Cronos, 248, 252, 254
Ctesippus (*Euthydemus*), 47
cubes, volume of, 229
Cyclical Argument, *Phaedo*, 255
Cynics, 420, 426
Cyrenaic school, 31

Daedalus' statues, 151, 153
daimōn, 219, 251
Damascius, 442, 443, 444
Dancy, R. M., 83
death, 110, 255, 256, 280–1
deficiency, judgment of, 124
definition
  dialogues, 105, 108
  ethical matters, 106–7
  kalos k'agathos concept, 106
  triangle, 156